Hymns of Our Faith

Hymns of Our Faith

A HANDBOOK FOR THE *BAPTIST HYMNAL*

William Jensen Reynolds

BROADMAN PRESS

Nashville, Tennessee

DEWEY DECIMAL CLASSIFICATION: 783.9
Library of Congress catalog card number: 64-14049
Printed in the United States of America

To Mary Lou

Foreword

In 1956 the Sunday School Board of the Southern Baptist Convention published *Baptist Hymnal*. *Hymns of Our Faith* has been written primarily as a companion to this hymnal, whose content furnishes the list of texts, tunes, authors, and composers for discussion. Mention of "the Hymnal" or "the Hymnal Committee" refers to *Baptist Hymnal* or the committee that prepared it. Hymn numbers from this hymnal also occur in the headings of the hymn discussions and elsewhere.

While *Hymns of Our Faith* is thus significantly related to a particular hymnal, most of the hymns it discusses are in general use among evangelical Christians of the United States. The book is organized so that it may be used conveniently with *Baptist Hymnal* or any other hymnbook. Part I contains hymn and tune discussions arranged alphabetically by first lines. Since tunes are discussed along with the hymns with which they are used, an Index of Tunes is provided at the back of the book to aid in locating tune discussions. Part II discusses authors and composers, and is arranged in a single alphabetical sequence.

Due to the limitation of space, it has been necessary to restrict all of the material to essential facts, reluctantly omitting at times interesting details of human interest. In the biographical treatment of authors and composers, the length of an individual sketch is not in any way a measure of the importance or significance of the person involved. Somewhat abbreviated treatment has been given persons who are well-known and for whom additional details are easily available. For persons whose identities are less familiar, more space has been given. A number of references are made of *The Hymn,* suggesting that additional helpful information may be secured from this valuable source.

The author would acknowledge his indebtedness to the several hymnal handbooks which have preceded this work: *Our Hymnody* (Methodist) by Robert Guy McCutchan; *The Story of Our Hymns* (Evangelical and Reformed) by Armin Haeussler; and *The Hymnal 1940 Companion* (Episcopal) largely prepared by Leonard Ellinwood. These have been invaluable guides, and instances of original research of these authors have been noted in numerous places. Also helpful have been three hand-books from England: *Companion to Congregational Praise* by K. L. Parry and Erik Routley; *The Baptist Hymn Companion,* Hugh Martin, editor; and *Historical Companion to Hymns Ancient and Modern,* Maurice Frost, editor. An indispensable source of reference has been John Julian's *A Dictionary of Hymnology.*

Most sincere gratitude is expressed to Dr. Davis C. Woolley of the Southern Baptist Historical Commission and to Miss Helen Conger of the Dargan-Carver Library, Nashville, for valuable assistance in secur-ing helpful materials; to Gordon D. Shorney of the Hope Publishing Company for making available the resources of the collections held by this company; to Ellen Jane Lorenz of the Lorenz Publishing Company for permission to use the valuable library of the late E. S. Lorenz; to James E. Thomas of the Rodeheaver, Hall-Mack Company for per-mission to quote from *Forty Gospel Hymn Stories* (copyright 1943 by George W. Sanville) and *Modern Gospel Song Stories* (copyright 1952 by Haldor Lillenas, assigned to the Rodeheaver Company).

Of great assistance has been the keen interest and continued en-couragement of Dr. W. Hines Sims, secretary of the Church Music Department of the Sunday School Board, chairman of the Hymnal Committee and editor for the *Baptist Hymnal.*

Genuine appreciation is expressed to Ernest K. Emurian for his generous sharing of data collected in his own research; to Andrew Hayden for providing heretofore unavailable data concerning several English authors and composers; and to Mr. and Mrs. Edmond D. Keith for their critical reading of this manuscript and helpful suggestions.

A word of personal gratitude must be recorded for the influence of the late Isham E. Reynolds, whose class in hymnology at Southwestern Baptist Theological Seminary first brought to the author an increased awareness of the richness of our hymnody, and of the late Robert G. McCutchan, whose personal counsel and confidence at the outset of this project provided needed encouragement and motivation.

Finally, to a host of friends, many known only through correspond-ence, the author expresses his indebtedness for their patient indulgence of a persistent inquirer. It is hoped that the appearance of this hand-book may bring to light, from sources now unknown, additional informa-tion which, up to this time, has eluded discovery. That this handbook might bring enrichment and greater understanding of our hymnody and a more meaningful experience in congregational singing is the earnest prayer of the author.

Contents

Introduction

Baptist Hymnody in America

The first Baptist church in the American colonies was organized in 1639—one year before the publication of the Bay Psalm Book.[1] However, one hundred and twenty-three years passed before the publication of the first Baptist collection of hymns, and this was a reprint of a collection which had been published a dozen years earlier in England. The first Baptist collection to be compiled on American soil appeared in 1766. To understand this long delay in any evident Baptist initiative to publish hymn collections, it will be helpful to sketch briefly the intriguing story of Baptist beginnings in America.

Early Beginnings

Baptist growth in the colonies was extremely slow and not without opposition. Many of those who settled in the New World seeking freedom for their own kind of religion were themselves intolerant of others. Following the organization of the Baptist church in Providence, Rhode Island, in 1639, other small groups of Baptists formed themselves into churches. The expansion of Baptist life may be seen from the following chronological list of the years in which Baptist churches were organized in various colonies, territories, and states:

Rhode Island	1639	Connecticut	1705
Massachusetts	1663	Virginia	1715
Pennsylvania	1684	New York	1724
New Jersey	1688	North Carolina	1724
South Carolina	ca.1690	Maryland	1742
Delaware	1703		

---

[1]This psalter, *The Whole Booke of Psalmes Faithfully Translated into English Metre* (1640), was the first book of any kind published in the English-speaking American colonies. It contained metrical versions of new translations of the psalms prepared by Puritan ministers in the Massachusetts Bay Colony who considered the psalter of Sternhold and Hopkins (1562) crude, unscholarly, and much too free.

New Hampshire	1755	Illinois	1796
Tennessee	ca.1765	Indiana	1798
Vermont	1768	Missouri	1806
Georgia	1772	Alabama	1808
Kentucky	1781	Louisiana	1812
Ohio	1790	Florida	1821
Mississippi	1791	Michigan	1824

By 1700 New England had only three hundred Baptists in ten small churches. As the early pioneers pushed south and west new Baptist churches appeared, but according to present-day methods, this was an extremely slow, tedious process. Almost two hundred years elapsed between the beginning of work in Rhode Island and the first organized church in Florida. By 1790, in sixteen states and territories, 867 churches had been organized with a total membership of 65,233. Most of this growth occurred in the latter half of the century, following the Great Awakening. John Asplund, whose faithfully compiled *Register* provides much information concerning the early Baptist churches, gave the following report as to the number of churches in each state in 1790.[2]

Virginia	204	New Hampshire	32
Massachusetts	107	Pennsylvania	28
North Carolina	94	New Jersey	26
South Carolina	70	Maryland	12
New York	57	Delaware	7
Connecticut	55	Western territories	
Kentucky	42	(including Tenn.)	19
Georgia	42		
Rhode Island	38	TOTAL	867
Vermont	34		

In England in the early seventeenth century Baptists were of two kinds. Those called the General Baptists were Arminian, teaching that Christ had died for all men. The Particular Baptists were Calvinistic. They taught that Christ had died only for those whom God had selected in advance to be saved. Baptist immigrants to the American colonies were from both groups. In England congregational singing had its beginning in Particular Baptist churches in the latter part of the seventeenth century, largely through the efforts of Benjamin Keach. General

---

[2]*The Annual Register of the Baptist Denomination in North America* (1791), p. 47.

Baptist churches permitted no congregational singing—psalms or hymns —until almost a century later.

Most of those English Baptists who opposed singing in public worship recognized scriptural authority for psalm singing. However, they opposed "promiscuous singing," the singing of believers and unbelievers together. Also, they opposed the use of "set forms," the metrical versions of the psalms, as being "man made" and unworthy of public worship. These beliefs left only the possibility that an individual might feel inspired to compose and sing a spontaneous song.

Singing in the Churches

Strangely enough it seems that at the middle of the seventeenth century singing in public worship may have existed in Baptist churches of the American colonies more generally than in those of England. Morgan Edwards reliably reports that psalm singing was practiced in the first Baptist church in Providence, Rhode Island,[3] where the small congregation, organized in 1639 "first met for worship in a grove, unless in wet and stormy weather, when they assembled in private houses."[4] Singing was also practiced from the first in the Newport church, established by 1644.[5]

Further evidence of singing in worship is given by John Clarke, pastor of the Newport church, who, together with John Crandall and Obadiah Holmes, had gone to Lynn, Massachusetts in July, 1651, to conduct a service in the home of William Witter, a member of Clarke's congregation. Two constables, who came to arrest these three for "disturbing the peace," waited until their "prayers, singing, and preaching was over" before they took them to prison in Boston.[6]

The Baptist cause was strengthened in the early years by Baptist immigrants who sought fellowship with those of like faith. However, some of these brought with them from their mother country a prejudice against singing in public worship.[7] This may explain the increased opposition to singing at Providence and Newport which resulted in the abandonment of this practice in these two churches in the 1650's. English Baptists settled in Delaware from 1675 on. In 1683 a company of Baptists arrived from Ireland, county of Tipperary, and they settled

---

[3]*History of the Baptists in Rhode Island* (1867), p. 314.
[4]David Benedict, *A General History of the Baptist Denomination in America* (1813), I, 476.
[5]Edwards, *op. cit.,* p. 324.
[6]John Clarke's report quoted in Benedict, *op. cit.,* I, 366.
[7]*Ibid.,* I, 218

in the neighborhood of Cohansey in New Jersey.[8] In spite of some opposition, these Irish Baptists practiced psalmody.[9]

While Benjamin Keach was persistently advocating congregational singing in his church at Southwark, England, his son Elias arrived in America in 1686. Two years later young Keach became pastor of the Pennepek church in Pennsylvania, which at the time had twelve faithful members.[10] Sharing his father's zeal for public singing, he led his church in this practice, but not without some opposition.[11]

It is not known from which collections or psalters these early Baptists sang. Possibly they used the Sternhold and Hopkins' *Psalter* (1562) or Ainsworth's *Psalter* (1612), which the Separatists knew in Amsterdam, or one of the editions of the *Anglo-Genevan Psalter* prepared for the English refugees in Switzerland in 1556 and later. Also possible is the use of hand-copied metrical versions taken from various sources. Only one copy would be needed by a congregation, for the psalms were "lined out" by the pastor or a deacon. Much research remains to be done in this regard; recent investigation certainly indicates that public singing among early Baptists was more widespread than has been reported previously.

Benson believed that "if the earliest New England Baptists practiced psalm singing at all, they probably, like their neighbors, lined the psalms out of the Bay Psalm Book."[12] However, that the Bay Psalm Book should have been found in Baptist hands in New England seems highly improbable—at least until many decades had erased from Baptist minds memories of the persecution they had suffered at the hands of Boston divines, some of whom were responsible for this psalter. John Cotton, who assisted in preparing it and wrote its preface, opposed the Baptists and engaged in extended controversy with Roger Williams. In 1644 a law was passed in Massachusetts primarily designed to stop the preaching of the Baptists.[13] Imprisonment, harsh fines, and public whippings meted out to faithful Baptist preachers are matters of record. Their only offense was preaching the gospel and worshiping God according to the dictates of their own consciences.

Welsh Baptists and Keach's Confession of Faith

A group of Welsh Baptists landed in New York in 1701. After a

---

[8]Edwards, *History of the Baptists in Delaware* (1885), p. 10.
[9]*Ibid.*, p. 52.
[10]Benedict, *op. cit.*, I, 580.
[11]*Ibid.*
[12]Louis F. Benson, *The English Hymn* (1915), p. 196.
[13]Benedict, *op. cit.*, I, 360.

brief stay at Pennepek, Pennsylvania, they settled in 1703 in New Castle, Delaware, about forty-two miles southwest of Philadelphia. This Welsh Tract church was the principal, if not the sole, means of introducing singing among the Baptists in the middle colonies.[14] Other Welsh Baptists settled in Pennsylvania, founding the Great Valley church, near Philadelphia, in 1711, and the Montgomery church in 1719.

To further affirm belief in the practice of public singing, the Welsh Tract church in 1716 adopted the Assembly Confession of Faith, prepared in England in 1689, to which Keach and his son Elias, in 1697, had added articles on singing psalms and the laying on of hands. Keach's firm belief in congregational singing is reflected in this statement, truly a monument in Baptist hymnody.

We believe that 'acts 16 25 eph 5 19 col 3 16' singing the praises of God, is a holy Ordinance of Christ, and not a part of natural religion, or a moral duty only; but that it is brought under divine institution, it being injoined on the churches of Christ to sing psalms, hymns, and spiritual songs; and that the whole church in their public assemblies, as well as private christians, ought to 'heb 2 12 jam 5 13' sing God's praises according to the best light they have received. Moreover, it was practiced in the great representative church, by 'matt 26 30 mat 14 26' our Lord Jesus Christ with his disciples, after he had instituted and celebrated the sacred ordinance of his Holy Supper, as a commemorative token of redeeming love.[15]

Abel Morgan, a Philadelphia minister, translated Keach's version of this confession into Welsh; and 122 members of the Welsh Tract church signed this document, the first confession of faith adopted by Baptists in America.

The so-called Keach's Confession was adopted by the Philadelphia Association, September 25, 1742, and a printing ordered of this new edition, which was done by Benjamin Franklin in 1743. For at least two decades prior to its formal adoption, the confession had been the accepted doctrinal standard among the churches of the middle colonies, which would indicate the use of singing.[16] It became known in America as the Philadelphia Confession of Faith. This Calvinistic document, with its provision for public singing, became widely accepted by early Baptist associations and was of unusual influence in the South.

Opposition to public singing gradually declined in the early eighteenth century. In churches where the practice had been discontinued, it was

---

[14]*Ibid.*, II, 6.

[15]William L. Lumpkin, *Baptist Confessions of Faith* (Philadelphia: Judson Press. 1959), p. 351; cf. pp. 348 ff.

[16]*Ibid.*, p. 349.

restored, and where it had thus far been forbidden, it was instituted for the first time. At the First church of Newport, during the brief ministry of John Comer, ordained co-pastor in May, 1726, congregational singing was restored,[17] probably using Tate and Brady's *New Version*.[18] The First church, Boston, introduced psalm singing by 1728, and in 1740 adopted Tate and Brady. Benson suggests that some Baptist demand in and around Philadelphia may have helped to encourage Benjamin Franklin to reprint Tate and Brady's *New Version* in 1733.[19]

The Great Awakening Popularizes Watts's Psalms and Hymns

Of major hymnological significance to the Baptist cause in America was the influence of the Great Awakening from about 1734 to about 1770. Originating within New England Congregationalism, under Jonathan Edwards, this movement received great assistance from the several visits to the colonies of George Whitefield, the great English evangelical preacher. The value of hymn singing in evangelical endeavor had been witnessed by Whitefield in England, and he was quick to employ similar methods in America. He loved the psalms and hymns of Isaac Watts; and largely through his efforts, these were introduced in the colonies where he preached. General Baptist churches of Arminian background, chiefly in New England, were less affected by this movement than the churches of Calvinistic tendencies. The Separate Baptists, which evolved out of this evangelical movement, became vigorous and enthusiastic hymn singers.

The fires of revival spread along the Atlantic seaboard, and the hymns and psalms of Watts became increasingly popular. Watts's *Hymns and Spiritual Songs,* which first appeared in England in 1707, was reprinted in Boston in 1739, in Philadelphia in 1742 (by Benjamin Franklin), and in New York in 1752. These and subsequent editions, combined with reprintings of Watts's *Psalms* (1719), found great favor among Baptist congregations, as well as among other groups.

Hymns for the Church Ordinances

Baptism and the Lord's Supper—the two church ordinances practiced by Baptists—have played an unusual role in the development of Baptist hymnody. In England, the introduction of hymn singing by Benjamin Keach to his church at Southwark in 1673 was accomplished using the scriptural basis that a hymn was sung by Christ and his disciples at the

---

[17]Benedict, *op. cit.,* I, 497.
[18]William L. Hooper, *Church Music in Transition* (Nashville: Broadman Press, 1963), p. 106.
[19]Benson, *op. cit.,* p. 197.

conclusion of the Lord's Supper. Here was argument for hymn singing that could not be disputed.

In America, the first emergence of Baptist distinctives in hymnody came through hymns written for one or both of these ordinances. The Newport Collection (1766), the first Baptist compilation made in the American colonies, opened with a section of sixteen hymns on baptism. This was followed by seventy-four hymns for the Lord's Supper. In 1791 a small collection, *Baptismal Hymns* by an unknown compiler, was published in Boston. Another anonymous compilation, *The Boston Collection* (1808), was compiled "principally with a view to accommodate the Baptist churches of Boston and its vicinity, who have long desired such a collection, for the purpose of singing at the administration of baptism."

The Influence of John Rippon

John Rippon, pastor of the Baptist church in Carter Lane, London, in 1787 published, *A Selection of Hymns from the best authors, intended to be an Appendix to Dr. Watts's Psalms and Hymns*. This collection of 588 hymns was reprinted in America in 1792. It became a standard for Baptist hymn singing and a major source for subsequent compilers. Jones and Allison had already drawn heavily on the London edition for their *Selection of Psalms and Hymns* (1790).

By the early years of the nineteenth century the psalms and hymns of Isaac Watts had become increasingly popular among Baptist congregations. James Winchell, pastor of the First Baptist Church, Boston, published in 1818 *An Arrangement of the Psalms, Hymns, and Spiritual Songs of Dr. Watts*. This collection, known as "Winchell's Watts," dominated Baptist hymn singing in New England for many years. Winchell acknowledged his indebtedness to John Rippon's arrangement of Watts which had been published in London in 1801. Rippon had removed the three divisions (books) set up originally by Watts which had been maintained in all printings up to this time, and the hymns were arranged according to subjects. "Rippon's Watts" was reprinted in Philadelphia in 1820, and became the most popular collection among Baptist churches in that area, while "Winchell's Watts" was almost universally accepted in New England.

Watts's popularity among the Baptists may be further evidenced from the fact that many collections which appeared at this time were not intended to replace Watts but were designed as a supplement or appendix, providing additional hymns especially for Baptist use. Among these "appendix" collections produced by Baptists were the anonymous collection published at Burlington, New Jersey (1807), and compilations by Staughton (1807), Parkinson (1809), Collins (1812), and Ripley (1821).[20] William Staughton, pastor of Philadelphia's First Baptist Church, and later president of Columbian College (1821-29), published an appendix to "Rippon's Watts" in 1813, using as his chief source John Newton and William Cowper's *Olney Hymns* (1779).

Baptist Associations Produce Hymnals

The role of the associational organization, a volunteer grouping of co-operating churches in a given vicinity, has had its influence on Baptist hymnody. The association provided a means for producing collections of hymns, when such an undertaking would have been impossible for a single church, and this operation was the forerunner of the denominational publishing house which developed in the mid-nineteenth century. The first such organization in America was the Philadelphia Association, organized in 1707. Second was the Charleston (South Carolina) Association, organized in 1751. By 1800 forty-eight associations had been formed. Thirty of these were located in the South, and six of the eight beyond the Alleghenies were in Kentucky.[21]

Philadelphia became a major center of Baptist activity, and in 1788 the Philadelphia Association requested Samuel Jones and Burgis Allison to prepare a hymnal "for the use of the associated churches."[22] This collection appeared in 1790. The Dover Association (Virginia), by 1830 the largest Baptist association in America, requested Andrew Broaddus to prepare a collection of hymns, and the *Dover Selection* appeared in 1828. In the preface Broaddus stated that this was "chiefly a selection of those compositions generally termed 'Spiritual Songs,' is principally intended for popular use and not as a standard book for the desk, or the leader of the hymn in public worship."

Spiritual Songs

While Baptist compilers drew heavily on English sources for the main body of their borrowed material, there was an increasing effort on the part of many to include native materials, marking the beginnings of American folk hymnody. One of the earliest examples is *Divine Hymns, or Spiritual Songs* (1784), compiled by Joshua Smith, a Baptist layman of Brentwood, New Hampshire. Though inferior to the literary quality of the borrowed English material, this collection had considerable popularity. Its eleventh edition (1803) happened to be the first hymnal

---

[20]Titles of these collections will be found in the chronological listing of Baptist hymnals given at the end of this section.

[21]*Encyclopedia of Southern Baptists* (1958), II, 985-6.

[22]Henry S. Burrage, *Baptist Hymn Writers and Their Hymns* (1888), p. 641.

which was adopted by the First Baptist Church, Portland, Maine.[23]

The acceptance of these "spiritual songs" is apparent by the fact that they appear in most Baptist collections from this time on. John Courtney's *The Christian's Pocket Companion* (1805) contained one hundred and eighty-one hymns and "one hundred and seventy-eight pages of choice Spiritual Songs."[24] An advertisement in a Richmond, Virginia, newspaper in 1803 describes Courtney's newest compilation, *Hymns and Spiritual Songs* (1803): "The Hymns are selected from the most approved authors and adapted to the different modes of Christian worship. The Spiritual Songs contained in our last publication are comprised in this also with some selected from pamphlets lately published in North and South Carolina and in Baltimore."[25]

Courtney, pastor of the First Baptist Church, Richmond, for thirty-eight years (1786-1824), and a leader among Virginia Baptists, was fond of hymn singing. In spite of the fact he published three successful collections, he would not permit the use of hymn books in his church, preferring to "line out" the hymns to his congregation.[26]

That there was much abuse and mutilation in corrupted versions of these spiritual songs both in manuscripts and in published collections is revealed in the prefaces of the collections of William Parkinson (New York, 1809), and George C. Sedgwick (Fredericksburg, Virginia, 1815). Parkinson was quite outspoken:

> This kind of composition has, for several years past been greatly abused— Songs have been circulated, not only in Ms. but also in print, which have been so barbarous in language, so unequal in numbers, and so defective in rhyme, as to excite disgust in all persons even of tolerable understanding in these things; which is infinitely worse, so extremely unsound in doctrine, that no discerning Christian can sing or hear them without pain.[27]

These are strong, forceful words expressing sincere critical judgment regarding hymnic material considered unworthy for intelligent Christian use. Surely this would merit for Parkinson, at that time pastor of the First Baptist Church of New York City, recognition as one of the earliest proponents among Baptists for a better type of hymnic literature.

The First Tune Books

Eighteenth-century Baptist collections contained only words of the

---

[23]*Ibid.*, p. 643.

[24]*Ibid.*, p. 644.

[25]Blanche Sydnor White, *First Baptist Church Richmond 1780-1955*, p. 18.

[26]*Ibid.*, p. 37.

[27]Preface to Parkinson's *A Selection of Hymns and Spiritual Songs* (1809), quoted in Benson, *op. cit.*, p. 202.

hymns printed in poetic form, and this was largely true well into the nineteenth century. John Rippon had published in England a tune book of two hundred tunes in 1791, but apparently this did not find favor in America. Samuel Holyoke's *The Christian Harmonist* (1804) appears to be the first American tune book designed for Baptists. It contained tunes "adapted to all the metres of Mr. Rippon's Selection of Hymns, in the Collection of Hymns by Mr. Joshua Smith, and in Dr. Watts's Psalms and Hymns." Designed for "use of the Baptist churches in the United States," the tune book gives evidence of the fact that these three collections were most widely used in those churches where Holyoke expected his tunes to be sung.

In 1817 Samuel Dyer published in Baltimore *Dyer's New Selection of Sacred Music.* The son of a New Hampshire Baptist preacher, Dyer was educated in England and studied music under Thomas Walker, who had assisted Rippon with his tune book and in 1814 published *Walker's Companion to Rippon's Tunebook.* Dyer's collection went through at least six editions, and the sixth edition, greatly enlarged, was called the *Philadelphia Collection of Sacred Music* (1828).

James Winchell, in 1819, published *Sacred Harmony* to provide tunes appropriate for his "Winchell's Watts," which appeared in the same year.

Oliver Shaw published several tune books before he joined the Second Baptist Church of Providence in 1834. The following year he published *The Social Sacred Melodist,* his last collection. The last fourteen years of his life were spent in the Baptist fellowship. Shaw was widely respected as a composer, organist, and music teacher, despite his blindness, which had begun when he was about twenty-one.

The tunes of Lowell Mason were widely sung by Baptists in many areas, and Baptists were familiar with his more successful collections. The two collections he designed especially for Baptists failed, however, to receive much acceptance. *Manual of Christian Psalmody* (1832), compiled by Mason and David Greene with the assistance of Rufus Babcock, Jr., pastor of the First Baptist Church of Salem, Massachusetts, was a "Baptist edition" of Mason and Greene's *Christian Psalmody,* which had appeared the previous year. Even less successful was *Union Hymns* (1834), also compiled by Mason, Greene, and Babcock.

Hymn Book Compilers (ca. 1780–ca. 1840)

Though Baptists seemingly got a late start in the publication of hymn collections, once this activity began, books appeared in almost every state. From the Newport Collection (1766) until well into the fourth decade of the next century many hands were busy making compilations. In addition to those individuals previously mentioned, this account would

In addition to those individuals previously mentioned, this account would include Thomas B. Ripley and John Butler of Maine; Benjamin Cleavland and James H. Linsley of Connecticut; Thomas Baldwin, Paul Himes, Jonathan Wilson, William Collier, Gustavus F. Davis, Enoch W. Freeman, Jonathan Howe, and Rufus Babcock, Jr., of Massachusetts; Ebenezer E. Cummins and Edmund Worth of New Hampshire; David Benedict of Rhode Island; John Stanford, Archibald Maclay, James Fenn, and Paris M. Davis of New York; Ebenezer Jayne of New Jersey; Daniel Dodge of Delaware; Lewis Skidmore and Stephen P. Hill of Maryland; Enoch Story, Jr., Lewis Baldwin, William Staughton, and John L. Dagg of Pennsylvania; Eleazer Clay, John Asplund, and Andrew Broaddus of Virginia. What a noble procession of Baptists, who, recognizing the value of congregational singing, devoted their energies to providing what they considered appropriate collections during this brief period of six decades.

Campmeeting Songs

Mention must be made of the campmeeting movement which began in Logan County, Kentucky, about 1800 and spread through Tennessee and the Carolinas, into Ohio, Georgia, Virginia, Maryland, Delaware, Pennsylvania, New York, Massachusetts, Connecticut, Vermont, and New Hampshire. Though begun by Presbyterians, both Methodists and Baptists shared in this sweeping evangelistic movement. Many collections of campmeeting songs were published, recording the spiritual songs which became popular in these meetings. However, the only Baptist collection yet found specifically designed for this purpose is Lewis Skidmore's *The Choice Collection of the Latest Social and Camp Meeting Hymns and Spiritual Songs* (Baltimore, 1825). Nevertheless, it is recognized that these campmeeting songs were welcomed by many Baptists, particularly along the western frontier and in the South, and their influence may be seen in subsequent compilations.

Southern Collections and Folk Hymnody

During this time collections began to appear in the South, the earliest being Jesse Mercer's *The Cluster of Spiritual Songs, Divine Hymns, and Sacred Poems* (Augusta, Georgia, 1813). First only a small pamphlet, subsequent editions were enlarged until by 1835 it contained over three hundred hymns. Other southern compilers are found in South Carolina—S. S. Burdett (1834) and William Dossey (1820); in Tennessee—Starke Dupuy (1818); in Kentucky—Silas Noel (1814) and Absalom Graves (1825); and in North Carolina—William P. Biddle and William J. Newborn (1825), and John Purifoy (1831).

Mention has already been made of the beginnings of folk hymnody in the late eighteenth century in New England. For these texts of folk origin a vast body of "unwritten music" accumulated as these hymns were "lined out" to the people. It was among the backwoods Baptists of New England that the first collection of these tunes appeared.[28] Jeremiah Ingalls, a devoted Congregational layman, published *The Christian Harmony,* in Exeter, New Hampshire, in 1805, and this is recognized as the first publication of these "Old Baptist" folk melodies. Many of the other oblong tune books with similar contents used the shaped notation developed by William Smith and William Little in 1801. The solmization system employed was the same four-note syllables, *fa, sol, la, mi,* which had first appeared in America in the 1698 edition of the Bay Psalm Book,[29] the earliest edition of this book to provide tunes. The use of shape notes as a teaching method for music reading spread rapidly and became immensely popular. It is interesting to note that one of the shape note collections of Andrew Law, published about 1812, carried the hearty endorsement and recommendation of William Staughton, pastor of the First Baptist Church of Philadelphia.

In the South, Baptist collections of hymns, more than any other factor, prompted tune book compilers to publish the tunes to which these hymns were being sung and to compose new tunes for others. Of the numerous oblong shape note tune books which appeared in the South, the two most widely used were William Walker's *Southern Harmony* (1835) and B. F. White's *Sacred Harp* (1844). Both Walker and White were Baptists—Walker lived at Spartanburg, South Carolina; and White lived at Hamilton, Harris County, Georgia. By present-day standards, both of these books were very poorly edited. Authors of the texts are not included. Names given for composers often indicate persons who wrote down existing melodies for the first time. In some instances the source from which the compiler selected the text is given. An examination of these two books from this standpoint is most revealing and indicates the influence of Baptist collections on the compilers.

	Southern Harmony (1835)	*Sacred Harp* (1844)
The Psalmist (1843)		38
Baptist Harmony (1834)	28	28
Dover Selection (1828)	12	9
Zion Songster (1829)	2	15

---

[28]George Pullen Jackson, *The Story of the Sacred Harp, 1844-1944,* p. 10.
[29]William Jensen Reynolds, *A Survey of Christian Hymnody* (New York: Holt, Rinehart, & Winston, 1963), p. 82.

Mercer's *Cluster* (1813)	9	12
Methodist Hymn Book (1828)	7	8
Watts's *Hymns*	5	5
Dossey's *Choice* (1820)	1	1
Rippon's *Hymns*		1
The Christian Lyre (1832)	1	

The Psalmist

Of special interest is the fact that White drew so heavily for texts for the *Sacred Harp* from *The Psalmist,* which had appeared only the previous year. Compiled by Baron Stow and Samuel F. Smith, this hymnal is a milestone in Baptist hymnody in America, and White demonstrated unusual judgment in relying on this source. At the time *The Psalmist* was published, Smith was pastor of the First Baptist Church, Newton, Massachusetts, and Stow was pastor of the Baldwin Place Baptist Church, Boston. Both men were aware of the growing need for a more contemporary compilation to replace "Winchell's Watts" and "Rippon's Watts," and the results of their efforts became a unifying force in hymnody, particularly in New England and the middle states.

However, the work of Stow and Smith was not favorably received in the South; for many of the hymns most popular in that area were omitted. Richard Fuller and Jeremiah B. Jeter attempted to remedy the situation by publishing a *Supplement to the Psalmist,* adding 106 hymns. While this supplemented edition was welcomed by the urban churches and the more educated congregations, it was somewhat advanced for the South and West. Much more appropriate for popular acceptance in these areas were W. C. Buck's *The Baptist Hymn Book* (Louisville, 1842), H. Miller's *New Selection of Psalms, Hymns, and Spiritual Songs* (Cincinnati, 1835), and J. M. Peck's *Dupuy's Hymns and Spiritual Songs* (Louisville, 1843), as well as Jesse Mercer's *Cluster* and Staunton S. Burdett's *Baptist Harmony.*

Denominational Publishing Begins

The controversy over slavery among Baptists resulted in the forming of the Southern Baptist Convention in 1845, and in the years that followed congregations in the southern states relied chiefly on their own collections. Up to this time hymnals found in Baptist churches were prepared and published by individuals. From this time on, however, denominational publishing agencies, both in the North and South, took on greater significance.

The Southern Baptist Publication Society was established in Charleston, South Carolina, in 1847; and several collections were issued. *Bap-*

tist Psalmody (1850), compiled by Basil Manly and Basil Manly, Jr., and containing 1295 hymns, was a collection of excellent quality; and the Southern Baptist Convention at the 1851 meeting in Nashville, voted to recommend it to the churches. It met with as much favor in the South as the *Psalmist* enjoyed in the North. In 1855 the Society published I. B. Woodbury's *The Casket,* and Edwin T. Winkler's *The Sacred Lute.*

Basil Manly, Jr., pastor of the First Baptist Church, Richmond (1850-54) and president of the Richmond Female Institute (1854-59) published *Baptist Chorals: A Hymn and Tune Book* (1859). The preface of this collection states:

The object of this volume is not to come in competition with hymn books now in circulation, but to render them more useful by supplying tunes adapted expressly to some of the choicest hymns. . . . hymns have been selected almost exclusively which are to be found in both the *Baptist Psalmody* and *The Psalmist,* the two books most extensively used in the Baptist churches in the United States.

Considerably removed from Charleston and Richmond were the less densely populated and more rural areas of Tennessee and Kentucky. Among the collections which enjoyed considerable regional popularity were J. M. D. Cates's *The Baptist Companion* (Nashville, 1850?) and *The Sacred Harp* (Nashville, 1867), A. B. Cates's *Baptist Songs, with Music* (Louisville, 1879), and J. R. Graves's *The New Baptist Psalmist* (Memphis, 1873). Graves, the leader of the Landmark movement among Southern Baptists and one of the most controversial denominational leaders of his day, pointed to the theological purity of his collection in the preface, stating: "In this collection there will be found no hymns that teach the doctrine of baptismal remission or ritual efficacy, no praises to be sung to dead relatives or friends, nor are children taught to pray to the angels, or desire to be angels."

The three most significant hymnals published for Baptists in the North during the last half of the nineteenth century were *The Baptist Hymn and Tune Book* (1871), *The Baptist Hymnal* (1883), and *Sursum Corda* (1898). All of these were the work of the American Baptist Publishing Society in Philadelphia. The first of these, a large collection of 980 hymns, failed to meet with general acceptance, largely because of the generally inferior quality of the tunes. The second collection is of better quality, and while it gives evidence of the rapidly emerging gospel song, it also reveals the initial impact among Baptists of *Hymns Ancient and Modern,* the most significant English hymnal of the nineteenth century. *Sursum Corda,* compiled by E. H. Johnson went even further in this direction. The compiler's disregard for the gospel song and his excessive borrowing of Anglican hymns and tunes resulted in a hymnal of the highest quality, but one unacceptable to the majority of Baptist congregations. All of this plus the Latin title was too much for too many, even among Baptists of the North.

In 1891 Basil Manly, Jr., now nearing the end of his life, published *Manly's Choice*. The Preface of this collection issued at the close of the century reveals Manly's great concern for the hymnody of Southern Baptists:

> For some years it has been apparent that the rage for novelties in singing, especially in our Sunday Schools, has been driving out of use the old, precious, standard hymns. They are not memorized as of old. They are scarcely sung at all. They are not contained in the non-denominational song books, which in many churches have usurped the places of our old hymn books.
>
> We cannot afford to lose these old hymns. They are full of the Gospel; they breathe the deepest emotions of pious hearts in the noblest strains of poetry; they have been listed and approved by successive generations of those who love the Lord; they are the surviving fittest ones from thousands of inferior productions; they are hallowed by abundant usefulness and tenderest memories. But the young people today are unfamiliar with them, and will seldom hear any of them if the present tendency goes on untouched.
>
> . . . To meet that need, the present work is offered. It is cheap and of convenient size; it contains no trash and no unreal sentiment or unsound doctrine . . . not one is inserted which is not judged worthy of a special place among the choice hymns of the language . . . Some modern tunes which are familiar and excellent would gladly have been used; but they are held under the laws of copyright and could not be procured, except at heavy expense, if at all. Two great ends have been kept in view. . . . to promote congregational singing . . . to do something toward the elevation and general culture of musical tastes among the Baptist people, whom I love.

The Gospel Song

Though Manly died shortly after this collection was published, he had felt the initial impact on Southern Baptists of the gospel song— that phenomenon which emerged in the late nineteenth century and continues to the present time. In addition to the influence of folk hymnody and campmeeting songs already mentioned, one of the major contributing factors in the rise of the gospel song was the innumerable collections of Sunday school songs. First designed solely for children, these songs were simple in character, popular in design and intended for immediate appeal. Jonathan Howe published the earliest Baptist collection of these songs in Boston in 1829. However, much more significant and influential were later collections by three Baptists—

William B. Bradbury, William H. Doane, and Robert Lowry. In New York, Bradbury compiled numerous collections from 1841 to 1867. Doane's first compilation appeared in 1861, and following Bradbury's death in 1868, Lowry was invited by Biglow and Main, Bradbury's successor, to compile and edit these collections. Some of the most widely used of these were jointly compiled by Doane and Lowry, and it is rather surprising to know that a great number of the currently favorite gospel songs first appeared in these Sunday school collections. This may be partially explained by the fact that by 1870 many Sunday schools were making provisions for adults as well as children. As evidence of this fact and the broadening scope of these collections, the introductory "Salutation" of Lowry and Doane's *Pure Gold for the Sunday School* (New York, 1871) states:

The hymns in this work are not all projected on the plane of childhood. That quiet revolution by which our Sunday Schools for children are passing up to the higher level of Bible Schools for all ages, has not been overlooked. Keeping that strictly in view, we have inserted hymns of Heaven which veteran saints can sing, hymns of Activity for the strong and buoyant, hymns of new Experience for the Christian child; as well as hymns of invitation to the unconverted, and hymns of Confession for the penitent. All through these leaflets of *Pure Gold* will be found soul-stirring hymns of Praise to God and to Christ, which the whole School can sing.

Apparently Southern Baptists felt that they should provide collections for their own Sunday schools, for in 1863 the Sunday School Board at Greenville, South Carolina, published *The Little Sunday School Hymn Book* and also C. J. Elford's *Confederate Sunday School Hymn Book*.[30] In reporting these two collections to the 1866 meeting of the Southern Baptist Convention in Russellville, Kentucky, the Sunday School Board stated that it had been unsuccessful in securing the printing of a collection of Sunday school songs with music, thereby justifying the publication of these two books.[31] *Kind Words,* a Sunday school paper for children, established in 1866, frequently contained new songs. In 1871, the Sunday School Board published *Kind Words in Melody,* made up of 59 tunes and 121 hymns which had appeared in the Sunday school paper.

To understand the significance of the Sunday school songs, it must be recognized that until even a few decades ago the Sunday school operated as a distinct organization under lay leadership, and was frequently considered a "competitor" to the church. Sunday school offerings were not considered church funds and were handled independently

---

[30]Hooper, *op. cit.,* p. 126.
[31]*Southern Baptist Convention Annual* (1866), p. 26.

of the church treasury. It is reasonable to expect that the pastor, the deacons, and the church treasurer looked with much disfavor on this siphoning off of funds which might have been received in the church services. As the Sunday school pupils were provided with literature and other materials, it is only natural that they should have their own song books.

The simple, singable Sunday school songs found a warm welcome in those churches where the regular hymn singing of the congregation had declined into a meaningless experience, lacking in vitality and warmth. When educational standards were low and cultural advantages meager, the absence of a traditional hymnody and the freedom and independence of the local congregation all joined together to provide a fertile climate for the gospel song.

Philip P. Bliss, a Baptist layman, compiled several Sunday school collections for George F. Root in Cincinnati. It was the singing of Bliss in a religious service in Chicago that first impressed Dwight L. Moody with the power of music in his evangelistic efforts. Moody secured the services of Ira D. Sankey, whose name became synonymous with the gospel song, which he popularized in both America and England.[32]

Lesser-known evangelists and lesser-known song leaders traveled throughout the southern states, and in revivals, tent meetings, camp-meetings, and street services, the gospel songs swept through village and hamlet. In many respects the gospel song may be considered a variant expression of American folk hymnody, and nowhere was there more fertile soil than among Southern Baptists.

One of these lesser known evangelists who exerted unusual influence among Baptists of the Southwest was Major W. E. Penn. A native Tennessean and an officer in the Confederate Army, Penn moved to Texas after the war and became a successful attorney at law. About 1875 he began conducting revivals as a lay-evangelist and experienced unusual success. During the next twenty years he traveled extensively throughout the Southwest, chiefly in Texas, and also preached in England and Scotland. Always, he confined his evangelistic efforts to Baptist churches and was one of the first among Baptists to have his own song leader. His insistence upon having a reed organ for his services introduced this instrument to many Baptist churches which previously had unaccompanied congregational singing. In 1881 he published his own collection of songs, *Harvest Bells,* and after this date used it exclusively in his meetings, making it the most widely used collection in the Southwest.

---

[32]In England, where *Sankey's Sacred Songs and Solos* is still published, these songs are referred to as "Sankeys."

He composed many songs for this collection and its several editions, and of unusual interest is the fact that this book has little in common with the Bliss and Sankey collections. Appropriate for his use and the people to whom he preached, this book was published in shape notes.

The Twentieth Century

The earliest publishing of gospel song collections by Southern Baptists seems to have occurred at Louisville. The Baptist Book Concern, an independent publishing firm owned by several Baptist leaders in Kentucky, published *Glorious Praise* (1904), compiled by William H. Doane and William J. Kirkpatrick, and *Song Evangel* (1906), compiled by Doane. At this same time the Sunday School Board (established in Nashville in 1891), published *The Baptist Hymn and Praise Book,* its first hymnal publication. Lansing Burrows, pastor of the First Baptist Church, Nashville, compiled this hymnal in conjunction with' a committee of denominational leaders. To the 1905 convention in Kansas City, the Board reported this book in its second printing and stated that it considered this hymnal "the very crown of its book publication."[33] The Board's report in 1911 indicated that ninety thousand copies had been circulated. In 1921 the Board published *Kingdom Songs,* compiled by I. E. Reynolds and Robert H. Coleman, and six years later reported that 333,000 copies had been circulated.

During the twenties and thirties the greatest single hymnic influence among Southern Baptists was the publishing activity of a Baptist layman in Dallas, Texas. Beginning in 1909, Robert H. Coleman published thirty-three collections, ranging from full-sized hymnals to small paper-back collections of songs.[34] The most far-reaching of these.were *The Modern Hymnal* (1926) and *The American Hymnal* (1933). The former of these is still being published by the Sunday School Board, which purchased Colemen's publishing firm in 1945. Sensitive to the hymn-singing practices of the churches he desired to serve, Coleman designed his compilations for popular appeal. Tremendous assets were his association with George W. Truett, his pastor, and his friendship with B. B. McKinney, destined to become Southern Baptists' most prolific gospel song writer. While he was no reformer of church music and proclaimed no high ideals of hymnody, he included a fine selection of standard hymns in the two hymnals mentioned above. Southern Baptist congregations in no small numbers first became acquainted with some of these hymns through his books.

---

[33]*Southern Baptist Convention Annual* (1905), p. 207.
[34]A complete listing of the publications of Colemen will be found included with his biographical sketch.

Between the two world wars a few voices championed the cause of a higher type hymnody for Southern Baptists. Like Parkinson and Manly of the previous century they spoke out against the triteness and shallowness of many of the gospel songs and pointed to the sturdiness and maturity of a nobler song. These welcomed the appearance in 1926 of *The New Baptist Hymnal,* jointly produced by the Northern and Southern conventions. It was published simultaneously in Philadelphia and Nashville by the respective publishing boards. Later Nashville editions contained three alterations which reflect differences in the usage of tunes. The tune for "Amazing grace! how sweet the sound" in the Philadelphia edition was WARWICK. In the Nashville edition this was changed to AMAZING GRACE, the Southern folk melody which had become in two brief decades unanimously accepted in Southern churches. Also, one hymn was completely deleted to make room for FOUNDATION for "How firm a foundation," whereas the Philadelphia edition provided only ADESTE FIDELIS. And for "Take my life and let it be," YARBROUGH was added as an alternate tune for HENDON.

While *The New Baptist Hymnal* was widely used in the North, it was too "new" for popular acceptance in the South. Even though it included a section of eighty-six gospel songs and a splendid selection of nineteenth-century standard hymns, there was little evidence of twentieth-century American or English hymnody. Yet, the book was simply ahead of its time, for an examination of its contents will reveal a surprising number of hymns which had to await the 1956 *Baptist Hymnal* to be discovered by Southern Baptist congregations. In spite of the fact that this hymnal was by no means widely used in Southern Baptist churches, it exerted influence in the South through its continued use for thirty years in the chapel services at the seminaries at Fort Worth and Louisville. Year after year seminary students sang from it in daily chapel services, and though few introduced it to their congregations, it is reasonable to assume that its influence helped prepare the way for the 1956 hymnal.

During this period of extraordinary denominational growth, a wide variety of hymnals could be found in churches throughout the Southern Baptist Convention. Since a local congregation is free to select its own hymnal, the publications of many independent publishers have found their way into Southern Baptist churches. Among the firms were Tabernacle Publishing Company, Hope Publishing Company, Rodeheaver Hall-Mack Company, Tullar-Meredith Company, and others. The shape note collections of "convention music" published by James D. Vaughn Company, Stamps-Baxter Music Company, and the Hartford Music Company enjoyed tremendous popularity in rural communities in many states; and the "fifth Sunday singings" were part of community life.

The first hymnal to bring about any degree of unanimity in the congregational singing of Southern Baptists was *The Broadman Hymnal* (1940), a hymn book still used by many congregations. This was compiled by B. B. McKinney, music editor of the Baptist Sunday School Board. Independent publishers who held the publishing rights to many copyrighted gospel songs looked with disfavor upon the Sunday School Board's entrance into the hymnal publishing field. They felt sure that for this hymnal's success, McKinney would have to draw heavily on their copyrighted materials. With the exception of Coleman, these publishers granted permission for the use of only two copyrights each, and this with the usual permission fee. The absence of many long-time favorite gospel songs is thereby explained. Because of this restriction McKinney was forced to rely on gospel songs no longer under copyright protection and also on his own writing. This field he knew well; for he was of the gospel song tradition, having composed in its idiom for more than twenty years.

No accurate records of distribution are available on *The Broadman Hymnal,* but on the basis of incomplete existing records, a conservative estimate indicates that seven or eight million copies have been circulated since 1940, making this one of the most popular hymnals ever published in America. It was published in both round and shape note editions, the latter edition helping to introduce this hymnal particularly to those areas where shape note singing was enthusiastically practiced. So extensively was it used that it became, more that any other previous collection, the most generally used hymnal among Southern Baptist churches. As such, it became a unifying force in congregational singing and gradually displaced other collections.

In spite of the acceptance which *The Broadman Hymnal* received, within a decade there was a growing need for a new hymnal. The growing awareness of the significance of music in the churches, the increasing influence of the seminary music schools, and the appearance of better-trained leadership in church music all furthered this cause. In 1953 plans for a new hymnal were launched by the Sunday School Board, the publishing agency of the Southern Baptist Convention. A representative committee of thirty-seven people—pastors, theologians, teachers, church musicians, state music secretaries, and other denominational leaders—was selected to begin work on the new hymnal.

W. Hines Sims, editor of the hymnal and chairman of the committee, guided the work of the committee, always aware of the responsibility of providing a compilation suitable to the needs of more than thirty thou-

sand Southern Baptist churches scattered throughout the nation. The
Baptist Hymnal was published in 1956, the largest and most eclectic
compilation for Southern Baptists in this century. In eight years since
its initial appearance, more than four million copies have been circulated,
and many more churches each year join the ranks of Southern Baptists
who sing from the *Baptist Hymnal*

> Praise God, from whom all blessings flow;
> Praise Him, all creatures here below;
> Praise Him above, ye heavenly host;
> Praise Father, Son, and Holy Ghost.

Baptist Collections of Hymns
Published in America[35]

Date	Title	Compiler	Place Published
1762	*Evangelical Hymns and Songs* (reprint of 1750 English ed.)	Benjamin Wallin	Boston
1766	*Hymns and Spiritual Songs*	Unknown	Newport, R. I.
1773	*Hymns and Spiritual Songs*	Unknown	Williamsburg, Va.
1782	A collection (title unknown)	Philip Hughes	Wilmington, Del.
1782	*A Choice Collection of Hymns*	Unknown	Philadelphia
1784	*Divine Hymns, or Spiritual Songs*	Joshua Smith	Norwich, Conn.
1784	*A Choice Collection of Hymns*	Enoch Story, Jr.	Philadelphia
1786	*Hymns on Different Spiritual Subjects*	Benjamin Cleavland	Norwich, Conn.
1787	*The Works of David Culy* (reprint of 1726 English ed.)	David Culy	Boston
1790	*Collection of Sacred Ballads*	Andrew Broaddus	Virginia
1790	*A Selection of Psalms and Hymns*	Samuel Jones and Burgis Allison	Philadelphia
1791	*Baptismal Hymns*	Unknown	Boston
1792	*A Selection of Hymns* (reprint of 1787 English ed.)	John Rippon	Elizabeth Town, New Jersey
1792	*A Collection of Evangelical Hymns*	John Stanford	New York
1793	*Hymns and Spiritual Songs*	Eleazer Clay	Richmond, Va.
1796	*Hymns* (reprint of 1783 English ed.)	Richard Burnham	Boston
1798	*Selection of Hymns and Spiritual Songs*	Andrew Broaduus	Richmond, Va.
1799	*A Collection of Evangelical Hymns*	A. Harpending	Mount Holly, N. J.
1801	*Hymns* (reprinted from Medley's English editions, 1785-1800)	Samuel Medley	Boston
1801	*The Christian's Pocket Companion*	John Courtney	Richmond, Va.

---

[35]Because of space limitations only abbreviated titles are used. The listing includes
collections published by or for Baptists but does not include the many Sunday school
collections by Robert Lowry, W. H. Doane and others, nor the collections of splinter
groups which developed in the nineteenth century.

Year	Title	Author	Location
1803	*Hymns and Spiritual Songs*	John Courtney	Richmond, Va.
1804	*Christian Harmonist*	Samuel Holyoke	Salem, Mass.
1807	*Selection of Evangelical Hymns*	William Staughton	Philadelphia
1807	*Selection of Evangelical Hymns*	Unknown	Burlington, N. J.
1808	*Original Hymns and Spiritual Songs*	Lewis Baldwin	Philadelphia
1808	*Hymns and Poems on Various Subjects*	James Fenn	Schenectady, N. Y.
1808	*Selection of Hymns and Psalms*	Daniel Dodge	Wilmington, Del.
1808	*Boston Collection of Sacred and Devotional Hymns*	Unknown	Boston
1809	*Hymns and Spiritual Songs*	Ebenezer Jayne	Morristown, N. J.
1809	*Selection of Hymns and Spiritual Songs*	William Parkinson	New York
1810	*New Selection of Seven Hundred Evangelical Hymns* (reprint of 1806 English ed.)	John Dobell	Morristown, N. J.
1812	*New Selection of Hymns*	William Collier	Boston
1813	*Cluster of Spiritual Songs, Divine Hymns and Sacred Poems*	Jesse Mercer	Augusta, Ga.
1813	*An Appendix, from the Olney Hymns, with Additional Hymns*	William Staughton	Philadelphia
1814	*Selection of Hymns, Psalms and Spiritual Songs*	Silas M. Noel	Frankfort, Ky.
1815	*Selection of Hymns and Spiritual Songs*	George C. Sedgwick	Fredericksburg
1816	*Selection of Hymns for Public Worship*	Archibald Maclay	New York
1817	*Selection of Hymns*	Paul Himes and Jonathan Wilson	Greenfield, Mass.
1817	*Pawtucket Collection of Conference Hymns*	David Benedict	Providence, R. I.
1817	*Dyer's New Selection of Sacred Music*	Samuel Dyer	Baltimore
1818	*Hymns and Spiritual Songs*	Starke Dupuy	West Tennessee
1819	*An Arrangement of . . . Watts*	James Winchell	Boston
1819	*Sacred Harmony*	James Winchell	Boston
1820	*Psalms and Hymns of Dr. Watts Arranged by Dr. Rippon*	John Rippon	Philadelphia
1820	*The Choice*	William Dossey	Philadelphia
1821	*Selection of Hymns*	Thomas B. Ripley	Portland, Me.
1823	*A Selection of Hymns*	John Purify	Raleigh, N. C.
1824	*Baptist Hymn Book*	James Fenn	Unknown
1825	*Baptist Hymn Book*	Wm. P. Biddle and Wm. P. Newborn	Washington
1825	*Choice Collection of the Latest Social and Camp Meeting Hymns and Spiritual Songs*	Lewis Skidmore	Baltimore
1825	*Hymns, Psalms, and Spiritual Songs*	Absalom Graves	Louisville, Ky.
1826	*Young Christian's Companion*	G. F. Davis	Boston

Year	Title	Author/Editor	Place
1827	Rippon's *Watts* with Rippon's *Selections*	C. G. Sommers and John L. Dagg	Philadelphia
1828	*Dover Selection of Spiritual Songs*	Andrew Broaddus	Richmond
1828	*Conference Hymns* (2nd ed.)	Daniel Greene	Providence
1828	*Philadelphia Collecton of Sacred Music*	Samuel Dyer	New York
1829	*Selection of Hymns*	Enoch W. Freeman	Exeter, N. H.
1829	*The Baptist Songster*	R. Winchell	Wethersfield, Conn.
1829	*Selection of Favorite Hymns*	J. A. Burke	Albany, N. Y.
1829	*Choice Hymns*	Jonathan Howe	Boston
1830	*Baptist Conference and Prayer Meeting Hymn Book*	Paris M. Davis	Binghamton, N. Y.
1830	*A Selection of Hymns*	C. M. Fuller	Auburn, N. Y.
1831	*Collection of Psalms, Hymns and Spiritual Songs*	Luke Barker	New York
1831	*Selection of Hymns*	John Courtney	Richmond
1832	*Hymns of Zion*	B. M. Hill	New York
1832	*Manual of Christian Psalmody*	Rufus Babcock, Jr.	Boston
1834	*Union Hymns*	Rufus Babcock, Jr. and Lowell Mason	Boston
1834	*Baptist Harmony*	Staunton S. Burdett	Philadelphia
1835	*Social Sacred Melodist*	Oliver Shaw	Providence, R. I.
1835	*New Selection of Psalms, Hymns and Spiritual Songs*	H. Miller	Cincinnati
1835	*Conference Manual*	Ebenezer E. Cummins and Edmund Worth	Concord, N. H.
1835	*Southern Harmony*	William Walker	New Haven, Conn
1836	*Select Hymns*	J. H. Linsley and Gustavus F. Davis	Hartford, Conn.
1836	*Christian Melodies*	Stephen P. Hill	Baltimore
1836	*Virginia Selection of Psalms, Hymns and Spiritual Songs*	Andrew Broaddus	Richmond, Va.
1839	*Revival Hymns*	John Butler	Boston
1841	*Hymns for the Vestry and Fireside*	Sewall S. Cutting	Boston
1842	*Baptist Hymn Book*	William C. Buck	Louisville, Ky.
1842	*Hymns for Social and Private Worship*	J. B. Hague	Unknown
1843	*Dupuy's Hymns and Spiritual Songs*	J. M. Peck	Louisville, Ky.
1843	*A Collection of Hymns*	A. A. Guernsey	Strongsville, Ohio
1843	*Hymns for Social Meetings*	A. D. Gillette	Philadelphia
1843	*The Psalmist*	Baron Stow and Samuel F. Smith	Boston

Year	Title	Author/Editor	Place
1844	Sacred Harp	B. F. White and E. J. King	Philadelphia
1845	The Evangelical Harp	Jacob Knapp	Utica, N. Y.
1846	The Companion	J. M. D. Cates	Nashville
1848	The Social Psalmist	Smith and Stow	Boston
1848	Ocean Melodies	J. H. Hanaford	Boston
1849	Conference Hymns	John Dowling	New York
1849	Christian Melodist	Joseph Banvard	Boston
1849	Baptist Harp	George B. Ide and Edgar M. Levy	Philadelphia (ABPS)*
1849	Manual of the Sacred Choir	Eli Ball	Richmond
1850	Supplement to The Psalmist	Fuller and Jeter	Philadelphia
1850	A Collection of . . . Hymns	L. Burkitt	Philadelphia
1850?	The Baptist Companion	J. M. D. Cates	Nashville
1850?	Select Hymns for Public and Private Worship	Second Baptist Church Committee	Philadelphia
1850	Baptist Psalmody	Basil Manly and Basil Manly Jr.	Charleston, S. C.
1851	Southwestern Psalmist	Sidney Dyer	Louisville
1855	Social *Harp*	John G. McCurry	Philadelphia
1855	The Casket	I. B. Woodbury	Charleston, S. C.
1855	The Sacred Lute	Edwin T. Winkler	Charleston, S. C.
1856	Congregational Psalmist	Unknown	Rochester, N. Y.
1857	Baptist Hymn and Tune Book	John Stanford Holme	New York
1857	Prayer Meeting Hymn Book	William Crane	Baltimore
1858	Baptist edition of the *Sabbath Hymn Book*	Francis Wayland	New York
1858	Revival Gems	Joseph Banvard	Boston
1858	The Sacred Lyre	J. Aldrich	Boston
1858	The Vestry Harp	N. M. Perkins	Boston
1858	Southern Psalmist	J. R. Graves and J. M. Pendleton	Nashville
1859	Church Melodies	Hastings and Turnbull	New York
1859	Baptist Chorals	Basil Manly Jr.	Richmond
1859	Melodies of Zion	H. D. Phinney	Oswego, N. Y.
1860	The Psalmist, with Music	B. F. Edmands	Boston
1860	Spiritual Songs	James Inglis	Detroit
1861	Union Harp	Edwin Burnham	Philadelphia
1862	Baptismal Harmonies	Edmund Turney	New York
1863	The Little Sunday School Hymn Book	Unknown	Charleston, S. C.
1863	Confederate Sunday School Hymn Book	C. J. Elford	Charleston, S. C.
1864	Devotional Hymn and Tune Book	William B. Bradbury	Philadelphia

*This is the first hymnal published by the American Baptist Publication Society, Philadelphia.

Year	Title	Author/Editor	Place
1865	*Revival Hymns*	A. B. Earle	Boston
1865	*Sunday School Hymn Book*	C. J. Elford	Greenville, S. C.
1865	*The Baptist Vocalist*	C. A. Worley	Carrollton, Illinois
1866	*Christian Harmony*	William Walker	Philadelphia
1867	*Sacred Harp*	J. M. D. Cates	Nashville
1867	*Revival Hymns*	Edwin Burnham	Boston
1868	*Conference and Revival Hymns*	John Dowling	New York
1868	*Chapel Melodies*	Vail and Lowry	New York
1869	*Songs of the Sanctuary* (Baptist edition)	T. S. Griffiths	New York
1870	*Revival Songs*	Emerson Andrews	Boston
1870	*Songs of Devotion*	William H. Doane	New York
1871	*Service of Song for Baptist Churches*	S. L. Caldwell and A. J. Gordon	Boston
1871	*Baptist Hymn and Tune Book*	H. G. Weston and John M. Evans	Philadelphia
1871	*The Baptist Praise Book*	Committee	New York
1871	*Kind Words in Melody*	Unknown	Greenville, S. C.
1872	*Vestry Hymn and Tune Book*	A. J. Gordon	Boston
1873	*Heaven in Song*	H. C. Fish	New York
1873	*New Baptist Psalmist*	J. R. Graves	Memphis
1873	*The Little Seraph*	J. R. Graves	Memphis
1874	*Christian Praise*	Charles D. Bridgman	New York
1878	*Calvary Selection of Spiritual Songs*	R. S. MacArthur	New York
1879	*Gospel Hymn and Tune Book*	Robert Lowry and W. H. Doane	Philadelphia
1879	*Baptist Songs, with Music*	A. B. Cates	Louisville
1881	*Songs for the Lord's House*	C. D. Bridgman and Henry Camp	New York
1881	*Harvest Bells*	W. E. Penn	Unknown
1883	*Baptist Hymnal*	Committee	Philadelphia
1884	*Harvest Bells No. 2*	Penn and Hunt	Cincinnati
1886	*A Collection of Old and New Songs*	Brown and Hunt	St. Louis
1886	*Harvest Bells No. 3*	Penn and Lincoln	Cincinnati
1892	*Manly's Choice*	Basil Manly Jr.	Richmond
1892	*Soul Songs*	Committee	Waco, Texas
1894	*Life Songs*	Theron Brown	Boston
1894	*The Coronation Hymnal*	A. J. Gordon	Boston
1896?	*Harvest Bells* (from Nos. 1,2,3)	A. B. P. S.	Philadelphia
1896	*Songs of the Kingdom*	W. H. Doane	Philadelphia
1897	*In Excelsis* (Calvary edition)	R. S. MacArthur	New York
1898	*Sursum Corda*	E. H. Johnson	Philadelphia
1902	*Hymns New and Old*	T. T. Eaton	New York
1902	*The Endeavor Hymnal*	H. B. Grose	New York
1904	*Baptist Hymn and Praise Book*	Lansing Burrows	Nashville

Year	Title	Editor/Compiler	Place
1904	*Glorious Praise*	W. H. Doane and W. J. Kirkpatrick	Louisville
1906	*Church Hymns and Tunes*	Turner, Tupper, and Biddle	New York
1906	*The Praise Book*	H. B. Grose	Boston
1906	*Song Evangel*	W. H. Doane	Louisville
1909	*The Evangel**	Robert H. Coleman	Philadelphia
1910	*Heart Praise*	J. A. Brown	Fort Worth
1914	*The New Baptist Praise Book*	Shepard and Lawrence	Philadelphia
1918	*Popular Hymnal*	Robert H. Coleman	Dallas
1920	*Songs of Redemption*	W. Plunkett Martin and J. W. Jelks	Atlanta, Ga.
1921	*Victorious Praise*	S. S. Board	Nashville
1921	*Kingdom Songs*	I. E. Reynolds and Robert H. Coleman	Nashville
1923	*The Chapel Book*	John L. Hill	Nashville
1923	*Living Hymns*	Committee	Philadelphia
1925	*Jehovah's Praise*	Reynolds and McKinney	Fort Worth
1925	*Service Hymnal*	S. W. Beazley	Chicago
1926	*The Modern Hymnal*	Robert H. Coleman	Dallas
1926	*The New Baptist Hymnal*	Committee	Philadelphia and Nashville
1933	*Songs of Faith*	George W. Card	Nashville
1933	*The American Hymnal*	Robert H. Coleman	Dallas
1935	*Hymns for Creative Living*	Judson Press	Philadelphia
1936	*Abiding Songs*	George W. Card	Nashville
1937	*Songs of Victory*	B. B. McKinney	Nashville
1940	*The Song Evangel*	B. B. McKinney	Nashville
1940	*The Broadman Hymnal*	B. B. McKinney	Nashville
1941	*Christian Worship*	Committee	Philadelphia
1945	*Look and Live Songs*	B. B. McKinney	Nashville
1946	*Songs of Life*	B. B. McKinney	Nashville
1947	*Voice of Praise*	B. B. McKinney	Nashville
1954	*Crusade Songs*	W. Hines Sims	Nashville
1956	*Baptist Hymnal*	Committee	Nashville

---

*This is the first collection of Robert H. Coleman. Of his other publications, only the major ones are listed here. The complete listing of his publications may be found included in his biographical account.

Part I

Hymn Texts and Tunes

A charge to keep I have 358

This hymn by Charles Wesley first appeared in *Short Hymns on Select Passages of Holy Scriptures* (Vol. I, 1762, No. 188), in two eight-line stanzas. It is based on Leviticus 8:35.

Boylston, composed by Lowell Mason, first appeared in his *The Choir, or Union Collection of Church Music* (1832, No. 165), where it was set to "Our days are as grass." Boylston is the name of a town in Massachusetts, and also a well-known street in Boston.

It is most interesting to note the similarity between this tune and Hobart which, indicated as "arranged from an Ancient Chant," appears in I. B. Woodbury's *New Lute of Zion* (1853, p. 149) and in the 1857 tune edition of the *Methodist Hymnal* of 1849:

UNISON.
1. Give to the winds thy fears; Hope, and be un - dis - may'd;

UNISON.
God hears thy sighs and counts thy tears; God shall lift up thy head;

"A Child of the King"—*see* My Father is rich in houses and lands

1

William Cowper's hymn first appeared in the *Olney Hymns,* Book II (1779). Originally in five stanzas, the present version begins with the second stanza. The first stanza begins, "The spirit breathes upon the word."

BURLINGTON was composed by John F. Burrowes. It is believed that this tune first appeared in 1830 in England. The earliest American usage the writer has found is J. Ireland Tucker's *Hymnal with Tunes Old and New* (New York, 1872, No. 363).

A mighty fortress is our God   40

Martin Luther's mighty hymn of the Reformation, "Ein' feste Berg ist unser Gott," inspired by Psalm 46, first appeared, undoubtedly with this tune, in Klug's *Gesangbuch* (Wittenburg, 1529). No copies of this collection are now extant. In all probability the hymn was written at the time of the Diet of Speyer, when the German princes made their formal protest against the attacks on their liberties and hence gained the name "Protestants." In 1539, ten years after the hymn first appeared, Miles Coverdale published an English translation in his *Goostly Psalmes and Spiritualle Songes,* which begins:

> Oure God is a defence and towre
> A good armour and good weapen,
> He hath ben ever oure helpe and sucoure
> In all the troubles that we have ben in.
> Therefore wyl we never drede
> For any wonderous dede
> By water or by londe
> In hilles or the sea-sonde.
> Our God hath them al i his hond.

Thomas Carlyle published a translation in 1831, "A safe stronghold our God is still," which is generally used in England and Canada today. Our translation, the most widely known in America, is by Frederick H. Hedge. Written in 1852, this translation first appeared in W. H. Furness's *Gems of German Verse* (Philadelphia, 1853), and later the same year in *Hymns for the Church of Christ* (Boston), edited by Hedge and F. D. Huntington. Julian gives a detailed account of the translations of this hymn, revealing that by 1900 over eighty translations in more than fifty-three languages had appeared. In the *Handbook to the Church Hymnary* (London, 1927) James Moffatt describes this as being the "greatest hymn of the greatest man of the greatest period of German history."

EIN' FESTE BURG appeared in *Kirchen Gesänge* (Nuremberg, 1531) and four years later in the second edition of Klug's *Gesangbuch*, 1535. The present version is based on the arrangement and harmonization of J. S. Bach.

Here is a stalwart, sturdy tune of unusual virility which has been incorporated in major works of several composers with striking effectiveness. It appears in a cantata by the same name by J. S. Bach, in Meyerbeer's opera *Les Huguenots*, in Mendelssohn's *Reformation Symphony*, in Wagner's *Kaisermarsch*, and in Nicolai's *Fest Ouvertüre*.

A parting hymn we sing 397

This hymn was one of seven contributed by Aaron R. Wolfe under the signature "A. R. W." to Thomas Hastings' *Church Melodies* (1858). The author has stated:

I can remember nothing definitely about it, except that in looking over the topics in the hymn-books with the idea of endeavoring to supply deficiencies, I thought something of this kind might be suitable in rising from the Lord's table.

LABAN was composed by Lowell Mason in 1830.

A ruler once came to Jesus by night 215

William T. Sleeper is the author of this hymn. The composer, George C. Stebbins, in his *Memoirs and Reminiscences* (pp. 76-77), relates the following account of the writing in August, 1877, when he was assisting Dr. George F. Pentecost in an evangelistic campaign in Worcester, Massachusetts.

During those meetings, one of the subjects preached upon was the "New Birth." While presenting the truth, enforcing it by referring to various passages of Scripture, Dr. Pentecost quoted our Lord's words to Nicodemus, "Verily, verily, I say unto you, ye must be born again," John 3:3-7. It occurred to me that by taking the line, "Verily, verily, I say unto thee," from the third verse, and putting it with the line, "Ye must be born again," and by transferring the word "I" from the middle of the first line to the beginning, so it would read, "I verily, verily, say unto thee, Ye must be born again," those passages would then fall into rhythmical form, and by the use of some repetitions could be made available for a musical setting, and also for a chorus to a hymn, if some suitable verses could be found. . . . I spoke to Reverend W. W. [*sic*.] Sleeper, one of the pastors of the city who sometimes wrote hymns, of my impression and asked him if he would write me some verses on the subject. He acted at once upon my suggestion and soon after came to me with the hymn that bears his name. Before the meetings closed a musical setting was made.

The hymn first appeared in *Gospel Hymns No. 3* (1878).

BORN AGAIN is the name given this tune by the Hymnal Committee.

A wonderful Saviour is Jesus my Lord 272

Fanny J. Crosby wrote this text, and the musical setting was composed by William J. Kirkpatrick. It first appeared in *The Finest of the Wheat No. 1,* compiled by George D. Elderkin, R. R. McCabe, John R. Sweney, and Kirkpatrick (Chicago: R. R. McCabe, 1890, No. 49).

KIRKPATRICK is the name given this tune by the Hymnal Committee.

Abide with me: fast falls the eventide 295

Henry F. Lyte, the author of this hymn, had served for twenty-four years as curate at Lower Brixham in Devonshire, England. Because of failing health, he had been advised by his physician to move to another climate, and on September 4, 1847, he preached his final sermon to his congregation. In the preface to Lyte's *Remains,* his daughter, Anna Maria Maxwell Hogg writes: "In the evening of the same day he placed in the hands of a near and dear relative the little hymn, 'Abide with me,' with the air of his own composing, adapted to the words."

H. T. Bindley, in a letter published in *The Spectator* (Oct. 3, 1925), claimed that the hymn was written in 1820, shortly after Lyte had visited a dying friend, William Augustus Le Hunte. Bindley offered as evidence a copy of this hymn said to have been given to Le Hunte's brother. Some authorities have accepted Bindley's evidence since, there is no apparent conflict with Mrs. Hogg's statement, which does not emphatically state that the hymn was *first* written on September 4, 1847.

The author's great-grandson, Walter Maxwell-Lyte, in an article in the *London Times* (Nov. 1, 1947), attempted to resolve the controversy by giving all the known information. The Le Hunte manuscript is not an autograph but a copy, and it bears evidence of being written in 1847. The article reproduced a letter dated August 25, 1847, written by Lyte to Julia Bolton, who later married Lyte's youngest son. The poem is included with the letter and is referred to as "my latest effusion." This evidence seems to point to the conclusion that the hymn was written in the summer—July or August—of 1847, and before September 4. The hymn was first published in Lyte's *Remains* (London, 1850). Its first appearance in America was in Henry Ward Beecher's *Plymouth Collection* (1855), with the notation that the hymn was meant to be read and not sung. This hymn has enjoyed widespread usage and perhaps has been most helpful to Christian hearts in times of trial and distress. It was the last hymn Edith Cavell sang before she suffered martyrdom in Belgium, October 12, 1915, during World War I.

EVENTIDE was composed by William H. Monk for this hymn for the first edition of *Hymns Ancient and Modern* (London, 1861). At least two versions of the writing of this tune have been circulated. One version set forth in some of the most reliable writings states that this tune was composed in ten minutes at the close of a meeting of the committee compiling *Hymns Ancient and Modern,* in spite of a piano lesson being given in an adjoining room. After the composer's death, his widow reportedly said that her husband wrote this tune "in her company out-of-doors at a time of great sorrow, after they had stood some time watching the glory of the setting sun."

Alas! and did my Saviour bleed   101

Isaac Watts included this hymn in his *Hymns and Spiritual Songs* (1707) in six four-line stanzas, entitled "Godly sorrow arising from the sufferings of Christ." The omitted stanzas two and five are:

> Thy body slain, sweet Jesus, Thine—
> And bathed in its own blood—
> While the firm mark of Wrath Divine
> His soul in anguish stood.

> Thus might I hide my blushing face
> While his dear cross appears;
> Dissolve my heart in thankfulness,
> And melt mine eyes to tears.

All of the stanzas except the final one have been subjected to alterations. The fourth line of stanza one, originally "For such a worm as I," has been changed in some collections to read "For such a one as I" and in others, "For sinners such as I." This latter alteration, found in most hymnals today, is the one adopted for use in the hymnal. Deleting the word "worm" involves a literary expression and in no way implies any theological compromise.

In her autobiography, Fanny J. Crosby tells how "my soul flooded with celestial light" at the time of her conversion, when this hymn was sung.

AVON, sometimes called MARTYRDOM, has also been known as FENWICK, DRUMCLOG, INVERNESS, and ALL SAINTS. This tune appeared toward the end of the eighteenth century, printed on leaflets for use in music classes. It was in common or duple time. In triple time, it appeared in R. A. Smith's *Sacred Music Sung in St. George's Church,* second edition (Edinburgh, 1825), where it is called an "old Scottish melody." In the same form, it was included in J. Robertson's *The*

Seraph, a Selection of Psalms and Hymns (Glasgow, 1827) with the footnote, "The above tune, FENWICK, or MARTYRDOM, and by some called DRUMCLOG, was composed by Mr. Hugh Wilson, a native of Fenwick." After the tune appeared in Smith's collection, Wilson's heirs brought legal action after his death to validate Wilson's ownership of copyright. In view of the fact that this verdict involved only ownership and not composership, and because of the similarity of this tune to a Scottish ballad, "Helen of Kirkconnel," as pointed out by Miss Anne Gilchrist in *The Choir* (July, 1934), it is quite possible that Wilson adapted an old Scottish melody. In *Companion to Congregational Praise*, Erik Routley says:

> The tune seems therefore to be owed in equal measure to three sources— a Scottish traditional melody, Hugh Wilson's arrangement of it in duple time, and R. A. Smith's rearrangement in triple time. Since the triple rhythm is . . . indispensable to the tune, the contribution of Smith seems to us at least as great as that of Wilson. It remains one of the finest, most dignified, and most celebrated of all psalm-tunes.

Alas! and did my Saviour bleed ("At the Cross")   94

Isaac Watts's text is discussed above. The words of the refrain

> At the cross, at the cross where I first saw the light,
>   And the burden of my heart rolled away,
> It was there by faith I received my sight,
>   And now I am happy all the day!

were added or more probably adapted by Ralph E. Hudson when he composed the tune HUDSON.

HUDSON, in its present version, first appeared in *Songs of Peace, Love and Joy,* compiled and published by Hudson (Alliance, Ohio, 1885, No. 81). Two years later Hudson included this in his *Songs for the Ransomed.*

Because of the difference in character of the music for the stanzas and that of the refrain, it is quite likely that the refrain melody was known at this time and was used by Hudson in completing this hymn. Further evidence supports this possibility by the fact that this refrain melody appears as a separate tune in *Glad Hallelujahs,* edited by J. R. Sweney and William J. Kirkpatrick (Philadelphia: Thos. T. Tasker, 1887, No. 123). It is set to Charles Wesley's "O how happy are they who the Saviour obey," with a da capo refrain using the text, "At the cross, at the cross where I first saw the light." The tune is said to be "arranged by E. E. Nickerson." The same treatment is used for this refrain melody in the *Emory Hymnal* (Philadelphia: John J. Hood,

1887, No. 98), with original stanzas provided by R. Kelso Carter and the same refrain text as above.

While it is recognized that songbook compilers of this period were not always careful in giving accurate information concerning authors and composers of hymns and tunes, it is unlikely that Hudson's name would have been omitted in the two compilations published by Tasker and Hood if he had been the composer of the refrain melody. The most plausible answer seems to be that the refrain, both words and melody, emerged from the camp meeting tradition, and were added by Hudson to his original tune, using Watts's hymn for the stanzas. A comparison of the central theme of the stanzas with that of the refrain text is most revealing.

All creatures of our God and King   3

The childlike delight of Francis of Assisi in the wonderful works of God is clearly reflected in this paraphrase of his "Canticle of the Sun." The original text was written during the unusually hot summer of 1225, when he was very ill and suffering the loss of his sight. His misery was increased by a swarm of field mice in his straw hut. How extraordinary that such a masterpiece should come from such circumstances! This paraphrase was written for a children's Whitsuntide festival at Leeds, England, by William H. Draper, while he was rector of Adel, Yorkshire, 1899-1919. It was first published in a small collection of Draper's hymns in 1926 and was included in *School Worship* (London, 1926).

LASST UNS ERFREUEN. This tune first appeared in *Geistliche Kirchengesang,* a Roman Catholic hymnal published in Cologne (1623). Apparently it was well known in the seventeenth century among Roman Catholics in southern Germany, but it was not included in the Protestant hymnals of Germany. This forgotten German tune was revived in the present century and appeared in *The English Hymnal* (London, 1906), harmonized by Ralph Vaughan Williams. If the fermata at the end of the second line is disregarded, this melody may be sung as a two-, three-, or four-part canon at the unison, and its possibilities for antiphonal singing are obvious.

All glory, laud, and honor   151

It is generally accepted that the original Latin hymn, "Gloria, laus, et honor," consisting of thirty-nine couplets, is the work of Theodulph, Bishop of Orleans. It was probably written about 820 while he was imprisoned at Angers by King Louis I. There is unfounded legend that Theodulph's release from prison was occasioned by his singing of this hymn from the window of his cell while the king was passing by.

7

Numerous English translations of this hymn for Palm Sunday have been made. John Mason Neale's first translation appeared in his *Medieval Hymns* (1851), "Glory and honour and laud." His second effort, "Glory and laud and honour," in his *Hymnal Noted* (1854), was altered to our present first line in the 1859 trial edition of *Hymns Ancient and Modern* (London).

ST. THEODULPH first appeared in a small twelve-page pamphlet, *Ein andachtiges Gebet* (Leipzig, 1615), as the second of two five-part tunes for the hymn "Valet will ich dir geben" by Herberger. Haeussler's *The Story of Our Hymns* (p. 190) notes that prior to World War II, a copy of this original pamphlet was preserved in the city library of Breslau. This tune was first associated with the present hymn in *Hymns Ancient and Modern* (London, 1861).

All hail the power of Jesus' name 132, 133, 134

This hymn by Edward Perronet has become the traditional opening hymn for the meetings every five years of the Baptist World Alliance. The initial stanza of this hymn first appeared in the *Gospel Magazine* (VI, Nov., 1779), with the tune by William Shrubsole, later known as MILES LANE. In the April, 1780, issue of this publication, this stanza with seven additional stanzas was published under the title, "On the Resurrection, the Lord Is King." The complete hymn was included in Perronet's *Occasional Verses, Moral and Sacred, Published for the Instruction and Amusement of the Candidly Serious and Religious* (1785). This hymn has undergone many alterations, the most extensive of which occurred in John Rippon's *Selection of Hymns* (1787). The present version is based on Rippon's alteration, which in stanza one involves one word; in stanza two, two lines; in stanza three, three lines. The fourth stanza is original with Rippon. This is one of two hymns in the hymnal which is provided with three tunes, and the singing of this stalwart hymn to any of these tunes is a thrilling experience. Percy Dearmer's succinct comment in his *Songs of Praise Discussed* is: "C.M., but not when it is sung!"

CORONATION (132) was composed for this hymn by Oliver Holden in 1792 and first appeared in Holden's *Union Harmony, or Universal Collection of Sacred Music* (Boston, 1793). The tune name is from the repeated fourth line of each stanza, "And crown Him Lord of all."

MILES LANE (133) first appeared anonymously in the *Gospel Magazine* (Nov., 1779) with the first stanza of this hymn. Soon after this it appeared in Addington's *Collection of Psalm Tunes* (London, 1780) where it was named MILES LANE and the composer given as William Shrubsole.

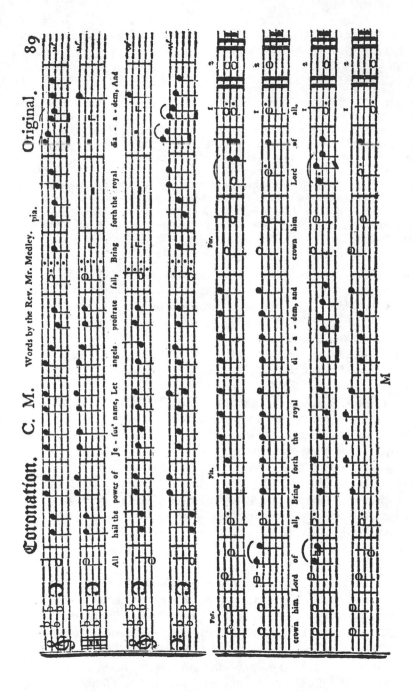

FROM HOLDEN'S *Union Harmony*

9

Ralph Vaughan Williams, in an article in the *Manchester Guardian* in 1943, describes Shrubsole as a "one-tune man" remembered by a single melody.

Of course, "Miles Lane" owes something to the splendid words to which it is set . . . But it was left to Shrubsole to add the coping-stone to the structure with his twofold repetition of the words "Crown Him". . . Elgar is credibly reported to have pronounced this tune the finest in English hymnody. . . . Without Veit Bach there would never have been John Sebastian. Would the *Magic Flute* ever have existed without the spade-work of Adam Hiller? These lesser people, with their limited but intense vision, can concentrate that vision into sixteen bars better than those great ones whose minds are occupied with symphonies forty minutes long, and it is certainly true that whereas Shrubsole could not have written *Gerontius,* Elgar could not have written "Miles Lane."

Stephen Addington, who named this tune, was minister of Miles' Lane Meeting House, London, when he prepared his *Collection of Psalm Tunes.* Miles' Lane is a shortened corruption of "St. Michael's Lane," and McCutchan (*Hymn Tune Names,* p. 103) states that this corruption is first mentioned in the 1758 *London Guide.*

DIADEM (134) was written for this hymn in 1838 by James Ellor when he was only nineteen years of age. Ellor was a hat maker by trade and directed the music at the Wesleyan Chapel, Droylsden, near Manchester, England. After writing this tune, Ellor took it to the hat factory, where it was sung and enthusiastically received. Sufficient copies were made so that it might be sung at the forthcoming Sunday school anniversary at the Wesleyan Chapel, and very soon the singing of this tune became a custom for all anniversary events throughout the area.

Those who attended the Baptist World Alliance meeting in Rio de Janeiro in 1960 will long remember the thrill of the closing session in the Maracana Stadium as two hundred thousand joined in singing this hymn with this tune.

All people that on earth do dwell   13

Rowland E. Prothero in *The Psalms in Human Life* says that this hymn and tune "survives all the changes of thought and fashion that the progress of four centuries has witnessed." This metrical version of Psalm 100, ascribed to William Kethe, appeared in *Fourscore and Seven Psalms of David* (Geneva, 1561) and in Day's *Psalter* (published in London the same year). The only alteration from the original in our text is the word "flock" in stanza two, which was "folck", an old spelling of "folk". However, the word "folk" is a better translation of the Hebrew, which is equivalent to "people" in the familiar translation "we are his people and the sheep of his pasture."

This hymn is mentioned in Shakespeare's *The Merry Wives of Windsor* (Act II, Sc. I): "They do no more adhere and keep peace together than the Hundredth Psalm to the tune of Greensleeves." Longfellow, in *The Courtship of Miles Standish,* calls it "that grand old Puritan anthem." It was the first congregational hymn used at the coronation of Queen Elizabeth II, June 2, 1953.

OLD 100TH was composed or adapted by Louis Bourgeois for the 1551 edition of the *Genevan Psalter,* where it was set to the French version of Psalm 134. The first English words to which it was set were Kethe's version of Psalm 100, and it has been sung to this text for four hundred years. The original form of the tune was:

All the way my Saviour leads me 268

This hymn was written by Fanny J. Crosby. She had been the recipient of unexpected good fortune, and as she sat in her room meditating upon the goodness of God, the lines of this hymn flashed into her mind. It was written out and sent to Robert Lowry who composed the tune, ALL THE WAY. It first appeared in a Sunday school collection, *Brightest and Best,* compiled by William H. Doane and Lowry (Chicago, 1875, No. 64), with the Scripture text, "The Lord alone did lead him" (Deut. 32:12).

All things are Thine; no gift have we 403, 536

John Greenleaf Whittier wrote this hymn for the opening of Plymouth Church, St. Paul, Minnesota, in 1872. It was published in Whittier's *Complete Poetical Works* (1876), and the first hymnal inclusion was in W. Garrett Horder's *Congregational Hymns* (London, 1884).

GERMANY (403) appeared in William Gardiner's *Sacred Melodies* (1815), attributed to Beethoven. Gardiner stated, in his *Music and Friends* (1838), that this tune is "somewhere in the works of Beethoven, but I cannot point it out." Most authorities reject the attributing of this tune to Beethoven, and it has been suggested by some that the tune is based on a German folk melody. However, Ellinwood calls attention to the resemblance of the theme of the *Allegro ma non troppo* movement of Beethoven's *Piano Trio* (Op. 70, No. 2) with the beginning and ending of this hymn tune. The present harmonization seems to be from J. Ireland Tucker's *Hymnal with Tunes Old and New* (New York, 1872).

HERR JESU CHRIST (536) is an early seventeenth-century German melody of unknown origin. It appeared in *Pensum Sacrum* (Görlitz, 1648), as one of eighty melodies given in the Appendix. Apparently it was a favorite of J. S. Bach, for he used it several times in his organ writing.

All things bright and beautiful 8

This hymn by Mrs. Cecil F. Alexander first appeared in her *Hymns for Little Children* (1848). It is based on the phrase "maker of heaven and earth" in the Apostle's Creed and also Genesis 1:31a, "God saw every thing that he had made, and, behold, it was very good." Originally of seven four-line stanzas, the hymn now appears with four of the seven stanzas combined into two eight-line stanzas with the other three stanzas omitted.

SPOHR is taken from a solo in Louis Spohr's oratorio *Des Heilands letze Stunden* (1834). An English version entitled *Calvary,* prepared by Edward Taylor and presented at the Norwich Festival in 1839, contained the solo "Though all Thy friends prove faithless," sung by Mary. James Stimpson's anthem arrangement of the melody with the text "As pants the hart" brought it great popularity, and the opening strains were adopted as the hymn tune. The writer has found this hymn tune in Edwin P. Parker's *Song Flowers for the Sunday School* (Hartford, 12th ed., 1874, No. 67), set to this text.

All to Jesus I surrender 363

According to the account of the author, Judson W. Van DeVenter, this hymn was written

in memory of the time when, after a long struggle, I had surrendered and dedicated my life to active Christian service. The song was written while I was conducting a meeting at East Palestine, Ohio, and in the home of George Sebring, who later founded the city of Sebring, Florida. The Sebring camp meeting at Sebring, Ohio, was also founded by him.

SURRENDER was composed by Winfield S. Weeden for this text, and it was first published in *Gospel Songs of Grace and Glory,* compiled by Weeden, Van DeVenter, and Leonard Weaver (Philadelphia: Hall-Mack Co., 1896, No. 83). Of the original five four-line stanzas, the present version uses stanzas one, three, and four. The original form of the tune was written for a duet between the soprano and tenor lines in the stanzas and four-part singing in the refrain. The Hymnal Committee altered the music of the stanzas to provide for four-part singing throughout.

Almost persuaded now to believe   248

In Whittle's *Memoirs of P. P. Bliss,* the following account is given:

Rev. Mr. Brundage tells of the origin of "Almost Persuaded," in a sermon preached by him many years ago. The closing words of the sermon were—"He who is almost persuaded is almost saved, but to be almost saved is to be entirely lost." Mr. Bliss being in the audience was impressed with the thought, and immediately set about the composition of what proved one of his most popular songs, deriving his inspiration from the sermon of his friend, Mr. Brundage.

The present version is unaltered from the original which was first published in *The Charm,* a Sunday school songbook compiled by Bliss (Cincinnati: John Church & Co., 1871, No. 69). Later it was included in Bliss's *Gospel Songs* (1874, No. 37). The use of this hymn in the *Gospel Hymn* series and in *Sacred Songs and Solos,* together with its use by Sankey in the evangelistic campaigns with Moody, made it an extremely popular and effective invitation hymn.

Am I a soldier of the cross   405

This hymn appeared in Isaac Watts' *Sermons* (1721-24, Vol. III), following a sermon on "Holy Fortitude" based on 1 Corinthians 16:13, "Stand fast in the faith, quit you like men, be strong." Originally consisting of six four-line stanzas, the omitted stanzas five and six are:

> Thy saints, in all this glorious war,
> Shall conquer, though they die;
> They view the triumph from afar,
> And seize it with their eye.

> When that illustrious day shall rise,
> And all thy armies shine
> In robes of victory through the skies,
> The glory shall be thine.

13

ARLINGTON is adapted from the minuet in the overture to Thomas A. Arne's *Artaxerxes,* an opera produced in London in 1762. It first appeared as a hymn tune in Ralph Harrison's *Sacred Harmony,* Volume I (1784). The original form of the melody is:

Amens—*see* Responses and Amens.

Amazing grace! how sweet the sound 188

John Newton's hymn first appeared in the *Olney Hymns* (1779), in six four-line stanzas entitled, "Faith's Review and Expectation." The first three stanzas in the present version are unaltered from the original. The three omitted stanzas are:

> 4. The Lord has promised good to me,
>   His word my hope secures;
> He will my shield and portion be
>   As long as life endures.
>
> 5. Yea, when this flesh and heart shall fail,
>   And mortal life shall cease,
> I shall possess within the veil,
>   A life of joy and peace.
>
> 6. The earth shall soon dissolve like snow,
>   The sun forbear to shine;
> But God, who called me here below,
>   Will be for ever mine.

The fourth stanza of the present version, beginning "When we've been there ten thousand years," is not by Newton. This appears as the final stanza in a version of the anonymous hymn "Jerusalem, my happy home" found in numerous nineteenth-century American collections, i.e., *The Baptist Songster,* compiled by R. Winchell (Wethersfield, Conn., 1829, Hymn 38). Together with the first three stanzas of Newton's hymn, this anonymous quatrain appears as the fourth and final stanza in E. O. Excell's *Coronation Hymns* (Chicago, 1910, No. 282). Newton's hymn had appeared in Excell's collections prior to this date, but

NEW BRITAIN. C. M.

Baptist Harmony, p. 123.

1 Amazing grace! (how sweet the sound) That saved a wretch like me! I once was lost, but now am found, Was blind, but now I see

2 'Twas grace that taught my heart to fear, And grace my fears relieved: How precious did that grace ap - pear, The hour I first believed!

3 Through many dangers, toils, and snares,
I have already come:
'Tis grace has brought me safe thus far,
And grace will lead me home.

4 The Lord has promised good to me,
His word my hope secures;
He will my shield and portion be,
As long as life endures.

5 Yes, when this flesh and heart shall fail,
And mortal life shall cease,
I shall possess, within the veil,
A life of joy and peace.

6 The earth shall soon dissolve like snow,
The sun forbear to shine;
But God, who call'd me here below,
Will be for ever mine.

FROM WALKER'S *Southern Harmony*

15

this marks his first use of this fourth stanza. It appeared the following year in Robert H. Coleman's *The New Evangel* (Dallas, 1911), which was printed by Excell in Chicago. This was the second songbook issued by Coleman. The inclusion of this hymn in this form with this tune in this and all subsequent collections issued by Coleman over the following thirty years largely accounts for its popularity among Southern Baptists.

AMAZING GRACE is an early American melody of unknown origin. The earliest appearance of this tune seems to be in the *Virginia Harmony* (1831), an oblong tune book compiled by James P. Carrell and David S. Clayton, Lebanon, Virginia. It became exceedingly popular and, bearing such names as NEW BRITAIN, HARMONY GROVE, SYMPHONY, SOLON, and REDEMPTION, it appeared in most of the oblong tune books published in the South in the nineteenth century. The transfer of this tune from the "oblong" to the "upright" collections may have been the work of R. M. McIntosh (*q.v.*), for he included a number of these old shaped note tunes in the many collections he edited and published in the latter part of the nineteenth century. The present form of the tune is usually credited to E. O. Excell, whose arrangement first appeared in his *Make His Praise Glorious* (Chicago, 1900, No. 235).

"America"—*see* My country, 'tis of thee

"America the Beautiful"—*see* O beautiful for spacious skies

Angels, from the realms of glory   **76**

James Montgomery's hymn first appeared in the *Iris* (Dec. 24, 1816), a Sheffield, England, newspaper edited by Montgomery, where it was entitled "Nativity." A slightly altered version appeared in his *Christian Psalmist* (1825) and has been very popular ever since. The omitted fifth stanza is:

> Sinners, wrung with true repentance,
>   Doomed for guilt to endless pains,
> Justice now revokes the sentence,
>   Mercy calls you—break your chains;
>   *Refrain*

REGENT SQUARE—*see* Praise, my soul, the King of heaven.

Angels we have heard on high   **64**

This best known of all French carols was first published, text and tune, in the *Nouveau recueil de cantiques* (1855). Jan R. H. de Smidt, in his *Les noëls et la tradition populaire* (1932), believes that this carol dates from the eighteenth century. There have been numerous versions of the text, but all evidently stem from the same source, beginning "Les anges dan nos campagnes." Some of the more familiar are "Bright angels we have heard on high," "Bright angel hosts are heard on high," "Hearken all! what holy singing," and "Shepherds in the fields abiding."

GLORIA. The first appearance of this melody has already been noted. In R. R. Chope's *Carols for Use in Church* (1875) it appeared for the first time in an English book, with Grantham's translation of the French original beginning "When the crimson sun had set." The tune is characteristic of many French carol melodies in its narrow compass, its almost monotonous opening phrases, and its childlike mirth and unsophisticated grace. The sequential "gloria" in the refrain is an expression of sheer joy and delight. The harmonization found here was made for this hymnal by Warren M. Angell at the request of the editor.

"Anniversary Hymn"—*see* O God of our fathers, we praise and adore Thee

Another year is dawning   497

This hymn by Frances R. Havergal was written in 1874. In a letter to her family in England, written from Ormont Dessous, Switzerland, and dated September, 1874, the author includes a listing of "what I have written, and what I am going to write." Among those things listed as already written is the item, " 'New Year's Wishes,' by Caswell's request, for a very pretty card." It was first published in Miss Havergal's *Under the Surface* (1874).

AURELIA—*see* I lay my sins on Jesus.

"Are ye able," said the Master   351

In a letter to the writer dated July 21, 1962, Earl Marlatt, the author of this text, provides the following information:

The tune BEACON HILL was composed by Harry S. Mason in April, 1924, while he was a graduate student at Boston University School of Religious Education. It was written as a musical setting for Harry Wright's entry into a school song contest. Mr. Wright half read and half sang the text of the song to broken phrases of a tune he had remembered from his school days. Mr. Mason took the basic theme as it was hummed by Mr. Wright, supplied the missing measures and elaborated the whole into stirring music for Mr. Wright's text. The song was then submitted for the contest, but surprisingly to many who had heard and admired it did not rate with the judges. Among those especially disappointed in this

17

result was Professor Earl Marlatt, at that time head resident of the men's dormitory, called "The Hermitage"; he had overheard the song-making in the music room and remembered the arresting tune. Consequently, when he was asked the following spring to write a hymn for the consecration of the officers of the Student Association at the School of Religious Education, he found that the expression, "Are ye able," from a sermon he had preached the preceding Sunday, sang exactly to the first measure of Harry Wright's text and the tune Harry Mason had arranged for it. After that the music miraculously seemed to suggest the words until the whole hymn was finished in a single evening.

BEACON HILL, composed by Harry S. Mason, was named for a section of Boston, located north of Boston Common.

"Are You Washed in the Blood?"—*see* Have you been to Jesus for the cleansing power

Arise, O youth of God! 423

William P. Merrill's original hymn (cf. "Rise up, O men of God!") was altered and a refrain was added by B. B. McKinney in 1937, when he composed this tune. A comparison with the original hymn will reveal the changes. The present version first appeared in *Songs of Victory* (Nashville, 1937, No. 14).

LEAVELL is the name given this tune by the Hymnal Committee. Frank H. Leavell (1884-1949) was an outstanding youth leader among Southern Baptists during the first half of the twentieth century. For many years he was secretary of the Student Department of the Sunday School Board, ministering to Baptist students on college campuses.

Art thou weary, heavy laden 245

This hymn first appeared in John Mason Neale's *Hymns of the Eastern Church,* first edition (1862) and given as a translation from Stephen the Sabaite (725-794). In the preface to the third edition (1866), Neale says that this hymn "contains so little that is from the Greek" that it should not have been included in this collection and in the fourth edition (1882), it is shifted to the Appendix. In its original form, the first line read, "Art thou weary, art thou languid," and this is frequently used as the initial line. An omitted fourth stanza reads:

> If I find him, if I follow,
>   What his guerdon here?
> Many a sorrow, many a labour,
>   Many a tear.

The last two lines of the final stanza originally were:

> Angels, martyrs, prophets, virgins
> Answer, "Yes."

This is said to have been the favorite hymn of Franklin D. Roosevelt.

STEPHANOS was composed by Henry W. Baker for this text for inclusion in the Appendix to *Hymns Ancient and Modern* (1868, No. 209). Baker, general editor for this collection, composed the melody and the harmonization was made by William H. Monk, musical editor.

As with gladness men of old 68

William C. Dix wrote this hymn in about 1858, while recovering from a serious illness. It first appeared in a privately circulated small collection, *Hymns of Love and Joy,* and later appeared in the original edition of *Hymns Ancient and Modern* (1860). It first appeared in America in the Episcopal *Hymnal* (1874) and in the *Methodist Episcopal Hymn Book* (1878).

DIX was arranged for this text in the musical edition of *Hymns Ancient and Modern* (1861, No. 64). For further discussion of the tune *see* For the beauty of the earth.

Ask ye what great thing I know 161

Johann C. Schwedler wrote this German hymn, which is based on 1 Corinthians 2:2 and Galatians 6:14. It was first published eleven years after the author's death in the *Hirschberger Gesangbuch* (1741) in six four-line stanzas, beginning, "Wollt ihr wissen, was mein Preis?" with the refrain, "Jesu, der Gekreuzigte." Benjamin H. Kennedy's English translation first appeared in his *Hymnologia Christiana, or Psalms and Hymns Selected and Arranged in the Order of the Christian Seasons* (1863). In 1869, this hymn was included in two collections, *Hymns of the Church* (Dutch Reformed) and Schaff's *Christ in Song* (New York), making its first appearance in America.

HENDON, composed by Henri A. C. Malan, first appeared in one of his collections for which he wrote both words and music, the first of which appeared in 1823. The date of this tune is usually given as 1827. The first American inclusion was Lowell Mason's *Carmina Sacra* (1841).

"At Calvary" —*see* Years I spent in vanity and pride

"At the Cross" —*see* Alas, and did my Saviour bleed ("At the Cross")

Awake, my soul, in joyful lays   **26**

This hymn by Samuel Medley first appeared in J. H. Meyer's *Collection of Hymns for Lady Huntingdon's Chapel, Cumberland Street, Shoreditch* (London, 1782). It was included in Medley's *Hymns* (Bristol and Bradford, 1785), in eight four-line stanzas. The version in common usage is from Rippon's *Selection, 1787.*

LOVINGKINDNESS is one of forty-two tunes by William Caldwell found in his *Union Harmony* (Maryville, Tennessee, 1837). It appears in numerous collections after this date, where it is often given without Caldwell's name and labeled "Western Melody," reflecting the fact that Tennessee was then the western frontier.

Awake, my soul, stretch every nerve   **309**

This hymn by Philip Doddridge first appeared in Job Orton's edition of Doddridge's *Hymns* (1755), in five four-line stanzas entitled "Pressing On in the Christian Race." The hymn is based on Philippians 3:12-14, and the omitted fourth stanza is:

> That prize with peerless glories bright,
> Which shall new lustre boast,
> When victor's wreaths and monarch's gems
> Shall blend in common dust.

CHRISTMAS, sometimes called LUNENBURG or SANDFORD, is an adaptation of the soprano aria "Non vi piacque ingiusti Dei" in the second act of George Frederick Handel's opera *Siroe,* written in 1728. The hymn tune version of this melody first appeared in David Weyman's *Melodia Sacra* (1815), where it is set to Psalm 132 and attributed to Handel. It was also included in Lowell Mason's *Boston Handel and Haydn Society Collection of Church Music* (1821), and no doubt its initial popularity can be credited to this inclusion. The tune name CHRISTMAS comes from its association with Nahum Tate's Christmas hymn "While shepherds watched their flocks by night."

Awake, my tongue, thy tribute bring   **24**

This hymn by John Needham first appeared in *Hymns Devotional and Moral* (Bristol, England, 1768), entitled "The Divine Perfections." This collection, published by S. Farley, contained 263 hymns and was published while Needham was co-pastor of the Callowhill Street Baptist Church in Bristol.

Away in a manger, no crib for a bed   **77**

A great deal of mystery which long surrounded this familiar and well-loved song of the Christ child has been cleared away by Richard S. Hill in a splendid article entitled, "Not So Far Away in a Manger, Forty-one Settings of an American Carol," in the Music Library Association *Notes* (III, No. 1). While the authorship of the words is still unknown, Hill removes any reason for associating the carol with Martin Luther.

The earliest appearance of the text which Mr. Hill was able to locate is in J. C. File's *Little Children's Book* (Philadelphia, 1885), published by the Evangelical Lutheran Church in North America. Here the words were set to a tune ST. KILDA by J. E. Clark. The second appearance of the text is found in James R. Murray's *Dainty Songs for Little Lads and Lasses* (Cincinnati: The John Church Co., 1887), with the notation: "Luther's Cradle Hymn (composed by Martin Luther for his children and still sung by German mothers to their little ones)." His initials "J. R. M." seem to indicate that he is the composer of the tune MUELLER which is found in our hymnal.

Subsequent compilers have used Murray's caption and have popularized the idea that Luther wrote both words and music. In many collections the tune is attributed to an unknown and unidentified "Carl Mueller." The irony of finding this name as the tune name in our hymnal may serve as a reminder of the unfounded myth which has grown around this carol.

The third stanza was found in *Gabriel's Vineyard Songs,* (Louisville, 1892), a collection by Charles H. Gabriel, with no author given.

The tune most popular in England is CRADLE SONG by William J. Kirkpatrick from his "Around the World with Christmas," 1895, a pamphlet containing seven songs. It is also found in the Episcopal *Hymnal 1940*.

Be known to us in breaking bread   **398**

This metrical grace appeared in James Montgomery's *Christian Psalmist* (1825) in two four-line stanzas entitled, "The Family Table."

DUNDEE is one of twelve "common tunes" (not assigned to a particular hymn) which appeared in *The One Hundred Fifty Psalms of David,* edited by A. Hart (Edinburgh, 1615), where it is called FRENCH TUNE. In 1621 it appeared in England in Ravenscroft's *Psalter* where it is indexed among the Scottish tunes and called DUNDY.

This hymn was written by Civilla D. Martin, and the tune, GOD CARES, was composed by her husband, W. Stillman Martin. Mrs. Martin gives the following information concerning the writing of this hymn in 1904.

I was confined to a sick bed in a Bible school in Lestershire, New York. My husband was spending several weeks at the school, making a songbook for the president of the school. "God Will Take Care of You" was written one Sunday afternoon while my husband went to a preaching appointment. When he returned I gave the words to him. He immediately sat down to his little Bilhorn organ and wrote the music. That evening he and two of the teachers sang the completed song. It was then printed in the songbook he was compiling for the school.

The hymn was first published in *Songs of Redemption and Praise* (1905) compiled by evangelist John A. Davis, founder of the Practical Bible Training School, Lestershire, N. Y.

Be present at our table, Lord 396

This metrical grace to be sung before partaking of the Lord's Supper was written by John Cennick. It first appeared in his *Sacred Hymns for the Children of God* (London, 1741, No. 130), with the heading "Before Meat." John Wesley was very fond of using this grace and had these words engraved on the family teapot used in his home.

UXBRIDGE is an original hymn tune composed by Lowell Mason "in the spirit of Gregorian," in 1830. It was first published in *The Boston Handel and Haydn Society Collection of Church Music,* ninth edition (Boston, 1830). The tune was named for a town in Massachusetts.

Be Thou my vision 62

This ancient Irish poem probably dates from the eighth century. Mary Byrne made the translation into English prose, and it was published in *Erin* (Vol. II, 1905). The versification of Miss Byrne's prose was made by Eleanor Hull and appeared in her *Poem-book of the Gael* (1912). Its first appearance as a hymn is in the revised *Church Hymnary* (Edinburgh, 1927).

SLANE is a traditional Irish air from Patrick W. Joyce's *Old Irish Folk Music and Songs* (1909), set to the text "With my love on the road." It was harmonized by David Evans and set to this text for the revised *Church Hymnary* (Edinburgh, 1927). Slane is a hill some ten miles from Tara in County Meath where Ireland's patron saint, Patrick (*ca.* 389-461), lit the paschal fire on Easter eve, challenging King Loegaire.

This hymn by Isaac Watts is from his *Hymns and Spiritual Songs, Book II* (1707), where it is entitled, "The faithfulness of God in His promises." Originally it consisted of nine four-line stanzas.

MANOAH first appeared in Henry W. Greatorex's *Collection of Church Music* (Hartford, Conn., 1851) with no source given. It is thought that Greatorex arranged or adapted this tune from some source now unknown.

Beneath the cross of Jesus 345

This hymn by Elizabeth C. Clephane first appeared anonymously in the *Family Treasury* (1872), a Scottish Presbyterian magazine published in Edinburgh. Under the general title, "Breathings on the Border," eight of the author's hymns appeared in this magazine during the years 1872-74. It is interesting to note that this was the first of two hymns included in the 1872 issue; and the eighth hymn, found in the 1874 issue, is "There were ninety and nine that safely lay."

In publishing the first of these hymns, the editor, Rev. W. Arnot, wrote:

These lines express the experiences, the hopes, and the longings of a young Christian lately released. Written on the very edge of this life, with the better land fully in view of faith, they seem to us footsteps printed on the sands of Time, where these sands touch the ocean of Eternity. These footprints of one whom the Good Shepherd led through the wilderness into rest, may, with God's blessing, contribute to comfort and direct succeeding pilgrims.

In 1869, three years before, the author had passed away at the age of thirty-nine.

ST. CHRISTOPHER was composed by Frederick C. Maker for this hymn when it was included in the supplement to the *Bristol Tune Book* (1881).

"Benediction"—*see* May the grace of Christ our Saviour

Blessed assurance, Jesus is mine 269

Fanny J. Crosby, the author of this hymn, provides the following account:

In the year 1873 I wrote "Blessed Assurance." My friend, Mrs. Joseph F. Knapp, composed a melody and played it over to me two or three times on the piano. She then asked what it said. I replied:

Blessed assurance, Jesus is mine!
O What a foretaste of glory divine!
Heir of salvation, purchase of God,
Born of His spirit, washed in His blood.

The first appearance of this hymn seems to have been in John R. Sweney's *Gems of Praise* (Philadelphia: Methodist Episcopal Book Room, 1873, No. 66). It was included in the *Gospel Hymn* series in America and in Sankey's *Sacred Songs and Solos* in England and through these collections became immensely popular on both sides of the Atlantic.

"Blessed Redeemer"—*see* Up Calvary's mountain one dreadful morn

"Blessed Be the Name"—*see* O for a thousand tongues to sing ("Blessed Be the Name")

Blessed Saviour, we adore Thee   138

Written in 1942, this hymn by B. B. McKinney was first published in the *Teacher* (July, 1942), a Sunday school periodical. Its first appearance in a song collection was in *Look and Live Songs* (1945, No. 124).

GLORIOUS NAME is the name given this tune by the Hymnal Committee. It is interesting to compare the form of this tune, both stanza and refrain, with that of the French carol GLORIA (*see* Angels we have heard on high).

Blest be the tie that binds   366

John Fawcett, an English Baptist preacher, is the author of this hymn. An apocryphal story associates the writing of this hymn with Fawcett's pastorate of the Baptist church at Wainsgate. However, in John Gadsby's *Memoirs of the Principal Hymn Writers and Compilers of the 17th, 18th, and 19th Centuries* (London, 1861, p. 54), there is the following account:

In 1772 he [Fawcett] went to London, to supply for Dr. Gill, [at Carter's Lane Chapel] who, through age and infirmities, was incapacitated from preaching. After Dr. Gill's decease, Mr. Fawcett was invited to become the regular pastor, which, by the advice of some friends, and seeing that he had an increasing family, with only £25 a year from the people at Wainsgate, he consented to do; but, after a portion of his furniture and books had been sold he relented, and told his flock that if they would raise him to £40 a year, it would be the extent of his wishes. This, however, they declined to do. He nevertheless decided upon remaining, and throwing himself upon the providence of God.

No mention is made of this hymn or its association with this event at Wainsgate. In Fawcett's *Life and Letters* (1818) and *Miscellaneous Writings* (1826) there is no evidence that relates this hymn to this event. Josiah Miller, in *Singers and Songs of the Church* (1869, p. 273), is the first to mention that this hymn was "written in 1772 to commemorate the determination of its author to remain with his attached people at Wainsgate."

The hymn was included in Fawcett's *Hymns Adapted to the Circumstances of Public Worship* (Leeds, England, 1782, No. 104), and consisted of six four-line stanzas. The omitted stanzas five and six read:

> This glorious hope revives
>   Our courage by the way;
> When each in expectation lives,
>   And longs to see the day.
>
> From sorrow, toil, and pain,
>   And sin, we shall be free;
> And perfect love and friendship reign
>   Throughout eternity.

DENNIS first appeared in *The Psaltery,* edited by Lowell Mason and George J. Webb (1845), where it was set to Doddridge's "How Gentle God's Commands", with the statement that it is "Arranged from J. G. Nägeli." Ellinwood, in *The Hymnal 1940 Companion* (p. 304), reports having found in Nägeli's *Christliches Gesangbuch* (1828) a tune set to "O selig, selig, wer vor dir," which is possibly the original source of Mason's arrangement.

Blow ye the trumpet, blow!   250

This is one of seven hymns by Charles Wesley which appeared in *Hymns for New Year's Day* (1750). Originally consisting of six six-line stanzas, the present version uses stanzas one, two, and six without alteration, except for the final line of each stanza which originally read, "Return to your eternal home." The year of jubilee, as described in Leviticus 25:8-17, was celebrated each fifty years—the year following seven sabbaticals. It was a time of liberty and freedom from slavery and forgiveness of indebtedness. Using the year of jubilee as a backdrop, Wesley pictures vividly salvation through Christ as he sings joyfully

> Jesus, our great High Priest
>   Hath full atonement made
> Ye weary spirits, rest;

Ye mournful souls, be glad:
The year of jubilee is come!
Return, ye ransomed sinners, home.

LENOX, sometimes called TRUMPET, was composed by Lewis Edson, a New England singing school teacher. It first appeared in Simeon Jocelyn's *The Chorister's Companion* (New Haven, Conn., 1782 or 1783). This was originally a fuguing tune, a type of hymn tune which became very popular in New England in the latter part of the eighteenth century, largely through the efforts of William Billings.

Bread of heav'n, on Thee we feed 395

This hymn first appeared in Josiah Conder's *The Star in the East* (1821) and is based on John 6:51-54; 15:1. Originally consisting of two six-line stanzas, the present version of three four-line stanzas was made by using lines five and six of both stanzas to make our stanza three. The original form of the hymn was written in first person singular, beginning, "Bread of heav'n, on Thee I feed." The three-stanza plural version first appeared in Pratt's *Psalms and Hymns* (1829).

HOLLEY was composed by George Hews for "Softly now the light of day," and was first published in the *Boston Academy Collection of Church Music,* third edition (1835). McCutchan suggests that the tune name came from a village in Orleans County, New York.

Bread of the world, in mercy broken 394

This hymn first appeared in Reginald Heber's posthumous *Hymns Written and Adapted for the Weekly Church Service of the Year* (1827). It consisted of two four-line stanzas and was headed "Before the Sacrament."

EUCHARISTIC HYMN was composed by John S. B. Hodges for this hymn in 1868 while Hodges was rector of Grace Episcopal Church, Newark, New Jersey. It first appeared in the *Book of Common Praise* (1869).

Break Thou the bread of life 178

Mary A. Lathbury wrote the first two stanzas of this hymn (at the request of Dr. John H. Vincent) in the summer of 1877 at Lake Chautauqua.

Stanzas three and four in the present version were added to Miss Lathbury's hymn by Alexander Groves and these first appeared in the *Wesleyan Methodist Magazine* (London, Sept., 1913).

BREAD OF LIFE was composed by William F. Sherwin for Miss Lathbury's stanzas in 1877, and it was first included in publications which he prepared for use at Lake Chautauqua. Its first hymnal inclusion is found in *The Calvary Selection of Spiritual Songs,* edited by Charles S. Robinson and Robert S. MacArthur (New York, 1878, No. 145).

"Breathe on Me"—*see* Holy Spirit, breathe on me

Breathe on me, Breath of God   167

This hymn, based on "When he had said this, he breathed on them, and saith unto them, Receive ye the Holy Ghost" (John 20:22), was written by Edwin Hatch and was first published by the author in a privately printed leaflet entitled *Between Doubt and Prayer* (1878). Its first appearance for congregational use was in Allon's *The Congregational Psalmist Hymnal* (London, 1886).

TRENTHAM—*see* O Love of God most full.

Brethren, we have met to worship   368

In many early collections George Atkins is credited as being the author of this hymn. However, no information has been found concerning either the hymn or the author.

HOLY MANNA, composed by William Moore, first appeared in *Columbian Harmony* (No. 122), which he compiled. It was registered in the District of West Tennessee, April 2, 1825, and printed in Cincinnati by Morgan, Lodge and Fisher. It is one of eighteen tunes by Moore which appear in this oblong collection of shaped-note tunes in the four-shape tradition. HOLY MANNA became very popular and is found in most of the subsequent oblong tune books that appeared throughout the South in the nineteenth century.

Brightest and best of the sons of the morning   67

Reginald Heber wrote this hymn while he was vicar of his family parish, Hodnet, Shropshire, and it was first published in *The Christian Observer* (Vol. X). It was later included in Heber's *Hymns Written and Adapted to the Weekly Church Service of the Year* (1827).

MORNING STAR was originally part of an anthem composed by James P. Harding in June, 1892, to be sung at Gifford Hall Mission, located in Islington, then one of London's worst slum districts. Its first appearance in America seems to have been in *The Church Hymnal* (1894), Charles L. Hutchins' musical edition of the Episcopal *Hymnal* (1892).

Brightly beams our Father's mercy   300

This hymn by Philip P. Bliss was suggested by the following illustration in a sermon by the evangelist, Dwight L. Moody.

On a dark, stormy night, when the waves rolled like mountains and not a star was to be seen, a boat rocking and plunging, neared the Cleveland harbor. "Are you sure this is Cleveland?" asked the captain, seeing only one light from the light-house. "Quite sure, sir," replied the pilot. "Where are the lower lights?" "Gone out, sir." "Can you make the harbor?" "We must, or perish, sir!" And with a strong hand and a brave heart, the old pilot turned the wheel. But alas, in the darkness he missed the channel, and with a crash upon the rocks the boat was shivered, and many a life lost in a watery grave. Brethren, the Master will take care of the great light-house: *let us keep the lower lights burning!*

Bliss supplied both the text and this tune, LOWER LIGHTS, which first appeared in *The Charm, a Collection of Sunday School Music,* which he compiled (Cincinnati: John Church & Co., 1871, No. 14).

"Bring Them In"—*see* Hark! 'tis the Shepherd's voice I hear

Bring ye all the tithes into the storehouse   **404**

This hymn, both words and music, was written in 1923 by Lida Shivers Leech and copyrighted that year by Charles H. Gabriel. It appeared the following year in Robert H. Coleman's *Harvest Hymns* (No. 235). In Coleman's *The Modern Hymnal* (1926, No. 449), it is indicated that the hymn had become the property of Coleman.

GIVING is the name suggested for this tune by the composer.

"Bringing In the Sheaves"—*see* Sowing in the morning, sowing seeds of kindness

Cast thy burden on the Lord   **254**

George Rawson's hymn appeared in the *Leeds Hymn Book* (1853) and was actually a rewritten version of an earlier hymn found in Rowland Hill's *Psalms and Hymns* (1783) . Rawson's version has suffered considerable alteration by unknown editors, to the extent that some lines bear no resemblance to either Rawson or Hill.

SEYMOUR—*see* Softly now the light of day.

"Child's Morning Hymn"—*see* Father, we thank Thee for the night

"Christ Arose"—*see* Low in the grave He lay, Jesus my Saviour

Christ for the world we sing   **458**

This hymn was written while the author, Samuel Wolcott, was pastor of the Plymouth Congregational Church, Cleveland, Ohio. The following is his own account of its writing: "The Young Men's Christian

Association of Ohio met in one of our churches, with their motto, in evergreen letters over the pulpit, "Christ for the World, and the World for Christ." This suggested the hymn, 'Christ for the World We Sing.' " On his way home from that service, February 7, 1869, Wolcott wrote the hymn. Almost thirty years before this Wolcott had spent two years as a missionary to Syria, but ill health forced his return home. His hymn bears evidence of the evangelistic zeal which burned in his heart and his concern for the worldwide spread of the gospel. The hymn seems to have first appeared in William H. Doane's *Songs of Devotion* (New York: Biglow & Main, 1870, No. 76), set to ITALIAN HYMN.

CUTTING was composed by William F. Sherwin for this hymn. The earliest appearance the writer has found is in a small pamphlet "Forest Songs for Chatauqua Assemblies," compiled by Sherwin and H. R. Palmer (New York: Biglow & Main, 1888, No. 11).

Christ has for sin atonement made   **130**

This hymn and tune by Elisha A. Hoffman first appeared in *Gospel Hymns No. 6* (1891). The omitted stanzas four and six are:

> He walks beside me all the way,
> What a wonderful Saviour!
> And keeps me faithful day by day;
> What a wonderful Saviour!

> To Him I've given all my heart,
> What a wonderful Saviour!
> The world shall never share a part;
> What a wonderful Saviour.

BENTON HARBOR is the name given this tune by the Hymnal Committee. For a number of years Hoffman was pastor of the First Presbyterian Church, Benton Harbor, Michigan.

"Christ Receiveth Sinful Men"—*see* Sinners Jesus will receive

"Christ Returneth"—*see* It may be at morn, when the day is awaking

Christ, the Lord, is risen today   **115**

Charles Wesley's great hymn of Christ's resurrection first appeared in *Hymns and Sacred Poems* (1739), entitled "Hymn for Easter Day," where it consisted of eleven four-line stanzas. The present version consists of stanzas one, four, the first half of stanza two with the last two lines of stanza three, and stanza five of the original.

EASTER HYMN appeared anonymously in *Lyra Davidica* (London, 1708), where it was set to "Jesus Christ Is Risen Today," a translation of a fourteenth-century century Easter carol. It appeared in its present form in John Arnold's *The Compleat Psalmodist* (London, 1741). The original form is given below:

Believed by many to be one of Charles Wesley's finest hymns, this appeared in *A Collection of Psalms and Hymns* (1740), prepared by John and Charles Wesley. It was entitled "Morning Hymn" and is based on "Unto you that fear my name shall the Son of righteousness arise" (Mal. 4:2).

SPANISH HYMN. The origin of this tune or its name is unknown. A version of the melody with variations for the piano was copyrighted in 1825 by Benjamin Carr. He also made a choral arrangement about the same time for solo voice, quartet, full chorus, and accompaniment. Hauessler gives its first appearance in *A Collection of Metrical Versions* by M. Burgoyne (London, 1827), where it was entitled SPANISH CHANT, which indicates that it was a melody known both in America and England. When it is used with the metrical form 6.6.6.6.6.6., it is usually called MADRID, and SPANISH HYMN for 7.7.7.7.7.7.

"Close to Thee"—*see* Thou, my everlasting portion

Come, every soul by sin oppressed **235**

This hymn—both words and music by John H. Stockton—appeared in Stockton's *Salvation Melodies No. 1* (Philadelphia: Perkinpine & Higgins, 1874, p. 1), in five stanzas. The omitted stanza is

> O Jesus, blessed Jesus, dear,
> I'm coming now to Thee;
> Since Thou hast made the way so clear
> And full salvation free.

The original refrain was

> Come to Jesus, come to Jesus, come to Jesus now;
> He will save you, He will save you, He will save you now.

This was altered by Ira D. Sankey to its present form. Apparently Sankey had secured a manuscript copy of this hymn prior to its first publication mentioned above, for he relates that he had this song on his trip in England in 1873.

One day in mid-ocean, as I was looking over a list of hymns in my scrapbook, I noticed one commencing, "Come every soul by sin oppressed," by the Rev. John Stockton, with the familiar chorus, "Come to Jesus." Believing that these words had been so often sung that they were hackneyed, I decided to change them and tell how to come to Jesus by substituting the words, "Only Trust Him." In this form it was first published in *Sacred Songs and Solos* in London.

It was also included in Bliss and Sankey's *Gospel Hymn and Sacred Songs* (1875, No. 94). Later in his use of this invitation hymn, Sankey frequently changed the words of the refrain to "I will trust him."

STOCKTON is the name given this tune by the Hymnal Committee.

Come, Holy Spirit, Dove divine 385

This hymn is made up of stanzas taken from Adoniram Judson's hymn, "Our Saviour bowed beneath the wave," written about 1829, during the time Judson was translating the Bible into the Burmese language. The present version first appeared in Winchell's *Collection* (1832).

MARYTON was composed by H. Percy Smith for "Sun of my soul, thou Saviour dear," and it first appeared in *Church Hymns with Tunes* (London, 1874).

Come, Holy Spirit, heavenly Dove 169

Written by Isaac Watts, this hymn first appeared in his *Hymns and Sacred Songs* (1707), in five four-line stanzas entitled "Breathing After the Holy Spirit, or Fervency of Devotion Desired." Although many alterations have been made in this text, the present version is unaltered from the original. The omitted stanza two is:

> Look how we grovel here below,
> Fond of these trifling toys;
> Our souls can neither fly nor go
> To reach eternal joys.

BALERMA, or BALLERMA, is of the same origin as AUTUMN (*see* Mighty God, while angels bless Thee) and is an adaptation made by Robert Simpson of "Belerma and Durandarte" by Barthélémon. Shortly after Simpson's death in 1832, this adaptation was found among his papers and was published in *A Selection of Original Sacred Music . . . Intended to Form the Sixth Vol. of Steven's Selection of Sacred Music,* edited by John Turnbull (Glasgow, 1833), where it is attributed to Simpson.

Come, let us tune our loftiest song 128

Written by Robert A. West, this hymn first appeared in *Hymns for the Use of the Methodist Episcopal Church* (New York, 1849). Though more than a century old, this is the first appearance of the hymn in a denominational hymnal other than Methodist.

DUKE STREET—*see* Jesus shall reign where'er the sun.

Come, says Jesus' sacred voice 244

Anna L. Barbauld's hymn first appeared in the revised edition of her *Poems* (London, 1792).

HORTON is listed in Henry L. Mason's *Hymn-Tunes of Lowell Mason* as an undated hymn tune arrangement made by Mason from Xavier Schnyder (von Wartensee).

Come, Thou Almighty King 12

The authorship of this hymn is unknown even though it has been attributed to Charles Wesley. John Wesley began publishing hymns in small tracts or pamphlets as early as 1737 and had issued many of these by 1780, when he compiled the large *Collection of Hymns for the Use of the People Called Methodists.* One four-page pamphlet, published about 1757, contained this hymn and one by Charles Wesley, "Jesus, Let Thy Pitying Eye." This tract appeared bound with copies of George Whitfield's *Collection of Hymns* (1757, 1759, and 1760 editions). Haeussler, in *The Story of Our Hymns,* sets forth three valid reasons for not attributing this hymn to Charles Wesley. First, the fact that this hymn is not found in any of the older hymnals of English Methodism; second, the odd meter of this hymn was not used by the Wesleys in any of their hymnic writing; and third, Charles Wesley never claimed the hymn. It has been thought that this hymn with its unusual meter was written for the tune to "God Save the King," which came into general use in 1745. For some time the hymn was sung to this tune (which is known to us as AMERICA).

ITALIAN HYMN, sometimes called TRINITY or MOSCOW, was one of several tunes contributed by Felice de Giardini to *The Collection of Psalm and Hymn Tunes Sung at the Chapel of the Lock Hospital,* (London, 1769), published by Martin Madan. In this collection the tune appeared written in three part harmony. The original form of the melody was

The inconsistency of hymnal compilers has resulted in the three tune names (as well as others). ITALIAN HYMN has been used, no doubt, because it was composed by "the Italian," as Giardini was known in England. TRINITY refers to the content of the text and MOSCOW, to the place where Giardini died.

Come, Thou Fount of every blessing 313

Robert Robinson wrote this hymn in 1758, and it first appeared in *A Collection of Hymns used by the Church of Christ in Angel Alley, Bishopsgate* (1759), in four eight-line stanzas. Madan, in his *Psalms and Hymns* (1760), omitted the fourth stanza and this pattern has been followed ever since. There has been some speculation that this hymn might have been written by the Countess of Huntingdon; however, it is generally agreed to be the work of Robinson. The second stanza, beginning "Here I raise mine Ebenezer," refers to an incident related in 1 Samuel 7:12, "Then Samuel took a stone, and set it between Mizpeh and Shen, and called the name of it Ebenezer, saying, Hitherto hath the Lord helped us." "Ebenezer" is Hebrew for "stone of help."

NETTLETON first appeared as a two-part tune in John Wyeth's *Repository of Sacred Music, Part Second* (1813, p. 112), where it was named HALLELUJAH. In the Index it is indicated as being a new tune, and no composer's name is given. The tune has been attributed by some to Asahel Nettleton (1783-1844), a well-known evangelist of the early nineteenth century, who compiled *Village Hymns* (1825). However, this compilation contained no music, and there is no evidence that Nettleton wrote any tunes during his life. Also, it seems that Wyeth was not a tune composer, but published this tunebook "for the use of Christian churches" strictly as a business venture. It is not known where the tune name first appeared nor who was responsible for it.

Come to Jesus, ye who labor 246

Edwin P. Parker wrote this hymn in 1898, and it first appeared in the *Pilgrim Hymnal* (Boston, 1904).

BULLINGER was composed by Ethelbert W. Bullinger in 1874 while he was curate at Walthamstow, Essex, England. It first appeared in *Wesley's Hymns and New Supplement* (London, 1877), where it was set to "Jesu, Refuge of the Weary."

Come to the Saviour now 226

John M. Wigner, a Baptist layman, wrote this hymn in 1871. It was first published in the 1880 Supplement to *Psalms and Hymns* (1st ed.,

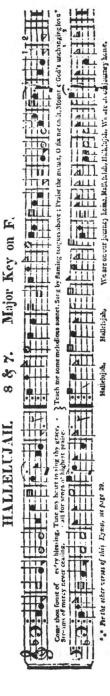
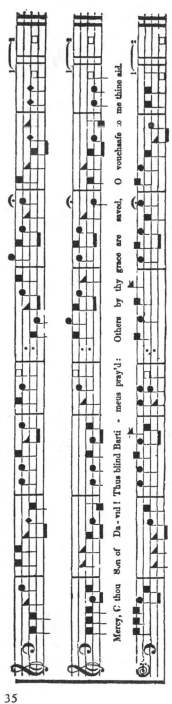

"Hallelujah" from Wyeth's *Repository*

"Restoration" from Walker's *Southern Harmony* (See "Come, Ye Sinners, Poor and Needy")

1858), a Baptist collection. This supplement was prepared by the author's father, John Thomas Wigner, a Baptist minister.

INVITATION was composed for this hymn by Frederick C. Maker and first appeared in the *Bristol Tune Book* (1881, No. 723).

"Come unto me, ye weary" 227

This hymn by William C. Dix first appeared in Littledale's *The People's Hymnal* (London, 1867). Concerning its writing Dix has said:

I was ill and depressed at the time, and it was almost to idle away the hours that I wrote the hymn. I had been ill for many weeks, and felt weary and faint, and the hymn really expresses the languidness of body from which I was suffering at the time. Soon after its completion I recovered, and I always look back to that hymn as the turning point in my illness.

MEIRIONYDD is a Welsh hymn melody, probably composed by William Lloyd. It appeared in manuscript form in *Caniadau Seion* (1840), which belonged to William Lloyd. In this manuscript form it was called BERTH. Meirionydd is the name of the county south of Caernarvon, Wales, where Lloyd lived.

Come, we that love the Lord 308

Isaac Watts's short meter hymn, "Come, we that love the Lord," first appeared in his *Hymns and Sacred Songs* (1707), in ten four-line stanzas entitled "Heavenly Joy on Earth." The text of the refrain was added by Robert Lowry when he composed the tune MARCHING TO ZION in 1867. It first appeared in *Silver Spray* (1868), a collection of Sunday school songs.

Come, ye disconsolate, where'er ye languish 297

This hymn first appeared in Thomas Moore's *Sacred Songs, Duets, and Trios*, 1824 edition, entitled "Relief in Prayer." Considerable alteration was made in the hymn for its inclusion in Mason and Hastings' *Spiritual Songs for Social Worship* (Boston, 1831). The second line of stanza one, and the second and third lines of stanza two were changed from the original, and a new third stanza was added. These changes were presumably made by Thomas Hastings.

CONSOLATION first appeared in Samuel Webbe's *A Collection of Motetts or Antiphons* (London, 1792), arranged for solo voice. It appeared with this text in *Spiritual Songs for Social Worship* (1831).

This ode, written by John of Damascus about the middle of the eighth century, is based on the Song of Moses, Exodus 15. It was a portion of the Greek Canon for St. Thomas' Sunday, the traditional name used in the Eastern Orthodox Church (Greek) for the Sunday following Easter, sometimes referred to as Little Easter or Low Sunday. John Mason Neale's translation in four eight-line stanzas first appeared in an article on Greek mythology in the *Christian Remembrancer* (Apr., 1859) and later in Neale's *Hymns of the Eastern Church* (1862). In 1868 it was included, with the substitution of a doxology for stanza four in the Appendix to *Hymns Ancient and Modern* (No. 291).

With some alterations, the first stanza in the present version is made up of the first four lines of the first stanza and the second four lines of the third stanza of the original translation. The second stanza is substantially Neale's second stanza, and the third stanza is the new stanza in a form of doxology which was added in 1868.

St. Kevin was composed for this text by Arthur S. Sullivan and first appeared unnamed in *The Hymnary* (London, 1872), edited by Joseph Barnby. It was given the name it now bears in Sullivan's *Church Hymns with Tunes* (London, 1902).

Come, ye sinners, poor and needy 241

"I Will Arise and Go to Jesus," which appears in the hymnal as the title of the hymn, is taken from the first line of the refrain text, which does not occur in the original hymn. Joseph Hart's hymn was first published in his *Hymns Composed on Various Subjects* (1759) in seven six-line stanzas with the heading "Come, and Welcome, to Jesus Christ." The original form of the first stanza reads

> Come, ye sinners, poor and wretched,
>   Weak and wounded, sick and sore;
> Jesus ready stands to save you,
>   Full of pity, love and power;
> He is able, he is able,
>   He is willing: doubt no more.

The source of the refrain text is from an anonymous hymn which appears in American collections in the nineteenth century.

> Far, far away from my loving Father,
>   I had been wandering, wayward, wild,
> Fearing only lest His anger
>   Overtake His sinful child.

Fain had I fed on the husks around me,
  Till to myself I came, and said,
"Plenty have my Father's servants,
  Perish I for want of bread."

"I will arise, though faint and weary,
  Home to my Father I will go;
Woe is me that e'er I wandered,
  Ah, that I such need should know."

"Father," I'll say, "I have sinned before Thee,
  No more may I be called Thy son:
Make me only as Thy servant,
  Pity me, a wretch undone!"

Then I arose and came to my Father—
  Mercy amazing! Love unknown!
He beheld me, ran, embraced me,
  Pardoned, welcomed, called me "son!"

Refrain
  I will arise and go to Jesus,
    He will embrace me in His arms;
  In the arms of my dear Saviour,
    O there are ten thousand charms.

The above refrain with the present tune appears in P. P. Bliss's *Gospel Songs* (1874, No. 111), with the four stanzas of the anonymous "Prodigal Son" hymn printed below the music. Below the tune is this comment by the compiler:

This chorus may be sung after each of the following stanzas, or as a response to "Come, ye sinners, poor and needy," "Jesus sought me when a stranger," etc. It is one of the old-fashioned camp-meeting "spirituals," and well deserves a place among *Gospel Songs*. P.P.B.

From Bliss's comment it is not clear whether the combining of this refrain text with Hart's hymn was an original suggestion or merely a statement of current practice at this date 1874. However, this is the first mention of the association of the two which the writer has found.

Arise is an American folk tune of unknown origin. Named Resto-ration and set to the hymn "Mercy, O Thou Son of David," it appears in William Walker's *Southern Harmony* (1835, p. 5), as shown above on page 35.

Come, ye thankful people, come 490

This harvest hymn by Henry Alford first appeared in his *Psalms and Hymns* (1844) and again, after some revision, in his *Poetical Works* (1865). It originally consisted of seven eight-line stanzas.

ST. GEORGE'S WINDSOR was composed by George J. Elvey for "Hark, the song of Jubilee" and first appeared in Thorne's *A Selection of Psalm and Hymn Tunes* (London, 1858). Its association with Alford's hymn dates from *Hymns Ancient and Modern* (London, 1861). The tune name was taken from St. George's Chapel, Windsor, where the composer was organist for forty-seven years.

Coming now to Thee, O Christ my Lord 342

This hymn, words and music, was written in 1925 by B. B. McKinney and first published by Robert H. Coleman in *The Little Evangel* (Dallas, 1925, No. 4).

TRAVIS AVENUE is the name given this tune by the Hymnal Committee. The composer was music director at the Travis Avenue Baptist Church, Fort Worth, Texas, 1931-35.

"Count Your Blessings"—*see* When upon life's billows you are tempest tossed

Crown Him with many crowns 152

The original form of this hymn by Matthew Bridges first appeared in his *Hymns of the Heart,* second edition (1851), consisting of six stanzas. In the present version, stanzas one and three are from this original. Godfrey Thring wrote some additional stanzas which appeared in his *Hymns and Sacred Lyrics* (1874). The present second stanza is from this work. The first four lines of stanza four are from Bridges, and the last four from Thring.

DIADEMATA was composed by George J. Elvey for this hymn, and it first appeared in the Appendix to *Hymns Ancient and Modern* (London, 1868, No. 318). The name is taken from the Greek word for "crowns" found in Revelation 19:12.

Dare to be brave, dare to be true 411

The writer has been unable to find any information concerning this hymn by W. J. Rooper or this tune, COURAGE, by Duncan Hume.

Day is dying in the west 29

Mary A. Lathbury wrote this hymn, originally consisting of two stanzas with refrain, in 1877 at the request of Dr. John H. Vincent, founder of the Chautauqua Assembly, New York. It was first sung at a vesper service at Chautauqua Lake. It was copyrighted in 1877 by Vincent, and its first hymnal inclusion was in *The Calvary Selection of Sacred Songs,* compiled by Charles S. Robinson and Robert S. Mac-Arthur (New York, 1878, p. 405). At the insistence of many friends, the third and fourth stanzas were added by the author in 1890.

CHAUTAUQUA was composed in 1877 for this text by William F. Sherwin, a Baptist musician whom Vincent had chosen to be music director at the Chautauqua Assembly.

Dear Lord and Father of mankind 335

This hymn is taken from the final stanzas of John Greenleaf Whittier's poem, "The Brewing of Soma," first published in the *Atlantic Monthly* (April, 1872, p. 474). The poem tells of the brewing of an intoxicating drink, a ritual practiced by a religious sect in India. Whittier contrasts practices of modern man with these pagan rites.

> As in that child-world's early year,
> Age after age has striven
> By music, incense, vigils drear,
> And trance, to bring the skies more near,
> Or lift men up to heaven.

> And yet the past comes round again,
> And new doth old fulfil;
> In sensual transports wild as vain
> We brew in many a Christian fane
> The heathen Soma still.

He then concludes the poem with the lines of our hymn. These stanzas were first adapted as a hymn by W. Garrett Horder for his *Worship Song* (London, 1884).

REST, also called ELTON, was composed by Frederick C. Maker for this text for inclusion in G. S. Barrett's *The Congregational Church Hymnary* (London, 1887).

"Dedicatory Hymn"—*see* To Him who hallows all our days

Depth of mercy! can there be 242

This hymn by Charles Wesley first appeared in *Hymns and Sacred Poems* (1740) in thirteen four-line stanzas, entitled "After a Relapse into Sin."

SEYMOUR—*see* Softly now the light of day.

Down at the cross where my Saviour died 95

Nothing is known about the writing of this hymn by Elisha A. Hoffman and the tune, GLORY TO HIS NAME, composed by John H. Stockton. This first appeared in *Joy to the World*, compiled by T. C. O'Kane, C. C. McCabe, and John R. Sweney (Cincinnati: Hitchcock & Walden, 1878, No. 34).

"Doxology"—*see* Praise God, from whom all blessings flow.

Draw Thou my soul, O Christ 314

Lucy Larcom's hymn first appeared in her own compilation of verse *At the Beautiful Gate* (1892).

ST. EDMUND, composed by Arthur S. Sullivan, first appeared in *The Hymnary* (London, 1872), of which the composer was music editor.

Encamped along the hills of light 256

This is one of several texts which John H. Yates sent to Ira D. Sankey, for which Sankey composed tunes. In *My Life and the Story of the Gospel Hymns*, Sankey states that he published this hymn first in *The Christian Endeavor Hymnbook*. However, in *Gospel Hymns No. 6* (1891), it appeared with the copyright notice in the same year held by Biglow and Main. If Sankey's statement above is correct, then both collections would have to have appeared the same year. The original manuscript of Sankey's life story was completely destroyed in a fire in Battle Creek, Michigan, and the present book was rewritten from memory shortly thereafter. By this time Sankey was blind; and he dictated this material, relying on other sources for additional information and data. It was a most amazing feat, and it is surprising that the errors are so few.

Eternal Father, strong to save 61

William Whiting wrote this hymn in 1860 and it was first published somewhat revised in *Hymns Ancient and Modern* (1861, No. 222) under the heading "For those at sea. 'These [men] see the works of the Lord, and his wonders in the deep (Psalm 107:24).' " There exists another version, which is a revision by the author published in the appendix to the SPCK *Psalms and Hymns* (London, 1869). The present version is the one first published and is most commonly used today.

MELITA, composed by John B. Dykes for this hymn, was first published in the musical edition to *Hymns Ancient and Modern* (1861). It is named for the island, now called Malta, where the apostle Paul was shipwrecked. "When they were escaped, then they knew that the island was called Melita" (Acts 28:1).

Americans know this century-old hymn and tune of English origin as "The Navy Hymn." On November 24, 1963, as the body of the late President John F. Kennedy was borne up the steps of the Capitol Building to lie in state in the rotunda, the hymn was played by the Navy Band. Again the following day, it was played by the Marine Band at the conclusion of the burial service at Arlington National Cemetery.

Face to face with Christ, my Saviour   475

Grant Colfax Tuller first wrote this tune for his own text which began, "All for me the Saviour suffered." This was written shortly before an evening service in Rutherford, New Jersey, in 1898, where Tullar was assisting in an evangelistic meeting in the Methodist Episcopal Church. In that evening service this hymn was sung by Rev. Charles L. Mead, the pastor of the church. The following morning, Tullar received by mail several poems from Mrs. Frank A. Breck, and one of these poems, "Face to face with Christ my Saviour," fitted perfectly to the tune Tullar had written the previous evening. He was so pleased by this coincidence and delighted with the new text that he discarded his own poem and replaced it with Mrs. Breck's poem. It was published the following year in a collection published by the Tullar-Meredith Company of New York.

FACE TO FACE is the name given this tune by the Hymnal Committee.

Fairest Lord Jesus   159

The association of this hymn or tune with the Crusades is completely erroneous. Armin Haeussler in *The Story of Our Hymns* cites an article by Hoelscher in *Oesterreichische Viertelsjahrsschriften fuer Katholishe Theologie* (Vienna, IV, 222-56), which states that the text

seems to have come originally from Jesuit circles, having six verses under the Latin heading "Suspirium ad Jesum." In Muenster, Westphalia, where the Anabaptists established their famous but short-lived theocracy, the Roman Catholics published a hymnal in Low German and one in High German in 1674, a third collection appearing in 1677 under the title (abbreviated) *Muensterisch Gesangbuch,* a compilation of 304 hymns and 199 tunes. In this book this misnamed "Crusaders' Hymn" made its first appearance. . . . The text of the hymn originated at least fifteen years before its publication, for it is contained in a manuscript which has been found in Muenster, dated 1662.

The English translation by Richard Storrs Willis first appeared in his

42

Church Chorals and Choir Studies (New York, 1850). In this collection is the notation that this hymn was "sung by the German knights on their way to Jerusalem," which gave rise to the fanciful but untrue legend. For a similar erroneous notation, see "Away in a manger" (77).

CRUSADER'S HYMN is sometimes called ST. ELIZABETH. In spite of all efforts to set an earlier date on this tune, it first appeared in Hoffmann and Richter's *Schlesische Volkslieder* (Leipzig, 1842), a collection of folk songs found in Silesia by the compilers. Here it appeared with the German text of this hymn. The tune first appeared in England in Allon and Gauntlett's *The Congregational Psalmist,* second edition (London, 1861), where it was set to Watts's "How pleased and blest was I."

Franz Liszt used this tune as part of the Crusaders' March in his oratorio *The Legend of St. Elizabeth* (1862). In the preface of this work, Liszt acknowledges his gratitude to Herr Kantor Gottschlag for acquainting him with the "Pilgrims' Song."

"Faith Is the Victory"—*see* Encamped along the hills of light

Faith of our fathers! living still   **252**

In Frederick W. Faber's *Jesus and Mary; or Catholic Hymns for Singing and Reading* (London, 1849) the hymn first appeared in two versions—one for England and one for Ireland. The present version, following the four-stanza hymn for England, omits the second stanza and alters the third. Originally the second and third stanzas read:

> Our fathers, chained in prisons dark,
>   Were still in heart and conscience free:
> How sweet would be their children's fate,
>   If they, like them, could die for thee.
> Faith of our fathers, holy faith!
>   We would be true to thee till death.
>
> Faith of our fathers! Mary's prayers
>   Shall win our country back to thee;
> And through the truth that comes from God,
>   England shall then indeed be free.
> Faith of our fathers, holy faith!
>   We would be true to thee till death.

The altering of these lines, removing the obvious traces of Roman Catholic teaching, makes the present version acceptable and usable for all Christians. The hymn speaks effectively of the faith described in Hebrews 11. In *The Story of Our Hymns,* Haeussler says:

There have been martyrs of the Christian faith in every century since Hebrews 11 was written. There were those who, like our Lord, were nailed to the cross, or sent, like Paul, to the block, or were weighted down with stones like Symphorosa and drowned in rivers or seas, or were burned to death like Polycarp, or were done to death in other brutal ways. . . . Some writers and historians have estimated that at least 50,000,000 people have suffered a martyr's death since the crucifixion of Christ. In our times many have died in the Boxer Rebellion in China, and during the earlier years of the Communist regime in Russia, because of their faith in Christ. "In spite of dungeon, fire, and sword," they made secure for us "the rich heritage of a living faith, a heroic spirit, and a free church."

ST. CATHERINE, composed by Henri F. Hemy, first appeared in *Crown of Jesus Music* (London, 1864), where it was set to a Roman Catholic hymn entitled, "St. Catherine, Virgin and Martyr," which began,

> Sweet St. Catherine, maid most pure,
> Teach us to meditate and pray.

Catherine of Alexandria was a fourth-century Christian martyr. Hemy's tune consisted of the first sixteen measures of the present version. The final eight measures of the present version were added by James G. Walton when he made this arrangement for his *Plain Song Music for the Holy Communion Office* (1874).

Father, I stretch my hands to Thee   46

This hymn by Charles Wesley first appeared in his *Collection of Psalms and Hymns* (1741) with the title, "A Prayer for Faith." Originally of six stanzas, the present version contains stanzas 1, 2, 5, and 4.

ST. AGNES was composed by John B. Dykes for the hymn "Jesus, the very thought of Thee" and was first published in Grey's *Hymnal for Use in the English Church* (London, 1866).

Father in heaven, who lovest all   460

This is "The Children's Song" in Rudyard Kipling's *Puck of Pook's Hill* (1906). It first appeared as a hymn in *School Praise* (London, 1907), edited by J. M. E. Ross, and published by the English Presbyterian Church. The present version begins with the second stanza. The first stanza begins, "Land of our birth, we pledge to thee."

SAXBY was composed by Timothy R. Matthews for "Sun of my soul, Thou Saviour dear," for a hymn tune competition in which he was awarded fourth place. It was first published in Matthews' *Twenty-four Hymn Tunes* (London, 1867). The tune was named for a small town in the midlands of England.

Father, let me dedicate 498

This hymn first appeared in Lawrence Tuttiett's *Germs of Thought on the Sunday Special Services* (1864). Originally consisting of four eight-line stanzas, the omitted stanza four is

> If Thou callest to the cross,
>   And its shadow come,
> Turning all my gain to loss,
>   Shrouding heart and home;
> Let me think how Thy dear Son
>   To His glory came,
> And in deepest woe pray on:
>   "Glorify Thy Name."

NEW YEAR was composed by Joseph Barnby.

Father, we thank Thee for the night 341

The writer has been unable to locate any information concerning the author of this hymn, Rebecca J. Weston, the composer of the tune, WE THANK THEE, Daniel Batchellor, or the first appearance of text and tune. It seems that the hymn with this tune appeared in a collection published in Philadelphia about 1885.

Fight the good fight with all thy might! 406

This hymn, which first appeared in John S. B. Monsell's *Hymns of Love and Praise for the Church's Year* (1863), is based on 1 Timothy 6:12. The original form of the third stanza is

> Cast care aside, upon thy Guide
> Lean, and his mercy will provide;
> Lean, and the trusting soul shall prove
> Christ is its life, and Christ its love.

PENTECOST was composed by William Boyd in 1864. The composer describes the circumstances in the *Musical Times* (XLIX, 1908).

Baring-Gould asked me to compose a tune to "Come, Holy Ghost, our souls inspire" to be sung at a large meeting of Yorkshire colliers. I walked, talked, slept and ate with the words, and at last evolved the tune which I naturally named PENTECOST.

In the same article Boyd tells how this tune was first associated with Monsell's hymn.

One day, as I was walking along Regent Street I felt a slap on my back,

45

and turning round I saw my dear old friend Arthur Sullivan. "My dear Billy" he said, "I've seen a tune of yours which I must have." (He was then editing *Church Hymns*) "All right," I said, "Send me a cheque and I agree." No copy of the book, much less a proof was sent to me, and when I saw the tune I was horrified to find that Sullivan had assigned it to "Fight the good fight!" We had a regular fisticuffs about it, but judging from the favour with which the tune has been received, I feel that Sullivan was right in so mating words and music.

Fling out the banner! let it float   446

This hymn was written by George W. Doane for a flag-raising at the request of the students in St. Mary's School, Burlington, New Jersey. Doane, the founder of this school for girls, wrote these lines in December, 1848, at his home, "Riverside." It was published in *Verses for 1851 in Commemoration of the Third Jubilee of the S.P.G.* and was included in the posthumous second edition of his *Songs by the Way* (1859).

WALTHAM, sometimes called CAMDEN or DOANE, was composed by John B. Calkin for this hymn for *The Hymnary* (London, 1872).

"Footsteps of Jesus"—*see* Sweetly, Lord, have we heard Thee calling

For all the blessings of the year   495

No information has been found concerning this hymn or its author, Albert H. Hutchinson.

OLDBRIDGE was composed by Robert N. Quaile in 1903 and first appeared in *The English Hymnal* (London, 1906).

For the beauty of the earth   153

This hymn by Folliott S. Pierpoint first appeared in Orby Shipley's *Lyra Eucharistica,* second edition (1864), entitled, "The Sacrifice of Praise." It consisted of eight six-line stanzas, of which four are omitted, and the original final line of each stanza was "This our sacrifice of praise." In stanza four, "For Thy church that evermore" was originally "For Thy Bride that evermore," and "Her pure sacrifice of love" was "This pure sacrifice of love."

DIX is an adaptation from a chorale which appeared in Conrad Kocher's *Stimmen aus dem Reiche Gottes* (Stuttgart, 1838). The adaptation was made by W. H. Monk for *Hymns Ancient and Modern* (1861, No. 64), for the text "As with gladness men of old," by William C. Dix. The tune name is derived from the name of the author of the hymn with which it was first used.

Forward through the ages 463

Frederick L. Hosmer wrote this hymn in 1908 for an installation service, while he was pastor of the First Unitarian Church, Berkeley, California. It first appeared in the author's *The Thought of God,* Third Series (1918).

ST. GERTRUDE—*see* Onward, Christian soldiers.

Free from the law, O happy condition 199

Philip P. Bliss is the author of both words and music. Major D. W. Whittle, in his *Memoirs of Philip P. Bliss,* gives the following account of the writing of this song.

Just before Christmas, 1871, Mrs. Bliss asked a friend, "What shall I get for my husband as a Christmas present?" and, at the suggestion of this friend, purchased and presented him with the bound volume of a monthly English periodical called *Things New and Old.* Many things in these books of interpretation of Scripture and illustrations of Gospel truth were blessed to him, and from the reading of something in one of these books, in connection with Romans 8, and Hebrews 10:10, suggested this glorious gospel song.

In his *Memoirs and Reminiscences,* George C. Stebbins says that this hymn

is conceded to be the clearest statement of the doctrine of grace in distinction from the law to be found in hymnology. Indeed, it was said at the time of Moody and Sankey's first visit to Scotland in 1873 that the singing of that hymn had more to do in breaking down the prejudice that existed against Gospel hymns up to that time than anything else, as its teaching was so Scriptural and in such perfect accord with the teaching of the Scottish divines. The music setting of it, too, could not have been improved upon.

The hymn first appeared in Bliss's *Sunshine for Sunday Schools* (Cincinnati: John Church & Co., 1873, No. 82), and was included in his *Gospel Songs* (Cincinnati, 1874, No. 13).

Friend of the home, as when, in Galilee 376

This hymn by Howell E. Lewis, beloved English Congregational minister, first appeared in the *Congregational Hymnary* (London, 1916). It is one of nine hymns by Lewis included in this collection.

ELLERS—*see* Saviour, again to Thy dear name we raise.

Mary B. C. Slade, the wife of a Massachusetts Methodist minister, is the author of this text. The tune THE KINGDOM IS COMING was composed by Rigdon M. McIntosh for these words, and it first appeared in *The School Festival* (1873).

From every stormy wind that blows 296

This hymn by Hugh Stowell first appeared in the 1828 volume of *The Winter's Wreath, a Collection of Original Compositions in Prose and Verse,* an illustrated annual published by Stowell in London and Liverpool from 1828 to 1832. It was rewritten in 1831 for the author's *Selection of Psalms and Hymns Suited to the Services of the Church.* Originally in six four-line stanzas, the present version is made up of stanzas one, two, three, and five. The omitted stanzas four and six are

> Ah! whither could we flee for aid,
> When tempted, desolate, dismayed?
> Or how the hosts of hell defeat,
> Had suffering saints no mercy-seat?
>
> Oh! may my hand forget her skill,
> My tongue be silent, stiff, and still;
> My bounding heart forget to beat,
> If I forget the mercy-seat.

RETREAT, composed by Thomas Hastings for this text, first appeared in his *Sacred Songs for Family and Social Worship* (1842, No. 173).

From Greenland's icy mountains 449

This hymn was written by Reginald Heber in the early summer of 1819 at Wrexham, England, where his father-in-law, Dr. Shipley, was vicar. As Dr. Shipley discussed with Heber on Saturday the missionary sermon Shipley was to deliver the following day, he asked Heber to provide an appropriate hymn for the service. In twenty minutes the hymn was written, and Heber chose a tune from *The Beggar's Opera,* " 'Twas when the seas were roaring," to which it was sung the next day. The hymn was first published in *The Evangelical Magazine* (July, 1821), with the heading "Hymn composed for a missionary meeting." Its first appearance in America was in Asahel Nettleton's *Village Hymns for Social Worship* (1824).

MISSIONARY HYMN was composed by Lowell Mason in 1824 for this text. Following Heber's appointment as Bishop of India, the hymn appeared in the American edition of *The Christian Observer*

(Feb., 1823). Perhaps it was through this publication, or Nettleton's *Village Hymns,* that it came to the attention of Miss Mary W. Howard of Savannah, Georgia, who requested Mason to provide a suitable tune for it. At this time Mason worked as a bank clerk in Savannah and served as Sunday school superintendent and organist at the Independent Presbyterian Church. Miss Howard was also a member here and taught in the Negro Sunday school sponsored by this church. She later married Rev. Francis R. Goulding, a Presbyterian minister. Mason's tune was first published in Boston as a soprano solo in the key of F, "Composed and dedicated to Miss Mary W. Howard of Savannah, Georgia." Its first publication as a hymn tune was in the *Boston Handel and Haydn Society Collection of Church Music,* seventh edition (1829).

From ocean unto ocean 450

This hymn emphasizing home missions was written by Robert Murray, an eminent Canadian Presbyterian minister. It was first published in *The Hymnal of the Presbyterian Church in Canada* (1880). Although the author was thinking of his native Canada when he wrote these lines, they are equally appropriate for use in the United States.

LANCASHIRE—*see* Lead on, O King Eternal.

From over hill and plain 407

This hymn was written by E. Taylor Cassel and the tune by his wife, Flora H. Cassel, at the request of the Baptist Young People's Union of the Northern (now American) Baptist Convention. According to Phil Kerr in *Music in Evangelism,* the song was not accepted by the BYPU leaders and Cassell asked that it be returned. He then sent the manuscript to the Epworth League through which organization it became immediately quite popular. At the time this hymn was written, Dr. and Mrs. Cassel lived in Hastings, Nebraska, where he practiced medicine and both were active members of the Baptist Church. The hymn first appeared in E. O. Excell's *Triumphant Songs No. 4* (1894, No. 52). It is found in most of the compilations of Robert H. Coleman since *The Evangel* (1909), which accounts for its popularity among Southern Baptists.

LAMBDIN is the name given this tune by the Hymnal Committee. J. E. Lambdin was for thirty-five years secretary of the Training Union Department of the Sunday School Board of the Southern Baptist Convention, and was one of the leaders in the development of the Southern Baptist Training Union program which grew out of the BYPU work.

Gentle Jesus, meek and mild 510

This hymn by Charles Wesley first appeared in *Hymns and Sacred Poems* (London, 1742) and was later included in *Hymns for Children* (1763).

SEYMOUR—*see* Softly now the light of day.

Gentle Mary laid her Child 73

This hymn was written by Joseph Simpson Cook. Alta Linda Cook, the author's daughter, has provided the writer with the following information in a letter dated December 13, 1954:

The carol was written for a carol competition in *The Christian Guardian,* Christmas, 1919, and won first prize. It was published that year in *The Christian Guardian,* by the Methodist Book and Publishing House, Toronto, with three musical settings also entered in the competition, (1) E. L. Ashford, (2) Dr. Herbert Sanders, and (3) V. Virtino Morris.

TEMPUS ADEST FLORIDUM is a melody which appeared in *Piae Cantiones,* compiled by Theodoricus Petrus of Nyland, Finland, 1582, where it is set to a Latin carol of spring. In 1853, J. M. Neale made a metrical version of the legend of Good King Wenceslaus for this tune which has resulted in the association of this tune with the Christmas season. The present harmonization was made by Sir Ernest MacMillan for the *Hymnary of the United Church of Canada* (Toronto, 1930), where this text and tune appeared together for the first time.

Give of your best to the Master 353

Howard B. Grose is the author of the text, and the tune was composed by Charlotte A. Barnard. BARNARD is the name given the tune by the Hymnal Committee.

"Glorious Is Thy Name"— *see* Blessed Saviour, we adore thee

Glorious things of thee are spoken 381

This hymn by John Newton appeared in the *Olney Hymns,* Book I (1779, No. 60), in five eight-line stanzas. It is based on Psalm 87:3, "Glorious things are spoken of thee, O city of God." The present version omits stanzas four and five of the original, and the last four lines of stanza three. To complete the third stanza, the first four lines of the first stanza are repeated.

AUSTRIAN HYMN—*see* Word of God, across the ages.

"Glory to His Name"—*see* Down at the cross where my Saviour died

Go to dark Gethsemane 105

There are two versions of this hymn, both by James Montgomery. The first appeared in Cotterill's *Selection of Psalms and Hymns* (1820) and the second in the Leeds *Selection of Hymns* (1822). The latter version is more generally used and is the one found in the hymnal.

GETHSEMANE first appeared unnamed in Richard Redhead's *Church Hymn Tunes, Ancient and Modern* (1853), set to "Rock of Ages, Cleft for Me," the hymn for which it was written. It is sometimes called REDHEAD or PETRA, this latter name (meaning "rock") from the hymn with which it was first used.

God be with you till we meet again! 372

The author, Jeremiah E. Rankin, gives the following information concerning the writing of this hymn:

It was written as a Christian good-bye, and first sung in the First Congregational Church [Washington, D.C.] of which I was minister for fifteen years. We had Gospel meetings on Sunday nights, and our music was intentionally of the popular kind. I wrote the first stanza, and sent it to two gentlemen for music. The music which seemed to me best suited to the words was written by W. G. Tomer, teacher of public schools in New Jersey, at one time on the staff of General O. O. Howard. After receiving the music (which was revised by Dr. J. W. Bischoff, the organist of my church) I wrote the other stanzas.

The hymn was first published in *Gospel Bells,* compiled by Bischoff, Otis F. Presbrey, and Rankin (Chicago: The Western Sunday School Publishing Co., 1880, No. 50).

GOD BE WITH YOU was composed by William G. Tomer.

God calling yet! shall I not hear? 223

Gerhard Tersteegen's hymn, "Gott rufet noch; sollt' ich nicht endlich hören," was first published in the second edition of his *Geistliches Blumengärtlein* (meaning "Spiritual Flower Garden," 1735) and consisted of eight four-line stanzas. It was based on "Today if ye will hear his voice, harden not your heart" (Psalm 95:7-8). The English translation in 11. 11. 11. 11. meter appeared in *Hymns from the Land of Luther* (1855), a collection of translations of German hymns by two sisters, Jane L. Borthwick and Sarah Borthwick Findlater. Mrs. Findlater made this translation beginning, "God calling yet! and shall I never harken?" It was altered to long meter form (8.8.8.8.), by the editors of the Andover *Sabbath Hymn Book* (1859), with the first line altered as it now appears.   This Andover revision is found in most American hymnals.

WOODWORTH—*see* Just as I am, without one plea

God, give us Christian homes!   377

This hymn, written in 1949, first appeared in *Home Life* (May, 1950, p. 4), with the following notation:

A SONG FOR CHRISTIAN HOME WEEK—This new song by the popular writer and singer, B. B. McKinney, is published for the first time as a theme song for Christian Home Week. Later to be published in hymn-books, it is offered now through *Home Life* as a suitable musical message in special services focusing on Christian family living.

Dr. Joe W. Burton, editor of *Home Life,* says,

My recollection is that McKinney told me in private conversation that he had this song and that I asked to see it and then requested permission to publish it. We held it deliberately for the May issue to tie in with Christian Home Week. Also, we introduced it at the Southern Baptist Convention which met that year (1950) in Chicago as a presentation by the Oklahoma Baptist University Bison Glee Club.

The hymn was printed in single sheets and had a widespread usage in this form.

CHRISTIAN HOME is the name given this tune by the Hymnal Committee.

God is love, His mercy brightens   50

This hymn by John Bowring appeared in his *Hymns* (1825) in five four-line stanzas, the first stanza being repeated as stanza five.   *The Leeds Hymn Book* (1853) omitted the repetition of the first stanza, a practice commonly found in later hymnals.   In Thring's *Collection* (1880) "mist" was changed to "gloom" in stanza three, line three.

STUTTGART is an adaptation from a melody in *Psalmodia Sacra* (Gotha, 1715), which was composed or arranged by Christian Frederick Witt, one of the coeditors.   The present adaptation was made by Henry Gauntlett for *Hymns Ancient and Modern* (1861, No. 59), where this name is given.   McCutchan (*Hymn Tune Names,* p. 159) gives evidence that the association of this name with this tune was well known early in the nineteenth century.

William Cowper's hymn first appeared anonymously in John Newton's *Twenty-Six Letters on Religious Subjects: to Which Are Added Hymns* (London, 1774). In the *Olney Hymns* (1779) Newton included the hymn and acknowledged Cowper's authorship. Cowper, who suffered great mental affliction, attempted suicide by drowning in October, 1773. There has been much speculative discussion as to whether this hymn was written before or after this tragic event in his life. However, no positive information is available.

ST. ANNE first appeared anonymously in the *Supplement to the New Version of the Psalms,* sixth edition (London, 1708), as a setting for Psalm 62, and named "St. Anne." In Philip Hart's *Collection* (London, 1720), William Croft is named as composer. The tune is named for St. Anne's Church, Soho, where Croft was organist. Handel used the tune in his Chandos Anthem. "O Praise the Lord." The opening phrase of the melody appears in J. S. Bach's "Fugue in E flat," more popularly known now as "St. Anne Fugue."

God of grace and God of glory 465

In anticipation of the opening of the Riverside Church, New York City, Harry Emerson Fosdick, the pastor, wrote this hymn in the summer of 1930, while at his summer home on the coast of Maine. It was first sung at the opening service, October 5, 1930, and at the dedication service, February 8, 1931. Its first appearance in a hymnal was in *Praise and Service* (New York: The Century Company, 1932). The widespread acceptance of this hymn throughout the English-speaking world reflects the sturdy character of these lines and their usefulness in contemporary Christian living. This is one of the finest hymns produced in the twentieth century and a valuable contribution to our hymnody.

CWM RHONDDA—*see* Guide me, O Thou great Jehovah.

God of our fathers, whose almighty hand 54

Daniel C. Roberts wrote this hymn in 1876 while he was rector of St. Thomas Episcopal Church, Brandon, Vermont. It was written for a celebration of the centennial Fourth of July and sung on this occasion to RUSSIAN HYMN. Roberts submitted the hymn anonymously to the committee appointed to revise the Episcopal hymnal, and it was included in the *Hymnal* (1892).

NATIONAL HYMN was composed by George W. Warren for this text to be used at the centennial celebration of the United States Constitution.

It was later included in Tucker and Rousseau's *Hymnal Revised and Enlarged* (1894), a musical edition of the Episcopal *Hymnal* (1892).

God, our Father, we adore Thee   5

The first appearance of this hymn by George W. Frazer in America was in *Hymns of Grace and Truth,* published by Loizeaux Brothers (New York, 1904). Gordon Shorney of the Hope Puplishing Company, Chicago, wished to include this hymn in his *Tabernacle Hymns No. 5,* and inquired of Alfred H. Loizeaux if there was any omitted stanza addressed to the Holy Spirit. Since there was none, Loizeaux wrote several alternative stanzas and submitted them to Shorney, who chose one for his hymnal. In a letter to the writer dated November 23, 1954, concerning this added third stanza, Loizeaux states:

> I believe that the reason no stanza on the Holy Spirit appeared in the *Grace and Truth Book* is that the Brethren, so called "Plymouth Brethren" have felt quite strongly that we have no precedent in Scripture for directing worship personally to the Holy Spirit, even though we believe definitely that He is the third person of the Trinity. Personally, I do not hold invariably to this rule and thought that the hymn would be more complete with a stanza addressed to the Holy Spirit.

LOVE DIVINE—*see* Love divine, all loves excelling.

God, that madest earth and heaven   30

Originally this hymn consisted only of Reginald Heber's first stanza and was published in Heber's *Hymns* (1827). A traditional story maintains that Heber wrote these words after hearing the tune AR HYD Y NOS in a Welsh home where he was staying.

Our third stanza by Richard Whately, archbishop of Dublin, was added to Heber's stanza and the two appeared together in *Sacred Poetry* (Dublin, 1838). Whately's stanza is a free translation of the Compline Antiphon.

Our second stanza is by William Mercer and appeared in his *Church Psalter and Hymn Book,* Oxford edition (1864), with the above two stanzas plus a fourth stanza also by Mercer, beginning, "Holy Father, throned in heaven."

AR HYD Y NOS, so well known as "All Through the Night," is a traditional Welsh melody which was included in Edward Jones's *Musical Relicks of the Welsh Bards* (1784, p. 56). The writer has been unable to locate the first appearance of this harmonization attributed to L. O. Emerson.

This hymn is the result of the efforts of two men that wrote words to the same tune. Henry F. Chorley's hymn of four stanzas appeared in John Hullah's *Part Music* (1842), set to this tune. Following Chorley's style, John Ellerton wrote his hymn of four stanzas in 1870, and it first appeared in Brown-Borthwick's *Select Hymns for Church and Home* (1871). From these two hymns a combined version first appeared in the SPCK *Church Hymns* (1871). A number of alterations have been made in various collections. In our version stanzas one and three are from Ellerton and stanza two from Chorley.

RUSSIAN HYMN was written by Alexis F. Lwoff in 1833 at the command of Czar Nicholas I to furnish a hymn for Russia. In his memoirs the composer speaks of his great fear for the responsibility given him, for the tune would need to be "majestic, powerful, full of sentiment, comprehensible to all, suitable to the army and suitable to the people from the learned to the illiterate." Joukovsky provided the text; when it was first publicly performed on November 23, 1833, the Czar was so impressed that he ordered that the opening words, "God protect the Czar," be added to the Lwoff family coat of arms. First appearance of the melody as a hymn tune was in John Hullah's *Part Music* (1842). Tschaikovsky, in an interesting anachronism, used this tune in his *1812 Overture*.

God, who touchest earth with beauty   **45**

Mary S. Edgar wrote this hymn for campers in 1925. It was awarded first prize in a contest conducted by the American Camping Association in 1926.

GENEVA was composed for this text by C. Harold Lowden while he was musical editor for the Sunday School Board of the Reformed Church in the U.S.A. The text had been brought to his attention by a Miss Miller who was in charge of Young People's work. It was first sung from single sheets at an International Sunday School Association meeting in Chicago.

"God Will Take Care of You"—*see* Be not dismay'd whate'er betide

Good Christian men, rejoice   **74**

John Mason Neale's free rendering of a fourteenth-century macaronic carol (employing a mixture of two or more languages), first appeared in Neale's *Carols for Christmastide* (London, 1853). This carol came out of an era when the practice of using the vernacular, the language of the people, in sacred song was beginning. Adding lines in the vernacular to existing Latin texts was a device used by early reformers in the introduction of congregational singing in the language of the people, and helped pave the way for Luther's reforms of congregational song. Ellinwood records (*The Hymnal 1940 Companion,* p. 26) that the "macaronic character of the text was fully tested on September 14, 1745, at the Moravian Mission in Bethlehem, Pennsylvania, where the mission diary records that it was sung simultaneously in thirteen languages, European and Indian."'

IN DULCI JUBILO. This fourteenth-century melody is found in an early fifteenth century manuscript in the University Library at Leipzig. The first published version appeared in Klug's *Geistliche Lieder* (Wittenburg, 1535), but it is much older than this. The name freely translated means "in sweet shouting."

"Grace Greater than Our Sin"—*see* Marvelous grace of our loving Lord

Gracious Saviour, who didst honor   503

No information has been found concerning this hymn by Emily Shirreff or this tune, MOTHERHOOD, composed by L. Meadows White.

Great is Thy faithfulness, O God my Father   47

Thomas O. Chisholm, the author of this hymn, in a letter to the writer, dated June 9, 1955, states:

There is no circumstantial background for "Great Is Thy Faithfulness." I sent it, with a number of lyrics to Rev. W. M. Runyan and he used several, among them this one. This was in 1923, and I was then living in Vineland, New Jersey. It went rather slowly for several years, but was taken up by Dr. Houghton, then president of Moody Bible Institute, and began its wider usefulness there. He once wrote me that, while it was not the official theme song for the Institute, it was by long odds the most popular. He went away on a health errand and returned apparently relieved and in the chapel service that morning he said, "Well, I think we shall have to sing 'Great Is Thy Faithfulness.'" He died soon after and at his funeral service where many were gathered the hymn was sung, his wife joining with the large audience in the singing.

This hymn—words and music—first appeared in *Songs of Salvation,* compiled by William M. Runyan (Chicago, 1923, No. 70).

FAITHFULNESS was composed by William M. Runyan, and in a letter to the writer, dated August 3, 1954, he stated:

There is no special circumstance connected with the writing of this particular hymn other than the fact that Mr. Chisholm and I were very devoted co-workers, and I wrote harmonies to some twenty or twenty-five of his poems. This particular poem held such an appeal that I prayed most earnestly that my tune might carry over its message in a worthy way, and the subsequent history of its use indicates that God answered prayer. It was written in Baldwin, Kansas, in 1923, and was first published in my private song pamphlets.

Regarding the naming of the tune, Dr. Runyan wrote in October 14, 1954: "I appreciate the courtesy of your submitting to me the opportunity for suggesting the name for "Great Is Thy Faithfulness." We have made it something of a subject for family discussion. It is often referred to as "The Faithfulness Song," and my impulse is to call it 'Faithfulness.' "

Great Redeemer, we adore Thee   154

John Roy Harris wrote this hymn in December, 1934, while he was on the faculty of Oklahoma Baptist University. It is based on Isaiah 47:4, "As for our redeemer, the Lord of hosts is his name."

REDENTORE (Italian for "redeemer") was composed by Paolo Conte for this text in 1936, replacing an earlier tune composed by Harris. The manuscript was purchased by the Sunday School Board, and it was first published in *The Broadman Hymnal* (1940).

Guide me, O Thou great Jehovah   55, 56

This Welsh hymn by William Williams first appeared in his *Halleluiah* (Bristol, England 1745) in five six-line stanzas entitled "Strength to pass through the wilderness." Stanzas 1, 3, and 5 were translated into English by Peter Williams in his *Hymns on Various Subjects* (Carmarthen, 1771). A year later the original author, William Williams, or possibly his son John, made another English version using Peter Williams' first stanza, then translating stanzas three and four of the original hymn and adding a new fourth stanza. It was first published in a leaflet, then included in the Lady Huntingdon *Collection,* fifth edition (1772 or 1773). Our hymnal uses this version, omitting the fourth stanza.

CWM RHONDDA (55) was written in 1907 for the annual Baptist Cymanfa Ganu (singing festival) at Capel Rhondda, Pontypridd, Wales, and was printed in leaflets for that occasion. In the quarter century following its writing, it was used in more than five thousand festivals. Its first appearance in England was in the *Fellowship Hymn Book* (Revised, 1933) and in the *Methodist Hymn Book* of the same year. It appeared in America in *The Hymnal* (Presbyterian, U.S.A., 1933), set to the text above.

ZION (56) was written in 1830, according to McCutchan, when in the preparation of the manuscript for a new collection, a new tune was needed for Thomas Kelly's

On the mountain's top appearing
Lo! the sacred herald stands,
Welcome news to Zion bearing,
Zion long in hostile lands:
Mourning captive
God himself will loose thy bands.

Thomas Hastings composed this tune on the spur of the moment, taking the name ZION from this text. It appeared in *Spiritual Songs for Social Worship* (Utica, 1832, p. 16), edited by Hastings and Lowell Mason. As will be seen by the illustration below as it first appeared, the tune was written in two sections, and each section was repeated. A comparison of our tune with this original shows that our melody is like the "air" except for the final line. In this repeat, the "alto" line is used in our melody. Apparently this alteration was done by Hastings, for it appears as we have it in his *Church Melodies* (New York, 1858).

Hail, Thou long-expected Jesus   **70**

This hymn by Charles Wesley first appeared in *Hymns for the Nativity of our Lord* (1744). It was originally in two eight-line stanzas, with the first line beginning, "Come, thou long expected Jesus." The alteration of this beginning line first appeared in the Protestant Episcopal *Hymnal* (1871).

HARWELL was composed by Lowell Mason in 1840 and first appeared in his *Carmina Sacra* (1841, No. 218).

Hail, Thou once despised Jesus   **149**

The original form of this hymn in two stanzas first appeared in a seventy-two page pamphlet entitled *A Collection of Hymns Addressed to the Holy, Holy, Holy, Triune God, in the Person of Christ Jesus, Our Mediator and Advocate* (London, 1757). Here the author is not given and the compiler is unknown. However all subsequent inclusions of this hymn have credited it to John Bakewell. Our version, with slight alterations, is that which appeared in Martin Madan's *Collection of Psalms and Hymns* (London, 1760).

AUTUMN—*see* Mighty God, while angels bless Thee.

Hail to the brightness of Zion's glad morning!   **453**

Thomas Hastings and Lowell Mason were coeditors of *Spiritual Songs for Social Worship* (1832), a collection designed to raise the standards of music in that day. Hastings had written this hymn in 1830, and Mason supplied the tune, WESLEY, for this text to be included in this collection. It is interesting to observe that this compilation included for the first time such hymns as Palmer's "My faith looks up to Thee," and Smith's "The morning light is breaking." Hastings' tune, TOPLADY, written for "Rock of ages, cleft for me," appeared first in this book and brought worldwide attention to Toplady's hymn which had gone almost unnoticed for nearly a half century in England. The only alteration from Hastings' original text is the substitution of "engines" for "weapons" in stanza four, line three. Perhaps the anonymous alterer would have been wiser to have left this unaltered.

"Hallelujah! Christ Is Risen"—*see* Hallelujah! hallelujah! Heart and voice to heaven raise

Hallelujah! hallelujah! Heart and voice to heaven raise   **114**

This hymn by Christopher Wordsworth first appeared in his *The Holy Year, or, Hymns for Sundays and Holy-days and Other Occasions*

(1862). Three of the original five stanzas are used here and these have been considerably altered. The first stanza originally began:

> Alleluia! Alleluia!
> Hearts to heaven and voices raise;

The title "Hallelujah! Christ Is Risen" was given by McGranahan, when it was included in *Gospel Hymns No. 6* (1891) with the Scripture reference, "Who according to his abundant mercy hath begotten us again" (1 Peter 1:3).

McGRANAHAN was written for this text by James McGranahan and first appeared in *Gospel Hymns No. 6* (1891), edited by Ira D. Sankey, George C. Stebbins, and McGranahan.

"Hallelujah! What a Saviour"—*see* "Man of sorrows," what a name

Happy the home when God is there　　　　　　　　　374

This hymn by Henry Ware, the Younger, first appeared in *Selection of Hymns and Poetry for the Use of Infant and Juvenile Schools and Families,* third edition (1846), compiled by Mrs. Herbert Mayo.

ST. AGNES—*see* Father, I stretch my hands to Thee.

Hark, hark, my soul! angelic songs are swelling　　　469

Entitled "The Pilgrims of the Night," this hymn first appeared in Frederick W. Faber's *Oratory Hymns* (1854), in seven four-line stanzas. Its inclusion in the Appendix to *Hymns Ancient and Modern* (London, 1868), brought it widespread popularity.

PILGRIMS was composed by Henry Smart for this hymn for the Appendix to *Hymns Ancient and Modern* (London, 1868, No. 325).

Hark, ten thousand harps and voices　　　　　　　145

This hymn by Thomas Kelly first appeared in his *Hymns on Various Passages of Scripture,* second edition, (1806), in seven six-line stanzas, with the heading, "Let all the angels of God worship Him." Lowell Mason added the "Hallelujahs" and "Amens" when he wrote the tune for this text. In *Our Hymnody* McCutchan writes: "The Joint Commission charged with compiling the *Methodist Hymnal,* 1935, not always wisely softened all the 'Hallelujahs' into 'Alleluias.' Sometimes a Methodist feels the need of shouting 'Hallelujah!' " This goes for Baptists, too!

HARWELL was first written for this text (*see* Hail, Thou long-expected Jesus).

Hark! the herald angels sing

This hymn by Charles Wesley first appeared in *Hymns and Sacred Poems* (1739), with the first stanza beginning

Hark, how all the welkin rings,
Glory to the King of Kings!

This was altered to its present form in George Whitefield's *Collection* (1753). Various alterations and versions have appeared, and these are dealt with in detail by Julian. In its original version the hymn consisted of ten four-line stanzas. In the Supplement to the *New Version* (1782) of Tate and Brady it appeared in three eight-line stanzas with the first two lines of the hymn repeated as a refrain. With slight alterations this version appears in the hymnal.

MENDELSSOHN is an adaptation of a theme from the second movement of Felix Mendelssohn's *Festgesang,* composed in 1840 in commemoration of the invention of the art of printing, scored for men's voices and brass instruments. The adaption was made by William H. Cummings in 1855 and published by him the following year. The first hymnal inclusion was Richard Chope's *Congregational Hymn and Tune Book* (London, 1857). It is interesting to note that in *Hymns for the Use of The Methodist Episcopal Church with Tunes for Congregational Worship* (1857) the first hymn and tune book published by Methodists in America, this Wesleyan hymn is given in five four-line stanzas and used with the hymn tune HENDON (*see* Ask ye what great thing I know).

Hark, the voice of Jesus calling 440

Daniel March, a Congregational minister, was invited to deliver a sermon to the Philadelphia Christian Association meeting in the Clinton Avenue Church, Philadelphia, on October 18, 1868. His text was, "Here am I; send me" (Isa. 6:8), and he was unable to find a suitable hymn for the occasion. Shortly before the service he wrote this hymn in four stanzas, and it was used in the service. It was first published in the 1878 *Hymnal* of the Methodist Episcopal Church. Originally, the first stanza began: "Hark, the voice of Jesus crying."

ELLESDIE—*see* Jesus, I my cross have taken.

Hark! 'tis the Shepherd's voice I hear 429

Alexcenah Thomas is the author of this text; and William A. Ogden composed the tune, which first appeared in *Notes of Victory for Sunday Schools,* compiled by Ogden and E. S. Lorenz (Chicago: Fleming H.

Revell Co., 1885, No. 4), with the reference, "The Lamb which is in the midst of the throne shall feed them" (Rev. 7:17).

SHEPHERD is the name given this tune by the Hymnal Committee.

Have faith in God when your pathway is lonely 253

B. B. McKinney was assisting in a revival meeting at the First Baptist Church, Muskogee, Oklahoma. Dr. C. C. Morris, pastor of the First Baptist Church, Ada, Oklahoma, was the evangelist during this meeting, January 21, to February 4, 1934. The depression of the early thirties had taken a serious toll. Family fortunes and even meager savings were wiped out unexpectedly as businesses failed and banks closed. In these days of uncertainty, McKinney felt keenly the need of secure faith in God. One evening during the sermon he began the writing of this hymn; and it was completed, both words and music, later that evening after he returned to his room in the Severs Hotel. The manuscript was sent to Robert H. Coleman (*q.v.*), who copyrighted it in 1934 and first published it in his *Leading Hymns* (Dallas, 1936, No. 28).

The tune was named MUSKOGEE by the Hymnal Committee for the town where it was written.

Have Thine own way, Lord! 355

Adelaide A. Pollard wrote the hymn after she had returned home from a prayer meeting service. The experience of the prayer meeting had brought about in her own heart a reconciliation to God's will at a time of great distress of soul. In all probability this occurred during the time Miss Pollard was associated with a group headed by an evangelist named Sandford, which made an unsuccessful effort in the late 1890's to secure funds to finance a missionary trip to Africa.

POLLARD was composed by George C. Stebbins for this text, and he included it in his *Northfield Hymnal with Alexander's Supplement* (1907). In the same year it also appeared in Sankey's *Hallowed Hymns New and Old,* and Sankey and Clement's *Best Endeavor Hymns.* All three of these collections were published by Biglow and Main.

Have you been to Jesus for the cleansing power 192

Elisha A. Hoffman wrote both words and music for this gospel song; and it first appeared in *Spiritual Songs for Gospel Meetings and the Sunday School,* edited by Hoffman and J. H. Tenney (Cleveland: Barker & Smellie, 1878, p. 15). Three years later, it appeared in England in Sankey's *Sacred Songs and Solos.* It is interesting to note that this song is not found in any of the four editions of *Gospel Hymns* which appeared after the writing of this song.

The Hymnal Committee believed this hymn by B. B. McKinney to have been written in Lubbock, Texas, and thus the tune name LUBBOCK. After the hymnal was published, Dr. Ray Summers, professor of New Testament, Southern Baptist Theological Seminary, Louisville, Kentucky, supplied the following information:

The true situation is that this hymn was written in my home town of Allen, Texas. I have heard Mr. McKinney tell the story frequently in assemblies and conferences, and one day when I met him personally and mentioned that my home was at Allen, he told me again face-to-face the story of the writing of the song. He was teaching in Southwestern Seminary and came to Allen, which is about fifty miles from Fort Worth, for a Sunday school conference. He had planned to go back to Fort Worth after the evening session of the conference but was prohibited from doing so because of a storm which interrupted all transportation. He spent the night in the home of Mr. and Mrs. Elzir Leach. During that night there was a terrific storm which endangered the little town. During that storm Mr. McKinney wrote this song. The next morning he went back to the morning session of the conference and sang the song for the first time.

In some recently discovered notes of McKinney, there is a brief statement which reinforces the above information, with the additional statement concerning the evening service of this conference:

The preacher had brought a wonderful message of salvation and had given the invitation for lost people to accept Christ. The first plea had been rejected, no one came. The preacher reinforced his invitation with a powerful appeal to the lost which closed with these words, "Place your hand in the nail-scarred hand," gripping me like a vice. I wrote the statement down on an envelope. As the service closed a storm cloud came up and we all rushed to our homes. I went to my room. The storm struck in a moment after I arrived. During the storm I wrote the first stanza of "The Nail-scarred Hand." Before retiring I completed the song—words and music.

The manuscript was sent to Robert H. Coleman who first published it in *Harvest Hymns* (Dallas, 1924, No. 46).

"He Hideth My Soul"—*see* A wonderful Saviour is Jesus my Lord

"He Included Me"—*see* I am so happy in Christ today

"He Is Able to Deliver Thee"—*see* 'Tis the grandest theme thro' the ages rung

This song first appeared in *Gospel Hymns No. 5* (1887, p. 18), where the author is given as "Alice Monteith," one of the many pseudonyms used by Fanny J. Crosby. This is the first appearance of this hymn with the correct name of the author.

NEWCASTLE is the name given this tune by Ira D. Sankey. It is named for the town in Pennsylvania to which the Sankey family moved in 1857, when Ira D. Sankey was seventeen years of age. Here he attended high school, during which time he joined the Methodist Episcopal Church and began his first choir work.

"He Is So Precious to Me"—*see* So precious is Jesus, my Saviour, my King

"He Keeps Me Singing"—*see* There's within my heart a melody

He leadeth me! O blessed tho't   58

As a young man who recently had been graduated from Brown University and Newton Theological Institution, I was supplying for a couple of Sundays the pulpit of the First Baptist Church in Philadelphia. At the midweek service—on the 26th of March, 1862—I set out to give the people an exposition of the 23rd Psalm, which I had given before on three or four occasions; but this time I did not get further than the words "He Leadeth Me." Those words took hold of me as they had never done before. I saw in them a significance and beauty of which I had never dreamed.

It was the darkest hour of the War of the Rebellion. I did not refer to that fact—that is, I don't think I did—but it may subconsciously have led me to realize that God's leadership is the one significant fact in human experience, that it makes no difference how we are led, whither we are led, so long as we are sure God is leading us.

At the close of the meeting a few of us in the parlor of my host, good Deacon Wattson, who resided next door to the church, kept on talking about the thoughts which I had emphasized; and then and there, on a back page of the brief from which I had intended to speak, I penciled the hymn, handed it to my wife and thought no more about it.

It occurred to her months afterward to send the hymn to the *Watchman and Reflector,* a paper published in Boston, where it was first printed. In that paper it attracted the attention of William B. Bradbury, who slightly modified the refrain and set the hymn to the music which has done so much to promote its popularity. As I wrote the hymn, the refrain consisted of only two lines. Mr. Bradbury added the other two. In other respects the hymn stands just as I wrote it in Deacon Wattson's parlor, talking and writing at the same time.

I did not know until 1865 that my hymn had been set to music. I went to Rochester to preach as a candidate before the Second Baptist Church. Going into their chapel on the day I reached the city, I took up a hymnal to see what they sang, and opened it at my own hymn "He Leadeth Me."

I accepted it as an indication of divine guidance and have no doubt I was right.

The hymn has been translated into many different languages, perhaps more than any other modern hymn, as it appeals especially to the wanderer and the outcast, and I have received many touching testimonials to the comfort and help it has rendered God's dear children. It was to that end, I take it, that He put it into my mind and heart when, as it must be seen, I hadn't the faintest conception of what I was doing.

One of my former students writes me that it is the favorite hymn of the Japanese Christians. The hymn was actually sung in a Chinese court of justice by a Chinaman who had never seen a white missionary, to show the presiding justice what a Christian hymn was like. The man was on trial for renting a building to some Christians who had opened an opium refuge, and, having told the judge that at their meetings the Christians prayed and sang hymns, he was asked for a specimen hymn. He sang "He Leadeth Me."

Such is Joseph H. Gilmore's story of this hymn, as given in the November, 1926, issue of the *UGI Circle*, published by the United Gas Improvement Company, Philadelphia. This company's building was erected on the location of the house where this hymn was written. On June 1, 1926, the company erected a bronze tablet on the side of the building which gives the first stanza of the hymn together with the following:

"He Leadeth Me" sung throughout the world was written by the Rev. Dr. Joseph H. Gilmore, a son of a governor of New Hampshire, in the home of Deacon Wattson, immediately after preaching in the First Baptist Church, N.W. corner Broad and Arch Streets, on the 26th day of March, 1862. The church and Deacon Wattson's home stood on the ground upon which this building is erected.

The hymn first appeared in the *Watchman and Reflector* (XLIII, No. 49, 4) in four six-line stanzas, entitled, "He Leadeth Me Beside Still Waters" and is signed CONTOOCOOK. No reason is known for the use of this pseudonym, apparently given by the author's wife. It would seem to be of Algonquin origin, and there is a river by this name in New Hampshire.

HE LEADETH ME was written by William B. Bradbury for this text and it first appeared in Bradbury's *The Golden Censer* (New York, 1864, No. 105). Apparently the appearance of this text in the *Watchman and Reflector* came to Bradbury's attention, causing him to compose this tune. He used the first four lines of each stanza of the poem for the stanzas of the hymn. The fifth and sixth lines of each stanza of Gilmore's original were the same and were used by Bradbury as the first two lines of the refrain. The third line of the refrain, "His faithful follower I would be," seems to have been added by Bradbury, for it does not occur in Gilmore's original. The final line of the refrain is an alteration of the final line of each stanza of the original.

"He Lifted Me"—*see* In loving-kindness Jesus came

"He Lives"—*see* I serve a risen Saviour

Hear, hear, O ye Nations, and hearing, obey 467

Frederick L. Hosmer wrote this hymn in 1909, and it was included in the Unitarian *New Hymn and Tune Book* (Boston, 1914). It later appeared in Hosmer's *The Thought of God,* Third Series (1918).

JOANNA—*see* Immortal, invisible God only wise.

Hear ye the Master's call 437

This text by S. C. Kirk with this tune by Grant Colfax Tullar first appeared in *Sunday School Hymns No. 2,* compiled by I. H. Meredith and Tullar (New York: Tullar-Meredith Co., 1912, No. 12). It was originally in the key of C.

TULLAR is the name given this tune by the Hymnal Committee.

Heralds of Christ, who bear the King's commands 452

Laura S. Copenhaver, the author of this hymn, was a frequent lecturer and teacher at summer church conferences. Because of personal reasons, it was necessary for her to cancel an engagement at Northfield, Massachusetts, in the summer of 1894. She wrote this poem and sent it to the conference, asking that it be "accepted in my place," according to her daughter, Eleanor Copenhaver Sherwood of Marion, Virginia. The Women's Missionary Society of the United Lutheran Church in America, which holds the copyright to this hymn, states that it was first published as a poem in 1915, entitled "The King's Highway." The earliest hymnal inclusion seems to be H. Augustine Smith's *Hymns for the Living Age* (New York, 1925, No. 401).

NATIONAL HYMN—*see* God of our fathers, whose almighty hand.

Here at Thy table, Lord 392

No information has been found concerning this hymn for the observance of the Lord's Supper written by May P. Hoyt.

BREAD OF LIFE—*see* Break Thou the bread of life (178).

"Hiding in Thee"—*see* O safe to the Rock that is higher than I

"Higher Ground"—*see* I'm pressing on the upward way

"His Way with Thee"—*see* Would you live for Jesus, and be always
   pure and good

Here, O my Lord, I see Thee face to face   391

Once each year Horatius Bonar visited his brother, Dr. John J.
Bonar, and assisted him at a communion service. It was for such a
service, and at the request of his brother, that Bonar wrote this hymn.
It was first printed in the service leaflet for the first Sunday in October,
1855, at St. Andrew's Free Church, Greenock, Scotland. It was published in the author's *Hymns of Faith and Hope* (1857).

PENITENTIA was composed by Edward Dearle for Samuel J. Stone's
"Weary of earth, and laden with my sin" and first appeared in *Church
Hymns with Tunes* (1874). *Penitentia* is a Latin word meaning peni-
tence.

Holy Bible, Book divine   179

John Burton, Sr., an English Baptist Sunday school teacher, is the
author of this hymn. It first appeared in Burton's *Youth's Monitor in
Verse, a Series of Little Tales, Emblems, Poems and Songs* (1803). In
the *Evangelical Magazine* (June, 1805) it appeared with the signature,
"Nottingham—J.B." At this time Burton lived at Nottingham. In
1806 he included the hymn in his *Hymns for Sunday Schools, or In-
centives for Early Piety.*

ALETTA, composed by William B. Bradbury, first appeared in his
The Jubilee (New York, 1858), where it was set to "Weary sinner,
keep thine eyes" and is indicated as being a new tune.

Holy Ghost, with light divine   170

Andrew Reed, the author of this hymn, included it in his *Supplement
to Watts's Psalms and Hymns* (1817) and later in his *Hymn Book, Prepared from Dr. Watts's Psalms and Hymns, and Other Authors, with
Some Originals* (1842). It was entitled "Prayer to the Holy Spirit."

MERCY is an adaptation by Edwin P. Parker of Louis M. Gottschalk's
"The Last Hope" (1854), a composition for piano. It first appeared in
one of Charles S. Robinson's collections.

Holy holy, holy! Lord God Almighty   1

This paraphrase of Revelation 4:8-11 by Reginald Heber written
while he was vicar of Hodnet, Shropshire, 1807-23, was first published
in *A Selection of Psalms and Hymns of the Parish Church of Banbury,*

third edition (1826) and later, in his posthumous *Hymns* (1827). Heber was one of the pioneers in the early nineteenth century who sought the literary refinement of the English hymn, and this hymn is one of his finest examples of this new hymnic expression in highest poetic style.

NICAEA. The beauty and usefulness of the hymn have been greatly enhanced by this tune written for it by John B. Dykes. It is the finest of all his hymn tunes; and it first appeared, along with six other tunes by him, in *Hymns Ancient and Modern* (London, 1861). Dykes named this tune in recognition of the Council of Nicaea, A.D. 325, whose summary of Christian doctrine contains an important affirmation of the doctrine of the Trinity.

Holy Spirit, breathe on me 174

The original form of this hymn is by Edwin Hatch (*see* Breathe on me, Breath of God). B. B. McKinney's considerable alteration was made in 1937, and this hymn, words and music, first appeared in *Songs of Victory* (Nashville, 1937, No. 5), of which McKinney was editor.

TRUETT was composed by B. B. McKinney, and the tune was named by the Hymnal Committee. George W. Truett (1867-1944) served as pastor of the First Baptist Church, Dallas, Texas, forty-seven years, and was one of the outstanding preachers of his day. A quotation for which he was widely known is "To know the will of God is the greatest knowledge, and to do the will of God is the greatest achievement."

Holy Spirit, faithful guide 165

Marcus M. Wells gives the following account of his writing of this text and tune.

On a Saturday afternoon in October, 1858, while at work in my corn-field, the sentiment of the hymn came to me. The next day, Sunday, being a very stormy day, I finished the hymn and wrote a tune for it and sent it to Professor I. B. Woodbury.

When the tune arrived in New York, Woodbury had gone south because of his health. Sylvester Main, his associate, was at the time preparing the material for the November, 1858, issue of the *New York Musical Pioneer,* Woodbury's monthly musical periodical, and this hymn with this tune, FAITHFUL GUIDE, was included.

Holy Spirit, from on high 171

This hymn was written by William H. Bathurst and first appeared in his *Psalms and Hymns for Public and Private Use* (1831), entitled

"Holy Spirit's direction implored."
SEYMOUR—*see* Softly now the light of day.

Hope of the world, Thou Christ of great compassion 282

In August, 1954, the Second Assembly of the World Council of Churches met at Evanston, Illinois. Prior to this meeting the Hymn Society of America, after consultation with representatives of the World Council, invited the submitting of new hymn texts suitable for use at Evanston. From nearly five hundred texts received, this hymn written by Georgia Harkness was first choice of the committee. It was first published by the Hymn Society of America in a pamphlet with ten other hymns written for the same occasion entitled, "Eleven Ecumenical Hymns" (1954). The omitted third stanza is

> Hope of the world, afoot on dusty highways,
>   Showing to wandering souls the path of light;
> Walk Thou beside us lest the tempting byways
>   Lure us away from Thee to endless night.

Dr. Harkness has written that there is nothing particular to say about the writing of this hymn.

O PERFECT LOVE, chosen for this hymn by the Hymnal Committee, was arranged from an anthem composed by Joseph Barnby for the marriage of the Duke and Duchess of Fife, July 27, 1889. As a hymn tune it first appeared in Stainer's *Church Hymnary* (Edinburgh and Oxford, 1898).

How beauteous were the marks divine 84

This hymn is a portion of a poem of seven eight-line stanzas entitled "Hymn to the Redeemer" by A. Cleveland Coxe, which appeared in the 1847 edition of his *Christian Ballads*. In the present version, with some alterations, the first stanza is the last half of stanza one, the second stanza is the first half of stanza two, the third stanza is the last half of stanza two, and the fourth stanza is the first half of stanza six. In the Preface to the 1847 edition, Coxe comments on the thirteen poems added to this edition.

They lack the boyish exhilaration of his early verses; but on that very account may better suit the taste of many. The critic indeed will be pleased with little that the book contains. But if, like a pointed arch that delights in the moss and ivy which would spoil a Grecian column, it exhibits more of Gothic rudeness than of *Doric delicacy*, it may perhaps be allowed the merit of being in keeping with the architectural symbolism of the holy

Faith. May it be approved by Christians, as it will doubtless be despised by the World.

CANONBURY is taken from Robert Schumann's "Nachtstüke" (Op. 23, No. 4), composed in 1839. The earliest collection in which the writer has found this hymn tune adaptation is J. Ireland Tucker's *Hymnal with Tunes, Old and New* (1872, No. 522).

How firm a foundation, ye saints of the Lord   262, 263

The authorship of this well-known hymn remains an unsolved mystery. In 1787, while John Rippon was pastor of the Carter Lane Baptist Church, Tooley Street, London, he published *A Selection of Hymns from the Best Authors*. This hymn appeared in the first edition, bearing simply the signature "K—". In the 1822 edition this became "Kn," in the 1835 edition, "Keen," and in the 1844 edition it became "Kirkham." Robert Keene (or Keen) was a close friend of Rippon, serving as precentor of the Carter Lane Baptist Church, 1776-93, and no doubt he may have assisted in compiling Rippon's *Selection*. An examination of early editions of this collection reveals no hymn whose authorship is credited to Keene. However, Rippon's *Selection of Hymns and Hymn Tunes* (1791), while published under Rippon's auspices, seems from internal evidence, on the authority of Dr. W. T. Whitley (*Baptist Quarterly*, London, October, 1941), to have been compiled by Robert Keene. In this tune book are six tunes—BOURTON, SALEM NEW, CARTER LANE, GEARD (assigned to this hymn), PAINSWICK, and FAWCETT—all of which are signed "R. Keene" or "Keene." Since these tunes bear his name, it is likely that this hymn would have been credited to him had he been the author. Since no other hymn in any of these collections bears his name, it seems highly probable that he was not a hymn writer at all but a tune composer. Until more conclusive proof is found, this hymn will remain anonymous, bearing its original mark, "K—."

Originally, the hymn consisted of seven four-line stanzas and was entitled, "Exceeding Great and Precious Promises." The present version, with slight alterations, is made up of stanzas one, three, five, and seven. The omitted stanzas two, four, and six are:

> In every condition, in sickness, in health,
> In poverty's vale, or abounding in wealth;
> At home and abroad, on the land, on the sea,
> As thy days may demand, shall thy strength ever be!

When through the deep waters I call thee to go,
The rivers of woe shall not thee overflow;
For I will be with thee, thy troubles to bless
And sanctify to thee thy deepest distress.

Even down to old age, all my people shall prove
My sovereign, eternal, unchangeable love;
And when hoary hairs shall their temples adorn,
Like lambs they shall still in my bosom be borne.

Rippon's *Selection* was exceedingly popular and became a standard of Baptist hymnody. Eleven editions appeared in England before Rippon's death in 1836 and an American edition was printed in Philadelphia in 1820. This hymn soon became well known throughout the North and South and was included in many collections. It was the favorite hymn of Theodore Roosevelt, and Andrew Jackson requested that it be sung at his bedside shortly before he died at the Hermitage. By his own request, it was sung at the funeral of Robert E. Lee "as an expression of his full trust in the ways of the Heavenly Father."

ADESTE FIDELIS (262)—*see* O come, all ye faithful, joyful and triumphant.

The source of the tune FOUNDATION (263) has been as baffling as the hymn to which it is sung. An overcrowded page in the *Hymn and Tune Book of the Methodist Episcopal Church, South* (1889) made it appear that Anne Steele, the hymn writer, was the composer of this tune, and this error has been duplicated in untold collections. Actually, this is one of the sturdy folk hymn tunes which appeared in the South. It seems to have made its first appearance in William Caldwell's *Union Harmony, or Family Musician, Being a Choice Selection of Tunes, Selected from the Works of the Most Eminent Authors Ancient and Modern Together with a Large Number of Original Tunes Composed and Harmonized by the Author* (Maryville, Tennessee, 1837, p. 58). Seven years later the tune appeared in *The Sacred Harp,* compiled by B. F. White and E. J. King (Hamilton, Georgia, 1844, p. 72), where it is called BELLEVUE and is credited to "Z. Chambless."

In his discussion of this tune in *Our Hymnody,* Robert G. McCutchan states that it "appeared in a pamphlet compilation entitled, *The Cluster of Spiritual Songs, Divine Hymns and Sacred Poems,* by the Rev. Jesse Mercer, D. D., and which, by 1817, reached a third edition"; and this has been repeated in other accounts. There were, however, no tunes in Mercer's *Cluster,* for it was a collection of hymns only. Evidently McCutchan's statement was based on the fact that in *The Sacred Harp,* along with the name "Z. Chambless," mentioned above, appears the

71

notice "Mercer's *Cluster*, p. 411." This is intended to indicate the source of the text and has no reference to the tune.

How sweet the name of Jesus sounds
160

Written by John Newton, this hymn first appeared in the *Olney Hymns* (1779), entitled "The Name of Jesus," with the text "Thy name is as ointment poured forth" (Song of Sol. 1:3). In stanza four, line one, "shepherd" was originally "husband." One verse is omitted:

> By Thee my prayers acceptance gain,
> Although with sin defiled;
> Satan accuses me in vain
> And I am owned a child.

ORTONVILLE—*see* Majestic sweetness sits enthroned.

How tedious and tasteless the hours
306

This hymn by John Newton first appeared in the *Olney Hymns* (London, 1779). It was entitled "Fellowship with Christ" and was based on Psalm 73:25, "None upon earth I desire beside thee."

This hymn seems to have enjoyed tremendous popularity among Baptists of the South. When Baron Stow and Samuel Francis Smith, two Baptist preachers from New England, compiled *The Psalmist* (1843), vigorous protest came from the South because of the omission of this hymn and others equally popular in that area. To overcome this opposition, a supplement was issued four years later by Richard Fuller of Baltimore and J. B. Jeter of Richmond, which included among others this hymn and also "Amazing grace, how sweet the sound." In the preface to this supplement these two Southern Baptist preachers made the following explanation:

Old songs, like old friends, are more valued than new ones. A number of the hymns best known, most valued, and most frequently sung in the South are not found in the *Psalmist*. Without them, no hymnbook, whatever may be its excellences, is likely to become generally or permanently popular in that region. To supply this deficiency in the *Psalmist,* as far as may be, is the design of the following Supplement.

CONTRAST, listed by several names and credited to numerous composers or sources, has appeared in American tune books since the early nineteenth century. It was particularly popular among the southern tune books, and the earliest appearance found by George Pullen Jackson was in Ananias Davisson's *Supplement to Kentucky Harmony* (1820). Although it has long been accepted as an American folk melody, Jackson contends that the earliest form of this tune seems to have been "Es nehme zehn-tausend Ducaten," in J. S. Bach's cantata, *Mer habn en neue Oberkeet* (cf. *Bach-Gesellschaft,* XXIX, 195). Jackson quotes Sabine Baring-Gould in stating that the earliest printed form of the Bach tune in England was in *The Tragedy of Tragedies, or Tom Thumb* (1734), as the setting of the song, "In Hurry Posthaste for a License." Jackson further notes that this tune is found in *Vocal Music, or the Songster's Companion,* second edition (1782), to the text, "Farewell, Ye Green Fields and Sweet Groves," and suggests that Newton's hymn is a parody on this secular text. Furthermore, the name GREEN FIELDS, quite commonly found attached to this tune in the southern tune books, is taken from this secular text.

I am a stranger here, within a foreign land   433

Dr. E. Taylor Cassel wrote this text for which his wife, Flora H. Cassel, provided the tune. It was written in 1902 when they made their home in Hastings, Nebraska, and Dr. Cassel practiced medicine there. It was first published in *International Praise,* compiled and published by E. O. Excell (Chicago, 1902, No. 90).

CASSEL is the name given this tune by the Hymnal Committee.

I am coming to the cross   243

William McDonald's account of the writing of the hymn is given by McCutchan in *Our Hymnody.*

The hymn was written in 1870, in the city of Brooklyn, New York, while I was pastor in that city. I had felt the need of a hymn to aid seekers of heart purity while at the altar. I had desired something, simple in expression, true to experience, and ending in the fullness of love. The tune composed by Mr. Fischer, with the first two lines of the chorus, I had seen, and was much pleased with their simplicity. And as I was sitting in my study one day, the line of thought came rushing into my mind, and I began to write, and in a few minutes the hymn was on paper. It was first sung at a National Campmeeting, held at Hamilton, Mass., June 22, 1870.

It appeared in the *Baptist Praise Book* (1871) and in the 1872 edition of Joseph Hillman's *The Revivalist.* It was included in a pamphlet for camp meetings issued in 1872 by the *Advocate of Christian Holiness.*

TRUSTING was composed by William G. Fischer.

I am happy today and the sun shines bright   209

J. Edwin McConnell wrote both words and music for this hymn. In a letter to the writer dated April 25, 1955, Mrs. Jean McConnell Larkin of St. Petersburg, Florida, a sister of the author, provides the following information.

> One very cold, below zero, day in a hotel in Spirit Lake, Iowa, an eighteen-year-old youth was at the piano and humming to himself. His father, who had been opening his mail nearby, asked what he was playing. "Oh, just another song aborning, Dad," answered the boy. . . . That night they introduced "Whosoever Surely Meaneth Me" to the audience of their evangelistic meeting, where it soon became their "theme song" of the campaign.

The manuscript of the song was purchased by Charlie D. Tillman, who copyrighted it in 1914.

McCONNELL is the name given this tune by the Hymnal Committee.

"I Am Praying for You"—*see* I have a Saviour, He's pleading in glory

I am resolved no longer to linger   **216**

In a letter to the writer dated January 28, 1955, Mrs. J. L. Toll, daughter of the composer, James H. Fillmore, states that this tune

> was written in 1896 as a delegation song for Ohio—fourteen train loads— for the World Christian Endeavor Convention in San Francisco, honoring Frances E. Clarke, founder of Christian Endeavor. The song became so popular Mr. Hartsough wrote new words for it for our hymnals.

With Palmer Hartsough's new text, the hymn first appeared in *The Praise Hymnal,* compiled by Gilbert J. Ellis and Fillmore (Cincinnati: Fillmore Bros., 1896, No. 228).

RESOLUTION is the name given this tune by the Hymnal Committee.

I am satisfied with Jesus   **436**

B. B. McKinney has given the following account:

> This song was written in 1926 in my office at the Southwestern Baptist Theological Seminary during my days as a teacher in that great institution.
> I shall never forget the Saturday afternoon when this song was written. I had been thinking about the beautiful life of Christ and His unfailing love. I thought of His greatness to me as a Saviour, Comforter and Friend As I thought of His greatness, I thought of my littleness. When I thought of what He had done for me and how little I had done for Him I became dissatisfied with my own little life. I was altogether satisfied with Jesus but was altogether dissatisfied with my own life.
> I composed "Satisfied with Jesus" with deep consciousness of my own

need of a more consecrated life in Christ. Out of a sincere longing for this deeper life, I wrote with little effort the words and music. The whole song was written with very tender emotion and completed with tears. I had a new fellowship with Christ that afternoon. I dedicated my life anew to Him. I am still dissatisfied with my life. No Christian should ever be satisfied until we awake in His likeness.

The hymn w..s first published in Robert H. Coleman's *The Modern Hymnal* (Dallas, 1926. No. 427).

ROUTH, the name given this tune by the Hymnal Committee, is well known to Southern Baptists. McKinney married Leila Routh. Her brother, Dr. E. C. Routh, preacher, journalist, author, was for many years editor of the *Baptist Messenger,* the Oklahoma Baptist weekly. Dr. Porter Routh, son of E. C. Routh, is the executive secretary of the Executive Committee of the Southern Baptist Convention.

I am so glad that our Father in heaven 509

Philip P. Bliss wrote both words and music in Chicago, in June, 1870, while he and his wife were staying in the home of Major Daniel W. Whittle. It was first published in Bliss's *The Charm for Sunday Schools* (Cincinnati: John Church Co., 1871).

JESUS LOVES EVEN ME, the name of this tune, is sometimes used as the title for this hymn.

I am so happy in Christ today 194

Johnson Oatman, Jr., was a prolific writer of gospel song texts and supplied many of the composers of his day with song material. Hall, in *Biography of Gospel Song and Hymn Writers* (p. 359), states that "He has constantly on hand more orders for songs [texts] than he can possibly fill." Among the gospel song composers who used his texts were Sweney, Hugg, Gabriel, Excell, Gilmour, and many others.

SEWELL was composed for this text by Hampton H. Sewell. In a letter to the writer dated May 2, 1955, Mrs. Bettie M. Sewell, widow of the composer, states that Sewell became a singing evangelist with Rev. Charles Dunaway in January, 1909.

In April, 1909, they had a wonderful revival in Waycross, Georgia, and many souls were saved. It was in this meeting that Bishop Arthur Moore was brought to Christ. It was also in this meeting that my husband was inspired to write the hymn "He Included Me."

This song first appeared in Sewell's *Hymns of Glory, No. 2* (Atlanta, Ga., 1914, No. 65). SEWELL was the name given this tune by the Hymnal Committee.

I am Thine, O Lord, I have heard Thy voice 349

Fanny J. Crosby wrote this hymn in Cincinnati, Ohio, while visiting in the home of William H. Doane. One evening their conversation dealt with the nearness of God. Before retiring, the author wrote the words of this hymn. Doane later supplied the tune, I AM THINE, and the hymn first appeared in *Brightest and Best,* a Sunday school songbook compiled by Doane and Robert Lowry (New York: Biglow & Main, 1875). It was entitled, "Draw Me Nearer," and is based on "Let us draw near with a true heart" (Heb. 10:22).

I am thinking today of that beautiful land 470

Eliza E. Hewitt wrote the text and John R. Sweney composed the tune which first appeared in *Songs of Love and Praise, No. 4,* compiled by Sweney, Henry L. Gilmour, and J. H. Entwisle (Philadelphia: John J. Hood, 1897, No. 172).

STARS IN MY CROWN is the name given this tune by the Hymnal Committee.

I can hear my Saviour calling 361

It is not known when this hymn first appeared. In many collections it bears the notice, "Copyright 1890, J. S. Norris." If this indicates the approximate date of the writing of this hymn, it occurred during or immediately following a two-year pastorate by Norris of the Congregational church in Webster City, Iowa. No information has been found concerning E. W. Blandy, the author of the words.

NORRIS was composed by J. S. Norris. The tune was named by the Hymnal Committee.

I gave My life for thee 399

Frances R. Havergal had jotted down the motto, "I did this for thee; what hast thou done for Me?" which had been placed under a picture of Christ in the study of an eminent German pastor. The author's sister has provided the following account:

On January 10, 1858, she had come in weary, and sitting down she read the motto, and the lines of her hymn flashed upon her. She wrote them in pencil on a scrap of paper. Reading them over she thought them so poor that she tossed them on the fire, but they fell out untouched. Showing them some months after to her father, he encouraged her to preserve them, and wrote the tune BACA specially for them. The hymn was printed on a leaflet, 1859, and in *Good Words,* February, 1860.

KENOSIS was composed by Philip P. Bliss for this hymn and dedicated to the "Railroad Chapel Sunday School, Chicago." It first appeared in *Sunshine for Sunday Schools* by P. P. Bliss (Cincinnati: John Church & Co., 1873, p. 56). The word "kenosis" comes from Greek and refers to Christ's self-emptying (cf. Phil. 2:7).

I have a Saviour, He's pleading in glory   232

Dwight L. Moody and Ira D. Sankey were in Scotland from November, 1873, until the last of January, 1874. Horatius Bonar, the eminent Scottish Presbyterian preacher was in attendance at these meetings. Sankey's first attempt at song writing occurred at Edinburgh when he composed a tune for Bonar's "Yet There Is Room." It was also during these days in Edinburgh that news reached Moody and Sankey of the tragedy at sea involving the wife and children of Horatio Spafford (*see* When peace, like a river, attendeth my way). Weeks later in Ireland, Sankey found the words of this hymn by S. O'Malley Cluff, written in 1860 and printed in a leaflet. Shortly afterward he wrote his second tune. Within a few weeks they were in London, and this hymn became immensely popular in these meetings. There is no evidence to the fact that Sankey ever knew the identity of the author. This text with Sankey's tune, INTERCESSION, appeared in England in Sankey's *Sacred Songs and Solos* and in America in *Gospel Hymns and Sacred Songs* (1875, No. 11). Originally in five stanzas, the omitted fourth stanza is:

> I have a peace; it is calm as a river—
> A peace that the friends of this world never knew;
> My Saviour alone is its Author and Giver,
> And oh, could I know it was given to you!

I have a song I love to sing   208

Edwin O. Excell wrote both words and music, and they first appeared in *Echoes of Eden for the Sunday School,* compiled and published by E. O. Excell (Chicago, 1884, No. 26). Originally consisting of five stanzas, the omitted stanza is:

> I have a joy I can't express,
> Since I have been redeemed,
> All through His blood and righteousness,
> Since I have been redeemed.

OTHELLO is the name given this tune by the Hymnal Committee, using the composer's middle name.

Brigadier Gordon Avery of the Salvation Army publishing house in London has supplied the information concerning this hymn and its author, Charles W. Fry. Soon after Fry's death on August 24, 1882, the manuscript of these words, written to a secular melody, was found among his personal effects by his widow. Attached to the song was a note stating that this had been written at a Mr. Wilkinson's home in Lincoln, England, in June 1881, where Fry was a guest during his service with the Salvation Army in that city. The words were first published in *The War Cry* for December 29, 1881. Words and music first appeared in *Salvation Music, Vol. 2* (1883). The first appearance of this song in America was in *Gospel Hymns No. 5* (1887) and was included in this collection after Ira D. Sankey, one of the compilers, had become acquainted with it in England. The text is credited to Fry and the music is given as "Arr. by Ira D. Sankey." It is in 6/8 rhythm.

SALVATIONIST is an adaptation of a minstrel song written by William S. Hays in Louisville, Kentucky, in 1871, entitled "The Little Old Log Cabin down the Lane." Apparently this minstrel song became quite popular in England, and Fry, attracted by its secular popularity, sought to capitalize on its melodic appeal and used it with a sacred text. There is considerable alteration in Fry's version of the tune. Possibly, Fry jotted it down from memory, and the alterations were unintentional; or it may be that he made the melodic changes on purpose. Arch R. Wiggins in *Father of Salvation Army Music: Richard Slater* (London: Salvationist Publishing & Supplies, 1945, p. 24), tells of the work of Fry and his three sons who made up the Fry Family Band:

> The Frys made up their parts as they went along; they required no printed music. Fred (the eldest son) and his brothers all knew shorthand, so whenever they heard a fresh song they would take down the words and Fred would write the music in tonic sol-fa. Once, when the Founder's (General Booth) Sunday night meeting was unusually stiff, he dropped on Fred Fry for a vocal solo, and as suddenly Fry had the inspiration to sing "Depth of Mercy" to the then popular secular air, "It is years since last we met," which resulted in completely changing the atmosphere of the gathering and a number of people deciding for Christ.

In a letter to the writer dated November 2, 1954, Brigadier Frank Longino, secretary of the Music and Education Department of the Salvation Army regional headquarters, Atlanta, Georgia, writes that the Salvation Army

was not the first to use secular tunes with "converted" words as it was the practice of the Wesleys also, and for the same purpose—to attract people so they might hear the Gospel. The tune of "Lily of the Valley" was a popular ditty heard in dance-halls of that time. Another still sung and much loved by the Salvationists was "The blood of Jesus cleanses white as snow" to the tune of "I traced her little footsteps in the snow."

I might add that this song is not entirely typical of the Army songs because, paradoxically, in our worship services we still use the stately and formal hymns of the church. In our street services, however, we use the gay and rollicking sort, and so have become identified with this type alone.

I hear the Saviour say   225

Elvina M. Hall wrote this hymn in 1865 during a Sunday morning service at the Monument Street Methodist Church in Baltimore, Maryland. While the pastor was leading in prayer, Mrs. Hall wrote the hymn on the flyleaf of a copy of a hymnal, *New Lute of Zion*. Later she gave a poem to her pastor with little thought that it one day would become so well known.

ALL TO CHRIST was composed by John T. Grape. The Monument Street Methodist Church was undergoing repairs to the building, and the cabinet organ had been placed in the care of Mr. Grape, the church organist. He had been greatly impressed with a song entitled, "Jesus Paid It All," which appeared in Bradbury's *Golden Censer* (1864) and set out to write another tune on the same model. Grape has stated that

Soon after, the Rev. George W. Schrick called on me to select anything new I had to offer. On hearing this piece he expressed his pleasure with it and stated that Mrs. Elvina M. Hall had written some words that would just suit the music. I gave him a copy of it and it was soon sung in several churches here in Baltimore and well received. At the suggestion of friends I sent a copy to Professor Theodore Perkins and it was published in *Sabbath Chords* (New York: Brown and Perkins, 1868, no. 93).

It is not inconceivable that Mrs. Hall was also familiar with Bradbury's tune, and possibly had it in mind when she wrote the words. This hymn appeared in Bliss's *Gospel Songs* (1874) and became a familiar hymn in the *Gospel Hymn* series. Because of the many alterations in the original text, Mrs. Hall's five stanzas are given here as they first appeared.

> I hear my Saviour say
>   Thy strength indeed is small,
> Thou hast nought thy debt to pay,
>   Find in me thy all in all.

Yea, nothing good have I,
    Whereby thy grace to claim;
I'll wash my garments white
    In the blood of Calvary's Lamb.

And now complete in Him,
    My robe his righteousness,
Close sheltered 'neath His side,
    I am divinely blest,

When from my dying bed
    My ransomed soul shall rise,
Jesus paid it all
    Shall rend the vaulted skies.

And when before the throne
    I stand in Him complete,
I'll lay my trophies down
    All down at Jesus feet.

The writer has endeavored to identify George W. Schrick, the Methodist minister mentioned in the above account, who was supposedly the pastor of the Monument Street Methodist Church in Baltimore. An inquiry directed to the Baltimore Annual Conference of the Methodist Church has brought this reply dated May 9, 1955, from Dr. William H. Best, conference historian;

I have gone over the lists of the ministers of the Methodist Episcopal, Methodist Episcopal South, and the Methodist Protestant church which we have compiled in our Baltimore Conference Minutes of the Methodist Church concerning the Reverend Mr. Schrick referred to in your letter, but none of these older men have any recollection of this brother. He may have been a local preacher or an unordained supply and as such his name would not appear in any of these lists.

I hear Thy welcome voice   224

This hymn and this tune, WELCOME VOICE, were written in 1872 while the author, Lewis Hartsough, was conducting a revival meeting in Epworth, Iowa. It first appeared in the 1872 edition of *The Revivalist* (No. 464 [1st ed., 1868]), of which Hartsough was musical editor. Apparently it was published shortly afterward in a monthly magazine, *The Guide to Holiness,* for Ira D. Sankey reports finding this hymn in a copy of this magazine which was sent to him in England in 1873. Sankey included it in *Gospel Hymns and Sacred Songs* (1875, No. 63), which led to its widespread popularity. Originally in six stanzas, the omitted stanzas four and five are:

80

'Tis Jesus who confirms
The blessed work within,
By adding grace to welcomed grace,
Where reigned the power of sin.

And He the witness gives
To loyal hearts and free,
That every promise is fulfilled,
If faith but brings the plea.

I heard the bells on Christmas day   78

This hymn is made up of stanzas one, two, six, and seven of a poem
of seven stanzas entitled, "Christmas Bells," which was written by Henry
Wadsworth Longfellow in 1864 for the Sunday school of the Unitarian
Church of the Disciples, Boston. These four stanzas were included in
the Unitarian *New Hymn and Tune Book* (Boston, 1914). References
to the Civil War, in progress at the time this poem was written, are found
in the omitted stanzas.

WALTHAM—*see* Fling out the banner! let it float

I heard the voice of Jesus say   302

Horatius Bonar wrote this hymn while he was pastor at Kelso, Scotland. It first appeared in his *Hymns, Original and Selected* (1846)
and later in his *Hymns of Faith and Hope* (1862), entitled "The Voice
from Galilee." It is based on John 1:16.

SPOHR—*see* All things bright and beautiful.

I know not how that Bethlehem's Babe   276

In 1910, Harry W. Farrington, a graduate student at Harvard University, submitted this hymn in a competition for a Christmas hymn
sponsored by the school, and it was the unanimous choice of the judges
as the winning hymn. It was first published in a collection of the
author's poems, *Rough and Brown* (1921). In *Valleys and Visions,* a
collection of his works published posthumously by his widow, Dora
Davis Farrington, the author gives the following information about this
hymn:

I do not know the "mystery of Godliness" anymore than did Paul; but I
believe in the Virgin Birth, the Atonement, and the Resurrection, because
I cannot conceive of God in any but the terms of Christ, nor of Christ of
anything else than God in earthly form. Not from logic, nor history, nor
dogmatic theology, but from the witness of His spirit in my own personal
experience do I know the Saviour. This is all crystallized in the story of my
poem.

Its first hymnal inclusion seems to be *The Abingdon Hymnal* (New York, 1928).

St. Agnes (*see* Father, I stretch my hands to Thee) was used for this text in *The Methodist Hymnal* (1935), at the suggestion of the author's widow.

I know not why God's wondrous grace 275

In many collections this hymn is credited to "El Nathan," the pseudonym of Daniel W. Whittle. James McGranahan, Whittle's music director, composed the tune. This first appeared in *Gospel Hymns No. 4* (1883).

El Nathan is the name given this tune by the Hymnal Committee.

I know that my Redeemer liveth 127

Jessie Brown Pounds is the author of the text, and James H. Fillmore is the composer of the tune, Hannah. This hymn first appeared as part of an Easter cantata, *Hope's Messenger,* by Fillmore, published by the Fillmore Music House (Cincinnati, 1893). Its first hymnal inclusion was *The Praise Hymnal* (1896), compiled by Gilbert J. Ellis and Fillmore. The Hymnal Committee named this tune Hannah for the composer's mother, Hannah Lockwood Fillmore.

"I Know the Bible Is True"—*see* I know the Bible was sent from God

I know the Bible was sent from God 184

This hymn by B. B. McKinney first appeared in *The Modern Hymnal,* published by Robert H. Coleman (Dallas, 1926, No. 237), where the author of the text was given as Gene Routh, a pseudonym used several times by McKinney. "Gene" is the name of his second son, and "Routh" is his wife's family name.

Grice is the name given this tune by the Hymnal Committee and is named for Dr. Homer L. Grice, who was for many years the leader in Vacation Bible school activity among Southern Baptists.

"I Know Whom I Have Believed"—*see* I know not why God's wondrous grace

I lay my sins on Jesus 210

This hymn, thought to be Horatius Bonar's first effort at hymn writing, appeared in his *Songs for the Wilderness,* first series (1843), in four eight-line stanzas entitled "The Fulness of Jesus."

Aurelia was composed by Samuel S. Wesley for "Jerusalem the

golden," and first appeared in *A Selection of Psalms and Hymns* (London, 1864), edited by Wesley and Charles Kemble. The name of the tune was suggested by the composer's wife and was taken from *aureus,* the Latin word for "golden."

I love Thee, I love Thee, I love Thee, my Lord   150

The author of this text and the composer of this tune are anonymous. These stanzas set to this tune, called CHARITY, appeared in *The Christian Harmony, or Songsters Companion,* compiled by Jeremiah Ingalls (Exeter, N. H.: Henry Ranlet, 1805, No. 44).

This was the last hymn to be included in the hymnal. It was brought to the attention of the editor by the writer of this handbook, who had discovered it in the *Free Methodist Hymnal* (1910). The contents of the hymnal had been selected, and the initial plates were being made. By some oversight, one hymn appeared twice, being listed in two different categories. The vacancy caused by the removal of this duplicate left room for one additional hymn, and "I love Thee" was chosen by the editor.

I love Thy kingdom, Lord   382

It was not until after the Revolutionary War that Isaac Watts's *Psalms of David Imitated in the Language of the New Testament* (1719) came into widespread usage in America. Louis Benson states that "to make the *Imitations* palatable at that epoch to the newly won liberties of America, some changes were necessary in those passages in which Watts had made David appear as a patriotic Englishman." This resulted in *The Psalms of David . . . by I. Watts,* D.D. *A New Edition in which the Psalms Omitted by Dr. Watts Are Versified, Local Passages Are Altered, and a Number of Psalms Are Versified anew in Proper Metres. By Timothy Dwight,* D.D. *President of Yale College. At the Request of the General Association of Connecticut* (Hartford, 1801). The present hymn is Timothy Dwight's version of a portion of Psalm 137, and originally consisted of eight four-line stanzas. This is probably the earliest American hymn which remains in common usage.

ST. THOMAS is the second quarter of a sixteen-line quadruple short meter tune called HOLBORN which appeared in Aaron Williams' *Universal Psalmodist,* second edition (London 1763). This fragment appears as a separate tune in the fifth edition (1770) and the same year appeared in Isaac Smith's *Collection of Psalm Tunes.*

"I Love Thee" from Ingalls' *Christian Harmony*

This hymn is taken from a long poem by Katherine Hankey written in 1866 and based on the life of Christ. The first section of the poem is entitled "The Story Wanted," and was written on January 29. The hymn "Tell Me the Old, Old Story" (222) is from this first section. The second section—written in November, 1866, entitled "The Story Told"—contained the stanzas used in this hymn. The text of the refrain was written by the composer of the tune.

HANKEY, composed by William G. Fischer, was first published in a pamphlet, entitled *Joyful Songs, Nos. 1 to 3* (Philadelphia: 1869 Methodist Episcopal Book Room). Twenty-four of the forty-one tunes in this pamphlet were composed or arranged by Fischer. Five years later it appeared in Bliss's *Gospel Songs* (Cincinnati, 1874), and in 1875 it was included in Bliss and Sankey's *Gospel Hymns and Sacred Songs.* These two collections brought the hymn to the attention of multitudes, and it became extremely popular.

I must needs go home by the way of the cross   196

This text by Jessie Brown Pounds, set to Charles H. Gabriel's tune, was written in 1906. In his *Singers and Their Songs,* Gabriel gives the following explanation:

There is nothing of particular interest concerning "The Way of the Cross Leads Home," except that the author was quite innocent of any controversial spirit. She had heard it urged that this hymn teaches that there is no safety beyond the line of conservative theology. The intention was merely to give emphasis to the truth so constantly held up in the teachings of Christ, that heroic Christianity does not follow the line of least resistance.

The hymn first appeared in *Living Praises No. 2,* compiled by Gabriel and W. W. Dowling (St. Louis: Christian Publishing Co., 1906, No. 52).

I must tell Jesus all of my trials   298

Elisha A. Hoffman wrote both words and music for this hymn, and it first appeared in the 1894 edition of *Pentecostal Hymns* (Chicago: Hope Publishing Co., No. 4), of which Hoffman was one of the music editors. In the same year it appeared in Hoffman's *Christian Endeavor Hymnal.*

ORWIGSBURG is the name given this tune by the Hymnal Committee for the town in Pennsylvania where Hoffman was born.

Concerning the writing of these words, the author, Annie S. Hawks, has said, "I was so filled with the sense of nearness to the Master that, wondering how one could live without Him, either in joy or pain, these words, 'I Need Thee Every Hour,' were ushered into my mind, the thought at once taking full possession of me." Mrs. Hawks wrote the stanzas; and Dr. Robert Lowry, her pastor, composed the tune NEED and wrote the words of the refrain.

The hymn was first published in a small collection compiled for use in the National Baptist Sunday School Convention at Cincinnati in November, 1872. It next appeared in *Royal Diadem for the Sunday School,* compiled by Lowry and William H. Doane (New York: Biglow & Main, 1873, No. 35), with the heading "Without me ye can do nothing" (John 15:5). The original fourth stanza omitted in our hymnal is

> I need Thee every hour;
> Teach me Thy will;
> And Thy rich promises
> In me fulfil.

It was first sung in England by Ira D. Sankey in the D. L. Moody meetings held in the East End of London in 1874.

I need Thee, precious Jesus 221

This hymn by Frederick Whitfield first appeared as a single hymn sheet in 1855, consisting of six eight-line stanzas. It was included in Whitfield's *Sacred Poems and Prose* (1861), and its first hymnal inclusion was in Ryle's *Hymns for the Church* (1860).

AURELIA—*see* I lay my sins on Jesus.

I saw the cross of Jesus 190

This hymn by Frederick Whitfield first appeared in his *Sacred Poems and Prose* (1861).

WHITFIELD is the name given this tune by the Hymnal Committee. It is also known as CALCUTTA. In *The Choir* (LI, No. 5, 91) the following explanation concerning this tune is given by Maurice Frost:

It is generally attributed to Bishop Heber, but it was certainly not written by him. An article in the *Oxford Diocesan Magazine* for August, 1932, by the late Rev. C. C. Inge, gave its source, and also related its history. It appeared in a manuscript book of tunes belonging to his family set to his grandfather's version of Psalm 61 (*The Cleveland Psalter,* by Archdeacon Churton), 8.8.8.3.8.7. Mr. W. W. Inge of Rugby kindly looked up the

manuscript for me and sent me a copy of the tune. It is harmonized, and
the melody is as follows:

It goes back to a benefit concert arranged by Thomas Moore at the
Theatre Royal, Dublin, in 1811, where it appears in a "Melologue upon
National Music" as a "Greek Air resumed," with a note, "For this pretty
Greek melody I am indebted to Mr. Gell who brought it with him from
Athens." A copy is in the British Museum, G. 806.c.(66), and the melody
is given thus:

The harmonization suggests that the first version in the manuscript book
was taken direct from the concert programme.

The final line of the tune has been considerably altered in our version.
It is not known who first arranged this as a hymn tune, or who made
these alterations. The earliest appearance of this hymn tune the writer
has found is in *The Sunday-Scholar's Tune Book* (London: The Sunday
School Union, 1869, No. 132), where it is called PATNA.

I serve a risen Saviour, He's in the world today   279

Alfred H. Ackley wrote both words and music to this hymn. According to George W. Sanville's account in *Forty Gospel Hymn Stories*,
this hymn was written following an experience Ackley had with a young
Jew whom he tried to win to Christ. The young man's startling question, "Why should I worship a dead Jew?" brought forth Ackley's im-

mediate reply, "He lives!" Reflecting upon this discussion, and rereading the account of the resurrection of Christ, he wrote both words and music. The hymn first appeared in *Triumphant Service Songs* (Chicago: The Rodeheaver Co., 1934, No. 286).

ACKLEY is the name given this tune by the Hymnal Committee.

I stand amazed in the presence   139

Charles H. Gabriel wrote both words and music of this hymn, and it first appeared in *Praises,* compiled and published by E. O. Excell (Chicago, 1905, No. 3).

"I Surrender All"—*see* All to Jesus I surrender

I think when I read that sweet story of old   506

In 1841, while visiting the Normal Infant School, Grey's Inn Road, London, Jemima T. Luke heard a Greek melody used as a marching tune which captured her interest. Later, while riding alone in a stage coach to attend a missionary meeting in Wellington, she penciled the first two stanzas of this hymn on the back of an old envelope. A third stanza was added later. The hymn with this tune first appeared in the *Sunday School Teachers' Magazine* (March, 1841). The first hymnal inclusion was in *The Leeds Hymn Book* (1853, No. 874), where it appeared unsigned. Originally consisting of three eight-line stanzas, the present version uses stanza one for the first and second stanzas, and the present third stanza uses the first four lines of the original stanza two. The last half of stanza two and the third stanza mentioned above read as follows:

> In that beautiful place he has gone to prepare
>   For all who are washed and forgiven,
> And many dear children are gathering there
>   For of such is the kingdom of heaven.
>
> But the thousands and thousands who wander and fall
>   Never heard of that heavenly home.
> I should like them to know there is room for them all
>   And that Jesus has bid them to come.
> I long for the joy of that glorious time,
>   The sweetest and brightest and best,
> When the dear little children of every clime
>   Shall crowd to his arms and be blest.

SWEET STORY is an arrangement by William B. Bradbury of the original Greek melody and first published in his collection for Sunday schools, *Oriola* (dated 1859, but not published until the following year). The Greek origin of this melody is unknown.

I was sinking deep in sin 212

In a letter to the writer dated May 23, 1955, Mrs. Louise Rowe Mayhew, daughter of the author, James Rowe, writes:

Howard E. Smith was a little man whose hands were so knotted with arthritis that you would wonder how he could use them at all, much less play the piano, but he could and did. I can see them now, my father striding up and down humming a bar or two and Howard E. playing it and jotting it down. Thus was "Love Lifted Me" composed. That was in Saugatuck, Connecticut, a good many years ago.

This occurred in 1912, and the hymn was copyrighted that same year by Charlie D. Tillman. Shortly afterward Tillman sold the copyright to Robert H. Coleman, and the song appeared in Coleman's *Select Gospel Songs,* edited by J. P. Scholfield, E. L. Wolslagel, and I. E. Reynolds (1916, No. 6).

SAFETY is the name given this tune by the Hymnal Committee.

"I Will Arise and Go to Jesus"—*see* Come, ye sinners, poor and needy

"I Will Not Forget Thee"—*see* Sweet is the promise, "I will not forget thee,"

I will sing of my Redeemer 143

This text by Philip P. Bliss was found in his trunk, which escaped damage in the tragic train wreck which claimed the lives of Bliss and his wife. It is not known when it was written or whether Bliss had composed a tune for the words.

MY REDEEMER was composed by James McGranahan while on a visit to Chicago, after Bliss's death, to consider Major D. W. Whittle's invitation to carry on Bliss's work as Whittle's song leader. McGranahan showed the song to Whittle, and, according to George C. Stebbins in *Reminiscences and Gospel Hymn Stories,*

Before his [McGranahan's] leaving Chicago it was decided to have it sung in the tabernacle services, and also that it would be well to have it sung by four men's voices. The music was arranged accordingly and two of the most prominent baritone soloists of the city were secured, they singing the lower parts, Mr. McGranahan taking the alto, an octave higher, and I the melody.

A great audience was present in the tabernacle. The Major related the finding of the words among Mr. Bliss's effects, and Mr. McGranahan's setting them to music, which awakened a keen interest among the people, thus preparing the way for a sympathetic hearing.

Some months after this, Stebbins tells of "making a record" in New York City where an Edison phonograph was being exhibited. He sang "My Redeemer," giving it the distinction of being one of the first songs recorded on Edison's new invention.

> The record was made on a cylinder wrapped in tinfoil, which was turned by hand both in recording and reproducing, . . . and when it was made I stepped aside and heard myself sing. . . . the hearing of my own voice, and every word with striking distinctness enunciated, and even my characteristic manner of singing, modulation of voice and phrasing, produced a unique sensation.

This hymn with this tune first appeared in *Welcome Tidings, A New Collection for Sunday School,* compiled by Robert Lowry, William H. Doane, and Ira D. Sankey (1877, No. 52). The following year it appeared in McGranahan's *The Gospel Male Choir* (Cincinnati: John Church & Co., 1878, No. 42), and in *Gospel Hymns No. 3.*

I will sing the wondrous story 144

Armin Haeussler in *The Story of Our Hymns* gives an account of a visit with Francis H. Rowley, the author of this hymn, in Boston in September, 1947, in which the details of the writing of this hymn are given by the author.

> We were having a revival at the First Baptist Church at North Adams, Mass., in 1886, the third year of my pastorate there, which was one of the richest and most blessed experiences of my entire ministry. I was assisted by a young Swiss musician named Peter Bilhorn who suggested that I write a hymn for which he would compose the music. The following night the hymn came to me without any particular effort on my part.

Numerous alterations in the original text were made without the author's knowledge or consent. Apparently, Ira D. Sankey made these changes when the manuscript was prepared for publication. The copyright, registered in 1887, was held by Sankey. In the present version, stanzas one and five are unaltered. Originally, stanzas two, three and four were as follows:

> I was lost: but Jesus found me,
>   Found the sheep that went astray,
> Raised me up and gently led me
>   Back into the narrow way.

Faint was I, and fears possessed me,
    Bruised was I from many a fall;
Hope was gone, and shame distressed me:
    But his love has pardoned all.

Days of darkness still may meet me,
    Sorrow's paths I oft may tread;
But His presence still is with me,
    By His guiding hand I'm led.

WONDROUS STORY was composed for this hymn by Peter P. Bilhorn and first appeared in *Gospel Hymns No. 5* (1887). In the same year it was included in Sankey's *Sacred Songs and Solos*. George C. Stebbins tells how Bilhorn's song came to Sankey's attention in Haldor Lillenas' *Modern Gospel Songs Stories*.

Peter Bilhorn came to Brooklyn, where I was then living, and was introduced to me by a friend. He informed me that he was converted in a meeting Dr. Pentecost and I had conducted in Chicago. At my request he sang a song, which impressed me most favorably. As a result I invited him to remain with me as a guest until he could find a suitable place, and also I offered to render any possible assistance in regard to his voice and interpretation, and that without cost to him. He accepted the offer.

During the winter Bilhorn wrote his first song, so far as I know, and I harmonized it for him, as he had not studied harmony up to that time. The song was entitled, "I Will Sing the Wondrous Story." I took Peter with me to call on Ira D. Sankey, and showed him the song. It impressed him as being serviceable and he accepted it as a gift. It was published in his next book and became one of the most popular numbers in the collection.

I would be true, for there are those who trust me   315

Howard A. Walter sent to his mother the first two stanzas of his poem "My Creed," which he had written on January 1, 1907, while teaching English at Waseda University, Tokyo, Japan. His mother, Mrs. Henry S. Walter, submitted the poem to *Harper's Bazaar,* where it first appeared in the May, 1907, issue. The third stanza was written by Walter sometime later and sent to his cousin, the Rev. Theodore A. Greene, minister of the First Church of Christ (Congregational), New Britain, Connecticut. In this, the author's home church, a memorial tablet was placed on February 14, 1926, on which was inscribed the first two stanzas of the hymn.

PEEK was composed by Joseph Y. Peek with the assistance of Grant Colfax Tullar (*q.v.*), an organist and composer. Peek had met Walter during the summer of 1909, and had been given a copy of "My Creed." Although he possessed no technical knowledge of music or composition, the words of this text brought forth this melody in his mind. He whistled it to Dr. Tullar, who wrote it down and harmonized the tune. These facts concerning this tune were long unknown. The late Reginald L. McAll, secretary of the Hymn Society of America, requested the Hon. Edgar M. Doughty, an official referee of the New York State Supreme Court and an accomplished musician and active member of a Baptist church, to assist in locating this information. Doughty, after much inquiry, completed this research shortly before his death in 1947 at the age of eighty.

If you are tired of the load of your sin   230

Both words and music of this hymn of invitation were written by Mrs. C. H. Morris. In *Forty Gospel Hymn Stories* George Sanville gives the following account of events which occurred in 1898.

At the Sunday morning service, Mountain Lake Park, Maryland, camp meeting, the minister preached with apostolic fervor. His zeal for saving souls charged his message with spiritual power. His handling of his theme, "Repentance," brought many to the altar. One was a woman of culture and refinement. As she knelt and prayed, she gave evidence of the inner struggle taking place. She wanted to do something—to give, not receive. Mrs. C. H. Morris quietly joined her at the altar, put her arms around her, and prayed with her. Mrs. Morris said, "Just now your doubtings give o'er." Dr. H. L. Gilmour, song leader of the camp meeting, added another phrase, "Just now reject Him no more." L. H. Baker, the preacher of the sermon, earnestly importuned, "Just now throw open the door." Mrs. Morris made the last appeal, "Let Jesus Come Into Your Heart."

These phrases remained in the mind of Mrs. Morris and immediately a melody tied them all together. Before the close of the camp meeting she completed the song. Dr. Gilmour purchased the manuscript and copyrighted it in that same year. It was first published in *Pentecostal Praises,* compiled by William J. Kirkpatrick and Gilmour (Philadelphia: Hall-Mack Co., 1898, No. 72).

McCONNELSVILLE is the name given this tune by the Hymnal Committee for the town in Ohio where Mrs. Morris made her home.

"I'll Go Where You Want Me to Go"—*see* It may not be on the mountain's height

"I'll Live For Him"—*see* My life, my love I give to Thee

I'm pressing on the upward way   319

Johnson Oatman, Jr., is the author of the words, and the tune HIGHER GROUND was composed by Charles H. Gabriel. According to Gabriel's own account given in his *Sixty Years of Gospel Song,* he composed this tune shortly after his return to Chicago in September, 1892, and sold it for five dollars. It was purchased by J. Howard Entwisle, a Philadelphia songbook compiler, who published it in *Songs of Love and Praise No. 5,* compiled by John R. Sweney, Frank M. Davis, and Entwisle (Philadelphia: John J. Hood, 1898, No. 89). Commenting on this hymn in *Biography of Gospel Song and Hymn Writers,* J. H. Hall says: "This song once took high rank among the holiness people, and secured a lasting place in American hymnology. Nothing can bring forth more shouts at camp-meeting of 'Glory' and 'Hallelujah' than the singing of 'Higher Ground.'"

Immortal, invisible God only wise 43

This hymn by Walter Chalmers Smith is based on 1 Timothy 1:17, "Now unto the King eternal, immortal, invisible, the only wise God, be honour and glory for ever and ever. Amen." It was first published in Smith's *Hymns of Christ and Christian Life* (1867). Garrett Horder persuaded the author to make a few alterations and included the hymn in his *Congregational Hymns* (1884). The present form appeared in Horder's *Worship Song* (London, 1905), except that the fourth stanza is made up of the open couplets of the fourth and fifth stanzas of the original.

JOANNA, sometimes called ST. DENIO, first appeared as a hymn tune in Wales in John Roberts' *Caniadau y Cyssegr* (Sacred Songs, 1839), where it is called PALESTRINA. It is based on a Welsh folk song, "Can Mlynedd i 'nawr" ("A hundred years from now"), well known in the early nineteenth century. Gustav Holst introduced it in *The English Hymnal* (Oxford, 1906), where it was used with this text.

Immortal Love, forever full 277

This hymn is made up of a selection of stanzas from John Greenleaf Whittier's "Our Master," a poem of thirty-eight stanzas, written in 1866, and first published in his *Tent on the Beach and Other Poems* (1867). The present version uses stanzas one, five, fourteen, and sixteen of the original poem.

SERENITY is an arrangement from William V. Wallace's "Ye Winds That Waft," composed in 1856. It is not known who made this hymn tune adaptation, nor when it first appeared. The earliest appearance may have occurred in Charles S. Robinson and Robert S. MacArthur's *The Calvary Selection of Spiritual Songs* (New York: The Century Co., 1878, p. 189).

The author, John Oxenham, has provided the following information concerning this hymn:

The hymn was written as part of "The Pageant of Darkness and Light," which proved the chief attraction at the London Missionary Society's exhibition, "The Orient in London," in 1908. I was asked to do the book. Harris L. McCunn set it all to very charming music. Hugh Moss staged it. It ran in the Agricultural Hall for a month and was seen by over a quarter of a million people. . . . The four sections of the pageant were North America, Africa, the South Seas, and India. "No East or West" was in the latter.

One of the London newspapers carried this comment concerning the exhibition by the London Missionary Society:

One got a vivid conception of the heroic stuff missionaries are made of when they were seen penetrating the frozen lands of the north and the untrodden depths of darkest Africa. It was easier to realize what Mr. Winston Churchill meant in his speech, when he opened the Exhibition, when he spoke of the civilizing and humanitarian work of the missionaries, which has for its motive force their zeal to win the savage and superstitious hearts of the heathen to the rule of Christ.

The hymn was first published in Oxenham's *Bees in Amber* (1913) and later in *Selected Poems of John Oxenham* (1924). The first American hymnal which the writer has found to include this hymn is H. Augustine Smith's *Hymns of the Living Age* (1925).

St. Peter—*see* In memory of the Saviour's love.

In heavenly love abiding 303

Anna L. Waring's hymn entitled, "Safety in God," first appeared in *Hymns and Meditations by A. L. W.* (1850), a small book containing nineteen hymns.

Nyland is a Finnish hymn melody. In *The Story of Our Hymns,* Armin Haeussler presents a detailed discussion of this tune and states that it appeared in the Appendix of the 1909 edition of the *Suomen Evankelis Luterilaisen Kirken Koraalikirja* (Finland's Evangelical Luthern Church Chorale Book). In a recent revision of the *Koraalikirja,* Nyland appears with the statement that it is a folk tune which was first sung near Kuortane, a small village in Etalapohjanmaa (South Ostrobothnia). The present harmonization was made by David Evans for the *Revised Church Hymnary* (Edinburgh, 1927), for which he was musical editor. Millar Patrick, one of the joint editors of this same hymnal, named the tune for one of the provinces of Finland.

In loving-kindness Jesus came 202

This hymn—the tune by Charles H. Gabriel and the text credited to Charlotte G. Homer, Gabriel's pseudonym—first appeared in *Revival Hymns,* compiled by D. B. Towner and Charles M. Alexander (Chicago: Bible Institute Colportage Assn., 1905, No. 28).

HE LIFTED ME, the tune name, is sometimes used as a title for the hymn.

In memory of the Saviour's love 393

This hymn is made up of stanzas three, five, and six of Thomas Cotterill's hymn "Blest with the presence of their God," which first appeared in the *Uttoxeter Selection* (1805). This three-stanza version appeared in Whittingham's *Collection* (1835).

ST. PETER, composed by Alexander R. Reinagle, first appeared in his *Psalm Tunes for the Voice and Pianoforte* (Oxford, 1836), set to Psalm 118, "Far better 'tis to trust in God." In Reinagle's *Collection of Psalm and Hymn Tunes* (1840) it was named ST. PETER after the church, St. Peter's-in-the-East, Oxford, where the composer served as organist.

In the cross of Christ I glory 100

This hymn by John Bowring, based on Galatians 6:14, first appeared in the author's *Hymns* (1825). The fifth stanza, a repetition of the first, is omitted in the hymnal.

There is a fascinating and oft-told story that this hymn was inspired by the ruins of a once great cathedral on the island of Macao, near Hong Kong. The building had been destroyed save for the front wall topped by a great metal cross, blackened with age. It has been said that Bowring, inspired by the sight of this old cross, "towering o'er the wrecks of time," wrote this hymn. If this is true, and it is doubtful, Bowring must have learned about this old cathedral from some other source, for he did not go to China until 1849, twenty-four years after the hymn was written.

RATHBUN was composed by Ithamar Conkey for this hymn in 1849 while he was organist of the Central Baptist Church, Norwich, Connecticut. The tune was first published in Greatorex's *Collection of Psalm and Hymn Tunes* (1851), set to Mühlenberg's "Saviour, who thy flock art feeding." In *Our Hymnody,* McCutchan gives the following account of the writing of this tune, quoting an article in the *Norwich Bulletin* (1907).

> Doctor Hiscox was . . . pastor of the church. He had prepared a series of seven sermons from "The Words on the Cross."
>
> One Sunday during the series it was a very rainy day. Mr. Conkey was sorely disappointed that the members of the choir did not appear, as only one soprano came. Mr. Conkey was so discouraged and disheartened that after the prelude he closed the organ and locked it and went to his home on Washington Street. The pastor and choir gallery were at opposite ends of the church, and he could leave without attracting the attention of the congregation.
>
> That afternoon he sat down at the piano for practice, the thoughts suggested in the series of sermons Doctor Hiscox had prepared and the words of the hymn suggested to be sung, "In the cross of Christ I glory," passing and repassing through his mind. He then and there composed the music which is now so universally familiar in churches of every denomination, known as RATHBUN. He admitted afterward the inspiration was a vivid contradiction of his feelings at the morning service.

In the hour of trial 317

James Montgomery's manuscript of this hymn is dated October 13, 1834, and with it are the names of twenty-two friends to whom he sent copies. However, it was not published until 1853, when it appeared in Montgomery's *Original Hymns for Public, Private, and Social Devotion.* Originally in four stanzas, the omitted third stanza is:

> If, with sore affliction,
>   Thou in love chastise,
> Pour thy benediction
>   On the sacrifice;
> Then, upon thine altar,
>   Freely offered up,
> Though the flesh may falter,
>   Faith shall drink the cup.

The final stanza of the present version was considerably altered by Frances A. Hutton for W. H. Hutton's *Supplement and Litanies,* published in London in the last half of the nineteenth century.

PENITENCE was hurriedly composed by Spencer Lane in 1875, one Sunday noon while his wife prepared dinner. At the close of the morning church service at St. James Episcopal Church, Woonsocket, Rhode Island, the minister had given Lane, the choirmaster, the hymns for the evening service. One of the tunes did not appeal to him, so he wrote this as a substitute. It was sung in the evening service that same Sunday, and was first published in Charles L. Hutchins' *The Church Hymnal* (1879).

Into the woods my master went 90

Sidney Lanier wrote this hymn in Baltimore in November, 1880, less than a year before his death. It was entitled, "A Ballad of Trees and the Master." It appeared in his posthumous *Poems* (New York, 1901). It's first hymnal inclusion was the *Methodist Hymnal* (1905).

LANIER was composed for this hymn by Peter C. Lutkin for the *Methodist Hymnal* (1905), for which he was one of the musical editors.

"Is Your All on the Altar"—*see* You have longed for sweet peace, and for faith to increase

Is your life a channel of blessing 438

Harper G. Smyth wrote both words and music of this hymn in 1903. The earliest collection in which it has been found is James McGranahan's *Hymns, Psalms, and Gospel Songs* (Pittsburg: H. H. McGranahan, 1904, No. 312).

EUCLID is the name given this tune by the Hymnal Committee. For a number of years Smyth served as music director for the Euclid Avenue Baptist Church, Cleveland, Ohio.

It came upon the midnight clear 71

Edmund H. Sears wrote this hymn in 1849 while he was minister of the Unitarian Church at Wayland, Massachusetts. It first appeared in the *Christian Register* (XXVIII, Dec. 29, 1849). McCutchan, in *Our Hymnody,* states that it is one of "the first of the carol-like hymns that seem to have sprung from American poets. Hymns stressing the social message of Christmas—'peace on earth, good will toward men'—are distinctly American." When Sears wrote this hymn about the song of the heavenly host, the storm clouds of strife were gathering which erupted a dozen years later in the Civil War. Stanza three contains references to the social upheaval in New England which resulted from the industrial revolution there. In some hymnals, stanza four has been altered because, as Henry Wilder Foote points out in his *American Unitarian Hymn Writers and Hymns,* "its 'backward look' to a golden age is not Biblical but is derived from the Fourth Eclogue of the poet Virgil."

CAROL is an arrangement of the twenty-third Study in Richard S. Willis' *Church Chorals and Choir Studies* (New York, 1850). In its original form it is a hymn tune set to "See Israel's gentle shepherd stand." The present arrangement of Willis' tune has been credited to

Uzziah C. Burnap. However, in *The Hymnal 1940 Companion,* Ellinwood notes that in a letter to Hubert P. Main, dated October 25, 1887, written from Detroit, Willis states that he made this arrangement adapting it to "While shepherds watched their flocks by night." At this time, Willis was a vestryman in the Church of the Transfiguration (The Little Church Around the Corner) in New York City.

"It Is Well with My Soul"—*see* When peace, like a river, attendeth my way

It may be at morn, when the day is awaking   120

This hymn by H. L. Turner with this tune by James McGranahan first appeared in *Gospel Hymns No. 3* (1878, p. 18), with the Scripture reference, "I will come again, and receive you unto myself" (John 14:3).

CHRIST RETURNETH is the name given this tune by the Hymnal Committee. In many collections this appears as the title of the hymn.

It may not be on the mountain's height   425

The first stanza of this hymn was written by Mary Brown during or shortly before 1894. Charles E. Prior is the author of stanzas two and three.

MANCHESTER was composed by Carrie E. Rounsefell in 1894, while assisting in a revival meeting in the Baptist church in Lynn, Massachusetts. The pastor of the church had given her Mary Brown's stanza, and suggested that she compose a tune for it. She later said, "I took the words, got down before the Lord with my little autoharp, asked Him to give me a tune, and this music was the answer." It was sung that evening in the service, and the following Sunday it was used in Bowdoin Square Church, Boston. First printed in song sheet form, it soon began to appear in many collections and has been widely used. The earliest appearance that has been found is *Best Hymns No. 2,* compiled by Harold F. Sayles and Elisha A. Hoffman (Chicago: Evangelical Publishing Co., 1895, No. 74). The tune was named by the Hymnal Committee for the home town of the composer.

I've found a friend, oh, such a friend   261

This hymn by James G. Small was first published in *The Revival Hymn Book,* second series (1863) and then included in Small's *Psalms and Sacred Songs* (1866), published in Scotland.

FRIEND was composed by George C. Stebbins in January, 1878, while he was assisting Dr. George F. Pentecost in a revival meeting held in the Music Hall at Providence, Rhode Island. It was first published in *Gospel Hymns No. 3* (1878), the first of this series with which Stebbins was associated. It was during this engagement at Providence that Stebbins also wrote "Must I go, and empty-handed" (430), and first used his tune EVENING PRAYER to the hymn "Saviour, breathe an evening blessing" (34).

I've found a friend who is all to me   197

In a letter to the writer dated August 6, 1954, Jack P. Scholfield, who wrote both words and music, states that it was written in 1911 while he was assisting Dr. Mordecai F. Ham in evangelistic meetings. "The melody just came to me, almost as a gift. Then I tried to make the words fit the tune. It was popular from the start and Robert H. Coleman told me some years ago it had been published in several foreign languages." It was first published in Robert H. Coleman's *The New Evangel* (Dallas, Texas, 1911, No. 89).

RAPTURE is the name suggested for this tune by the composer and first appears in this hymnal.

I've wandered far away from God   237

Both words and music of this well-known hymn of invitation were written by William J. Kirkpatrick. It first appeared in *Winning Songs,* compiled by John R. Sweney, H. L. Gilmour, and Kirkpatrick (Philadelphia: John J. Hood, 1892, No. 141).

COMING HOME is the name given this tune by the Hymnal Committee.

Jehovah the Lord, our Saviour and King   494

Edwin McNeely wrote this hymn in November, 1946, for the Wednesday evening prayer meeting service before Thanksgiving at the Evans Avenue Baptist Church, Fort Worth, Texas, where he served as music director. It was used in that service for the first time, sung to LYONS, which the author had selected. The following year, while Dr. McNeely was serving as interim music director for the First Baptist Church, San Antonio, Texas, the hymn was again used at Thanksgiving. This is the first hymnal inclusion for this text.

LYONS—*see* O worship the King, all glorious above.

Jerusalem, the golden   477

About 1145 Bernard of Cluny wrote *De Contemptu Mundi* (On the Contemptibleness of the World), a long poem of 2,966 lines, which began: "Hora novissima tempora pessima sunt: vigilemus!" It was written in Latin hexameters and employed a rhyme scheme so difficult to maintain that Bernard attributed his success in writing the poem to a special gift of the Holy Spirit. In Trench's *Sacred Latin Poetry* (1849), John M. Neale discovered a cento of ninety-five lines from this poem, and without trying to reproduce the original meter, translated portions of it in his *Mediaeval Hymns and Sequences* (1851). Because of the splendid response to his efforts, Neale translated 218 lines of the original poem in his *Rhythm of Bernard de Morlaix, Monk of Cluny, on the Celestial Country* (1858). Eight hymns have been taken from Neale's translation, four of which have been used extensively. Only this one appears in the Hymnal.

EWING was composed by Alexander Ewing for "For thee, O dear, dear country," another hymn taken from Neale's translation mentioned above. First written in triple rhythm, it was printed in a single sheet in 1853, and published in John Grey's *A Manual of Psalm and Hymn Tunes* (London, 1857), where it was called ST. BEDE'S. The original form of the rhythm was:

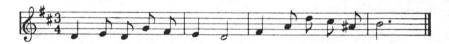

The change of rhythm to its present form was made by William H. Monk for *Hymns Ancient and Modern* (London, 1861). Ewing was never pleased with this alteration of his tune and said, "It now seems to me a good deal like a polka." In spite of the composer's opinion, the widespread acceptance of this tune has proved the wisdom of Monk's judgment.

Jesus calls us o'er the tumult   **360**

This hymn by Mrs. Cecil F. Alexander was first published in the Society for the Propagation of Christian Knowledge Tract No. 15, "Hymns for Public Worship" (1852, No. 116), in five four-line stanzas. The present version is unaltered from the original. The omitted second stanza is

> As, of old, Saint Andrew heard it
> By the Galilean lake,
> Turned from home and toil and kindred,
> Leaving all for His dear sake.

GALILEE was composed by William H. Jude for this hymn and first appeared in *The Congregational Church Hymnal* (London, 1887), edited by G. S. Barrett and E. J. Hopkins.

"Jesus, I Come"—*see* Out of my bondage, sorrow, and night

Jesus, I my cross have taken   **387**

This hymn appeared signed "G" in Henry F. Lyte's *Sacred Poetry,* third edition (Edinburgh, 1824), in six eight-line stanzas with the heading, "Lo, we have left all, and followed thee" (Mark 10:28). In *Poems Chiefly Religious* (1833) Lyte claimed authorship of the hymn.

ELLESDIE has been attributed to Wolfgang A. Mozart in many hymnal collections. In *Winnowed Hymns,* compiled by C. C. McCabe and D. T. MacFarlan (1873), its source is given as "Air, Mozart, Arr. by H. P. M." In later collections with which Hubert P. Main was associated, this tune is again found. Main left no information about its source; but since the melody with bass line appeared in Joshua Leavitt's *The Christian Lyre* (Vol. II, 1831), it is assumed that Main simply harmonized it. There seems to be no evidence that will support crediting the tune to Mozart. McCutchan, in *Hymn Tune Names,* states that ELLESDIE "is said to be a 'made name'—from the initial letters 'L. S. D.' of some person unknown."

Jesus is all the world to me   **155**

This hymn and tune by Will L. Thompson first appeared in the *New Century Hymnal* (East Liverpool, Ohio: Will L. Thompson Co., 1904).

ELIZABETH is the name given this tune by the Hymnal Committee. Thompson married Miss Elizabeth Johnson in 1891 at East Liverpool, Ohio.

"Jesus Is Calling"—*see* Jesus is tenderly calling thee home

Jesus is coming to earth again   **125**

Mrs. C. H. Morris wrote both the words and music of this hymn. It first appeared in *The King's Praises No. 3,* compiled by H. L. Gilmour, George W. Sanville, William J. Kirkpatrick, and Melvin J. Hill (Philadelphia: The Praise Publishing Co., 1912).

Jesus is tenderly calling thee home   **229**

Fanny J. Crosby is the author of the text of this familiar hymn of invitation.

CALLING TODAY was composed for this text by George C. Stebbins. In his *Memoirs and Reminiscences* (pp. 105-6) Stebbins states that there was no incident that occasioned the setting made to Fanny Crosby's words, "Jesus Is Tenderly Calling," nor did either the words nor the music impress me as possessing more than ordinary merit, even for evangelistic work. The music was written with the view of making the song available as an invitation hymn; but that it would meet with instant favor, and in a few years would become generally known, did not enter my mind.

With the Scripture reference, "Arise, he calleth thee," (John 11:28), this hymn first appeared in *Gospel Hymns No. 4* (1883).

"Jesus Is the Friend You Need"—*see* When the sun shines bright and your heart is light

Jesus, keep me near the cross 97

The tune was first written by William H. Doane and given to Fanny J. Crosby to provide the text. The hymn appeared in *Bright Jewels,* compiled by W. B. Bradbury, W. H. Doane, W. F. Sherwin, and Chester G. Allen (New York: Biglow & Main, 1869, No. 130).

Jesus, lover of my soul 156, 157, 158

This well-loved hymn by Charles Wesley, written in 1738, first appeared in *Hymns and Sacred Poems* (1740) in five eight-line stanzas. The omitted stanza is:

> Wilt thou not regard my call?
> Wilt thou not accept my prayer?
> Lo, I sink, I faint, I fall—
> Lo, on thee I cast my care;
> Reach me out thy gracious hand,
> While I of thy strength receive,
> Hoping against hope I stand,
> Dying, and behold I live!

Because of the intimate expression found in the first stanza, many attempts at alteration have been made. However, Wesley's original form is found in most collections today.

Regarding the many "dramatic" stories regarding this hymn, John Julian (*A Dictionary of Hymnology,* p. 591) says:

Many charming accounts of the origin of this hymn are extant, but unfortunately, some would add, they have no foundation in fact. The most that we can say is that it was written shortly after the great spiritual change which the author underwent in 1738; and that it was published within a few months of the official date (1739) which is given as the founding of Methodism. It had nothing whatever to do with the struggles, and dangers with lawless men, in after years. Nor with a dove driven to Wesley's bosom by a hawk, nor with a sea-bird driven to the same shelter by a pitiless storm. These charming stories must be laid aside until substantiated by direct evidence from the Wesley books; or from original mss. or printed papers as yet unknown.

Dr. Louis F. Benson, perhaps America's most outstanding hymnologist, has written:

> We are dealing with the best-loved hymn in the language; the favorite of learned and illiterate, high and humble. And why is it so? No critic urged its acceptance. Average Christians could not analyze its appeal; its tenderness is a part of the explanation, but the hymns in general have as much. And after due tribute to these qualities the suspicion remains that the secret of its appeal lies in a poetic beauty that the average man feels without analyzing it, and in a perfection of craftsmanship that makes him want to *sing* it simply because it awakens the spirit of song in him rather than a mood of reflection. . . .
>
> John Wesley desired that the texts of his brother's and his own hymns, furnished in his large *Collection* . . . (1780), should be final. As for hymn tinkerers, he said in the Preface: "I desire that they would not attempt to mend them; for they really are not able. None of them is able to mend either the sense or the verse." The reference here very likely was to Whitefield or Toplady, both of whom had altered the hymns they had appropriated. After Wesley's death his wishes were disregarded even by the publishers of his own book. Charles Wesley's hymns suffered long at editorial hands that were all thumbs. His "Jesus, Lover of my Soul," being the most lyrical, suffered the most, and only in our day has been restored to its original beauty. . . . How intolerable have been the changes in "Jesus, Lover of My Soul."

MARTYN (156) was written in the fall of 1834 while Simeon B. Marsh was on his way on horseback from Amsterdam to Johnstown, New York, to conduct a singing school. He stopped his horse, dismounted, and sketched the melody of this tune. It was first published in Thomas Hastings' *Musical Miscellany* (1836), set to John Newton's hymn "Mary, at her Saviour's tomb." McCutchan and Haeussler both credit Thomas Hastings with the initial association of this tune with "Jesus, Lover of My Soul," but fail to give any source. In Hastings' *Church Melodies* (New York, 1859), this hymn is set to LIBNAH (p. 10), quite a different melody. If, as McCutchan says, Hastings "discovered its affinity" for this text, he must have changed his mind, for in this same collection MARTYN is set to Anna L. Barbauld's hymn, "Come, said Jesus' sacred voice" (p. 189). It is interesting to note that in the first Methodist hymn and tune book published in America, *Hymns for the Use of the Methodist Episcopal Church with Tunes for the Congregation* (New York, 1857, p. 162), Wesley's text appears with this tune, giving evidence of the acceptance by Methodists of this text and tune by this date.

REFUGE (157) was composed by Joseph P. Holbrook and first appeared in Charles H. Robinson's *Songs of the Church, or Hymns and Tunes for Christian Worship* (Chicago: A. S. Barnes, 1862, No. 378).

ABERYSTWYTH (158) composed by Joseph Parry was first published in Stephen and Jones's *Ail Llyfr Tonau ac Emynau* (Wales, 1879), where it was set to the Welsh hymn "Beth sydd i mi yn y byd." Later, in h's cantata *Ceridwen,* Parry used this tune set to "Jesus, lover of my soul." The tune is named for the town where Parry was teaching—at Welsh University College—when he wrote this tune.

"Jesus Loves Even Me"—*see* I am so glad that our Father in heav'n

Jesus loves me! this I know   512

The words of this favorite children's song by Anna B. Warner first appeared in a novel, *Say and Seal,* written in 1860 by the author in collaboration with her sister, Susan B. Warner.

CHINA was composed by William B. Bradbury for this text, and it first appeared in his *The Golden Shower* (1862, No. 68). It has been reported by missionaries that this is the favorite hymn of the children in China, which accounts for the tune name assigned by the Hymnal Committee. Because of the popularity of this song, it has been appropriated by other religious sects. While on a visit to Hawaii in 1954, Dr. W. Hines Sims, editor of the *Hymnal,* visited a Buddhist temple and heard children singing, "Yes, Buddha loves me, Yes, Buddha loves me."

"Jesus Paid It All"—*see* I hear the Saviour say

"Jesus Saves"—*see* We have heard the joyful sound

Jesus, Saviour pilot me   337

This hymn first appeared anonymously in *The Sailor's Magazine* (Vol. 43, Mar. 3, 1871, p. 119) and in *The Baptist Praise Book* (1871). Following its appearance in *Spiritual Songs* (1875), Edward Hopper revealed that he was the author. Hopper, who was pastor of the Church of the Sea and Land in New York City, wrote it for sailors who attended his church. Originally in six six-line stanzas, our version consists of stanzas one, five, and six. The omitted three stanzas of the original are

When the Apostles' fragile bark
Struggled with the billows dark,
On the stormy Galilee,
Thou didst walk upon the sea;
And when they beheld Thy form,
Safe they glided through the storm.

Though the sea be smooth and bright,
Sparkling with the stars of night,
And my ship's path be ablaze
With the light of halcyon days,
Still I know my need of Thee;
Jesus, Saviour, pilot me.

When the darkling heavens frown,
And the wrathful winds come down,
And the fierce waves, tossed on high,
Lash themselves against the sky,
Jesus, Saviour, pilot me
Over life's tempestuous sea.

PILOT was composed by John E. Gould for this hymn in 1871, and it appeared the same year in *The Baptist Praise Book*.

Jesus shall reign where'er the sun 116

This is probably the earliest hymn with an emphasis on world missions. Written by Isaac Watts, it first appeared in his *Psalms of David, Imitated in the Language of the New Testament* (1719) as the second part of his metrical version of Psalm 72. The present version is made up of stanza one, the last half of stanza two coupled with an alteration of the last half of stanza three, and stanzas four and five of the original eight stanzas.

A striking account of the use of this hymn is given in Stevenson's *Methodist Hymn Book Notes* (1883, pp. 351-52):

Perhaps one of the most interesting occasions on which this hymn was used was that on which King George, the sable [*sic*], of the South Sea Islands, but of blessed memory, gave a new constitution to his people, exchanging a heathen for a Christian form of government. Under the spreading branches of the banyan trees sat some five thousand natives from

105

Tonga, Fiji, and Samoa, on Whitsunday, 1862, assembled for divine worship. Foremost amongst them all sat King George himself. Around him were seated old chiefs and warriors who had shared with him the dangers and fortunes of many a battle,—men whose eyes were dim, and whose powerful frames were bowed down with the weight of years. But old and young alike rejoiced together in the joys of that day, their faces most of them radiant with Christian joy, love, and hope. It would be impossible to describe the deep feeling manifested when the solemn service began, by the entire audience singing Dr. Watts's Hymn—"Jesus shall reign where'er the sun" . . . Who, so much as they, could realise the full meaning of the poet's words? for they had been rescued from the darkness of heathenism and cannibalism; and they were that day met for the first time under a Christian constitution, under a Christian king, and with Christ Himself reigning in the hearts of most of those present! That was indeed Christ's kingdom set up in the earth.

DUKE STREET first appeared in Henry Boyd's *A Select Collection of Psalm and Hymn Tunes* (Glasgow, 1793) and was marked for use with Addison's nineteenth Psalm. No composer's name was given. It is found under its present name and attributed to John Hatton in *Euphonia*, a collection of tunes edited by William Dixon (Liverpool, 1805). The tune was named for a street where Hatton lived in St. Helen's, England.

Jesus, the very thought of Thee 135

"Dulcis Jesu memoria," the Latin hymn from which this translation was made, has long been attributed to Bernard of Clairvaux, but this claim has been seriously questioned. In the Hymn Society of Great Britain and Ireland *Bulletin* (Oct., 1945) Dr. F. J. E. Raby points out that the earliest and best texts were copied in England, and that the poem passed from England to France, Italy, and Germany, and that it was known to John of Hoveden and Richard Rolle. Dr. Raby concludes that in view of these known facts, "it is difficult to resist the conclusion that the poem is the work of an Englishman and was written about the end of the Twelfth century." This translation by Edward Caswall first appeared in his *Lyra Catholica* (London, 1849). Originally in ten stanzas, the present version uses stanzas 1, 2, 3, and 4.

ST. AGNES—*see* Father, I stretch my hands to Thee.

Jesus, Thou joy of loving hearts 136

This hymn, like the preceding, is taken from "Dulcis Jesu Memoria." Here we have stanzas four, three, twenty-four, and ten of the original, as translated by Ray Palmer for the *Sabbath Hymn Book* (1858). Edwards A. Park and Austin Phelps, both professors at Andover Seminary, together with Lowell Mason, edited this collection. This is one of seven hymns which Palmer contributed to this collection at the request of the editors.

QUEBEC, sometimes called HESPERUS, was composed by Henry Baker in 1854 when he was a student at Exeter College, Oxford. Lightwood states that it was submitted unsigned to the *Penny Post* (London), which in 1861 conducted a search for a new tune for Keble's "Sun of my soul." It is thought that some college classmate of Baker submitted the tune without his knowledge. It was first published anonymously in John Grey's *A Hymnal for Use in the English Church* (1866), set to Keble's hymn, and later in Bickersteth's compilation in 1871, after which Baker acknowledged his authorship of the tune.

Jesus, Thy boundless love to me 288

Paul Gerhardt's hymn, "O Jesu Christ, mein schönstes Licht," first appeared in Crüger's *Praxis Pietatis Melica,* fifth edition (Berlin, 1653). There have been several translations of this hymn, the most popular being the one by John Wesley, which appared in his *Hymns and Sacred Poems* (1739) and is used in the Hymnal.

ST. CATHERINE—*see* Faith of our fathers! living still.

Joy to the world! the Lord is come 65

This hymn by Isaac Watts first appeared in his *Psalms of David Imitated in the Language of the New Testament* (1719) in four four-line stanzas, as the second part of his version of Psalm 98 (vv. 4-9). It appears here unaltered. Some regrettable alterations have appeared which quite distort the original meaning of the hymn or the psalm on which it is based. A Seventh-Day Adventist hymn focuses on the second coming of Christ by changing the present tense to the future: "Joy to the world, the Lord *will* come." Even worse is the alteration made in *Social Hymns for Use of Friends of the Rational System of Society* (1838).

> Joy to the world! the light has come,
> The only lawful King:
> Let every heart prepare it room
> And moral nature sing.

ANTIOCH appeared in Lowell Mason's *Modern Psalmist* (Boston, 1839) with the indication that it is "from Handel." It is further indicated that this is one of the tunes in this collection that has "either been arranged, adapted, or composed for this work, or taken from other recent works of the Editor." Henry L. Mason (*Hymn-Tunes of*

107

Lowell Mason, p. 65) dates the tune as having been written in 1836.

The first four notes of the tune are identical with the opening notes of the chorus "Lift up your heads," and the notes sung to "and heaven and nature sing" are like the introduction to the tenor recitative "Comfort Ye My People," both from Handel's *Messiah.* Mason's association of the tune with Handel thus seems to be, as Haeussler says, "gaining a maximum of fiction from a minimum of fact." Ebenezer Prout is of the opinion that it is "very far from Handel." James T. Lightwood believes it to be of American origin. Hamilton C. MacDougall says that it has the earmarks of a Methodist revival tune of the later eighteenth century and is "good fun to sing unless you are a highbrow or a fraid cat." Nevertheless, regardless of the genuine source of the tune, it has become a permanent part of our congregational repertoire at the Christmas season as a joyful song of our Saviour's birth.

Joyful, joyful, we adore Thee   44

Tertius Van Dyke has said that this hymn was written by his father Henry Van Dyke when he was a guest preacher at Williams College. He handed the manuscript to President Garfield at the breakfast table saying, "Here is a hymn for you. Your mountains (the Berkshires) were my inspiration. It must be sung to the music of Beethoven's 'Hymn to Joy.'" It is included in his *Poems,* third edition (1911), where it is dated 1908.

HYMN TO JOY is taken from the last movement of Ludwig van Beethoven's *Symphony No. 9,* composed 1817-23, and published in 1826. The adaptation of this melody into a hymn tune was made by Edward Hodges.

Just as I am, Thine own to be   249

This hymn by Marianne Hearn was suggested by Charlotte Elliott's hymn (*see* Just as I am, without one plea). It first appeared in *Voice of Praise* (1887, No. 348), published by the Sunday School Union of London. Originally consisting of six stanzas, the omitted stanzas five and six are:

> With many dreams of fame and gold,
> Success and joy to make me bold,
> But dearer still my faith to hold,
>   For my whole life, I come.

> And for thy sake to win renown,
> And then to take the victor's crown,
> And at Thy feet to cast it down,
>   O Master, Lord, I come.

JUST As I AM was composed by Joseph Barnby for this hymn, and it first appeared in *Home and School Hymnal* (London, 1892).

Just as I am, without one plea 240

Charlotte Elliott wrote this hymn in 1834, while she was living at Westfield Lodge, Brighton, England. Her brother, an Anglican minister, and other members of her family were assisting with a bazaar on behalf of the building fund of St. Mary's Hall, Brighton. Charlotte was not well enough to go with the family. She had lain awake all night, oppressed with her own physical weakness and "tossed about with many a doubt." In the midst of this restlessness, she took pencil and paper and "deliberately set down for her own comfort the formulas of her faith." The poem first appeared without the author's knowledge in a leaflet in 1835 and was published in the *Invalid's Hymn Book* (1836) in six four-line stanzas with the Scripture text "Him that cometh to me I will in no wise cast out" (John 6:37).

WOODWORTH first appeared in Bradbury and Hastings' *Mendelssohn Collection, or Third Book of Psalmody* (New York, 1849, p. 60), where it is in the key of C and set to "The God of love will sure indulge," and signed with the initials "W. B. B.," for W. B. Bradbury.

Just when I need Him, Jesus is near 267

This text was one of a group of poems which William C. Poole submitted to Charles H. Gabriel in 1907, the first attempt the author had made at writing hymn texts. Gabriel composed the tune and copyrighted both words and music in 1907. The following year the song was purchased by E. O. Excell and was first published in Excell's *Service in Song* (Chicago, 1909). The same year it appeared in *The Evangel,* compiled by Robert H. Coleman and W. W. Hamilton; E. O. Excell, editor (Philadelphia: American Baptist Publication Society, No. 37). This collection was Coleman's first venture in songbook publishing, an operation which continued for thirty years with significant influence upon the hymn singing of Southern Baptists.

GABRIEL was the name given this tune by the Hymnal Committee for the composer.

"Just When I Need Him Most"—*see* Just when I need him, Jesus is near

Lead, kindly light! amid th' encircling gloom 60

John Henry Newman wrote this poem on June 16, 1833, aboard a ship which was becalmed for a whole week in the Straits of Bonifacio, between Corsica and Sardinia, as he was en route from Palermo to

Marseilles. He had been seriously ill in Sicily and had grave concern about his work in England. The uncertainty of his future work hung heavily on him. His faith in the divine purpose of God is evident in this hymn written under these circumstances. The popularity of the hymn was quite surprising to Newman, and he attributed its success to Dykes's tune. The text first appeared in *The British Magazine* (February, 1834) with the heading "Faith," and was published later in *Lyra Apostolica* (1836). The first American use of this hymn was in *A Book of Hymns for Public and Private Devotions* (Cambridge, 1846), edited by Samuel Longfellow and Samuel Johnson.

LUX BENIGNA was composed by John B. Dykes for this hymn on August 29, 1865, while the composer was walking through the Strand in London. It first appeared in Barry's *Psalms and Hymns for the Church, School and Home* (London, 1867), where it was called ST. OSWALD, after Dyke's parish in Durham and was in the key of G. In the Appendix of *Hymns Ancient and Modern* (London, 1868, No. 342) it was written in A flat and the name changed to LUX BENIGNA (meaning "kindly light") to avoid confusion with another tune by Dykes by the first name.

Lead on, O King Eternal 417

This was written by Ernest W. Shurtleff as the graduation hymn for the class of 1887 at Andover Theological Seminary, of which the author was a member. It was published the same year in Shurtleff's *Hymns of the Faith*.

LANCASHIRE was composed by Henry Smart for a musical festival at Blackburn, England, on October 4, 1835, observing the three-hundredth anniversary of the Reformation in England. Set to "From Greenland's Icy Mountains," it was printed in a leaflet for the occasion. The first hymnal inclusion was Smart's *Psalms and Hymns for Divine Worship* (London, 1867). The tune seems to have been first used with Shurtleff's hymn in *The Methodist Hymnal* (1905). Lancashire is the county location of Blackburn, where Smart was organist at the time he wrote this tune.

"Leaning on the Everlasting Arms"—*see* What a fellowship, what a joy divine

Let all mortal flesh keep silence 80

The Liturgy of St. James of Jerusalem, one of the earliest forms of Christian liturgical worship, was used in the Eastern Orthodox churches probably as early as the fifth century. This metrical translation of a prayer from the liturgy was made by Gerard Moultrie for *Lyra Euchar-istica,* second edition (1864).

PICARDY is a French carol, probably from the seventeenth century. It is found in *Chansons populaires des provinces de France,* Volume IV (Paris, 1860, p. 6), where it is given as being sung by Mme. Pierre Dupont to the words "Jesus Christ s'habille en pauvre," a folk song she remembered from her childhood in Picardy. It was adapted for the present text in *The English Hymnal,* 1906.

Let all on earth their voices raise 7

This metrical version of Psalm 96 by Isaac Watts entitled "The God of the Gentiles" first appeared in Watts's *Psalms of David Imitated in the Language of the New Testament* (1719). Originally consisting of four six-line stanzas and the meter 8.8.8.D., this hymn has undergone considerable alteration.

ARIEL appeared in an early edition of the *Boston Academy Collection of Church Music* (1st ed., 1836), credited to Lowell Mason with the footnote: "This tune is taken from *Occasional Psalm and Hymn Tunes* (1836), by permission of the proprietor of that work." Apparently this is one of many tunes which Mason arranged and adapted for his needs from European sources. Henry L. Mason, in his *Hymn Tunes of Lowell Mason,* states that the source of this tune is Mozart.

"Let Jesus Come Into Your Heart"—*see* If you are tired of the load of your sin

"Let Others See Jesus in You"—*see* While passing thro' this world of sin

"Let the Lower Lights Be Burning"—*see* Brightly beams our Father's mercy

Let there be light, Lord God of hosts 444

In a letter to the writer, dated November 3, 1954, the author, William M. Vories, states:

In 1908, three years after I began the work of the "Omi Mission" in Japan (which is now officially "The Omi Brotherhood") I read an article in a magazine from America which told of various European preparations for war. I was so much disgusted by that news that I wrote some sarcastic verses about it, as a sort of safety valve for my feelings. Then, to return to a constructive attitude, I wrote the words, "Let there be light." Then I sent both verses to the *Advocate of Peace.* The editor promptly replied, asking permission to use the second part only. Several religious publications copied the words, and one of them suggested, editorially, that these words should be used in hymnals, since there were not enough hymns on peace. As far as I remember, the *Century Hymnal* (1921) was the first to use it.

PENTECOST—*see* Fight the good fight with all thy might!

Lift up your heads, ye mighty gates 247

Georg Weissel's hymn, "Macht hoch die Thür, das Thor macht weit," first appeared in the *Preussische Fest-Lieder,* Part I (1642). It is based on Psalm 24, and consisted of five eight-line stanzas. Catherine Winkworth's translation of this German hymn first appeared in her *Lyra Germanica* (1855). The present version is made up of the first half of her stanzas one, four, and five.

TRURO—*see* Ride on! ride on in majesty!

Light of the world, we hail Thee 454

This missionary hymn by John S. B. Monsell was first published in the author's *Hymns of Love and Praise* (1863). The omitted third stanza is:

> Light of the world, before Thee
> Our spirits prostrate fall;
> We worship, we adore Thee,
> Thou Light, the Life of all;
> With Thee is no forgetting
> Of all Thine hand hath made;
> Thy rising hath no setting,
> Thy sunshine hath no shade.

SALVE DOMINE (meaning, "Hail, Lord") was composed by Lawrence W. Watson and first appeared in *The Book of Common Praise* (1909), the hymnbook of the Church of England in Canada. In a letter to Robert G. McCutchan, the composer's son states that his father's tune was first published locally in Charlottetown, Prince Edward Island.

He wrote it as an alternative tune to the words of the hymn, "Hail to the Lord's Anointed" [Montgomery] . . . and it was sung in St. Peter's Cathedral for a year or two until the Canadian Hymnal of the Church of England was published and the tune was then published in this book and used throughout England.

Like a river glorious 294

Frances R. Havergal wrote this hymn at Leamington, England, in November, 1874. It was first published in her *Loyal Responses* (1878).

WYE VALLEY was composed by James Mountain for this hymn, and it first appeared in his *Hymns of Consecration and Faith* (London, 1876, No. 272), entitled "Perfect Peace."

Like radiant sunshine that comes after rain 285

In a letter to the writer, dated August 6, 1954, Alfred Barratt, author of this hymn, states that it was written on September 18, 1919, and purchased by the composer on January 1, 1920.

> I was thinking of peace as interpreted by many writers, but I was not satisfied. For instance, "When peace like a river." Then there is "Peace, peace, wonderful peace, Like billows flooding my soul," etc. I thought peace was different—calm, quiet, soothing, gentle, noiseless. In my moments of quiet meditation, I discovered that peace is just like sunshine after rain— like rest after sorrow and pain, like hope in the depths of despair, like comfort in loneliness, like sweet, gentle, refreshing dew. Furthermore, I found out that peace is a promise, a light to shine in darkness, a refuge in trouble, a guardian in danger, a defender in strife, and a guide to that heavenly home. With these thoughts in my mind, I sat down and wrote "Wonderful Peace of My Saviour."

VENTING was composed by Isham E. Reynolds for this text in 1924 and was first published in Robert H. Coleman's *Harvest Hymns* (Dallas, 1924, No. 68). The tune was named by the Hymnal Committee for Dr. Albert Venting, a friend of the composer for many years, who, after many years service as seminary professor and pastor, was professor of Church Music at Baylor University.

Living for Jesus a life that is true 352

C. Harold Lowden composed the tune about 1915, and it was first published under the title "Sunshine Song" in a Children's Day Service that he wrote. Early in 1917, while preparing a collection of hymns for publication, he came across this song and was impressed that the tune needed a stronger text. He substituted "Living for Jesus" for the original title and sent the tune to Thomas O. Chisholm, then living at Winona Lake, Indiana, for a new text. Chisholm returned the copy, saying that he had never "made a poem to order" and did not think he could do this. Lowden insisted that he try and informed Chisholm that he "believed God had led me to select him" to write the text. Chisholm was impressed by this earnest appeal and shortly returned the copy with the text of the four stanzas and refrain.

This hymn was published by the composer in single sheets in the spring of 1917, and it was first used in this form in a number of summer youth conferences. Later the same year it appeared in

Uplifting Songs, compiled by Lowden and Rufus W. Miller and published by the Heidelberg Press.

LIVING is the name given this tune by the composer at the request of the Hymnal Committee.

Lo, He comes with clouds descending 123

The story of this hymn is unique for it involves the efforts of three men—two hymn writers and one compiler who pieced together this version. In 1750 John Cennick wrote a hymn, "Lo, He cometh, countless trumpets," consisting of six six-line stanzas. In 1758 Charles Wesley published in his *Hymns of Intercession for All Mankind* a four-stanza hymn, "Lo, He comes with clouds descending" in the same meter as Cennick's hymn and was no doubt inspired by this hymn. The present version is a combination of these two which appeared with alterations in Madan's *Collection of Psalms and Hymns* (1760). Stanzas one and two are from Wesley, stanza three from Cennick, and stanza four from Wesley, with the exception of "O come quickly" which is Cennick's line.

REGENT SQUARE—*see* Praise, my soul, the King of heaven.

Look, ye saints! the sight is glorious 148

Thomas Kelly incuded this hymn in his *Hymns on Various Passages of Scripture,* third edition (1806), in which also appeared his "Hark, Ten Thousand Harps and Voices" (145). It is unaltered from the original.

REGENT SQUARE—*see* Praise, my soul, the King of heaven.

Lord, as of old at Pentecost 173

Charles H. Gabriel wrote both words and music for this hymn. It first appeared in *Great Revival Hymns, No. 2,* compiled by Homer Rodeheaver and B. D. Ackley (Chicago: The Rodeheaver Co., 1912), with the author of the words given as "Charlotte G. Homer," Gabriel's pseudonym.

OLD-TIME POWER is the name given this tune by the Hymnal Committee.

Lord, dismiss us with Thy blessing 31

This hymn first appeared anonymously in *A Supplement* to the *Shawbury Hymn Book* (Shrewsbury, England, 1773) and was included in several other compilations where no author's names were given. In the Harris *Collection of Psalms and Hymns,* seventh edition (York, 1791), it is credited to John Fawcett. Since the editors of these hymnals were, like Fawcett, all Nonconformists and no doubt knew Fawcett during his long pastorate of the Baptist chapel at Wainsgate, Hebden Bridge, Yorkshire, Julian concludes that Fawcett is very probably the author. We have the original three stanzas with some slight alterations in the first and third.

SICILIAN MARINERS' HYMN is of folk tune tradition and served as a setting for the Latin hymn "O sanctissima, O piissima." It is generally believed that the German poet Herder discovered this song on a visit to Italy in 1788-89, and published it in *Stimmen der Völker in Liedern* (1807). In the meantime, it had appeared almost simultaneously in Ralph Shaw's *The Gentleman's Amusement* (Philadelphia, 1794-95), and in Merrick and Tattersall's *Improved Psalmody* (1794). No connection has ever been established between this tune and Sicily or the sea as the name would imply. Ellinwood suggests the possibility that the song is an air from an obscure Neapolitan opera of the eighteenth century.

Lord, for tomorrow and its needs 339

Sybil F. Partridge is the author of this hymn. Her account of its writing is given by Frederick M. Steele in *The Continent* (Nov. 11, 1920).

I came here (The Convent of Notre Dame) as a young girl. Soon after I had got into the routine of my duties, one of the elderly sisters fell seriously ill, and though death seemed not far distant and though she longed to be released, the end was continually delayed. While strength seemed swiftly ebbing it was necessary to keep up her courage for at least one day more.

With these thoughts running through my mind, one night in 1876 while sitting by her bedside, between midnight and 3 o'clock in the morning, I wrote the poem.

I sent a copy of the verses to my mother, which some time later, without my knowledge, she published in a religious paper of London. If it has helped any other soul, in this or any other country, I am deeply grateful, and to the Lord be all the praise.

This poem of eight four-line stanzas first appeared in *The Messenger of the Sacred Heart of Jesus* (London, Jan. 1880, p. 29), a Roman Catholic monthly publication. According to McCutchan, its first appearance in America seems to have been in Fred A. Fillmore's *Songs of Rejoicing* (Cincinnati, 1888, p. 81).

VINCENT was composed by Horatio R. Palmer for this text and first appeared in his *Garnered Gems of Sunday School Song* (Cincinnati: John Church Co., 1892, No. 45), where the author of the text is erroneously given as "E. R. Wilberforce."

"Lord, I'm Coming Home"—*see* I've wandered far away from God

Lord Jesus, I long to be perfectly whole 201

This text by James L. Nicholson and tune by William G. Fischer were first published in a sixteen-page pamphlet entitled "Joyful Songs No. 4" (Philadelphia: Methodist Episcopal Book Room, 1872). Seven of the twelve songs contained in this pamphlet were by Fischer. This hymn is based on "Wash me, and I shall be whiter than snow" (Psalm 51:7). Of the six stanzas in the original hymn, the present version uses one, three, five, and four, in that order. Each of the original stanzas began "Dear Jesus," instead of "Lord Jesus." Other alterations occur in stanza two, line one, "look down" was "come down"; stanza three, line one, "most humbly" was "must humbly"; and stanza four, line one, "Thou knowest" was "Thou see'st." No doubt the popularity of this hymn can be attributed to its inclusion in *Gospel Hymns No. 2,* from which the present version is taken. It is not known who made these alterations.

FISCHER is the name given this tune by the Hymnal Committee.

Lord, lay some soul upon my heart 332

This hymn was written in 1939 and was first published in *The Broadman Hymnal* (Nashville, 1940, No. 451). The first stanza is anonymous and the second and third stanzas were written by Mack Weaver and B. B. McKinney, who also composed the tune.

LEILA is the name given this tune by the Hymnal Committee for Lelia Routh McKinney, wife of the composer.

"Lord, Send a Revival"—*see* Send a revival, O Christ, my Lord

Lord, speak to me, that I may speak 340

This hymn by Frances R. Havergal was written on April 28, 1872, at Winterdyne, Bewdley, England, and was first printed that same year in one of Parlane's musical leaflets under the heading, "A Worker's Prayer. None of us liveth unto himself, Romans 14:7." It was published in the author's *Under the Surface* (1874). Originally in seven four-line stanzas, the present version consists of stanzas one, four, six, and seven. The omitted stanzas are:

Oh, lead me, Lord, that I may lead
The wandering and the wavering feet;
Oh, feed me, Lord, that I may feed
Thy hungering ones with manna sweet.

O strengthen me, that while I stand
Firm on the Rock, and strong in Thee,
I may stretch out a loving hand
To wrestlers with the troubled sea.

O give Thine own sweet rest to me,
That I may speak with soothing power
A word in season, as from Thee,
To weary ones in needful hour.

CANONBURY is an arrangement of a melody from Schumann's *Nachtstücke* in F (Op. 23, No. 4), written in 1839. McCutchan suggests that the tune was named for the street or square bearing this name in Islington, London.

Love divine, all loves excelling 2

Written by Charles Wesley in 1743, this hymn first appeared in *Hymns for Those That Seek and Those That Have Redemption in the Blood of Jesus Christ* (London, 1747), where it was entitled "Jesus, show us Thy salvation" and consisted of four eight-line stanzas. So few of the earlier hymns dealt with the idea of God as love that this hymn was a welcomed contribution to the Wesleyan hymn singing, for it mirrored a major emphasis of their preaching. Several changes from the original appear in our text. In stanza two, line four, the original was, "Let us find that second rest"; stanza two, line five, "take away our power of sinning"; stanza three, line two, "let us all Thy life receive"; and in stanza four, line two, "pure and sinless let us be."

LOVE DIVINE (also called ZUNDEL or BEECHER) was composed for these words in 1870 by John Zundel, Henry Ward Beecher's organist at the Pilgrim Congregational Church in Brooklyn, New York. It was published in the same year in *Christian Heart Songs, A Collection of Solos, Quartettes and Choruses of All Meters* (New York, 1870, No. 91). In the index Zundel attempted to indicate the right tempo for each tune by giving the number of seconds required for singing one stanza. The time indicated for this tune is sixty-five seconds.

"Love Is the Theme"—*see* Of the themes that men have known

"Love Lifted Me"—*see* I was sinking deep in sin

Low in the grave He lay, Jesus my Saviour   **112**

The text and tune of this hymn of the resurrection were written in 1874 by Robert Lowry. It was first published in *Brightest and Best,* a Sunday school songbook edited by W. H. Doane and Lowry (New York: Biglow & Main, 1875). It is based on "He is not here, but is risen" (Luke 24:6).

"Loyalty to Christ"—*see* From over hill and plain

Majestic sweetness sits enthroned   **118**

This hymn by Samuel Stennett, an English Baptist pastor, first appeared in John Rippon's *A Selection of Hymns from the Best Authors* (London, 1787), with the heading, "Chief Among Ten Thousand; or, the Excellences of Christ." It is based on Song of Solomon 5:10-16. The present version uses stanzas three, four, five, and seven of the original hymn. The omitted stanzas are:

1. To Christ, the Lord, let every tongue
   Its noblest tribute bring;
   When he's the subject of the song,
   Who can refuse to sing?

2. Survey the beauties of his face,
   And on his glories dwell;
   Think of the wonders of his grace
   And all his triumphs tell.

6. His hand a thousand blessings pours
   Upon my guilty head:
   His presence gilds my darkest hours,
   And guards my sleeping bed.

8. To heaven, the place of his abode,
   He brings my weary feet,
   Shows me the glories of my God,
   And makes my joys complete.

9. Since from his bounty I receive
   Such proofs of love divine,
   Had I a thousand hearts to give,
   Lord, they should all be thine.

ORTONVILLE was written for this hymn by Thomas Hastings and first appeared in his *The Manhattan Collection* (New York, 1837), where it was in the key of C.

"Make Me a Blessing"—*see* Out in the highways and byways of life

"Make Me a Channel of Blessing"—*see* Is your life a channel of blessing

"Man of sorrows," what a name   163

Both words and music, written by Philip P. Bliss, first appeared in the *International Lessons Monthly* (1875), entitled "Redemption." The hymn was included in *Gospel Hymns No. 2* (1876, No. 9), in five stanzas. The omitted third stanza is:

> Guilty, vile and helpless, we;
> Spotless Lamb of God was He;
> "Full atonement!" can it be?
> Hallelujah, what a Saviour!

March on, O soul, with Strength!   422

This hymn by George T. Coster, written in Bedford Park, London, on August 3, 1897, first appeared in *The Evangelical Magazine* (London, Feb. 1898). The first hymnal inclusion was in *Hessle Hymns* (1901), where it was entitled "Battle Song" and consisted of six eight-line stanzas. Its first appearance in America was in *The Pilgrim Hymnal* (Boston, 1904).

ARTHUR'S SEAT appeared with the credit line, "Arranged from Sir John Goss, 1800—," in *Hymns and Songs of Praise,* compiled by John K. Paine and Uzziah C. Burnap (New York, 1874). Arthur's Seat is the name of a hill overlooking Edinburgh, Scotland, which is supposed to have been named for Arthur, the British prince who defeated the Saxons in that region. The reason for the tune name and the work of Goss from which the tune was taken both remain unknown.

Marvelous grace of our loving Lord   200

Julia H. Johnson is the author of this text, and the tune was composed in 1910 by Daniel B. Towner. MOODY is the name given this tune by the Hymnal Committee. For many years Towner was the head of the Music Department of Moody Bible Institute in Chicago. The earliest appearance of this hymn the writer has found is in *Hymns Tried and True*, compiled by Towner (Chicago: The Bible Institute Colportage Association, 1911, No. 2).

Edwin P. Parker wrote these stanzas to be read at the close of a sermon while he was pastor of the Center Church, Hartford, Connecticut. He also composed the tune, LOVE'S OFFERING, and the hymn and tune first appeared in *The Christian Hymnal* (1889).

Mighty God, while angels bless Thee   **4**

The writing of this hymn by Robert Robinson resulted from an experience he had with a young lad, Benjamin Williams, who later became a deacon in the Baptist church at Reading, England. One day, while holding the boy on his lap, and under the influence of that affectionate feeling which a child's love inspires, Robinson wrote

> Mighty God, while angels bless Thee,
>   May an infant lisp Thy name?
> Lord of men as well as angels,
>   Thou art every creature's theme.

After completing the hymn, he read it to the child and put it playfully into his hand. Joseph Belcher, in *Historical Sketches of Hymns and Their Writers* (1859), relates, "Well do we remember the deep feeling with which Deacon Williams described to us the scene, as we sat with him by his own fireside." Originally in nine four-line stanzas with the refrain, "Hallelujah, hallelujah, hallelujah, amen," it now appears with one stanza omitted and the other eight stanzas combined into four eight-line stanzas. The word "infant" has been changed to "mortal." The hymn first appeared in J. Middleton's *Hymns* (1793) and later, in Robinson's *Miscellaneous Works* (1807), edited by Benjamin Flower, father of Sarah Flower Adams (*q.v.*).

AUTUMN. The authorship or source of this tune has been a matter of considerable dispute. In various collections it has been attributed to Louis von Esch, François H. Barthélémon, and Ludovich Nicholson. It has been called a melody arranged from Psalm 42 in the *Genevan Psalter* (1551). In his detailed discussion of this tune in *Our Hymnody,* McCutchan carefully disposes of all other claims except that of Barthélémon. As to the initial appearance of the melody, McCutchan states that "sometime after 1796, a song with harp accompaniment, ascribed to F. H. Barthélémon, the eminent violinist, was published with words taken from 'The Monk' by Matthew Gregory Lewis." An American edition of the song entitled "Durandarte and Belerma," a Spanish ballad, appeared in Benjamin Carr's *Musical Journal,* (III, No. 63. Philadelphia, 1801-2).

In the fall of 1861, Julia Ward Howe, with her husband, Dr. Howe, their pastor, Dr. James Freeman Clarke, and Governor Andrews of Massachusetts, were visiting Washington, D. C., and were invited to watch a military review of federal troops some distance from the city. On their return to Washington on a road congested with troops, the soldiers began singing "John Brown's body lies a-mouldering in the grave." Dr. Clarke commented on the stirring character of the tune and suggested that Mrs. Howe write a better text for it. During that night the words came to her and the stanzas were completed before daybreak. On her return to Boston, she showed the poem to James T. Fields, editor of the *Atlantic Monthly,* who suggested the title, "Battle Hymn of the Republic," and published it in the February, 1862, issue. Originally in five stanzas, the omitted third stanza is:

> I have read the fiery gospel writ in burnished rows of steel:
> "As ye deal with my contemners, so with you my grace shall deal."
> Let the Hero, born of woman, crush the serpent with His heel,
>   Since God is marching on.

In *American Unitarian Hymn Writers and Hymns,* Henry Wilder Foote states:

It attracted little attention until it caught the eye of Chaplain C. C. McCabe (later a Methodist bishop) who had a fine singing voice and who taught it first to the 122nd Ohio Volunteer Infantry regiment to which he was attached, then to other troops, and to prisoners in Libby Prison after he was made prisoner of war. Thereafter it quickly came into use throughout the North as an expression of the patriotic emotion of the period.

BATTLE HYMN is of obscure origin. It has been attributed to a William Steffe, but his identity, or the reason for crediting him with this melody remain unknown. It is generally agreed that it is a variant of an old camp meeting tune, one form of which was:

Say, broth-ers will you meet us? Say, broth-ers will you meet us?

Say, broth-ers will you meet us on Ca - naan's hap - py shore?

Apparently originating in South Carolina, this song was well known many years prior to the Civil War. During the war it became a favorite among the northern troops as the religious words were replaced by impromptu lines. (Numerous popular songs were given the same parody-like treatment during World War II.) The John Brown text really involves two people by the same name. The first was an obscure private in the northern troops. By the time of John Brown's raid on Harper's Ferry, October 16, 1859, and his execution on December 2, of the same year, this text, made up for Pvt. John Brown, was used for John Brown, the ardent abolitionist, and it was in this form that it came to Mrs. Howe's attention.

It has been said that this was the favorite hymn of Gen. George S. Patton, Jr., and that he requested that it be played before sending his men into action in Europe during World War II.

More about Jesus would I know 321

Eliza E. Hewitt, the author of this hymn, was an invalid for a number of years. Later her health greatly improved, and she became interested in writing poetic verse. Some of her children's poems came to the attention of John R. Sweney, and he set a number of them to music. As the result of this initial contact, they collaborated on many hymns. In addition to the present hymn, with its tune SWENEY, they also wrote "There is sunshine in my soul today" (273) and "I am thinking today of that beautiful land" (470).

More holiness give me 338

This hymn, words and music by Philip P. Bliss, first appeared in *Sunshine for Sunday Schools* (Cincinnati: John Church & Co., 1873, No. 15). This was the second collection compiled by Bliss.

MY PRAYER, the tune name, is the original name given the hymn by the author-composer.

More like Jesus would I be 316

Fanny J. Crosby's text with this tune by William H. Doane first appeared in Doane's *Silver Spray* (Cincinnati: John Church Co., 1867, No. 15). This collection was one of the most popular Sunday school songbooks of its day. Doane donated the profits from its sale to purchase a large pipe organ which was placed in the YMCA Hall in Cincinnati. The organ, which was used for many years, was called "Silver Spray."

MORE LIKE JESUS is the name given this tune by the Hymnal Committee.

More like the Master I would ever be 325

Charles H. Gabriel wrote both words and music of this hymn in 1906, and it first appeared in his *Praise and Service* (Philadelphia: American Baptist Publication Society, 1907, No. 120). HANFORD is the name given this tune by the Hymnal Committee.

More love to Thee, O Christ 292

Elizabeth Prentiss wrote this hymn in 1856 at a time when she was experiencing physical suffering and mental anguish. Her husband has given the following information.

Like most of her hymns, it is simply a prayer put into the form of verse. She wrote it so hastily that the last stanza was left incomplete, one line having been added in pencil when it was printed. She did not show it, not even to her husband, until many years after it was written; and she wondered not a little that, when published, it met with so much favor.

It was first printed in a leaflet in 1869. The omitted third stanza in the present version is:

> Let sorrow do its work,
>   Come grief or pain;
> Sweet are thy messengers,
>   Sweet their refrain,
> When they can sing with me,
> More love, O Christ, to Thee,
>   More love to Thee!

MORE LOVE TO THEE was composed by William H. Doane for this text, and it first appeared in Doane's *Songs of Devotion* (1870, No. 379).

Must I go, and empty-handed 430

According to the account given by George C. Stebbins in his *Memoirs and Reminiscences,* the author of this hymn, Charles C. Luther, was inspired by the words of a dying young man who said, "I am not afraid to die; Jesus saves me now, but, oh! must I go empty-handed?" Luther, a Baptist minister, wrote this hymn in 1877, and with the present tune it first appeared in *Gospel Hymns No. 3* (1878).

PROVIDENCE was composed by George C. Stebbins shortly after the author had given him the words. At this time Stebbins was engaged in a series of meetings in Providence, Rhode Island, with Dr. George F. Pentecost. The tune was named by the Hymnal Committee for the city in which it was written.

The present version of this hymn appeared unsigned in *The Oberlin Social and Sabbath School Hymn Book* (1844), compiled by George N. Allen; and the three stanzas may be traced to three different sources. The first stanza is an alteration of a quatrain in Thomas Shepherd's *Penitential Cries* (1693), one of several collections of lyric poetry which appeared late in the seventeenth century. In its original form, this stanza read:

> Shall Simon bear the Cross alone,
> And other Saints be free?
> Each Saint of thine shall find his own,
> And there is one for me.

Stanza two seems to date from a missionary collection published at Norwich, England (*ca.* 1810), and stanza three apparently dates from Allen's 1844 collection, for it has not been found earlier.

MAITLAND was composed by Allen for this text for his 1844 Oberlin collection mentioned above. In Henry Ward Beecher's *Plymouth Collection* (1855) it is called CROSS AND CROWN and is said to be a "Western Melody." The appearance of the hymn and tune in Beecher's collection helped to make them widely known.

My country, 'tis of thee 487

Samuel Francis Smith, who was to become one of the outstanding Baptist preachers of the nineteenth century, wrote this hymn when he was a young man. Usually the year 1832 is given as the date, and autographic transcripts written some years later by the author carried the notation, "Written in 1832" (see cut of holograph). However, the facts are to the contrary.

During the time Smith was a student at Andover Seminary, William C. Woodbridge returned from a visit to Germany and gave Lowell Mason a number of German hymnals and tune books. Since Mason could not read German, he showed them to Smith. One of these collections contained the tune now known as AMERICA. At the home of Rev. William Jenks in Boston, Smith wrote this hymn of five stanzas to fit this tune. A few days later Jenks showed the hymn to Rev. Dr. Wisner, pastor of Park Street (Congregational) Church, and recommended its use at a celebration of American independence by the Boston Sabbath School Union to be held at the church on July 4, 1831.

Two copies of the program for this service are known to exist, which are in the Chapin Collection of Williams College and the American

HOLOGRAPH BELONGING TO DR. J. W. STORER

Antiquarian Society, Boston. The copy in the Chapin Collection was the personal copy of William Jenks on the reverse side showing the notes he made of Wisner's sermon. The program carries the five stanzas of the hymn with the indication that it was to be sung by the Juvenile Choir.

The account of this service in the *Christian Watchman* (XII No. 29, 106) does not mention the hymn. However, it does state that Lowell Mason directed the Juvenile Choir, and its report of Dr. Wisner's sermon coincides with Jenks' notes mentioned above. All of this evidence definitely establishes that the hymn was written and first used in 1831.

The first collection to include the hymn was Lowell Mason's *The Choir, or Union Collection of Church Music* (Boston, 1832), where four stanzas are given. The original third stanza does not seem to have survived in any printings but the Park Street program. Here are found words of strong conviction against England's treatment of the colonies and the resulting War of Independence.

> No more shall tyrants here
> With haughty steps appear,
>   And soldier bands;
> No more shall tyrants tread
> Above the patriot dead—
> No more our blood be shed
>   By alien hands.

It is a strange coincidence that the tunes of our two most frequently sung patriotic songs—"The Star-spangled Banner" and "My country, 'tis of thee"—have unknown origins. Ironically, both tunes came from England, the country from which this nation won its independence almost two hundred years ago. The tune AMERICA is sung today to "My country, 'tis of thee" and also throughout the British Commonwealth for "God save the Queen." Unsuccessful attempts have been made to attribute it to several individuals. The first appearance seems to have been in the *Gentleman's Magazine* (Oct., 1745), with the words "God save great George, our King." In the German collection in which Smith found the tune, it was set to a patriotic text, seeming to indicate that its use for patriotic expression had not been confined to England.

My dear Redeemer and my Lord   83

This hymn by Isaac Watts first appeared in *Hymns and Spiritual Songs, Book II,* (1707), entitled "The example of Christ."

FEDERAL STREET was composed by Henry K. Oliver in 1832 for "So fades the lovely blooming flower" by Anne Steele and was first published in Lowell Mason's *Boston Academy Collection of Church Music* (1836). It is named for the street in Boston where stood the church Oliver attended as a boy.

My faith looks up to Thee   257

The author, Ray Palmer, gives this full account of the writing of the hymn:

Immediately after graduating at Yale College, in September, 1830, the writer went to the city of New York to spend a year teaching in a select school for young ladies. This private institution, which was patronized by the best class of families, was under the direction of an excellent Christian lady connected with Saint George's Church. . . . The writer resided in the family of the lady who kept the school, and it was there that the hymn was written. It had no external occasion whatever. Having been accustomed from childhood, through an inherited propensity perhaps, to the occasional expression of what his heart felt, in the form of verse, it was in accordance with this habit, and in an hour when Christ, in the riches of his grace and love, was so vividly apprehended as to fill the soul with deep emotion, that the lines were composed. There was not the slightest thought of writing for another eye, least of all writing a hymn for Christian worship. Away from outward excitement, in the quiet of his chamber, and with a deep consciousness of his own needs, the writer transferred as faithfully as he could to paper what at the time was passing within him. Six stanzas were composed and imperfectly written, first on a loose sheet, and then accurately copied into a small morocco-covered book, which for such purposes the author was accustomed to carry in his pocket. This first complete copy is still [1875] preserved. It is well remembered that when writing the last line, "A ransomed soul," the thought that the whole work of redemption and salvation was involved in those words, and suggested the theme of eternal praises, moved the writer to a degree of emotion that brought abundant tears.

A year or two after the hymn was written, and when no one, so far as can be recollected, had ever seen it, Dr. Lowell Mason met the author in the street in Boston, and requested him to furnish some hymns for a Hymn and Tune Book, which in connection with Dr. Hastings of New York, he was about to publish. The little book containing the hymn was shown him, and he asked for a copy. We stepped into a store together, and a copy was made and given to him, which, without much notice, he put into his pocket. On sitting down at home and looking it over, he became so much interested in it that he wrote for it the tune OLIVET, to which it has almost universally been sung. Two or three days afterward we met again in the street, when, scarcely waiting to salute the writer, he earnestly exclaimed: "Mr. Palmer, you may live many years and do many good things, but I think you will be best known to posterity as the author of "My Faith Looks Up to Thee!"

And history has proved that Mason was right!

This hymn, with Mason's tune OLIVET, first appeared in *Spiritual Songs for Social Worship*, edited by Mason and Thomas Hastings (Boston, 1832).

My Father is rich in houses and lands 270

This hymn was written by Harriet E. Buell, and the circumstances concerning the writing of the hymn are related by Frank J. Metcalf in *American Writers and Compilers of Sacred Music* (p. 352-53):

The hymn . . . was suggested to her during a Sunday-morning service which she was attending in 1878 at Thousand Island Park, New York, and the stanzas were largely composed while she was walking home to her cottage after the service. She had no thought of its ever being used as a hymn. She was a constant contributor for something like fifty years to the Northern Christian Advocate, published at Syracuse, New York, and the poem was sent, as were most of her writings, to that paper. It was first published in 1878, and she received, much to her surprise, a copy of the hymn and music in the autumn of that year, from the Rev. John B. Sumner, a total stranger to her. He found it in the Advocate.

With regard to the year 1878 Metcalf is in error, for the poem first appeared in the *Northern Christian Advocate* (Feb. 1, 1877, p. 2), where it is given in this form:

CHILD OF A KING

by Hattie E. Buell

"And if children, then heirs"

My Father is rich in houses and lands,
He holdeth the wealth of the world in His hands;
Of rubies and diamonds, of silver and gold,
His coffers are full, He has riches untold.

The kings of the earth may boast, in their pride,
Of their glory and honor, their riches beside;
When the "King of all kingdoms" for tribute shall call,
They must pay the full price, for He ruleth them all.

My Father's own Son, the "Savior of Men"
Once wandered o'er the earth as the poorest of them,
But now He is reigning forever on high,
And will give us a home in the sweet bye and bye.

I once was an outcast, a stranger on earth,
A "sinner" by choice, and an "alien" by birth,
But I've been "adopted". My name's written down
As an heir to a mansion, a robe, and a crown.

It matters not, then, what my station may be,
The few days that on earth are allotted to me;
Since when at the last my kingdom I gain,
Forever and ever with Him I shall reign.

A tent or a cottage, then, why should I care,
While they're building a palace for me "over there?"
Though an exile from home, yet still I may sing,
All glory to God, I'm the child of a King!

BINGHAMTON was composed by John B. Sumner in 1877, while he was
pastor in Binghamton, New York.

My hope is built on nothing less   283

This hymn seems to have been written in 1834. The author, Edward
Mote, wrote the following account in *The Gospel Herald* (London).

One morning it came into my mind as I went to labour, to write an hymn
on the "Gracious Experience of a Christian." As I went up Holborn I had
the chorus,

On Christ the solid Rock I stand,
All other ground is sinking sand.

In the day I had four first verses complete, and wrote them off. On the
Sabbath following I met Brother King as I came out of Lisle Street Meeting,
. . . who informed me that his wife was very ill, and asked me to call and
see her. I had an early tea, and called afterwards. He said that it was his
usual custom to sing a hymn, read a portion, and engage in prayer, before
he went to meeting. He looked for his hymnbook, but could find it nowhere.
I said, "I have some verses in my pocket; if he liked, we would sing them."
We did; and his wife enjoyed them so much, that after service he asked me,
as a favour, to leave a copy of them for his wife. I went home, and by the
fireside composed the last two verses, wrote them off, and took them to
Sister King. . . . As these verses so met the dying woman's case, my attention to them was the more arrested, and I had a thousand of them printed
for distribution. I sent one to the *Spiritual Magazine,* without my initials,
which appeared some time after this. Brother Rees, of Crown Street, Soho,
brought out an edition of hymns (1836), and this hymn was in it. David
Denham introduced it (1837) with Ree's name, and others after. . . . Your
inserting this brief outline may in future shield me from the charge of
stealth, and be a vindication of truthfulness in my connection with the
Church of God.

In 1836 it appeared in Rees' collection, and later the same year in
Mote's *Hymns of Praise,* London. The original form of the hymn is:

Nor earth, nor hell, my soul can move,
I rest upon unchanging love;
I dare not trust the sweetest frame,
But wholly lean on Jesus' name;
On Christ, the solid Rock, I stand,
All other ground is sinking sand.

My hope is built on nothing less
Than Jesus' blood and righteousness;
'Midst all the hell I feel within,
On his completed work I lean;
On Christ, the Solid Rock, I stand,
All other ground is sinking sand.

When darkness veils his lovely face,
I rest upon unchanging grace;
In every rough and stormy gale,
My anchor holds within the veil;
On Christ, the solid Rock, I stand,
All other ground is sinking sand.

His oath, his covenant, and his blood,
Support me in the sinking flood;
When all around my soul gives way,
He then is all my hope and stay.
On Christ, the solid Rock, I stand,
All other ground is sinking sand.

I trust his righteous character,
His council, promise, and his power;
His honor and his name's at stake
To save me from the burning lake;
On Christ, the solid Rock, I stand,
All other ground is sinking sand.

When I shall launch in worlds unseen,
O may I then be found in him,
Dressed in his righteousness   alone,
Faultless to stand before the throne.
On Christ, the solid Rock, I stand,
All other ground is sinking sand.

SOLID ROCK, composed by William B. Bradbury for this text in 1863, first appeared in his *The Devotional Hymn and Tune Book* (Philadelphia: American Baptist Publication Society, 1864, No. 52). This collection was the only new Baptist hymnal to appear in our country during the Civil War.

Benjamin Schmolck's hymn "Mein Jesu! wie du willst," with eleven stanzas, first appeared in his *Heilige Flammen der himmlisch gesinnten Seele, in 50 Arien* (Striegau, 1704). It is based on "He said, Abba, Father, all things are possible unto thee; take away this cup from me: nevertheless not what I will, but what thou wilt" (Mark 14:36). Jane L. Borthwick's translation first appeared in her *Hymns from the Land of Luther* (1854).

JEWETT is based on the familiar section for horns in the overture to Carl Maria von Weber's opera, *Der Freischütz,* written in 1820. In *Our Hymnody,* McCutchan states that

Weber's favorite motto was "As God wills." It is said his last words when dying in London were, "Let me go back to my own home and then 'God's will be done.'" One wonders if this were known to whoever first used this tune with this hymn.

This arrangement as a hymn tune was made by Joseph P. Holbrook and first appeared in Charles S. Robinson's *Songs of the Church, of Hymns and Tunes for the Christian Worship* (Chicago: A. S. Barnes, 1862, No. 376).

My Jesus, I love Thee 289

Usually the date of this hymn is given as 1858, with the statement that the author, William Ralph Featherston, was sixteen years old at the time. However, if the date is correct, the author was only twelve years old. If the age of the author is correct, then the date should be 1862. McCutchan states that the author sent the hymn to his aunt, Mrs. E. Featherston Wilson, who then lived in Los Angeles, California, who approved of it and suggested that it be published. David J. Beattie, in *The Romance of Sacred Song* (London, 1931), states that "the original copy of the hymn, in the author's handwriting, is still a cherished treasure in the family." The first appearance of the hymn seems to have been in England in *The London Hymn Book* (1864). By 1870 it had found its way into American collections.

GORDON was composed for this text by Adoniram J. Gordon. It first appeared in the 1876 edition of *The Service of Song for Baptist Churches,* compiled by S. L. Caldwell and Gordon (Boston: Gould & Lincoln, No. 1105 [1st ed., 1871]). The preface to the 1876 edition indicates that among the new materials added are "the increasingly popular gospel songs of Sankey, Lowry, Doane, Fischer, and Bliss."

My life, my love I give to Thee 359

This hymn by Ralph E. Hudson with this tune by C. R. Dunbar first appeared in *Salvation Echoes,* R. E. Hudson compiler and publisher (Alliance, Ohio, 1882, No. 62).

DUNBAR is the name given this tune by the Hymnal Committee.

My soul, be on thy guard 420

This hymn by George Heath first appeared in his *Hymns and Poetic Essays Sacred to the Public and Private Worship of the Diety* (Bristol, 1781), where it was entitled "Steadfastness."

LABAN—*see* A parting hymn we sing.

"My Prayer"—*see* More holiness give me

"My Redeemer"—*see* I will sing of my Redeemer

"My Saviour First of All"—*see* When my life-work is ended, and I cross the swelling tide

"My Saviour's Love"—*see* I stand amazed in the presence

My soul in sad exile was out on life's sea 228

Henry Lake Gilmour wrote the text and the tune was composed by George D. Moore. It first appeared in *Sunlit Songs,* compiled by John R. Sweney, William J. Kirkpatrick, and Gilmour (Philadelphia: John J. Hood, 1890, No. 158). Originally in five stanzas, the omitted fourth stanza reads

> How precious the thought that we all may recline,
> Like John, the beloved so blest,
> On Jesus' strong arm, where no tempest can harm,
> Secure in the "Haven of Rest."

HAVEN OF REST, the name given this tune by the Hymnal Committee, is frequently used as the title of the hymn.

"Near the Cross"—*see* Jesus, keep me near the cross

"Near to the Heart of God"—*see* There is a place of quiet rest

Nearer, my God, to Thee 322

This was one of thirteen hymns Sarah F. Adams wrote in 1840 which were submitted to the Rev. William Johnson Fox for his *Hymns and Anthems* (1841), compiled for the use of his congregation at the

Unitarian South Place Chapel, Finsbury, England. In America the hymn first appeared in James Freeman Clarke's *The Disciples' Hymn Book: a Collection of Hymns and Chants for Public and Private Devotions, prepared for the use of the Church of the Disciples* (Boston, 1844). The hymn is based on the story of Jacob at Bethel as given in Genesis 28:10-22.

BETHANY was composed by Lowell Mason for this hymn in 1856 and first appeared in the Andover *Sabbath Hymn and Tune Book* (1859). In 1868 Mason related to a friend the following account:

When we were compiling the collection known as the *Sabbath Hymn and Tune Book,* they [that is, Edward A. Park and Austin Phelps] applied to me for a musical setting for the hymn, "Nearer, My God, to Thee." The metre was irregular. But one night some time after, lying awake in the dark, eyes wide open, through the stillness of the house the melody came to me, and the next morning I wrote down the notes of BETHANY.

The story of the singing of this hymn by the passengers of the ill-fated English ship *Titanic,* which sank on April 14, 1912, with a loss of 1,635 passengers, has become legendary. The presumption that Mason's tune BETHANY was sung by the *Titanic* passengers and played by the ship's band has been further imbedded by the use of the tune in the recent motion picture production of this experience. Strong protests have come from England, saying that BETHANY has never been associated with this text in England and that at the sinking of the *Titanic,* another tune was sung and played.

Nearer, still nearer, close to Thy heart   281

Mrs. C. H. Morris wrote both words and music for this hymn and it first appeared in *Pentecostal Praises,* compiled by William J. Kirkpatrick and H. L. Gilmour (Philadelphia: Hall-Mack Co., 1898, No. 117).

No, not despairingly   206

This hymn by Horatius Bonar first appeared in his *Hymns of Faith and Hope,* third series (1866), with the heading, "Confession and Peace."

Very little is known concerning this tune, KEDRON, and its composer, Ann B. Spratt. James Edmund Jones says that this tune is one of two tunes by Miss Spratt which appeared in the *Book of Common Praise* (1866). In J. Ireland Tucker's *The Parish Hymnal* (New York, 1870) it is set to "Nearer, My God, to Thee," and simply called "Hymn 51 First Tune." In Tucker's *Tunes Old and New* (1872) it appears as

Number 507, where it is called KEDRON and set to the same hymn as his earlier collection. Its first association with the present hymn seems to have been in *The Methodist Hymnal* (1905).

"Nothing but the Blood"—*see* What can wash away my sin

Now, on land and sea descending 28

This hymn by Samuel Longfellow first appeared in *Vespers* (1859), a collection of hymns for use in the vesper services at the second Unitarian Church, Brooklyn, where Longfellow served as pastor, 1857-60.

VESPER HYMN first appeared as a glee for four voices in *A Selection of Popular National Airs* (London, 1818) by Sir John Stevenson. It was called "Russian Air," and there was a notation that the fourth line of our tune was added to the original melody by Stevenson. It appeared the following year in America in Oliver Shaw's *Melodia Sacra, A Providence Selection of Sacred Music* (Providence, 1819, No. 147). Ellinwood (*The Hymnal 1940 Companion,* p. 130) was unable to find any valid reason to credit Bortniansky as composer, even though most hymnals carry this ascription, and states that a careful examination of the published works of Bortniansky does not reveal any lines which remotely resemble this "Russian Air" of Stevenson. It is interesting to note that in the version of this tune which appears in *The Hymnal 1940,* the original Stevenson final line appears as the third line, while the third line of the original tune appears as the final fourth line.

Now thank we all our god 491

This hymn of gratitude, "Nun danket alle Gott," was written by Martin Rinkart during the Thirty Years' War, 1618-1648, while he was pastor at Eilenburg in Saxony. Though severely attacked three times, the town served as a haven for refugees, causing famine and pestilence. For some time Rinkart was the only pastor in the city, and during the great pestilence of 1637 he conducted about 4,500 burial services—sometimes as many as forty or fifty a day. In the midst of these circumstances, he wrote these lines of thanksgiving to God. The first stanza is an expression of thanksgiving for the blessings of God. The second is a petition for God's care and keeping. The final stanza is a doxology, praising the Father, Son, and Holy Spirit. The hymn was probably first published in Rinkart's *Jesu-Hertz-Büchlein* (1636), no copy of which is now known. The hymn is found in the extant 1663 edition of this collection. With this tune, the hymn appeared in the 1647 edition of Johann Crüger's *Praxis Pietatis Melica* (Berlin). Catherine Winkworth's translation first appeared in her

Lyra Germanica, second series (1858), and again in her *Chorale Book for England* (1863).

NUN DANKET composed by Johann Crüger first appeared in his *Praxis Pietatis Melica,* (Berlin, 1647 edition [first edition, *ca.* 1644]). The present version is a reduction to four-part harmony of the six-part version in Felix Mendelssohn's *Lobgesang* (Hymn of Praise; Op. 52, 1840).

Now the day is over   35

Sabine Baring-Gould wrote this hymn in eight stanzas for the children of Horbury Bridge, near Wakefield, England, while he was curate in charge of that mission district. It was first published in *The Church Times* (February 16, 1865). In 1868 it appeared in the Appendix to *Hymns Ancient and Modern,* set to the tune EUDOXIA which Baring-Gould wrote for it. The hymn is based on "When thou liest down, thou shalt not be afraid: yea, thou shalt lie down, and thy sleep shall be sweet" (Prov. 3:24).

MERRIAL was composed by Barnby in 1868 and first published in his *Original Tunes to Popular Hymns* (1869). It appeared in America in Charles S. Robinson's *Spiritual Songs for Social Worship* (1878), named EMMELAR. McCutchan (*Hymn Tune Names,* p. 102) states that Robinson made up this name from the initials of his daughter's name, M. L. R., but later substituted the present name as a spelling of his daughter's name, Mary L.

Now to the Lord a noble song   19

This hymn by Isaac Watts first appeared in *Hymns and Spiritual Songs* (1707), entitled "Christ All and in All."

DUKE STREET—*see* Jesus shall reign where'er the sun.

O beautiful for spacious skies   489

Katherine Lee Bates wrote this hymn one summer evening in 1893 at Colorado Springs, Colorado, after she had visited the summit of Pike's Peak with a group of friends. It remained in her notebook until she chanced upon it again in 1899 and sent it to a publisher in Boston.

MATERNA, meaning "motherly," was composed by Samuel A. Ward for the hymn "O mother dear, Jerusalem." Ward is said to have composed the tune, jotting it down on his cuff, while crossing New York harbor after a day's outing at Coney Island. An employee in Ward's music store has stated that this occurred in 1882, and that the tune was first performed by a choir of two hundred men and boys at Grace Episcopal Church, Newark, New Jersey, where Ward was organist. However, Ward's son-in-law, Rev. Henry W. Armstrong, has stated that the tune was composed in memory of Ward's eldest daughter, Clara, who died in 1885. The tune was first published in *The Parish Choir* (VIII, No. 378), and its first hymnal inclusion was in Charles L. Hutchins' *The Church Hymnal* (1894, No. 403), as the first setting for "O Mother Dear, Jerusalem." In 1912 the president of Massachusetts Agricultural College requested permission of the composer's widow to set this tune to Miss Bates's text, and this happy marriage of words and music became immensely popular during World War I.

O blessed day of motherhood!   504

Concern over the lack of hymnic literature appropriate for Mother's Day use prompted Ernest F. McGregor to write this hymn in 1925.

MATER was composed by Arthur Depew for this text. Shortly after the hymn was written, Dr. McGregor brought it to his organist friend, Depew, who was at the time serving as organist at the Collegiate Church of St. Nicholas, New York City, and requested him to write a suitable tune.

O brother man, fold to thy heart thy brother!   447

This hymn is made up of stanzas thirteen, eleven, and fourteen from John Greenleaf Whittier's poem "Worship," written in 1848. It was first published in his *Labor and Other Poems* (1850), with the heading, "Pure religion and undefiled before God and the Father is this, To visit the fatherless and the widows in their affliction, and to keep himself unspotted from the world," (James 1:27). The first of the fifteen original stanzas begins:

> The pagan's myths through marble lips are spoken,
>   The ghosts of o!d Beliefs still flit and moan,
> Round fane and altar overthrown and broken,
>   O'er tree-grown barrow and gray ring of stone.

Robert G. McCutchan comments that the poem was written

to show his opposition to, and contempt for, elaborate rites and ceremonies in worship. His Quaker simplicity prompted him to emphasize "the holier worship" which "feeds the widow and the fatherless," and which is the essence of "Brotherhood" in the "Kingdom of God."

ILONA was composed for this text by Joseph W. Lerman in 1908 as he was completing twenty-eight years of service as organist at the Olivet Memorial Church, Brooklyn, New York.

O come, all ye faithful 66

Seven manuscripts of this famous Latin hymn, all from the middle of the eighteenth century have been known. The most recent discovery was made in 1946 by Maurice Frost. These manuscripts bear the signature of John Francis Wade, a layman, who made his living by copying and selling music at Douai, France. The problem that has bothered hymnologists has been whether the words and music should be credited to Wade or whether he copied them from some now unknown source. After examining these existing manuscripts, Dom John Stéphan in *Adeste Fideles: A Study on Its Origin and Development* (1947) presents convincing evidence for crediting this hymn to Wade.

The original Latin hymn had four stanzas and four others were subsequently added. The present version, using stanzas 1, 3 and 4, was based on a translation made in 1841 by Frederick Oakeley for use by his congregation at Margaret Street Chapel, London, beginning "Ye faithful approach ye." The first line was changed to "O come, all ye faithful" in F. H. Murray's *A Hymnal for Use in the English Church* (London, 1852), and this version has become the most popular throughout the English speaking world.

The tune, in all the manuscripts in triple time, first appeared in duple time in Samuel Webbe's *Essay on the Church Plain Chant* (London, 1782). The tune became very popular immediately and made its first American appearance in Benjamin Carr's *Musical Journal* (II, No. 29).

ADESTE FIDELES is the generally accepted name for this tune and is taken from the beginning of the original Latin text. Because of the fact that Webbe was organist at the chapel of the Portuguese Embassy in London, and that this tune became known because of its use there, it has been sometimes called PORTUGUESE HYMN. The use of this latter name has been deceiving, at least by implication, in suggesting a Portuguese source or background.

O could I speak the matchless worth 146

Written by Samuel Medley, this hymn first appeared in his *Hymns,* third edition (1789), entitled "Praise of Jesus." The present version is made up of stanzas two, four, six, and eight of the original. The omitted first stanza begins, "Not of terrestrial mortal themes."

ARIEL—*see* Let all on earth their voices raise.

O day of rest and gladness 36

This is the opening hymn in Christopher Wordsworth's *Holy Year* (1862). It was originally in six stanzas.

MENDEBRAS was arranged by Lowell Mason from an anonymous melody, possibly a German folk melody. It first appeared in *The Modern Psalmist* (1839), set to "I love Thy kingdom, Lord."

O do not let the Word depart 234

Eliza Reed's hymn, "O do not let the Word depart," with the heading, "The Accepted Time," first appeared in *The Hymn Book* (1842), compiled by her husband, Andrew Reed (*q.v.*). Here the original hymns by Reed and his wife were anonymous, but in Reed's *Wycliffe Chapel Supplement* (1872) the authors' names are given. The alterations in the hymn and the text for the refrain were probably the work of the composer.

CALVIN was composed by J. Calvin Bushey for this text. The tune was named by the Hymnal Committee, using the middle name of the composer.

O for a faith that will not shrink 255

This hymn by William H. Bathurst was first published in his *Psalms and Hymns* (1831), in six four-line stanzas entitled "The Power of Faith."

ARLINGTON—*see* Am I a soldier of the cross.

O for a thousand tongues to sing 129

Charles Wesley wrote these lines in 1739 as he approached the anniversary date of his conversion of May 21, 1738. The original hymn contained eighteen stanzas and began, "Glory to God, and praise, and love," and was entitled "For the Anniversary Day of One's Conversion." It first appeared in *Hymns and Sacred Poems* (1740). Stanza seven begins "O for a thousand tongues to sing," which is the present first stanza, and these words are based on the statement of the Moravian missionary, Peter Böhler, to Wesley, "Had I a thousand tongues, I would praise him with them all." The use of this seventh stanza as the initial stanza is first found in R. Conyers' *Psalms and Hymns* (1767). Apparently this met with John Wesley's approval, for this form was adapted by him in his *Collection of Hymns* (1780), where it was the first hymn. The present version is made up of stanzas seven, eight, nine, and ten of Wesley's original hymn.

AZMON first appeared anonymously in Lowell Mason's *The Modern*

Psalmist (Boston, 1839).   In the preface of this book, Mason states that his recent European tour was primarily

to obtain materials for a work like this.   In the prosecution of this design he [Mason] visited many of the most important cities and obtained from distinguished composers of different nations much manuscript music; and also a great variety of recent musical publications—English, German, and French, which had not before reached this country.

The list of names in this preface includes "Glaser, J. M., German, 1780." In *The Sabbath Hymn and Tune Book* (1859) Mason named this tune DENFIELD and credited it to C. G.

O for a thousand tongues to sing ("Blessed be the Name")   140

Charles Wesley's hymn "O for a thousand tongues to sing," discussed above, forms the basis for this hymn. The adaptation here was made by Ralph E. Hudson, in which he substituted "Blessed be the name of the Lord," for the second and fourth lines of each stanza.   The adapted text and this tune, BLESSED NAME, first appeared in *Songs for the Ransomed,* compiled and published by Hudson (Alliance, Ohio, 1887).

BLESSED NAME is the name given this tune by the Hymnal Committee.   It is highly probably that this tune has a similar origin to that of OH, HOW I LOVE JESUS (*see* There is a name I love to hear). Hudson likely arranged it from a tune existing early in the nineteenth century.   This tune appears in *Hymns of the Christian Life,* compiled by R. Kelso Carter and A. B. Simpson (1891, No. 385), set to "All praise to Him who reigns above," with the tune "arr. by Wm. J. Kirkpatrick" (copyrighted 1888 by Kirkpatrick).   In William Rosborough's *Celestial Showers No. 2* (Texarkana, Texas, 1900, No. 10), with the anonymous text, "O come, let us, in songs to God" the tune is given as "Arranged" and the notation "Used by permission of E. A. Hoffman, owner of copyright."   Other illustrations could be given, but this indicates that the tune was widely known, and the variance in crediting composership suggests folk origin.   It is interesting to note that this tune does not appear in *Gospel Hymns* numbers 1 through 6, nor in Sankey's *Sacred Songs and Solos.*   It seems most likely that the tune is of camp meeting origin and that various common meter hymns were used for the stanzas, keeping the same text for the refrain.

O God of light, Thy Word, a lamp unfailing   185

Written by Sarah E. Taylor, this was chosen as the winning hymn of more than five hundred texts submitted to The Hymn Society of America in 1951-52, coincident with the publication of the new Revised

Standard Version of the Bible. It was first published by The Hymn Society of America in a pamphlet entitled, "Ten New Hymns on the Bible" (New York, 1953).

ANCIENT OF DAYS was composed by J. Albert Jeffery in 1886 at the request of Bishop William C. Doane for his hymn "Ancient of days, who sittest throned in glory," to be sung at the bicentennial celebration of the granting of the city charter of Albany, New York, the first chartered city in America. The tune appeared in 1894 in two musical editions of the 1892 Episcopal *Hymnal*. In Hutchins' edition it is called ANCIENT OF DAYS, and in Tucker and Rousseau's edition it is called ALBANY, the name it bears in *The Hymnal 1940*.

O God of our fathers, we praise and adore Thee   **500**

Edward Hughes Pruden, pastor of the First Baptist Church of Washington, D. C., is the author of this hymn. Dr. Pruden has provided the following information:

The Anniversary Hymn was written in connection with our observance of the One Hundred and Fiftieth Anniversary of our church here in 1952. I actually wrote the hymn one evening while visiting my mother in my home town of Chase City, Virginia. The hymn is used in our church on the first Sunday in each March, which is the Sunday nearest our anniversary date. Our church was founded in 1802 during the administration of Thomas Jefferson.

KREMSER—*see* We praise Thee, O God, our Redeemer, Creator.

O God, our help in ages past   **286**

This hymn is the first part of Isaac Watts's metrical version of Psalm 90, covering verses 1-5. It appeared in his *Psalms of David* (1719) in nine stanzas. The present version uses stanzas one, two, three, five, and nine of the original. The original first line, "Our God," was changed to "O God" by John Wesley in his *Psalms and Hymns* (1738). The omitted stanzas are

> 4. Thy word commands our flesh to dust,
>   "Return ye sons of men:"
> All nations rose from earth at first,
>   And turn to earth again.

> 6. The busy tribes of flesh and blood
>   With all their lives and cares
> Are carried downwards by thy flood,
>   And lost in following years.

140

7. Time, like an ever-rolling stream,
   Bears all its sons away;
   They fly, forgotten, as a dream
   Dies at the opening day.

8. Like flowery fields the nations stand
   Pleased with the morning light;
   The flowers beneath the mower's hand
   Lie withering ere 'tis night.

St. Anne—*see* God moves in a mysterious way.

O God, we pray for all mankind 456

This hymn of world missions was written by Howard J. Conover. No information has been found concerning its origin or source.

Ortonville—*see* Majestic sweetness sits enthroned.

O happy day that fixed my choice 389

Philip Doddridge is the author of this hymn. Entitled "Rejoicing in our Covenant engagements to God" (2 Chron. 15:15), it appeared without the refrain in Orton's edition of Doddridge's *Hymns* (1755).

Happy Day appeared in William McDonald's *The Wesleyan Sacred Harp* (Boston, 1854), set to "Jesus, my All to heaven is gone" with the present refrain, "Happy day, happy day, When Jesus washed my sins away!" Doddridge's hymn was given as an alternate text. It is quite possible that the tune was known prior to this date and appeared in earlier collections. McCutchan indicates that the hymn tune refrain is from a song by Edward F. Rimbault entitled "Happy Land." More than likely the rest of the tune was the work of some anonymous musician or musicians.

O happy home where Thou art loved the dearest 373

Carl J. P. Spitta's original German hymn, "O selig Haus, wo man dich aufgenommen," written in 1826, first appeared in Spitta's *Psalter und Harfe* (Pirna, Saxony, 1833), in five eight-line stanzas. Sarah B. Findlater's translation appeared in her *Hymns from the Land of Luther,* third series (1858), with the first line, "O happy house! where Thou art loved the best." The altered version which we have was made with Mrs. Findlater's permission and appeared in the Scottish *Church Hymnary* (1898). The hymn is based on Luke 19:9, "Jesus said unto him, This day is salvation come to this house, forsomuch as he also is a son of Abraham."

Two omitted stanzas of Mrs. Findlater's translation are:

O happy home, where two in heart united
In holy faith and blessed hope are one,
Whom death a little while alone divideth,
And cannot end the union here begun!

O happy home, where little ones are given
Early to Thee, in humble faith and prayer,
To Thee, their Friend, who from the heights of heaven
Guides them, and guards with more than mother's care.

ALVERSTOKE was first published in 1883 in a collection of original tunes by Barnby. Apparently the first hymnal to include it was the *Methodist Free Church Tune-Book* (1892), where it was set to "Still, Still with Thee."

O Holy Saviour, friend unseen 287

This hymn by Charlotte Elliott was written soon after the death of her father in 1834, and published that year in her *Invalid Hymn Book.*

FLEMMING was composed by Friedrich F. Flemming in 1811 as a song for men's voices set to "Integer vitae scelerisque purus" from the ode of Horace. It appeared as a hymn tune in the revised edition of the *Congregational Psalmist* (London, 1875), and in the *Bristol Tune Book,* second series (Bristol, 1876).

O Jesus, I have promised 386

John E. Bode wrote this hymn about 1866 for the confirmation of his daughter and two sons in the Church of England, and it was printed as a leaflet in 1868 by the Society for the Promotion of Christian Knowledge. It was first published in the SPCK's *Psalms and Hymns* (1869) and consisted of six eight-line stanzas. The present version is made up of stanzas one, five, two, and three of the original.

ANGEL'S STORY was composed by Arthur H. Mann for the hymn "I love to hear the story which angel voices tell," and first appeared in *The Methodist Sunday School Hymnbook* (London, 1881). The tune name was taken from the first line of this hymn for which it was composed.

O Jesus, Master, when today 466

This hymn was written by Charles S. Newhall in 1913, and first appeared in *The Survey* (Jan. 3, 1914). Its first appearance in a hymnal was in *Social Hymns of Brotherhood and Aspiration* (1914).

HUMILITY was composed by Samuel P. Tuckerman and was published in *The National Lyre* (1848), edited by Tuckerman, Bancroft, and Oliver.

O Jesus, Thou art standing   346

The author, William W. How, has given this information concerning the writing of this hymn:

I composed the hymn early in 1867, after I had been reading a very beautiful poem entitled, "Brothers, and a Sermon" [Jean Ingelow]. The pathos of the verses impressed me very forcibly at the time. I read them over and over again, and finally, closing the book, I scribbled on an old scrap of paper my first idea of the verses beginning, "O Jesus, Thou art standing."

The hymn is based on Revelation 3:20, "Behold, I stand at the door, and knock," and was first published in 1867 edition of *Psalms and Hymns* (1st ed., 1854), compiled by the author and Thomas B. Morrell.

ST. HILDA is the work of two men. The first two phrases of the tune first appeared in *Vollständige Sammlung* (Stuttgart, 1799), edited by Johann Friedrich Christmann and Justin Heinrich Knecht. In this collection, to which Knecht contributed ninety-eight tunes, this tune is called KNECHT after the composer and is dated 1793. The final two phrases were added by Edward Husband in 1871. The tune is named for a devoted woman who lived in England in the seventh century and had great influence in the religious and political life of her day.

O land of rest for thee I sigh   284

John Julian, in his *Dictionary of Hymnology,* states that he had traced this hymn to *Songs for the Sanctuary* (1865), where it appeared as "Anon." with the first line beginning, "Sweet land of rest, for thee I sigh." In later collections the name of Elizabeth Mills is frequently found. While there is insufficient proof to credit or discredit the claim of Miss Mills's authorship, the writer would be inclined to believe that this text is of American folk hymn tradition.

LAND OF REST is usually attributed to William Miller. In the Seventh-Day Adventist *Hymnal* (1940) this tune is found among the "Early Adventist Hymns."

O little town of Bethlehem   75

Phillips Brooks wrote this hymn in 1868 for the children of the Sunday school of Holy Trinity Episcopal Church, Philadelphia, after his visit to Bethlehem in 1865. It was first printed in leaflets and became very well known locally. Originally in five stanzas, the fourth is usually omitted, as in the present version. It was first published in William R. Huntington's *Church Porch* (1874).

ST. LOUIS was composed in 1868 by Lewis H. Redner for these words at the request of Brooks when Redner was organist at Holy Trinity Church. Words and music first appeared in Huntington's collection mentioned above where the tune was named ST. LOUIS. Ernest K. Emurian, in his *Stories of Christmas Carols,* relates that when Phillips Brooks asked Lewis Redner to compose this tune, he suggested that if it was a suitable tune he would call it ST. LEWIS. Redner replied that perhaps it should be called ST. PHILLIPS. Emurian then comments:

Brooks paid his organist a worthy tribute without embarrassing him by naming the new tune "St. Louis," changing the spelling of the Superintendent's first name from "Lewis" to "Louis," an alteration which gave rise to many conjectures about a possible but non-existent connection between the mid-western city of that name and the name of the tune.

O love of God most full   52

This hymn by Oscar Clute first appeared in the *Pilgrim Hymnal* (1904) in three eight-line stanzas. In *The New Hymn and Tune Book* (1914) the hymn was reduced to five four-line stanzas by the omission of the last half of the first stanza. Our version first appeared in the Presbyterian *Hymnal* (1933), which omitted the first half of the original second and third stanzas and altered the first stanza, lines three and four, which were originally:

> Thou warm'st my heart, thou fill'st my soul,
> With might thou strengthenest me.

TRENTHAM was composed by Robert Jackson for Henry W. Baker's "O perfect life of love" and first appeared, according to James T. Lightwood, in *Fifty Sacred Leaflets* (1888). It was first used with this text in the Presbyterian *Hymnal* (1933). This tune was named for a village in the county of Staffordshire, England.

O Love that wilt not let me go   290

George Matheson wrote this hymn on June 6, 1882, while he was pastor of the Innellan Church, Argyllshire, Scotland. It first appeared in *Life and Work* (Jan., 1883), a Church of Scotland monthly magazine, and was included in the *Scottish Hymnal* (Edinburgh, 1885). Matheson's own account of the writing of this hymn is as follows:

I was at that time alone. . . . Something had happened to me, which was known only to myself, and which caused me the most severe mental suffering. The hymn was the fruit of that suffering. It was the quickest bit of work I ever did in my life. I had the impression rather of having it dictated to me by some inward voice than of working it out myself. I am quite sure that the whole work was completed in five minutes, and equally sure that it never received at my hands any retouching or correction. The Hymnal Committee of the Church of Scotland desired the change of one word. I had written originally "I climbed the rainbow in the rain." They objected to the word "climb" and I put in "trace."

ST. MARGARET was composed by Albert L. Peace for this text in 1884, and first appeared in the *Scottish Hymnal* (Edinburgh, 1885). The composer has written that this tune was composed

during the time the music of *The Scottish Hymnal,* of which I was the musical editor, was in preparation. I wrote it at Brodick Manse, where I was on a visit to my old friend, Mr. M'Lean. There was no tune of that particular metre available at that time, so I was requested by the Hymnal Committee to write one especially for Dr. Matheson's hymn. After reading it over carefully, I wrote the music straight off, and may say that the ink of the first note was hardly dry when I had finished the tune.

O Master, let me walk with Thee   426

Washington Gladden wrote this poem in 1879 for the magazine *Sunday Afternoon,* which he edited. Entitled, "Walking with God," it was included in "The Still Hour," a column designed for devotional reading. It consisted of three eight-line stanzas. The author has stated:

Dr. Charles H. Richards found the poem . . . and made a hymn of it by omitting the second stanza, which was not suitable for devotional purposes.
It had no liturgical purpose and no theological significance, but it was an honest cry of human need, of the need of divine companionship.

The omitted second stanza is:

> O Master, let me walk with Thee
> Before the taunting Pharisee;
> Help me to bear the sting of spite,
> The hate of men who hide Thy light,
> The sore distrust of souls sincere
> Who cannot read Thy judgments clear,
> The dullness of the multitude,
> Who dimly guess that Thou art good.

The hymn was first published in *Christian Praise* (New York, 1880 [in later editions the title was changed to *Songs of Christian Praise*]), compiled by Charles H. Richards.

MARYTON (*see* Come, Holy Spirit, Dove divine) was the choice of Dr. Gladden for his hymn.

O Master Workman of the race 441

Jay T. Stocking wrote this hymn shortly after receiving a request from the Pilgrim Press for a new hymn to be included in a forthcoming hymnal. Dr. Stocking was visiting his summer camp in the Adirondacks for a brief fishing trip and at the camp he found carpenters and workmen making necessary repairs on the building. When not engaged in fishing, he watched with keen interest the carpenters at their work. Later, he said, "The figure of the carpenter, as applied to Jesus, flashed on me as never before, and I sat down and wrote the hymn, almost, if not quite, in the exact form in which it now appears. It first appeared in *The Pilgrim Hymnal* (Boston, 1912).

AMESBURY was composed by Uzziah C. Burnap and first appeared in the Presbyterian *Hymnal* (1895).

O my soul, bless God the Father 51

This is a metrical version of Psalm 103, which appeared anonymously in the United Presbyterian *Book of Psalms* (1871), a psalter published for use in North America. Originally it had sixteen stanzas.

STUTTGART—*see* God is love, his mercy brightens.

O perfect Love, all human thought transcending 501

Dorothy B. Gurney wrote this hymn in 1883 at Pull Wyke, Windermere, England, for the marriage of her sister. In the wedding it was sung to Dyke's STRENGTH AND STAY, the bride's favorite tune. The author has stated that the writing of the hymn, which she did in fifteen minutes, "was no effort whatever after the initial idea had come to me of the two-fold aspect of perfect union, love and life, and I have always felt that God helped me write it." It first appeared in the Supplement to *Hymns Ancient and Modern* (1889).

O PERFECT LOVE—*see* Hope of the world, Thou Christ of great compassion.

O sacred Head, now wounded 91

While the Latin text, "Salve mundi salutare," is sometimes attributed to Bernard of Clairvaux, there seems to be insufficient evidence to support this belief. The earliest Latin manuscripts of this text are from the fourteenth century. Paul Gerhardt, the great German hymn writer, used Part VII of the Latin poem as the basis for his free translation, which first appeared in Crüger's *Praxis pietatis melica* (Frankfort, 1656). The English translation, based on Gerhardt's German version, was made by James W. Alexander. It first appeared in *The Christian Lyre* (New York, 1830), compiled by Joshua Leavitt, a Congregational minister. Dr. Philip Schaff has written that this hymn "has shown imperishable vitality in passing from the Latin into the German and from the German into the English, and proclaiming in three tongues . . . with equal effect, the dying love of our Saviour, and our boundless indebtedness to him."

PASSION CHORALE first appeared in Hans Leo Hassler's *Lustgarten* (Nürnberg, 1601), set to a love song, "Mein G'muth ist mir verwirret von einer Jungfrau zart" (My heart is distracted by a gentle maid). It first appeared as a hymn tune in *Harmoniae Sacrae,* third edition (Görlitz, 1613), set to "Herzlich thut mich verlangen." In Crüger's *Praxis pietatis melica,* it appeared with Gerhardt's hymn and has been associated with this text both in German and English ever since. J. S. Bach seems to have been very fond of this melody, for he used it five times in his *St. Matthew Passion* (1729). The present version is a combination of harmonizations made by Bach.

O safe to the Rock that is higher than I 271

William O. Cushing, the author of this hymn, has given the following information:

"Hiding in Thee" was written in Moravia, New York, in 1876. It must be said of this hymn that it was the outgrowth of many tears, many heart-conflicts and soul-yearnings, of which the world can know nothing. The history of many battles is behind it. But the occasion which gave it being was the call of Mr. Sankey. He said, "Send me something new to help me in my gospel work." A call from such a source, and for such a purpose, seemed a call from God. I so regarded it, and prayed: "Lord, give me something that may glorify Thee." It was while thus waiting that "Hiding in Thee" pressed to make itself known. Mr. Sankey called forth the tune, and by his genius gave the hymn wings, making it useful in the master's work.

Cushing's text with Sankey's tune HIDING IN THEE first appeared in *Welcome Tidings,* compiled by Robert Lowry, William H. Doane, and Sankey (1877, No. 60), with the heading, "My strong rock for a house of defence." (Psalm 31:2).

O sometimes the shadows are deep **320**

This hymn was written by Erastus Johnson, and William G. Fischer composed the tune ROCK OF REFUGE. Johnson's account of the writing of this hymn is given by McCutchan in *Our Hymnody:*

At a convention of the Y.M.C.A. in 1873 at Carlisle, Pennsylvania, which I attended as a delegate from Pittsburgh, Pennsylvania, John Wanamaker was president. About the close of the first session a telegram came from Philadelphia announcing the failure of Jay Cook, in whose bank Wanamaker had $70,000, which to him at that time was a serious matter and the loss of which might result in his financial undoing.

Soon followed reports of other failures throughout the country, indicating a general panic and, of course, throwing a pall of gloom over the convention. As an expression of the common feeling I wrote this hymn.

Mr. William Fisher [Fischer] was at the convention, who with my brother, William (since Reverend), led the singing. Mr. Fisher set the hymn to music and it immediately became popular in the convention.

The first publication of this hymn was in John R. Sweney's *Gems of Praise* (Philadelphia: Methodist Episcopal Book Room, 1873, No. 55).

"O That Will Be Glory"—*see* When all my labors and trials are o'er

O they tell me of a home far beyond the skies **484**

Josiah K. Alwood, a circuit riding preacher, is the author and composer of this hymn. Returning home from a preaching appointment on a cloudless moonlight night, the words of this hymn came to him as he rode alone on horseback. The next morning he wrote down the words and picked out the melody on a little Estey parlor organ. Later he met J. F. Kinsey who harmonized the tune and sent it to a publisher. It seems to have first appeared in Kinsey's *Living Gems* (Chicago: The Echo Music Co., *ca.* 1890).

O think of the home over there **480**

DeWitt C. Huntington wrote this text and Tullius C. O'Kane composed the tune which first appeared in O'Kane's *Additional Fresh Leaves, a Supplement to Fresh Leaves* (New York: Phillips & Co., 1868).

HOME OVER THERE is the name given this tune by the Hymnal Committee.

O Thou God of my salvation **164**

This hymn, usually attributed to Thomas Olivers, appeared at the end of *A Short Account of the Death of Mary Langson of Taxall, in*

Cheshire, Who Died January the 29, 1769 (printed in 1771). Olivers was the superintendent of the Methodist Circuit in which Taxall was included, in 1769-71, and is usually regarded as the author of this pamphlet and the hymn appended to it. John Wesley included it in his *Pocket Hymn Book,* fifth edition (1786). Olivers is best known for his hymn, "The God of Abraham praise."

REGENT SQUARE—*see* Praise, my soul, the King of heaven.

O Thou who in Jordan didst bow Thy meek head   388

George Washington Bethune wrote this hymn in 1857, and it has been widely used by Baptists as a baptismal hymn.

ST. MICHEL's—*see* Our Father, in heaven, we hallow Thy name.

O Thou whose gracious presence blest   375

Louis F. Benson wrote this hymn for the dedication of the pastor's new home of the Grace Presbyterian Church, Jenkintown, Pennsylvania. Mrs. Francis Palmer, the pastor's wife and a niece of the author, suggested to Benson in December, 1925, that he write a hymn for the occasion. Later he wrote:

Nothing could seem more unpropitious than to be asked to write a hymn on a particular subject and to be asked at a particular time a week hence; but for some reason the hymn came without conscious effort, probably on account of my love for the home, and because of my sharing the joy of my niece just about to go into a new home.

The hymn was sung on this occasion on January 1, 1926, to this tune. It was first published in *Christian Song* (1926), set to this tune.

REST (ELTON) (335)

O Thou whose hand hath brought us   379

Frederick W. Goadby, an English Baptist preacher, wrote this hymn for the opening of a new church building at Beechen Grove, Watford. With the heading "Opening of a Place of Worship," it first appeared in the *Baptist Hymnal* (London, 1879). The omitted stanzas four and five are:

> And as the years roll onward
>   And strong affections twine,
> And tender memories gather
>   About this sacred shrine,
> May this its chiefest honor,
>   Its glory, ever be,
> That multitudes within it
>   Have found their way to Thee.

Lord God, our fathers' helper,
Our joy, and hope, and stay:
Grant now a gracious earnest
Of many a coming day.
Our yearning hearts Thou knowest;
We wait before Thy throne:
O come, and by Thy presence
Make this new house Thine own.

WEBB was composed for a secular text beginning, " 'Tis dawn, the lark is singing," while the composer was on board ship bound for America. It first appeared in *The Odeon,* a collection of secular melodies compiled by George J. Webb and Lowell Mason (Boston, 1837). It appeared as a hymn tune set to Samuel Francis Smith's "The Morning Light Is Breaking," in Moses L. Scudder's *The Wesleyan Psalmist* (1842). In Mason and Webb's *Cantica Laudis* (1850) it is used to Smith's hymn and named GOODWIN.

O where are kings and empires now 383

This hymn is a portion of A. Cleveland Coxe's "Chelsea," a poem of ten eight-line stanzas, which first appeared in *The Churchman* (1839) and was included the following year in the author's *Christian Ballads.* In the present version the first stanza is first half of stanza six, the second stanza is the last half of stanza eight, the third stanza is the first half of stanza seven, and the fourth stanza is the last half of stanza seven. At the time he wrote this poem, Coxe was a student at the General Theological Seminary, Chelsea Square, New York City, for whose location he named this poem.

ST. ANNE—*see* God moves in a mysterious way.

"O Why Not Tonight"—*see* O do not let the Word depart

O Word of God Incarnate 183

This hymn by William W. How is based on Psalm 119:105, "Thy word is a lamp unto my feet, and a light unto my path." It first appeared in the 1867 supplement to *Psalms and Hymns,* edited by T. B. Morrell and How.

MUNICH is adapted from a melody which is found in the *Neuvermehrtes Gesangbuch* (Meiningen, 1693), where it is set to "O Gott, du frommer Gott." The present version is based on an adaptation made by Felix Mendelssohn and used as a chorale, "Cast Thy Burden on the Lord," in his *Elijah* (1847).

This hymn by Robert Grant was first published in Henry Bickersteth's *Christian Psalmody* (1833), the year before Grant became governor of Bombay. Based on Psalm 104, it is too free to be called a mere paraphrase. Furthermore, it is based on Kethe's version of this Psalm which appeared in the *Anglo-Genevan Psalter* (1561). A comparison of the two is most interesting.

Lyons appeared in the second volume of William Gardiner's *Sacred Melodies* (London, 1815), where it is set for mixed voices and orchestra to the text "O praise ye the Lord, Prepare a new song," and is attributed to "Haydn." In the works of Franz Joseph Haydn and his younger brother, Johann Michael Haydn, there are a number of themes which begin like this melody, but none can be identified as the source of Gardiner's adaptation. Most authorities list the first American appearance of this tune in the *Boston Handel and Haydn Society Collection* (1822, ed. Lowell Mason). However, J. William Thompson has found this tune in Oliver Shaw's *Sacred Melodies* (Providence, 1818) in the same form and to the same text as in Gardiner's collection.

O Zion, haste, thy mission high fulfilling   **451**

The author, Mary Ann Thomson, has stated:

> I wrote the greater part of the hymn, "O Sion, Haste," in the year 1868. I had written many hymns before, and one night, while I was sitting up with one of my children who was ill with typhoid fever, I thought I should like to write a missionary hymn to the tune of the hymn, "Hark, Hark My Soul! Angelic Songs are Swelling," as I was fond of that tune, but as I could not then get a refrain I liked, I left the hymn unfinished and about three years later I finished it by writing the refrain which now forms a part of it.

Originally in six stanzas, the omitted stanzas three and six are:

> 'Tis thine to save from peril of perdition
>   The souls for whom the Lord His life laid down;
> Beware lest, slothful to fulfill thy mission,
>   Thou lose one jewel that should deck His crown.

> He comes again, O Sion, ere thou meet Him,
>   Make known to every heart His saving grace;
> Let none whom He hath ransomed fail to greet Him,
>   Through thy neglect, unfit to see His face.

The first hymnal inclusion was in the Protestant Episcopal *Hymnal* (1892, No. 249).

TIDINGS was composed by James Walch in 1875 as a setting for Faber's "Hark, Hark My Soul," because he felt that the currently used tunes of Smart and Dykes were unsuitable for this hymn. It was first published in *The Hymnal Companion to the Book of Common Prayer* (London, 1877). The first appearance of this tune in America occurs in Charles L. Hutchins' *The Church Hymnal* (New York, 1894, No. 249), where it is set to this text.

Of the themes that men have known   293

Albert C. Fisher, a well-known Texas Methodist pastor and evangelist, wrote both words and music. It first appeared in Robert H. Coleman's *The World Evangel* (Dallas, 1913, No. 7).

FISHER is the name given this tune by the Hymnal Committee.

Oh, for a closer walk with God   365

William Cowper wrote the hymn on December 6, 1769, during the illness of a close friend, Mrs. Unwin. It was included in a letter written the following day, with the notation: "I began to compose the verses yesterday morning before daybreak but fell asleep at the end of the first two lines; when I awakened again, the third and fourth were whispered to my heart in a way which I have often experienced." It was first published in Conyers' *Collection of Psalms and Hymns,* second edition (1772). It was included in *Olney Hymns,* Book I (1779, No. 3), with the heading, "Walking with God," and is based on Genesis 5:24, "Enoch walked with God."

BALERMA, sometimes BALLERMA, is another version of Barthelémon's tune discussed under AUTUMN (*see* **Mighty God, while angels bless Thee**). This hymn tune arrangement was found posthumously among the papers of Robert Simpson and was published in *A Selection of Original Sacred Music . . . Intended to Form the Sixth Vol. of Steven's Selection of Sacred Music* (ed. John Turnbull, 1833). It is interesting to compare the melodic form of the tunes BALERMA and AUTUMN.

"Oh, How I Love Jesus"—*see* There is a name I love to hear

Oh, say, can you see, by the dawn's early light   486

Because of persistent British interference against American commerce, the United States declared war on England on June 18, 1812, and the War of 1812 lasted for two and a half years. Late in August,

1814, the British under General Ross landed at Chesapeake Bay and set fire to the Capitol, the White House, and other public buildings in Washington. During this attack a Dr. Beanes of Upper Marlborough, Maryland, was taken prisoner. Because of his political influence, Francis Scott Key, later district attorney, District of Columbia, was persuaded to negotiate Beanes's release. Key and his party reached the British fleet in Chesapeake Bay off the mouth of the Potomoc River on September 7, and were successful in securing the agreement for the release of Beanes. However, fearing that Key's party might alert the American forces of the proposed attack on Baltimore, the British detained them. After the British fleet had arrived at Baltimore, Key's party was returned to their sloop under guard, and they fearfully witnessed the British bombardment of Fort McHenry on September 13, which lasted all day and into the night. Although the firing ceased shortly after midnight, it was not until they saw the United States flag flying over Fort McHenry in the early morning mist that they knew the British had been unsuccessful in this attack. Still on the sloop, Key, inspired by this experience, began sketching these lines beginning, "O say can you see, by the dawn's early light." In his hotel room in Baltimore that evening, he wrote out a clean copy, which is now preserved in the Walters Art Gallery, Baltimore. The following day it was printed in handbill form, and within a week it had been reprinted in two Baltimore papers. About a month later, Joseph Carr published the song in sheet music form.

The present version uses stanzas one and four of Key's original poem. The omitted stanzas two and three are:

On the shore dimly seen through the mist of the deep,
　Where the foe's haughty host in dread silence reposes,
What is that which the breeze o'er the towering steep,
　As it fitfully blows, half conceals, half discloses:
Now it catches the gleam of the morning's first beam,
In full glory reflected, now shines in the stream;
'Tis the star-spangled banner. Oh! long may it wave
O'er the land of the free, and the home of the brave.

And where is that band who so vauntingly swore,
　'Mid the havoc of war and the battle's confusion,
A home and a country they'd leave us no more?
　Their blood has washed out their foul footsteps' pollution;
No refuge could save the hireling and slave
From the terror of flight, or the gloom of the grave,
And the star-spangled banner in triumph shall wave
O'er the land of the free, and the home of the brave.

NATIONAL ANTHEM is of unknown origin. It appeared in the *Vocal Magazine* (London, 1778), set to the text "To Anacreon in Heaven," by Ralph Tomlinson, president of the Anacreontic Society in London. Apparently the tune had existed for several years prior to this time. The following year a sheet music edition appeared in London. In these early appearances of the tune no composer is given. The association of John Stafford Smith with this tune is due to an arrangement for three voices which he published in 1799. The tune was apparently known in America in the early 1790's, for within that decade it appeared in several American collections set to Tomlinson's text, as well as other texts of a patriotic nature. Key himself wrote a set of words to this tune, which he sang at a dinner in honor of Stephen Decatur at Georgetown, District of Columbia, in December, 1805. Since he had already written words for this stirring melody, it is natural to presume that writing another text came easily nine years later. Many patriotic songs have been written and publicized, but this song has outlived them all, and was acclaimed our national anthem by public acceptance long before the Act of Congress, March 3, 1931, gave it official recognition, 117 years after it was first written.

On a hill far away stood an old rugged cross   93

The circumstances surrounding the writing of this hymn in 1913, are given by the author, George Bennard. (George W. Sanville, *Forty Gospel Hymn Stories,* p. 15).

I was praying for a full understanding of the cross, and its plan in Christianity. I read and studied and prayed. I saw Christ and the Cross inseparably. The Christ of the Cross became more than a symbol. The scene pictured a method, outlined a process, and revealed the consummation of spiritual experience. It was like seeing John 3:16 leave the printed page, take form, and act out the meaning of redemption. While watching this scene with my mind's eye, the theme of the song came to me, and with it the melody; but only the words of the theme, "The Old Rugged Cross," came. An inner voice seemed to say, "Wait"!

I was holding evangelistic meetings in Michigan, but could not continue with the poem. After a series of meetings in New York state, the following week, I tried again to compose the poem, but could not. It was only after I had completed the New York meeting, and returned to Michigan for further evangelistic work, that the flood-gates were loosed.

Many experiences of the redeeming grace of God through our Lord Jesus Christ during those meetings had broken down all barriers. I was enabled to complete the poem with facility and dispatch. A friend aided in putting it into manuscript form.

This hymn was written by Samuel Stennett, an English Baptist preacher, and it first appeared in John Rippon's *Selection of Hymns* (London, 1787), with the heading, "Heaven Anticipated." Originally it consisted of eight four-line stanzas. It has long been a favorite among the evangelical denominational groups in America. Neither of the refrains appearing in the hymnal is part of Stennett's original hymn.

O'KANE (478) was composed by Tullius C. O'Kane for this hymn and first appeared in his *Jasper and Gold* (Chicago: Hitchcock & Walden, 1877, No. 58).

PROMISED LAND (479) is found in many of the oblong tune collections of the shaped note tradition which were widely used in the southern part of the United States in the nineteenth century. Its first appearance seems to have been in William Walker's *Southern Harmony* (1835), where it is attributed to "Miss M. Durham." No information has been found to identify this person. A prominent singing-school teacher, Walker was a devoted Baptist layman, whose musical influence extended far beyond his native South Carolina.

The altering of the key of this tune from F sharp minor to F major was the work of Rigdon M. McIntosh, at one time head of the music department of Vanderbilt University, Nashville and for many years music editor of the Methodist Episcopal Church, South, publishing house, Nashville. Although a great deal of the folk character of the original tune was lost in this alteration, the tune has enjoyed immense popularity and in this degree has far surpassed O'Kane's tune. The altered version seems to have first appeared in *The Gospel Light,* edited by H. R. Christie (Atlanta, Ga.: R. M. McIntosh Co., 1895).

"Once for All"—*see* Free from the law, O happy condition

Once to every man and nation **418**

In December, 1845, as a protest against the war with Mexico, James Russell Lowell wrote "The Present Crisis," a poem of eighteen five-line stanzas. It was his deep conviction that the war was unjust and that the acquisition of new territory would only enlarge the area of slavery. It was first published in his *Poems* (1849). The hymn version first appeared in England when Garrett Horder took sixteen lines from this poem of ninety long lines and made them into four eight-line stanzas. Horder published this first in his *Hymns Supplemental to Existing Collections* (1896) and again in his *Worship Song* (1905). The omitted third stanza of Horder's version is:

By the light of burning martyrs
    Jesus' bleeding feet I track,
Toiling up new Calvaries ever
    With the cross that turns not back;
New occasions teach new duties,
    Time makes ancient good uncouth;
They must upward still and onward
    Who would keep abreast of truth.

AUSTRIAN HYMN—*see* Word of God, across the ages.

One day when heaven was filled with his praises   85

There seems to be no information concerning the writing of this hymn by J. Wilbur Chapman. A letter from the composer, Charles H. Marsh, to the writer gives the following information:

I had been invited by Dr. J. Wilbur Chapman to be the organist and accompanist of the Winona Lake Chautauqua and Bible Conference (Indiana). I was just out of high school and it seemed to me a fabulous job—$100 per month and all expenses paid. This was for the three summer months. I think it was about 1908 or 1909 that Dr. Chapman was invited to conduct a Bible Conference at Stony Brook, Long Island, and he took me with him. It was at Stony Book that he gave me the poem "One Day" and another entitled "All Hail the Power." I set them both that summer and as I remember they were copyrighted in my name. Within a year or two Dr. Parley E. Zartmann (Dr. Chapman's assistant) persuaded me to sell my interest in the two songs to him. I wanted to go to college, so I left my association with Dr. Chapman, much as I enjoyed it. Soon after that Dr. Chapman joined forces with Charles M. Alexander and the next time I saw "One Day" in print, it had at the bottom "Charles M. Alexander, owner of the copyright." In the meantime, Dr. Zartmann had sold the two songs to the Hope Publishing Company. I don't know who won out in the mess that was raging at the time, but I do think Dr. Zartmann and the Hope Publishing Company were in the right and that Alexander had simply appropriated the song because of Dr. Chapman having written the words. The Rodeheaver Company came into the picture by claiming they had bought the song from Alexander. When the copyright came up for renewal, the Rodeheaver Company bought the renewal from me as the copyright had reverted to the composer.

CHAPMAN is the name given this tune by the Hymnal Committee.

"Only Trust Him"—*see* Come, ev'ry soul by sin oppressed

Onward, Christian soldiers   412

Sabine Baring-Gould wrote this hymn in 1864 for a children's festival at Horbury Bridge, Yorkshire, England, "for procession with cross and banners." Its first publication was in *The Church Times* (Oct. 15, 1864), where is consisted of six stanzas.

ST. GERTRUDE was composed by Arthur S. Sullivan for this hymn in 1871 for inclusion in Sullivan's *The Hymnary* (London, 1872). However, before this collection was published, the tune appeared in the *Musical Times* (London, Dec. 1871). In a letter to the *Musical Times* (London, July 1902.), Mrs. Gertrude Clay-Ker-Seymer, for whom the tune was named, gives the circumstances as she recalls them concerning the writing of the tune in her home in Dorsetshire, while Sullivan was visiting there. The first appearance of the tune in America sems to be in John R. Sweney's *Gems of Praise* (Philadelphia: Methodist Episcopal Book Room, 1873).

Open my eyes that I may see   312

Clara H. Scott wrote both words and music for this hymn, and it first appeared in *Best Hymns No. 2,* compiled by E. A. Hoffman and Harold F. Sayles (Chicago: Evangelical Publishing Co., 1895, No. 82). It was originally in the key of G.

SCOTT is the name given this tune by the Hymnal Committee.

"Our Best"—*see* Hear ye the Master's call

Our Father in heaven, we hallow Thy name   343

This hymn by Sarah J. Hale first appeared in *Church Psalmody,* compiled by Lowell Mason and David Greene (Boston: Perkins & Marvin, 1831).

ST. MICHEL'S, sometimes called GOSHEN, BEULAH, HINTON, PALESTINE, or ST. MARIA appeared anonymously in *The Hymns and Psalms used at the Asylum or House of Refuge for Female Orphans* (London, 1785-88), compiled by William Gawler.

Our Lord Christ hath risen   112

This hymn was written in 1873 by William C. Plunket for inclusion in the Irish *Church Hymnal* (Belfast, 1873), where it was set to the tune "O Ursprung des Lebens," by T. Selle.   This seems to be Plunket's only contribution to hymnic literature.

KIRN, composed by John P. Taylor, first appeared in *The Revised Church Hymnary* (Edinburgh, 1927), where it was used with this hymn. The composer's sister, Miss Mary Taylor, in a letter to the writer dated December 19, 1954, states:

The Taylor family originally belonged to the island of Sanda, off the coast of Southend Kintya Argyll, and, as a matter of fact, my brother had intended to call the tune for this Easter hymn "Sanda," but out of deference for the minister of Kirn Parish Church, where he was organist for a time, he named it "Kirn."

Out in the highways and byways of life 431

According to the composer, George S. Schuler, the words for this hymn were written by Ira B. Wilson about 1909, and the tune was not composed until 1924.

Oddly enough, neither of us can recall how we came to write the song. To this day he [Wilson] claims to have no part in authoring the work, but I do know he wrote it. When the song was in manuscript it was submitted to a publisher. It was rejected as "being unsuited for our need." I had plates made and one thousand copies printed, costing me a sum I could ill afford at the time. George Dibble, well known as an evangelist in those days, introduced the number at an International Sunday School Convention at Cleveland, Ohio. Here it became a great favorite, and it is needless to say that within a short time I received many offers for the song.

It was later published in *Voice of Thanksgiving No. 2.*
The tune was named SCHULER by the Hymnal Committee for the composer.

Out of my bondage, sorrow, and night 233

In 1877 William T. Sleeper and George C. Stebbins had collaborated in writing "Ye Must Be Born Again" (215). A number of years later, Sleeper sent the words for this hymn to Stebbins, who provided this tune, JESUS I COME. It first appeared in *Gospel Hymns No. 5* (1887), with the Scripture text subtitle, "Deliver me, O my God" (Psalm 71:4).

Pass me not, O gentle Saviour 219

Fanny J. Crosby wrote this text for which William H. Doane provided the tune, PASS ME NOT. Written in 1868, it first appeared in Doane's *Songs of Devotion* (New York, 1870, No. 102).

"Pentecostal Power"—*see* Lord, as of old at Pentecost

"Power in the Blood"—*see* Would you be free from the burden of sin

Praise God, from whom all blessings flow 514

A doxology is an expression of praise to God. In the Old Testament the term "alleluia" or "hallelujah" is the Hebrew expression for "Praise ye the Lord" and is used as a brief doxology at the beginning or end of Psalms 104, 113, 115, 116, 117, 135, 146, 147, 148, 149, and 150. In the New Testament early Christian expressions of praise may be found in Romans 16:27, Ephesians 3:21, Jude 25, and Revelation 5:13. In the practice of the early Christian church the *Gloria in excelsis,* known as the "Greater Doxology," was used in the Eastern (Greek) church in the second century. The *Gloria Patri,* known as the "Lesser Doxology," was known in its present form by the end of the fourth century. To combat the rising influence of Arian heresy, congregations were exhorted to join together in praise of God the Father, God the Son, and God the Holy Spirit.

This well-known doxology, written by Thomas Ken, is the most widely used throughout the English-speaking world. It is the final stanza of three famous hymns—"Morning Hymn," "Evening Hymn," and "Midnight Hymn,"—which Ken wrote about 1673 and included in *A Manual of Prayers for the Use of the Scholars of Winchester College* (1695 edition). In this original version the third line read "Praise him above y' Angelic Host." The present form was made by Ken in 1709. It has been said that this doxology has done more to teach the doctrine of the Trinity than all the theological books ever written.

OLD 100TH—*see* All people that on earth do dwell.

Praise Him, praise Him, all ye little children   511

The anonymous text with this tune appeared in Carey Bonner's *Child Songs* (London, 1908). The composer of the tune, GOD IS LOVE, is given as E. Rawdon Bailey, a pseudonym used by Bonner.

Praise Him! praise Him! Jesus, our blessed Redeemer   137

This hymn, words by Fanny J. Crosby and tune by Chester G. Allen, was first published in *Bright Jewels,* a Sunday school songbook edited by W. B. Bradbury, W. H. Doane, W. F. Sherwin, and Allen (New York: Biglow & Main, 1869, p. 82), where it was titled, "Praise, Give Thanks."

JOYFUL SONG is the name given this tune by the Hymnal Committee and is taken from the last two words of the refrain.

Praise, my soul, the King of heaven   18

Based on Psalm 103, this hymn by Henry F. Lyte first appeared in his *The Spirit of the Psalms* (1834), a collection of new paraphrases of the psalms, as the second of two versions of this psalm. The fifth line of each stanza has been changed from "Praise Him, praise Him" to "Alleluia! alleluia!" At the wedding of Queen Elizabeth II at Westminster Abbey, November 20, 1947, which occurred on the one hundredth anniversary of Lyte's death, this was used at her request as the opening processional hymn.

REGENT SQUARE was composed by Henry Smart for the English Presbyterian hymnal *Psalms and Hymns for Divine Worship* (London, 1867), where it was set to Bonar's "Glory be to God the Father." The tune is named for the Regent Square Presbyterian Church, known as the "cathedral of Presbyterianism in London." Dr. Hamilton, minister of this church, served as editor of the above collection and gave this tune the name it bears.

Praise the Lord! ye heavens, adore Him 9

This hymn first appeared in a four-page tract pasted at the end of some of the copies of the music edition of *Psalms, Hymns, and Anthems of the Foundling Hospital* (London, 1796) and of the words edition of 1801. The authorship is unknown. However, it likely was written after 1801 and pasted in both editions at the same time. The tract, containing five hymns in all, was entitled *For Foundling Apprentices Attending Divine Service to Return Thanks*. This hymn is entitled "Hymn from Psalm CXLVIII, Haydn." Hymn singing by the inmates of charitable institutions was a well-established practice of the late eighteenth century.

The Foundling Hospital, an orphanage in London, was founded in 1739 by Thomas Coram to care for deserted and orphaned children. Musical concerts given as benefits for the hospital contributed greatly to its financial support over a period of many years. In 1749 George F. Handel gave a benefit concert in the Foundling Chapel for which he composed the anthem, "Blessed are they that consider the poor." In 1750, at the completion of the chapel, Handel gave the organ.

HYFRYDOL is a jubilant tune, most fitting for this hymn of praise. It is interesting to observe that the range of the tune, with the exception of one note, lies within the compass of the first five tones of the scale. The tune was composed about 1830 by Rowland H. Prichard, who was less than twenty years of age, and was first published in Griffith Roberts' *Haleliwiah Drachefn* (literally, "Hallelujah Again," Carmarthen, Wales, 1855).

Praise to God, immortal praise 14

This hymn by Anna L. Barbauld first appeared in *Hymns for Public Worship* (Warrington, Eng., 1772) in nine four-line stanzas, entitled "Praise to God in Prosperity and Adversity." It was included in the author's *Poems* with the Scripture reference, Habakkuk 3:17-18.

DIX—*see* For the beauty of the earth.

Praise to the Lord, the Almighty, the King of creation 6

This stalwart hymn, based on Psalm 103:1-6 and Psalm 150, was written by Joachim Neander when he was thirty years of age, the last year of his life. It was published in his *A und Glaub- und Liebesübung* (Bremen, 1680), with the tune set here. Catherine Winkworth's excellent translation appeared in her *Chorale Book for England* (1863). It has been widely accepted and may be found in most contemporary hymnals. This is the first inclusion of the hymn and tune in a hymnal of general use among Southern Baptist churches.

LOBE DEN HERREN first appeared in the *Ander Theil des erneuerten Gesangbuch,* second edition (Stralsund, 1665). Its appearance in the 1904 edition of *Hymns Ancient and Modern* and *The English Hymnal* (1906) added greatly to its popular acceptance. The present version is from the *Chorale Book for England,* second edition (1864), and the harmonization is by Sterndale Bennett. The tune name is taken from the first line of Neander's German text, "Lobe den Herren" (Praise to the Lord).

Prayer is the soul's sincere desire 336

James Montgomery wrote this hymn in 1818 at the request of Edward Bickersteth for his *Treatise on Prayer* (1819). It was first published in a pamphlet in 1818 with three other hymns by Montgomery for use in the Nonconformist Sunday schools in Sheffield, England. In 1819 it also appeared in Cotterill's *Selection,* eighth edition, London. Originally consisting of eight four-line stanzas, our version is made up of stanzas one, three, five, and eight. The omitted stanzas two, four, six, and seven are

> Prayer is the burden of a sigh,
>   The falling of a tear,
> The upward glancing of an eye
>   When none but God is near.

> Prayer is the Christian's vital breath
>   The Christian's native air,
> His watchword at the gates of death:
>   He enters heav'n with prayer.

> The saints in prayer appear as one
>   In word, and deed, and mind,
> While with the Father and the Son
>   Sweet fellowship they find.

No prayer is made by man alone,
The Holy Spirit pleads,
And Jesus, on the eternal throne,
For sinners intercedes.

CAMPMEETING has its origin in the folk hymnody of America. It was a well-known tune sung in the camp meetings of the early nineteenth century, where the tune was used for both stanza and refrain. Many common meter hymns were used to this tune, but the refrain text usually remained the same.

I do believe, I now believe
That Jesus died for me,
And that He shed His precious blood,
From sin to set me free.

Robert G. McCutchan made this harmonization and named this tune for the *Methodist Hymnal* (1935), of which he was editor.

Purer in heart, O God   369

Mrs. A. L. Davison is the author of the text, and the tune, PURER IN HEART, was composed by James H. Fillmore. The hymn first appeared in *Songs of Gratitude,* compiled by Fillmore (Cincinnati: Fillmore Bros., 1877, No. 67).

Ready to suffer grief or pain   439

This text appears in the English *Keswick Hymn-Book* credited to A. C. Palmer. The identity of this author, and the source of this text remain unknown. The only use of this text in America has been with the present tune, and since it first appeared in 1903, the author has been given as "S.E.L." Attempts to identify the owner of these three initials proved futile. In 1955, the writer received a song manuscript from James C. Moore, with these same initials given for the author of the text. An inquiry was addressed to him, calling his attention to the same initials on this hymn, "Ready." Moore replied that "S.E.L." stood for "selected." In other words, the text was anonymous. Moore added that he had adopted this practice from Tillman, who used it for the same purpose. The mystery was solved! Apparently, the author of this hymn was unknown to Tillman.

TILLMAN was composed by Charles D. Tillman for this hymn, and it first appeared in *The Revival No. 4,* compiled and published by Tillman (Atlanta, 1903, No. 7), with the Scripture reference, "Behold, thy servants are ready to do whatsoever my lord the king shall appoint"

(2 Sam. 15:15). Originally the text was in five four-line stanzas. Tillman used stanza one for the refrain, and in its original form it read:

> Ready to go, ready to wait,
> Ready a gap to fill;
> Ready for service, small or great,
> Ready to do His will.

Redeemed, how I love to proclaim it 203

Fanny J. Crosby's text with this tune by William J. Kirkpatrick was first published in *Songs of Redeeming Love,* edited by John R. Sweney, C. C. McCabe, T. C. O'Kane, and Kirkpatrick (Philadelphia: John J. Hood, 1882, No. 7). The omitted stanza five is:

> I know there's a crown that is waiting,
> In yonder bright mansion for me,
> And soon, with the spirits made perfect,
> At home with the Lord I shall be.

REDEEMED is the name given this tune by the Hymnal Committee.

Rejoice, the Lord is King 108

Based on Philippians 4:4, "Rejoice in the Lord alway: and again I say, Rejoice," this hymn by Charles Wesley first appeared in John Wesley's *Moral and Sacred Poems* (1744) and later in Charles Wesley's *Hymns for our Lord's Resurrection* (1746). The present version uses the first three stanzas of the original six.

DARWALL, sometimes called DARWALL'S 148TH, was composed by John Darwall for Psalm 148, "Ye boundless realms of joy" in Aaron Williams' *New Universal Psalmodist* (1770). It was written in two parts—melody and bass, and the initial note of the melody was A. This initial note was changed to D in Williams' *Psalmody in Minature* (1778).

Rejoice, ye pure in heart 17

Edward H. Plumptre wrote this hymn, based on Psalm 20:4 and Philippians 4:4, for the annual choir festival at Peterborough Cathedral, England, in May, 1865, and it was published with a special music setting that same year. Without music it appeared in Plumptre's *Lazarus and Other Poems,* second edition (1865), in eleven stanzas. It first appeared as a hymn in the 1868 Appendix to *Hymns Ancient and Modern* (No. 386) and has enjoyed widespread popularity. The present version uses stanzas 1, 2, 7, and 10.

MARION, named for the composer's mother, was written by Arthur

H. Messiter in 1883 for this hymn and was first published in the *Hymnal with Music As Used in Trinity Church* (New York, 1893), which was ed'ted by Messiter.

Rescue the perishing 207

Fanny J. Crosby's account of the writing of this hymn is given in *Fanny Crosby's Story of Ninety-Four Years* (pp. 76-78):

It was written in the year 1869, when I was forty-nine years old. . . . Many of my hymns were written after experiences in New York mission work. This one was thus written. I was addressing a large company of working men one hot summer evening, when the thought kept forcing itself on my mind that some mother's boy must be rescued that night or not at all. So I made a pressing plea that if there were a boy present who had wandered from his mother's home and teaching, he would come to me at the close of the service. A young man of eighteen came forward and said, "Did you mean me? I promised my mother to meet her in heaven, but as I am now living that will be impossible." We prayed for him and he finally arose with a new light in his eyes and exclaimed in triumph: "Now I can meet my mother in heaven, for I have found God."

A few days before Mr. Doane had sent me the subject, "Rescue the Perishing," and while I sat there that evening, the line came to me, "Rescue the Perishing, care for the dying." I could think of nothing else that night. When I arrived home I went to work on the hymn at once, and before I retired it was ready for the melody. The next day my song was written out and forwarded to Mr. Doane, who wrote the beautiful and touching music as it now stands to my hymn.

RESCUE was composed for this text by William H. Doane, and the text and tune first appeared in Doane's *Songs of Devotion* (New York: Biglow & Main, 1870, No. 642).

Responses and Amens 515-554

The Lord is in his holy temple (515)—a setting of Habakkuk 2:20 composed by George F. Root.

The Lord is in his holy temple (516)—Warren M. Angell composed this setting of Habakkuk 2:20, and it first appeared in *The Church Musician* (Sept., 1951). The tune was named SHAWNEE by the Hymnal Committee.

O Father, unto Thee (517)—this prayer response by Warren M. Angell first appeared in *The Church Musician* (Dec., 1954, p. 11).

Create in me a clean heart (518)—a setting of Psalm 51:10 composed by William J. Reynolds in 1948, which first appeared in *The Church Musician* (Oct., 1951, p. 11).

We would worship Thee (519)—composed in 1949, this response by James Bigelow first appeared in *The Church Musician* (Oct., 1951, p. 11).

O Lord of love, Thou light divine (520)—authorship unknown. VICTORY—*see* The strife is o'er, the battle done.

O worship the Lord (521)—this setting of Psalm 96:9 was composed by Robert G. McCutchan and first appeared in *The Methodist Hymnal* (1935) with McCutchan's pseudonym "John Porter."

Lead me, Lord (522)—this is taken from an anthem of the same title by Samuel Sebastian Wesley.

Spirit of the living God (523)—both words and music were written by Daniel Iverson. B. B. McKinney's arrangement first appeared in *Songs of Victory* (1937, No. 79).

Glory be to the Father (524-526)—*see* discussion of Praise God, from whom all blessings flow.

GLORIA PATRI, first setting (524), was composed by Charles Meineke and is taken from the "Evening Prayer" in *Music for the Church, Containing Sixty-two Psalm and Hymn Tunes in Four Parts Together with Chants, Doxologies, and Responses . . . Composed for St. Paul's Church, Baltimore* by C. Meineke, Organist (1844).

The second setting (525) is from Henry W. Greatorex's *Collection of Sacred Music* (1851), where it appears as *Gloria Patri* No. 1.

The third setting (526), known as the Old Scottish Chant, is of unknown origin, possibly originally based on a plain chant.

Now for each yearning heart (527)—this prayer response was composed by James Bigelow in 1948.

In Jesus' name we pray (528)—written in 1949 for use by the choir of the First Baptist Church, Oklahoma City, Oklahoma, where the composer, William J. Reynolds, served as minister of music.

Almighty Father, hear our prayer (529)—the source of this text is unknown. The tune appears at the close of the dramatic "Baal scene" in Felix Mendelssohn's oratorio *Elijah,* composed in 1846.

Hear our prayer, O Lord (530)—this prayer response, written by George Whelpton about 1900, was first printed in a four-page leaflet containing other responses and a dismissal hymn which Whelpton had prepared. Shortly afterward it was included in one of the hymnals he edited for The Century Company.

Hear our prayer, O heavenly Father (531)—the source of the text is unknown. A hymn tune called ST. FAVIAN, credited to Chopin and arranged by Henry Wilson appears in J. Ireland Tucker's *Hymnal with Tunes Old and New* (New York, 1872, No. 310), with the indication·

that the arrangement was made for this hymnal. With slight alterations, the response uses only the last four measures of Wilson's arrangement. The source of Chopin's melody is not known.

Let the words of my mouth (532)—Adolph Baumbach's setting of Psalm 19:14 first appeared in *Baumbach's Sacred Quartets, A Collection of Pieces for the Opening and Close of Service* (Boston, 1862).

Bless Thou the gifts (533)—this is a stanza from Samuel Longfellow's hymn, "Thou Lord of life, our saving health," written in 1886. CANONBURY—*see* How beauteous were the marks divine.

All things come of Thee (534)—the text of this offertory response is taken from 1 Chronicles 29:14*b*. The identity of the person who made this arrangement and the source of the Beethoven melody remain unknown.

We give Thee but Thine own (535)—*see* alphabetical listing.

All things are Thine (536)—*see* alphabetical listing.

Grant us, Lord, the grace of giving (537)—the authorship of this text is unknown. STUTTGART—*see* God is love; His mercy brightens.

May the grace of Christ our Saviour (538)—this is the first half of a one-stanza hymn of eight lines by John Newton which appeared in the *Olney Hymns,* Book III (1779). It is a paraphrase of 2 Corinthians 13:14, and the final four lines of Newton's text read:

> Thus may we abide in union
>   With each other and the Lord,
> And possess, in sweet communion,
>   Joys which earth cannot afford.

DORRNANCE was composed by Isaac B. Woodbury and named CHESTER. It first appeared in Woodbury's *The Choral* (1845), as a setting for "Sweet the Moments, Rich in Blessing."

Grace, love, and peace abide (539)—W. Hines Sims wrote the music of this benediction to words provided by Ann Brown, who is Mrs. W. Hines Sims. Dr. Sims has stated: "My wife and I were discussing on one occasion the need for choral benedictions to be sung in our churches. It seemed that the same one or two were being used all of the while. She suggested the words and I set them to music." This first appeared in *The Church Musician* (Mar., 1951, p. 23). Dr. Sims named this tune MERIDIAN for Meridian, Mississippi, the birthplace of Mrs. Sims.

Benediction—*see* discussion of 538 above. BRYSON CITY was composed by B. B. McKinney for this text, and it first appeared in *The Broadman Hymnal* (1940, No. 497). The Hymnal Committee named the tune for the town in North Carolina where Dr. McKinney died.

The Lord bless thee and keep thee (541)—the text is from Numbers 6:24-26, and the tune was composed by B. B. McKinney. It first appeared in *The Broadman Hymnal* (1940, No. 498).

The Lord bless you and keep you (542)—this setting of Numbers 6:24-26 was composed by Peter C. Lutkin and dedicated "to my friend, William Smedley." It was first published in octavo form (Clayton F. Summy Company, 1900). The first hymnal inclusion was in *The Methodist Hymnal* (1905), and the sevenfold Amen with which it closes was omitted, as Dean Lutkin did not feel it was suitable for congregational use.

Amens—Amen is a Hebrew word meaning "so be it," and was taken over from the Jewish liturgy by the early Christian church. The re-affirming character of the Amen led to the writing of extensive finales in fugal style in the choral music of the seventeenth and eighteenth centuries, such as Handel's "Amen Chorus" at the conclusion of his *Messiah*. As a congregational expression the word is a solemn and heartfelt avowal of faith. The singing of Amens should be voiced in a hearty manner and should never be sung in a weak, apologetic spirit. Walford Davies, in his preface to *A Student's Hymnal,* says, "An Amen cannot be too good. It is music's chance to embody the great Christian affirmative. In singing an Amen it is well to pretend you may never sing another, and put everything into it, recalling St. Paul's great saying: 'In Him was Yea.' "

DRESDEN (543)—it is believed that this was composed by Johann Gottlieb Naumann, 1741-1801. The name comes from its long association with the Royal Chapel at Dresden. Mendelssohn used this melody in his *Reformation Symphony,* and Wagner employed it as a recurring theme in his *Parsifal.*

THREEFOLD (544)—traditional. Composer and source unknown.

THREEFOLD (545)—traditional. Composer and source unknown.

FOURFOLD (546)—composed by John Stainer.

SEVENFOLD (547)—composed by John Stainer and first published in his *Choir-Book for the Office of Holy Communion* (1873), to be sung following the prayer of consecration.

ST. PETER (548)—composed by Ellen Kett.

CHOLMONDELY (549)—composed by Ellen Kett.

GUNNAR (550)—composed by A. Gunnar.

PACEM (551)—composed by John Storer.

RESTARE (552)—composed by John Storer.

THE BELL CADENCE (553)—composed by T. S. Tearne.

FINIR (554)—composed by John Storer.

In the search for hymns on the Bible, (*see* O God of light), this hymn was submitted by M. Elmore Turner. The author, in a letter dated November 14, 1954, states that the hymn was written in 1951, "in the Shenandoah National Park near Luray, Virginia, while our family was enjoying a brief camping trip there in the uplifting atmosphere of the Blue Ridge Mountains and the Shenandoah Valley of Virginia." At the time of the writing of this hymn, the author was pastor of the Broad Street Christian Church, New Bern, North Carolina.

ST. PETERSBURG was written by Dimitri S. Bortniansky a few years before his death in 1825. It first appeared in the *Choralbuch* (Moscow, 1825) edited by Johann Heinrich Tscherlitzky. In the edition of Bortniansky's sacred works, compiled by Tschaikovsky in 1884, this tune (No. 116) is set to a Russian hymn. There seems to be no evidence to support the fact that this tune is an arrangement or adaptation from a larger work. It first appeared in England in Montague Burgoyne's *Collection of Psalms and Hymns* (London, 1827).

"Revive Us Again"—*see* We praise Thee, O God! for the Son of Thy love

Ride on! ride on in majesty   102

Henry H. Milman wrote this hymn while he was professor of poetry at Oxford University. It was first published as a hymn for Palm Sunday in Heber's *Hymns Written and Adapted to the Weekly Church Services of the Year* (1827). Originally the hymn consisted of five four-line stanzas. The fourth stanza is

> Ride on! ride on in majesty!
> The last and fiercest strife is nigh;
> The Father on His sapphire throne
> Expects His own anointed Son.

When Heber received the manuscript of this hymn, he wrote to Milman: "You have indeed sent me a most powerful reinforcement to my projected hymn book. A few more such hymns and I shall neither need nor wait for the aid of Scott and Southey."

TRURO first appeared anonymously in Thomas Williams' *Psalmodia Evangelica* (1789), set to the hymn "Now to the Lord a noble song."

Ring out the old, ring in the new   495

This hymn is made up of selected stanzas from Alfred Tennyson's, *In Memorian,* published in 1850. Originally consisting of eight four-line stanzas, the present version uses stanzas two, four, seven, and eight. It is interesting to note the *abba* rhyme scheme in these stanzas, which is rarely found in hymnic literature.

WALTHAM—*see* I heard the bells on Christmas day.

Rise, my soul, and stretch thy wings   122

Written by Robert Seagrave, this hymn first appeared in his *Hymns for Christian Worship, Partly Composed and Partly Collected from Various Authors* (1742). It consisted of four eight-line stanzas, and was entitled "The Pilgrim's Song."

AMSTERDAM appeared in the *Foundery Collection* (London, 1742), the first compilation of tunes published by John Wesley. In this collection for reasons unknown, Wesley credited this tune to James Nares, an eighteenth-century English church music composer. Actually, AMSTERDAM was one of six tunes Wesley adapted for his collection from Freylinghausen's *Geistreiches Gesangbuch* (Halle, 1st ed., 1704; re. 1714; complete and augmented ed. 1741). Associating this tune with Nares is an error which many hymnals have copied.

Rise up, O men of God!   445

The author, William Pierson Merrill, gives the following account of the writing of this hymn.

Nolan R. Best, then editor of *The Continent,* happened to say to me that there was urgent need of a brotherhood hymn. . . . The suggestion lingered in my mind, and just about that time (1911) I came upon an article by Gerald Stanley Lee, entitled "The Church of the Strong Men." I was on one of the Lake Michigan steamers going back to Chicago for a Sunday at my own church, when suddenly this hymn came up, almost without conscious thought or effort.

Entitled "To the Brotherhood," it first appeared in *The Continent* (Feb. 16, 1911), a Presbyterian publication published in Chicago. The first hymnal inclusion was *The Pilgrim Hymnal* (Boston, 1912).

ST. THOMAS—*see* I love Thy kingdom, Lord

Rock of Ages, cleft for me   103

In *The Gospel Magazine* (Oct., 1775) a single stanza of this hymn by Augustus M. Toplady first appeared in an article entitled "Life a Journey" and was signed "Minimus." In the March, 1776, issue, this hymn appeared in four six-line stanzas following an article by Toplady dealing with the absolute impossibility of one's paying his indebtedness to God. He discussed the number of sins possible for a man to commit by the day, the hour, the minute, and the second—and calculated that in eighty years a man would commit 2,522,880,000 sins. The hymn was entitled "A living and dying prayer for the holiest believer in the world." The allusion to the "holiest believer" is thought by George John Stevenson to refer to John Wesley and "can only be designed by Mr. Toplady as a sneer at the doctrine of entire holiness, which both the Wesleys so strongly enforced in their preaching and hymns."

Numerous alterations have been inflicted upon this hymn, and the present version is basically that which appeared in Cotterill's *Selection of Psalms and Hymns* (1815). Our first stanza is substantially like the original, and the third is like the original fourth. Our second stanza is a selection of lines from the original second and third stanzas given here:

> Not the labors of my hands
>   Can fulfill the Law's demands:
> Could my zeal no respite know,
>   Could my tears forever flow,
> All for Sin could not atone:
>   Thou must save, and Thou alone.
>
> Nothing in my hand I bring;
>   Simply to the Cross I cling;
> Naked, come to Thee for Dress;
>   Helpless, look to thee for grace;
> Foul, I to the fountain fly;
>   Wash me, Saviour, or I die!

There is no evidence to substantiate the well-known story that this hymn was written during a thunderstorm when Toplady had taken refuge in a cleft of rock at Burrington Coomb in the Mendip Hills in southern England. Much more probable is the suggestion set forth by E. J. Fasham in *The Baptist Quarterly* (April, 1940, pp. 94-96) that the inspiration for the hymn came from the following lines from a sermon by Dr. Daniel Brevint, "The Christian Sacrament and Sacrifice" (1673), some of which were quoted in the preface to Charles Wesley's *Hymns on the Lord's Supper* (1745):

Let not my heart burn with less zeal, to follow and serve Thee now, when this bread is broken at this table, than did the hearts of Thy disciples when Thou didst break it at Emmaus, O Rock of Israel, Rock of Salvation, Rock struck and cleft for me, let those two streams of blood and water which once gushed out of Thy side . . . and let not my soul less thirst after them at this distance, than if I stood upon Horeb, whence sprang this water and near the very cleft of rock, the very wounds of my Saviour whence gushed out this sacred blood.

A. C. Benson, having heard this hymn sung at William Gladstone's funeral at Westminster Abbey, said, "To have written words which should come home to people in moments of high, deep, and passionate emotion, consecrating, consoling, uplifting—there can hardly be anything worth better doing than that."

TOPLADY was written in 1830 by Thomas Hastings and was first published in *Spiritual Songs for Social Worship* (Utica, 1832). It was written in three parts and in the key of D.

Safely through another week 37

This hymn by John Newton appeared in Conyer's *Psalms and Hymns* (1774) and in *Olney Hymns,* Book II (1779), in five stanzas. It was given under the heading, "Saturday evening." Because of the desirability for using this hymn on Sunday morning, alterations were made to make it more suitable.

SABBATH was composed by Lowell Mason for this hymn in 1824. It first appeared in the *Boston Academy's Collection of Church Music* (1835, p. 253). Henry L. Mason, in his *Hymn-Tunes of Lowell Mason,* indicates that this tune was written in 1824 and that it is an arrangement of a German melody.

"Satisfied With Jesus"—*see* I am satisfied with Jesus

"Saved, Saved"—*see* I've found a friend who is all to me

Saviour, again to Thy dear name 27

John Ellerton wrote this hymn for a choral festival at Nantwich, Cheshire, England, in 1866. It was later revised and abridged to its present form for inclusion in *Hymns Ancient and Modern* (1868, No. 279). Ellerton organized the first choral society in the Midlands, which met at Nantwich for many years.

ELLERS was composed for this hymn by Edward J. Hopkins for Brown-Borthwick's *Supplemental Hymn and Tune Book,* third edition (1869), where it appeared as a unison setting with varied accompaniment for each stanza. The present harmonization was made by Hopkins for the *Appendix to the Bradford Tune Book* (1872), at the request of the editor, Samuel Smith. A slightly different harmonization by Arthur S. Sullivan made for *Church Hymns* (1874) is found in some hymnals today.

Saviour, breathe an evening blessing 34

James Edmeston was so impressed by the following statement from Salte's *Travels in Abyssinia,* "At night their short evening hymn 'Jesu Mahaxaroo' (Jesus, forgive us) stole through the camp," that he wrote this hymn. It was first published in his *Sacred Lyrics* (1820) in two eight-line stanzas. One of the earliest collections to adapt it for congregational use was Bickersteth's *Christian Hymnody* (1833).

EVENING PRAYER. George C. Stebbins wrote this tune in 1876 as a response to be sung after prayer in the morning service at Tremont Temple Baptist Church, Boston, while he was music director there. Two years later, while engaged in evangelistic services at Providence, he first discovered the appropriateness of Edmeston's text for this tune. It was first published with these words in *Gospel Hymns No. 3,* (1878, edited by Ira D. Sankey, James McGranahan, and Stebbins).

Saviour, like a shepherd lead us 344

Although usually ascribed to Dorothy A Thrupp, the authorship of this hymn is quite uncertain. The hymn first appeared unsigned in *Hymns for the Young,* fourth edition (1836), compiled by Dorothy A. Thrupp. It appeared in Carus Wilson's *Children's Friend,* June, 1838, signed "Lyte." In the same year it appeared, again unsigned, in Mrs. Herbert Mayo's *Selection of Hymns and Poetry for the use of Infant and Juvenile Schools.* Miss Thrupp contributed other hymns and poems to this collection and they are signed "D. A. T." The fact that these initials did not appear with this hymn seem to indicate that Mrs. Mayo did not credit it to Miss Thrupp. Regarding the authorship of this hymn in the presence of the known facts, Julian states that the "evidence is decidedly against Miss Thrupp, and somewhat uncertain with regard to Lyte."

BRADBURY was composed by William B. Bradbury for this hymn and first appeared in the 1859 edition of Bradbury's *Oriola,* a Sunday school collection.

Saviour, more than life to me 326

Fanny J. Crosby is the author of the text, and the tune, EVERY DAY AND HOUR, was composed by William H. Doane. This first appeared in a Sunday school collection, *Brightest and Best,* compiled by Robert Lowry and Doane (1875). Ira D. Sankey, in *My Life and the Story of the Gospel Hymns* (1907), states that the tune was written before the text.

It was in 1875 that Mr. Doane sent the tune to Fanny Crosby, and requested her to write a hymn entitled "Every day and hour." Her response in the form of this hymn gave the blind hymn-writer great comfort and filled her heart with joy. She felt sure that God would bless the hymn to many hearts. Her hope has been most fully verified, for millions have been refreshed and strengthened as they have sung it. At the suggestion of Mr. D. W. McWilliams, who was superintendent of Dr. Cuyler's Sunday-school for twenty-five years, it was put into *Gospel Hymns*.

Saviour, teach me day by day 291

This hymn by Jane E. Leeson first appeared in her *Hymns and Scenes of Childhood, or A Sponsor's Gift* (London, 1842). Originally in four eight-line stanzas, the last four lines of stanzas one and two and the first four lines of stanzas three and four are omitted in the present version.

INNOCENTS appeared in *The Parish Choir* (III, No. 59), a magazine published by the Society for Promoting Church Music. William H. Monk was for a time the musical editor of this periodical. The origin of this tune is quite obscure. Efforts have been made to attribute it to such sources as a Handelian theme from *Siroe* (cf. CHRISTMAS—Awake, my soul, stretch every nerve), an unpublished song by Joseph Smith entitled "The Sun," and a song by Samuel Webbe the Younger. There are admitted similarities between the hymn tune and each of these three sources but insufficient evidence to credit any one of these as the original source. The tune name was given from its first use in *The Parish Choir* with an Innocents' Day hymn, "Little flowers of martyrdom," concerning the infants which Herod massacred at Bethlehem.

Saviour, Thy dying love 400

This hymn was written in 1862 by Sylvanus D. Phelps, a Baptist minister. It first appeared unsigned in the *Watchman and Reflector* (Boston, Vol. XLV, No. 11, Mar. 17, 1864, p. 4), in the following version entitled, "Something for Thee."

> Something, my God, for Thee,
> Something for Thee:
> That each day's setting sun may bring
> Some penitential offering:
> In Thy dear name some kindness done;
> To Thy dear love some wanderer won;
> Some trial meekly borne for Thee
> Dear Lord, for Thee.

Something, my God, for Thee,
    Something for Thee:
That to Thy gracious throne may rise
Sweet incense from some sacrifice—
Uplifted eyes undimmed by tears,
Uplifted faith unstained by fears,
    Hailing each joy as light from Thee,
        Dear Lord, from Thee.

Something, my God, for Thee,
    Something for Thee:
For the great love that Thou hast given,
For the great hope of Thee and heaven,
My soul! her first allegiance brings,
And upward plumes her heavenward wings,
    Nearer, my God, to Thee,
        Nearer to Thee.

Apparently this hymn was rewritten by the author in its present form, when, at the invitation of Robert Lowry, it was submitted along with other poems for a forthcoming collection being compiled by Lowry and William H. Doane. It was included in this collection, *Pure Gold,* a Sunday school songbook, published by Biglow and Main (New York, 1871, No. 21), with the heading, "Lord, what wilt Thou have me to do?" (Acts 9:6).

On his seventieth birthday, Phelps received the following letter from Robert Lowry:

It is worth living 70 years even if nothing comes of it but one such hymn as

Saviour! Thy dying love
    Thou gavest me;
Nor should I aught withhold,
    Dear Lord, from Thee.

Happy is the man who can produce one song which the world will keep on singing after its author shall have passed way. May the tuneful harp preserve its strings for many a long year yet, and the last note reach us only when it is time for the singer to take his place in the heavenly choir.

SOMETHING FOR JESUS was composed by Robert Lowry for these words when included in *Pure Gold.*

Seal us, O Holy Spirit 175

In a letter to the writer dated November 23, 1954, Isaac H. Meredith gave the following information:

Many years ago I was the musical director in the Central Presbyterian Church of Brooklyn, New York, of which Dr. John F. Carson was the pastor. During this period I frequently led the singing in three-day Bible conferences for the deepening of the spiritual life. The speakers usually were Dr. Arthur T. Bersia, Dr. Cornelius Wolfking [Woelfkin?], and Dr. Carson. This hymn is built on the outline of a Bible reading on the Holy Spirit by Dr. Carson. It was sung first in Dr. Carson's church. It is my first choice of all the hymns I have written. In the many years I spent in evangelistic work it was one of my most effective solos. It first appeared in one of our early hymnbooks *Sermons in Song No. 3,* no. 77.

This collection was published by Tuller-Meredith Company, New York, in 1901.

CARSON was suggested as the name for this tune by the composer in honor of his former pastor in Brooklyn.

"Send a Great Revival"—*see* Coming now to Thee, O Christ my Lord

Send a revival, O Christ, my Lord   333

Words and music were written by B. B. McKinney and were first published by Robert H. Coleman in *Evangel Bells* (Dallas, 1927, No. 1).

MATTHEWS is the name given this tune by the Hymnal Committee. Dr. Charles E. Matthews was secretary of the Department of Evangelism of the Home Mission Board, 1947-56. Prior to this time he had served for twenty-four years as pastor of the Travis Avenue Baptist Church, Fort Worth, Texas. McKinney served as music director for the church during part of Matthews' pastorate.

"Send the Light"—*see* There's a call comes ringing o'er the restless wave

Serve the Lord with gladness   434

Concerning the writing of this song, B. B. McKinney has written:

In the summer of 1930, Miss Mary Virginia Lee, Southwide Intermediate secretary, requested me to write an Intermediate song on their adopted theme, "Serve the Lord with Gladness," taken from Psalm 100. While on my way to New Orleans, Louisiana, by train, this song, words and music came to me. It was a clear summer day, rich with the beauties of "lovely Louisiana," pond lilies and moss-covered trees. The click of the car wheels over the rails seemed to form a rhythmic sensation for the melody. All nature seemed to be praising God. In my vision I could see great multitudes of happy Intermediates singing a "new song" unto the Lord. How my heart burned within me to write for them a singable song. After reading again Psalm 100, the melody and words came quickly to me. When I reached my destination the theme song for Southern Baptist Intermediates had been composed.

The hymn was first published by Robert H. Coleman in *Service Songs* (Dallas, 1931, No. 2).

LEE is the name given this tune by the Hymnal Committee for Miss Mary Virginia Lee, now Mrs. J. E. Kirk of Oklahoma City, Oklahoma.

Shall we gather at the river 481

Robert Lowry, who wrote both words and music, gives the following account:

One afternoon in July, 1864, when I was pastor at Hanson Place Baptist Church, Brooklyn, the weather was oppressively hot, and I was lying on a lounge in a state of physical exhaustion. I was almost incapable of bodily exertion, and my imagination began to take to itself wings. Visions of the future passed before me with startling vividness. The imagery of the apocalypse took the form of a tableau. Brightest of all were the throne, the heavenly river, and the gathering of the saints. My soul seemed to take new life from that celestial outlook. I began to wonder why the hymn-writers had said so much about the "river of death" and so little about "the pure water of life, clear as crystal, proceeding out of the throne of God and of the Lamb." As I mused the words began to construct themselves. They came first as a question of Christian inquiry, "Shall we gather?" Then they broke out in a chorus, as an answer of Christian faith, "Yes, we'll gather." On this question and answer the hymn developed itself. The music came with the hymn.

It was first published in Lowry and Doane's Sunday school collection, *Happy Voices* (New York: Biglow & Main, 1865, No. 220), in five four-line stanzas with a refrain.

Aaron Copland has included this hymn in a set of American folk songs arranged for solo voice, *Old American Songs,* Second Set (1954). In a nation-wide telecast in 1962, featuring the Philadelphia Orchestra with Eugene Ormandy conducting, three songs from this group were performed with William Warfield as soloist. In his commentary, Ormandy stated that this was a southern camp meeting song from American folk tradition. Aside from the fact that the song was written in Brooklyn and is not of folk tradition, was published in New York, not in the South, and was a Sunday school song, not a camp meeting song, Mr. Ormandy was right!

HANSON PLACE is the name given the tune by the Hymnal Committee for the church in Brooklyn where Dr. Lowry was pastor when he wrote it.

Shepherd of tender youth 162

This is a paraphrase by Henry M. Dexter of a hymn which was appended to a book known as *The Instructor,* or *The Tutor,* by Clement of

Alexandria and written in the second century. In the preparation of a sermon on the characteristics of early Christians, Dexter translated this Greek hymn of Clement into prose, and then made this metrical paraphrase. It first appeared in *The Congregationalist* (Dec. 21, 1849), a denominational paper of which he was editor. Its first appearance for congregational usage was in Hedge and Huntington's *Hymns for the Church of Christ* (1853).

KIRBY BEDON was written in 1887 and first appeared in *The Congregational Church Hymnal* (London, 1887). McCutchan (*Hymn Tune Names*, p. 89), says that the name means "the church near Bedon."

Silent night, holy night 72

This famous carol has had a most interesting history. It all began on December 24, 1818, in the little village of Oberndorf in the Alpine section of Austria. When it was discovered that the organ in St. Nicholas Church would not function and the music planned for the Christmas Eve service could not be used, Father Joseph Mohr, the assistant priest, decided to write a new song to be used instead. He prepared the text and asked the acting organist, Franz Gruber, to compose a tune. The resultant composition, written for two voices and guitar, was sung in the service that evening.

Later, when Karl Mauracher of Zillerthal came to repair the organ, he heard about the "organless" Christmas Eve service and of the new carol composed in the emergency. Mauracher secured a copy of the carol and in the next few years was responsible for spreading it through the Tyrol, referring to it simply as a "Tiroler Volkslied." The Strasser family of Zillertal, who were glove makers and also folk singers, became familiar with the song, and when they visited the Leipzig fair in 1831, they sang it there. A year later they gave a concert at Leipzig and included it on their program. A Dresden musician named Friese who was in the audience copied it down and took the carol with him to Berlin. It is not known whether or not there was ever an original manuscript, but the earliest manuscript by the composer himself, dated 1833, is scored for chorus, organ, and orchestra. Haeussler notes that its first published appearance was in *Katholisches Gesang- und Gebetbuch für den öffentlichen und häuslichen Gottesdienst zunächst zum Gebrauche der katholischen Gemeinden im Königreiche Sachsen* (Leipzig, 1838), usually referred to as the *Leipziger Gesangbuch.* In 1840 it was published in a collection of "four genuine Tyrolean songs, sung by the Strasser sisters from Zillerthal," at Dresden. The popularity of Tyrolean songs and singers in the middle nineteenth century no doubt helped popularize this carol both in Europe and America.

It was first used in America by German-speaking congregations. The first English version published in America seems to have been J. W. Warner's free paraphrase of the German text, "Silent night! Hallow'd night," which appeared in a Methodist compilation, *The Devotional Harmonist* (1849).

In the version given here, stanzas 1 and 3 are from the three-stanza English version by John Freeman Young, which first appeared in John Clark Hollister's *The Sunday-School Service and Tune Book* (New York, 1863). The identification of the author of this widely used translation, which has remained a mystery for almost a century, has been definitely established by Bryon E. Underwood in his "Bishop John Freeman Young Translator of 'Stille Nacht!' " in *The Hymn* (VIII, No. 4). Young's second stanza is:

> Silent night, holy night,
> Shepherds quake at the sight,
> Glories stream from heaven afar,
> Heavenly hosts sing alleluia;
> Christ, the Saviour, is born!
> Christ, the Saviour, is born!

Stanzas 2 and 4 in the present version are from other sources.

Simply trusting every day 259

This hymn was written by Edgar Page Stites and apparently first appeared in a newspaper.

TRUSTING JESUS was composed by Ira D. Sankey for this text. He has stated that

the words of this hymn were handed to Mr. Moody at Chicago in 1876, in the form of a newspaper clipping. He gave them to me, and asked me to write a tune for them. I assented, on condition that he should vouch for the doctrine taught in the verses, and he said he would.

It was first published in *Gospel Hymns No. 2* (1876, No. 35).

"Since I Have Been Redeemed"—*see* I have a song I love to sing

"Since Jesus Came into My Heart"—*see* What a wonderful change in my life has been wrought

Sing the wondrous love of Jesus 483

Both the author, Eliza E. Hewitt, and the composer, Emily D. Wilson, attended regularly the Methodist camp meetings at Ocean Grove, New Jersey, and apparently their collaboration in writing this hymn resulted from this mutual interest. It first appeared in *Pentecostal Praises,* compiled by William J. Kirkpatrick and Henry L. Gilmour Philadelphia: Hall Mack Co., 1898, No. 148).

HEAVEN is the name given this tune by the Hymnal Committee.

Sing them over again to me 181

Philip P. Bliss is the author of both words and music. It first appeared in *Words of Life* (1874), the first issue of a Sunday school paper published by Fleming H. Revell (New York). It was later included in *Gospel Hymns No. 3* (1878). George C. Stebbins, in his *Memoirs and Reminiscences,* tells of using this hymn in an evangelistic campaign with Dr. George F. Pentecost in New Haven, Connecticut, in 1878. Two years before Mr. Revell had given Stebbins a copy of the Sunday school paper which contained this hymn.

I carried that song through two seasons of evangelistic work, never thinking it possessed much merit, or that it had the element of special usefulness, particularly for solo purposes. It occurred to me to try it one day during the campaign in New Haven, and, with the help of Mrs. Stebbins, we sang it as a duet. To our surprise the song was received with the greatest enthusiasm and from that time on to the close of the meetings was the favorite of all the hymns used. As an illustration of the hold it got upon the people all about that section of the country, I received a letter from the Secretary of the Connecticut State Sunday School Association offering me what seemed an absurdly large sum of money, if I would, with Mrs. Stebbins, come to the State Convention and sing that one song.

Sinners Jesus will receive 195

Erdmann Neumeister is the author of the German hymn beginning, "Jesus nimmt die Sünder an! Saget doch dies Trostwort allen." It first appeared in Neumeister's *Evangelischer Nachklang* (Hamburg, 1718), a collection of eighty-six original hymns written to conclude the author's sermons. This hymn in eight six-line stanzas was designed to be sung at the close of a sermon based on Luke 15:1-7. Emma F. Bevan's translation appeared in her *Songs of Eternal Life* (London, 1858, p. 23). The first stanza of her translation is:

Sinners Jesus will receive;
Tell this word of grace to all
Who the heavenly pathway leave,
All who linger, all who fall;
This can bring them back again:
"Christ receiveth sinful men."

NEUMEISTER was originally composed by James McGranahan for men's voices, and first appeared in his *The Gospel Male Choir No. 2* (Cincinnati: The John Church Co., 1883, No. 6). In adapting this text, McGranahan used only the first four lines of each stanza with some alterations, and chose the final couplet from stanza six as the text for the refrain. The tune was named by the Hymnal Committee.

So let our lips and lives express   323

This hymn by Isaac Watts first appeared in his *Hymns and Spiritual Songs* (1707).

WAREHAM first appeared in William Knapp's *A Sett of New Psalm Tunes and Anthems* (London, 1738). One of the unusual characteristics of this tune is that with one exception the melody moves degreewise from beginning to end.

So precious is Jesus, my Saviour, my King   304

Charles H. Gabriel wrote both words and music of this hymn, and it first appeared in his *Joyful Praise* (Chicago: Jennings & Pye, 1902, No. 2). The first stanza has been altered from the original which read:

I'm happy in Jesus, my Saviour, my King,
And all the day long of His goodness I sing,
To Him in my weakness I lovingly cling,
For He is so precious to me.

Apparently these alterations were made by E. O. Excell, who purchased the hymn from Gabriel (Feb. 4, 1907) and six weeks later filed a new copyright registration under the title "He Is So Precious to Me."

PRECIOUS TO ME is the name given the tune by the Hymnal Committee.

Softly and tenderly Jesus is calling   236

Will L. Thompson wrote both words and music for this well-known invitation hymn. In many early collections which include this hymn, the copyright date is given as 1880, which would indicate that it first appeared in that year. The writer has been unable to find this hymn in any collection earlier than J. S. Inskip's *Songs of Triumph* (Philadelphia: National Publishing Association for the Promotion of Holiness, 1882, No. 87).

THOMPSON is the name given this tune by the Hymnal Committee.

Softly now the light of day 33

This hymn by George W. Doane was published in his *Songs by the Way* (1824) and entitled "Evening," with the quotation "Let my prayer be set forth . . . as incense; and the lifting up of my hands as the evening sacrifice" (Psalm 141:2).

SEYMOUR, sometimes called WEBER, is taken from the theme of the opening chorus of *Oberon,* Weber's last opera, composed during 1825-26 and first performed at Covent Garden, London, on April 12, 1826.

It was arranged as a hymn tune by Henry W. Greatorex and first appeared in his *Collection of Psalm and Hymn Tunes, Chants Anthems and Sentences for the use of the Protestant Episcopal Church in America* (1851), where it was set to "Jesus, Lover of my soul" (No. 415).

Soldiers of Christ, arise 416

This hymn by Charles Wesley, based on Ephesians 6:11-18, first appeared in *Hymns and Sacred Poems* (1749). Originally consisting of sixteen eight-line stanzas, the present version makes use of stanzas one, two, and sixteen.

DIADEMATA—*see* Crown Him with many crowns.

"Something for Thee"—*see* Saviour, Thy dying love

Sowing in the morning, sowing seeds of kindness 432

This text by Knowles Shaw with a tune which he also composed first appeared unsigned in his *The Golden Gate for the Sunday School* (Cincinnati: John Church Co., 1874, No. 9). In *The Morning Star, a New Collection of Sunday School Music* by Shaw (St. Louis: Christian Publishing Co., 1877, No. 82), this hymn is credited to Shaw.

HARVEST was composed by George A. Minor for this text, and it first appeared in his *Golden Light No. 1, for Sunday Schools* (Richmond: J. J. Shotwell, 1879, No. 6), with the reference, "The harvest is the end of the world" (Matt. 13:39). The original key was B flat.

In this thirty-two page collection, six tunes and four texts are credited to Minor, a Baptist layman, who led the Sunday school music in the First Baptist Church of Richmond, Virginia. In the preface it is stated that this pamphlet "will be followed every six months by other numbers." Apparently this plan did not materialize, for the Library of Congress has a copy of *Golden Light No. 3,* dated April 21, 1884. The writer has not found a copy of *No. 2.*

Speak to my heart, Lord Jesus 331

B. B. McKinney wrote this hymn in 1927, and it first appeared in Robert H. Coleman's *Evangel Bells* (Dallas, 1927, No. 12).

HOLCOMB is the name given this tune by the Hymnal Committee. Dr. T. L. Holcomb served as executive secretary-treasurer of the Sunday School Board, 1935-53. He was responsible for McKinney's association with this publishing agency of the Southern Baptist Convention. Together with Dr. J. O. Williams and Dr. W. Hines Sims, he selected the Hymnal Committee.

Spirit divine, attend our prayer 172

This hymn by Andrew Reed first appeared in the *Evangelical Magazine* (June, 1829), with the heading "Hymn to the Spirit. Sung on the late Day appointed for solemn Prayer and Humiliation in the Eastern District of the Metropolis." The meeting referred to had been held on Good Friday, 1829, and it had been called by the London Board of Congregational Ministers in the interest of "a revival of religion in the British churches." The hymn later appeared in Reed's *Hymn Book* (London, 1842). Samuel Longfellow's adaptation appeared as "Anon." in the Unitarian *Hymns of the Spirit* (1864), edited by Samuel Johnson and Longfellow. For a comparison of Longfellow's revision with Reed's original, the latter is given here:

> Spirit divine, attend our prayers,
> And make this house thy home;
> Descend with all thy gracious powers,
> O come, great Spirit, come!
>
> Come as the light; to us reveal
> Our emptiness and woe,
> And lead us in those paths of life
> Whereon the righteous go.
>
> Come as the fire, and purge our hearts
> Like sacrificial flame;
> Let our whole soul an offering be
> To our Redeemer's Name.

Come as the dew, and sweetly bless
  This consecrated hour;
May barrenness rejoice to own
  Thy fertilizing power.

Come as the dove, and spread thy wings,
  The wings of peaceful love;
And let thy Church on earth become
  Blest as the Church above.

Come as the wind, with rushing sound
  And pentecostal grace;
That all of woman born may see
  The glory of thy face.

Spirit divine, attend our prayers;
  Make a lost world thy home;
Descend with all thy gracious powers;
  O come, great Spirit, come.

BRECON was composed by Nicholas Heins in 1900. The earliest appearance that has been found is in *Hymns of the Centuries,* edited by Benjamin Shepard (New York: A. S. Barnes & Co., 1911).

Spirit of God, descend upon my heart 166

Written by George Croly, this hymn first appeared in his *Psalms and Hymns for Public Worship* (London, 1854), with the heading "Holiness Desired."

LONGWOOD, composed by Joseph Barnby, first appeared in Novello's *The Hymnary* (London, 1872), which was edited by Sir Arthur Sullivan. It was set to Ellerton's "Saviour, again to Thy dear name we raise."

Stand up, and bless the Lord 16

James Montgomery wrote this hymn for the Red Hill Wesleyan Sunday school anniversary, Sheffield, England, March 15, 1824, and it began:

> Stand up and bless the Lord,
> Ye children of His choice.

Montgomery changed "children" to "people" when it was published in his *Christian Psalmist* (1825).

OLD 134TH, sometimes called ST. MICHAEL, is an adaptation of a Genevan psalm tune. In its original form it first appeared in the 1551 *Genevan Psalter* as a tune composed or adapted by Louis Bourgeois and

ORIGINAL FORM OF MELODY, OLD 134TH

set to Psalm 101. As with many of the Genevan psalm tunes, it underwent considerable alteration to conform to the common meter, short meter, and long meter forms of the Old Version of Sternhold and Hopkins. In the 1561 *Anglo-Genevan Psalter,* this tune was adapted to short meter and set for Psalm 134, which accounts for the tune name. After 1595, it seems to have been dropped from popular usage. In its present form it appeared in William Crotch's *Psalm Tunes* (London, 1836), where it was called ST. MICHAEL.

Stand up, stand up for Jesus 415, 419

The story of this hymn is given by the author, George Duffield, Jr.:

"Stand Up for Jesus" was the dying message of the Rev. Dudley A. Tyng, to the Young Men's Christian Association, and the ministers associated with them in the Noon-Day Prayer Meeting during the great revival of 1858, usually known as "The Work of God in Philadelphia."

A very dear personal friend, I knew young Tyng as one of the noblest, bravest, manliest men I ever met. . . . The Sabbath before his death he preached in the immense edifice known as Jaynes' Hall, one of the most successful sermons of modern times. Of the five thousand men there assembled, at least one thousand, it was believed, were "the slain of the Lord." His text was Exodus 10:11, and hence the allusion in the third verse of the hymn.

The following Wednesday, leaving his study for a moment, he went to the barn floor, where a mule was at work on a horse-power, shelling corn. Patting him on the neck, the sleeve of his silk study gown caught in the cogs of the wheel, and his arm was torn out by the roots! His death occurred in a few hours. . . .

The following Sunday the author of the hymn preached from Eph. 6:14, and the above verses were written simply as the concluding exhortation. The superintendent of the Sabbath school had a fly-leaf printed for the children—a stray copy found its way into a Baptist newspaper—and from that paper it has gone in English, and in German and Latin translations all over the world.

The hymn first appeared in *The Psalmist* (1858 edition). Originally in six eight-line stanzas, the version at 415 uses stanzas one, four, and six; 419 also uses stanza three.

WEBB (415)—see O Thou whose hand hath brought us. The first association of this hymn with this tune seems to have been in William B. Bradbury's *The Golden Chain* (New York, 1861).

GEIBEL (419) was composed by Adam Geibel for this hymn, and it first appeared in his *Uplift Voices* (New York: Geibel & Lehman, 1901, No. 18).

Standing on the promises of Christ my King 266

This hymn—words and music by R. Kelso Carter—was first published in *Songs of Perfect Love,* compiled by John R. Sweney and Carter (Philadelphia: John J. Hood Publisher, 1886, No. 120). Originally consisting of five stanzas, the omitted stanza three is:

> Standing on the promises I now can see
> Perfect, present cleansing in the blood for me;
> Standing in the liberty where Christ makes free,
>   Standing on the promises of God.

PROMISES is the name given this tune by the Hymnal Committee.

Still, still with Thee, when purple morning breaketh 25

This was written by Harriet B. Stowe, who is perhaps best known as the author of *Uncle Tom's Cabin,* a novel so well known a century ago. Based on Psalm 139:18, this hymn was written in the summer of 1853, while the author was visiting in the home of a friend. She enjoyed walking in the early morning hours, seeing the dawn break. Out of such experiences of meditation came the inspiration for these words.

CONSOLATION is based on the melody of "Consolation" (*Songs Without Words,* Book 2, No. 3), by Felix Mendelssohn. In Charles L. Hutchins' 1894 musical edition of the Episcopal hymnal, this tune is called BRIGHTEST AND BEST, and in the index the arrangement is credited to A. Levy and dated 1880. The tune appears, however, in Charles S. Robinson's *Spiritual Songs* (1875).

Sun of my soul, Thou Saviour dear 15

This hymn is a selection from the fourteen stanzas of John Keble's poem entitled "Evening" in *The Christian Year* (1827). It was written on November 25, 1820, with the first stanza beginning " 'Tis gone, that bright and orbed blaze," and is based on Luke 24:29. It first appeared in America in the *Collection of Songs and Hymns* (Boston, 1835).

HURSLEY evolved from a melody which appeared in the *Katholisches Gesangbuch* (Vienna, *ca.* 1774), set to the hymn "Grosser Gott, wir loben dich." Its first appearance in a Protestant hymnal was Schicht's *Allgemeines Choralbuch* (Leipzig, 1819), set to the same text. Five years later it appeared in France in *Choix de Cantiques*. It was included in David Weyman's *A Sequel to Melodia Sacra* (Dublin, *ca* 1844), set to "Jesus and shall it ever be." The present form of this tune was the choice of Keble and his wife as a suitable tune for "Sun of my soul," and it first appeared with this text in the *Metrical Psalter* by W. J. Irons and Henry Lahee (1855). The tune was named for the parish where Keble served for many years.

"Sunshine in My Soul"—*see* There is sunshine in my soul today

"Sweet By and By"—*see* There's a land that is fairer than day

Sweet hour of prayer, sweet hour of prayer   **327**

The four stanzas of this hymn first appeared in *The New York Observer* (Sept. 13, 1845), with this explanation:

During my residence at Coleshill, Warwickshire, England, I became acquainted with W. W. Walford, the blind preacher, a man of obscure birth and connections and no education, but of strong mind and most retentive memory. In the pulpit he never failed to select a lesson well adapted to his subject, giving chapter and verse with unerring precision and scarcely ever misplacing a word in his repetition of the Psalms, every part of the New Testament, the prophecies, and some of the histories, so as to have the reputation of "knowing the whole Bible by heart." He actually sat in the chimney corner, employing his mind in composing a sermon or two for Sabbath delivery, and his hands in cutting, shaping, and polishing bones for shoe horns and other little useful implements. At intervals he attempted poetry. On one occasion, paying him a visit, he repeated two or three pieces which he had composed, and having no friend at home to commit them to paper, he had laid them up in the storehouse within. "How will this do?" asked he, as he repeated the following lines, with a complacent smile touched with some slight lines of fear lest he should subject himself to criticism. I rapidly copied the lines with my pencil, as he uttered them, and sent them for insertion in the *Observer,* if you should think them worthy of preservation.

The above was written by the Rev. Thomas Salmon (1800-54), who came to the United States in 1842 following a four-year pastorate at Coleshill. Efforts to further identify the man described in Salmon's communication have been unsuccessful. An examination of the Warwickshire Poll Books and early directories in the Birmingham Public

Libraries by V. H. Woods, city librarian, "did not reveal that Walford was a Coleshill name at that time." In a letter dated October 3, 1955, the Rev. Canon H. Douglas Barton, vicar of Coleshill, says, "I have not found any entry of the name 'Walford' in my Church Registers—Baptism, Marriage and Burial around the years 1845."

There was a Rev. William Walford (1772-1850), a Congregational minister, who was president of Homerton Academy and the author of several books. This man does not fit Salmon's description. He was educated, and there is no evidence that he was blind. It is highly probable that Salmon knew of this man, although there is no evidence that Salmon was ever a student at Homerton Academy. *The Autobiography of the Rev. William Walford,* edited by John Stoughton (1851), reveals no suggestion of blindness, nor is there any hint that Walford ever wrote a hymn or had any poetic gift. There are, however, some vague references to a period of prolonged and serious illness that seem to imply what today might be called a "nervous breakdown." Walford evidently could not carry on his work at Homerton during this period, but there is no mention of where he stayed at the time (cf. biographical sketch). On the basis of all this evidence, it would seem reasonable to assume that this William Walford is not the man who wrote this hymn. However, Joseph F. Green, Jr., has made a careful study of *The Manner of Prayer* (1836) by William Walford of Homerton Academy and on the basis of internal evidence notes striking similarities between the book and the hymn. Throughout both is the recurring theme that prayer is the answer to Christian problems and needs. Definite points of emphasis common to both the book and hymn as noted by Dr. Green are:

1. The present life is one of great care and temptation.
2. The Christian desires release through fellowship with God.
3. God invites the Christian to enter such fellowship.
4. Christians receive God's blessings in praying together.
5. Christians look forward to shedding the body in death and coming into a realization of blessedness not known here.

Furthermore, there are a number of distinctive words and phrases, and a likeness of terminology indicating that a similar spirit prevails in both writings. The book was published in 1836, and the hymn was written sometime during the four-year pastorate of Salmon at Coleshill, 1838-42. Could Walford of Coleshill and Walford of Homerton be one and the same person? Certainly not from the biographical information available. On the basis of this internal criticism, it would seem highly possible. Could it be that Salmon's communication to the *New York*

Observer might have contained some slightly "exaggerated" data? So far as is known, Salmon left no other record of this information.

The writer has shared the evidence of this research with Armin Haeussler and Erik Routley. Dr. Haeussler states that he is inclined to believe that they are one and the same person. Dr. Routley, on the other hand, states that "It is only too likely that the hymn was falsely ascribed to somebody else of almost the same name; but it seems very unlikely that Walford of Coleshill had anything to do with Homerton." In the face of these irreconcilable facts, we shall await further information to resolve the mystery of the identity of the author of this hymn. One plausible conjecture is that Salmon or someone else read Walford's book on prayer to the blind preacher of Coleshill, accounting for the literary similarities between the book and the hymn. Salmon's calling the hymn writer "Walford" may have involved a slip of memory.

In 1859 Thomas Hastings and Robert Turnbull published a Baptist edition of their collection *Church Melodies* (1858). This hymn—words only—appears as Number 890 in a section of hymns on baptism and miscellaneous subjects added for this Baptist edition. The long meter tune suggested for this text is THE BETTER LAND, which appears on page 30. This is the earliest hymnal inclusion of this text which the writer has found.

SWEET HOUR was composed by William B. Bradbury for this hymn. The earliest book which the writer has found to contain this tune is Bradbury's *The Golden Chain* (New York, 1861, No. 10). Bradbury's *Cottage Melodies* (1859), is usually given as the source of this tune. While this tune does appear in later editions of this collection, it does not appear in the first edition in 1859. It seems to have been the common custom of such compilers as Bradbury, Mason, and Hastings that when a particular tune was published in a new collection and began to be popular, this tune was immediately inserted into subsequent editions and printings of earlier collections with which they were associated. SWEET HOUR appears in the thirtieth edition of Bradbury's *Oriola,* which appeared in 1862. Such practice has resulted in considerable confusion in accurately designating sources for many of these tunes.

Sweet is the promise "I will not forget thee"   278

This hymn—both words and music by Charles H. Gabriel—first appeared in *Triumphant Songs No. 2,* compiled and published by E. O. Excell (Chicago, 1889).

SWEET PROMISE is the name given this tune by the Hymnal Committee.

"Sweet Peace, the Gift of God's Love"—*see* There comes to my heart one sweet strain

Sweetly, Lord, have we heard Thee calling   **362**

Mary B. C. Slade wrote this hymn, originally in seven four-line stanzas, and Asa B. Everett composed the tune FOOTSTEPS. The omitted stanzas four, five and six are:

> Though, dear Lord, in Thy pathway keeping,
>   We follow Thee;
> Through the gloom of that place of weeping,
>   Gethsemane!

> If Thy way and its sorrows bearing,
>   We go again,
> Up the slope of the hill-side, bearing
>   Our cross of pain.

> By and by, through the shining portals,
>   Turning our feet,
> We shall walk with the glad immortals,
>   Heaven's golden streets.

This text with this tune seems to have first appeared in *The Amaranth*, compiled by Atticus G. Haygood and R. M. McIntosh (Nashville, 1871, p. 124), a Sunday school collection for the Methodist Episcopal Church, South, prepared by instruction of the General Conference of 1870.

Take my life, and let it be   **356, 357**

Frances R. Havergal wrote this hymn on February 4, 1874, after an unusual experience in prayer. She has given the following account:

I went for a little visit of five days [to Areley House, Worcestershire, in December 1873]. There were ten persons in the house, some unconverted and long prayed for, some converted but not rejoicing Christians. He gave me the prayer, "Lord, give me *all* in this house." And He just *did*. Before I left the house everyone had got a blessing. The last night of my visit I was too happy to sleep, and passed most of the night in praise and renewal of my own consecration, and these little couplets formed themselves and chimed in my heart, one after another till they finished with "ever, only, all, for Thee."

The hymn was first published in the Appendix of Snepp's *Songs of Grace and Glory* (1874) and later in Miss Havergal's *Loyal Responses* (1878).

YARBROUGH (356) is credited to William B. Bradbury in the collections of recent decades which include this tune. A search through many of the collections of Bradbury has failed to reveal this tune, and the earliest that it has been found is *New Life, or Songs and Tunes for Sunday School, Prayer Meeting, and Revival Occasions,* compiled by R. M. McIntosh and W. G. E. Cunnyngham (Nashville: Southern Methodist Publishing House, 1879, No. 166), where this tune is given as "arr. by R. M. McIntosh," and there is no mention of Bradbury.

HENDON (357)—*see* Ask ye what great thing I know.

Take the name of Jesus with you 305

This hymn was written by Lydia Baxter in 1870 for William H. Doane, who composed the tune PRECIOUS NAME. It first appeared in *Pure Gold,* edited by Doane and Robert Lowry (New York: Biglow & Main, 1871, No. 13).

Take time to be holy 367

Two different accounts of the writing of this hymn by William D. Longstaff have been given. Ira D. Sankey has stated that Longstaff wrote it after hearing a sermon preached at New Brighton, England, on the text, "Be ye holy; for I am holy" (1 Peter 1:16). George C. Stebbins, composer of the tune, has stated that at a meeting at Keswick, England, a speaker told of Dr. Griffith John, a missionary to China, and quoted a statement the missionary had made at a conference in China, "Take time and be holy." Stebbins says that the hymn was written that evening at Keswick. It is possible that there is no conflict in these two accounts; however, the writer is inclined to discount Sankey's story and place more confidence in Stebbins' version. According to McCutchan, the hymn first appeared in an English publication about 1882, and later in *Hymns of Consecration,* used at Keswick.

HOLINESS was composed by George C. Stebbins in 1890 for this text, while he was in India. The poem had been clipped from a periodical by a friend and given to Stebbins some months before. While assisting Dr. George F. Pentecost and Bishop Thoburn in meetings and conferences in Bombay, Calcutta, Madras, and other cities in India, Stebbins discovered this poem among the papers he had with him. He composed this tune and mailed it to Ira D. Sankey in New York. It was first published in Sankey's *Winnowed Songs for Sunday School* (1890, No. 40), and the following year appeared in *Gospel Hymns No. 6.*

This hymn was written in Clanton, Alabama, after the author, B. B. McKinney, had had dinner with R. S. Jones, a friend of many years. They were attending the Alabama Sunday School Convention (southern section), January 15-17, 1936, where Jones was a featured speaker and McKinney was leading the music. Jones had served as a missionary in Brazil for several years but had returned home because of his health. A few days prior to this convention, Jones had learned that because of his health he would not be able to return to Brazil. In the conversation at dinner, McKinney expressed his deepest sympathy and inquired as to Jones's future plans. Jones replied, "I don't know, but wherever He leads I'll go." The words lingered in McKinney's mind. He returned to his hotel room and wrote both words and music before leaving for the convention session that evening. At the close of the evening session, after Jones had spoken, McKinney told the audience of the dinner conversation with Jones and said he had been inspired to write a song. He handed a manuscript copy to the organist and sang it as a solo.

Shortly afterwards, Jones became associated with the Southern Baptist Relief and Annuity Board, Dallas, Texas, where he served faithfully until his retirement in 1957. He died at Murray, Kentucky, May 19, 1960.

In the comments about this convention found in the *Alabama Baptist* (Jan. 13, 1936, p. 3), the editor, L. L. Gwaltney, says: "The music was under the direction of Mr. B. B. McKinney of the Sunday School Board who conducted it well. We believe in his case common sense and music are well blended." This hymn was copyrighted as a separate title on May 14, 1936, and first appeared in *Songs of Victory* (Nashville, 1937, No. 4), the first collection prepared by McKinney for the Sunday School Board.

FALLS CREEK is the name given this tune by the Hymnal Committee. Falls Creek Baptist Assembly is located in the Arbuckle Mountains in southern Oklahoma, and was founded in 1917. From 1925 to 1945, McKinney directed the music at this annual summer assembly for Oklahoma Baptists and wielded a great influence in the church music throughout the state. More than twenty thousand people attend this assembly now each year, and the congregational singing begun by McKinney has become a tradition of Falls Creek, now under the direction of Gene Bartlett, Oklahoma Baptist state music secretary. This hymn was introduced at the assembly by McKinney in 1936, prior to its publication the following year.

The words and music of this hymn were written by Albert S. Reitz in 1925, and he has provided the following information about this hymn:

When I was pastor of the Rosehill Baptist Church in Los Angeles we had a heart-warming Day of Prayer under the leadership of the Evangelical Prayer Union of Los Angeles. The next morning in my study the Lord gave me the words and the music then followed. As I remember it Dr. Herbert G. Tovey first published it in a booklet of hymns, then it appears in one of Rodeheaver's *Solos and Duets*.

This first appearance was in Tovey's *Gospel Solos and Duets No. 2*, fifth edition (Los Angeles: The Biola Book Room, 1925).

Tell me the old, old story 222

Katherine Hankey wrote a lengthy poem, "The Old, Old Story," which was a life of Christ in verse. The first part, entitled, "The Story Wanted," was written on January 29, 1866, and this hymn was taken from this section. The second section was written on November 18, 1866, from which "I love to tell the story" (p. 85) was taken. A comparison of these two hymns is most interesting, particularly the similarity of the first stanzas of each.

OLD, OLD STORY was composed by William H. Doane, who provides the following information about this tune.

In 1867 I was attending the International meeting of the Young Men's Christian Association in Montreal. Among those present was Major-General Russell, then in command of the English forces during the Fenian excitement. He arose in the meeting and read the words of the song from a sheet of foolscap paper, the tears streaming down his bronzed cheeks as he read. I was much impressed, and immediately requested the privilege of making a copy. He gave me the copy from which he had read. I wrote the music for the song while on the stagecoach one hot summer afternoon between the Glen Falls House and the Crawford House in the White Mountains. That evening we sang it in the parlors of the hotel and thought it pretty, though we scarcely anticipated the popularity which was subsequently accorded it. It was afterwards published in sheet form in Cincinnati.

The same year it appeared in Doane's *Silver Spray* (Cincinnati, 1867, No. 67). It is in H. R. Palmer's *Sabbath School Songs* (Chicago, 1868, No. 23). It is interesting to note that the companion hymn (p. 85) had appeared a year earlier, and it is quite possible that Doane was unaware of Fischer's tune at the time he wrote this tune.

The author of this hymn is William H. Parker, an English Baptist layman, who was greatly interested in Sunday school work. One Sunday afternoon in 1885, after he had returned from Sunday school, he sat alone thinking over his experiences of the day. Recalling the oft-repeated request of the children, "Teacher, tell us another story," he composed the lines of this hymn. In speaking of this hymn, Carey Bonner comments:

> It is not to be wondered at that boys and girls love these verses, for they form a series of concrete word-pictures in varied and vivid style, enabling young singers to realize outstanding events in our Lord's life from Galilee to Calvary.

STORIES OF JESUS was the prize-winning tune submitted by Frederic A. Challinor in a competition sponsored by the National Sunday School Union of England in its centennial year, 1903, for new hymn tunes for several texts which it printed in a leaflet. Parker's hymn was one of those included. Sir Frederick Bridge, organist at Westminster Abbey, was the judge, and when he had examined the manuscripts submitted, he handed Challinor's manuscript to Carey Bonner, secretary of the National Sunday School Union, and remarked, "This is the best. A fine hymn, too. In a few years both will be sung all over the kingdom." Its first hymnal inclusion was the *Sunday School Hymnary* (1905).

Tell me the story of Jesus 211

Fanny J. Crosby's text with this tune, STORY OF JESUS, by John R. Sweney, first appeared in *The Quiver of Sacred Song,* compiled by William J. Kirkpatrick and Sweney (Philadelphia: John J. Hood, 1880, No. 52).

Ten thousand times ten thousand 476

This hymn by Henry Alford first appeared in *Good Words* (March, 1867). Later the same year it was included in the author's *The Year of Praise*. A fourth stanza, not included in the present version, was added in 1870, when the hymn was printed in Pickersgill and Alford's *The Lord's Prayer Illustrated.*

ALFORD was composed by John B. Dykes for this hymn and first appeared in *Hymns Ancient and Modern,* Revised Edition (London, 1875).

"Thanksgiving Hymn"—*see* Jehovah the Lord, our Saviour and King

"The Banner of the Cross"—*see* There's a royal banner given for display

The church's one foundation 380

In 1866, Bishop John William Colenso of Natal attacked the historicity of the Pentateuch in his book, *The Pentateuch and Book of Joshua, Critically Examined,* and a great controversy ensued in the Church of England. Bishop Gray of Capetown deposed Colenso and issued a strong defense of the church. Samuel J. Stone, then curate at Windsor, became an active supporter of Bishop Gray and published *Lyra Fidelium* (1866), twelve credal hymns based on the Apostles' Creed. The ninth article of the Creed was the basis for this hymn. Originally in seven eight-line stanzas, the present version is made up of stanzas one, two, five, and the first four lines each of stanzas six and seven. This form of the hymn, with one additional stanza, appeared in the Appendix to *Hymns Ancient and Modern* (London, 1868), set to the present tune.

AURELIA—*see* I lay my sins on Jesus.

The day of resurrection 111

This is a translation of the first of eight odes which make up the Golden Canon for Easter Sunday by John of Damascus. John Mason Neale's free translation appeared in his *Hymns of the Eastern Church* (1862), together with this account of the singing of this "glorious old hymn of victory" in the Greek church:

The circumstances under which the Canon is sung are thus eloquently described by a modern writer. The scene is at Athens.
"As midnight approached, the Archbishop, with his priests, accompanied by the King and Queen, left the Church, and stationed themselves on the platform. . . . Everyone now remained in breathless expectation, holding their unlighted tapers in readiness when the glad moment should arrive, while the priests still continued murmuring their melancholy chant in a low half-whisper. Suddenly a single report of a cannon announced that twelve o'clock had struck, and that Easter day had begun; then the old Archbishop elevating the cross, exclaimed in a loud, exulting tone, 'Christos anesti,' 'Christ is risen!' and instantly every single individual of all that host took up the cry, and the vast multitude broke through and dispelled forever the intense and mournful silence which they had maintained so long, with one spontaneous shout of indescribable joy and triumph, 'Christ is risen! Christ is risen!' At the same moment the oppressive darkness was succeeded by a blaze of light from thousands of tapers, which communicating one from another, seemed to send streams of fire in all directions, rendering the minutest objects distinctly visible, and casting the most vivid glow on the expressive faces full of exultation, of the rejoicing crowd; bands of music struck up their gayest strains; the roll of the drum through the town, and

further on the pealing of the cannon announced far and near these 'glad tidings of great joy'; while from hill and plain, from the sea-shore and the far olive-grove, rocket after rocket ascending to the clear sky, answered back with their mute eloquence, that Christ is risen indeed, and told of other tongues that were repeating those blessed words, and other hearts that leap for joy; everywhere men clasped each other's hands, congratulated one another, and embraced with countenances beaming with delight, as though to each one separately some wonderful happiness had been proclaimed;—and so in truth it was; and all the while rising above the mingling of many sounds, each one of which was a sound of gladness, the aged priests were distinctly heard chanting forth a glorious old hymn of victory in tones so loud and clear, that they seemed to have regained the youth and strength to tell the world how 'Christ is risen from the dead, having trampled death beneath His feet, and henceforth they that are in the tombs have everlasting life!' "

Neale's original translation began " 'Tis the day of resurrection." This was altered to the present first line in *The Parish Hymn Book* (London, 1863), the first appearance of this hymn in a hymnal for congregational singing.

GREENLAND first appeared as a hymn tune in Jacob's *National Psalmody,* which was published while Jacob was organist at Surrey Chapel, London, 1817. In Jacob's collection it was called SALZBURG. No doubt Jacob's source for this tune was Latrobe's *Selection of Sacred Music from the Work of the Most Eminent Composers of Germany and Italy,* Volume I (1806, p. 128), where it is indicated that it is from one of Michael Haydn's "Services for Country Churches." The use of this tune with Heber's "From Greenland's icy mountains" accounts for its name.

"The Divine Gift"—*see* O God of light, Thy Word, a lamp unfailing

The first Noel the angel did say 63

The first appearance of this anonymous text is found in Davies Gilbert's *Some Ancient Christmas Carols* (1823). It appeared somewhat altered and in the version from which our four stanzas are taken in William Sandys' *Christmas Carols, Ancient and Modern* (London, 1833). The second stanza, while traditionally found in even the most carefully edited hymnals, is not true to the scriptural account; for the shepherds did not see the star.

The French "Noël" is supposed to have come from the Provençal "nadal," a corruption of the Latin "natalis" (birthday). There is also a possible association with "novella" (news). "Nowell" is an old English spelling. It was an expression of joy originally shouted or sung to commemorate the birth of Christ. It is mentioned in "Franklin's Tale" in Chaucer's *Canterbury Tales*.

> Biforn him stant braun of the tusked swyn,
> And "Nowell" cryeth every lusty man.

THE FIRST NOEL, the traditional tune for these words appeared in Sandys' *Christmas Carols, Ancient and Modern* (London, 1833). Millar Patrick, in the *Handbook to the Church Hymnary Supplement* (1935), states that the tune is believed to have originally been the treble part (above the melody) of a tune by Jeremiah Clark to "An Hymn for Christmas Day," which is an elaborated form of ST. MAGNUS (*see* The Lord will come and not be slow). The strange position the tune occupies in the octave and the unusual economy of phrase lends support to this "descant theory." With the exception of the initial measure in each phrase, the entire tune lies between the third of the scale and the upper octave.

The great Physician now is near 86

William Hunter, a Methodist minister, wrote more than 125 hymns and published them in three collections. This hymn, entitled "Christ, the Physician," appeared in Hunter's *Songs of Devotion* (1859). Originally in seven stanzas, the omitted stanzas four, five, and seven are:

> The children too, both great and small,
>   Who love the name of Jesus,
> May now accept the gracious call
>   To work and live for Jesus.
>
> Come, brethren, help me sing His praise,
>   Oh, praise the name of Jesus;
> Oh, sisters, all your voices raise,
>   Oh, bless the name of Jesus.
>
> And when to that bright world above,
>   We rise to see our Jesus,
> We'll sing around the throne of love
>   His name, the name of Jesus

GREAT PHYSICIAN was written for this text by John H. Stockton. The earliest collection in which the writer has found this tune is in *Joyful Songs, Nos. 1, 2, and 3 Combined* (Philadelphia: Methodist Episcopal Book Room, 1869), with the notation, "arr. by J. H. Stockton. Harm. Prof. Garland." It later appeared in Stockton's *Salvation Melodies No.*

1, for the Friends of Jesus (Philadelphia: Perkinpine & Higgins, 1874, No. 16). The following year it was included in Bliss and Sankey's *Gospel Hymns and Sacred Songs,* and through this channel became widely known.

"The Haven of Rest"—*see* My soul in sad exile was out of life's sea

The head that once was crowned with thorns   117

This hymn by Thomas Kelly first appeared in his *Hymns on Various Passages of Scripture,* fifth edition (Dublin, 1820), with the heading "Perfect Through Sufferings." It is based on "For it became him, for whom are all things, and by whom are all things, in bringing many sons unto glory, to make the captain of their salvation perfect through sufferings" (Heb. 2:10). The present version uses stanzas one, three, four, and six of the original.

AZMON—*see* O for a thousand tongues to sing.

The heavens declare Thy glory, Lord   187

Isaac Watts's metrical version of Psalm 19 first appeared in his *The Psalms of David Imitated in the Language of the New Testament* (1719), entitled, "The Book of Nature and of Scripture Compared."

DUKE STREET—*see* Jesus shall reign where'er the Sun.

The Holy Ghost is here   168

This hymn was written by Charles Haddon Spurgeon, the outstanding English Baptist preacher of the nineteenth century. With the heading, "Prayer," it first appeared in Spurgeon's *Our Own Hymnbook, a Collection of Psalms and Hymns for Public, Social, and Private Worship* (London, 1866). This collection, made primarily to be used at Spurgeon's Tabernacle in London, contained twenty hymns and psalm versifications by Spurgeon.

BOYLSTON—*see* A charge to keep I have.

The King of love my Shepherd is   280

This splendid metrical version of Psalm 23 by Henry W. Baker first appeared in the Appendix to *Hymns Ancient and Modern* (London, 1868).

DOMINUS REGIT ME was composed by John B. Dykes for this text for inclusion in the above collection. The title of the tune is the first three words of Psalm 23 in the Vulgate (Latin version of the Bible).

"The King's Business"—*see* I am a stranger here, within a foreign land

"The Kingdom Is Coming"—*see* From all the dark places

The light of God Is falling   **442**

The author, Louis F. Benson, served as the editor for the revision of the 1905 Presbyterian *Hymnal,* and it was in this connection that this hymn came to be written. The following information from Benson is given by Calvin Laufer in *Hymn Lore:*

When the revision was nearly completed, at a meeting held at my home, Delancey Place, Philadelphia, on April 8, 1910, I reported among other things these two: First, that in studying the draft of the revised hymnal I noticed that the fine and effective tune "Greenland" was set to nothing except a hymn for harvest, which meant that the tune could never be used in the ordinary church service. Secondly, that I thought we ought to have a hymn of human brotherhood, in plain human speech, with the emphasis in everyday living rather than on doctrine in church relationship; that I had tried to find such a hymn, but could not and had then tried to write one, but without good results.

After the meeting the chairman of the committee, Judge Robert N. Willson, called me aside and in a warm, sympathetic way said that there was a great opportunity for any man who could fill it to write a hymn on modern lines that should go into our churches; that he believed I could do it and trusted I would. I was a bit touched by his kindly interest and confidence and out of the quickened state of feeling . . . the hymn came. The next day I wrote it pretty much as it stands and on October 11 I finished it off, and the next day sent it to Judge Willson. Oddly enough the hymn did not first appear in "The Hymnal," Revised, for which it was written, but in the new "Westminster Hymnal," which was being prepared by another committee and was published April 1, 1911, "The Hymnal," Revised, not being published till September.

MISSIONARY HYMN—*see* From Greenland's icy mountains.

"The Light of the World Is Jesus"—*see* The whole world was lost in the darkness of sin

"The Lily of the Valley"—*see* I have found a friend in Jesus

The Lord is my shepherd, no want shall I know   **57**

This paraphrase of Psalm 23 by James Montgomery first appeared in his *Songs of Zion, Being Imitations of Psalms,* (1822).

POLAND is an adaptation of a song, "Verlassen bin i," from a collection of Carinthian folk songs by Thomas Koschat (Vienna, *ca.* 1880) and first performed in Vienna, March 22, 1880. This tune appears in *Koschat-Album, a Selection of the Most Popular Carinthian Songs by Thomas Koschat* (Milwaukee, 1888), arranged for two voices with piano accompaniment.   With the German text is given this English translation:

> Forsaken, forsaken, forsaken am I!
> Like the stones in the causeway, my buried hopes lie.
> I go to the churchyard, my eyes fill with tears,
> And kneeling I weep there, Oh my love loved for years,
> And kneeling I weep there, Oh my love loved for years,
>
> A mound's in the churchyard, that blossoms hang o'er;
> It is there my love's sleeping, to waken no more.
> 'Tis there all my footsteps, my passions all lead,
> And there my heart turneth, I'm forsaken indeed,
> And there my heart turneth, I'm forsaken indeed.

It is not known who adapted this melody as a hymn tune, but the earliest appearance found by the writer is in E. O. Excell's *Triumphant Songs No. 3* (Chicago, 1892, No. 77), where it is given as "Arr. from Koschat" and set to Josiah Hopkins' "O Turn Ye, O Turn Ye."

The Lord will come and not be slow   126

John Milton, the great English poet of the seventeenth century, translated two of the Psalms, 114 and 136, from Hebrew into English when he was fifteen years old.   In 1648, greatly distressed by the Civil War, he made metrical translations of nine Psalms, 80-88.   All of these translations appear in his *Poems* (1673).   The hymn given here is, with one stanza omitted, a selection of stanzas which appeared in Garrett Horder's *Worship Song* (London, 1905) and in *The English Hymnal* (1906).   Stanza one is based on Psalm 85:13; stanza two, Psalm 85:11; stanza three, Psalm 82:8; and stanza four, Psalm 86:10.

ST. MAGNUS first appeared anonymously in Henry Playford's *The Divine Companion, or David's Harp New Tun'd,* second edition (London, 1707).   In this collection there is the note: "The three following tunes by Mr. Jer. Clarke." ST. MAGNUS is the fourth tune following this note which has raised some question about its authorship.   Nevertheless, Jeremiah Clarke is generally accepted as having written this tune.   William Riley, in his *Parochial Harmony* (London, 1762), first named this tune in honor of St. Magnus Church, built by Christopher Wren in 1676 and located on Lower Thames Street near London Bridge.

The Master hath come, and He calls us to follow   427

This hymn by Sarah Doudney appeared in the Sunday School Union's *Songs of Gladness* (London, 1871), with the heading, "Jesus and Mary of Bethany."   Miss Doudney was a prolific writer and contributor to magazines and periodicals of her day, and it is quite possible that this hymn appeared in such a publication prior to the above named collection.

ASH GROVE is a Welsh folk tune of secular origin. The tune name is from the original text which told of the lovers who strolled in the grove of Ash trees.

The morning light is breaking 448

Samuel Francis Smith wrote this hymn in 1832, during his senior year at Andover Theological Seminary. At the time he was preparing to be a foreign missionary. He had become greatly interested in the work of Adoniram Judson in Burma. As this surge of missionary zeal stirred within him, reports came from Judson that after long anguish and discouragement, the light was breaking and multitudes were accepting Christ as Saviour. Smith was jubilant with this exciting news and during this experience penned this vibrant missionary hymn. It was first published in *Spiritual Songs for Social Worship,* compiled by Lowell Mason and Thomas Hastings (Boston, 1832), and was later included in *The Psalmist* (1843), a hymnal compiled for Baptists by Smith and Baron Stow.

WEBB—*see* O Thou whose hand hath brought us.

"The Nail-scarred Hand"—*see* Have you failed in your plan of your storm-tossed life

"The Old Rugged Cross"—*see* On a hill far away stood an old rugged cross

The radiant morn hath passed away 32

Godfrey Thring wrote this hymn in 1864 and it was first published in his *Hymns* (1866) under the heading, "The Lord shall be thine Everlasting Light." Thring wrote that it

was composed as an "afternoon" hymn, as in most of the parishes in that part of Somersetshire in which I lived, the sacred service was nearly always held in the afternoon and not in the evening, whilst all the hymns in the hymnbooks in common use were for the late evening or night. I wrote "The radiant morn hath passed away" to supply this want.

It was included in the Appendix to *Hymns Ancient and Modern* (London, 1868, No. 274). The second stanza originally began "Our life is but a fading dawn," but was revised by the author when a friend wrote to him that the dawn does not fade but grows brighter.

THE RADIANT MORN was composed by Charles F. Gounod. The work from which it is taken and the identity of the person who made this adaptation remain unknown. The earliest appearance of the hymn tune the writer has found is in Tucker and Rousseau's *Hymnal Revised and Enlarged* (1894), where it is set to this text.

"The Rock That Is Higher than I"—*see* O sometimes the shadows are deep

"The Solid Rock"—*see* My hope is built on nothing less

The Son of God goes forth to war   414

Reginald Heber wrote this hymn for St. Stephen's Day, the day following Christmas. Stephen, the first Christian martyr (Acts 6:5 to 7:60), is referred to in the second stanza. The hymn of eight four-line stanzas first appeared in Heber's *Hymns Written and Adapted to the Weekly Church Service of the Year* (1827). The omitted quatrains (stanzas five and six of the original hymn) are:

> A glorious band, the chosen few,
>   On whom the Spirit came;
> Twelve valiant saints, their hope they knew,
>   And mocked the cross and flame.

> They met the tyrant's brandished steel,
>   The lion's gory mane;
> They bowed their necks the death to feel:
>   Who follows in their train?

ALL SAINTS, NEW was composed by Henry S. Cutler for this text and first appeared in J. Ireland Tucker's *Hymnal with Tunes Old and New* (New York, 1872, No. 176). The "new" was used in the tune name because other tunes had been named ALL SAINTS.

The spacious firmament on high   10

Joseph Addison's hymn was first published in *The Spectator* (London) in its issue of Saturday, August 23, 1712. Addison was the editor of this nonpolitical paper issued daily from March 1, 1711, to December 6, 1712, whose purpose it was to "bring philosophy out of the closets and libraries, schools and colleges, to dwell in the clubs and assemblies, at tea tables, and in coffee houses." The hymn appeared at the end of "An Essay on the Proper Means of Strengthening and Confirming Faith in the Mind of Man," and is based on Psalm 19:1-6, which is quoted in the essay.

CREATION is an adaptation from the chorus "The Heavens Are Telling," from Franz Joseph Haydn's oratorio *The Creation*. Haydn said, "Never was I so pious as when composing *The Creation*. I knelt every day and prayed God to strengthen me for my work." The identity of the person who made this adaptation is unknown, but it appears as early as 1845 in *The Choral,* compiled by B. F. Baker and I. B. Woodbury. The use of this melody as a hymn tune is rarely found outside the United States.

"The Star-Spangled Banner"—*see* Oh, say, can you see, by the dawn's early light

The strife is o'er, the battle done   107

This anonymous Latin hymn has been traced to the Jesuit *Symphonia Sirenum Selectarum* (Cologne, 1695). The translation by Francis Pott was made in 1859 and was first published in his *Hymns Fitted to the Order of Common Prayer* (1861).

VICTORY is an adaptation from the "Gloria Patri et Filio" of Giovanni P. da Palestrina's *Magnificat Tertii Toni* (1591), which William H. Monk made for the original musical edition of *Hymns Ancient and Modern* (1861, No. 114). In making this adaptation Monk used the first two phrases, repeated the first phrase and added original Alleluias for the beginning and the end. For this hymnal the committee changed the rhythm at the beginning of each of the three lines of the hymn in order that the accent of the tune might more nearly fit the spoken inflection of the text.

"The Unclouded Day"—*see* O they tell me of a home far beyond the skies

The voice that breathed o'er Eden   502

This hymn, dated July 12, 1857, was written by John Keble as a protest against the Divorce Act of 1857. First printed as a tract, it appeared the same year in the *Salisbury Hymn Book*.

BLAIRGOWRIE was composed by John B. Dykes for this hymn in February, 1872, for the wedding of a friend.

"The Way of the Cross Leads Home"—*see* I must needs go home by the way of the cross

The whole world was lost in the darkness of sin   88

D. W. Whittle in *Memoirs of Philip P. Bliss* (New York: A. S. Barnes & Co., 1877, p. 137), states:

"The Light of the World is Jesus" was written in the summer of 1875, at his home, No. 664 West Monroe Street, Chicago. It came to him all together, words and music, one morning while passing through the hall to his room, and was at once written out.

This hymn and tune by Philip P. Bliss first appeared in *The International Lessons Monthly* (1875). It is based on John 9:5, "I am the light of the world." It is found in *Gospel Hymns and Sacred Songs No. 1* (1875, p. 41).

The wise may bring their learning 513

This hymn appeared anonymously in *The Book of Praise for Children* (London, 1881).

ELLON was composed by George F. Root for Emily H. Miller's hymn "I love to hear the story which angel voices tell." It seems to have first appeared in L. H. Dowling's *The Crown of Sunday School Songs* (1871), where the tune is called ANGEL'S STORY.

There comes to my heart one sweet strain 299

Peter P. Bilhorn wrote this text as well as the tune, SWEET PEACE. It first appeared in *Crowning Glory,* compiled and published by Bilhorn (Chicago, 1888, No. 23).

There is a fountain filled with blood 92

This hymn by William Cowper is based on Zechariah 13:1, "In that day there shall be a fountain opened to the house of David and to the inhabitants of Jerusalem for sin and for uncleanness." It was probably written in 1771, and it first appeared in Conyer's *Collection of Psalms and Hymns* (1772) in seven four-line stanzas and was included in the *Olney Hymns* (1779). Cowper's original second stanza is

> The dying thief rejoiced to see
> That fountain in his day;
> And there have I, as vile as he,
> Washed all my sins away.

Various alterations have been made in the hymn. James Montgomery completely rewrote the first stanza because he felt that Cowper represented the fountain as being filled up instead of springing up. Julian feels that these alterations have "changed the whole meaning and character of the hymn, so far as Cowper was concerned. . . . the sustained confidence and rapture of Cowper are entirely lost." The omitted stanzas six and seven are:

Lord, I believe thou hast prepared,
  Unworthy though I be,
For me a blood-bought free reward,
  A golden harp for me.

'Tis strung and tuned for endless years,
  And formed by power divine,
To sound in God the Father's ears
  No other name but Thine.

In the hymnal, the two couplets of stanza five have been reversed. It is not known when this shifting of lines first occurred, nor the reason, if any. It may be found in this order in a number of compilations, including the *Broadman Hymnal* (1940). The original order of stanza five seems much more logical:

Then in a nobler, sweeter song
  I'll sing Thy power to save,
When this poor lisping, stammering tongue
  Lies silent in the grave.

CLEANSING FOUNTAIN is marked "Western Melody" or "Unknown" in most of the nineteenth-century American tune books. It is quite characteristic of the camp meeting songs of the early nineteenth century, and in all probability, crediting the arrangement to Lowell Mason is erroneous. Mason wrote a tune for this text in 1830 which is called COWPER, and there is some similarity. McCutchan suggests that Mason had probably heard CLEANSING FOUNTAIN before he wrote COWPER. In some collections this tune is noted as being "arranged *from* Mason."

There is a green hill far away   98

This is one of a series of hymns written by Cecil F. Alexander for her Sunday school and is based on a passage in the Apostle's Creed: "Suffered under Pontius Pilate, was crucified, dead, and buried." It first appeared in her *Hymns for Little Children* (1848, p. 31), in five four-line stanzas.

GREEN HILL was written by George C. Stebbins in 1878, and first appeared the same year in *Gospel Hymns No. 3*, edited by Ira D. Sankey, James McGranahan, and Stebbins. Stanza five was used for the text of the refrain.

There is a name I love to hear   131

Written by Frederick Whitfield, this hymn was first published in hymn sheets and leaflets in 1855 and appeared in Whitfield's *Sacred Poems*

The Palace.
Londonderry.

7 Sep^t
1891

There is a green hill far away
  Without a city wall
Where the dear Lord was crucified
  Who died to save us all.

We do not know, we cannot tell
  What pains He had to bear.
But we believe it was for us.
  He hung and suffered there.

There was none other good enough
  To pay the price of sin,
He only could unlock the gate
  Of Heaven, and let us in.

He died that we might be forgiven
  He died to make us good
That we might go at last to Heaven
  Saved by His precious blood.

O dearly dearly has He loved
  And we must love Him too
And trust in His redeeming blood
  And try His works to do. C. F. Alexander

HOLOGRAPH BELONGING TO MRS. J. W. STORER

and Prose (1861). The words of the refrain are not a part of the original text.

OH, HOW I LOVE JESUS is a tune of unknown origin. It is found in many nineteenth-century American collections with a variety of common meter hymns for the stanzas. Among those most frequently found are Newton's "Amazing grace! how sweet the sound," Watts's "Alas! and did my Saviour bleed," and the present text. All of these use the "Oh, how I love Jesus" text for the refrain. The tune has the simplicity and lilting style typical of the folklike camp meeting songs which emerged in America in the early nineteenth century.

There is a place of quiet rest 301

This hymn was written by Cleland B. McAfee in 1901 while he was pastor of the First Presbyterian Church of Chicago, Illinois. The death of his nephew had brought great sorrow to his heart, and in the midst of this tragedy he wrote these lines and composed this tune. It was sung the following Sunday in the communion service at his church. McAfee submitted the manuscript of this hymn to the Lorenz Publishing Company of Dayton, Ohio, and it first appeared in *The Choir Leader* (Oct., 1903).

MCAFEE is the name given this tune by the Hymnal Committee.

There is never a day so dreary 142

A number of years after these words and music were written Ernest O. Sellers, who composed the tune, wrote to Anna B. Russell, the author of the text, asking for the story of the writing of the hymn. Miss Russell replied that there was no information which she could give.

NEW ORLEANS was composed in 1921 while Dr. Sellers was teaching at the Baptist Bible Institute (now New Orleans Baptist Theological Seminary), New Orleans, Louisiana. Entitled "A Song in the Heart," it first appeared in *Hosanna in the Highest* compiled by Gipsy Smith and William McEwan (Brooklyn: Hosanna Publishing Co., n.d. [1921?], No. 7). A favorite hymn of evangelist Gipsy Smith, it was widely used in his evangelistic meetings.

NEW ORLEANS is the name given this tune by the Hymnal Committee for the city where Dr. Sellers taught for so many years.

"There Is Power in the Blood"—*see* Would you be free from the burden of sin

There is sunshine in my soul today 273

This hymn was written by Eliza E. Hewitt while she was teaching school in Philadelphia. One day as she was attempting to correct an incorrigible boy, he struck her across the back with a heavy slate, causing severe injury. She was placed in a heavy cast for six months. After the long confinement, her doctor permitted her to go for a short walk in nearby Fairmount Park on a warm spring day. With her heart overflowing with joy for her recovery, she returned home and wrote these lines.

SUNSHINE was composed by John R. Sweney for this text, and it first appeared in *Glad Hallelujahs,* edited by William J. Kirkpatrick and Sweney (Philadelphia: Thos. T. Tasker, Sr., 1887, No. 84). In its original form all stanzas began "There's" instead of "There is," and the first line of stanza three began, "There's springtime in my soul today." The tune was named by the Hymnal Committee.

There shall be showers of blessing 264

This text was written by the well-known American evangelist of the late nineteenth century, Major Daniel W. Whittle. The tune, SHOWERS OF BLESSING, was composed by James McGranahan, who served as music director for Major Whittle after the death of Bliss. This song first appeared in *Gospel Hymns No. 4* (1883).

There's a call comes ringing o'er the restless wave 457

Charles H. Gabriel wrote both words and music for this hymn in 1890, shortly after he had accepted the position of chorister at the Grace Methodist Episcopal Church, San Francisco, California. It was included in *Scripture Songs,* compiled and published by Gabriel (San Francisco, 1891, No. 203), with the inscription, "Written expressly for the Easter service of the Grace M. E. Sunday School, San Francisco, California." In *Sixty Years of Gospel Song,* Gabriel provides the following information:

It was here, at the urge of our Sunday school superintendent, that I wrote "Send the Light" for the occasion of his "golden offering" on Missionary Day. A field secretary of missions attended the service and carried the song east, where, through the singing of Chaplain McCabe, it immediately became popular.

It is possible that the Missionary Day mentioned in Gabriel's own account and the Easter service referred to in the inscription were the same. However, it is quite likely that they were not the same, and that the error in Gabriel's account is due to the fact that his account of this was written at least twenty-five years after the hymn first appeared.

The first publication seems to have been in *The Finest of the Wheat,* edited by George D. Elderkin (Chicago: R. R. McCabe and Company, 1890, No. 60).

In its original form, the refrain consisted of sixteen measures. In the first eight measures a new melodic line featuring a bass solo is used, and the final eight measures contain the refrain as it now is known. McCABE is the name given this tune by the Hymnal Committee.

There's a glad new song ringing in my heart   311

In 1954, W. Hines Sims discovered the manuscript of this hymn by Albert C. Fisher in the files of B. B. McKinney, his predecessor as secretary of the Church Music Department of the Baptist Sunday School Board. Apparently Fisher had submitted this manuscript to McKinney in the early 1940's. It was added to the hymnal by Dr. Sims shortly before publication.

REDEEMING LOVE is the name given this tune by the Hymnal Committee.

There's a land that is fairer than day   471

Sanford F. Bennett wrote this hymn shortly after the close of the Civil War, when he was a druggist in Elkhorn, Wisconsin. Joseph P. Webster, composer of the tune SWEET BY AND BY, was a music teacher in the same town. Bennett has given the following account of the writing of the hymn.

Mr. Webster, like many musicians, was of an exceedingly nervous and sensitive nature, and subject to periods of depression, in which he looked upon the dark side of all things in life. I had learned his peculiarities so well that on meeting him I could tell at a glance if he was melancholy, and had found that I could rouse him by giving him a new song to work on.

He came into my place of business, walked down to the stove, and turned his back on me without speaking. I was at my desk writing. Turning to him I said, "Webster, what is the matter now?" "It's no matter," he replied, "it will be all right by and by." The idea of the hymn came to me like a flash of sunlight, and I replied, "The Sweet By and By! Why would not that make a good hymn?" "Maybe it would," said he indifferently. Turning to my desk I penned the words of the hymn as fast as I could write. I handed the words to Webster. As he read his eyes kindled, and stepping to the desk he began writing the notes. Taking his violin, he played the melody and then jotted down the notes of the chorus. It was not over thirty minutes from the time I took my pen to write the words before two friends with Webster and myself were singing the hymn.

It first appeared in *The Signet Ring, a New Collection of Music and*

Hymns, Composed for Sabbath Schools, compiled by Webster (Chicago: Lyon & Healy, 1868, No. 90).

There's a light upon the mountains   124

This hymn by Henry Burton was written in 1910, and was first published in *The Hymnal of Praise* (London, 1913).

AUTUMN—*see* Mighty God, while angels bless Thee.

There's a royal banner given for display   408

In *Gospel Hymns No. 5* (1887) this hymn appears with the text credited to "El Nathan," a pseudonym frequently used by Daniel W. Whittle. It is based on Psalm 60:4, "Thou hast given a banner to them that fear thee, that it may be displayed because of the truth."

ROYAL BANNER was composed by James McGranahan for this text. The tune was named by the Hymnal Committee.

There's a song in the air   69

This hymn by Josiah G. Holland appeared as early as 1874 in W. T. Giffe's Sunday school collection, *The Brilliant* (p. 107), set to BETHLEHEM by Josiah Osgood. It later appeared in Holland's *Complete Poetical Writings* (1879). Its first hymnal inclusion was in the *Methodist Hymnal* (1905).

CHRISTMAS SONG was composed for these words by Karl P. Harrington in July, 1904, while the composer was vacationing at North Woodstock, New Hampshire. A letter from the composer's widow, Mrs. Jennie E. Harrington, to the writer dated October 29, 1954, gives a quotation from Harrington concerning the writing of this tune:

In the latter part of my father's life, he secured a new and larger cabinet organ for our home in Middletown, and gave me the original Estey organ, for which I had a sentimental fondness. This old instrument, in due time, found its resting-place in our cottage in the White Mountains, North Woodstock, New Hampshire. One day I sat down to it and played off an air to Holland's hymn.

The tune was selected by the Methodist Hymnal Commission, of which the composer was a member, for inclusion in the *Methodist Hymnal* (1905).

There's a wideness in God's mercy   48

This is a selection of stanzas from Frederick W. Faber's hymn, "Souls of men, why will ye scatter?" which first appeared in his *Hymns,* 1862. The present version makes use of stanzas 4, 6, 8, and 12.

WELLESLEY was composed by Lizzie S. Tourjee before her graduation from high school at Newton, Massachusetts. She had been asked to write a tune for the graduation hymn. It was first published in the *Hymnal of the Methodist Episcopal Church with Tunes* (1878). The composer's father, Dr. Eben Tourjee, founder of the New England Conservatory of Music, was one of the musical editors of this Methodist collection. The tune was named for Wellesley College.

There's within my heart a melody   307

Luther B. Bridgers, a Georgia Methodist preacher, wrote both words and music, presumably following the tragic loss of his wife and children who were burned to death in a house fire while he was conducting a revival in Kentucky. It first appeared in *The Revival No. 6,* compiled and published by Charlie D. Tillman (Atlanta, 1910, No. 21), one of seven songs by Bridgers in this collection, all bearing a 1910 copyright notice. Robert H. Coleman purchased the hymn from Bridgers in 1917 and first used it in his *Popular Hymnal* (1918, No. 181).

SWEETEST NAME is the name given this tune by the Hymnal Committee.

This is my Father's world   59

The three eight-line stanzas of this hymn are made up of six quatrains from a poem of sixteen stanzas by Maltbie D. Babcock, first published in *Thoughts for Every-Day Living,* (New York: Charles Scribner's Sons, 1901). The first line of each of the sixteen stanzas begins "This is my Father's world." Haeussler (*The Story of Our Hymns,* p. 117) says

Babcock brings us the message of God's presence, God's personality, God's power, and God's purpose, through this inspired bit of verse. It is thus not a mere outburst of song about nature, but a seasoned appreciation, beautifully worded, of unfailing trust in the ways and judgments of God.

TERRA PATRIS (the Father's Earth) composed by Franklin L. Sheppard, first appeared in his *Alleluia* (1915), a Presbyterian Sunday school songbook. Because he thought it to have been a tune unconsciously carried over from his childhood, Sheppard designated it as an "English melody." However, it is commonly accepted now as an original tune. Sheppard and Babcock were close friends for many years and from their friendship came this splendid text and tune.

This is the day the Lord hath made   39

This hymn by Isaac Watts is from his *Psalms of David Imitated in the Language of the New Testament* (1719). This is the last of four parts of Psalm 118 and has the heading "Hosanna: or, the Lord's Day."

ARLINGTON—*see* Am I a soldier of the cross.

This rite our blest Redeemer gave   384

This hymn by Sylvanus D. Phelps first appeared in *The Devotional Hymn Book* (1864) and was written while the author was pastor of the First Baptist Church, New Haven, Connecticut.

McCOMB was composed by W Hines Sims for this text for the hymnal. Concerning this tune, Dr. Sims has stated:

> I took this poem with me to a revival meeting in the First Baptist Church, McComb, Mississippi. Dr. Wyatt Hunter was the pastor and Dr. H. Leo Eddleman was the evangelist. The revival was held April 4-11, 1954. During the week I had opportunity for some work and made the music setting of the poem. I gave it the tune name McCOMB for the city where it was written.

Tho' the way we journey may be often drear   474

Lewis E. Jones wrote both words and music in 1906 while he was serving as general secretary of the YMCA in Fort Worth, Texas. The manuscript was sold to Charles H. Gabriel who included it in his *Praise and Service* (Philadelphia: American Baptist Publication Society, 1907, No. 93).

JONES is the name given this tune by the Hymnal Committee.

Tho' your sins be as scarlet   213

This text by Fanny J. Crosby with William H. Doane's tune first appeared in *Gospel Music,* compiled by Robert Lowry and Doane (New York: Biglow & Main, 1876, No. 44). In his *Memoirs and Reminiscences,* George C. Stebbins, explains that he discovered this song in this collection which had not come into popular usage (pp. 123-24):

> I was impressed with the possible usefulness of the song—if some slight changes were made—in my work. I found various repetitions that seemed unnecessary. These I eliminated and, without materially changing the author's theme, began singing it, as a duet, with Mrs. Stebbins. . . . Satisfying myself as to the usefulness of the hymn, as thus arranged, I submitted the changes to Dr. Doane, and he very cordially consented to its use in that form.

Stebbins' arrangement first appeared in *Gospel Hymns No. 5,* (1887), where it is arranged for soprano and tenor duet and quartet. The present four-part arrangement throughout was made for the hymnal.

CRIMSON is the name given this tune by the Hymnal Committee.

Privately printed by the author, Emily E. S. Elliott, for use by the choir and children of St. Mark's Church, Brighton, England, in 1864, this hymn is based on Luke 2:7, "Because there was no room for them in the inn." It was published in the *Church Missionary Juvenile Instructor* (1870), which Miss Elliott edited and in her *Chimes for Daily Service* (1880). The refrain for the final stanza was not in the original version, and its source is unknown.

MARGARET, sometimes called ELLIOTT, was composed for these words by Timothy R. Matthews and appeared in *Children's Hymns and Tunes* (London, 1876).

Thou hast said, exalted Jesus 390

John E. Giles was pastor of the Baptist church in Salter's Hall, London, in 1830, when he wrote this baptismal hymn. It was written during a time of serious illness, as he anticipated administering the ordinance of baptism upon his recovery. The hymn first appeared in the Baptist *Psalms and Hymns* (London, 1858), and the first line originally read, "Hast Thou said, exalted Jesus."

GREENVILLE is adapted from a pantomime (an instrumental number) in Jean J. Rousseau's opera *Le Devin du Village,* written in 1752, and first performed before the king of France at Fontainebleau, October 18, 1752. In 1733 a group of Italian "buffa" singers gave a performance of Pergolesi's *La Serva Perdrona* in Paris. This performance resulted in a bitter controversy in France between the intelligensia and the nationalistic elements concerning the superiority of French or Italian music. Rousseau, siding with the intelligensia in favor of Italian music, wrote this opera—both words and music—to support his argument of the inferiority of French music and the "unsingableness" of the French language.

J. B. Cramer arranged Rousseau's pantomime melody as a piano solo with variations and called it "Rousseau's Dream." It was published in London about 1818. The melody became well known in America in the early part of the nineteenth century and was published in sheet music for solo voice with accompaniment. The first appearance of the hymn tune seems to be in the *Handel and Haydn Collection of Church Music,* second edition (Boston, 1823), where it is called GREENVILLE. It also appeared in England in Thomas Walker's *Companion to Dr. Rippon's Tune-Book (ca. 1825)*. It is not known whether Cramer first named this tune "Rousseau's Dream," but among the oft-told unfounded stories of our hymnody is the legend that Rousseau dreamed of a visit to heaven where he heard the angels singing this tune.

Thou, my everlasting portion 354

In 1874 Silas J. Vail brought a tune to Fanny Crosby and asked her to provide a text for it. As he played it for her, she said that the melody of the refrain suggested to her the words "close to Thee." She immediately wrote the entire hymn. It first appeared in *Songs of Grace and Glory for Sunday Schools,* compiled by W. F. Sherwin and Vail (New York: Horace Waters & Son, 1874, No. 17). Later the hymn became the property of Biglow and Main, and was included in *Gospel Hymns No. 2* (1876).

Vail's tune CLOSE TO THEE takes its name from the refrain of the hymn.

Thou, O Christ of Calvary 189

The hymn and tune by James C. Moore appear for the first time in this hymnal. It was submitted to the Hymnal Committee and accepted for this collection.

MOORE was named by the Hymnal Committee for the author-composer.

Thou, whose almighty word 461

John Marriott wrote this hymn about 1813. Like his other hymns, it was never published by him during his lifetime. A few of his hymns appeared in print, but without his permission. Based on Genesis 1:3, this hymn originally began "Thou, whose eternal word" and consisted of four seven-line stanzas. It was quoted by Thomas Mortimer at a meeting of the London Missionary Society in Great Queen Street Chapel, London, May 12, 1825, six weeks after the author's death and was printed with a digest of Mortimer's speech in the *Evangelical Magazine* (June, 1825, p. 262). It was printed again in *The Friendly Visitor* (July, 1825), unsigned and entitled "Missionary Hymn."

ITALIAN HYMN (TRINITY)—*see* Come, Thou Almighty King.

Though . . .—*see* Tho' . . .

Throw out the lifeline across the dark wave 217

Edward S. Ufford wrote this hymn and tune in 1886 while he was pastor of the Baptist church in Westwood, Massachusetts, a small community near Boston. He frequently visited Nantucket Beach, a particularly treacherous coastal area, where many ships had been dashed to pieces on the rocks. Here was located a lifesaving station, which had a Lyle gun to shoot out a lifeline to ships in peril. In the author's *Lily of the Valley* (1895) the following information is given.

A friend of mine portrayed for me a scene on that famous beach, where afterwards I saw eight vessels cast ashore, which laid the basis of my song. An account of it was published in the Boston *Globe*. A schooner was thrown by the raging element on the coast there, where it lay exposed to the cutting wind and icy waves, all the while bumping and dragging itself along, threatening to go to pieces every minute. Soon the wreckers appeared, joined by willing hands. There through the breakers they could see the large schooner with two chain cables out. In the rigging were the crew of eight men and one woman, holding on for their lives, as the huge waves broke over them amid the blinding snow and fearful gale. Now came the life-line, which was shot out toward the vessel, but the distance was too great. Shot after shot was fired, but the rope of silk fell too short of the doomed craft. At last a shot was fired which went over the vessel, and with loud cheers those on shore began to make preparation to haul the shipwrecked men in. It was a perilous undertaking, but it was successfully accomplished.

In the autumn of 1887, George C. Stebbins was assisting Dr. George F. Pentecost in a series of meetings in Lawrence, Massachusetts, and during this time Ufford showed his hymn to Stebbins. Its value was apparent to Stebbins, for he purchased the manuscript, reharmonized the tune, and first published it in *The Male Chorus,* compiled by Ira D. Sankey and Stebbins (1888), where it was arranged for men's voices. The first appearance for congregational singing was in *Winnowed Songs for the Sunday School*, compiled by Sankey (1890, No. 130). The following year it appeared in *Gospel Hymns No. 6.*

LIFELINE is the name given this tune by the Hymnal Committee.

Thy Word is a lamp to my feet   180

This hymn, written in 1908 by Ernest O. Sellers, is a paraphrase of portions of Psalm 119. Stanza one is based on verse 105, stanza two on verses 89 and 90, stanza three on verses 164, 62, and 57, and the refrain on verse 11. The first appearance seems to have been in *The Ideal Song and Hymn Book,* compiled by D. B. Towner (New York: Fleming H. Revell Co., 1909, No. 54).

EOLA was composed by Sellers for this text in 1908. The tune was named by the Hymnal Committee for Eola, Louisiana, where Dr. Sellers spent the last years of his life.

Thy Word is like a garden, Lord **182**

Written by Edwin Hodder, this hymn first appeared in his *New Sunday School Hymn Book* (1863), entitled "Holy Scripture" and consisting of seven four-line stanzas. The present version is made up of stanzas one, two, three, and six of the original.

CLONMEL is an Irish folk song known as "The Flight of the Earls." The melody first appeared as a hymn tune in the *Church and School Hymnals* (London, 1926). This arrangement by William J. Reynolds appeared as a unison anthem for children in *The Church Musician* (Mar., 1952, pp. 18-19). In *Congregational Praise* (London, 1951) Eric H. Thiman, the musical editor, named the tune CLONMEL for a small town in Ireland.

'Tis midnight and on Olive's brow **104**

William B. Tappan's hymn first appeared in his *Poems* (Philadelphia, 1822), entitled "Gethsemane."

OLIVE'S BROW was written for this hymn by William B. Bradbury and was first published in *The Shawm* (New York, 1853, p. 94), compiled by Bradbury and George F. Root. The name of the tune is from the first line of the hymn.

'Tis so sweet to trust in Jesus **258**

This hymn was written by Louisa M. R. Stead, but the date it was written is not known. Ernest K. Emurian, in *Famous Stories of Inspiring Hymns,* states that the hymn was written in 1890 a few months after the tragic death of Mr. Stead. This seems to be in error, for Mrs. Stead was widowed when she went to South Africa as a missionary in 1880, and this hymn with this tune was copyrighted and published by the composer in 1882. Nevertheless, Mr. Stead's death occurred during or before 1880, and it is altogether possible that this hymn was written out of this experience of sorrow, but no definite evidence has been found to support this hypothesis. In a short time the hymn became widely used and loved. After the author's death in Southern Rhodesia in 1917, E. H. Greeley, a fellow missionary, wrote:

We miss her very much, but her influence goes on as our five thousand native Christians continually sing:

> Zwakanaka kuda Yesu,
> Ku mu kudza iye wo,
> Ku zorora ne ku fara,
> Ne ku ziwa iye zwe.

(Chorus)
Yesu, Yesu, ndino imba
Iye ano ndida wo,
Yesu, Yesu, wakanaka,
Une nyasha hur wo.

TRUST IN JESUS was composed by William J. Kirkpatrick for this text, and it first appeared in *Songs of Triumph,* compiled by John R. Sweney and Kirkpatrick (Philadelphia: Thos. T. Tasker, Sr., Publisher, 1882, No. 46).

'Tis the blessed hour of prayer, when our hearts lowly bend   329

This is another of the many hymns which resulted from the collaboration of Fanny J. Crosby and William H. Doane. It first appeared in *Good as Gold,* a Sunday school collection compiled by Robert Lowry and Doane (New York: Biglow & Main, 1880). The tune was named BLESSED HOUR by the Hymnal Committee.

'Tis the grandest theme thro' the ages rung   198

This gospel song, words and music by William A. Ogden, first appeared in E. O. Excell's *Triumphant Songs for Sunday Schools and Gospel Meetings* (Chicago and New York, 1887, No. 64).

To God be the glory, great things He hath done   41

Fanny J. Crosby wrote the words and the tune was composed by William H. Doane. It was one of the new gospel songs which made their first appearance in a Sunday school collection, *Brightest and Best* (1875), compiled by Doane and Robert Lowry. Among the other songs which made their initial appearance in this collection were "All the way my Saviour leads me," "I am Thine, O Lord," "Saviour, more than life to me," and "Christ Arose." These four songs were included in the popular *Gospel Hymns* series and have been among the most widely known gospel songs to the present day. It seems strange that "To God Be the Glory" was not included in the six volumes of *Gospel Hymns,* and this omission no doubt accounts for its being totally unknown in America until recently. Ira D. Sankey (*q.v.*) included it in his *Sacred Songs and Solos* which was published in England and is still in use today.

Cliff Barrows, music director of the Billy Graham Crusade team, has provided the writer with the following information:

I first heard the hymn during one of our early visits to England around 1952. Then in compiling our song book for the Harringay Crusade it was suggested by Rev. Frank Colquhoun that it be included in our *Greater*

London Crusade Song Book. This was done, and from the very outset of the meetings in Harringay, it became one of the favorites and was used almost every night during the last month of those meetings. Upon our return to the states, I began looking through some of the old hymn books and saw that it had been included several years ago in those earlier publications but had been omitted in recent hymnals. We began using it right away in our crusades here and found that people loved to sing it, as well as they did in London. I believe the first crusade we used this hymn in America upon our return was in Nashville in 1954. This was the first crusade upon our return from the meetings at Harringay.

It is most extraordinary that this long forgotten American gospel song should have been imported from England and become immensely popular during the last decade. An examination of Fanny J. Crosby's text reveals an expression of objectivity not usually found in gospel hymnody. Here is a straight-forward voicing of praise to God, not simply personal testimony nor sharing some subjective aspect of Christian experience.

To Him who hallows all our days 499

This hymn by John L. Rosser was written for the dedication of the new building of the First Baptist Church, Selma, Alabama, while the author was pastor. After going to his room following an evening service, he wrote these stanzas, and they were first sung at the dedicatory service.

ELLACOMBE first appeared in the *Gesangbuch der Herzoglichen Wirtembergischen Katholischen Hofkapelle* (1784). Its first appearance in England was in the 1868 appendix to *Hymns Ancient and Modern.* The tune is named for a village in Devonshire, England.

To the work! to the work! we are servants of God 435

Fanny J. Crosby wrote this text in 1869, and two years later William H. Doane composed the tune. It was first published in Doane's *Pure Gold* (1871), with the heading "Home Missions" and was included in Bliss and Sankey's *Gospel Hymns and Sacred Songs* (1875).

TOILING ON is the name given this tune by the Hymnal Committee.

Trials dark on every hand 473

Charles A. Tindley, distinguished Negro Methodist pastor in Philadelphia, wrote both words and the tune BY AND BY. The present version with slight alterations in both text and harmonization was made by B. B. McKinney for inclusion in *The Broadman Hymnal* (1940).

Truehearted, wholehearted, faithful, and loyal

Frances R. Havergal wrote this hymn at Ormont Dessous, Switzerland, September, 1874, while touring with a group of friends. During this trip a great deal of her time was devoted to her writing. In one of her "circular" letters to her family she lists " 'True Hearted!' New Year's Address (in verse) for Y.W.C.A. for January 1875," among a number of things she had recently written. The hymn consisted of ten four-line stanzas, and the present version is made up of stanzas one, two, and four, with stanza ten being the refrain. The fourth stanza originally began: "Wholehearted! Saviour, beloved and glorious." The hymn was first published in Miss Havergal's *Loyal Responses* (1878).

TRUEHEARTED was composed by George C. Stebbins for this text during a revival meeting in New Haven, Connecticut. It first appeared as a four-part song for men's voices in *The Male Chorus,* compiled by Ira D. Sankey and Stebbins (New York and Chicago: Biglow & Main, 1888, No. 16). Stebbins rearranged the tune for mixed voices and in this form it first appeared in *Winnowed Songs for Sunday School* (1890, No. 30). The following year it was included in *Gospel Hymns No. 6.*

"Trust and Obey"—*see* When we walk with the Lord

"Trust, Try and Prove Me"—*see* Bring ye all the tithes into the store-house

"Trusting Jesus"—*see* Simply trusting every day

Up Calvary's mountain one dreadful morn **106**

While listening to a sermon on the subject "Our Blessed Redeemer," Harry Dixon Loes was inspired to write this tune. He sent the music and the suggested title to Avis Burgeson Christiansen, a friend of many years and a capable writer of song poems. Mrs. Christiansen wrote the three stanzas and the refrain as they now stand. The hymn first appeared in *Songs of Redemption* (No. 117), compiled by W. Plunkett Martin and James W. Jelks, published by the Baptist Home Mission Board, Atlanta, Georgia, with the notice, "Copyright 1920, Martin and Jelks."

REDEEMER is the name suggested by the composer to the Hymnal Committee and appears for the first time in this hymnal.

Walk in the light! so shalt thou know **370**

This hymn by Bernard Barton first appeared in his *Devotional Verses* (London, 1826). It is based on 1 John 1:7, "But if we walk in the light, as he is in the light, we have fellowship one with another, and the blood of Jesus Christ his Son cleanseth us from all sin.

MANOAH appeared in the *Collection of Church Music* (1851), compiled by Henry W. Greatorex, but there is no information in the Tune Index of this collection that sheds any light regarding the composer, arranger, or source of the tune. Manoah was the name of Samson's father.

Watchman! tell us of the night   462

Written as a dialogue between the "watchman" and the "traveler," this hymn first appeared in John Bowring's *Hymns* (1825), in three eight-line stanzas. The conversational style reflects the author's travels and experiences in the service of the British Colonial government. The hymn may be sung antiphonally with great effectiveness.

ST. GEORGE'S, WINDSOR—*see* Come, ye thankful people, come.

We are living, we are dwelling   421

Grave concern over national affairs prompted the writing of this poem by A. Cleveland Coxe, when he was twenty-two years of age. It first appeared in his *Athanasion* (1840). It is interesting to compare this hymn with Lowell's "Once to every man and nation" (418), which was written five years later.

AUSTRIAN HYMN—*see* Word of God, across the ages.

We gather together to ask the Lord's blessing   492

This anonymous Dutch hymn and tune were written late in the sixteenth century celebrating the country's freedom from Spain. They first appeared in Adrianus Valerius' *Nederlandtsche Gedenckclanck* (1626 edition), which was published in Haarlem one year after his death. From this collection, Edward Kremser, a Vienna musician, published six songs entitled, *Sechs Altniederländische Volkslieder* (1877), one of which was this text with this tune. An American edition of Kremser's work was published by Wm. Rohlfing & Sons (Milwaukee, 1895). Theodore Baker's English translation was made in 1894.

KREMSER takes its name from the musician whose publication of the tune and the hymn recovered them for modern use.

We give Thee but Thine own   402, 535

William W. How wrote this hymn in 1858, and it was first published in How and Morrell's *Psalms and Hymns,* second edition (1864).

ST. ANDREW was composed by Joseph Barnby in 1866 for Monsell's hymn, "Sweet is Thy mercy, Lord," while the composer was organist at St. Andrew's Church, London, and was published unnamed in Barnby's *Hymn Tunes* (London, 1869). It is named ST. ANDREW in his posthumous *Hymn Tunes* (1897).

We have heard the joyful sound 191

Priscilla J. Owens wrote this hymn for a Sunday school mission anniversary in Baltimore. It was adapted to the chorus of "Vive le Roi" in Meyerbeer's opera, *Les Huguenots.*

JESUS SAVES was composed by William J. Kirkpatrick for this text, and it first appeared in *Songs of Redeeming Love*, edited by John R. Sweney, C. C. McCabe, T. C. O'Kane, and Kirkpatrick (Philadelphia, 1882).

We plow the fields and scatter 493

This hymn is the "Peasants' Song" from *Paul Erdmanns Fest,* a descriptive account of a harvest festival in a farmhouse in northern Germany written by Matthias Claudius and published in 1782. The "Peasants' Song" was in seventeen four-line stanzas with a refrain. Jane M. Campbell's translation, first published in C. S. Bere's *Garland of Songs, or an English Liederkranz* (London, 1861), is based on stanzas three, five, seven, nine, ten, and thirteen of the original.

ST. ANSELM was composed by Joseph Barnby in 1868, and first appeared in his *Original Tunes* (London, 1869), set to "O day of rest and gladness."

We praise Thee, O God! for the Son of Thy love 205

William P. Mackay wrote this hymn in 1863, and revised it four years later. In 1875, it was included in Bliss and Sankey's *Gospel Hymns and Sacred Songs* (No. 25) with the heading, "O Lord, revive Thy work" (Hab. 3:2). Originally consisting of five stanzas and refrain, the omitted stanza four is:

> All glory and praise to the God of all grace,
> Who has brought us; and sought us, and guided our ways.

REVIVE US AGAIN, composed by John J. Husband, appeared early in the nineteenth century, and seems to have been first used with some other text. In *Gospel Hymns and Sacred Songs* (1875) it appears as Number 24, set to Bonar's "Rejoice and be glad!" Mackay's text is given below as an alternate text. In later collections Bonar's hymn was discarded and Mackay's hymn became inseparably wedded to this tune.

This hymn was written by Julia Cady Cory when J. Archer Gibson, organist of the Brick Presbyterian Church, New York, expressed a desire for a new text for the tune KREMSER. In a letter to the writer. dated October 21, 1954, Mrs. Cory states that the hymn

was written in 1902, soon after I was out of school. My family then attended the Brick Presbyterian Church, New York City, and the organist came to me, asking for a hymn to the old tune, KREMSER, for Thanksgiving use. I struggled along for two weeks and finally produced what we have today.

The hymn was first sung at Thanksgiving, 1902, at two New York City churches—Brick Presbyterian Church and the Church of the Convenant. A month later the author's father, J. Cleveland Cady, wished to use this hymn at the annual Christmas service at the Church of the Covenant. For the occasion the author added the following Christmas stanza which is not generally known.

> Thy love Thou didst show us, Thine only Son sending,
> 　Who came as a babe and whose bed was a stall,
> His blest life He gave us and then died to save us;
> 　We praise Thee, O Lord, for Thy gift to us all.

While this hymn was written as a substitute for "We gather together to ask the Lord's blessing" (492), it is not another translation or version of the Dutch original, as indicated in at least one hymnal companion.

KREMSER is a Dutch folk song which appeared in *Nederlandtsch Gedenckclanck,* edited by Adrian Valerius, and published in Haarlem in 1626, one year after his death. This collection of Dutch folk songs remained virtually unnoticed until it was discovered by Edward Kremser, a musician living in Vienna. He published six tunes from this collection in his *Sechs Altniederländische Volkslieder* (Leipzig, 1877), including KREMSER, used with a German translation of the Dutch text, "We gather together to ask the Lord's blessing."

"We Shall See the King Someday"—*see* Tho' the way we journey may be often drear

We would see Jesus, for the shadows lengthen　　　　　**324**

This hymn by Anna B. Warner, based on John 12:20-23, first appeared in a novel, *Dollars and Cents* (1852), by Amy Lathrop, a pseudonym of Miss Warner. Its first hymnal inclusion was in Miss Warner's *Hymns of the Church Militant* and Thomas Hastings' *Church Melodies,* both published in 1858. Originally consisting of six stanzas, the omitted stanzas three and four are:

> We would see Jesus: other lights are paling,
>> Which for long years we have rejoiced to see;
> The blessings of our pilgrimage are failing;
>> We would not mourn them, for we go to Thee.

> We would see Jesus: yet the spirit lingers
>> Round the dear objects it has loved so long,
> And earth from earth can scarce unclose its fingers;
>> Our love to Thee makes not this love less strong.

CONSOLATION—*see* Still, still with thee, when purple morning breaketh.

We would see Jesus; lo! His star is shining 89

In a letter to the writer dated October 14, 1954, the author of this hymn, J. Edgar Park, stated that it was "written in 1913 in connection with two books I had published at that time on the Sermon on the Mount. This hymn was an attempt to capture the youthful enthusiasm for Jesus as contrasted with the more usual middle-aged nostalgia usually represented in hymns." The first appearance of the hymn was in *Worship and Song* (Boston: Pilgrim Press, 1921).

CUSHMAN, composed by Herbert B. Turner, first appeared in *Hymns and Tunes for Schools* (Hampton, Va.: 1907), for which the composer served as editor. He wrote this tune for Anna B. Warner's hymn, "We would see Jesus, for the shadows lengthen."

Welcome, delightful morn 21

This hymn first appeared in John Dobell's *A New Selection of Seven Hundred Evangelical Hymns for Private, Family, and Public Worship* (London, 1806, No. 548) with the heading, "Sunday Morning." The hymn was signed "Hayward," but the identity of the author has never been discovered. The first American collection to include this hymn seems to have been N. S. S. Beman's *Sacred Lyrics* (Troy, N. Y., 1841), a hymnal for Presbyterian churches.

LISCHER is an arrangement by Lowell Mason of a tune by Friedrich Schneider, and it first appeared in Mason's *Carmina Sacra: or Boston Collection of Church Music* (1841, No. 186).

This hymn is a paraphrase of "Salve Festa dies," written near the end of the sixth century by Venantius Fortunatus. John Ellerton's translation first appeared in Brown-Borthwick's *Supplemental Hymn and Tune Book* (London, 1868), in six stanzas, with the first stanza used as a refrain.

HERMAS was written by Frances R. Havergal for her children's hymn, "Golden harps are sounding," and was first published in *Havergal's Psalmody* (London, 1871). In the preface of this collection Miss Havergal states the reasons for the selection of the tune names found in the book. The tune is named for Hermas, the friend of Paul (Rom. 16:14).

"We'll Work till Jesus Comes"—*see* O land of rest, for thee I sigh

"We're Marching to Zion"—*see* Come, we that love the Lord

We've a story to tell to the nations **455**

This hymn—words and music—was written by H. Ernest Nichol in 1896, and published the same year in *The Sunday School Hymnary* (London). Many early collections credit this tune, MESSAGE, to "Colin Sterne," a pseudonym used by Nichol for many of his hymn tunes. It is a "made up" name, a rearrangement of the letters of his middle and last names.

What a fellowship, what a joy divine **371**

Haldor Lillenas, in *Modern Gospel Song Stories,* states that prior to the writing of this hymn, A. J. Showalter had received letters from two friends, both of whom had lost their wives. In an effort to express his heartfelt sympathy, he wrote to them, quoting the Scripture passage, "The eternal God is thy refuge, and underneath are the everlasting arms." As he pondered these words, he was impressed that they would make the basis for a song. He wrote the music and the words of the refrain, and asked his friend, Elisha A. Hoffman, to provide appropriate stanzas.

This hymn, words and music, first appeared in *The Glad Evangel for Revival, Camp, and Evangelistic Meetings,* compiled by Showalter, L. M. Evilsizer, and S. J. Perry (Dalton, Ga.: A. J. Showalter & Co., 1887, No. 1).

What a friend we have in Jesus **328**

Joseph Scriven, who lived near Port Hope, Ontario, wrote this hymn in 1855 to comfort his mother in a time of sorrow. A friend visiting Scriven when he was ill, saw the manuscript of the poem, and Scriven admitted having written it. To another friend Scriven once explained that "the Lord and I did it between us." Its first appearance seems to have been in Horace L. Hastings' *Social Hymns, Original and Selected* (Boston, 1865), where it appeared unsigned.

CONVERSE, sometimes called ERIE, was composed by Charles C. Converse in 1868 and first appeared in *Silver Wings,* compiled by Karl Reden, Converse's pseudonym (Boston, Oliver Ditson, 1870, No. 98), where the tune is credited to Reden. Ira D. Sankey, in *My Life and the Story of the Gospel Hymns,* tells how this hymn first came to his attention.

Returning from England in 1875, I soon became associated with P. P. Bliss in the publication of what later became known as "Gospel Hymns No. 1." After we had given the completed compilation to our publishers I chanced to pick up a small paper-covered pamphlet of Sunday-school hymns, published in Richmond, Virginia. I discovered this and sang it through, and determined to have it appear in "Gospel Hymns." As the composer of the music was my friend, C. C. Converse, I withdrew from the collection one of his compositions and substituted for it, "What a Friend We Have in Jesus." Thus the last hymn that went into the book became one of the first in favor.

What a wonderful change in my life has been wrought 310

Rufus H. McDaniel wrote the words in 1914 as an expression of his own faith following the untimely death of his son.

McDANIEL was composed the same year by Charles H. Gabriel and was first introduced in pamphlet form by Gabriel and Homer Rodeheaver in the Billy Sunday campaign in Philadelphia in 1915. Rodeheaver purchased the manuscript and published it in his *Songs for Service* (Chicago, 1915, No. 3). The tune was named by the Hymnal Committee.

"What a Wonderful Saviour"—*see* Christ has for sin atonement made

What can I give to Jesus 508

This anonymous hymn appears in E. Thompson Baird's *Hymns of the Voice of Praise* (Richmond, 1872, No. 96). The text was altered considerably by Loren R. Williams.

DEDICATION is an adaptation of a melody from Alfred R. Gaul's cantata *The Holy City.* This adaptation with the present version of the text was made by Loren R. Williams and first appeared as a unison anthem in *The Church Musician* (June, 1954). At the request of the Hymnal Committee it was adapted as a hymn tune for the hymnal.

What can wash away my sin 204

Robert Lowry wrote both words and music of this hymn, and it was first published in *Gospel Music,* compiled by William H. Doane and Lowry (New York: Biglow & Main, 1876, No. 7), with the reference, "Without the shedding of blood there is no remission of sin" (Heb. 9:22). Originally consisting of six stanzas, the omitted stanzas five and six are:

> Now by this I'll overcome—
> Nothing but the blood of Jesus,
> Now by this I'll reach my home—
> Nothing but the blood of Jesus.

> Glory! Glory! this I sing—
> Nothing but the blood of Jesus,
> All my praise for this I bring—
> Nothing but the blood of Jesus.

PLAINFIELD is the name given this tune by the Hymnal Committee. Lowry became pastor of the Park Avenue Baptist Church, Plainfield, New Jersey, in 1875. He resigned in 1885 because of ill health and made his home in Plainfield until his death in 1899.

"What If It Were Today"—*see* Jesus is coming to earth again

When all of my labors and trials are o'er 485

Charles H. Gabriel was inspired to write both words and music of this hymn by Ed Card, superintendent of the Sunshine Rescue Mission, St. Louis, Missouri, who was known as "Old Glory Face." His radiant personality and his frequent use of the jubilant expression "Glory" made him an inspiration to all who knew him. His fervent, earnest, prayers always ended with "and that will be glory for me." Gabriel's hymn first appeared in *Make His Praise Glorious,* compiled and published by E. O. Excell (Chicago, 1900, No. 54).

GLORY SONG, the name given this tune, is the name by which this hymn has been affectionately known.

This hymn by Isaac Watts first appeared in his *Hymns and Spiritual Songs* (1707), in four four-line stanzas, with the heading, "The Hopes of Heaven our Support under Trials on Earth." William Cowper refers to the opening lines in his poem "Truth" 1782), when he contrasts the hope of Voltaire with that of the poor and believing cottager, who

> Just knows, and knows no more, her Bible true—
> A truth the brilliant Frenchman never knew:
> And in that charter reads with sparkling eyes,
> Her title to a treasure in the skies.

PISGAH appeared in Ananias Davisson's *Kentucky Harmony* (1817), credited to J. C. Lowry. It also appeared in Alexander Johnson's *Tennessee Harmony* (*ca.* 1819), where it is called CHRISTIAN TRIUMPH and in the index is credited to Johnson. The first eight measures of this melody appear as a separate tune in the Presbyterian *Hymnbook* (1955), where it is called COVENANTERS. PISGAH is quite typical of the religio-folk tunes which appeared in the South in the early nineteenth century. To hear this tune sung by the "fasola" syllables at a *"Sacred Harp* singing" is an exciting experience.

When I survey the wondrous cross **99**

Considered by many to be the finest English hymn, this hymn by Isaac Watts first appeared in his *Hymns and Spiritual Songs* (1707). It is based on Galatians 6:14 and was entitled "Crucifixion to the World, by the Cross of Christ." The first two lines of the original first stanza were

> When I survey the wondrous cross
> Where the young Prince of Glory died.

In 1709 an enlarged edition of the above collection was published in which Watts altered the first stanza as we now have it. There were five stanzas in the original hymn, the fourth was bracketed by Watts indicating that it could be omitted. The four stanza form of this hymn first appeared in George Whitefield's 1757 supplement to his *Collection of Hymns,* and has been most used since that time. The omitted stanza is

> His dying crimson, like a robe,
> Spreads o'er his body on the tree;
> Then I am dead to all the globe,
> And all the globe is dead to me.

HAMBURG was written by Lowell Mason in 1824 while he was living in Savannah, Georgia, and was first sung in the First Presbyterian Church in that city. It first appeared in *The Boston Handel & Haydn Society Collection of Church Music,* third edition (1825). In this collection Mason indicated that it was arranged from a Gregorian chant.

When Jesus comes to reward His servants 119

This song of the second coming of Christ first appeared in *Gospel Music* (1876), entitled "Watching." Fanny J. Crosby wrote the hymn and William H. Doane composed the tune.

WOODSTOCK, the name given this tune by the Hymnal Committee, is for Woodstock Academy, a Congregational school which Doane attended as a teen-age boy. His Christian experience of conversion occurred during his final year at this school.

When morning gilds the skies 23

The German hymn "Beim frühen Morgenlicht" is anonymous. Various versions have been found in the *Katholiches Gesangbuch* (Würzburg, 1828) and *Fränkische Volkslieder* (Leipzig, 1855), as well as other collections. Edward Caswall's translation first appeared in Formby's *Catholic Hymns* (London, 1854). In Caswall's *Masque of Mary,* eight additional stanzas were added. It is a hymn of joyous praise to Jesus Christ.

LAUDES DOMINI was composed by Joseph Barnby for this hymn when it appeared in the Appendix to *Hymns Ancient and Modern* (London, 1868, No. 314).

When my life work is ended, and I cross the swelling tide 472

This hymn—words by Fanny J. Crosby and tune by John Sweney—first appeared in *Songs of Love and Praise,* compiled by Sweney, W. J. Kirkpatrick, and Henry L. Gilmour (Philadelphia: John J. Hood, 1894, No. 128).

I SHALL KNOW HIM is the name given this tune by the Hymnal Committee.

When peace, like a river, attendeth my way 265

Horatio G. Spafford, the author of this hymn, was a successful Chicago lawyer who enjoyed a close friendship with Moody, Sankey, Pentecost, Bliss, and numerous other evangelistic leaders of his day. In 1873, upon the advice of the family physician, for the benefit of his wife's health, he planned a European trip for his family. Due to unexpected last minute business developments, he had to remain in Chicago, but sent his wife and four daughters on ahead as scheduled on the S.S. *Ville du Havre* in November, 1873. He expected to follow in a few days. On November 22, the *Ville du Havre* was struck by the *Lochearn,* an English ship, and twelve minutes later it sank. Mrs. Spafford was saved, but her daughters perished. On December 1, the survivors were landed at Cardiff, Wales, and Mrs. Spafford cabled her husband "Saved alone." Shortly afterward, Spafford left by ship to meet his wife, and on the high seas near the scene of the tragedy wrote this hymn. The details of this experience, as well as the account of this extraordinary family, are related by Spafford's daughter, Bertha Spafford Vester, in her book, *Our Jerusalem* (1950).

VILLE DU HAVRE was composed for this text by Philip P. Bliss and it first appeared in *Gospel Hymns No. 2* (1876, No. 76), compiled by Ira D. Sankey and Bliss.

"When the Morning Comes"—*see* Trials dark on every hand

"When the Roll Is Called up Yonder"—*see* When the trumpet of the Lord shall sound, and time shall be no more

When the sun shines bright and your heart is light   214

This hymn, both words and music by Isham E. Reynolds, first appeared in Robert H. Coleman's *The Popular Hymnal* (Dallas, Tex., 1918, No. 213). At the time Coleman was compiling this book, he examined several new songs recently composed by Reynolds. This song was among the group. Reynolds did not feel that it had particular merit, but it attracted the attention of Coleman. He purchased it and included it in his forthcoming collection.

LURA is the name given this tune by the Hymnal Committee for Lura Hawk Reynolds, wife of the composer.

When the trumpet of the Lord shall sound, and time shall be no more   482

James M. Black, who wrote both words and music of this hymn, was a songbook compiler of considerable reputation and was appointed on the Joint Commission for the *Methodist Hymnal* of 1905. His account of the writing of this hymn, as given by Ira D. Sankey in *My Life and the Story of the Gospel Hymns,* is as follows:

While a teacher in a Sunday-school and president of a young people's society, I one day met a girl, fourteen years, poorly clad and the child of

228

a drunkard. She accepted my invitation to attend the Sunday-school, and joined the young people's society. One evening at a consecration meeting, when members answered the roll call by repeating Scripture texts, she failed to respond. I spoke of what a sad thing it would be, when our names are called from the Lamb's Book of Life, if one of us should be absent; and I said, "O God, when my own name is called up yonder, may I be there to respond!" I longed for something suitable to sing just then, but I could find nothing in the books. We closed the meeting, and on my way home I was still wishing that there might be a song that could be sung on such occasions. The thought came to me, "Why don't you make it?" I dismissed the idea, thinking that I could never write such a hymn. When I reached my house my wife saw that I was deeply troubled, and questioned me, but I made no reply. Then the words of the first stanza came to me in full. In fifteen minutes more I had composed the other two verses. Going to the piano, I played the music just as it is found today in the hymn-books, note for note, and I have never dared to change a single word or a note of the piece since.

In a letter written from Williamsport, Pennsylvania, January 7, 1913, to Robert H. Coleman, granting permission for $20.00 to use the hymn in Coleman's *World Evangel,* Black says:

Everybody else are raising the prices of their great songs and why should not I? It is the common consent of all people everywhere that "When the Roll Is Called Up Yonder" is the greatest song that has been written for the last twenty-five years. I am of that opinion myself. It goes into more books than any other one gospel song in the English language. That tells the story. Hereafter the price of that song shall be $25.00. Do you blame me?

The hymn was written in 1893 and first appeared in *Songs of the Soul,* compiled by Black and Joseph F. Berry (1894). The same year it appeared in Henry Date's *Pentecostal Hymns* (Chicago: Hope Publishing Co.).

ROLL CALL is the name given this tune by the Hymnal Committee.

When upon life's billows you are tempest tossed   318

This hymn by Johnson Oatman, Jr., with this tune by Edwin O. Excell, first appeared in *Songs for Young People,* compiled and published by Excell (Chicago, 1897, No. 34). The hymn became extremely popular, both in the United States and in England, and has been a great favorite in evangelistic campaigns.

BLESSINGS is the name given this tune by the Hymnal Committee.

"When We All Get to Heaven"—*see* Sing the wondrous love of Jesus

This hymn was written by John H. Sammis. Concerning the writing of the hymn and tune, Daniel B. Towner, the composer, has given the following information.

Mr. Moody was conducting a series of meetings in Brockton, Massachusetts, and I had the pleasure of singing for him there. One night a young man rose in a testimony meeting and said, "I am not quite sure—but I am going to trust, and I am going to obey." I just jotted that sentence down, and sent it with the little story to the Rev. J. H. Sammis, a Presbyterian minister. He wrote the hymn, and the tune was born. The chorus

> Trust and obey,
> For there's no other way
> To be happy in Jesus
> But to trust and obey

was written before the hymn was.

This text, with this tune, TRUST AND OBEY, first appeared in *Hymns Old and New* (Chicago: Fleming H. Revell Co., 1887, No. 59).

Where cross the crowded ways of life   **464**

In 1903 Caleb T. Winchester, a member of the committee preparing the *Methodist Hymnal* of 1905, suggested to Frank Mason North that he write a new missionary hymn for the hymnal. Dr. North wrote the hymn, basing it on Matthew 22:9, which he had used shortly before as the text for a sermon. The hymn was first printed in *The Christian City* (June, 1903), of which Dr. North was the editor. It reflects his great concern for city missions, and the author's own account gives further insight into the background of his experience.

My life was for long years, both by personal choice and official duty, given to the people in all phases of their community life. New York was to me an open book. I spent days and weeks and years in close contact with every phase of the life of multitudes, and at the morning, noon, and evening hours was familiar with the tragedy, as it always seemed to me, of the jostling, moving currents of the life of the people as revealed upon the streets and at great crossings of the avenues; and I have watched them by the hour as they passed, by tens of thousands. This is no more than many another man, whose sympathies are with the crowd and with the eager, unsatisfied folk of the world, has done . . . that [the hymn] has found its way into so many of the modern hymnals and by translation into so many of the other languages is significant, not as to the quality of the hymn itself, but as to the fact that it is an expression of that tremendous movement of the soul of the gospel in our times which demands that the follower of Christ must make the interest of the people his own, and must find the heart of the world's need if he is in any way to represent his Master among men.

GERMANY—*see* All things are Thine; no gift have we.

"Where He Leads Me"—*see* I can hear my Saviour calling

"Wherever He Leads I'll Go"—*see* Take up thy cross and follow Me

While passing thro' this world of sin   348

The refrain of this hymn by B. B. McKinney was written first and appeared in Robert H. Coleman's *The Pilot* (Dallas, Texas, 1922, No. 248). Two years later the words and music of the stanzas were added, and the complete hymn first appeared in Coleman's *Harvest Hymns* (1924, No. 7).

COLEMAN is the name given this tune by the Hymnal Committee for Robert H. Coleman (*q.v.*).

While shepherds watched their flocks by night   79

This hymn by Nahum Tate first appeared in the Supplement to the *New Version of the Psalms* (1700) by Tate and Brady. All of Tate's hymns in this collection have been forgotten except this metrical version of Luke 2:8-14.

CHRISTMAS—*see* Awake, my soul, stretch every nerve.

While we pray and while we plead   218

This hymn by Daniel W. Whittle, with Charles C. Case's tune, WHY NOT NOW, first appeared in *Gospel Hymns No. 6* (1891).

"Whiter Than Snow"—*see* Lord Jesus, I long to be perfectly whole

Who is on the Lord's side?   413

Frances R. Havergal's hymn based on 1 Chronicles 12:1-18 and entitled, "Home Missions," was written in October, 1877, and first published in the author's *Loyal Responses* (1878). Originally consisting of five twelve-line stanzas, the present version uses stanzas one, four, and five unaltered. The omitted stanzas two and three are

> Not for weight of glory,
>   Not for crown and palm,
> Enter we the army,
>   Raise the warrior-psalm;

231

But for love that claimeth
Lives for whom He died:
He whom Jesus nameth
Must be on His side.

Response: By Thy love constraining,
By Thy grace divine,
We are on the Lord's side;
Saviour, we are Thine.

Jesus, Thou hast bought us,
Not with gold or gem,
But with Thine own life-blood,
For thy diadem.
With Thy blessing filling
Each who comes to Thee,
Thou hast made us willing,
Thou hast made us free.

Response: By Thy grand redemption,
By Thy grace divine,
We are on the Lord's side
Saviour, we are Thine.

ARMAGEDDON is an adaptation of a German melody which appeared in Layriz's *Kern des deutschen Kirchengesangs,* Part III (Berlin, 1853), and credited there to Luise Reichardt. The tune was set to the hymn "Wenn ich Ihn nur habe" by Hardenburg. John Goss's adaptation of this melody first appeared in the 1872 revision of William Mercer's *The Church Psalter and Tune Book* (London; 1st ed., 1864), when it was set to "Onward, Christian Soldiers." The tune name, found in Revelation 16:16, is a Greek word meaning "the plain of Megiddo."

"Whosoever heareth," shout, shout the sound!   238

Philip P. Bliss wrote both words and music for this hymn. During the winter of 1869-70, the English evangelist, Henry Moorhouse, conducted a series of meetings in Chicago. For seven consecutive services he preached on the text John 3:16. Bliss attended these services, and from the inspiration of this experience came this hymn. It was first published in George F. Root's *The Prize* (Cincinnati: John Church & Co., 1870, No. 7). Four years later Bliss included it in his *Gospel Songs.*

" 'Whosoever' Meaneth Me"—*see* I am happy today and the sun shines bright

"Whosoever Will"—*see* "Whosoever heareth," shout, shout the sound

Why do you wait, dear brother   **220**

George F. Root wrote both words and music for this hymn, and it first appeared in *Gospel Hymns No. 3* (1878, No. 19).

SHEFFIELD is the name given this tune by the Hymnal Committee for the town in Massachusetts where Root was born.

"Why Not Now"—*see* While we pray and while we plead

"Will Jesus Find Us Watching"—*see* When Jesus comes to reward his servants

"Will There Be Any Stars"—*see* I am thinking today of that beautiful land

With happy voices ringing   **507**

William G. Tarrant wrote this hymn in 1888, and it first appeared in the 1892 supplement to the *Essex Hall Hymnal* (London), a collection made especially for the Unitarian Christian Church, Wandsworth, London, where the author was pastor for thirty-seven years.

BERTHOLD, also called TOURS, was composed by Berthold Tours in 1872 and first appeared in Arthur S. Sullivan's *The Hymnary* (London, 1872).

With joy we hail the sacred day   **38**

This hymn by Harriet Auber first appeared in her *Spirit of the Psalms* (London, 1829), where it was entitled "Sunday." This collection consisted mainly of psalm versifications, this hymn being one of the few exceptions. About twenty of these psalm versions appeared in Charles Haddon Spurgeon's *Our Own Hymn Book* (London, 1866), a collection made for use in his church.

BROWN, composed by William B. Bradbury, first appeared in *The Psalmodist* (1844, p. 89), set to "I love to steal awhile away."

"Wonderful Peace of My Saviour"—*see* Like radiant sunshine that comes after rain

"Wonderful, Wonderful Jesus"—*see* There is never a day so dreary

"Wonderful Words of Life"—*see* Sing them over again to me

Word of God, across the ages   **176**

During 1951 the Hymn Society of America solicited new hymns on the Bible in connection with the publication in 1952 of the Revised

Standard Version of the Bible. This was chosen as one of the winning hymns and was first published by the Hymn Society of America in a pamphlet entitled "Ten New Hymns on the Bible" (New York, 1953).

Most of the hymn tunes by classical composers found in hymnals today are adaptations from their sacred or secular works. AUSTRIAN HYMN is an exception, for it was written as a hymn tune by Franz Joseph Haydn for Hauschka's national anthem, "Gott erhalte Franz den Kaiser." It was first sung on February 12, 1797, on the birthday of the emperor, Franz II. Later the tune appeared as a theme for variations in the slow movement of Haydn's string quartet known as the "Emperor" or "Kaiser" (Op. 76, No. 3). Apparently Haydn based this hymn tune on a Croatian folk song, "Vjatvo rano se ja vstanem," for the first three bars of both tunes are identical. Five years after its composition in Germany, this tune appeared in England in Edward Miller's *Sacred Music* (London, 1802). Its earliest use as a hymn tune in Germany dates from a Breslau collection of 1804.

Work, for the night is coming   424

This hymn was written when the author, Annie Louise Walker (later Coghill), an English girl eighteen years old, was visiting her brothers in Canada. It was published in a Canadian newspaper in 1854, and appeared in the author's collection of poems, *Leaves from the Backwoods* (Montreal, 1861). Armin Haeussler has found an autographed first edition copy in the Parliamentary Library in Ottawa. Originally the fourth line of each stanza had six syllables instead of five, and the eighth line of each stanza was, "Night, when man's work is done." The author was greatly displeased with Lowell Mason's alterations, but was unsuccessful in her efforts to restore the original form of the hymn.

WORK SONG, composed by Lowell Mason, first appeared in his *The Song Garden,* Second Book (Boston and New York, 1864, p. 81), one of a series of public school music books edited by Mason.

Would you be free from the burden of sin   193

Both words and music were written by Lewis E. Jones while he was attending the camp meeting at Mountain Lake Park, Maryland. Dr. H. L. Gilmour purchased the manuscript and it was first published in *Songs of Praise and Victory,* compiled by William J. Kirkpatrick and Gilmour (Philadelphia: Pepper Publishing Co., 1899, No. 58). It also appeared in *Gospel Praises,* compiled by Kirkpatrick, Gilmour, and J. L. Hall (Philadelphia: Hall Mack Co., 1899, No. 69).

POWER IN THE BLOOD is the name given this tune by the Hymnal Committee.

Would you live for Jesus, and be always pure and good 239

Cyrus S. Nusbaum wrote both words and music in 1898, and his own account of this experience is given in Haldor Lillenas' *Modern Gospel Song Stories* (p. 147).

I had spent my first year in pastoral work. Having been appointed to serve as pastor on one of the poorest circuits in our district, I had struggled hard during the year to take care of the seven preaching places and congregations. It had been a most difficult task, strenuous and discouraging, and the income was pitifully small. At the end of the conference year my wife and I gathered our few necessary belongings and, with the assistance of one of our members, we arrived at the railway station in order to take the train to the place where the conference was to meet that year.

Naturally, we had prayed and hoped that at this conference I might be appointed to a better charge, but when the Bishop read the appointments the last night of the conference I was named as pastor of the same old "hard scrabble circuit." It was with heavy hearts that we repaired to our lodging place that night. Mrs. Nusbaum sensibly retired early, but I remained in the little parlor with no one to disturb me. I was very unhappy and a spirit of rebellion seemed to possess me. About midnight I finally knelt in prayer beside my chair. After some struggles a deep peace came stealing into my heart. I told the Lord I would be willing to let Him have His way with me regardless of the cost. With that feeling of surrender to the will of God came the inspiration for the song now so well known throughout Christendom.

Nusbaum sold the manuscript of this hymn to Dr. H. L. Gilmour, who included it in *Gospel Praises,* compiled by William J. Kirkpatrick, J. Lincoln Hall, and Gilmour (Philadelphia: Hall-Mack Company, 1899, No. 17). NUSBAUM is the name given this tune by the Hymnal Committee.

Ye Christian heralds! go, proclaim 459

This hymn uses the last three stanzas of a poem of seven stanzas entitled, "Farewell to Missionaries," which first appeared in an English newspaper about 1803. It was reprinted in *Hymns for the Use of Christians* (Portland, Maine, 1805), compiled by Elias Smith and Abner Jones, with the heading, "On the Departure of the Missionaries, By a Bristol Student." Bourne Hall Draper, then a student for the ministry at the Baptist Academy, Bristol, has been identified as the author of this poem. In its original form, the poem read:

Ruler of worlds! display thy power,
Be this thy Zion's favored hour;
Bid the bright morning star arise,
And point the nations to the skies.

Set up thy throne where Satan reigns,
On Afric shores, on India's plains;
On wilds and continents unknown,
And be the universe thine own!

Speak and the world shall hear thy voice;
Speak and the deserts shall rejoice!
Scatter the shades of mortal night;
Let worthless idols flee the light!

Trusting in him, dear brethren, rear
The gospel standard void of fear:
Go seek with joy your destined shore,
To view your native land no more.

Yes, Christian heroes! go, proclaim
Salvation through Emmanuel's name!
To India's clime the tidings bear,
And plant the Rose of Sharon there.

He'll shield you with a wall of fire,
With flaming zeal your hearts inspire;
Bid' raging winds their fury cease,
And hush the tempests into peace.

And when our labors all are o'er,
Then we shall meet to part no more;
Meet with the blood-bought throng to fall
And crown our Jesus, Lord of all!

DUKE STREET—*see* Jesus shall reign where'er the sun.

"Ye Must Be Born Again"—*see* A ruler once came to Jesus by night

Ye servants of God, your Master proclaim   **147**

This hymn by Charles Wesley first appeared in *Hymns for Times of Trouble and Persecution* (1744) in six four-line stanzas in the section entitled "Hymns to Be Sung in Tumult."

LYONS—*see* O worship the King, all glorious above.

Years I spent in vanity and pride   **96**

This hymn was written by William R. Newell while he was associated with Moody Bible Institute in Chicago. The words had been vaguely in his mind for a few weeks and then one day on his way to lecture they suddenly began crystallizing in his mind. He stepped into an unoccupied classroom and wrote them down quickly on the back of an envelope as they now appear. Proceeding to his class he met Daniel B. Towner, then director of music at the Institute, handed him the verses and suggested that he compose suitable music for them. When the author returned from his class, Dr. Towner had completed the tune, and they sang it together. It first appeared in *Famous Hymns* (1895, No. 79).

CALVARY is the name given this tune by the Hymnal Committee.

Yield not to temptation 364

Regarding the writing of this hymn and tune, Horatio R. Palmer has written:

This song is an inspiration. I was at work on the dry subject of "Theory" when the complete idea flashed upon me, and I laid aside the theoretical work and hurriedly penned both words and music as fast as I could write them. I submitted them to the criticism of a friend afterward, and some changes were made in the third stanza, but the first two are exactly as they came to me. The music was first written in A flat; but I soon saw that B flat was better, and for many years it has appeared in that key. I am reverently thankful it has been a power for good.

Time has proved the original key more acceptable, for the tune appears in A flat in most collections. This hymn and tune first appeared in Palmer's *Sabbath School Songs* (Chicago: Adams, Blackmer, & Lyon, 1868, No. 43).

You have longed for sweet peace, and for faith to increase 350

Elisha A. Hoffman wrote both words and music in 1900. No other information has been found concerning this hymn. HOFFMAN is the name given the tune by the Hymnal Committee.

Zion stands with hills surrounded 378

This hymn by Thomas Kelly first appeared in his *Hymns on Various Passages of Scripture,* second edition (Dublin, 1806), in five six-line stanzas. It is based on Psalm 125:2. The original first line read "Zion stands by hills surrounded."

ZION—*see* Guide me, O Thou great Jehovah

Part II

Authors and Composers

Ackley, Alfred Henry (b. Spring Hill, Bradford Co., Pa., Jan. 21, 1887; d. Whittier, Calif., July 3, 1960), received his first musical instruction from his father and later studied harmony and composition in New York and London. He was an accomplished cellist. In 1914 he was ordained to the Presbyterian ministry and served churches in Elmhurst and Wilkes-Barre, Pennsylvania, and Escondido, California. Throughout his ministry he maintained a keen interest in the writing of hymns and hymn tunes, and he has stated that his hymns, gospel songs, children's songs, secular songs, and college glee club songs number approximately fifteen hundred. He was the brother of Benton D. Ackley, who was for many years pianist for Homer Rodeheaver during his work with Billy Sunday. Both Ackley brothers were associated with the Rodeheaver Publishing Company in the compilation of hymnals and gospel songbooks, and they contributed many songs to these collections.

HE LIVES—I serve a risen Saviour (279)

Adams, Sarah Flower (b. Harlow, Essex, Eng., Feb. 22, 1805; d. London, Eng., Aug. 14, 1848), was the second daughter of Benjamin Flower, editor of *The Cambridge Intelligencer* and later of *The Political Review*. She married William Bridges Adams, a civil engineer, in 1834. Her portrayal of "Lady MacBeth" in the Richmond Theater in London in 1837 was most successful; however, she abandoned any aspiration for the theater because of her health. She contributed both verse and prose to *The Repository,* a periodical edited by her minister, William Johnson Fox, of the South Place Unitarian Church, Finsbury, London. For use in his church, Fox published *Hymns and Anthems* (1841), to which she contributed thirteen hymns, among which was "Nearer, my God, to Thee." Her sister, Eliza, who served as music editor of this collection, was the inspiration for Browning's *Pauline.* Her major literary work was *Vivia Perpetua* (1841), a religious dramatic poem in five acts, dealing with the conflict of heathenism and Christianity. In 1845 she

238

published *The Flock at the Fountain,* a catechism for children, interspersed with hymns.

Nearer, my God, to Thee (322)

Addison, Joseph (b. Milston, Wiltshire, Eng., May 1, 1672; d. London, Eng., June 17, 1719). The son of Lancelot Addison, an Anglican clergyman, he was educated at Charterhouse and at Queen's and Magdalen Colleges, Oxford, where he exhibited unusual literary talent as a writer of Latin verse. He abandoned his preparation for the ministry and turned his interest to literature and politics. He joined the Whig party and through influential friends, held several important offices. His chief fame rests upon his literary contributions to *The Tatler, The Spectator, The Guardian,* and *The Freeholder.* All of his hymns appeared in *The Spectator,* a daily paper which he founded in 1711.

The spacious firmament on high (10)

Alexander, Cecil Francis Humphreys (b. Tyrone Co., Ire., 1823; d. Londonderry, Ire., Oct. 12, 1895), was the daughter of Major John Humphreys. In 1850 she married William Alexander, an Irish clergyman, who in 1893 became Primate of all Ireland. Prior to her marriage she published *Verses from the Holy Scripture* (1846) and *Hymns for Little Children* (1848). This latter collection, her best-known work, contained but thirty pages, but it was printed in more than one hundred editions. Among her later books were *Narrative Hymns for Village Schools* (1853), *Poems on Subjects in the Old Testament* (Part I, 1854; Part II, 1857), and *Hymns Descriptive and Devotional* (1858). (Cf. *The Hymn,* Vol. 5, No. 2, 37)

All things bright and beautiful (8)
Jesus calls us o'er the tumult (360)
There is a green hill far away (98)

Alexander, James Waddell (b. Hopewell, Va., Mar. 13, 1804; d. Sweetsprings, Va., July 31, 1859), was educated at the College of New Jersey (now Princeton University) and at Princeton Theological Seminary and later taught at both schools. He was ordained to the Presbyterian ministry and served as pastor of the First Presbyterian Church, Trenton, New Jersey, 1829-32; was professor of rhetoric at the College of New Jersey, 1832-44; pastor of the Duane Street Presbyterian Church, New York City, 1844-49; professor of church history, Princeton Theological Seminary, 1849-51; and pastor of the Fifth Avenue Presbyterian Church, New York City, 1851-59. He had a great interest in hymnology, and his translations of Latin and German hymns were published posthumously in 1861 under the title, *The Breaking Crucible and Other Translations.*

O sacred Head, now wounded (tr.) (91)

Alford, Henry (b. London, Eng., Oct. 7, 1810; d. Canterbury, Eng., Jan. 12, 1871). Educated at Ilminster Grammar School, and Trinity College, Cambridge, he was ordained in the Church of England in 1833 and served as curate to his father at Winkfield, Wiltshire, and at Ampton. For eighteen years he was vicar at Wymeswold, Leicestershire. In 1853 he was called to Quebec Chapel, London, and in 1857 made Dean of Canterbury. His most famous work was his commentary on the Greek New Testament, which was recognized as the standard critical commentary of the late nineteenth century. He was a member of the New Testament Revision Committee. He wrote a number of original hymns and made many translations.

Come, ye thankful people, come (490)
Ten thousand times ten thousand (476)

Allen, Chester G. (1838-78). No information has been found concerning this composer, other than the fact that he collaborated in compiling several collections of Sunday school songs, such as *Bright Jewels* (New York, 1869, with William B. Bradbury, W. H. Doane, and W. F. Sherwin).

JOYFUL SONG—Praise Him! praise Him! (137)

Allen, George Nelson (b. Mansfield, Mass., Sept. 7, 1812; d. Cincinnati, Ohio, Dec. 9, 1877). After graduating from Oberlin College in 1838, he taught music there until his retirement in 1864. His work as a music educator laid the foundation for what became, in 1865, the Oberlin Conservatory of Music. He compiled *The Oberlin Social and Sabbath Hymn Book* (1844), to which he contributed several tunes.

MAITLAND—Must Jesus bear the cross alone (428)

Alwood, Josiah Kelley (b. Harrison Co., Ohio, July 15, 1828; d. Morenci, Mich., Jan. 13, 1909). Ordained a minister in the church of the United Brethren in Christ, he spent many years as a circuit rider, traveling on horseback to his many appointments. He would be gone from his family for weeks at a time, holding revival meetings and lecturing on Christian doctrine. Later, he became a presiding elder in the North Ohio Conference and was a delegate to several general conferences of the United Brethren Church. Always a staunch supporter of the original constitution of his denomination, he was a delegate to the general conference at the time of the separation of the church into two groups at York, Pennsylvania, in 1889. His son, Rev. O. G. Alwood, was ordained a minister in the Church of the United Brethren in Christ, and served his denomination as pastor, presiding elder, and also as bishop. This information has been furnished the writer by Mrs. Marjorie Alwood Johnson of Hillsdale, Michigan, the daughter of O. G. Alwood and granddaughter of Josiah Kelley Alwood.

THE UNCLOUDED DAY—O they tell me of a home far beyond the skies (484)

Angell, Warren Mathewson (b. Brooklyn, N.Y., May 13, 1907). The son of Earl Warren and Lily (Ward) Angell, he was educated at Syracuse University (B.M., 1929, M.M., 1933) and Teachers' College of Columbia University (Ed.D., 1944). He studied piano with Severin Eisenberger, 1931, Max Landow, 1936, and Abram Chasins, 1940; and voice with Harry Robert Wilson, 1942-44. After serving two years as head of the Piano Department, Murray State Teachers' College, Kentucky, he became dean of the College of Fine Arts, Oklahoma Baptist University, Shawnee, in 1936. During a two-year leave of absence, 1942-44, while working on his doctorate, he sang with Fred Waring's Pennsylvanians. In addition to his administrative and teaching responsibilities, he has for more than twenty years directed the Bison Glee Club, which has toured extensively. He has written a considerable amount of sacred choral music, and is the author of *Vocal Approach* (1950), *The Choir Clinic Manual* (1952), *The Beginning Vocalist* (1956), *The Progressing Vocalist* (1957), and *The Advanced Vocalist* (1959). Widely known as a choral clinician throughout the South, he has been named a Fellow of the National Association of Teachers of Singing.

GLORIA (arr.)—Angels we have heard on high (64)
Responses (516, 517)

Arne, Thomas Augustus (b. London, Eng., Mar. 12, 1710; d. London, March 5, 1778), was educated at Eton and after completing his law course, he finally obtained his father's consent and turned his efforts to music. He composed two oratorios, *Abel* (1774) and *Judith* (1764); thirteen masques and operas, among which were *Rosamond* (1733), *Comus* (1738), *Alfred* (1740, of which the finale is now known to patriotic Englishmen as "Rule Britannia"), and *Artaxerxes* (1762). He lived in a day when Handel's music far overshadowed in England all native composers, yet he was considered the outstanding English composer of the eighteenth century. His sister, Mrs. Susanna

241

Cibber, was an outstanding singer for whom Handel wrote the contralto solos in *The Messiah*.

ARLINGTON—Am I a soldier of the cross (405)
O for a faith that will not shrink (255)
This is the day the Lord hath made (39)

Atkins, George. The identity of this author is unknown.

Brethren, we have met to worship (368)

Auber, Harriett (b. London, Eng., Oct. 4, 1773; d. Hoddesdon, Hertfordshire, Eng., Jan. 20, 1862), was the daughter of James Auber, Anglican clergyman, and great-granddaughter of Pierre Auber of Normandy, who came to England in 1685 as a Huguenot refugee after the revocation of the Edict of Nantes. She lived a quiet life in the villages of Broxbourne and Hoddesdon, Hertfordshire, and was well known for the high literary quality of her poetry. In her *The Spirit of the Psalms* (1829), she wrote a number of metrical versifications of Psalms in an attempt to improve on the poetic character of existing versions. Included in this collection were some original hymns as well as hymns by other authors. Charles Haddon Spurgeon included twenty of her hymns in his *Our Own Hymnbook* (1866).

With joy we hail the sacred day (38)

Babcock, Maltbie Davenport (b. Syracuse, N.Y., Aug. 3, 1858; d. Naples, It., May 18, 1901). Of a socially prominent family, he was educated at Syracuse University and Auburn Theological Seminary. He was recognized as an outstanding student, a vigorous competitor on the athletic field, and a skilful musician at the organ, piano, and violin. Ordained to the Presbyterian ministry, he became pastor of the First Presbyterian Church, Lockport, New York. For fourteen years he was pastor of the Brown Memorial Church in Baltimore, and in 1899 was called to succeed Henry van Dyke as pastor of the Brick Presbyterian Church of New York City. He had served this church for only eighteen months when his untimely death occurred on a trip to the Holy Land. A collection of his writings, *Thoughts for Everyday Living,* appeared a few months after his death.

This is my Father's world (59)

Bach, Johann Sebastian (b. Eisenach, Ger., Mar. 21, 1685; d. Leipzig, Ger., July 28, 1750). The most outstanding member of the most extraordinarily musical family of all times, he was trained in the choir schools at Ohrdruf and Lüneburg and served briefly as organist at Arnstadt and Mühlhausen. The remainder of his life was spent at three places: Weimar (1708-17), Cöthen (1718-23), and Leipzig (1723-50). During the years at Leipzig, where he served as cantor of St. Thomas Church, he wrote his greatest works. His output was enormous, and his skill was unequalled in all areas of composition. Details of his life, analysis of his works, and listings of his compositions are easily available and need not be included here. He was not widely known as a composer in his day, and his music remained virtually unknown until it was introduced to the world by Mendelssohn almost a century after his death. The so-called "Bach chorales" as we know them today were not originally melodies but his harmonizations of existing melodies in the style of the eighteenth century. These were collected and published posthumously in 1769 by his son, C.P.E. Bach.

PASSION CHORALE (arr.)—O sacred Head, now wounded (91)
HERR JESU CHRIST (arr.)—All things are Thine: no gift have we (536)

Baker, Henry (b. Nuneham, Oxfordshire, Eng., 1835; d. Wimbledon, Eng., April 15, 1910). His father was an Anglican minister. He was educated at Winchester and Cooper's Hill, where he studied civil engineering. Because of his keen interest in music and at the urging of John Bacchus Dykes, he earned a music degree at Exeter College, Oxford, in 1867. For many years he was engaged in the construction of railroads in India. A number of his tunes appear in Garrett Horder's *Worship Song* (1905).

QUEBEC—Jesus, Thou joy of loving hearts (136)

Baker, Henry Williams (b. London, Eng., May 27, 1821; d. Monkland, Eng., Feb. 12, 1877). Educated at Trinity College, Cambridge, and ordained in 1844, he became vicar of Monkland, Hertfordshire, and remained there until his death. He was largely responsible for *Hymns Ancient and Modern* (1861) and for almost twenty years served as chairman of the Editorial Committee. In this position he used his editorial authority in deleting unworthy material and making editorial changes in material submitted for consideration. For this reason his critics remarked that *H. A. and M.* really meant "Hymns Asked for and Mutilated." Nonetheless, this hymnal stands as a monument today in English hymnody. It is the accepted hymnal of the Anglican church in spite of the fact that no hymnal has ever been officially adopted. Since its appearance more than one hundred years ago, its imprint is evident in the development of Christian hymnody. All subsequent hymnal compilers are debtors to this compilation, for they have reprinted its hymns, copied its format, and maintained the marriages of many texts and tunes which appeared here for the first time together.

The King of love my Shepherd is (280)
STEPHANOS—Art thou weary, heavy laden (245)

Baker, Theodore (b. New York, N.Y., June 3, 1851; d. Dresden, Ger., Oct. 13, 1934). His musical training was in Germany, and his doctoral dissertation at the University of Leipzig (1881) dealt with the music of the Seneca Indians of North America. From 1892 to 1926 he served as literary editor for G. Schirmer, Inc. In 1900 he published *Baker's Biographical Dictionary,* a fifth edition of which was issued in 1958. Upon his retirement in 1926, he returned to Germany, where he remained until his death.

We gather together to ask the Lord's blessing (tr.) (492)

Bakewell, John (b. Brailsford, Derbyshire, Eng., 1721; d. Lewisham, Eng., Mar. 18, 1819). One of the earliest local preachers of the Wesleyan movement, he was known as an ardent evangelist. He moved to London shortly after the first Methodist Conference (1744), and became acquainted with the Wesleys, Toplady, Madan, and other evangelical leaders of the day. For some years he conducted the Greenwich Royal Park Academy and is credited with introducing Methodism to Greenwich. He died at the age of ninety-eight and was buried in the Wesleyan burial ground at City Road Chapel, London.

Hail, Thou once despised Jesus (149)

Barbauld, Anna Letitia (b. Kibworth-Harcourt, Leicestershire, Eng., June 20, 1743; d. Newington Green, Eng., Mar. 9, 1825). Her father, John Aiken, was a dissenting minister, who became classical tutor at a dissenting academy in Warrington when she was ten years old. In this academic environment her interest and activity in literary ventures found opportunity for expression. In 1774 she married Rochemont Barbauld, a Unitarian minister of French descent. For more than eleven years she assisted her husband in conducting a school at Palgrave, Suffolk, in connection with his pastoral work in the local church. In addition to other literary works, she wrote twenty-one hymns, all of which were found in Unitarian hymnals at the end of the nineteenth century.

Come, says Jesus' sacred voice (244)
Praise to God, immortal praise (14)

Baring-Gould, Sabine (b. Exeter, Eng., Jan. 28, 1834; d. Lew-Trenchard, North Devonshire, Eng., Jan. 2, 1924). The son of an English squire, he spent much of his early life in Germany and France. He was educated at Clare College, Cambridge, and was a master in the choir school of St. Barnabas, Pimlico, London, and at Hurstpierpoint College, Sussex. Following his ordination in 1864, he became curate of Horbury with special charge of the mission at Horbury Bridge. His best known hymns were written for the children of this mission. After serving at Dalton, near Thirsk, Yorkshire, and East Mersea, Essex, he became Rector of Lew-Trenchard, in 1881, having inherited the family estate there after his father's death. He was an extraordinary man whose interests ranged over many areas and whose industry was inexhaustible. He wrote many books of history, biography, poetry, and fiction, and was said to have more works attached to his name in the British Museum catalog than any other writer of his time. He was a pioneer in the collection of folk songs, and in collaboration with H. Fleetwood Shephard he published *Songs and Ballads of the West* (1889-91), collected mainly in Devon and Cornwall. In 1894 he published *A Garland of Country Song.* His work in this area furnished the inspiration for the intensive research of Cecil J. Sharp, England's most outstanding authority on folk song. They collaborated on *English Folk-songs for Schools.*

Now the day is over (35)
Onward, Christian soldiers (412)

Barnard, Charlotte Alington (b. Eng., Dec. 23, 1830; d. Dover, Eng., Jan. 30, 1869), married Charles Cary Barnard in 1854. She was a student of William Henry Holmes, professor of piano of the Royal Academy of Music. Beginning about 1858, she published over one hundred ballads under the pseudonym "Claribel," the best known of which is "Come back to Erin."

BARNARD—Give of your best to the Master (353)

Barnby, Joseph (b. York, Eng., Aug. 12, 1838; d. London, Eng., Jan. 28, 1896). As a boy he was a chorister at York Minster, at the age of twelve, an organist, and fourteen, a choirmaster. He received his musical education at the Royal Academy of Music. His two most important posts of service as organist and choirmaster were at St. Andrew's, Wells Street, London (1863-71), where his choir was recognized as the outstanding choir in the city, and at St. Ann's Soho (1871-76), where he began the annual singing of Bach's passion music. From 1875 to 1892 he was precentor of Eton College and resigned to become principal of the Guildhall School of Music. From 1861 to 1876 he was musical adviser to Novello, Ltd., who in 1867 set up for him a choral group which came to be known as "Barnby's Choir." He was knighted in 1892. Five hymn books, the most noted of which was the *Hymnary* (1872), were edited by him. He wrote 246 hymn tunes, all of which were published in one volume after his death. He did not name any of his tunes, and the names which they now bear have been attached by subsequent hymnal editors and compilers.

ALVERSTOKE—O happy home where Thou art loved the dearest (373)
JUST AS I AM—Just as I am, Thine own to be (249)
LAUDES DOMINI—When morning gilds the skies (23)
LONGWOOD—Spirit of God, descend upon my heart (166)
MERRIAL—Now the day is over (35)
NEW YEAR—Father, let me dedicate (498)
O PERFECT LOVE—Hope of the world, Thou Christ of great compassion (282)
    O perfect Love, all human thought transcending (501)
ST. ANDREW—We give Thee but Thine own (402, 535)
ST. ANSLEM—We plow the fields and scatter (493)

Barratt, Alfred (b. Lancashire, Eng., Oct. 2, 1879), was educated for the ministry in England but came to America and attended Gordon College. He was ordained to the Presbyterian ministry in 1913 and retired in 1948. He received an honorary Litt.D. from Bob Jones University in 1937. Throughout the years of his active ministry he has written a large number of hymns. He makes his home in Pleasantville, New Jersey.

Like radiant sunshine that comes after rain (285)

Barthélémon, Francois Hippolyte (b. Bordeaux, Fr., July 27, 1741; d. London, Eng., July 23, 1808). His father was an official in the Colonial Department of the French government, and his mother was from a wealthy Queen's County, Ireland, family. After brief service in the Irish brigade, he left the army to study music in England and became one of the most distinguished violinists of his time. He became an operatic conductor at Marylebone and Vauxhall Gardens. He married a talented singer, Mary Young, a niece of the wife of Thomas Arne, and during 1776-77 they toured Germany, Italy, and France. He enjoyed the friendship of Joseph Haydn during the latter's visit to London in the 1790's. He wrote five operas, one oratorio, six symphonies, concertos, and violin sonatas. He was a member of the Swedenborgian Church. Ill health and misfortune came in his last years and he died a brokenhearted paralytic.

AUTUMN—Mighty God, while angels bless Thee (4)
  There's a light upon the mountains (124)
  Hail, Thou once despised Jesus! (149)
BALERMA—Come, Holy Spirit, heavenly dove (169)
  Oh, for a closer walk with God (365)

Barton, Bernard (b. London, Eng., Jan. 31, 1784; d. Woodbridge, Eng., Feb. 19, 1849). Known as England's "Quaker Poet," he was educated at a Quaker school at Ipswich. At the age of twelve he was apprenticed to a shopkeeper at Halstead, Essex, and ten years later joined his brother in a corn and coal business at Woodbridge, Suffolk. After the death of his wife, he spent a year in Liverpool as a tutor. He returned to Woodbridge in 1810 and served as a clerk in the local bank for almost forty years. During these years he enjoyed the friendship of Charles Lamb, Byron, and Shelley. From 1812 to 1845 he published ten books of verse from which some twenty hymns came into usage.

Walk in the light! so shalt thou know (370)

Batchellor, Daniel (b. Eng., Nov. 23, 1845; d. Philadelphia, Pa., Jan. 19, 1934), was a composer of children's songs, an author of books on musical instruction, and a member of the Society of Friends. With Thomas Charmbury he was coauthor of *The Tonic Sol-fa Music Course for Schools* (Chicago: S. R. Winchell & Co., 1884-86).

WE THANK THEE—Father, we thank Thee for the night (341)

Bates, Katherine Lee (b. Falmouth, Mass., Aug. 12, 1859; d. Wellesley, Mass., Mar. 28, 1929). Her father, William Bates, and her grandfather, Joshua Bates, were both Congregational ministers. The latter was president of Middlebury College, 1818-38. She attended Wellesley and Newton high schools, and graduated from Wellesley College in 1880. After six years of high school teaching, she taught at Wellesley College, where she later became head of the English Department. She was the author or editor of more than twenty works, among which are *History of American Literature* (1908); *America, the Beautiful* (1911), a collection of verse; *Fairy Gold* (1916); *The Pilgrim Ship* (1926). She was given a Litt.D. by Middlebury College in 1914 and by Oberlin College in 1916. An LL.D. was conferred on her by Wellesley College in 1925.

O beautiful for spacious skies (489)

Bathurst, William Hiley (b. Clevedale, near Bristol, Eng., Aug. 28, 1796; d. Lydney Park, Gloucestershire, Eng., Nov. 25, 1877), was the son of Charles Bragge, one-time member of parliament for Bristol, who took the name Bathurst when he succeeded to his uncle's estate at

Lydney Park, Gloucestershire. He was educated at Winchester and Christ Church, Oxford, where he graduated in 1818 and entered the ministry. He held the rectory of Barwick-in Elmet, near Leeds, from 1820 to 1852. He resigned from this position because he was unable to reconcile his doctrinal views with the Book of Common Prayer of the Anglican Church, particularly with regard to the baptismal and burial services. He retired to private life at Darley Dale, near Matlock, and succeeded to the family estate in 1863. Among his works are *Psalms and Hymns for Public and Private Use* (Leeds, 1830), *A Translation of the Georgics of Virgil* (1849), and *Metrical Musings* (1849).

Holy Spirit, from on high (171)
O for a faith that will not shrink (255)

Baumbach, Adolph (b. Ger., 1830; d. Chicago, Ill. Apr. 3, 1880), was reared in Germany, where he received his musical education. Sometime before 1855 he emigrated to the United States and taught music in Boston, later moving to Chicago. In addition to teaching piano and organ, he composed some piano music and published a collection of sacred music for quartet choirs.

Response (532)

Baxter, Lydia (b. Petersburg, N.Y., Sept. 8, 1809; d. New York, N.Y., June 22, 1874), and her sister were converted under the preaching of a Baptist missionary, Rev. Eben Tucker. Shortly afterward, the two sisters were largely responsible for the forming of a Baptist church in their home town of Petersburg. After her marriage, she moved with her husband to New York City, where she zealously carried on her Christian activity. Although she became an invalid and was confined to her bed much of the time, her home was a gathering place for preachers, evangelists, and Christian workers. The radiance of her Christian experience was an inspiration to all who knew her. She published a collection of religious verse, *Gems by the Wayside* (1855), and wrote a number of gospel songs which were widely used. The present hymn, the only one which remains in common usage, was written only four years before her death.

Take the name of Jesus with you (305)

Beethoven, Ludwig van (b. Bonn, Ger., Dec. 16, 1770; d. Vienna, Aust., Mar. 1827). His extraordinary musical talent made itself manifest during his early childhood. His father, a singer in the chapel and an excessive drinker, was abusive to his wife and family. Ludwig, the second child, was playing in public at the age of eight and composing when he was ten, and his father dreamed of great riches through the exploitation of his musical talents. Through his teacher, Neefe, he was introduced to Bach's *Well-tempered Clavichord,* still in manuscript. At the age of sixteen he visited Vienna and greatly impressed Mozart with his playing. Haydn invited him to study with him but became an indifferent teacher. The years that followed saw an ever-increasing output of music from his creative genius, both instrumental and vocal. Listings of these works are readily available and need not be included here. While he wrote no hymn tunes, quite a number have been adapted from his works. Of these adapted tunes, by far the most widely used is HYMN TO JOY, taken from his *Ninth Symphony.*

HYMN TO JOY—Joyful, joyful, we adore Thee (44)
Response (534)

Bennard, George (b. Youngstown, Ohio, Feb. 4, 1873; d. Reed City, Mich., Oct. 10, 1958). The son of a coal miner, Bennard moved with his family to Albia, Iowa, when he was a small child and later moved to Lucas, Iowa. While attending a meeting of the Salvation Army at Lucas, he was converted and wanted to be a gospel minister. However, when he was sixteen, his father died, leaving him to be the sole support of his mother and four sisters. Further education thus was impossible. He gained his theological knowledge through his association with other ministers and by his own reading and study. He moved his mother and sisters to Illinois, where he later married. He and his wife became Salvation Army workers, and he was a brigade leader of the corps. After several years he resigned this work, joined the Methodist Episcopal Church, and spent many years as an evangelist in the United States and Canada. Following the death of his first wife, he married Hannah Dahlstrom. Although he wrote more than three hundred gospel songs, he is remembered for the one song he wrote in 1913. For a number of years before his death he made his home at Reed City, Michigan, where there was erected a twelve-foot-high wooden cross bearing the words "Old Rugged Cross" and the notice "Home of Living Author, Rev. Geo. Bennard." He died at the age of eighty-five.

On a hill far away stood an old rugged cross—OLD RUGGED CROSS (93)

Bennett, Sanford Fillmore (b. Eden, Erie Co., N.Y., June 21, 1836; d. Richmond, Ind., June 12, 1898). When Bennett was two years old, his family moved to Plainfield, Illinois. He was educated at Waukegan Academy and the University of Michigan. Converted in a Methodist revival, he later declared himself as a Universalist, although for lack of opportunity he did not unite with that fellowship. After two years as superintendent of schools in Richmond, Illinois, he resigned to be associate editor of *The Independent,* a weekly newspaper at Elkhorn, Wisconsin. During the Civil War he served as a second lieutenant in the Fortieth Wisconsin Volunteers. After the war he returned to Elkhorn, where he opened a drugstore and began the study of medicine. Graduating from Rush Medical College in 1874, he practiced medicine for twenty-two years. He began writing as a youth, and his first poems appeared in the Waukegan *Gazette* in the early 1850's. He wrote a considerable amount of both prose and verse.

There's a land that is fairer than day (471)

Benson, Louis Fitzgerald (b. Philadelphia, Pa., July 22, 1855; d. Philadelphia, Oct. 10, 1930), received his law degree from the University of Pennsylvania and, for a period of seven years, enjoyed a very successful law practice. Under the compelling conviction that he should enter the ministry, he enrolled in Princeton Theological Seminary and was ordained to the Presbyterian ministry in 1886. After six years as minister of the Church of the Redeemer, Germantown, Pennsylvania, he resigned to edit a series of hymnals for the General Assembly of the Presbyterian Church, U.S.A. He edited *The Hymnal* (1895) and its revision (1911), *The Hymnal for Congregational Churches, The Chapel Hymnal,* and *The School Hymnal.* He was joint editor with Henry van Dyke of *The Book of Common Worship of the Presbyterian Church in the U.S.A.* Of his several hymnological works, the most significant is *The English Hymn: Its Development and Use in Worship* (1915). His large and valuable hymnological library was bequeathed to the Princeton Seminary (Cf. *The Hymn,* VI, 4, 113).

O thou whose gracious presence blest (375)
The light of God is falling (442)

Bernard of Clairvaux (b. Les Fontaines, near Dijon, Fr., 1091; d. Clairvaux, Fr., Aug. 20, 1153), was born in his father's castle at Les Fontaines. His father, a friend of the Duke of Burgundy, perished in the First Crusade. Bernard was educated at Chatillon. With a group of other noblemen, including an uncle and two brothers, he entered the Cistercian monastery at Citeaux in 1113. With twelve other monks he founded Clairvaux in 1115, from which he subsequently founded sixty-eight other monasteries. He was a highly respected person and achieved a position of great influence in his day. Luther called him "the greatest monk that ever lived." His authorship of the hymns listed below has been seriously questioned.

Jesus, the very thought of Thee (135)
Jesus, Thou joy of loving hearts (136)

Bernard of Cluny (twelfth century). Only fragments of information are known about this Bernard. He entered the abbey of Cluny and was there during the time that Peter the Venerable was abbot, 1122-56. This monastery was at its apex of cultural splendor during the twelfth century, and it was in this environment that Bernard wrote his *De Contemptu Mundi*, a satire against the vices and follies of his day. It was dedicated to the abbot.

Jerusalem, the golden (477)

Bethune, George Washington (b. New York, 1805; d. Florence, Italy, April 27, 1862), was educated at Dickinson College and Princeton Seminary. He was ordained to the Dutch Reformed ministry and was pastor in Rinebeck, New York (1827-30), Utica (1830-34), Philadelphia (1834-50), and Brooklyn Heights (1850-72). He was offered the chancellorship of New York University and the provostship of the University of Pennsylvania, both of which he declined. He wrote a number of hymns, most of which have passed from common usage. Among his published works are *The Fruits of the Spirit* (1839), Sermons (1847), *Lays of Love and Faith* (1847); and *The British Female Poets* (1848). He visited Italy in 1861-62, for his health, and died suddenly in Florence after having preached there.

O Thou who in Jordan didst bow Thy meek head (388)

Bevan, Emma Frances (b. Oxford, Eng., Sept. 25, 1827; d. Cannes, Fr., 1909), was the daughter of the Rev. Philip Nicholas Shuttleworth, warden of New College, Oxford, and later Bishop of Chichester. In 1856 she married R. C. L. Bevan, a London banker. Her greatest contribution to hymnic literature rests in her translations of German verse, which were published in her *Songs of Eternal Life* (1858) and in *Songs of Praise for Christian Pilgrims* (1859).

Sinners Jesus will receive (tr.) (195)

Bigelow, James, is the pseudonym of a Southern Baptist composer who prefers to remain anonymous.
Responses (519, 527)

Bilhorn, Peter Philip (b. Mendota, Ill., July 22, 1865; d. Los Angeles, Calif., Dec. 13, 1936), was of Bavarian descent, and the family name of Pulhorn was changed to Bilhorn by Abraham Lincoln, while the latter was a judge at Ottawa, Illinois. His father, George Bilhorn, a carriage maker by trade, was killed in the Civil War three months before his birth. In 1876 the Bilhorn family moved to Chicago, and some time after this he and his older brother, following their father's trade, established the Eureka Wagon and Carriage Works.

He possessed a fine singing voice and became a popular singer in the German concert halls and beer gardens of Chicago. In 1883, during a revival conducted by George F. Pentecost and George C. Stebbins, he was converted. He decided to pursue seriously his musical education and studied with Frederick W. Root, Jean de Reske, and George C. Stebbins. Leaving his brother to manage the family business, he traveled extensively in evangelistic work with evangelists D. D. O'Dell, George F. Pentecost, and John Currie. He spent some time among the cowboys of the Dakotas and returned to Chicago about 1887.

In need of a small portable musical instrument for his evangelistic work, he invented a small reed organ weighing less than seventy pounds, which could be carried in a folding case. These organs, manufactured by the Bilhorn Folding Organ Company, Chicago, became very popular for evangelistic and missionary work. Bilhorn donated the profits from this venture to religious work in Chicago. He composed quite a number of gospel songs and became a publisher of considerable stature in Chicago.

As an evangelistic song leader he achieved widespread fame, and preceded Homer Rodeheaver as Billy Sunday's song leader prior to 1908. At the World's Christian Endeavor Convention in London's Crystal Palace in 1900 he conducted a choir of four thousand voices. During this time, at the invitation of Queen Victoria, he sang several of his hymns in the chapel of Buckingham Palace. As a composer and hymn writer, he produced more than two thousand songs. The publications of the Bilhorn Publishing Company met with considerable success, and at the time of his death he owned the copyrights to more than fourteen hundred gospel songs. His published works include *Crowning Glory No. 1* (1888), *Crowning Glory No. 2*, *Soul-Winning Songs*, *Choice Songs: Hymns of Heavenly Harmony*, *Sunshine Songs*, *Songs of Peace and Power*, *Century Gospel Hymns*, *Songs for Male Choruses* (2 vols.), *Sacred and Secular Selections for Ladies' Voices* (1900), and three books of anthems.

There comes to my heart one sweet strain—SWEET PEACE (299)
WONDROUS STORY—I will sing the wondrous story (144)

Black, James Milton (b. South Hill, Sullivan Co., N.Y., Aug. 19, 1856; d. Williamsport, Pa., Dec. 21, 1938). Following an early music education in singing and organ playing, Black became a teacher of singing schools. He was the editor of more than a dozen gospel songbooks which were published by the Methodist Book Concern (New York and Cincinnati), McCabe Publishing Company (Chicago), and the Hall-Mack Company (Philadelphia). The most popular collection was *Songs of the Soul* (1894), which in the first two years sold more than four hundred thousand copies. An active Methodist, Black was appointed by the bishops of the Methodist Episcopal Church to serve on the Joint Commission for the *Methodist Hymnal* (1905). It is interesting to note that while he was the only gospel song composer to serve on the commission, not one of his songs was included in the hymnal. He was a member of the Pine Street Methodist Church, Williamsport, from 1904 until his death.

When the trumpet of the Lord shall sound—ROLL CALL (482)

Blanchard, Ferdinand Quincy (b. Jersey City, N.J., July 23, 1876). The son of Edward Richmond and Anna Winifred (Quincy) Blanchard, Blanchard was educated at Amherst College (A.B., 1898) and Yale Divinity School (B.D., 1901). He was ordained to the Congregational ministry and served as pastor at Southington, Connecticut, 1901-04, and at East Orange, New Jersey, 1904-15. From 1915 until his retirement he was pastor of the Euclid Avenue Congregational Church, Cleveland, Ohio. He has received many honors, including the honorary D.D. degree from Amherst College, 1918, and Oberlin University, 1919. A respected leader in his denomination, he was elected moderator of the Congregational Christian Churches of the U.S.A. He has written several hymns.

Word of God, across the ages (176)

Blandy, E. W. The identity of this author is unknown.

I can hear my Saviour calling (361)

Bliss, Philip Paul (b. Clearfield Co., Pa., July 9, 1838; d. near Ashtabula, Ohio, Dec. 29, 1876), was born in a log cabin. At the age of eleven he left home to work on farms and in lumber camps. He was converted about the age of twelve and joined the Baptist church near Elk Run, Pennsylvania. His first musical instruction was under J. G. Towner, the father of D. B. Towner. The same year he attended his first musical convention, which was conducted by W. B. Bradbury at Rome, Pennsylvania. He married Lucy J. Young in 1859 and for the following year worked on the farm for his father-in-law. In 1860, with the help of his horse, Old Fanny, and a twenty-dollar melodeon, he began work as a professional music teacher. He taught singing schools during the winter season and for several summers he attended the Normal Academy of Music at Geneseo, New York, conducted by T. E. Perkins, T. J. Cook, Bassini, and others. He sold his first song to Root and Cady, Chicago music publishers, in 1864, and shortly afterward became associated with this firm for four years. He taught singing schools and held musical conventions, and was widely known as a teacher, soloist and leader. The persistent encouragement of D. L. Moody and other friends caused him to give up his music teaching and become a singing evangelist. Beginning in March, 1874, he was associated with Major D. W. Whittle in twenty-five revival meetings in Illinois, Wisconsin, Michigan, Pennsylvania, Kentucky, Tennessee, Minnesota, Missouri, Alabama, and Georgia. Following a revival in Peoria in early December, 1876, he spent Christmas with his family in Rome, Pennsylvania. Leaving their children in Rome, Bliss and his wife left by train for Chicago for an engagement in Moody's Tabernacle the following Sunday. As the train crossed a ravine approaching Ashtabula, the bridge gave way and seven cars plunged into the icy river bed and the wreckage burst into flames. Bliss survived the fall and escaped through a window. He desperately returned to the wreckage to rescue his wife and both perished in the fire.

He furnished many songs for the collections of George F. Root, but the first compilation to bear his name was *The Charm, a Collection of Sunday School Music* (1871). This was followed by *Sunshine for Sunday Schools* (1873); *Gospel Songs, a Choice Collection of Hymns and Tunes, New and Old, for Gospel Meetings, Sunday Schools, Etc.* (1874); *Gospel Hymns and Sacred Songs* (1875); and *Gospel Hymns No. 2* (1876, compiled jointly by Bliss and Ira D. Sankey).

"Almost persuaded" now to believe—ALMOST PERSUADED (248)
Brightly beams our Father's mercy—LOWER LIGHTS (300)
Free from the law, O happy condition—ONCE FOR ALL (199)
I am so glad that our Father in heaven—JESUS LOVES EVEN ME (509)
I will sing of my Redeemer (143)
"Man of sorrows," what a name—HALLELUJAH! WHAT A SAVIOUR (163)
More holiness give me—MY PRAYER (338)
Sing them over again to me—WORDS OF LIFE (181)
The whole world was lost in the darkness of sin—LIGHT OF THE WORLD (88)
Whosoever heareth, "shout, shout the sound—WHOSOEVER (238)
KENOSIS—I gave my life for thee (399)
VILLE DU HAVRE—When peace, like a river, attendeth my way (265)

254

Bode, John Ernest (b. London, Eng., Feb. 23, 1816; d. Castle Camps, Cambridgeshire, Eng., Oct. 6, 1874), was educated at Eton and Christ Church, Oxford, where he was the first winner of the Hertford Scholarship in 1835. He was tutor in Christ Church for seven years and in 1847 became rector at Westwell, Oxfordshire. In 1860 he was appointed rector of Castle Camps, Cambridgeshire. He delivered the Bampton Lectures at Oxford in 1855. Among his published works are *Ballads from Herodotus* (1853), *Short Occasional Poems* (1858), and *Hymns from the Gospel of the Day* (1860).

O Jesus, I have promised (386)

Bonar, Horatius (b. Edinburgh, Scot., Dec. 19, 1808; d. Edinburgh, July 31, 1889), was educated at the University of Edinburgh. In 1837 at Kelso, he was ordained to the ministry of the Church of Scotland and was given charge of the North Parish. He and his church at Kelso were vigorously active in the movement which led to the founding of the Free Church of Scotland in 1843. He was one of the editors of *The Border Watch,* the official paper of the Free Church, and for many years, because of his keen interest in the second coming of Christ, he was editor of *The Journal of Prophecy.* In 1866 he became pastor of Chalmers Memorial Free Church, Edinburgh, named for Thomas Chalmers, the leader and first moderator of the Free Church Movement, who had been Bonar's teacher at the University of Edinburgh. In 1883, Bonar was elected moderator of the General Assembly of the Free Church of Scotland. Among his works are *Songs for the Wilderness* (1843); *The Bible Hymn Book* (1845); *Hymns, Original and Selected* (1846); *Hymns of Faith and Hope* (1857; second series, 1861); *The Song of the New Creation* (1872); and *Hymns of the Nativity* (1879).

Here, O my Lord, I see Thee face to face (391)
I heard the voice of Jesus say (302)
I lay my sins on Jesus (210)
No, not despairingly (206)

Borthwick, Jane Laurie (b. Edinburgh, Scot., Apr. 9, 1813; d. Edinburgh, Sept. 7, 1897), was the elder daughter of James Borthwick, manager of the North British Insurance Office, Edinburgh. With her sister, Sarah (Mrs. Eric Findlater), she published *Hymns from the Land of Luther* (four series, 1854, 1855, 1858, 1862), translations of German hymns. Sixty-one of the translations were by Jane and fifty-three by Sarah. Many of these hymns appeared in *The Family Treasury* signed "H. L. L.," the initials being derived from the title of the above collection. Charles Rogers, in his *Lyra Britannica* (1867), revealed "H. L. L."

as being Miss Borthwick, much to her displeasure, for she had used these initials for a good deal of prose and verse, as well as translations which she had contributed to various publications.

My Jesus, as Thou wilt! (tr.) (251)

Bortniansky, Dimitri Stepanovich (b. Gloukoff, Ukraine, Russ., Oct. 28, 1752; d. St. Petersburg, Russ., Oct. 7, 1825), studied in Moscow and later in St. Petersburg under Galuppi. In 1768 he followed his teacher to Venice with financial support from Catherine the Great, Empress of Russia. After further study in Bologna, Rome, and Naples, he returned to St. Petersburg in 1779 and was placed in charge of the Imperial Chapel Choir. He established a high degree of excellence in the performance of this group and wrote a great deal of church music for its use. Toward the end of the nineteenth century, his compositions were published in ten volumes, edited by Tschaikowsky.

ST. PETERSBURG—Revealing Word, thy light portrays (177)
VESPER HYMN—Now, on land and sea descending (28)

Bourgeois, Louis (b. Paris, Fr., *ca.* 1510; d. *ca.* 1561). A native of Paris, he became a follower of John Calvin and moved to Geneva in 1541. He was appointed cantor in St. Peter's Church and became master of the choristers in 1545. He was given the responsibility of providing tunes for the metrical psalms, at that time in gradual preparation, and produced a partial psalter in 1542. As a starting point for this work, he used the tunes in Calvin's Strassburg psalter in 1539, altering some and replacing some of the old tunes with new ones, and adding others. From 1542 to 1557 he served as music editor for the successive editions of the *Genevan Psalter*. It is not known how many original tunes he contributed to these editions. However, the significance of his workmanship is seen in the evidence presented by Douen, *Clément Marot et la Psautier Huguenot* (1878), and Pratt, *The Music of the French Psalter of 1562* (1939), that of the 125 tunes in the completed psalter, he was responsible for the final form of 85. He returned to Paris in 1557 and was last heard of in 1561, when he published a collection of harmonized psalm tunes.

OLD 100TH—All people that on earth do dwell (13)
Praise God from whom all blessings flow (514)

Bowring, John (b. Exeter, Eng., Oct. 17, 1792; d. Exeter, Nov. 23, 1872). The son of a woolen goods manufacturer, Bowring left school at the age of fourteen to assist his father. He became greatly interested in the mercantile business and because of the world trade involved, became interested in languages. One of the outstanding linguists of his day, he claimed to understand two hundred languages and to speak one hundred. He translated considerable verse from other languages. Because of his keen interest in politics and social reform, he was a contributor to the *Westminster Review,* and succeeded Jeremy Bentham as editor in 1825. Later he became active in the political life of England, serving in Parliament beginning in 1835; appointed consul at Canton, 1849; minister plenipotentiary to China in 1854; and later governor of Hong Kong. He was knighted by Queen Victoria in 1854. While he was a Unitarian, he has been described as being "nearer to orthodoxy than the radical wing of his own denomination." His extensive writings were published in thirty-six volumes. Among these are *Matins and Vespers* (1823), and *Hymns, as a Sequel to the Matins* (1825).

God is love; His mercy brightens (50)
In the cross of Christ I glory (100)
Watchman! tells us of the night (462)

Boyd, William (b. Montego Bay, Jamaica, 1847; d. London, Eng., Feb. 16, 1928). Tutored by Sabine Baring-Gould at Hurstpierpoint, he later attended Worcester College, Oxford. Ordained in the Church of England in 1877, he became vicar of All Saints Church, Norfolk Square, London, in 1893, serving in this position until his retirement in 1918. He. was one of fourteen contributors to *Thirty-two Hymn-Tunes composed by Members of the University of Oxford* (1868). Of these tunes, only PENTECOST remains in common usage.

PENTECOST—Fight the good fight with all thy might (406)
Let there be light, Lord God of hosts (444)

Bradbury, William Batchelder (b. York, Me., Oct. 6, 1816; d. Montclair, N.J., Jan. 7, 1868). In 1830 Bradbury's family moved to Boston, and he attended the Boston Academy of Music and sang in Lowell Mason's choir at Bowdoin Street Church. In 1840 he served as organist at the First Baptist Church, Brooklyn, and the following year held the same position at the Baptist Tabernacle, New York City, where he conducted singing classes after the pattern of Mason's work in Boston. In 1847 he took his family to Europe and spent two years in Leipzig studying with Wenzel, Boehm, and Hauptman. Returning to New York in 1849, he devoted his time to teaching, conducting musical conventions, composing, and editing books. In 1854 he joined his brother, E. G. Bradbury, in establishing the Bradbury Piano Company. This enterprise was later taken over by Knabe. Between 1841 and 1867 Bradbury was associated with the publishing of fifty-nine collections of sacred and secular music. Among the more important of these are *The Young Choir* (1841), *The Psalmodist* (1844), *The Mendelssohn Collection* (1849), *The Shawm* (1853), *The Jubilee* (1858), *The Golden Chain* (1861), *Devotional Hymn and Tune Book* (1864), and *The Golden Censer,* (1864).

ALETTA—Holy Bible, Book Divine (179)
BRADBURY—Saviour, like a shepherd lead us (344)
BROWN—With joy we hail the sacred day (38)
CHINA—Jesus loves me! this I know (512)
HE LEADETH ME—He leadeth me! O blessed thought (58)
OLIVE'S BROW—'Tis midnight, and on Olive's brow (104)
SOLID ROCK—My hope is built on nothing less (283)
SWEET HOUR—Sweet hour of prayer, sweet hour of prayer (327)
SWEET STORY—I think when I read that sweet story of old (506)
WOODWORTH—Just as I am, without one plea (240)
   God calling yet! shall I not hear (223)
YARBROUGH—Take my life, and let it be (356)

Breck, Carrie E. (Mrs. Frank A.; b. Vermont, Jan. 22, 1855; d. Portland, Ore., Mar. 27, 1934). After her childhood in Vermont and a short residence in New Jersey, she moved to Portland, Oregon. A devoted housewife, the mother of five daughters, she gave lyric expression to her Christian devotion as she carried out her routine duties of the day. Her poems were often written as she did the daily housework. She was a member of the Presbyterian church.

Face to face with Christ, my Saviour (475)

Bridgers, Luther Burgess (b. Margaretsville, N.C., Feb. 14, 1884; d. Atlanta, Ga., May 27, 1948), began preaching at the age of seventeen and was a student at Asbury College in Kentucky. For more than twelve years he served as a pastor in Methodist churches, during which time he was widely known for his evangelistic zeal. In 1910 he suffered the tragic loss of his wife and three sons who were burned to death in the fire which destroyed his father-in-law's home in Harrodsburg, Kentucky, where they were visiting. In 1914 he became a general evangelist for the Methodist Episcopal Church, South. He was engaged in evangelistic work for eighteen years, with the exception of a brief period following World War I in which he was engaged in mission work in Belgium, Czechoslovakia, and Russia. In 1914 he married Miss Aline Winburn of Gainesville, Georgia, a music teacher at Shorter College, Rome, Georgia. After 1932 he served as a pastor in Georgia and North Carolina for thirteen years, and lived in Gainesville, Georgia, after his retirement.

There's within my heart a melody—SWEETEST NAME (307)

Bridges, Matthew (b. Malden, Essex, Eng., July 14, 1800; d. Sidmouth, Devonshire, Eng., Oct. 6, 1894), was educated in the Church of England, and in 1828 he published a book against the Roman Catholic Church entitled *The Roman Empire Under Constantine the Great.* Later, however, he came under the influence of the Oxford Movement and followed John Henry Newman and others into the Roman Church in 1848. Beside his political works, he published several volumes of history. Several hymns from his *Hymns of the Heart* (1847; enlarged 1851) and *The Passion of Jesus* (1852) have found their way into common usage. Henry Ward Beecher introduced several of these in America in his *Plymouth Collection* (1855). Bridges spent the latter part of his life in Canada in the province of Quebec.

Crown Him with many crowns (152)

Brooks, Phillips (b. Boston, Mass., Dec. 13, 1835; d. Boston, Jan. 23, 1893). Educated at the Boston Latin School and Harvard University, Brooks studied for the ministry at the Virginia Theological Seminary (Episcopal), Alexandria. Ordained in 1859, he began his ministry in Philadelphia at the Church of the Advent and three years later became rector of Holy Trinity Church of that city. In 1869 he became rector of Trinity Church, Boston, where he had a most fruitful ministry for twenty-two years. He was recognized as one of America's outstanding preachers, and many volumes of his sermons have been published. He delivered the now famous *Lectures on Preaching* at Yale Divinity School in 1877, and received the D.D. degree from Oxford University in 1885. In 1891 he was appointed bishop of Massachusetts, in which capacity he served only two years before his untimely death in 1893.

O little town of Bethlehem (75)

, **Brown, Ann** (b. Meridian, Miss., Feb. 20, 1908), is the daughter of Wiley B. and Mary (Rives) Brown. At an early age her family moved to Shreveport, Louisiana, where she received her education in the public schools and Centenary College, graduating *summa cum laude* in 1927. Shortly after completing college she became a public school teacher in Shreveport. In 1936 she was married to Walter Hines Sims (*q.v.*), the editor of *Baptist Hymnal.* After moving to Nashville, Tennessee, in 1945, she became head of the Latin Department of Montgomery Bell Academy, a preparatory school for boys.

Grace, love, and peace abide (539)

Brown, Mary, is believed to have lived in Jewett City, Connecticut, during the last decades of the nineteenth century. Other than this, no information is known.

It may not be on the mountain's height (425)

Buell, Harriett Eugenia Peck (b. Cozenovia, N.Y., Nov. 2, 1834; d. Washington, D.C., Feb. 6, 1910), was a regular contributor to the *Northern Christian Advocate,* Syracuse, New York, for fifty years. Until 1898 she made her home in Manlius, New York, and was an active member of the Methodist church there. After this date she resided in Washington, D.C., but continued to make her summer home in Thousand Island Park, New York.

My Father is rich in houses and lands (270)

Bullinger, Ethelbert William (b. Canterbury, Eng., Dec. 15, 1837; d. London, Eng., June 6, 1913). An Anglican clergyman, Bullinger was educated at King's College, London. He was greatly interested in music and studied with John Hullah and William H. Monk. An able Greek and Hebrew scholar, he was given the honorary Doctor of Divinity degree by the Archbishop of Canterbury in 1881. He composed several hymn tunes, the one included here being the only one remaining in common usage.

BULLINGER—Come to Jesus, ye who labor (246)

Bunnett, Edward (b. Shipdham, Norfolk, Eng., June 26, 1834; d. Norwich, Eng., Jan. 5, 1923). As a lad of eight Bunnett became a chorister at Norwich Cathedral and began organ study at the age of fifteen. In 1855 he became assistant organist to his teacher, Dr. Zechariah Buck, and served in this position for twenty-two years. He was educated at Cambridge University and received his doctorate there in 1869. He served as the conductor of the Norwich Musical Union for more than twenty-one years. In 1877 he became organist at St. Peter's, Mancroft, where his skilful playing brought him much attention and an enviable reputation.

KIRBY BEDON—Shepherd of tender youth (162)

Burnap, Uzziah Christopher (b. Brooklyn, N.Y., June 17, 1834; d. Brooklyn, Dec. 8, 1900). As a young man Burnap studied music in Paris. In his business ventures he was most successful and became a well-known dry goods merchant in Brooklyn. His keen interest in music is evidenced by the fact that he served as organist in the Reformed Church on the Heights, Brooklyn, for thirty-seven years. He composed numerous hymn tunes and collaborated with John K. Paine of Harvard University in compiling *Hymns and Songs of Praise.* He served as musical editor for the Reformed Church hymnal, *Hymns of the Church: with Tunes* (New York, 1869).

AMESBURY—O Master Workman of the race (441)

Burrowes, John Freckleton (b. London, Eng., Apr. 23, 1787; d. London, Mar. 31, 1852). An English composer and organist, Burrowes served as organist at St. James's Church, Piccadilly, for nearly forty years. He was a prolific composer who devoted most of his creative efforts to the writing of popular ballads and simple piano pieces.

BURLINGTON—A glory gilds the sacred page (186)

Burton, Henry (b. Swannington, Leicestershire, Eng., Nov. 26, 1840; d. West Kirby, Cheshire, Eng., Apr. 27, 1930). The members of Burton's family were ardent Methodists, and he was converted at the age of fifteen at a service held in his father's barn. With his mother and father and nine brothers and sisters he emigrated to America in 1856 and settled in northern Illinois. After his graduation from Beloit College in Wisconsin, he returned to England and was ordained in the Wesleyan Methodist ministry in 1869. His active ministry was largely in Lancashire and London, spanning more than forty years. Among his published works are *Gleanings from the Gospels,* "St. Luke" in the *Expositor's Bible,* and a book of poems, *Wayside Songs* (1886).

There's a light upon the mountains (124)

Burton, John, Sr. (b. Nottingham, Eng., Feb. 26, 1773; d. Leicester, Eng., June 24, 1822). An active Baptist layman, Burton became interested in Sunday school work, and wrote his first hymns for the children of his Sunday school. A volume of his hymns was published in 1802, under the title *The Youth's Monitor in Verse, in a Series of Little Tales, Emblems, Poems and Songs.* He was one of the compilers of the *Nottingham Sunday School Union Hymn Book* (1810), which passed through twenty editions by 1861.

Holy Bible, Book divine (179)

Bushey, J. Calvin, was a singing school teacher who lived in Ohio in the second half of the nineteenth century. He compiled several collections, among which were *The Chorus Class* (1879) and *Choral Climax* (1886), both published by the publishing firm of Will Thompson (*q.v.*) in East Liverpool, Ohio. Bushey's *Magnetic Melodies* (1892) was published by Thompson's Chicago branch. No other information has been discovered concerning this composer.

CALVIN—O do not let the Word depart (234)

Byrne, Mary Elizabeth (b. Dublin, Ire., 1880; d. Dublin, 1931), was educated at the Dominican Convent, Dublin, and at the University of Ireland. She became a research worker in the Board of Intermediate Education and was one of the compilers of the *Catalogue* of the Royal Irish Academy. Her most important work was her contribution to the *Old and Mid-Irish Dictionary* and the *Dictionary of the Irish Language*.

Be Thou my vision, O Lord of my heart (tr.) (62)

Calkin, John Baptiste (b. London, Eng., Mar. 16, 1827; d. London, Apr. 15, 1905). Calkin's father, a well-known music teacher, gave him his first musical instruction. At the age of twenty the son succeeded E. G. Monk as organist at St. Columba's College, Rathfarnham, near Dublin. Returning to London six years later, he held various organ positions, including Woburn Chapel. In 1883 he was appointed to the faculty of the Guildhall School of Music. He was a member of the Council of Trinity College, London, and a Fellow of the Royal College of Organists.

WALTHAM—Fling out the banner! let it float (446)
I heard the bells on Christmas day (78)
Ring out the old, ring in the new (496)

Campbell, Jane Montgomery (b. Paddington, London, Eng., 1817; d. Bovey Tracey, South Devon, Eng., Nov. 15, 1878), was the daughter of the Rev. A. Montgomery Campbell, rector of St. James's Church, Paddington, Hyde Park, London. She taught singing to the children in her father's parish school and published a *Handbook for Singers,* which contained the musical exercises used in her teaching. She was quite proficient in German and translated a number of German hymns which she contributed to the Rev. Charles S. Bere's *Garland of Songs, or an English Liederkranz* (London, 1862).

We plow the fields and scatter (tr.) (493)

Carr, Benjamin (b. London, Eng., Sept. 12, 1769; d. Philadelphia, Pa., May 24, 1831), received a thorough musical education in England and was well known as a singer with the London Ancient Concerts before he came to America in 1793. With his brother, Thomas, and their father, Joseph Carr, the Carr family became successful music publishers and dealers with stores in Philadelphia, New York, and Baltimore. Benjamin Carr's significant contributions to the musical culture of America were made as a composer, arranger, organist, pianist, and, most of all, as publisher and editor. He edited the weekly *Musical Journal,* and was one of the founders of the Musical Fund Society of Philadelphia in 1820. Through his publications and in sponsoring public concern, Carr gave great encouragement to contemporary American composers and artists as well as musicians from England and Europe. Among his significant collections of sacred music are *Masses, Vespers, and Litanies* (1805); *A Collection of Chants* (1816); and *The Chorister* (1820). (Cf. "The Carrs, American Music Publishers," *Musical Quarterly,* XVIII, 150-77.)

SPANISH HYMN (arr.)—Christ, whose glory fills the skies (22)

Carter, Russell Kelso (b. Baltimore, Md., Nov. 18, 1849; d. Catonsville, Baltimore Co., Md., Aug. 23, 1926), graduated in the first class from Pennsylvania Military Academy, Chester, 1867, and was recognized as an outstanding baseball pitcher and gymnast during his student days. In this school he remained to become an instructor in 1869, a professor of chemistry and natural sciences in 1872, and professor of civil engineering and higher mathematics in 1881. He spent a brief time, 1873-76, in California where he engaged in sheep raising. In 1887 he resigned his teaching position and was ordained into the Methodist ministry, where he became identified with the Holiness movement and was quite active in camp meeting activities. His literary output was prolific in the areas of mathematics, science, and religion. He published several novels. *Hymns of the Christian Life,* which he edited with A. B. Simpson, was published in 1891. To this collection Carter contributed fifty-two hymns, for forty-four of which he provided original tunes. For texts by other writers he wrote twenty-four tunes, and is credited as the arranger or adapter for twenty-five other tunes. After a number of years in the ministry, he took up the study of medicine and became a practicing physician in Baltimore.

Standing on the promises of Christ my King—PROMISES (266)

Case, Charles Clinton (b. near Linesville, Crawford Co., Pa., June 6, 1843; d. Oberlin, Ohio, Dec. 1, 1918). When Case was four years of age his family moved to Gustavus, Ohio, where he made his home until the last few years of his life. While still in his teens he came under the influence of the singing schools of such teachers as C. A. Bentley, G. Frederick Wright, and William B. Bradbury. Shortly afterward he began teaching, and during the summers he attended music normals conducted by George F. Root, William Mason, H. R. Palmer, P. P. Bliss, L. O. Emerson, and George J. Webb, all outstanding teachers of the day. He became a close friend of James McGranahan, who lived nearby, and

263

together they attended music conventions, were associated as faculty members, and jointly compiled *The Choice* (1875), and *Harvest of Song* (1877). He compiled and edited a number of collections for use in his conventions, as well as several Sunday school songbooks, nearly all of which were published by the John Church Company of Cincinnati, Ohio. For twelve years he led the music at Chautauqua Lake, New York, and was active in other Chautauqua meetings. For three years he led the 150-voice choir at the Moody Memorial Church in Chicago. He was also music director at the First Methodist Episcopal Church, Akron, Ohio, and the Ruggles Street Baptist Church, Boston, Massachusetts. For ten years he spent a part of each season with Dwight L. Moody as soloist and music director.

WHY NOT NOW?—While we pray and while we plead (218)

Cassel, Elijah Taylor (b. Indiana, Nov. 27, 1849; d. South Gate, Calif., July 3, 1930). During Cassel's early childhood his family moved by ox cart to Nebraska. After completing his medical education, he practiced medicine at Hastings, Nebraska. He was an active Baptist layman and well respected for his musical ability. About 1910, after he was past sixty years of age, he abandoned his medical practice and entered the ministry. He was ordained in Denver, Colorado, and served as pastor of the Bethel Baptist Church, Denver, 1911-17, and the First Baptist Church, Fort Morgan, Colorado, 1919-21. Shortly after he began his pastoral work in Denver, his wife, Flora Hamilton Cassel (*q.v.*), was killed. He remarried about 1917, before moving to Fort Morgan. In 1922 he moved to California, residing at South Gate. He joined the First Baptist Church of Huntington Park, where he taught a Bible class until his death. A memorial window in this church honors his memory. His second wife, Mrs. Anna Mae Cassel, died in 1949.

From over hill and plain (407)
I am a stranger here, within a foreign land (433)

Cassel, Flora Hamilton (b. Otterville, Ill., Aug. 21, 1852; d. Denver, Colo., Nov. 17, 1911), spent most of her childhood in Whitehall, Illinois, where her father, Rev. B. B. Hamilton, was pastor of the Baptist church. After she was sixteen, she lived with an aunt in Brooklyn, where she continued her school work and studied voice with Madame Hartell of New York. She was graduated from Maplewood Institute, Pittsfield, Massachusetts, in 1873, and became head of the music department of Shurtleff College, Upper Alton, Illinois. While here she married Dr. E. Taylor Cassel (*q.v.*), of Nebraska.

264

She was active in the Woman's Christian Temperance Union and published a collection of 116 original temperance songs, *White Ribbon Vibrations* (1890). Her tragic death occurred shortly after the Cassels had moved to Denver, Colorado. She had driven a buggy to the post office in University Park to pick up the mail. Returning to the buggy, she untied the team and stepped on the step. Something frightened the horses; and with her long skirts wrapped around the buggy step, she was dragged to death.

CASSEL—I am a stranger here, within a foreign land (433)
LAMBDIN—From over hill and plain (407)

Caswall, Edward (b. Yately, Hampshire, Eng., July 15, 1814; d. Edgbaston, Birmingham, Eng., Jan. 2, 1878). A son of the vicar at Yately, Caswall was educated at Marlborough and Brasenose College, Oxford. In 1840, following his ordination, he was appointed curate of Stratford-sub-Castle, Wiltshire. He became greatly interested in Catholicism, resigned his position in 1847, and was received into the Roman Catholic Church. His wife, who shared his enthusiasm for Catholicism, died in 1849, and the following year Caswell became a priest and entered the Oratory of St. Philip Neri at Edgbaston under Cardinal Newman. His most significant publication was *Lyra Catholica* (London, 1849), which contained 197 translations of Latin hymns from the *Roman Breviary* and other sources. Because of doctrinal reasons, few of his original hymns have been used outside the Roman Catholic Church.

Jesus, the very thought of thee (tr.) (135)
When morning gilds the skies (tr.) (23)

Cennick, John (b. Reading, Berkshire, Eng., Dec. 12, 1718; d. London, Eng., July 4, 1755). Born of Quaker parents, Cennick was brought up in the Church of England. Under the influence of John Wesley, he gave up his work as a land surveyor, was appointed by Wesley to teach the children of the coal miners at Kingswood, and became one of the first lay preachers of the Methodist group. Because of doctrinal differences, he left the Wesleys and joined with George Whitefield. In 1845 he joined the Moravian Brethren and was ordained in 1849. As a Moravian Brethren preacher he traveled and preached in Germany and Ireland. Among his published works are: *Sacred Hymns for the Children of God* (1741); *Sacred Hymns for the Use of Religious Societies* (1743); and *Hymns to the Honour of Jesus Christ* (1754). (Cf. *The Hymn*, VI, No. 3, 87.)

Be present at our table, Lord (396)

Challinor, Frederick Arthur (b. Longton, Staffordshire, Eng., Nov. 12, 1866; d. Paignton, Eng., 1952). At the age of ten Challinor was working in a brickyard, a year later he was working in a coal mine, and at age fifteen he was employed in a china factory. His musical interests were greatly increased through a piano which his family received as part of a legacy. He received his bachelor's degree in music in 1897, and six years later he earned the doctor's degree in music. He was actively engaged in composition; more than one thousand of his works have been published.

STORIES OF JESUS—Tell me the stories of Jesus (505)

Chapman, J. Wilbur (b. Richmond, Ind., June 17, 1859; d. Jamaica, Long Island, N.Y., Dec. 25, 1918). The son of Alexander and Lorinda (McWhitney) Chapman, Wilbur was educated at Lake Forest University (Illinois), and Lane Theological Seminary. Ordained to the Presbyterian ministry, he served as pastor of the First Reformed Church, Albany, New York, 1884-90; Bethany Presbyterian Church, Philadelphia, 1890-93, 1896-1900; and the First Presbyterian Church, New York City, 1900-05. He became an outstanding evangelist and traveled extensively conducting revival meetings. He was assisted for several years by Charles M. Alexander, a well-known evangelistic singer. In 1917 he was elected moderator for the General Assembly of the Presbyterian Church, U.S.A. He conducted many Bible conferences and was the first director of the Winona Lake Bible Conference (Indiana). Later he was largely responsible for beginning similar conferences at Montreat, North Carolina, and Stony Brook, Long Island, New York. In addition to eight published books, he wrote a number of hymn texts.

One day when heaven was filled with His praises (85)

Chisholm, Thomas Obediah (b. near Franklin, Simpson Co., Ky., July 29, 1866; d. Ocean Grove, N.J., Feb. 29, 1960), without high school or any other advanced training, taught school at the age of sixteen in the little country schoolhouse where he received his own education. When he was twenty-one, he became the associate editor of his home town weekly newspaper, the *Franklin Favorite*. Six years later he was converted during a revival meeting conducted in Franklin by Dr. H. C. Morrison. At Dr. Morrison's invitation he moved to Louisville to become office editor and business manager of Morrison's *Pentecostal Herald*. He was later ordained to the Methodist ministry and in 1903 joined the Louisville Methodist Conference. His health failed after a one-year pastorate at Scottsville, Kentucky, and he spent the next five years with his family on a farm near Winona Lake, Indiana. After 1909 he became a life insurance agent in Winona Lake and continued this same work when he moved to Vineland, New Jersey, in 1916. He retired in 1953 and spent his remaining years at the Methodist Home for the Aged, Ocean Grove. He wrote more than twelve hundred poems, more than eight hundred of which have appeared in religious periodicals, with quite a number being used as hymn texts. Of these hymn texts only the two given here have become widely known.

Great is Thy faithfulness, O God my Father (47)
Living for Jesus a life that is true (352)

Chopin, Frederic (b. Zelazowa Wola, Pol., Feb. 22, 1810; d. Paris, Fr., Oct. 17, 1849). One of the greatest composers of music for the piano, Chopin was by parentage half Polish and half French. At an early age he exhibited unusual musical talent. As a child his piano teacher was Adalbert Zwyny. Later he studied composition with Joseph Elsner of the Warsaw Conservatorium. He made his Paris debut in 1832, and made this city his headquarters until his death at the age of thirty-nine. Details of his life and lists of his works are readily available and need not be included here.

Response (531)

Chorley, Henry Fothergill (b. Blackley, Lancashire, Eng., Dec. 15, 1808; d. London, Eng., Feb. 16, 1872), although lacking in formal education, early showed literary talent. He gave up his job in a merchant's office in Liverpool to become a musical journalist. He became associated with the London *Athenaeum* in 1830 and was its musical editor for thirty-five years. He was also music critic for *The Times* for many years. In addition to his writings on music, literature, and art, he wrote novels, dramas, and verse. His posthumous *Autobiography, Memoir and Letters* was published in 1873.

God the almighty One! wisely ordaining (42)

Christiansen, Avis Burgeson (b. Chicago, Ill., Oct. 11, 1895), has been actively engaged in writing sacred texts for more than forty years. Her husband has been affiliated with Moody Bible Institute of Chicago for more than thirty years. They are members of the Moody Memorial Church of Chicago.

Up Calvary's mountain one dreadful morn (106)

Clark, Jeremiah (b. England, *ca.* 1669; d. London, Eng., Dec. 1, 1707), early served as a chorister under John Blow in the Chapel Royal. He was organist at Winchester College, 1692-95, and in 1695 became organist at St. Paul's Cathedral. In 1704 he and William Croft were appointed joint organists of the Chapel Royal. In 1705 he became vicar choral at St. Paul's. Among his varied compositions are musical settings for stage plays, cantatas, anthems, hymn tunes, and some music for the harpsichord. These latter compositions were for Queen Anne, whom he served as music master. Because of an unfortunate love affair, resulting in complete despair and melancholia, he decided to take his life. He rode into the country to a pond of water surrounded by trees. Undecided as to whether drowning or hanging would be the means of suicide, he tossed a coin. The fact that the coin stuck on its edge in the mud only added to his confusion, and he mounted his horse, rode to his home in St. Paul's churchyard, and shot himself with a pistol.

St. Magnus—The Lord will come and not be slow (126)

Claudius, Matthias (b. Reinfeld near Lübeck, Holstein, Ger., Aug. 15, 1740, d. Hamburg, Ger., Jan. 21, 1815), the son of a Lutheran pastor, studied for the ministry at the University of Jena. However, because of poor health and the rationalistic influences which cooled his religious zeal, his interests turned to law and languages. In 1776 he was appointed one of the Commissioners of Agriculture and Manufacture of Hesse-Darmstadt, and the following year became editor of the official Hesse-Darmstadt newspaper. While living at Darmstadt, he became acquainted with Goethe and a group of freethinking philosophers. A serious illness in 1777 restored his faith and renewed his ardent interest in religion. He moved to Wandsbeck and edited the *Wandsbecker Bote*.

We plow the fields and scatter (493)

Clement of Alexandria (*ca.* 170—*ca.* 220). Titus Flavius Clemens, commonly called Clement of Alexandria, was probably a native of Athens. He was converted to Christianity by Pantaenus, founder of the Catechetical School in Alexandria, and later succeeded him as head of this significant school of theological training. Under his leadership, 190-202, the school became the center of Christian scholarship, as he applied Hellenistic culture and Gnostic speculations to the exposition of Christian teaching. Because of the persecution of Christians by Emperor Severus which began in 202, Clement fled from Alexandria and nothing is known of his later life.

Shepherd of tender youth (162)

Clephane, Elizabeth Cecilia (b. Edinburgh, Scot., June 18, 1830; d. Melrose, Scot., Feb. 19, 1869). After the death of Elizabeth's father, Andrew Clephane, Sheriff of Fife, the family moved to Melrose, near

Abbotsford, the home of Sir Walter Scott. She was well known for her humanitarian interests on behalf of the poor of her community. She wrote at least eight hymns, and these were published posthumously, 1872-74, in *The Family Treasury,* edited by William Arnot, a Free Church minister. "The Ninety and Nine," which appeared in this publication, came to the attention of Ira D. Sankey while he was in Edinburgh with D. L. Moody, in 1873.

Beneath the cross of Jesus (345)

Cluff, Samuel O'Malley Gore (b. Dublin, Ire., 1837; d. Timahoe, Queens' Co., Ire., 1910), the son of Benjamin Richard and Eliza (Gore) Cluff, was educated at Trinity College, graduating with distinction in 1862. Ordained a minister in the Church of Ireland, he became pastor at Torquay, Ireland. He published a series of songs under the title *Timogue Leaflets.* In 1874 he became associated with the Plymouth Brethren.

I have a Saviour, He's pleading in glory (232)

Clute, Oscar (b. Bethlehem, N.Y., Mar. 11, 1837; d. Los Angeles, Calif., Jan. 27, 1902), after graduation from Michigan Agricultural College, taught mathematics at this institution for several years. Surrendering to the call to the ministry, he studied for a year at Meadville Theological Seminary and for twenty years pastored Unitarian churches in New Jersey, Iowa, and California. He became a successful college administrator, serving as president of Michigan Agricultural College (now Michigan State College), 1889-93, and Florida Agricultural College, 1893-97. He spent the last five years of his life in retirement in California.

O love of God most full (52)

Coghill, Annie Louise Walker (b. Kiddermore, Staffordshire, Eng., 1836; d. Bath, Eng. 1907), with her family moved to Canada about 1857, where her father, Robert Walker, a civil engineer, was employed in the construction of the Canadian Grand Trunk Railway. During the six years spent in Canada, she and her two older sisters conducted a private school for girls. She returned to England about 1863 and obtained a position as a governess. In 1883 she married Harry Coghill, a successful merchant, and they made their home near Hastings. Her literary works include six novels, a book of children's plays, and collections of poems.

Work, for the night is coming (424)

Coleman, Robert Henry (b. Bardstown, Ky., Nov. 1, 1869; d. Dallas, Tex., Feb. 13, 1946). While no hymn or tune appears in the hymnal attributed to Robert H. Coleman, this biographical sketch is included in recognition of his significance and influence on the hymnody of Southern Baptists during much of this century. As an independent publisher of hymnals and gospel songbooks for more than three decades, he supplied many of the hymnals used by Baptist churches, particularly in the middle and western areas of the Southern Baptist Convention.

He was educated at Georgetown College in Kentucky. As a young man he moved to Plano, Texas, where he operated a drugstore and for three years edited the *Plano Courier*. Later he was assistant YMCA secretary in Dallas. In 1903 he became assistant to George W. Truett, pastor of the First Baptist Church, Dallas, and except for six years as business manager of the *Baptist Standard,* 1909-15, he remained in this position until his death. In addition to his other duties in the church, he directed the congregational singing. He led the singing for many annual meetings of the Southern Baptist Convention, and served as music director for the Baptist World Alliance in Stockholm, Sweden, in 1923. In his early ventures as a songbook publisher, Coleman had the counsel and guidance of E. O. Excell (*q.v.*), an established publisher in Chicago. Coleman's early publications were printed by Excell, using Excell's music plates, thereby giving Excell the advantage of introducing to Coleman's customers many of Excell's copyrighted songs. (*See* "Amazing grace, how sweet the sound.") The extent of Coleman's influence may be seen by the listing of his thirty-three publications from 1909 to 1939. *The Evangel* (1909), *The New Evangel* (1911), *The World Evangel* (1913), *The Herald* (1915), *Select Gospel Songs* (1916), *Treasury of Songs* (1917), *The Popular Hymnal* (1918), *Kingdom Songs* (1921), *Coleman's Male Quartets* (1921), *The Pilot* (1922), *Revival Selections* (1922), *Hosannas* (1923), *Harvest Hymns* (1924), *The Little Evangel* (1925), *Coleman's New Quartet Book* (1925), *The Modern Hymnal* (1926), *Evangel Bells* (1927), *Coleman's Male Choir* (1928), *Gospel Melodies* (1928), *Revival Songs* (1929), *Girls' Quartets* (1929), *Majestic Hymns* (1930), *Service Songs* (1931), *Coleman's Songs for Men* (1932), *The Reapers* (1932), *The American Hymnal* (1933), *Pilot Hymns* (1934), *Glad Tidings* (1935), *Leading Hymns* (1936), *Ladies' Quartets* (1937), *Precious Hymns* (1938), *World Revival Hymns* (1939), and *Special Convention Songs* (1939).

Conder, Josiah (b. Aldersgate, London, Eng., Sept. 17, 1789; d. St. John's Wood, London, Eng., Dec. 27, 1855), at the age of thirteen worked in his father's bookshop, and became proprietor in 1811. In 1814 he acquired the *Eclectic Review,* which he owned and edited for twenty years. He also edited a Nonconformist newspaper, *The Patriot.* His poetical writing began at an early age and he published several collections of verse. An outstanding Congregational layman of his day, he served as editor of the first official hymnbook of the Congregational Union, *The Congregational Hymn Book, a Supplement to Dr. Watts's Psalms and Hymns* (1836). This collection contained about sixty of his original hymns.

Bread of heav'n, on Thee we feed (395)

Conkey, Ithamar (b. Shutesbury, Mass., May 5, 1815; d. Elizabeth, N.J., Apr. 30, 1867). After serving as organist at the Central Baptist Church, Norwich, Connecticut, Conkey went to New York City in 1850, where he became a well-known bass soloist, singing in the choirs of Calvary Episcopal Church and Grace Church. From 1861 until his death he served as bass soloist and conducted the quartet choir in the Madison Avenue Baptist Church.

RATHBUN—In the cross of Christ I glory (100)

Conover, Howard John (b. Woodstone, N.J., Nov. 22, 1850; d. Elmer, N.J., June 29, 1922), was educated at Pennington Seminary and at Dickinson College and entered the ministry of the Methodist Episcopal Church in 1874. In his later years he became quite interested in hymnology and was a member of the Hymn Writers and Composers' Society of New York City.

O God, we pray for all mankind (456)

Conte, Paolo (b. Palermo, It., Feb. 24, 1891), was educated at Liceo Benedetto Marcello, Venice, Italy, and received his master's degree in 1913. He came to America in 1914 and taught at the University of North Dakota, 1914-23. He was dean of fine arts, Oklahoma Baptist University, 1923-36, and taught at the University of Wichita, 1936-52. Since 1952 he has made his home in Colorado Springs, Colorado, and has served as music director in the First Baptist Church of that city. His compositions include piano, organ, vocal, and orchestral works. He is well known as an organ recitalist.

REDENTORE—Great Redeemer, we adore Thee (154)

Converse, Charles Crozat (b. Warren, Mass., Oct. 7, 1832; d. Highwood, N. J., Oct. 18, 1918), received his early education in the academy at Elmira, New York. In 1855 he went to Germany, studying music under Plaidy, Richter, and Hauptmann, and enjoyed the friendships of

271

Franz Liszt and Louis Spohr. He returned to America in 1859, and secured his law degree from Albany University in 1861. He enjoyed a successful law practice in Erie, Pennsylvania, and Rutherford College conferred on him the degree of LL.D. in 1895. Among his compositions are two symphonies, overtures, string quartets, oratorios, and many hymn tunes. He was early associated with William B. Bradbury and others in editing various collections of songs and Sunday school songbooks. Most of his composing, editing, and compiling was done under the pseudonym "Karl Reden," the German form of his name.

CONVERSE—What a friend we have in Jesus (328)

Cook, Joseph Simpson (b. Durham Co., Eng., Dec. 4, 1859; d. Toronto, Can., May 27, 1933), had his early education in England. After he came to Canada, he graduated from Wesleyan College of McGill University in Montreal. He entered the Methodist ministry and later went into the United Church of Canada.

Gentle Mary laid her child (73)

Copenhaver, Laura Scherer (b. Marion, Va., Aug. 29, 1868; d. Marion, Dec. 18, 1940), for more than thirty years taught English literature at Marion College, a school founded by her father. Her interest in the people of the mountain communities led to the founding of craft industries, including the art of making hand-woven coverlets and hooked rugs. She is credited with the beginning of the southern mountain work being done by the Home Mission Board of the United Lutheran Church in America, of which she was a member.

Heralds of Christ, who bear the King's command (452)

Cory, Julia Bulkley Cady (b. Nov. 9, 1882), is the daughter of J. Cleveland Cady, who was a well-known architect of New York City and an active churchman. She was educated at Brearley School and Reynolds School in New York. With her family she attended the Brick Presbyterian Church of New York City. Her writing began at the age of eight and she wrote the hymn for which she is now well known before she was twenty. In 1911 she married Robert Haskell Cory. For a number of years she resided in Englewood, New Jersey. Her death occurred there May 1, 1963.

We praise Thee, O God, our Redeemer (11)

Coster, George Thomas (b. Chatham, Kent, Eng., Oct. 3, 1835; d. Rotherham, Yorkshire, Eng., Aug. 29, 1912), following his education at New College, London, was ordained to the Congregational ministry at Newport, Essex, in 1859. From his ordination until his retirement in 1902 he held a number of pastorates; these were interrupted, however, by periods of ill health. He was keenly interested in humanitarian endeavors and was largely instrumental in founding the Victoria Hospital for children in Hull, as well as a local branch of the "Guild of Brave Poor Things," a self-help organization for the physically handicapped. In addition to several volumes of homiletical and devotional works, he published *Temperance Melodies and Religious Hymns* (1868), *Poems and Hymns* (1882), and *Hessle Hymns* (1901).

March on, O soul, with strength (422)

Cotterill, Thomas (b. Cannock, Staffordshire, Eng., Dec. 4, 1779; d. Sheffield, Eng., Dec. 29, 1823), was educated at the Free School, Birmingham, and at St. John's College, Cambridge. Following his ordination in 1803, he served as curate at Tutbury, became incumbent of Lane End, Staffordshire, 1808, and perpetual curate of St. Paul's, Sheffield, 1817-23. It was at the church in Sheffield that the legal controversy occurred in 1819, regarding Cotterill's efforts to introduce the use for congregational singing of the eighth and enlarged edition of his *A Selection of Psalms and Hymns* (first edition, 1810). Those in the congregation who opposed hymn singing sought to have this hymnal prohibited. The Archbishop of York persuaded him to withdraw the hymnal and prepare another collection (ninth edition, 1820), which was officially accepted, and thus became the first hymnal so recognized for use in the Anglican church.

In memory of the Saviour's love (393)

Cowper, William (b. Berkhampstead, Hertfordshire, Eng., Nov. 15, 1731; d. East Dereham, Norfolk, Eng., Apr. 25, 1800), was the son of the chaplain to George II. His mother, a descendant of John Donne, the poet, died when he was six years old. He was sent to a boarding school at Markyate, and later attended Westminster School. After studying law, he was called to the Bar in 1754 but never practiced law. He was offered the post of Clerk of the Journals to the House of Lords, but the dread of appearing before the House to stand examination resulted in mental illness and deep melancholia from which he was never thereafter free. Later he made his home with the family of Reverend Morley Unwin, whose wife became his devoted friend and guardian. After Unwin's death in 1767, John Newton (*q.v.*) persuaded Mrs. Unwin and her family to move to Olney. Cowper joined them there and remained in Olney for nineteen years, working with Newton both in literary and church activities. Together they produced the *Olney Hymns*

(1779), one of the significant collections of English hymnody. His poem, *The Task* (1785) and his translation of Homer were widely acclaimed, and he became recognized as the greatest poet of his day. The death of Mrs. Unwin in 1796 added to the anguish of his soul and mind and he died four years later. (Cf. *The Hymn*, I, No. 4, 5.)

> A glory gilds the sacred page (92)
> God moves in a mysterious way (53)
> Oh, for a closer walk with God (365)
> There is a fountain filled with blood (92)

Coxe, Arthur Cleveland (b. Mendham, N.J., May 10, 1818; d. Clifton Springs, N.Y., July 20, 1896), was the son of Samuel Hanson Cox, a well-known Presbyterian minister in Brooklyn. Following his graduation from New York University in 1838, he changed the spelling of his name and left the Presbyterian church. After graduation from General Theological Seminary, he was ordained in 1842 in the Episcopal church. He served three churches: St. John's, Hartford, Connecticut; Grace Church, Baltimore; and Calvary Church, New York. After this he served as Bishop of Western New York. His poetical works, written mostly early in his life, include *Advent* (1837), *Christian Ballads* (1840), and *Athanasion* (1842). He was a member of the Episcopal Hymnal Commission (1879-81) but refused permission for any of his hymns to be included in the hymnal of his own church.

> How beauteous were the marks divine (84)
> O where are kings and empires now? (383)
> We are living, we are dwelling (421)

Croft, William (b. Nether Eatington, Warwickshire, Eng., Dec. 30, 1678; d. Bath, Eng., Aug. 14, 1727), served as a chorister under John Blow at St. James's Chapel Royal. He became organist at St. Anne's, Soho, in 1700 and remained in this position for eleven years. He and Jeremiah Clark were appointed joint organists at the Chapel Royal in 1704, and in 1707, on the death of Clark, he became sole organist. In 1708 he succeeded John Blow as organist at Westminster Abbey and composer to the Chapel Royal. His epitaph in Westminster Abbey concludes (as translated from Latin),

Having resided among mortals for fifty years, behaving with the utmost candor (not more conspicuous for any other office of humanity than the friendship and love truly paternal to all whom he had instructed) he departed to the heavenly choir on the fourteenth day of August, 1727, that, being near, he might add his own Hallelujah to the Concert of Angels.

In his earlier life he composed music for the theatre, as well as other secular music. However, in later life he devoted himself entirely to sacred music and became one of the greatest names in English sacred music history. Of particular significance are his psalm tunes which are the earliest examples of the English psalm tune as distinguished from the Genevan or French psalm tunes.

St. Anne—God moves in a mysterious way (53)
       O God, our help in ages past (286)
       O where are kings and empires now? (383)

Croly, George (b. Dublin, Ire., Aug. 17, 1780; d. Holborn, Eng., Nov. 24, 1860), was educated at the University of Dublin, received his Master of Arts degree in 1804, and was ordained in the Church of Ireland. At the age of thirty he went to London and devoted his efforts to literary endeavors, publishing numerous works, biographical, historical, and religious in character. An outspoken Conservative, both in religion and politics, he strongly opposed any form of liberalism. He was made rector of St. Bene't Sherehog and St. Stephen's, Walbrook, in 1835. This latter church was in a poor section of London where no services had been conducted for many years, and the boldness of his preaching attracted large crowds to the services.

Spirit of God, descend upon my heart (166)

Crosby, Fanny Jane (b. South East, Putnam Co., N.Y., Mar. 24, 1820; d. Bridgeport, Conn., Feb. 12, 1915), became blind at the age of six weeks after a country doctor applied hot poultices to her inflamed eyes. She was educated at the New York City School for the Blind. After her graduation she taught English grammar, rhetoric, and Roman and American history for eleven years in that school. During the 1850's she began writing verse and provided numerous texts for the minstrel songs of George F. Root, then a teacher at the School for the Blind. In 1858 she was married to Alexander Van Alstyne, a musician who was also blind. Beginning in the 1860's she began to write texts for gospel songs, and, more than any other author, she captured the spirit of the nineteenth-century American gospel song. Her texts are numbered in the thousands, as poetical verse of Christian expression flowed unending from her Braille writer. Her name came to have a kind of magic formula for success as composers of gospel songs sought for her poetic verse. Much of her writing was done to order. For Biglow and Main she produced three hymns a week for an indefinite period of time. She spent most of her life in New York City, where she frequently attended the John Street Methodist Episcopal Church. She used more than two hundred pseudonyms in signing her hymns.

A wonderful Saviour is Jesus my Lord (272)
All the way my Saviour leads me (268)
Blessed assurance, Jesus is mine (269)
He is coming, the "Man of Sorrows" (121)
I am Thine, O Lord, I have heard Thy voice (349)
Jesus is tenderly calling thee home (229)
Jesus, keep me near the cross (97)
More like Jesus would I be (316)
Pass me not, O gentle Saviour (219)
Praise Him! Praise Him! Jesus, our blessed Redeemer (137)
Redeemed, how I love to proclaim it (203)
Rescue the perishing (207)
Thou, my everlasting portion (354)
Though your sins be as scarlet (213)
'Tis the blessed hour of prayer (329)
To God be the glory, great things He hath done (41)
To the work! to the work! (435)
When Jesus comes to reward His servants (119)
When my life-work is ended (472),

Crüger, Johann (b. Gross-Briesen, Pruss., Apr. 9, 1598; d. Berlin, Pruss., Feb. 23, 1662), was educated at the Jesuit College of Olmutz and in a "Poet's School" at Regensburg, where he studied music under the cantor, Paul Homberger. He arrived in Berlin in 1615 and completed his theological studies at the University of Wittenburg. In 1622 he became cantor of the Lutheran Cathedral of St. Nicholas, Berlin, and remained until his death. His significant contribution to hymnody rests in his chorale melodies which were composed as settings for the hymns of such Lutheran hymn writers as Gerhardt (*q.v.*), Franck, Herrmann, Rinkart (*q.v.*), Rist, and others. His *Praxis Pietatis Melica*, which passed through forty-four editions from 1644 to 1736, was the outstanding hymnic collection of the seventeenth century.

NUN DANKET—Now thank we all our God (491)

Cummings, William Hayman (b. Sidbury, Devonshire, Eng., Aug. 22, 1831; d. London, Eng., June 6, 1915), at the age of seven, became a chorister at St. Paul's Cathedral, where he received his early musical training. He studied organ with Edward J. Hopkins and became organist at Waltham Abbey in 1847. This same year, on April 16, he sang in a performance of Mendelssohn's *Elijah* at Exeter Hall which the composer conducted. He possessed an excellent tenor voice and gave concerts throughout England, Ireland, Scotland, and Wales, and in 1871 he visited the United States. He was particularly skilled in the Bach passion music. From 1879-96 he was professor of singing at the Royal Academy of Music, after which he succeeded Joseph Barnby as principal of the Guildhall School of Music. In addition to his fame as a singer, he was a recognized musicologist, lecturer, and composer. He was founder of the Purcell Society, and an active leader in the Philharmonic Society, the Musical Association, and the Incorporated Society of Musicians. In 1900 the University of Dublin gave him the honorary degree of Mus.D.

MENDELSSOHN (arr.)—Hark! the herald angels sing (81)

Cushing, William Orcutt (b. Hingham Center, Mass., Dec. 31, 1823; d. Lisbon, N.Y., Oct. 19, 1902). For more than twenty years he was a successful pastor of Christian churches in Searsburg, Auburn, Brookley, Buffalo, and Sparta, New York. Following the death of his wife in 1870, ill health forced his retirement from the active ministry. During this time he became intensely interested in hymn writing and wrote more than three hundred hymns which have been set to music by George F. Root, Robert Lowry, Ira D. Sankey, and others. Among his better-known hymns are: "Ring the bells of heaven," "When He cometh," "Down in the Valley," "There'll be no dark valley," and "Hiding in Thee."

O safe to the Rock that is higher than I (271)

Cutler, Henry Stephen (b. Boston, Mass., Oct. 13, 1824; d. Boston, Dec. 5, 1902), after early music study in America, visited Europe in 1844. While in England he became greatly interested in cathedral choirs. Returning to Boston in 1846, he became organist at Grace Church, and later at the Church of the Advent. In this latter church he organized a choir of men and boys after the English tradition, the first robed choir in the United States. In 1858 he became organist at Trinity Church, New York, and used the visit of the Prince of Wales in 1860 as the opportunity to bring his choir of men and boys into the chancel wearing vestments. After seven years' service at Trinity Church, he held positions in Brooklyn, Providence, Philadelphia, and Troy. Columbia University conferred on him the Mus.D. degree in 1864. While he was at Trinity Church, he published the *Trinity Psalter* (1864) and *Trinity Anthems* (1865). He retired in 1885 and lived in Boston until his death.

ALL SAINTS, NEW—The Son of God goes forth to war (414)

Darwall, John (b. Haughton, Staffordshire, Eng., 1731; d. Walsall, Eng., Dec. 18, 1789), was educated at Manchester Grammar School and at Brasenose College, Oxford, where he graduated in 1756. He became curate, and in 1769 vicar of St. Matthew's Parish Church, Walsall, where he spent the rest of his life. He was an enthusiastic amateur musician, and in addition to two volumes of piano sonatas, he composed tunes for all of the 150 psalms of Tate and Brady's *New Version*. Several of these psalm tunes were published in eighteenth-century tune books, but only his setting of Psalm 148, given here, has survived.

DARWALL—Rejoice, the Lord is King (108)

Davison, Fannie Estelle (Mrs. A. L.) (b. Cuyahoga Falls, Ohio, 1851; d. Chicago, Ill., Mar. 10, 1887), was the daughter of Philo and Sarah Ann (Linsted) Church. Her father was killed when she was ten years old and her mother later married Henry Christian Warner, moving the family to Carthage, Missouri, where Mr. Warner owned a hotel. Fannie Estelle Church was married to Asa Lee Davison, a court reporter, and they settled in Chicago, later living in Madison, Wisconsin. Two daughters were born to this home—Myrtle Estelle Davison (1871-1946), who became Mrs. Samuel Morris Brogan, and Iva Belle Davison (1881-1951), who became Mrs. Charles M. Jewett. Mrs. Davison was in poor health during her last years and was cared for by her mother. Upon her death, in 1887, she was buried at Carthage, Missouri. She is the author of a number of hymns, most of which appeared in collections published by Fillmore Bros. (Cincinnati). Two of these collections which contain several of her songs are *Joy and Gladness* (1880) and *The Voice of Joy* (1882). She wrote the libretto for the cantata *Faith, Hope and Love* (1886), for which J. H. Rosecrans composed the music.

For almost a decade the writer of this handbook had searched for the identity of this author without any results. In response to a news story carried by several state Baptist papers in 1962, the above information was provided by Mrs. L. E. Sandlin, Jr., of Huntsville, Alabama, a daughter of Myrtle Davison Brogan, and a granddaughter of the author.

Purer in heart, O God (369)

Dearle, Edward (b. Cambridge, Eng., Mar. 2, 1806; d. Camberwell, London, Eng., Mar. 20, 1891), a chorister at King's College, Trinity, and at St. John's College, Cambridge, became organist at St. Paul's, Deptford, at the age of twenty-one. From 1835 to 1864, he was organist at Newark-upon-Trent, and after this long tenure of continuous service, he moved to Camberwell, London, where he resided until his death. In addition to a number of hymn tunes, his compositions include anthems, oratorios, and service music.

PENITENTIA—Here O my Lord, I see Thee face to face (391)

Depew, Arthur (b. Hamilton, Ont., July 24, 1869; d. South Orange, N.J., Sept. 24, 1940), was educated at Trinity College. For a number of years he was organist and choirmaster at the First Presbyterian Church, Detroit, Michigan. He went to New York about 1904 to be organist in the John Wanamaker Auditorium. He also served as organist at the Plymouth Church, Brooklyn, and the St. Nicholas Collegiate Church, New York. In addition to his church positions, he enjoyed considerable success as a theater organist, playing at both the Capitol and Strand Theaters in New York. A number of miscellaneous works were published, including a cantata, *Lead, Kindly Light*, and a state song for New Jersey, "Jersey, Home of the Fir, Elm and Myrtle."

MATER—O blessed day of motherhood (504)

Dexter, Henry Martyn (b. Plympton, Mass., Aug. 13, 1821; d. Boston, Mass., Nov. 13, 1890), was educated at Yale and Andover Theological Seminary. Following his graduation from Andover in 1844, he was ordained to the Congregational ministry and accepted his first pastorate at Manchester, New Hampshire. In addition to his pastoral duties, he served as editor of *The Congregationalist* and *The Congregational Quarterly*. After eighteen years as pastor of the Berkeley Street Congregational Church, Boston, he resigned to devote his full time as editor of *The Congregationalist and Recorder*. He was recognized as a careful scholar and devoted much time to the early history of Congregationalism. Of his many books, his major effort was *The Congregationalism of the Last Three Hundred Years, as Seen in Its Literature* (1880). He seldom engaged in the writing of verse, and the translation given here seems to be the only poetical venture of his to have been published.

Shepherd of tender youth (tr.) (162)

Dix, William Chatterton (b. Bristol, Eng., June 14, 1837; d. Clifton, Eng., Sept. 9, 1898), was the son of William John Dix, a Bristol surgeon, who wrote *Life of Chatterton*. The elder Dix named his son for this Bristol poet. The son was educated at the Bristol Grammar School for a mercantile career, and later became manager of a marine insurance company in Glasgow. He wrote a large number of hymns, some of which were translations from the Greek. His hymnic writings were published in *Hymns of Love and Joy* (1861), *Altar Songs, Verses on the Holy Eucharist* (1867), *A Vision of All Saints* (1871), and *Seekers of a City* (1878).

As with Gladness men of old (68)
"Come unto me, ye weary" (227)

Doane, George Washington (b. Trenton, N.J., May 27, 1799; d. Burlington, N.J., Apr. 27, 1859), graduated at Union College, Schenectady, New York, in 1818, and attended General Theological Seminary. He was ordained to the Protestant Episcopal ministry in 1821, and was assistant minister at Trinity Church, New York, until 1824, when he became professor of Belles-Lettres at Trinity College, Hartford, Connecticut. He was appointed rector of Trinity Church, Boston, in 1828, and bishop of New Jersey in 1832. One of the foremost promoters of the Episcopal missionary movement and the establishment of church schools, he founded St. Mary's Hall, Burlington, in 1837, and Burlington College in 1846. Many of his hymns appeared in his *Songs by the Way* (1824). He was greatly interested in the Tractarian Movement in England, and published an American edition of John Keble's *The Christian Year* (1834). The altar in St. Peter's Church, Morristown, New Jersey, is a memorial to him.

Fling out the banner! let it float (446)
Softly now the light of day (33)

Doane, William Howard (b. Preston, Conn., Feb. 3, 1832; d. South Orange, N.J., Dec. 24, 1915), was educated at Woodstock Academy, where, at the age of fourteen, he directed the school choir. In his final school year, he was converted and joined the Baptist church at Norwich, Connecticut. After three years' work in his father's cotton manufacturing business, he became associated with J. A. Fay & Co., manufacturers of woodworking machinery. In 1860 he moved with this firm to Cincinnati and later became president. He spent the remainder of his life in Cincinnati, and was a respected and beloved civic and church leader. For more than twenty-five years he was superintendent of the Sunday school of the Mount Auburn Baptist Church. In spite of his business interests, he was most active in his avocation of composing hymn tunes and editing collections. His more than twenty-two hundred tunes and more than forty collections were widely known and extremely popular. His most successful collaboration was with Fanny J. Crosby, who frequently provided texts for tunes Doane had composed and sent to her. A dedicated Christian businessman and generous benefactor, from the proceeds of his most popular song book, *Silver Spray* (1867), he donated the pipe organ in the Cincinnati Y.M.C.A. hall. Later he contributed large sums to Denison University, a Baptist school at Granville, Ohio, which conferred on him the honorary Mus.D. degree in 1875.

BLESSED HOUR—'Tis the blessed hour of prayer (329)

CRIMSON—"Though your sins be as scarlet" (213)

EVERY DAY AND HOUR—Saviour, more than life to me (326)

I AM THINE—I am Thine, O Lord, I have heard Thy voice (349)

MORE LIKE JESUS—More like Jesus would I be (316)

MORE LOVE TO THEE—More love to Thee, O Christ (292)

NEAR THE CROSS—Jesus, keep me near the cross (97)

OLD, OLD STORY—Tell me the old, old story—(222)

PASS ME NOT—Pass me not, O gentle Saviour (219)

PRECIOUS NAME—Take the name of Jesus with you (305)

RESCUE—Rescue the perishing (207)

TO GOD BE THE GLORY—To God be the glory, great things He hath done (41)

TOILING ON—To the work! to the work (435)

WOODSTOCK—When Jesus comes to reward His servants (119)

Doddridge, Philip (b London, Eng., June 26, 1702; d. Lisbon, Port., Oct. 25, 1751), the son of a London merchant, was the youngest of twenty children, eighteen of which had died in infancy. His paternal grandfather was a clergyman ejected from his pastorate by the 1622 Act of Uniformity. His maternal grandfather, John Bauman, a Lutheran pastor in Prague, Bohemia, was exiled because of his faith and came to London to escape persecution. After the death of his parents in 1715, he declined an offer of a university education for the ministry in the Church of England and enrolled in the Nonconformist academy at Kibworth. In 1729 he became minister at Northampton and conducted his own academy there, continuing this work for twenty-two years. In 1736 he received the D.D. degree from the University of Aberdeen. In 1751 he contracted consumption and sailed for Lisbon for a much-needed rest and died there. Doddridge was a man of great learning and wrote many theological works. He is the author of about 370 hymns, which were published posthumously in 1755 by his friend, Job Orton. While he wrote in the style of Watts, he did not possess Watts's poetical skill. However, his hymns reflect a greater awareness of the social message of the gospel than those of Watts, and reveal the first missionary zeal in hymnic writing, anticipating by more

281

than half a century the missionary movement of the early nineteenth century. (Cf. *The Hymn*. II, No. 3, 13)

Awake, my soul, stretch every nerve (309)
O happy day that fixed my choice (389)

Doudney, Sarah (b. Portsea, Eng., Jan. 15, 1841; d. Headingtoń, near Oxford, Eng., Dec. 15, 1926), at an early age revealed unusual literary ability and wrote "The Lessons of the Water-Mill" when she was fifteen. One of the well-known lines from this poem is, "The mill cannot grind with the water that is past." A prolific writer, she published a number of novels, and contributed numerous articles to the *Sunday Magazine*. She spent most of her life in quiet seclusion in the remote village of Cobham in Hampshire. In addition to the present hymn, her evening hymn, "Saviour, now the day is ending," may be found in some collections.

The Master hath come, and He calls us to follow (427)

Draper, Bourne Hall (b. Cumnor, near Oxford, Eng., 1775; d. Southampton, Eng., Oct. 12, 1843). Draper's parents were members of the Church of England, and they had hoped to educate their son for the ministry. However, because of the lack of sufficient funds, these plans were abandoned, and he became a printer's apprentice at the Clarendon Press, Oxford. While there he joined the Baptist church, and upon completion of his apprenticeship he was recommended by his church for admittance to the Baptist Academy at Bristol, of which John Ryland was then head. After two years at Bristol, he was ordained in 1804 as pastor of the Baptist church at Chipping-Norton, Oxfordshire. Later he became pastor at Southampton, where he remained until his death. He is credited with writing thirty-six books, devotional works, and sermons, as well as several books for children. A number of his hymns appeared in issues of the *Baptist Magazine* signed with his initials, "B.H.D."

Ye Christian heralds! go, proclaim (459)

Draper, William Henry (b. Kenilworth, Warwickshire, Eng., Dec. 19, 1885; d. Clifton, Bristol, Eng., Aug. 9, 1933), was educated at Cheltenham College and Keble College, Oxford. Ordained in the Church of England in 1880, he was curate at St. Mary's, Shrewsbury; vicar of Alfreton; vicar of the Abbey Church, Shrewsbury; rector of Adel, Leeds; Master of the Temple, London, 1919-30; and thereafter vicar of Axbridge, Somerset. Among his publications are *Hymns for Holy Week* (1899, translations of hymns of the Greek Church), *The*

Victoria Book of Hymns (1897), and *Hymns for the Tunes by Orlando Gibbons* (1925). He also edited *Seven Spiritual Songs by Thomas Campion* (1919). Altogether he wrote more than sixty hymns, some of the finest of which are translations from the Latin and Greek.

All creatures of our God and King (tr.) (3)

Duffield, George, Jr. (b. Carlisle, Pa., Sept. 12, 1818; d. Bloomfield, N.J., July 6, 1888), was the son and grandson of Presbyterian ministers, the grandfather having served as joint chaplain to the Continental Congress during the Revolutionary War. He was educated at Yale University (B.A., 1837) and at Union Theological Seminary, New York, where he was graduated in 1840 and ordained the same year. His life was spent in the active pastorate of Presbyterian churches at Brooklyn, New York, 1840-47; Bloomfield, New Jersey, 1847-52; Philadelphia, 1852-61; Adrian, Michigan, 1861-65, Galesburg, Illinois, 1865-69; Saginaw, Michigan, 1869; and Ann Arbor and Lansing, Michigan, 1869-84. Following this last pastorate, he retired to Bloomfield, New Jersey, and for some time made his home with his son, Rev. Samuel W. Duffield, the author of *English Hymns, Their Authors and History* (1886).

Stand up, stand up for Jesus (415, 419)

Dunbar, C. R. No information has been found concerning this composer.

DUNBAR—My life, my love I give to Thee (359)

Dwight, Timothy (b. Northampton, Mass., May 14, 1752; d. New Haven, Conn., Jan. 11, 1817), received his early education through the teaching of his mother, the third daughter of Jonathan Edwards. He entered Yale University at the age of thirteen and was graduated in 1769. Intense study in his youth permanently injured his eyesight, and in later years he endured constant pain, at times being able to read only fifteen minutes out of each day. In spite of this difficulty, he became a man of great influence. During the time he served as a chaplain in the Continental Army, he became a close friend of George Washington. In 1783 he became the pastor of the Congregational Church at Greenfield, Connecticut, and in 1795 was elected president of Yale. The extent of his scholarship and knowledge may be seen from the fact that in addition to his administrative duties he taught ethics, metaphysics, logic, theology, literature, oratory, and also served as college chaplain. At the request of the General Association of the Presbyterian Churches of Connecticut, he made a revision of Isaac Watts's

Psalms to which he added thirty-three hymns of his own, and this was published in 1801. During the early part of the nineteenth century *Dwight's Watts* was the most widely used hymnal among the Presbyterian and Congregational churches in Connecticut.

I love Thy kingdom, Lord (382)

Dykes, John Bacchus (b. Hull, Eng., Mar. 10, 1823; d. Ticehurst, Sussex, Eng., Jan. 22, 1876), was the son of a banker and revealed his unusual musical talent at an early age. When he was ten, he played the organ in the church in Hull, where his grandfather was minister. He was educated at Wakefield and at St. Catharine's College, Cambridge. After his graduation in 1847, he was ordained deacon and subsequently priest at Walton, Yorkshire, and two years later was appointed to Durham. Shortly thereafter he became the precentor in the Cathedral there. In 1861 Durham University gave him his doctorate, and the following year he became vicar of St. Oswald's, Durham, where he remained until his death. A prolific composer of hymn tunes he is credited with having written about three hundred, most of which first appeared in *Hymns Ancient and Modern* or Chope's *Congregational Hymn and Tune Book*. He stands today as the tallest of the Victorian tune composers, and among his tunes are the finest examples of the era which they represent. (Cf. *The Hymn,* XII, No. 3, 69-76.)

ALFORD—Ten thousand times ten thousand (476)
BLAIRGOWRIE—The voice that breathed o'er Eden (502)
DOMINUS REGIT ME—The King of love my Shepherd is (280)
LUX BENIGNA—Lead, kindly Light! amid th'encircling gloom (60)
MELITA—Eternal Father, strong to save (61)
NICAEA—Holy, holy, holy! Lord God Almighty (1)
ST. AGNES—Father, I stretch my hands to Thee (46)
    Jesus, the very thought of Thee (135)
    I know not how that Bethlehem's Babe (276)
    Happy the home when God is there (374)

Edgar, Mary Susanne (b. Sundridge, Ont., May 23, 1889), was educated at Havergal College, Toronto, and the National Training School of the Young Women's Christian Association in New York. For a number of years she was associated with the National Y.W.C.A. of Canada in Montreal. She has traveled extensively throughout the world. In 1922 she founded Camp Glen Bernard, a private camp for girls in northern Ontario, and was known to her campers as "Ogima-qua" (friend of children). She has been living in Toronto since her retirement in 1955. The author of *Woodfire and Candlelight* and

Under Open Skies (1955), she has written a number of hymns, most of which have been for special occasions.

God, who touchest earth with beauty (45)

Edmeston, James (b. Wapping, London, Eng., Sept. 10, 1791; d. Homerton, Eng., Jan. 7, 1867), an eminent English architect and surveyor, was a devoted layman in the Church of England and a loyal supporter of the London Orphan Asylum. He was particularly fond of children, and many of his two thousand hymns were written for use in Sunday school. For many years it was his custom to write a hymn each week to be read at his family devotions each Sunday morning.

Saviour, breathe an evening blessing (34)

Edson, Lewis (b. Bridgewater, Mass., Jan. 22, 1748; d. Woodstock, Conn., 1820), was a blacksmith by trade. During the Revolutionary War, because he was a Tory, he moved his family to a sparsely settled section of western Massachusetts; and in 1776 he moved to New York. Following the war he conducted singing schools in Massachusetts, New York, and Connecticut. He settled in Woodstock, Connecticut, in 1817, where he remained until his death. He composed a number of "fuguing tunes," the three most popular of which were BRIDGEWATER, GREENFIELD and LENOX, all named for villages in his native state of Massachusetts. These tunes appeared in Jocelyn and Doolittle's *The Chorister's Companion* (*ca.* 1782) and became well known not only in New England but in the South. One or more are found in the *Southern Harmony* (1835), the *Sacred Harp* (1844), and other oblong tune books of this type.

LENOX—Blow ye the trumpet, blow (250)

Ellerton, John (b. London, Eng., Dec. 16, 1826; d. Torquay, Eng., June 15, 1893), was educated at King William's College, Isle of Man, and at Trinity College, Cambridge. Soon after he was ordained in 1850, he was appointed curate of St. Nicholas', Brighton, where he wrote his first hymns for the children of his parish. While vicar of Crewe Green, Cheshire, he became interested in social welfare work and served as vice-president of the Mechanics' Institution, where he taught classes in England and Bible History. During this same time he compiled his *Hymns for Schools and Bible Classes* (1859). His hymns and his interest in hymnology earned for him a place of high respect in this area, to the extent that his advice and counsel were sought by compilers of every significant hymnal published in the last half of the nineteenth century. His own hymns were published in *Hymns, Original and Trans-*

lated (1888), and he assisted the committee in the compilation of both the 1875 and 1889 editions of *Hymns Ancient and Modern*. (Cf. *The Hymn*, XII, No. 4, 101-6.)

God, the almighty One! wisely ordaining (42)
Saviour, again to Thy dear name we raise (27)
"Welcome, happy morning" (110)

Elliott, Charlotte (b. Clapham, Eng., Mar. 18, 1789; d. Brighton, Eng., Sept. 22, 1871). A serious illness in 1821 left Miss Elliott an invalid for the rest of her life. The following year she met César Malan, the Genevan evangelist, and through his influence decided to devote her life to religious and humanitarian interests. Her friendship with Malan was of lasting influence, as they corresponded with each other for forty years. Through pain and suffering she continued her literary pursuits. She assisted in the compilation of *The Invalid's Hymn Book* (1834), and the sixth edition (1854) contained 112 of her hymns. In addition to this compilation, her 150 hymns may be found in *Psalms and Hymns for Public, Private and Social Worship* (1835-48, edited by her brother, Henry Elliott); *Hours of Sorrow* (1836); *Hymns for a Week* (1839); and *Thoughts in Verse on Sacred Subjects* (1869).

Just as I am, without one plea (240)
O Holy Saviour, friend unseen (287)

Elliott, Emily Elizabeth Steele (b. Brighton, Eng., July 22, 1836; d. Mildmay Park, London, Eng., Aug. 3, 1897), was the daughter of Edward B. Elliott, rector of St. Mark's Church, Brighton, a brother of Charlotte Elliott. She was active in mission work, and most of her hymns were first used in her father's church. They were later published in the *Church Missionary Juvenile Instructor* of which she was editor for six years. Seventy of her hymns appeared in her *Chimes of Consecration* (1873) and *Chimes for Daily Service* (1880).

Thou didst leave Thy throne (82)

Ellor, James (b. Droylsden, Lancashire, Eng., 1819; d. Newburgh, N.Y., Sept. 27, 1899), at an early age learned the trade of hat making, the major activity of his home town. His natural musical ability was soon evident; and by the time he was eighteen, he was leading the choir in the local Wesleyan Chapel. Later he abandoned the hat making trade and secured employment with the railroad being constructed between Manchester and Godley Junction in England. In 1843 he came to the United States. Little is known of his later years except that he returned to his trade of hat making, and for many years before his death he was nearly blind. He died at the home of his son in Newburgh, New York, and was buried at Bloomfield, New Jersey.

DIADEM—All hail the power of Jesus' name (134)

Elvey, George Job (b. Canterbury, Eng., Mar. 27, 1816; d. Windlesham, Surrey, Eng., Dec. 9, 1893), was educated as a chorister in Canterbury Cathedral and before the age of seventeen became an organist of unusual skill. At the age of nineteen he became organist and master of the boys at St. George's Chapel, Windsor, the home church of the royal family. During his forty-seven years of continuous service at St. George's Chapel, he played for many services involving the royal family. In 1863 he played at the wedding of the Prince of Wales, who became King Edward VII upon the death of Queen Victoria in 1901. He was knighted in 1871 after his writing of the *Festival March* for the wedding of Princess Louise.

DIADEMATA—Crown Him with many crowns (152)
      Soldiers of Christ, arise (416)
ST. GEORGE'S WINDSOR—Come, ye thankful people, come (490)
      Watchman! tell us of the night (462)

Emerson, Luther Orlando (b. Parsonfield, Me., Aug. 3, 1820; d. Boston, Mass., Oct. 1, 1915), was educated at Parsonfield Seminary and Effingham Academy, and began the study of medicine at Dracut Academy. His enthusiasm for music prevailed, however, and he studied music with I. B. Woodbury. After eight years as a teacher and choir director in Salem, Massachusetts, he moved to Boston and became associated with the Oliver Ditson Company. In this capacity he compiled more than seventy collections and conducted more than three hundred musical conventions in the United States and Canada. He was given the honorary Mus.D. degree by Findlay College in Ohio.

AR HYD Y NOS (arr.)—God, that madest earth and heaven (30)

Evans, David (b. Resolven, Glamorganshire, Wales, Feb. 6, 1874; d. Resolven, 1948), was educated at Arnold College, Swansea; University College, Cardiff; and Oxford University, where he received the Mus.D. degree. From 1903 until his retirement in 1939, he was professor of Music at University College, Cardiff, and was recognized as the outstanding Welsh musician of his day. He was a leading conductor of the great Welsh singing festivals—Gymnafa Ganu—begun by John Roberts in the nineteenth century. He also served as a foremost adjudicator at the National Eisteddfod. He composed many choral and orchestral works and served as musical editor of the revised *Church*

Hymnary (1927), prepared for the Presbyterian churches of Scotland, Ireland, England, Wales, Australia, New Zealand, and South Africa. Both of the tunes given below are from this source.

NYLAND (harm.)—In heavenly love abiding (303)

SLANE (harm.)—Be Thou my vision, O Lord of my heart (62)

Everett, Asa Brooks (b. Virginia, 1828; d. near Nashville, Tenn., Sept., 1875), after completing medical training, abandoned the practice of medicine for a musical career. With his brother, L. C. Everett, he spent some time in Boston studying music. Following a brief time of teaching music in his native state, he spent four years studying in Leipzig, Germany. He was associated with his brother and R. M. McIntosh (*q.v.*) in the L. C. Everett Company, first located in Richmond, Virginia, and later in Pennsylvania. Prior to the Civil War, this firm had more than fifty teachers of music in their employ in the southern and Middle Atlantic states. He wrote numerous gospel songs and edited a number of collections, the best known of which was *The Sceptre* (New York: Biglow and Main).

FOOTSTEPS—Sweetly, Lord, have we heard Thee calling (362)

Ewing, Alexander (b. Aberdeen, Scot., Jan. 3, 1830; d. Taunton, Eng., July 11, 1895), after first studying law at Marischal College, Aberdeen, decided to seek a musical education. He spent some time at the University in Heidelberg, Germany; and while he was not a professional musician, he became quite skilled as a pianist, cellist, violinist, and cornetist. At the outbreak of the Crimean War in 1855, he enlisted in the army, serving in the Commissariat Department, and was stationed for a while at Constantinople. He remained in the foreign service until 1867, serving in Australia and China, and attained the rank of lieutenant colonel. The present tune, apparently written after his return from Heidelburg University, is the only music he is known to have composed.

EWING—Jerusalem, the golden (477)

Excell, Edwin Othello (b. Stark Co., Ohio, Dec. 13, 1851; d. Louisville, Ky., June 10, 1921), was the son of a German Reformed Church minister. Following his early education he worked for twelve years as a plasterer and bricklayer. During this time he began to conduct country singing schools and was a popular teacher. While leading the music in a revival in the Methodist Episcopal Church, East Brady, Pennsylvania, he was converted and turned his efforts toward sacred music. During 1877-83 he attended the normal music schools, studying under George F. Root, and his son, Frederick W. Root. Moving to Chicago in 1883, he began the publication of gospel songbooks, which were widely used. He was active in Sunday school work, leading the music at Sunday school conventions. With Methodist Bishop John H. Vincent, he helped found the International Sunday School Lessons. His ability as a congregational song leader was well known, and for twenty years he assisted evangelist Sam P. Jones in all of his revival meetings. His death occurred in Louisville, Kentucky, where he was assisting Gypsy Smith in a city-wide revival. He composed more than two thousand gospel songs, and published about fifty songbooks. An additional thirty-eight compilations were made for other individuals. He assisted Robert H. Coleman (*q.v.*) in his early songbook ventures, providing the plates and doing the printing and binding in Chicago.

I have a song I love to sing—OTHELLO (208)
AMAZING GRACE (arr.)—Amazing grace! how sweet the sound (188)
BLESSINGS—When upon life's billows you are tempest tossed (318)

Faber, Frederick William (b. Calverley, Yorkshire, Eng., June 28, 1814; d. London, Eng., Sept. 26, 1863), was educated at Shrewsbury and Harrow Schools, and at Balliol and University Colleges, Oxford. He was reared in strict Calvinistic discipline and teaching, but later, under the influence of John Henry Newman, became an enthusiastic follower of the Oxford Movement. Ordained in the Church of England in 1842, he became rector of a parish in Elton, Huntingdonshire. Here he introduced auricular confession, penance, and other practices advocated by the Oxford Movement. In 1846 he entered the Roman Catholic Church, was rebaptized, and took the name Wilfrid. He founded in Birmingham the "Brothers of the Will of God," a community which came to be known as the "Wilfridians," which was merged in 1848 with the Oratory of St. Philip Neri, of which Newman was superior. A branch of this order was established in London in 1849, which developed into Brompton Oratory, where Faber served as superior until his death. He had been greatly impressed with the hymns of John Newton (*q.v.*) and William Cowper (*q.v.*), and desired, in his own hymn writing, to produce hymns for Roman Catholics with the same popular appeal as the *Olney Hymns*. He wrote 150 hymns, which were published after he became a Roman Catholic, and these appeared in his *Hymns* (1849); *Jesus and Mary—Catholic Hymns for Singing and Reading* (1849; second edition, 1852); *Oratory Hymns* (1854); and *Hymns* (1862).

Faith of our fathers! living still (252)
Hark, hark, my soul! angelic songs are swelling (469)
There's a wideness in God's mercy (48)

Farrington, Harry Webb (b. Nassau, B.W.I., July 14, 1879; d. Asbury Park, N.J., Oct. 27, 1930), whose mother died shortly after his birth, was brought as an orphan to Baltimore. He attended the Darlington Academy in Maryland, and while a student there he was converted and joined the Methodist church at Darlington. After his call to the ministry, he attended Dickinson Seminary, Syracuse University, Boston University, and Harvard University. At the latter school he majored in philosophy and education and received his M.A. degree. In 1914, as field secretary of the Methodist Board of Sunday Schools, he established a week-day church school program in Gary, Indiana, and two years later inaugurated a similar program in New York City. During World War I he was in France for the Foyers du Soldat. He had been an outstanding football and basketball player during his student days at Syracuse University, and because of his athletic ability he did effective work as athletic director for the French troops. After the war he held several pastorates in New York City and later served as director of education for the Methodist Church Welfare League. Among his published works are a collection of poems, *Rough and Brown* (1921), and his autobiography, *Kilts to Togs* (1930).

I know not how that Bethlehem's Babe (276)

Fawcett, John (b. Lidget Green, near Bradford, Yorkshire, Eng., Jan. 6, 1740; d. Hebden Bridge, Eng., July 25, 1817), at sixteen, was greatly impressed by the preaching of George Whitefield. For a while he was associated with the Methodists and with them attended the Church of England. In 1758 he joined the Baptist church at Bradford, was ordained to the Baptist ministry in 1763, and was pastor at Wainsgate, Yorkshire, and at Hebden Bridge. He declined the call to become pastor of the Carter Lane Baptist Chapel in 1772, and also the opportunity to be principal of the Baptist Academy at Bristol in 1793. He founded the Northern Education Society, which is now known as Rawdon College, and was author of a number of publications—essays, sermons, and other religious writings. His hymns were written to be sung at the conclusion of his sermons, and 166 of these were included in his *Hymns Adapted to the Circumstances of Public Worship and Private Devotion* (1782). The preface of this collection of hymns reveals an insight into the author's modest evaluation of his hymns.

I blush to think of these plain verses falling into the hands of persons of an elevated genius, and refined taste. To such, I know, they will appear flat, dull and unentertaining. . . . If it may be conducive, under divine blessing, to warm the heart or assist the devotion of any humble Christian in the closet, the family, or the house of God, I shall therein sincerely rejoice, whatever censure I may incur from the polite world.

He was given the honorary D.D. degree by Brown University, Providence, Rhode Island, in 1811.

Blest be the tie that binds (366)
Lord, dismiss us with Thy blessing (31)

Featherston, William Ralph (b. Montreal, Que., July 23, 1846; d. Montreal, May 20, 1873), was the son of John and Mary (Stephenson) Featherston, and seems to have spent his life in Montreal. No other information has been found about this author except that he and his parents were members of the Wesleyan Methodist Church of Montreal, which was later named the St. James Methodist Church, and now is the St. James United Church, from whose records the above information was secured.

My Jesus, I love Thee, I know Thou are mine (289)

Fillmore, James Henry (b. Cincinnati, Ohio, June 1, 1849; d. Cincinnati, Feb. 8, 1936), was the eldest of seven children, five sons and two daughters, born to Augustus Dameron and Hannah (Lockwood) Fillmore. His father, an ordained minister in the Christian Church, was also a composer, songbook compiler and publisher, who developed his own system of musical notation using numbers on the staff in place of note heads. When James was sixteen his father died, and he took over his father's singing school engagements to support his family. He had learned the printing trade and also music typesetting. Later with his brothers he founded the Fillmore Brothers Music House, which became a successful Cincinnati music firm, publishing church and Sunday school collections, anthems, sheet music, and later, band and orchestral music. For many years this firm issued a monthly periodical, *The Musical Messenger*. Beginning with his Sunday school songbook *Songs of Glory* (1874), there followed many Fillmore publications which became widely used throughout the Midwest. For these collections he composed a great deal of music—hymn tunes, anthems and cantatas. His son, Henry Fillmore (1881-1956), became famous as a band director and composer of marches, some of which appeared under his pseudonym "Harold Bennett."

HANNAH—I know that my Redeemer liveth (127)
PURER IN HEART—Purer in heart, O God (369)
RESOLUTION—I am resolved no longer to linger (216)

Findlater, Sarah Borthwick (b. Edinburgh, Scot., Nov. 26, 1823; d. Torquay, Scot., 1907), was the younger daughter of James Borthwick, manager of the North British Insurance Office, Edinburgh. She became the wife of Eric John Findlater, Scottish Free Church minister at Lochearnhead, Perthshire. Years later, her daughter, Jane, wrote concerning her mother:

> Her home life with my father was almost idyllically happy, in the small manse at Lochearnhead, where there never was enough of money, yet where my parents exercised unceasing hospitality—almost foolish hospitality. They were both great readers, and used to read aloud to each other for hours. . . . That simple little hymn of hers which begins "O happy home", is really an epitome of her home life with my father—they were so single-eyed in their longing to serve God: it came first with them always.

With her sister, Jane Borthwick (*q.v.*), she translated German hymns. These translations were published in *Hymns from the Land of Luther* (1854-62), fifty-three of which were her own work.

God calling yet! shall I not hear? (tr.) (223)
O happy home where Thou art loved the dearest (tr.) (373)

Fischer, William Gustavus (b. Baltimore, Md., Oct. 14, 1835; d. Philadelphia, Pa., Aug. 12, 1912), learned to read music in a church singing class, and later studied music at night while learning the bookbinding trade at J. B. Lippincott's in Philadelphia. He became widely known as a music teacher and choral conductor. At the bi-centennial of the landing of William Penn, he directed the chorus of the combined Welsh Societies. After ten years as professor of music at Girard College, 1858-68, he resigned to enter the piano business with J. E. Gould. Although he wrote a number of gospel songs, he did not publish any collections. However, under the firm name of Fischer and Gould, he issued several leaflets of Sunday school songs.

FISCHER—Lord Jesus, I long to be perfectly whole (201)
HANKEY—I love to tell the story (141)
ROCK OF REFUGE—O sometimes the shadows are deep (320)
TRUSTING—I am coming to the cross (243)

Fisher, Albert Christopher (b. New Bern, N.C., Mar. 10, 1886; d. Dallas, Tex., Feb. 6, 1946), was educated at Polytechnic College (Fort Worth, Texas), Vanderbilt University, and Southern Methodist University. In 1908 he moved to Fort Worth and was for ten years general evangelist for the Methodist Episcopal Church, South. He served as a chaplain during World War I. Twelve years of his ministry were spent in the East Oklahoma Conference, and in 1944 he was transferred to the North Texas Conference. He wrote a number of gospel songs and edited *Best Revival Hymns* (Cokesbury Press, 1923).

Of the themes that men have known—FISHER (293)
There's a glad new song ringing in my heart—REDEEMING LOVE (311)

Flemming, Friedrich Ferdinald (b. Neuhausen, Saxony, Feb. 28, 1778; d. Berlin, Prussia, May 27, 1813), after completing medical education at Wittenberg, Jena, Vienna, and Trieste, settled in Berlin. He became a successful physician and maintained a keen interest in music as an avocation, composing numerous part songs for men's choral groups.

FLEMMING—O Holy Saviour, friend unseen (287)

Fortunatus, Venantius (b. Treviso, It., *ca.* A.D. 530; d. Poitiers, Fr., 609), studied at Milan and Ravenna, and his major interests were in rhetoric and poetry. His recovery from a serious eye trouble was attributed to the oil taken from the lamp which burned before the altar of St. Martin's of Tours. As a result of this cure, he made a pilgrimage to Tours in 565, and spent the rest of his life in Gaul. He enjoyed the friendship of Queen Rhadegunda, who had left her husband, Clotaire II, the Frankish king, to establish the convent of St. Croix at Poiters. Through her influence he became a priest, and in 599 became bishop of Poiters. He is recognized as the chief Latin poet of the sixth century. He produced a considerable amount of literary work, including a collection of 250 poems.

"Welcome, happy morning" (110)

Fosdick, Harry Emerson (b. Buffalo, N.Y., May 24, 1878), was educated at Colgate University and Divinity School, Union Theological Seminary (B.D., 1904), and Columbia University (M.A., 1908). During his first pastorate, at the First Baptist Church, Montclair, New Jersey, 1904-15, he taught at Union Seminary, and in 1915 became professor of practical theology. From 1919 to 1926 he was associated with the First Presbyterian Church of New York City. He accepted the pastorate of the Park Avenue Baptist Church, which later became the famed Riverside Church. He is the author of many books, among the most popular being *The Meaning of Prayer* (1915), *A Guide to Understanding the Bible* (1938), *Living Under Tension* (1941), and *On Being a Real Person* (1943). His success as a preacher and an author has brought him world-wide acclaim, and he is recognized as one of the outstanding ministers of his day.

God of grace and God of glory (465)

Foundery Collection. *A Collection of Tunes, Set to Music, As They Are Commonly Sung at the Foundery* (1742) was the first Wesleyan collection to provide tunes for the Wesleyan hymns. The "Foundery" was the Wesleyan headquarters, located near Moorfields, a suburb of London. For a number of years it had been used by the government for the casting of cannon. However, in 1716, during the recasting of the guns captured by the Duke of Marlborough in his French wars, an explosion almost demolished it and killed several workmen. The site was abandoned and remained in ruins until 1739, when John Wesley purchased it to serve as the first Methodist meetinghouse in London. This collection contained forty-two tunes, which Wesley selected from several sources. Regarding the appearance of this collection, James Lightwood has stated in *Hymn-Tunes and Their Story:*

> The *Foundery Tune-Book* was one of the worst printed books ever issued from the press; and not only is the printing itself bad, but the work is full of the most extraordinary mistakes, such as wrong bars and notes and impossible music phrases, while in the tune from Handel's opera the editor has simply transcribed the first violin part from the score.

AMSTERDAM—Rise, my soul, and stretch thy wings (122)

Francis of Assisi (b. Assisi, It., 1182; d. Assisi, Oct. 4, 1226), was the son of Pietro Bernardoni, a wealthy cloth merchant; and his youthful years were spent in frivolous living. A serious illness in 1202 wrought a great change in his life. Following his recovery he dedicated his life to prayer and poverty and his energies to caring for the outcasts of society. With burning zeal he sought to imitate the life of Christ in all that he did. He loved flowers, birds, and beasts, and saw the handiwork of God in all nature. He founded the order of Franciscans, and sent forth those who followed him to preach the gospel and help the needy. He loved music, and his familiarity with the music of the French troubadours caused him to adapt the troubadour style for sacred song. Among his writings which remain are a number of sermons, poems, and letters.

All creatures of our God and King (3)

Frazer, George West (b. Bally, near Sligo, Ire., 1830; d. Cheltenham, Gloucestershire, Eng., Jan. 24, 1896). Frazer's father was of the Lovat-Frazer family of Inverness, Scotland, but was born in Tralee, Ireland, and became police inspector in the Royal Irish Constabulary. Young Frazer was converted at the age of twenty in a revival meeting in Dublin conducted by the evangelist, Grattan Guiness. He was employed in a bank in Dublin, and devoted a great deal of his time in evangelistic work, preaching and giving his testimony. Some years later he resigned his position at the bank to devote his entire time to the ministry, and the latter years of his life were spent chiefly in visiting and attending assemblies in England. He finally settled at Cheltenham, where he was a neighbor and intimate friend of C. H. Mackintosh, well-known author of *Notes on the Pentateuch*. His numerous hymns were published in three separate volumes: *Midnight Praises, Day-Dawn Praises,* and *The Day-Spring*.

God, our Father, we adore Thee (5)

Fry, Charles William (b. Salisbury, Eng., May 29, 1837; d. Park Hall, Polmont, Eng., Aug. 23, 1882), was converted at the age of seventeen at the Wesleyan Chapel in his home town. Following the vocation of his father and grandfather, he became a builder of considerable reputation in Salisbury. His three sons shared in the business operation with him. He learned to play the cornet with great skill and taught his sons to be brass players. The Salvation Army began its work in Salisbury in 1878, and in spite of the local opposition to this endeavor, Fry and his three sons offered their services to play for the outdoor meetings. This was the beginning of the brass band activity of the Salvation Army and was immediately successful. The Fry family band was in such demand that business began to suffer, and it became apparent that they could not continue both activities. After consultation with General Booth and much prayer, they closed the business and offered themselves for full-time service in the Salvation Army, arriving in London on May 14, 1880. After two years of service Fry became ill and was cared for in the home of Mr. Livingstone Learmouth in Park Hill, Polmont, where he died. He was buried in the Necropolis Cemetery, Glasgow, Scotland.

I have found a friend in Jesus (87)

Gabriel, Charles Hutchison (b. Wilton, Iowa, Aug. 18, 1856; d. Los Angeles, Calif., Sept. 15, 1932), spent the first seventeen years of his life on an Iowa farm. He expressed a keen interest in music as a lad; and when his family secured a small reed organ, he quickly taught himself to play. At sixteen he began teaching singing schools, and his fame as a teacher and composer became widely known. For two years he was music director of the Grace Methodist Episcopal Church, San Francisco, California, 1890-92, after which he settled in Chicago. From 1895-1912 he published a number of collections. In 1912 he became associated with the publishing firm of Homer Rodeheaver and maintained his relationship until his death. The extraordinary output of his musical writing can be seen by the fact that he edited thirty-five gospel songbooks, eight Sunday school songbooks, seven books for men's chorus, six for ladies voices, ten children's songbooks, nineteen collections of anthems, and twenty-three cantatas. He was equally talented in music and verse, and frequently provided texts for his own tunes. Most of these texts were signed by his pseudonym "Charlotte G. Homer," the initials of which are the same as his own name with the G and H reversed.

I stand amazed in the presence—MY SAVIOUR'S LOVE (139)
In loving-kindness Jesus came—HE LIFTED ME (202)
Lord, as of old at Pentecost—OLD-TIME POWER (173)
More like the Master I would ever be—HANFORD (325)
So precious is Jesus, my Saviour, my King—PRECIOUS TO ME (304)
Sweet is the promise, "I will not forget thee"—SWEET PROMISE (278)
There's a call comes ringing o'er the restless wave—McCABE (457)
When all my labors and trials are o'er—GLORY SONG (485)
GABRIEL—Just when I need Him, Jesus is near (267)
HIGHER GROUND—I'm pressing on the upward way (319)
McDANIEL—What a wonderful change in my life has been wrought
    (310)
WAY OF THE CROSS—I must needs go home by the way of the cross
    (196)

Gardiner, William (b. Leicester, Eng., Mar. 15, 1770; d. Leicester, Nov. 16, 1853), a successful hosiery manufacturer and enthusiastic amateur musician, was active in many musical festivals. He enjoyed the friendship of some of the most celebrated musicians of his day. From his Leicester mill he once sent Joseph Haydn six pairs of stockings with Haydn's melodies (one of them AUSTRIAN HYMN) woven into the design. On frequent business trips to the Continent, he collected materials for the two collections for which he is best known. He had great admiration for Beethoven and claimed to be the first to introduce Beethoven's music to England. In 1812, he published *Sacred Melodies from Haydn, Mozart, and Beethoven, Adapted to the Best English Poets and Appropriated to the Use of the British Church* (London). A second volume appeared in 1815. In these two volumes, Gardiner first introduced adapted melodies from classic works as hymn tunes. Lowell Mason, in his early collections, relied heavily on the works of Gardiner. Other compilers followed this pattern, and the appropriating of classic melodies with the necessary alterations to hymn tune requirements became a fashionable enterprise in the nineteenth century, both in England and America.

GERMANY—All things are Thine, no gift have we (403)
    Where cross the crowded ways of life (464)

Gaul, Alfred Robert (b. Norwich, Eng., Apr. 30, 1837; d. Birmingham, Eng., Sept. 13, 1913), at the age of nine, was a chorister at the Cathedral of Norwich and studied under Dr. Zechariah Buck, cathedral organist, famed for his training of choirboys. He later became organist at Fakenham, Birmingham, and Edgbaston. In 1887 he became conductor of the Walsall Philharmonic and later teacher and conductor at the Birmingham and Midland Institute. He also taught at King Edward's High School for Girls and at the Blind Asylum. He composed numerous works; among the most popular have been his two cantatas, *Ruth* and *The Holy City*.

DEDICATION—What can I give to Jesus (508)

Gawler, William (b. Lambeth, London, Eng., 1750; d. London, Mar. 15, 1809), was organist of the Royal Female Orphan Asylum in Lambeth. For the use of the girls in this orphanage, he published *Hymns and Psalms Used at the Asylum for Female Orphans* (1785). At least two supplements or editions added additional tunes to the original collection.

ST. MICHEL'S—Our Father in heaven, we hallow Thy name (343)
O Thou who in Jordan didst bow Thy meek head (388)

Geibel, Adam (b. Baden, Ger., Sept. 15, 1885; d. Philadelphia, Pa., Aug. 3, 1933), was brought to America as a child. When he was about eight years of age he developed a slight eye infection, and through the application of improper medication lost his sight. However, his interest in music was strong and he studied diligently in Philadelphia. He became a skilful organist and conductor and a prolific composer. For the publishing of his music, he formed the Adam Geibel Music Company, which later became the Hall-Mack Company, and this firm later became the Rodeheaver Hall-Mack Company. He composed both sacred and secular songs and was particularly successful in the writing of songs for four-part men's voices. The most popular of his secular songs are "Kentucky Babe" and "Sleep, Sleep, Sleep," the latter used as the theme song of the Fred Waring radio program of some years ago. In addition to his creative work and his publishing business, he served as organist for many years at the Stetson Mission, Philadelphia.

GEIBEL—Stand up, stand up for Jesus (419)

Genevan Psalter (1551) (*see* Louis Bourgeois.)

OLD 100TH—All people that on earth do dwell (13)
Praise God from whom all blessings flow (514)
OLD 134TH (ST. MICHAEL)—Stand up and bless the Lord (16)

Gerhardt, Paul (b. Gräfenhainichen, near Wittenberg, Ger., Mar. 12, 1607; d. Lübben, Ger., May 27, 1676), was educated in the Elector's school at Grimma, 1622-27, and the University of Wittenberg, 1628-42.

He went to Berlin in 1642, where he became family tutor in the home of Andreas Barthold, an attorney. During this time he began his hymn writing and made the acquaintance of Johann Crüger (*q.v.*), choirmaster at St. Nicholas' Church. Many of his hymns appeared in Crüger's *Praxis Pietatis Melica* (1648), and others were added in subsequent editions. During his youth he had experienced much suffering due to the rigors and disasters of the Thirty Years' War. It was not until he was forty-four that he was ordained to the Lutheran ministry and served in Lutheran parishes at Mittenwalde, Berlin, and Lübben. In Berlin he served for eleven years at St. Nicholas' Church and renewed his association with Crüger, who, no doubt, encouraged his hymn writing. Because of his refusal to sign an edict of Elector Friedrich Wilhelm I, which limited free speech regarding theological differences between Luthern and Calvinistic churches, he was deposed from office in 1666 and even prohibited from conducting private worship in his own home. Because of the intervention of devoted friends, he was reinstated the following year. The death of his wife in 1668 seemed to climax his personal sorrow, for four of his five children had died during childhood. In the Lutheran church at Lübben, his last pastorate, hangs a life-sized painting of Gerhardt, with the inscription "Theologus in cribro Satanae versatus" (A divine sifted in Satan's sieve). At least two different dates may be found for the death of Gerhardt. Dr. Armin Haeussler, in *The Story of Our Hymns* (p. 672) presents in detail the research of Dr. Hermann Petrich, first published in Germany in 1914, proving May 27, 1676, to be the correct date. Most other hymnal handbooks, including the *Historical Companion to Hymns Ancient and Modern* (London, 1962), retain the erroneous date, June 7, 1676.

Gerhardt wrote 123 hymns, and these mark the transition in Lutheran hymnody from the confessional and ecclesiastical hymns of an earlier era to the hymns of subjective, devotional piety. (Cf. *The Hymn*, V, No. 3, 84)

Jesus, Thy boundless love to me (288)
O sacred Head, now wounded (tr.) (91)

Gesangbuch der Herzogl (1784). This collection, the full title of which is *Gesangbuch der Herzoglichen Wirtembergischen Katholischen Hofkapelle,* was published for use in the Roman Catholic chapel of the Duke of Württemberg. Of unusual significance is the fact that most of the fifty-five hymns in this collection were written by German Protestant hymn writers. The fourteen melodies included in the Appendix were not original nor new, but arrangements of existing hymn tune melodies.

ELLACOMBE—To Him who hallows all our days (499)

Giardini, Felice de (b. Turin, It., Apr. 12, 1716; d. Moscow, Russ., June 8, 1796), was a chorister at the Milan Cathedral, and while there studied voice with Paladini and violin with Somis. As a young man he played in various orchestras in the opera houses of Rome and Naples. He became widely known through his playing in Italy, his tour in Germany in 1748, and his concerts in London, 1750. From 1752 to 1784 he lived in England as violinist, teacher, conductor, and impresario of the Italian Opera group in London. He was recognized as an artist of first rank. His reputation opened the doors of the aristocracy to him, and among those who befriended him was Lady Huntingdon. Through her influence he consented to write some hymn tunes for a compilation being made by Martin Madan, *A Collection of Psalms and Hymn Tunes* (1769), known as the "Lock Collection." Of the four tunes he provided, only the present one has remained in usage. In 1796, after several unsuccessful operatic seasons in London, he went to Moscow, and died less than three months after his initial concert there.

ITALIAN HYMN (TRINITY)—Come, Thou Almighty King (12)
Thou, whose almighty word (461)

Giles, John Eustace (b. Dartmouth, Eng., Apr. 20, 1805; d. London, Eng., June 24, 1875), received his early education in the private school of Rev. James Hinton at Oxford. He was converted at the age of twenty, and joined the Baptist church at Chatham, where his father was pastor. After attending the Baptist College at Bristol, he was ordained to the Baptist ministry in 1830 and was pastor of Salter's Hall Chapel, London. Among his subsequent pastorates were South Parade (Leeds), Sheffield, Rathmines (Dublin), and Clapham Common (London). He was a forceful preacher and a staunch defender of Baptist faith and fellowship. While he was pastor at Leeds, he visited Hamburg, Germany, on behalf of J. G. Oncken and the Baptists who were suffering persecution at that time. Later he went to Denmark to plead with the king on behalf of the Baptist cause in that country. Among his published works were *Lectures on Socialism, A Lecture on Popery,* and *A Circular Letter on the Spirit of Faith.*

Thou hast said, exalted Jesus (390)

Gilmore, Joseph Henry (b. Boston, Mass., Apr. 29, 1834; d. Rochester, N.Y., July 23, 1918), was educated at Phillips Academy, Andover, Massachusetts, Brown University, and Newton Theological Seminary. After his graduation at Newton in 1861, he remained for one year as instructor in Hebrew. Ordained to the Baptist ministry in 1862, he accepted the pastorate of the Baptist church in Fisherville, New

Hampshire. While his father was Governor of New Hampshire, 1863-64, he served as his private secretary and also served as editor of the Concord *Daily Monitor*. In 1865 he became pastor of the Second Baptist Church, Rochester, New York. In addition to his pastoral duties, he was invited in 1867 to be acting professor of Hebrew at the Rochester Theological Seminary. The following year he was appointed professor of logic, rhetoric, and English literature at the University of Rochester and remained in this position until his retirement in 1911. In addition to writing several hymns, he was the author of six books, among which were *The Art of Expression* (1876), *Familiar Chats on Books and Reading,* and *Outlines of English and American Literature* (1905). He was loved and respected both in religious and educational circles, and lived a long and useful life. However, he is best remembered for the hymn written when he was twenty-eight as a visiting preacher in Philadelphia.

He leadeth me! O blessed thought (58)

Gilmour, Henry Lake (b. Londonderry, Ire., Jan. 19, 1836; d. Delair, N.J., May 20, 1920), at sixteen went to sea to learn navigation. When his ship landed at Philadelphia, he decided to seek his fortune in America. He learned the painter's trade, and while painting the lighthouse at Cape May, New Jersey, he met and married Letitia Pauline Howard in 1858. During the Civil War he served with the 1st New Jersey Cavalry, was captured, and spent months at Libbey Prison as a Confederate prisoner. He graduated from Philadelphia Dental School in 1867 and carried on an active dental practice for many years. In 1869 he moved to Wenonah, New Jersey, and the Methodist Church of Wenonah was organized in his home in 1885. He was devoted to this church and served for many years as trustee, steward, Sunday school superintendent, class leader, and chorister, holding the latter office for twenty-five years. He was gifted as a soloist and greatly respected as a choir director. He was widely used in revivals and camp meetings, devoting his ten weeks' vacation each year to this work. For forty years he directed the large chorus choir at Pitman Grove Camp Meeting and did similar work at Mountain Lake Park, Maryland, and at Ridgeview Park, Pennsylvania. He was a frequent visitor to the Ocean Grove Camp Meeting and through these activities came to know personally many composers and writers of gospel songs. He was associated with William J. Kirkpatrick and George Sanville in the Praise Publishing Company of Philadelphia, organized in 1906. Dr. Gilmour was the author and composer of many gospel songs and assisted in the compilation of more than sixteen songbooks.

My soul in sad exile was out on life's sea (228)

Gladden, Washington (b. Pottsgrove, Pa., Feb. 11, 1836; d. Columbus, Ohio, July 2, 1918), was graduated from Williams College in 1859 and ordained to the Congregational ministry the following year. From 1860 to 1882 he pastored successively several Congregational churches in New York and Massachusetts. In 1882 he became pastor of the First Congregational Church, Columbus, Ohio, where he distinguished himself in his notable ministry covering thirty-two years. He wrote a number of books and contributed extensively to both religious and secular periodicals. He served as moderator of the National Council of Congregational Churches, 1904-7, and became widely known as a preacher and lecturer. He was an early exponent of the social implications of the gospel and did much to popularize through his speaking and writing the results of biblical criticism.

O Master, let me walk with Thee (426)

Gläser, Carl Gotthelf (b. Weissenfels, Ger., May 4, 1784; d. Barmen, Ger., Apr. 16, 1829), received his early musical training from his father, and later attended St. Thomas' School in Leipzig, where he studied with Johann Hiller and August Müller. His violin training was under the Italian master, Campagnoli, who taught for a number of years in Leipzig. Later he moved to Barmen, where he became a teacher of voice, piano, and violin. He composed a good deal of choral music and was a well-known choral conductor.

AZMON—O for a thousand tongues to sing (129)
The head that once was crowned with thorns (117)

Goadby, Frederick William (b. Leicester, Eng., Aug. 10, 1845; d. Watford, Eng., Oct. 15, 1879), was educated at Loughborough Grammar School; Regent's Park College, London; and London University. After receiving his M.A. degree from the latter school in 1868, he was pastor of the Baptist church at Bluntisham. In 1876 he accepted the pastorate of the Baptist church at Watford, where his death occurred three years later. Of the several hymns he wrote, only the present one remains in common usage.

O thou, whose hand hath brought us (379)

Gordon, Adoniram Judson (b. New Hampton, N.H., Apr. 19, 1836; d. Boston, Mass., Feb. 2, 1895), named for the pioneer Baptist missionary to Burma, was educated at Brown University and Newton Theological Seminary. Ordained to the Baptist ministry in 1863, he was called as pastor of the Baptist church at Jamaica Plain, Massachusetts, and six years later succeeded Dr. Baron Stow as pastor of the Clarendon Street

Baptist Church, Boston. He was one of the editors of *The Service of Song for Baptist Churches* (1871) and editor of *The Vestry Hymn and Tune Book* (1872). For a time, in addition to his pastoral work, he served as editor of the monthly publication *The Watchword*. In 1878 he received the D.D. degree from Brown University. He was a close friend of Dwight L. Moody and was of great assistance in Moody's evangelistic efforts in Boston.

GORDON—My Jesus, I love Thee, I know Thou art mine (289)

Goss, John (b. Fareham, Eng., Dec. 27, 1800; d. London, Eng., May 10, 1880), was the son of Joseph Goss, parish organist at Fareham. At the age of eleven John went to London to live with his uncle, a singer of considerable reputation. He became a chorister in the Chapel Royal and was a pupil of Thomas Attwood. Beginning in 1827, he was professor of harmony at the Royal Academy of Music for forty-seven years. In 1838 he succeeded Attwood as organist at St. Paul's Cathedral, London. Because of his compositional skill, he was appointed composer to the Chapel Royal in 1856, knighted in 1872, and given the honorary Mus.D. degree at Cambridge in 1876. Among English church composers of his day, he was second only to Samuel S. Wesley (*q.v.*). He edited *Parochial Psalmody* (1826) for his congregation at Chelsea; *Chants, Ancient and Modern* (1841); and was musical editor of Mercer's *Church Psalter* (1856).

ARMAGEDDON—Who is on the Lord's side? (413)
ARTHUR'S SEAT—March on, O soul, with strength (422)

Gottschalk, Louis Moreau (b. New Orleans, La., May 8, 1829; d. Rio de Janeiro, Braz., Dec. 18, 1869), showed extraordinary musical talent in childhood. At the age of thirteen he was sent by his parents to Paris, where he studied piano with Halle and Stamaty. He made a successful tour through France, Switzerland, and Spain in 1852. The following year he returned to America, enjoyed phenomenal success touring the United States, and was recognized as the first American-born piano virtuoso. His most popular compositions were among his ninety piano pieces, and such numbers as *The Dying Poet, La Mort,* and *The Last Hope* (from which his hymn tune was taken) were included in his concerts by popular demand. He toured South America, and became a great favorite in Panama, Peru, and Chile. Greatly weakened by yellow fever, he was unable to complete his concert schedule in Brazil and died at Rio de Janeiro.

MERCY—Holy Ghost, with light divine (170)

Gould, John Edgar (b. Bangor, Me., 1822; d. Algiers, Africa, Mar. 4, 1875), began composing at an early age, and while still a young man, together with Edward L. White, compiled *The Modern Harp* (1846); *The Wreath of School Songs* (1847); *The Tyrolian Lyre* (1847); and *The Sunday School Lute* (1848). In 1852 he opened a music store on Broadway in New York City, and later he had a similar establishment in Philadelphia. He later compiled *Harmonia Sacra* (1851) and *Songs of Gladness for the Sabbath School* (1869). About 1868 he and William G. Fischer (*q.v.*) established a successful piano business and music store in Philadelphia. Because of ill health, in September, 1874, he traveled to England, Europe, and Africa. Instead of improving, his health declined, and he died in Algiers the following spring. Of the numerous tunes he composed, only the present one has survived in common usage.

PILOT—Jesus, Saviour, pilot me (337)

Gounod, Charles Francois (b. Paris, Fr., June 17, 1818; d. Paris, Oct. 17, 1893). Gounod's mother, a capable and accomplished woman, supervised his early literary, artistic, and musical education. He entered the Paris Conservatory in 1836, and for his cantata *Fernand,* won the "Grand Prix de Rome" in 1839. His study of music in Rome greatly heightened his interest in church music. On his return to Paris, he became a serious student of theology, but after two years decided against entering the priesthood. He composed a number of operas, by far the most popular of which is his *Faust,* written in 1859. His creative ventures include almost every vocal and instrumental media.

THE RADIANT MORN—The radiant morn hath passed away (32)

Grant, Robert (b. Bengal, India, 1779; d. Dalpoorie, India, July 9, 1838), was the son of Charles Grant, a director of the East India Company. When he was six years old the family moved to London. He was educated at Magdalen College, Cambridge (B.A., 1801; M.A., 1804) and was called to the English Bar in 1807. He became King's Sergeant in the Court of the Duchy of Lancaster and one of the commissioners in bankruptcy. He entered Parliament in 1818, and in 1833 introduced a bill in Commons for the removal of the civil restrictions imposed against the Jews. He was made Judge Advocate General in 1832, and two years later he was appointed Governor of Bombay, at which time he was knighted. His death occurred at Dalpoorie, in western India, where a medical college which bears his name was erected as a memorial to him. He wrote twelve hymns which were published posthumously by his brother, Lord Glenelg, under the title *Sacred Poems* (1839).

O worship the King, all glorious above (20)

Grape, John T. (b. Baltimore, Md., May 6, 1835; d. Baltimore, Nov. 2, 1915), the son of George and Charlotte Grape, was a successful coal merchant in Baltimore. For many years he was active in the Sunday school and was choir director in the Monument Street Methodist Church; later he became choir director for the Harford Avenue Methodist Church. He wrote a number of hymn tunes, but only the one given here remains in common usage.

ALL TO CHRIST—I hear the Saviour say (225)

Greatorex, Henry Wellington (b Burton-on-Trent, Derbyshire, Eng., Dec. 24, 1813; d. Charleston, S.C., Sept. 10, 1858), after receiving his musical education in England, came to the United States in 1839 and served as organist at Center Church in Hartford, Connecticut. About 1846 he resided for seven years in New York City, serving as organist at St. Paul's Church, and later at Calvary Church. In 1853 he became organist in an Episcopal church in Charleston, where he later died of yellow fever. He compiled *Collection of Psalm and Hymn Tunes, Chants, Anthems and Sentences for the Use of the Protestant Episcopal Church in America* (Boston, 1851), which contained thirty-seven original tunes and a number of arrangements, from which the following tunes have been taken.

GLORIA PATRI—Glory be to the Father (525)
MANOAH—Begin, my tongue, some heavenly theme (49)
      Walk in the light! so thou shalt know (370)
SEYMOUR—Softly now the light of day (33)
      Holy Spirit, from on high (171)
      Depth of mercy! can there be (242)
      Cast thy burden on the Lord (254)
      Gentle Jesus, meek and mild (510)

Grose, Howard Benjamin (b. Millerton, N.Y., Sept. 5, 1851; d. May 19, 1939), the son of Rev. Henry Laurenz and Emma Louisa (Seward) Grose, was educated at the University of Chicago and the University of Rochester (A.B., 1876; A.M., 1880). Ordained to the Baptist ministry in 1883, he served as pastor of the First Baptist Church, Poughkeepsie, New York, 1883-87, and the First Baptist Church, Pittsburgh, Pennsylvania, 1888-90. He was president of the State University of South Dakota, 1890-92, and then served as recorder and assistant professor of history at the University of Chicago, 1892-96. He was assistant editor of *The Watchman,* Boston, 1896-1900, and editorial secretary of the American Baptist Home Mission Society, 1904-10. He served as editor of *Missions* from 1910 until his retirement in 1933. He is the author of *Aliens or Americans* (1906); *The Incoming Millions* (1906); *Advance* *to the Antilles* (1910); and *Never Man So Spake* (1924).

Give of your best to the Master (353)

Groves, Alexander (b. Isle of Wight, Eng., 1842; d. Henley, Eng., 1909). Other than this information given in *The Baptist Hymn Book Companion* (London, 1962), nothing has been found concerning this author.

Break Thou the bread of life (178—stanzas 3 and 4)

Gruber, Franz Xaver (b. Unterweizberg, near Hochburg, Aust., Nov. 25,1787; d. Hallein, near Salzburg, Aust., June 7, 1863), was the son of a poor linen weaver who discouraged his son's musical ambitions, desiring that he follow a more remunerative profession. Nonetheless, he learned to play the violin without his father's knowledge and later studied organ with Georg Hartdobler. From 1807 to 1829 he was a schoolteacher at Arnsdorf, and to supplement his income he accepted the position of organist in St. Nikolaus Church at nearby Oberndorf in 1816. From 1828 to 1832 he was headmaster at Berndorf, and from 1833 until his death he was organist and choirmaster at Hallein near Salzburg. He is credited with more than ninety compositions, but his fame is based on the Christmas song he wrote in 1818.

STILLE NACHT—Silent night, holy night (72)

Gunner, A. No information has been found about this composer.
Response (550)

Gurney, Dorothy Frances Blomfield (b. London, Eng., Oct. 4, 1858; d. London, June 15, 1932), was the daughter of the Rev. Frederick George Blomfield, rector of St. Andrew's Undershaft, London. In 1897 she married Gerald Gurney, at one time an actor but later ordained in the Church of England. She and her husband joined the Roman Catholic Church at Farnborough Abbey in 1919. She published two volumes of poetry.

O perfect love, all human thought transcending (501)

Hale, Sarah Josepha Buell (b. Newport N.H., Oct. 24, 1788; d. Philadelphia, Pa., Apr. 30, 1879), was the daughter of Captain Gordon and Martha (Whittlesey) Buell. She was married to David Hale, a lawyer, who died in 1822. Unsuccessful in operating a millinery shop, she turned her efforts to writing. She became one of the first women magazine editors in America, first for *The Ladies' Magazine,* Boston, in 1828, and nine years later for Godey's *Ladies' Book,* Philadelphia. Through her persistent efforts in behalf of making Thanksgiving Day, the last Thursday in November, a national holiday, she finally persuaded President Abraham Lincoln in 1863 to issue the official proclamation. For her efforts in this regard she was often referred to as "Mrs. Thanksgiving."

Our Father in heaven, we hallow Thy name (343)

Hall, Elvina Mable (b. Alexandria, Va., June 4, 1820; d. Ocean Grove, N.J., July 18, 1889), was the daughter of Captain David Reynolds. She first married Richard Hall, and after his death she married, in 1885, Rev. Thomas Myers of the Baltimore Conference of the Methodist Church. For more than forty years she was a member of the Monument Street Methodist Church in Baltimore.

I hear the Saviour say (225)

Handel, George Frederick (b. Halle, Ger., Feb. 23, 1685; d. London, Eng., Apr. 14, 1759), showed extraordinary musical talent at an early age; but his father, preferring that he follow the legal profession, greatly discouraged his musical interests. He studied organ, harpsichord, and violin, as well as counterpoint and fugue with F. W. Zachaw, organist at the Halle Cathedral. After playing in a Hamburg opera orchestra for four years, he went to Italy and won considerable acclaim there. After 1713 he made his home in England and became a British subject in 1727. He enjoyed great success as an operatic composer and impresario until his popularity waned and, in 1737, he became bankrupt. He abandoned his operatic endeavors in favor of oratorio, and, with the immediate success of his *Messiah* in 1741, he gained new heights of public favor and acclaim. After he became blind in 1752 he continued his musical performances, and served as organist for performances of his oratorios until his death. His enormous output included forty-six operas, thirty-two oratorios, numerous cantatas, and many organ, choral, and instrumental works, details of which may be found in music reference works. He wrote three hymn tunes, GOPSAL, CANNONS, and FITZWILLIAM, for Charles Wesley's hymns. The first of these is still found today in English hymnals. Far better known are a few tunes which have been arranged from his vocal works.

ANTIOCH—Joy to the world! the Lord is come (65)
CHRISTMAS—While shepherds watched their flocks by night (79)
  Awake, my soul, stretch every nerve (309)

Hankey, Katherine (b. Clapham, Eng., 1834; d. London, Eng., 1911), christened Arabella Catherine but usually known as Kate, was the daughter of Thomas Hankey, a banker and member of the evangelical "Clapham Sect," led by William Wilberforce. As the result of the influence of this group she became interested in religious work, and while still a young girl began teaching in a Croydon Sunday school. When she was eighteen she organized a large Bible class for shop girls in London, and later began a similar class for girls of her own social circle. As a result of a trip to South Africa to bring home an invalid brother, she became greatly interested in foreign missions. In later years the income from all her literary efforts was given to this cause. During her last years she was active in hospital visitation in London.

I love to tell the story (141)
Tell me the old, old story (222)

Harding, James Procktor (b. London, Eng., May 19, 1850; d. London, 1911), served in the Inland Revenue Department, Somerset House, London, from 1867 until he retired on January 6, 1909, in the grade of Principal Clerk, "a comfortably senior position well up in the hierarchy of the Department." For thirty-five years he was organist at St. Andrew's Church, Islington, London, and composed quite a bit of church music.

MORNING STAR—Brightest and best of the sons of the morning (67)

Harkness, Georgia Elma (b. Harkness, N.Y., Apr. 21, 1891), was graduated from Cornell University in 1912 and continued her education at Boston University, Harvard University, Yale University, and Union Theological Seminary. She has taught on the faculty of Elmira College, 1923-37; Mount Holyoke College, 1937-39; Garrett Biblical Institute, 1939-50; and is currently professor of applied theology of the Pacific School of Religion, Berkeley, California. Ordained to the Methodist ministry in 1926, she is a recognized scholar in the field of theology and the author of eighteen books in the field of religion.

Hope of the world, Thou Christ of great compassion (282)

Harrington, Karl Pomeroy (b. Somersworth, N.H., June 13, 1861; d. Nov. 14, 1953), the son of Calvin Sears and Eliza Cynthia (Chase) Harrington, was educated at Wesleyan University, Middletown, Connecticut (A.B., 1882; A.M. 1885). He became a well-known teacher of Latin and taught at the University of North Carolina, University of Maine, and Wesleyan University. He was a member of several learned societies and was the author of a number of scholarly works. He was a recognized musician, who served in various Methodist churches as organist and choir director. With Peter C. Lutkin, he was one of the musical editors for the *Methodist Hymnal* (1905), to which he contributed twelve tunes. He was also a member of the committee for the *Methodist Hymnal* (1935).

CHRISTMAS SONG—There's a song in the air (69)

Harris, John Roy (b. Fayetteville, Ark., Dec. 5, 1891), while still a child, moved to the Indian Territory, where his father was a United States marshal and a farmer in what is now Sequoyah County, Oklahoma. After meager schooling in this frontier community, he finished high school in Muskogee, Oklahoma, attended Oklahoma Baptist University, and later the University of Oklahoma. He was a pioneer music and education director in Baptist churches of Oklahoma, beginning his work at Bristow in 1922. After serving at Ardmore and Shawnee, he taught music for seven years at Oklahoma Baptist University and was principal of the academy (high school). At various times he was an evangelistic singer, traveling with several evangelists throughout Oklahoma, Texas, and Arkansas. His longest tenure of service was at the First Baptist Church, Ada, where he was associate pastor for many years to the Rev. Clyde C. Morris. In 1955 he became associated with the First Baptist Church, Lawton, as director of city mission work, and remained in this position until his retirement.

Great Redeemer, we adore Thee (154)

Hart, Joseph (b. London, Eng., 1712; d. London, May 24, 1768), was brought up in a Christian home and received a splendid education. He became a schoolteacher in London and, according to his own account, lapsed into dissolute ways. During this time he wrote a pamphlet entitled, "The Unreasonableness of Religion, Being Remarks and Animadversions on the Rev. John Wesley's Sermon on Romans 8:32." He was converted in 1757 in the Moravian Chapel, Fetter Lane, London, and two years later became pastor of the Jewin Street Independent Chapel, London. An ardent Calvinist, he was a powerful preacher, widely known and well loved. It is said that twenty thousand people attended his funeral at Bunhill Fields, where, in 1875, more than a century after his death, a monument was erected to his memory. He published *Hymns Composed on Various Subjects, with the Author's Experience* (1759), which was used at his Jewin Street Chapel.

Come, ye sinners, poor and needy (241)

Hartsough, Lewis (b. Ithaca, N.Y., Aug. 31, 1828; d. Mount Vernon, Iowa, Jan. 1, 1919), was graduated from Cazenovia Seminary in 1852, and ordained to the Methodist ministry the following year. For fifteen years he served churches in the Oneida Conference, New York. Because of his health he requested transfer to the West and was appointed the first superintendent of the Utah Mission. Later he was appointed presiding elder of the Wyoming District. After a two-year pastorate in Epworth, Iowa, he transferred in 1874 to the Northwest Iowa Conference which included the Dakotas. Upon his retirement in 1895 he moved to Mount Vernon, Iowa. According to his own summary of his work, he "served fifteen pastoral charges and five presiding elder districts; traveled about 400,000 miles; made 9,000 pastoral visits, led 7,000 prayer meetings, quarterly conferences and love feasts, and preached 1,500 sermons." He served as musical editor for Joseph Hillman's *The Revivalist* (*ca.* 1868), a popular collection of evangelistic hymns and tunes that went into eleven editions. He wrote a number of hymns and tunes for the various editions of this book, but only the one given here remains in common usage.

I hear Thy welcome voice—WELCOME VOICE (224)

Hartsough, Palmer (b. Redford, Mich., May 7, 1844; d. Plymouth, Mich., Oct. 24, 1932), was the son of Wells and Thankful (Palmer) Hartsough. His father, an active layman, had helped to organize the Michigan Baptist Convention in 1836. In 1856 the family moved to Plymouth, Michigan. For a time he attended Kalamazoo College, a Baptist school, and also Michigan State Normal. At the latter school he became greatly interested in music and, while still a student, began teaching in singing schools in rural areas. During the following ten years he traveled throughout Michigan, Illinois, and Iowa, also briefly in Ohio, Kentucky, and Tennessee as an itinerant singing school teacher. About 1877, with interest in singing schools in the wane, he settled in Rock Island, Illinois. Here he opened a music studio, teaching vocal and instrumental music, and served as music director at the Baptist church where he was a member. His poetic ability caught the attention of James H. Fillmore (*q.v.*), and in 1893 he became associated with the Fillmore publishing firm in Cincinnati, providing texts for Fillmore's music. During his ten years in Cincinnati he made his home at the Bethel Mission, leading the Sunday school singing, and working with the poor and needy there. He also served as music director for the Ninth Street Baptist Church. He became a prolific writer of texts for hymns, gospel songs, Sunday school songs, cantatas, and programs, producing more than a thousand texts for publication. For some of his writing he used the pseudonym "Uncle Frank." He left the Fillmore firm in 1903 and for a time engaged in evangelistic singing. In 1906 he was ordained to the Baptist ministry and, following several brief pastorates, became pastor of the Baptist church at Ontario, Michigan, at the age of seventy. Here he enjoyed a successful pastorate of thirteen years, 1914-27. Upon his retirement in 1927 he returned to

Plymouth, Michigan, where he remained until his death at the age of eighty-eight. Throughout his life he remained unmarried. He was devoted to his two sisters and for many years wrote them a weekly letter. From information gleaned from hundreds of these letters, Henry O. Severance, University of Missouri librarian, has written an unpublished biography (1937), from which the above information has been taken.

I am resolved no longer to linger (216)

Hassler, Hans Leo (b. Nuremberg, Ger., Oct. 25, 1564; d. Frankfurt, Ger., June 8, 1612), received his early music education from his father, Isaac Hassler, and later studied with Andrea Gabrieli in Venice. Returning to Germany, he was successively organist to Count Octavian Fugger at Augsburg; at Frauenkirche, Nuremberg; and at the court of Prince Christian II of Saxony. The most eminent organist of his day, he was the first notable German musician to be educated in Italy, and his compositions reflect the influence of this training.

PASSION CHORALE (harm.)—O sacred Head, now wounded (91)

Hastings, Thomas (b. Washington, Conn., Oct. 15, 1784; d. New York, N.Y., May 15, 1872), at twelve, moved with his family by ox sledge to Clinton, Oneida County, New York. Amid the hardships of living on the frontier, his only formal education was in a country school. An albino and afflicted with extreme nearsightedness, he taught himself the fundamentals of music. By the time he was eighteen, he was leading the choir in the country church his family attended. He became active in the Oneida County Musical Society, and for this group made his first collection, *The Utica Collection,* which, combined with Warriner's *Springfield Collection* in 1816, was known as *Musica Sacra.* From 1823 to 1832 he edited *The Western Recorder,* Utica, a religious periodical, and he used the columns of this paper to promote his ideas regarding the improvement of church song. He moved to New York City in 1832, at the invitation of twelve churches who sought his services in the leadership of their choirs. He was dedicated to the cause of good church music, and together with Lowell Mason (*q.v.*) did much to shape the development of church music in America in the nineteenth century. Through his more than six hundred hymns, one thousand hymn tunes, and more than fifty collections, he made an indelible imprint on the musical life of his day. He was given the Mus.D. degree by the University of the City of New York in 1858. (Cf. *The Hymn,* X, No. 4, 105-110.)

Come, ye disconsolate, where'er ye languish (alt.) (297)
Hail to the brightness of Zion's glad morning (453)

ORTONVILLE—Majestic sweetness sits enthroned (118)
>How sweet the name of Jesus sounds (160)
>O God, we pray for all mankind (456)

RETREAT—From every stormy wind that blows (296)

TOPLADY—Rock of Ages, cleft for me (103)

ZION—Guide me, O Thou great Jehovah (56)
>Zion stands with hills surrounded (378)

Hatch, Edwin (b. Derby, Eng., Sept. 4, 1835; d. Oxford, Eng., Nov. 10, 1889), was educated at King Edward's School, Birmingham, and Pembroke College, Oxford. After his ordination in the Church of England, he taught in Canada, 1859-67, first at Trinity College, Toronto, and later as rector of the high school, Quebec. Returning to England in 1867, he became vice-principal of St. Mary's Hall, Oxford; rector of Purleigh, Essex, in 1883. The following year he was university reader in ecclesiastical history at Oxford. In 1880 he delivered his famous Bampton Lectures on "The Organization of the Early Christian Churches," and in 1888 the Libbert Lectures on "The Influence of Greek Ideas and Usages upon the Christian Church."

Breathe on me, breath of God (167)
Holy Spirit, breathe on me (174)

Hatton, John (b. Warrington, Eng., ?; d. St. Helens, Eng., 1793). Very little is known about Hatton. He lived on Duke Street in St. Helens, in the township of Windle. Apparently he was a member of the Presbyterian Chapel at St. Helens, for his funeral service was held there on Dec. 13, 1793.

DUKE STREET—Jesus shall reign where'ere the sun (116)
>Awake, my tongue, thy tribute bring (24)
>Now to the Lord a noble song (19)
>Come, let us tune our loftiest song (128)
>The heavens declare Thy glory, Lord (187)
>Ye Christian heralds! go, proclaim (459)

Havergal, Frances Ridley (b. Astley, Eng., Dec. 14, 1836; d. Caswall Bay, near Swansea, Wales, June 3, 1879), began writing verses at the age of seven, and these soon appeared in *Good Words* and other religious periodicals. Her father, William H. Havergal, was rector of St. Nicholas, Worcester, and this was her home from 1841 to 1860, when he retired. With occasional visits to North Wales, Scotland, and Switzerland, her later years were spent at Leamington and Caswall Bay. Throughout her life she was frail and in delicate health. While this limited her education, she learned several modern languages, as well as Hebrew and Greek. In spite of her frailness, she was an incessant writer, and composed a number of tunes. A volume of *Memorials* (1882) contained a partial autobiography, and her collected *Poetical Works* was published in 1884. At the age of fourteen she underwent a deep religious experience and later wrote, "There and then I committed my soul to the Saviour—and earth and heaven seemed bright from that moment." All of her hymns reflect the joy of this experience of commitment and consecration.

Another year is dawning (497)
I give my life for thee (399)
Like a river glorious (294)
Lord, speak to me that I may speak (340)
Take my life, and let it be (356, 357)
Truehearted, wholehearted, faithful, and loyal (410)
Who is on the Lord's side (413)
HERMAS—"Welcome, happy morning" (110)

Hawks, Annie Sherwood (b. Hoosick, N.Y., May 28, 1836; d. Bennington, Vt., Jan. 3, 1918), was the daughter of Marvin and Caroline (Bradt) Sherwood. For many years she lived in Brooklyn and was a member of the Hanson Place Baptist Church. One of her pastors at this church, Robert Lowry (*q.v.*), greatly encouraged her hymn writing. In 1859 she was married to Charles H. Hawks and three children were born into this home. After her husband's death in 1888, she lived until her death in the home of her daughter and son-in-law, Dr. and Mrs. W. E. Putnam, Bennington, Vt. Of the more than four hundred hymns credited to her, only the present one remains in common usage.

I need Thee every hour (334)

Haydn, Franz Joseph (b. Rohrau, Aust., Mar. 31, 1732; d. Vienna, Aust., May 31, 1809), the son of a wheelwright, was brought up in the Roman Catholic school of St. Stephen's, Vienna. His creative genius was evident at an early age, and he soon established his reputation as a composer. In 1761 he became musical director to the Hungarian family of Esterhazy and remained in this position for thirty years. With orchestra, choir, and solo singers at his command for the services of the chapel, the theater, and the concert room of the palace, he was afforded an irresistible opportunity for musical creativity and experimentation. Among his compositions are more than a hundred symphonies, twenty-two operas, four oratorios, and a tremendous amount of chamber music. In 1797 he visited England, where he was immensely popular and richly honored by royalty and nobility during his stay of eighteen months. Oxford University gave him an honorary Mus.D. degree. His most famous choral work, *The Creation*, was composed for an English text by Lidley. It was translated into German and first performed in Vienna in 1798. Concerning the writing of this oratorio, Haydn said: "Never was I so pious as when I was composing this work; I knelt down daily and prayed God to strengthen me for it." A man of deep religious feeling, he began each of his manuscripts with the inscription, "In nomine Domini," and wrote at the end, "Laus Deo," or "Soli Deo Gloria."

AUSTRIAN HYMN—Word of God, across the ages (176)
   Glorious things of thee are spoken (381)
   Once to every man and nation (418)
   We are living, we are dwelling (421)
CREATION—The spacious firmament on high (10)

Haydn, Johann Michael (b. Rohrau, Aust., Sept. 14, 1737; d. Salzburg, Aust., Aug. 10, 1806), the younger brother of Franz Joseph Haydn, was also a chorister at St. Stephen's, Vienna. In 1757 he became chapelmaster at Grosswardein, and in 1762 musical director to Archbishop Sigismund of Salzburg, where he remained until his death. Most of his writing was in the realm of sacred works, and his brother considered them far superior to his own. In addition to more than four hundred sacred works, he wrote a number of oratorios and more than a hundred instrumental works for organ and orchestra. A devout Christian, he was respected and loved by all who knew him. He initialed each of his manuscripts with "O. a. M. D. Gl," (*Omnia ad Majorem Dei Gloriam*).

GREENLAND—The day of resurrection (111)
LYONS—O worship the King, all glorious above (20)
   Ye servants of God, your Master proclaim (147)
   Jehovah the Lord, our Saviour and King (494)

Hays, William Shakespeare (b. Louisville, Ky., July 19, 1837; d. Louisville, July 23, 1907), the son of Hugh and Martha (Richardson) Hays, was educated in the Louisville schools and also attended colleges at Hanover, Indiana; Clarksville, Tennessee; and Georgetown, Kentucky. In 1856, while a student at Georgetown College, he published his first song, "Little Ones at Home." He left Georgetown College in 1857 to become a river front reporter for the Louisville *Democrat*. For writing songs sympathetic to the Confederacy, he was imprisoned by the Union forces in New Orleans. For several years he worked on Ohio and Mississippi River steamboats, eventually becoming captain of the packet, Gray Eagle. In 1868 he joined the staff of the Louisville *Courier-Journal,* and for thirty years he wrote a daily column containing river news, gossip, witticisms, and light verse. Both as a journalist and a song writer, he was a well-loved figure in Louisville from Civil War days through the "gay nineties." A prolific writer and composer of minstrel songs, he is credited with more than three hundred fifty songs, and in his day was second only to Stephen C. Foster in popularity. His "Mollie Darling" sold over a million copies, and at least a hundred of his songs sold at least seventy-five thousand copies.

SALVATIONIST—I have found a friend in Jesus (87)

"Hayward" in John Dobell's *Selection* (1806). John Dobell (1757-1840), a native of Poole, Dorsetshire, England, was a Christian layman, a member of a Nonconformist Chapel in Poole. He held a position as port-gauger under the Board of Excise in this city. In 1806 he published a significant collection of hymns under the lengthy title: *A New Selection of Seven Hundred Evangelical Hymns for Private, Family, and Public Worship (Many Original) from More Than Two Hundred of the Best Authors in England, Scotland, Ireland, and America, Arranged in Alphabetical Order; Intended as a Supplement to Dr. Watts's Psalms and Hymns.* In the second edition the number of hymns was increased to eight hundred, and this was bound with Dobell's *Dr. Watts's Fourth Book of Spiritual Songs,* which he had meticulously gleaned from the writings and sermons of Watts. Of unusual significance is the fact that Dobell's *Selection* was one of the first collections to give the name of the author with each hymn. The popularity and influence of this collection is evident in the fact that American editions appeared in Morristown, New Jersey, in 1810, 1815, and 1822, and in Philadelphia in 1825. Dobell attributed the present hymn to Hayward, but further identification of this author has remained a mystery since 1806.

Welcome, delightful morn (21)

Hearn, Marianne (b. Farningham, Kent, Eng., Dec. 17, 1834; d. Barmouth, Eng., Mar. 16, 1909), made her home at Northampton, where she was an active member of the College Street Baptist Church and taught a large Bible class for young women. She was on the editorial staff of the *Christian World,* a religious newspaper, and also served as editor of the *Sunday School Times,* a weekly publication for the use of Sunday school teachers in England. A prolific writer and poet, she was best known to her readers during her lifetime by her pseudonym "Marianne Farningham." Her collected literary works were published in twenty volumes, under such titles as *Lays and Lyrics of* *the Blessed Life* (1861), *Poems* (1865), *Morning and Evening Hymns for the Week* (1870), *Songs of Sunshine* (1878), and *Harvest Gleanings and Gathered Fragments* (1903). At the time of her death she was one of the most greatly beloved and honored women in the Baptist churches of England.

Just as I am, Thine own to be (249)

Heath, George (1750-1822), was educated at the Dissenting Academy at Exeter, England, and became pastor of a Presbyterian church at Honiton, Devonshire, in 1770, but proved unworthy of his office and was dismissed for bad conduct. Later, it seems, he became a Unitarian minister. Among his published works are *Hymns and Poetic Essays* (1781) and a *History of Bristol* (1797).

My soul, be on thy guard (420)

Heber, Reginald (b. Malpas, Cheshire, Eng., Apr. 21, 1783; d. Trichinopoly, India, Apr. 3, 1826), after his early education at the grammar school at Whitchurch and Bristow's select school at Neasdon, attended Brasenose College, Oxford, and became a fellow at All Souls College. Following a tour of the European continent with his friend, John Thornton, he became vicar of his family's parish, Hodnet, Shropshire. During his sixteen years at Hodnet, he became greatly interested in hymn writing, and his earliest efforts appeared in the *Christian Observer* in 1811. About 1819 he set about compiling a collection of hymns suitable to the requirements of the Christian year, and solicited hymns from Scott, Southey, Milman, and other literary friends. He was unsuccessful in securing the ecclesiastical approval of the Bishop of London for his collection. In 1823 he was appointed Bishop of Calcutta and served in India for less than three years before his sudden death in Trichinopoly, where he had gone to confirm a class of forty-two converts. His *Hymns Written and Adapted to the Weekly Service of the Church Year*, published posthumously in 1827, marked a new era in English hymnody. The significance of Heber's *Hymns* lay not only in its literary expression and lyric quality, but in the accommodation of these hymns to the liturgical church year. Each Sunday and most Holy Days of the Anglican Church were provided with appropriate hymns, based generally on the teaching of the day as given by the Epistle or Gospel. (Cf. *The Hymn*, XI, No. 2, 37-44.)

Bread of the world, in mercy broken (394)
Brightest and best of the sons of the morning (67)
From Greenland's icy mountain (449)
God, that madest earth and heaven (stanza 1) (30)

Holy, holy, holy! Lord God Almighty (1)
The son of God goes forth to war (414)

Hedge, Frederick Henry (b. Cambridge, Mass., Dec. 12, 1805; d. Cambridge, Aug. 21, 1890), was sent to Germany to study when he was thirteen. After four years he returned to Harvard, where he graduated in 1825. He was ordained as a Unitarian minister in 1829 and served churches at West Cambridge, Massachusetts, Bangor, Maine, Providence, Rhode Island, and Brookline, Massachusetts. During these years he also taught at Harvard, serving as professor of ecclesiastical history, 1857-76, and professor of German, 1872-81. In addition to his fame as a minister and a teacher, he was a recognized scholar in the field of German literature and published *Prose Writers of Germany*, a monumental work in this area. His significant contribution to hymnody was *Hymns for the Church of Christ* (1853), which he compiled with F. D. Huntington.

A mighty fortress is our God. (tr.) (40)

Heins, Nicholas (1839-1910). No information has been found to identify this composer.

BRECON—Spirit divine, attend our prayer (172)

Hemy, Henri Frederick (b. Newcastle-upon-Tyne, Eng., Nov. 12, 1818; d. Hartlepool, Eng., 1888), was organist at St. Andrew's Roman Catholic Church at Newcastle. Later he taught music at Tynemouth, and became professor of music at St. Cuthbert's College, Ushaw, Durham. His collection for piano study, *Royal Modern Tutor for the Pianoforte* (1858) was widely used. In 1864 he compiled *Crown of Jesus Music*, a collection of sacred music arranged from many sources, which was popular among Roman Catholics.

ST. CATHERINE—Faith of our fathers! living still (252)
Jesus, thy boundless love to me (288)

Hewitt, Eliza Edmunds (b. Philadelphia, Pa., June 28, 1851; d. Philadelphia, Apr. 24, 1920), the daughter of Captain James S. and Zeruiah (Edmunds) Stites, was educated in public school of Philadelphia and graduated from the Girl's Normal School as valedictorian of her class. After graduation she taught school for a number of years. Greatly interested in Sunday school work, she was for many years superintendent of the Sunday school of the Northern Home for Friendless Children and an active member of the Olivet Presbyterian Church, Philadelphia. When she moved into another section of the city, she joined the Calvin Presbyterian Church and served as superintendent of the Primary department until her death. Her first hymns were published by John R. Sweney and William J. Kirkpatrick. Later she wrote texts for B. D. Ackley, Charles H. Gabriel, E. S. Lorenz, and Homer Rodeheaver. She was a first cousin of Edgar Pate Stites (*q.v.*).

I am thinking today of that beautiful land (470)
More about Jesus would I know (321)
Sing the wondrous love of Jesus (483)
There is sunshine in my soul today (273)

Hews, George (b. Massachusetts, 1806; d. Boston, Mass., July 6, 1873), at the age of about twenty-four, settled in Boston and became well known as a tenor soloist teacher, organist, and piano maker. He was active in the Handel and Haydn Society.

HOLLEY—Bread of heav'n, on Thee we feed (395)

Hodder, Edwin (b. Staines, Middlesex, Eng., Dec. 13, 1837; d. Henfield, Sussex, Eng., Mar. 1, 1904), at the age of nineteen, went to New Zealand with a group of idealistic pioneers in the interest of sociological experimentation. After his return to England, he entered the English Civil Service in 1861, and remained in this work until his retirement in 1897. Among his published works are *Memories of New Zealand Life* (1862) and *The Life of a Century* (1900). His *New Sunday School Hymn Book* (1862) contained twenty-three of his hymns, among which was the present hymn.

Thy Word is like a garden, Lord (182)

Hodges, Edward (b. Bristol, Eng., July 20, 1796; d. Clifton, Eng., Sept. 1, 1867), after serving as organist in Bristol and Clifton, left England in 1838 to become organist at the Toronto Cathedral. The following year he moved to New York, N.Y., where has was organist at St. John's Episcopal Church, 1839-46, and Trinity Church, 1846-63. He returned to England in 1863, where he spent his remaining years. In addition to composing a number of anthems and hymn tunes, he wrote *An Apology for Church Music and Musical Festivals,* (London, 1834), *An Essay on the Cultivation of Church Music* (New York, 1841), and numerous articles contributed to music journals.

HYMN TO JOY (Arr.)—Joyful, joyful, we adore Thee (44)

Hodges, John Sebastian Bach (b. Bristol, Eng., 1830; d. Baltimore, Md., May 1, 1915), came to the United States at the age of fifteen to join his father, Edward Hodges, who had preceded him in 1838. He was educated at Columbia University and General Theological Seminary. He was ordained in the Episcopal church in 1854 and served successively at Pittsburgh, Nashotah House, Wisconsin, and Newark, New Jersey. In 1870 he was made rector of St. Paul's Church, Baltimore, a position he held for thirty-five years. At St. Paul's he established a choir school, the first in the United States, and replaced the mixed choir of men and women with a choir of men and boys. He composed anthems and hymn tunes and compiled the *Book of Common Praise* (1868), *Hymn Tunes* (revised edition, 1903), and was influential in the 1874 and 1892 editions of the Episcopal hymnal.

EUCHARISTIC HYMN—Bread of the world, in mercy broken (394)

Hoffman, Elisha Albright. (b. Orwigsburg, Pa., May 7, 1839; d. 1929), was educated in the public schools of Philadelphia and attended the Union Seminary of the Evangelical Association. For eleven years he was connected with the Evangelical Association publishing house in Cleveland, Ohio. Ordained as an Evangelical minister, he was pastor of Evangelical churches for a number of years and later became pastor of the First Presbyterian Church in Benton Harbor, Michigan. In addition to editing numerous collections, he was a prolific writer of gospel songs, frequently writing both words and music.

Christ has for sin atonement made—BENTON HARBOR (130)
Down at the cross where my Saviour died (95)
Have you been to Jesus for the cleansing power—WASHED IN THE BLOOD (192)
I must tell Jesus all of my troubles—ORWIGSBURG (298)
What a fellowship, what a joy divine (371)
You have longed for sweet peace, and for faith to increase—HOFFMAN (350)

Holbrook, Joseph Perry (b. near Boston, Mass., 1822; d. 1888), was associated with Charles S. Robinson and served as music editor for Robinson's hymnals, the most popular of which were *Songs of the Church* (1862) and *Songs for the Sanctuary* (1865). He assisted Dr. Eben Tourjee in compiling the 1878 Methodist hymnal. His own *Worship in Song* (1880) did not prove successful.

REFUGE—Jesus, lover of my soul (157)

Holden, Oliver (b. Shirley, Mass., Sept., 18, 1765; d. Charlestown, Mass., Sept. 4, 1844), at the age of twenty-one, moved to Charlestown, which had been burned by the British during the Battle of Bunker Hill. Here he labored as a carpenter in helping to rebuild the town and served as justice of the peace. About 1790, having prospered and acquired

318

considerable property, he abandoned carpentry and opened a general store. He also dealt in real estate, and when a new Baptist church was organized in Charlestown, he gave the land in which to erect the building. He belonged to the Puritan church in the community, served as pastor, and erected its wooden building largely through his personal efforts. He was a prominent citizen, an active Mason, and served as the Charlestown representative in the Massachusetts House of Representatives for eight terms between 1818 and 1833. In addition to his activities as a minister, music teacher, state representative, and realtor, he was a successful tune book compiler and editor. He published *The American Harmony* (1792); *Union Harmony* (1793); *The Massachusetts Compiler* (with H. Gram and S. Holyoke, 1795); *The Worcester Collection* (sixth edition, ed. and rev. by Holden, 1797); *Sacred Dirges, Hymns and Anthems* (1800); *Modern Collection of Sacred Music* (1800); *Plain Psalmody* (1800); *Charlestown Collection of Sacred Songs* (1803). The small pipe organ which belonged to Holden, and on which he composed the tune CORONATION, is now in the rooms of the Bostonian Society in the Old State House, Boston. (Cf. *The Hymn,* XIV, No. 3, 69-77.)

CORONATION—All hail the power of Jesus' name (132)

Holland, Josiah Gilbert (b. Belchertown, Mass., July 24, 1819; d. New York, N.Y., Oct. 12, 1881), after graduation from Berkshire Medical College, practiced medicine for a short time in Springfield, Massachusetts. He abandoned his medical practice to establish a weekly newspaper, which lasted only six months. Later he joined the editorial staff of the Springfield, Massachusetts, *Republican*, and became widely known as the writer of the "Timothy Titcomb Letters." He helped establish *Scribner's Magazine* and served as its editor until his death.

There's a song in the air (69)

Hopkins, Edward John (b. Westminster, London, Eng., June 30, 1818; d. London, Feb. 4, 1901), was a chorister at the Chapel Royal, where he studied theory with T. F. Walmisley. He became organist at the parish church of Mitcham, Surrey, 1834; St. Peter's, Islington, 1838, and St. Luke's, Berwick Street, 1841. In 1843 he was organist at Temple Church, London, a position he held for fifty-five years. He retired in 1898 and was succeeded by H. Walford Davies. He received the honorary Mus.D. from the Archbishop of Canterbury in 1882, and four years later from Trinity College, Toronto. With Edward F. Rimbault (*q.v.*), he published *The Organ: Its History and Construction* (1855). In addition to composing service music, anthems, hymns, and chants, he was highly respected as a hymnal editor. He was requested to complete the *Wesleyan Tune Book* (1876), after the deaths of H. J. Gauntlett and George Cooper, who had begun the compilation, and also served as music editor for the *Congregational Church Hymnal* (1887).

ELLERS—Saviour, again to Thy dear name we raise (27)
    Friend of the home, as when, in Galilee (376)

Hopper, Edward (b. New York, N.Y., Feb. 17, 1816; d. New York, Apr. 23, 1888), graduated from New York University and completed his theological course at Union Theological Seminary in 1842. He was ordained to the Presbyterian ministry and with the exception of eleven years when he preached at Greenville, New York, and Sag Harbor, Long Island, spent his entire ministry in his native city. His last pastorate was at the Church of the Sea and Land. Lafayette College honored him with a D.D. degree in 1871.

Jesus, Saviour, pilot me (337)

Hosmer, Frederick Lucian (b. Framingham, Mass., Oct. 16, 1840; d. Berkeley, Calif., June 7, 1929), was educated at Harvard University and Divinity School and was ordained to the Unitarian ministry. His pastorates included Northboro, Massachusetts, 1869-72; Quincy, Illinois, 1872-77; Cleveland, Ohio, 1878-92; St. Louis, Missouri, 1894-99; and Berkeley, California, 1900-04. Among his works were *The Way of Life* (1877), a service book for Sunday schools; *Unity Hymns and Carols* (with W. C. Gannett and J. Vilas Blake, 1880); and *The Thought of God in Hymns and Poems* (with W. C. Gannett, 1885), which contained fifty-six of his hymns. In addition to being a hymn writer, he was a student of hymnology, and gave a series of lectures on this subject at the Harvard Divinity School in 1908 and at the Pacific Unitarian School in 1912.

Forward through the ages (463)
Hear, hear, O ye nations (467)

How, William Walsham (b. Shrewsbury, Eng., Dec. 13, 1823; d. Leenane, County Mayo, Ire., Aug. 10, 1897), was educated at Wadham College, Oxford, and was ordained in the Anglican church in 1845. After curacies at St. George's Kidderminster and Holy Cross, Shrewsbury, he was appointed rector of Whittington, 1851; rural dean of Oswestry, 1853; and honorary canon of St. Asaph, 1860, and in 1865 he was chaplain of the English church at Rome. In 1879 he became Suffragan Bishop of East London, with the title Bishop of Bedford, and in 1888 became the first bishop of Wakefield. He was a plain, unassuming man, who cared little for higher ecclesiastical positions, and is best known for his work among the poor of the poverty-stricken East London slum area, where he was known as the "Poor Man's Bishop." Among his works were *Daily Family Prayers for Churchmen* (1854) and *Psalms and Hymns* (with T. B. Morrell, 1854). He was joint editor of *Church Hymns* (1871), of which Arthur Sullivan was music editor. He wrote more than fifty hymns, a number of which have enjoyed widespread usage. His death occurred in Ireland while he was on a vacation.

O Jesus, Thou art standing (346)
O Word of God incarnate (183)
We give Thee but Thine own (402, 535)

Howe, Julia Ward (b. New York, N.Y., May 27, 1819; d. Newport, R.I., Oct. 17, 1910), in 1848 married Dr. Samuel Gridley Howe, who in his younger days had fought in the Greek War of Independence and wrote *Historical Sketches of the Greek Revolution*. He was greatly interested in humanitarian interests and served as director of the Perkins Institute for the Blind, Boston. She was greatly devoted to her husband's work and became a distinguished and influential public speaker. In 1870 she proposed that the women of the world organize to end war for all time. She was also active as a writer and published three volumes of verse: *Passion Flowers* (1854), *Words of the Hour* (1856), and *Later Lyrics* (1866). A member of the Unitarian church, she frequently preached in churches of her own faith, as well as others.

Mine eyes have seen the glory of the coming of the Lord (488)

Hoyt, May P. No information has been found to identify this author.

Here at Thy table, Lord (392)

Hudson, Ralph E. (b. Napoleon, Ohio, July 9, 1843; d. Cleveland, Ohio, June 14, 1901), during his childhood, moved to Pennsylvania. At the outbreak of the Civil War, he enlisted as a private at Camp Wilkins, Pennsylvania, on June 20, 1861, in Company K, 10th Pennsylvania Reserves (later renamed the 39th Pennsylvania Volunteers). He served as a nurse at the General Hospital, Annapolis, Maryland, from June 1862 to February 1863, and was married to Mary Smith of Annapolis on March 4, 1863. Following his honorable discharge at Pittsburgh, June 11, 1864, he taught music at Mount Vernon College, Alliance, Ohio, for five years. Quite active as a singer and song composer, he later became a music publisher at Alliance. He was a licensed preacher in the Methodist Episcopal Church and devoted much of his time to evangelistic work. He published *Salvation Echoes* (1882); *Gems of*

Gospel Song (1884); *Songs of Peace, Love and Joy* (1885); *Songs of the Ransomed* (1887). These four books were combined and printed as a single volume, *Quartette*. He was an ardent Prohibitionist, wrote several temperance songs, and published *The Temperance Songster* (1886).

Alas, and did my Saviour bleed (refrain)—HUDSON (94)
My life, my love, I give to Thee (359)
BLESSED NAME—O for a thousand tongues to sing (140)

Hughes, John (b. Dowlais, Wales, 1873; d. Llantwit, Fardre, Pontypridd, Wales, May 14, 1932), the year after his birth moved with his family to Llantwit Fardre, where he lived the rest of his life. At the age of twelve he went to work as a doorboy at Glyn Colliery, a local mine. Later, he became a clerk and an official in the traffic department of the Great Western Railway. He was a lifelong member of the Salem Baptist Church, Llantwit Fardre, and succeeded his father in the offices of deacon and precentor. He composed a number of Sunday school marches, anthems, and hymn tunes.

CWM RHONDDA—Guide me, O Thou great Jehovah (55)
God of grace and God of glory (465)

Hull, Eleanor Henrietta (b. Manchester, Eng., Jan. 15, 1860; d. London, Eng., Jan. 13, 1935), was the founder and secretary of the Irish Text Society, and served as president of the Irish Literary Society of London. She is the author of several books on Irish history and literature.

Be Thou my vision, O Lord of my heart (versification) (62)

Hume, Duncan. No information has been found concerning this composer.

COURAGE—Dare to be brave, dare to be true (411)

Hunter, William (b. near Ballymena, County Antrim, Ire., May 26, 1811; d. Cleveland, Ohio, Oct. 18, 1877), when six years old emigrated with his family to America and settled in York, Pennsylvania. He was educated at Madison College, ordained to the Methodist ministry and served in the Pittsburgh Conference. He was editor of the Pittsburgh *Conference Journal,* 1836-40, and after it became the *Christian Advocate* he served twice again as its editor, 1844-52 and 1872-76. He was presiding elder in the Virginia and East Ohio Conferences. In 1855 he was appointed professor of Hebrew and Biblical Literature at Allegheny College, and remained in this position for fifteen years. He compiled three collections of hymns: *Select Melodies* (1838-51), *The Minstrel of Zion* (1845), and *Songs of Devotion* (1859). One hundred twenty-five hymns of his own appear in these three collections. Because of his experience as an editor and a compiler, he was one of twelve appointed by the General Conference of 1876 to revise the Methodist hymnal, but he died before the hymnal appeared in 1878.

The great Physician now is near (86)

Huntington, Dewitt Clinton (b. Townsend, Vt., Apr. 27, 1830; d. 1912), was educated at Syracuse University and ordained to the Methodist ministry in 1853. In addition to holding pastorates in Rochester, Syracuse, and Alion, New York, Bradford, Pennsylvania, and Lincoln, Nebraska, he served three times as presiding elder in New York, Pennsylvania, and Nebraska. He became chancellor of Nebraska Wesleyan University 1898-1908, and was then appointed professor of Bible.

O think of the home over there (480)

Husband, Edward (1843-1908), was educated in St. Aidan's College, Birkenhead, and was ordained in the Church of England in 1866. He was curate at Atherton, 1866-1872, and then curate and later vicar at St. Michael's and All Angels, Folkstone. He was interested in church music and frequently lectured on this subject. He published *The Mission Hymnal* (1874) and served as editor for *Supplemental Tunes to Popular Hymns* (1882) and an *Appendix for Use at the Church of St. Michael and All Angels, Folkstone* (1885). He frequently lectured on church music and played many organ recitals at Folkstone.

St. Hilda (arr.)—O Jesus, Thou art standing (346)

Husband, John Jenkins (b. Plymouth, Eng., 1760; d. Philadelphia, Pa., Mar. 19, 1825), spent the early part of his life at Plymouth, England, and was clerk at Surrey Chapel. He came to the United States in 1809 and settled in Philadelphia, where he taught music and served as clerk at St. Paul's Protestant Episcopal Church until his death. He was buried in St. Paul's churchyard. The November 11, 1820, issue of *Poulson's Daily Advertiser,* published in Philadelphia, carries an advertisement by Husband, stating that he, "clerk of St. Paul's Church, continues his Singing School at his School, No. 197 South Fourth Street, on Tuesday and Friday evenings, where the first principles of Sacred Music are taught on reasonable terms. A select School for Young Ladies on Saturday afternoons at 2 o'clock." He composed a number of tunes and anthems, and contributed "an improved mode of teaching music to facilitate the progress of the learner" to a subsequent edition of Andrew Adgate's *The Philadelphia Harmony* (first edition, 1790).

REVIVE US AGAIN—We praise Thee, O God! for the Son of Thy love (205)

Hutchinson, Albert H. No information has been found concerning this author.

For all the blessings of the year (495)

Hutton, Frances A. (1811-1877). Other than the fact that she lived in England, little is known of this woman whose alteration of a hymn by James Montgomery seems to be her only hymnic venture.

In the hour of trial (alt.) (317)

Ingalls, Jeremiah (b. Andover, Mass., Mar. 1, 1764; d. Hancock, Vt., Apr. 6, 1828). When Jeremiah was thirteen, his father, Abijah Ingalls, died from the hardships and privations of the Revolutionary War. Jeremiah settled in Newbury, Vermont, and married Mary Bigelow, and at various times was a farmer, a cooper, a tavern keeper and a singing master. All their children were musical and played instruments—violin, flute, clarinet, and bassoon—with their father leading the family ensemble with his bass viol. At Newbury, Ingalls was a deacon in the Congregational Church and the leader of the choir. During this time he published his *Christian Harmony* (1805). In 1819 he moved to Rochester, Vermont, and later moved to Hancock, where he died at the age of sixty-four. He wrote a number of hymn tunes.

I LOVE THEE—I love Thee, I love Thee, I love Thee, my Lord (150)

Jackson, Robert (b. Oldham, Lancashire, Eng., 1842; d. Oldham, 1914), studied music at the Royal Academy of Music and began his organ career at St. Mark's, Grosvenor Square, London. For some time he was a member of the Halle Symphony Orchestra at Birmingham. In 1868, he succeeded his father as organist at St. Peter's Church, Oldham, a position which his father had held for forty-eight years. He remained in this position until his death, serving for forty-six years. The tenure of service of this father and son at St. Peter's Church, Oldham, covering almost a century, seems to be an unequaled record in the annals of church music.

TRENTHAM—O Love of God most full (52)
Breathe on me, Breath of God (167)

Jacob, Benjamin (b. London, Eng., Apr. 1, 1778; d. London, Aug. 24, 1829), served as organist at Surrey Chapel, London, 1794-1825, and became well known as an organ recitalist. He was greatly devoted to the works of J. S. Bach and is considered one of the first English "apostles" of Bach's works. He published a *Collection of Psalm Tunes* for the Surrey Chapel (*ca.* 1800) and his *National Psalmody* (London, 1819), the source of the tune given below.

GREENLAND—The day of resurrection (111)

Jeffrey, John Albert (b. Plymouth, Eng., Oct. 26, 1855; d. Brookline, Mass., June 14, 1929), after early musical training under his organist father, studied for several years in Europe, with Liszt at Weimar, Reinecke at Leipzig, and Pracger at Paris. About 1876 he came to America, where he settled at Albany, New York, and organized a choral society. Two years later he became head of the music department at St. Agnes School, and assumed the position of organist and choirmaster of All Saints' Cathedral, Albany. In 1893 he became organist of the First Presbyterian Church, Yonkers, New York, and later joined the faculty of the New England Conservatory of Music, Boston, where he taught piano. During this latter time he also served for a while as organist at the North Cambridge Universalist Church.

ANCIENT OF DAYS—O God of light, Thy Word, a lamp unfailing (185)

John of Damascus (d. *ca.* 780), Greek theologian and hymn writer, was born in Damascus and was educated by Cosmas, a learned Italian monk. For a while he was an official under the Mohammedan caliph, and later retired to the monastery of St. Sabas, near Jerusalem, where he devoted his time to the writing of theological works and hymns. Late in life he was ordained priest of the Church of Jerusalem. He is known as one of the last Fathers of the Eastern Church and one of the greatest of her poets. His role as the organizer of liturgical chants of the Eastern Church is similar to that of Gregory in the Western Church. A staunch defender of the orthodox faith, he urged the use of pictures and images in the church as devotional and worshipful aids. He wrote six canons for the great festivals of the Christian Year, and was a significant influence in the development of hymnody in the Eastern Church.

Come, ye faithful, raise the strain (109)
The day of resurrection (111)

Johnson, Alexander. No biographical information has been found concerning this composer, except that he was a singing school teacher in Tennessee in the early part of the nineteenth century. The preface to the second edition of his *Tennessee Harmony* (1821) reveals him to be a musician of practical judgment. This preface, dated "West Tennessee, October 9th, 1820," states in part,

In presenting to public notice a Second Edition of the "Tennessee Harmony," the Author begs leave just to notice such improvements as nearly two years constant use of the book in his own schools, with the advice of several eminent teachers, have suggested, and which make their appearance in the present impression. . . . The "Tennessee Harmony" having become nearly the only elementary music book used in West Tennessee, the author felt unwilling to enhance the price, by a large appendix, or by such intricate and dainty pieces, as would be useful to but few. It is believed that the whole of the book will be found to contain such matter as is best suited to the taste and capacities of a majority of learners in the western country.

According to the listing of composers in the Index, Johnson claims as his own six of the ninety-seven tunes from the first edition and five of the fifteen added in the second edition.

PISGAH—When I can read my title clear (468)

Johnson, Erastus (b. Lincoln, Me., Apr. 20, 1826; d. Waltham, Mass., June 16, 1909), at the age of fifteen, entered the Academy at Calais, Maine, where he remained for two years. After six years teaching school, he entered Bangor Theological Seminary. His diligent study resulted in poor health and possible loss of his eyesight. Upon the recommendation of his physician he took a sea voyage to California on the ship *Gold Hunter*. For almost two decades he lived in the West, eight years as a rancher in California and eleven years farming in Washington state. He returned East and for twenty years worked in the oil industry in Pittsburgh, Pennsylvania. After eight years farming near Jackson, Maine, and eleven years in the state of Washington, he retired to Waltham, Massachusetts. Throughout his vigorous and active life, he remained a devoted Christian and a student of the Bible.

O sometimes the shadows are deep (320)

Johnston, Julia Harriette (b. Salineville, Ohio, Jan. 21, 1849; d. Peoria, Ill., Mar. 6, 1919), when six years old, moved with her family to Peoria, Illinois, where she lived the rest of her life. Her father, Rev. Robert Johnston, was pastor of the First Presbyterian Church of Peoria from 1856 until his death in 1864. For forty-one years she was superintendent of the younger children's department of the Sunday school and teacher of the infant class. She was president of the Presbyterian Missionary Society of Peoria for twenty years, an organization founded by her mother. For a number of years she wrote Primary Sunday school lesson material for the David C. Cook Publishing Company. Among her published works are: *School of the Master* (1880), *Bright Threads* (1897), *Indian and Spanish Neighbors* (1905), and *Fifty Missionary Heroes* (1913). She is the author of about five hundred hymns, with tunes provided by a host of song composers. Of this group, only the one given here remains in common usage.

Marvelous grace of our loving Lord (200)

Jones, Lewis Edgar (b. Yates City, Ill., Feb. 8, 1865; d. Santa Barbara, Calif., Sept. 1, 1936), graduated from Moody Bible Institute in the same class with Billy Sunday and became active in YMCA work. He served as physical director in YMCA at Davenport, Iowa, general secretary in Fort Worth, Texas, and in 1915 became general secretary in Santa Barbara, California. He remained in this position until his retirement in 1925. Hymn writing was a hobby, and in his spare time he produced quite a number that were published. According to his daughter, Mrs. Virgil Wayman, Santa Barbara, California, some of these hymns appeared under various pseudonymns which he used, such as Lewis Edgar, Edgar Lewis, Mary Slater, and others. Usually he wrote both words and music for his hymns.

Tho' the way we journey may be often drear—JONES (474)
Would you be free from the burden of sin—POWER IN THE BLOOD (193)

Jude, William Herbert (b. Westleton, Suffolk, Eng., Sept., 1851; d. London, Eng., Aug. 7, 1922), began his career as organist at the Blue Coat Hospital, Liverpool, and in 1889 became organist at Stretford Town Hall, near Manchester. He was a popular lecturer and recitalist and traveled extensively throughout Great Britain and Australia. He served as editor of the *Monthly Hymnal, Minister of Music, Music and the Higher Life* (1904), *Mission Hymns* (1911), and *Festival Hymns* (1916). He wrote an operetta, *Innocents Abroad,* and composed many anthems and songs.

GALILEE—Jesus calls us o'er the tumult (360)

Judson, Adoniram (b. Malden, Mass., Aug. 9, 1788; d. at sea, Bay of Bengal, Apr. 12, 1850), the first Baptist foreign missionary from the United States and the son of a Congregational minister, was educated at Rhode Island College (Brown University) and Andover Theological Seminary. With his wife, Anne Hasseltine, he sailed for India in 1812 under the auspices of the Congregationalists' American Board of Commissioners for Foreign Missions. Through his study of the New Testament teaching of baptism on the sea voyage he adopted the Baptist view, and upon his arrival in Calcutta he was baptized by an English Baptist missionary, William Ward. Forced out of India in 1813 by the British East India Company, the Judsons settled in Burma, where they witnessed for six years before the first convert was baptized. Because of bitter conflict between the British and Burmese armies, Judson was imprisoned for many months. By 1834 he had completed the arduous task of translating the Bible into Burmese. His return to the United States for a year in 1845 resulted in greatly increasing Baptist interest in missionary activity. His latter years were spent largely in completing a Burmese-English dictionary. He died while on a sea voyage for his health and was buried at sea in the Bay of Bengal.

Come, Holy Spirit, dove divine (385)

Keble, John (b. Fairford, Gloucestershire, Eng., Apr. 25, 1792; d. Bournemouth, Eng., March 29, 1866), as a child, was tutored at home by his father, the vicar of Coln St. Aldwin's. At the age of fourteen he entered Corpus Christi College, graduating at the age of eighteen with double first class honors. After receiving his M.A. in 1813, he remained at Oriel as a tutor. In 1815 he was ordained in the Church of England and served several country churches in addition to his teaching responsibilities. His collection of sacred poetry, *The Christian Year: Thoughts in Verse for the Sundays and Holidays Throughout the Year* (1827), had extraordinary influence on nineteenth-century English hymnody. Not less than ninety-six editions were published during Keble's lifetime, and its first American edition was published in 1834. The profits from this book were used to restore the church building at Hursley, where he became vicar in 1836 and remained the rest of his life. On July 14, 1833, he preached his now famous "Assize Sermon" on the subject of national apostasy, which is credited as marking the beginning of the Oxford Movement. Along with John Henry Newman (*q.v.*), E. B. Pusey, and others, he became one of the leaders in this movement, sometimes known as the Tractarian Movement because of the series of popular tracts entitled, *Tracts for the Times* (1833-41), which these men wrote. In their attempt to revitalize the Anglican church through a purification of its service, great interest was aroused in the revival of the practices and ideals of the pre-Reformation Catholic Church.

Sun of my soul, Thou Saviour dear (15)
The voice that breathed o'er Eden (502)

Kelly, Thomas (b. Kellyville, Stradbally, County Queens, Ire., July 13, 1769; d. Dublin, Ire., May 14, 1855), the son of an Irish judge, was educated at Trinity College, Dublin, and intended to follow the legal profession like his father. However, his deep spiritual convictions changed his mind, and he was ordained in the Irish Episcopal Church in 1792. His fervent evangelical preaching brought him into disfavor with the Archbishop of Dublin, who prohibited him from further preaching in that diocese. He left the Irish church and established an independent sect. A splendid preacher and a man of means, he devoted his energies to the service of the poor and built churches at Athy, Portarlington, Wextord and other places. He was a thorough Bible scholar and was well versed in classical and Oriental languages. His 765 hymns were published in *A Collection of Psalms and Hymns,* Dublin, 1802; *Hymns on Various Passages of Scripture,* Dublin, 1804; *Hymns by Thomas Kelly, Not Before Published,* Dublin, 1815, and subsequent editions of the latter two collections. He also issued a companion volume of tunes which he composed to be used with his hymns. (Cf. *The Hymn,* VI, No. 2, 59.)

Hark, ten thousand harps and voices (145)
Look, ye saints! the sight is glorious (148)
The head that once was crowned with thorns (117)
Zion stands with hills surrounded (378)

Ken, Thomas (b. Berkhampstead, Hertfordshire, Eng., July, 1637; d. Longleat, Wiltshire, Eng., Mar. 19, 1711), after the death of his parents in his early childhood, was brought up by his half-sister, Anne, the wife of Izaak Walton, author of *The Compleat Angler.* He was educated at Winchester College, Hart Hall, and New College, Oxford. Ordained in 1662, he served several churches until 1666, when he returned as a fellow to Winchester College. The following year he was curate at Brightstone, Isle of Wight, and in 1669 returned to Winchester, remaining there for ten years with duties at the Cathedral, the college, and as bishop's chaplain. During this time he published his *A Manual of Prayers for the Use of the Scholars of Winchester College* (1674). In 1679 he received the appointment from the Duke of York as chaplain to his daughter, Princes Mary (afterwards Queen), wife of William II of Orange, who resided at The Hague. Dismissed from this position because of his frankness, he returned to England, and in 1683 was appointed Chaplain of the Fleet and went with Lord Dartmouth to Tangier. In 1685 he was made Bishop of Bath and Wells, and three years later he was one of seven bishops imprisoned in the Tower of London for their refusal to subscribe to James II's Declaration of Indulgence. Following his trial and acquittal, he resigned his bishopric in 1691 and made his home with a devoted friend, Lord Weymouth, at Longleat, Wiltshire, until his death. All of his poetical works were published in four volumes in 1721.

Praise God, from whom all blessings flow (514)

Kennedy, Benjamin Hall (b. Summer Hill, near Birmingham, Eng., Nov. 6, 1804; d. Apr. 6, 1889), was educated at King Edward's School, Schrewsbury School, and St. John's College, Cambridge. He was successively a fellow at St. John's College, 1828-36; headmaster of Shrewsbury School, 1836-66; professor of Greek at Cambridge, and canon at Ely, 1867. He was ordained in 1829, and served for a while as prebendary of Lichfield Cathedral and rector of West Felton, Salop; however, he devoted himself mainly to educational activities. Among his several hundred hymnic writings were numerous translations from the German and recasts of hymns by other writers. These appeared in his *The Psalter, or the Psalms of David, in English Verse* (1860); and *Hymnologia Christiana, or Psalms and Hymns Selected and Arranged in the Order of the Christian Seasons* (1863). This latter compilation, unsuccessful as a popular hymnal, became a significant source of reference to subsequent compilers and editors.

Ask ye what great thing I know (tr.) (161)

Kethe, William (d. *ca.* 1593). Although no definite information is known about the date and place of Kethe's birth, it has been generally accepted that he was a native of Scotland. Because of the Marian persecution, 1555-58, he was in exile on the Continent following 1555, first at Frankfurt, and later at Geneva. In 1558 he was sent on a mission to the English exiles in Basel, Strassburg, and other places, and returned to Geneva the following year with their communications. It is thought that he was one of the scholars among the English refugees who remained in Geneva after 1558 to complete the English translation of the Bible, known as the Geneva Bible (1560), sometimes referred to as the "Breeches Bible." Twenty-five of his metrical psalm versions appeared in the *Anglo-Genevan Psalter* (1561). After his return to England he was appointed vicar at Childe Okeford in Dorsetshire, 1561-93. He served as chaplain to the English troops under the Earl of Warwick at Havre in 1563, and again in 1569. His death is usually given as having occurred about 1593; however, some sources place the date as late as 1608.

All people that on earth do dwell (13)

Kett, Ellen. No information has been found concerning this composer.

Amens (548, 549)

Key, Francis Scott (b. Pipe's Creek, Frederick Co., Md., Aug. 9, 1779; d. Baltimore, Md., Jan. 11, 1843), the son of a Continental Army officer who served with distinction in the Revolutionary War, was educated at St. John's College, Annapolis. He studied law and served three terms as district attorney for the District of Columbia, holding that position at the time of his death. A devoted Christian and a member of the Protestant Episcopal Church, at one time he seriously considered entering the ministry. He was a vestryman of St. John's Church, and later Christ Church, Georgetown, D. C. He held a lay reader's license, and taught a Bible class in the Sunday school. He was among the organizers of the Domestic and Foreign Missionary Society in 1820 and served as a delegate to the General Convention, 1814-25. In 1823 he was appointed a member of the committee to prepare a new hymnal for the Protestant Episcopal Church. His poetical writings, which appeared in various works, were collected and published in 1857.

Oh, say, can you see, by the dawn's early light (486)

Kinsey, John F. (b. near Fort Wayne, Ind., Mar. 22, 1852; d. ?), was the founder and head of The Echo Music Company, Chicago (1899-1909), and served as editor of *The Echo,* a monthly musical journal. He composed a number of songs and published more than thirty collections of songs.

THE UNCLOUDED DAY (harm.)—O they tell me of a home far beyond the skies (484)

Kipling, Rudyard (b. Bombay, India, Dec. 30, 1865; d. London, Eng., Jan. 18, 1936). Both of Kipling's grandfathers were Wesleyan Methodist ministers: Rev. Joseph Kipling and Rev. George B. MacDonald. His father, J. Lockwood Kipling, was in the British government service in India when Rudyard was born, and he was named for Rudyard Lake, Staffordshire, where his father and mother, Alice MacDonald, became engaged to be married. Educated at the United Services College, Westward Ho, North Devonshire, he returned to India in 1882, and began his journalistic career on the staff of the *Civil and Military Gazette,* Lahore, and the Allahabad *Pioneer.* During this time he gathered much material and wrote many of his stories about India, the earliest of which first appeared in the above papers. He left India in 1889 and toured China, Japan, and America. In 1892 he married an American, Caroline Starr Balestier, and resided for four years near Brattleboro, Vermont, after which he returned to England where he remained the rest of his life. He was awarded the Nobel Prize for literature in 1907. From 1922-25 he served as rector of the ancient University of St. Andrews in Scotland.

Father in heaven, who lovest all (460)

Kirk, S. C., was a layman whose literary efforts seem to have been confined to writing pamphlets for special day services—Children's Day, Christmas, and Easter—about the turn of the twentieth century. He lived in Philadelphia, and most of his writing was done for the Hall-Mack Publishing Company. No other information has been found.

Hear ye the Master's call (437)

Kirkpatrick, William James (b. Duncannon, Pa., Feb. 27, 1838; d. Philadelphia, Pa., Sept. 20, 1921), the son of Thompson and Elizabeth Kirkpatrick, received his early music training from his father. He later studied with Pasquale Rondinella, Leopold Meignen, and T. Bishop. He moved to Philadelphia in 1855 and became a member of the Wharton Street Methodist Episcopal Church. At the age of twenty-one he edited his first collection, *Devotional Melodies* (1859), a collection of camp meetings songs published by A. S. Jenks, Philadelphia. In 1861 he married Miss S. J. Doak. During the Civil War he was a fife-major in the 91st Regiment of the Pennsylvania Volunteers. Following the war he was engaged in the furniture business in Philadelphia, 1862-78, and maintained an active interest in church music in his spare time. After the death of his wife in 1878, he resigned his business interests and devoted his full time to music activity. He served as music director at Grace Methodist Episcopal Church, Philadelphia, 1886-97, and remained an active member until his death. In 1893 he married Mrs. Sara Kellogg Bourne, who died about 1910. In 1917 he married Mrs. John R. Sweney of Williamsport, Pennsylvania. From 1880 until his death, in the role of editor or associate editor, he was associated with the publication of about one hundred collections of gospel songs which bore the imprints of more than a score of publishers. Among his frequent collaborators were John R. Sweney (*q.v.*), H. L. Gilmour (*q.v.*), John H. Stockton (*q.v.*), and J. Howard Entwisle. He served as president of the Praise Publishing Company, Philadelphia, which published many of his collections.

> I've wandered far away from God—COMING HOME (237)
> JESUS SAVES—We have heard the joyful sound (191)
> KIRKPATRICK—A wonderful Saviour is Jesus my Lord (272)
> REDEEMED—Redeemed, how I love to proclaim it (203)
> TRUST IN JESUS—'Tis so sweet to trust in Jesus (258)

Knapp, Mrs. Joseph Fairfield (Phoebe Palmer) (b. New York, N.Y., Mar. 9, 1839; d. Poland Springs, Me., July 10, 1908), was the daughter of well-known Methodist evangelist Walter C. Palmer and early gave evidence of unusual musical talent. At the age of sixteen she married Joseph Fairfield Knapp, a devoted Christian and a successful business-man who founded the Metropolitan Life Insurance Company. They were members of the John Street Methodist Church of New York City, whose membership also included Fanny J. Crosby. Upon the death of her hus-band in 1891, Mrs. Knapp was left an annual income of $50,000, much of which she gave generously to religious and charitable causes. In her later years she lived in an elegant apartment in New York City's Hotel Savoy, in which was installed a large pipe organ. Her son, Joseph Palmer Knapp, who died in 1951 at the age of eighty-six, was head of the Crowell-Collier Publishing Company. She published more than five hundred gospel songs, and of these only the one listed below survives in common usage. One other solo song remains a perennial favorite, "Open the Gates of the Temple," for which she provided the music and Fanny J. Crosby wrote the words.

ASSURANCE—Blessed assurance, Jesus is mine (269)

Knapp, William (b. Wareham, Dorsetshire, Eng., 1698; d. Poole, Dorsetshire, Eng., Sept. 26, 1768), was of German descent, and became an organist, a composer, and a tune book compiler. For thirty-nine years he served as parish clerk of St. James's Church, Poole, in which position it was his responsibility to sing the responses in the services, and at the time of hymn singing to cheerfully announce, "Let us all sing to the praise and glory of God." He published *A Sett of New Psalms and An-thems in Four Parts* (London, 1738) and *New Church Melody* (London, 1753), but is known today for only one tune which remains in common usage.

WAREHAM—So let our lips and lives express (323)

Knecht, Justin Heinrich (b. Biberach, Ger., Sept. 30, 1752; d. Biber-ach, Dec. 1, 1817), was educated at the convent of Esslingen, where he learned to play the flute, oboe, trumpet, cor anglais, violin, and organ. He became professor of belles-lettres at Biberach, and later took on the additional duties of musical director for the town. In 1807 he became conductor of the court and theater orchestra at Stuttgart, but after two years he returned to Biberach. With the assistance of J. F. Christmann, he published *Vollständige Sammlung . . . Vierstimmige choralmelodien* *für das neue Würtemburgisches Landgesangbuch, Stuttgart* (1799). Ninety-seven tunes by Knecht made their first appearance in this hymnal.

St. Hilda—O Jesus, Thou art standing (346)

Kocher, Conrad (b. Dietzingen, Württemberg, Dec. 16, 1786; d. Stuttgart, Mar. 12, 1872), went to St. Petersburg (Leningrad) in 1803, where he studied piano with Klengel and Berger, and composition with J. H. Müller. In 1819 he spent a year in Italy studying a cappella singing. He was greatly influenced by the work of Palestrina, and made church choral music the major interest of his musical career. He returned to Stuttgart in 1820, and the following year founded the School of Sacred Song there. He did much to popularize four-part singing in the churches, and helped bring about some much-needed reforms in German church music. He published *Die Tonkunst in der Kirche* (1823), a treatise on church music, and *Zionsharfe* (1855), a compilation of ancient and modern chorales.

Dix—For the beauty of the earth (153)
As with gladness men of old (68)
Praise to God, immortal praise (14)

Koschat, Thomas (b. Viktring, near Klagenfurt, Aust., Aug. 8, 1845; d. Vienna, Aust., May 19, 1914), out of a keen interest in music and experience as a church choir singer, turned his efforts toward musical composition. In 1871 he published a group of vocal quartets in the Carinthian dialect, and these become so successful that he published some one hundred more. In 1875 he organized the famous "Kärnthner Quintette" with four other singers, and their performances were exceedingly popular. His "Liederspiel," *Am Wörthersee,* first given in Vienna, March 22, 1880, contained many of his favorite vocal songs. He also wrote a four-act "Volksstück mit Gesang," *Die Rusenthaler Nachtigall,* and the "Singspiel," *Der Bürgermeister von St. Anna.*

Poland—The Lord is my Shepherd (57)

Kremser, Edward (b. Vienna, Aust., Apr. 10, 1838; d. Vienna, Nov. 27, 1914), in 1869 became chorusmaster of the Vienna Männergesangverein and also conducted various other choral groups. He composed numerous vocal and instrumental works. His popular *Sechs Altniederländische Volkslieder* (Leipzig, 1877) was one of several works for men's chorus and orchestra. He edited *Wiener Lieder und Tänze* (two volumes, 1912, 1913).

Kremser—We praise Thee, O God, our Redeemer (11)
We gather together to ask the Lord's blessing (492)
O God of our fathers, we praise and adore Thee (500)

Lane, Spencer (b. Tilton, N.H., Apr. 7, 1843; d. Readville, Va., Aug. 10, 1903), during the Civil War, served three years with the Union Army. After study at the New England Conservatory of Music, he became a teacher of voice and instrumental music in New York City. He later moved to Woonsocket, Rhode Island, where he established a music store and served for thirteen years as organist and choirmaster at St. James's Protestant Episcopal Church. During this time he wrote a number of anthems and hymn tunes. After he left Rhode Island, he served churches in Monson, Massachusetts, and Richmond, Virginia. He moved to Baltimore where he was associated with the music firm of Sanders & Stayman, and also served as organist and choirmaster of the All Saints' Protestant Episcopal Church.

PENITENCE—In the hour of trial (317)

Lanier, Sidney (b. Macon, Ga., Feb. 3, 1842; d. near Tryon, N.C., Sept. 7, 1881), was educated at Oglethorpe College, Milledgeville, Georgia. During the Civil War he served in the Confederate Army, was captured by the Union forces, and as a result of the privations of his imprisonment his health was never strong. Following a brief legal practice in Macon, Georgia, he spent a brief time in San Antonio, Texas. He became the first flutist in the Peabody Symphony Orchestra, Baltimore, and in 1879 was appointed lecturer on English literature at Johns Hopkins University. Ill health continued to plague him, and in the summer of 1881 he went to North Carolina hoping to gain physical strength. In a short time he died. His literary accomplishments in spite of his difficulties were quite remarkable. He left twenty-four volumes of his works, ten volumes of which are poetical verse.

Into the woods my Master went (90)

Larcom, Lucy (b. Beverly, Mass., Mar. 5, 1826; d. Apr. 17, 1893), whose father, a New England sea captain, died when she was a child, moved with her mother to Lowell, Massachusetts. After a brief grade school education she worked for eight years in the mills of Lowell. She was a rural schoolteacher for a time at Looking Glass, Illinois, and later attended Monticello Female Seminary, Alton, Illinois. After graduation she returned to Massachusetts, where she taught school and continued her studies at Wheaton Seminary at Norton. A prolific writer of verse, her poems attracted the attention of John Greenleaf Whittier who became a lifelong friend. Among her publications were: *Wild Roses of Cape Ann* (1881), *Poetical Works* (1885), *At the Beautiful Gate* (1892), *As It Is in Heaven* (1891), and *The Unseen Friend* (1892).

Draw Thou my soul, O Christ (314)

Lathbury, Mary Artemisia (b. Manchester, Ontario Co., N.Y., Aug. 10, 1841; d. East Orange, N.J., Oct. 20, 1913), the daughter of a Methodist preacher, became a professional artist. She was associated with Rev. John H. Vincent when he was secretary of the Methodist Sunday School Union, and served as general editor of publications for children and young people. Much of her poetic writing first appeared in these publications. In 1885 she founded the "Look-Up Legion," a youth movement in Methodist Sunday schools. She was active in the summer assemblies at Lake Chautauqua in New York, and her poetic ability earned recognition as the "Poet Laureate of Chautauqua."

Break Thou the bread of life (stanzas 1 and 2) (178)

Day is dying in the west (29)

Leech, Lida Shivers (b. Mayville, N.J., May 12, 1873; d. Long Beach, Calif., Mar. 4, 1962), during her childhood lived at Cape May Court House, New Jersey, and was educated at Columbia and Temple Universities. She was organist at Bethany Methodist Church, Camden, New Jersey, and traveled widely as pianist in evangelistic services. She wrote about five hundred gospel songs.

Bring ye all the tithes into the storehouse—GIVING (404)

Leeson, Jane Eliza (b. London, Eng., 1807; d. London, 1882). Very little is known about this hymn writer. For many years she was active in the Catholic Apostolic Church and contributed nine hymns and translations to its hymnal. Later in life she became a Roman Catholic. She published four collections of religious verse.

Saviour, teach me day by day (291)

Lerman, Joseph (b. London, Eng., Dec. 23, 1865; d. Brooklyn, N.Y., Oct. 24, 1935), when a child, came with his family to America. He joined the Olivet Memorial Church of New York City as a boy, and in 1880 became church organist, a position he held for twenty-eight years. He resigned in 1908 because of ill health but later served as organist for short intervals of time at the Sixth Avenue Baptist Church, Borough Park Christian Church, Fourth Avenue Methodist Church, all of Brooklyn. He was also pianist for the famous Bible Class of John D. Rockefeller, Jr. He wrote a considerable amount of music for church and Sunday school use—anthems, cantatas, and seasonal services—most of which was published by the Tullar-Meredith Publishing Company. Later he was on the editorial staff of the Theodore Presser Company. A number of his hymn tunes are found in publications of the Fillmore Music House.

ILONA—O brother man, fold to thy heart thy brother (447)

Lewis, Howell Elvet (b. Conwil Elvet, Carmarthenshire, Apr. 14, 1860; d. Penarth, Glamorganshire, Wales, 1953), was educated at Presbyterian College, Carmarthen, and entered the Congregational ministry in 1880. For thirty-six years he was pastor of the Welsh Tabernacle, King's Cross, London. From the University of Wales he received the honorary degree of M.A. in 1906 and of D.D. in 1933. He was chairman of the Congregational Union of England and Wales, 1933-34. In 1948 King George VI conferred upon him the Order of the Companion of Honour. He was an active member of the Hymn Society of Great Britain, and was a member of the editorial committee of the Congregational *Hymnary.* He published several devotional books and volumes of sermons, and wrote many hymns, both in English and in Welsh. He was a beloved minister and preached to within two weeks of his death at the age of ninety-three.

Friend of the home, as when, in Galilee (376)

Loes, Harry Dixon (b. Kalamazoo, Mich., Oct. 20, 1892;), at birth was named Harold Loes, but during his early childhood he became known as Harry and has retained this name in later life. During his student days he chose his own middle name after Dr. A. C. Dixon, who was pastor of Moody Church. After a brief period of work with Marshall Field and Company, Chicago, he studied at Moody Bible Institute. Under the guidance and inspiration of Dr. D. B. Towner (*q.v.*), he began composing gospel songs. Later he studied at the American Conservatory of Music, the Metropolitan School of Music, and the Chicago Musical College. He was engaged in evangelistic work for more than twelve years throughout the United States and Canada. From 1927 to 1939 he served as music and educational director in the First Baptist Church, Okmulgee, Oklahoma, and the First Baptist Church, Muskogee, Oklahoma. In 1939 he joined the music faculty of Moody Bible Institute. Since his retirement he remains in Chicago, is a part-time teacher at Moody Institute, and has become associated with the Rodeheaver Company.

REDEEMER—Up Calvary's mountain, one dreadful morn (106)

Loizeaux, Alfred Samuel (b. Vinton, Iowa, Feb. 12, 1877; d. Towson, Md., May 7, 1962), was for many years an executive with the Baltimore Consolidated Light, Heat, and Power Company. He maintained an active association with the Baltimore School of the Bible, and edited *Help and Food,* a monthly magazine for Christians, published by Loizeaux Brothers, Inc. New York City. His only daughter and her husband are missionaries in the Congo.

God, our Father, we adore Thee (stanza 3) (5)

Longfellow, Henry Wadsworth (b. Portland, Me., Feb. 27, 1807; d. Cambridge, Mass., Mar. 24, 1882), was the son of Stephen and Zilpah (Wadsworth) Longfellow, and his mother was a descendent of John Alden and Priscilla Mullins. After his graduation from Bowdoin College in 1825, he studied in Europe. He was professor of modern languages and literature at Bowdoin College, 1829-34, and then became professor of literature at Harvard University, where he taught for seventeen years. In addition to being an outstanding scholar and teacher, he was the most influential American poet of his day. Among his poetic works which became extremely popular are *Evangeline* (1847), *The Song of Hiawatha* (1855), *The Courtship of Miles Standish* (1858), *Tales of a Wayside Inn* (1863, 1872, and 1874).

I heard the bells on Christmas day (78)

Longfellow, Samuel (b. Portland, Me., June 18, 1819; d. Portland, Oct. 3, 1892), was educated at Portland Academy and was graduated from Harvard University in 1839 and Harvard Divinity School in 1846. Ordained to the Unitarian ministry, he held pastorates at Fall River, Massachusetts, 1848-51; Brooklyn, New York, 1853-60; and Germantown, Pennsylvania, 1878-83. In the intervening years between his pastoral work, he preached in various churches and devoted his time to literary endeavors as his health permitted. In 1886 he published a biography of his brother, Henry Wadsworth Longfellow. With Samuel Johnson he edited *A Book of Hymns for Public and Private Devotions* (1846) and *Hymns of the Spirit* (1864). He also published *Vespers* (1859), a small collection of hymns for the vesper services he instituted in his church in Brooklyn, and *A Book of Hymns and Tunes* (1860). In editing their hymnals, Johnson and Longfellow sometimes altered hymns of other writers to make them conform to their views. This practice called forth the following Limerick from a friend:

> There once were two Sams of Amerique
> Who belong to profession called cleric;
> They hunted up hymns
> And cut off their limbs
> These truculent Sams of Amerique.

Bless Thou the gifts our hands have brought (533)
Now, on land and sea descending (28)
Spirit divine, attend our prayer (adapted) (172)

Longstaff, William Dunn (b. Sunderland, Eng., Jan. 28, 1822; d. Sunderland, Apr. 2, 1894), was the son of a wealthy shipowner. Being a man of independent means, he was generous in his gifts to charitable and philanthropic interests. He was a close friend of the Rev. Arthur A. Rees, who left the Anglican church and established Bethesda Free Chapel. He served as treasurer for the chapel and looked after the maintenance and improvements of the building. He became a close friend of Moody and Sankey and was active in their work in England. It is not known that he wrote any hymns other than the one given here.

Take time to be holy (367)

Lowden, C. Harold (b. Burlington, N.J., Oct. 12, 1883), as a child, learned to play the violin and played in the church orchestra. He began writing songs at the age of twelve and sold his first song to the Hall-Mack Company, where he was later employed. For twelve years he was musical editor for the Reformed Church Board. Resigning this position, he went into business for himself in Camden, New Jersey. In addition to his business interests, he taught music for eight years at the Bible Institute of Pennsylvania, and for twenty-eight years was minister of music for the Linden Baptist Church of Camden. In 1961 he retired from his business interests and from his work as church organist and choir director, in which activity he had continuously served for sixty years. He died at Collingswood, New Jersey, February 27, 1963.

GENEVA—God, who touchest earth with beauty (45)
LIVING—Living for Jesus a life that is true (352)

Lowell, James Russell (b. Cambridge, Mass., Feb. 22, 1819; d. Cambridge, Aug. 12, 1891), graduated from Harvard in 1838 and for a while practiced law. He turned his interest to literature and became professor of modern languages at Harvard in 1855. He was United States minister to Spain 1877-80, served as ambassador to England, 1880-85. He edited the *Atlantic Monthly,* 1857-62, and the *North American Review,* 1863-72. His loyal patriotism is evidenced in his writing as he spoke out vigorously against slavery and the Mexican War. His works include *The Vision of Sir Launfal* (1848), *The Biglow Papers* (1848 and 1862), *Among My Books* (1870 and 1876), *Political Essays* (1888), and several volumes of verse. While he was widely known as an essayist, critic, and poet, he was not, strictly speaking, a hymn writer. Several hymns which are found bearing his name have been taken from his larger poetical works.

Once to every man and nation (418)

Lowry, Joseph C. In the second edition of Ananias Davisson's *Kentucky Harmony* (1817), in which PISGAH appears, this composer is mentioned as being one of the "gentlemen teachers" in Virginia,

Tennessee, and Kentucky. No other information has been found, and the writer is indebted for this to current research by Harry Eskew into music publishing in the Shenandoah Valley of Virginia prior to the Civil War. Davisson's statement suggests the possibility that Lowry was acquainted with Alexander Johnson (*q.v.*), also a singing school teacher in Tennessee. While Davisson attributes this tune to Lowry, Johnson in his *Tennessee Harmony,* two years later, claims the tune as his. Of course, Johnson may have learned the tune from Lowry or from the *Kentucky Harmony* and appropriated it for his collection, claiming it as his own, a frequent practice. On the other hand, Lowry may have learned the tune from Johnson in Tennessee and carried it back across the mountains to the Shenandoah valley where Davisson inserted it in his collection. A third possibility is that this may have been a folk tune independently transcribed by the two men.

PISGAH—When I can read my title clear (468)

Lowry, Robert (b. Philadelphia, Pa., Mar. 12, 1826; d. Plainfield, N.J., Nov. 25, 1899), was educated at Bucknell University, graduating with honor in 1854. Following pastorates at West Chester, Pennsylvania, 1854-58, and New York City, 1859-61, he became pastor of the Hanson Place Baptist Church, Brooklyn, 1861-69. During his pastorate at Lewisburg, Pennsylvania, 1869-75, he was also professor of belles-lettres at Bucknell University located there, and received the D.D. degree in 1875. He then became pastor of the Park Avenue Baptist Church, Plainfield, New Jersey, where he remained until his death. During his pastorate in Brooklyn he became intensely interested in writing hymns and tunes. He succeeded William B. Bradbury as editor of Sunday school song collections for Biglow and Main, New York, in 1868, and collaborated with William H. Doane in most of these publications, to which he and Doane contributed many songs. Among these publications are: *Happy Voices* (1865), *Gospel Melodies* (1868), *Bright Jewels* (1869), *Pure Gold* (1871), *Royal Diadem* (1873), *Temple Anthems* (1873), *Hymn Service* (1871, 1872, 1873), *Tidal Wave* (1874), *Brightest and Best* (1875), *Welcome Tidings* (1877), *Fountain of Song* (1877), *Chautauqua Carols* (1878), *Gospel Hymn and Tune Book* (1879), *Good as Gold* (1880), *Our Glad Hosanna* (1882), *Joyful Lays* (1884), and *Glad Refrain* (1886).

Come, we that love the Lord (refrain)—MARCHING TO ZION (308)
Low in the grave He lay—CHRIST AROSE (113)
Shall we gather at the river—HANSON PLACE (481)
What can wash away my sin—PLAINFIELD (204)

ALL THE WAY—All the way my Saviour leads me (268)
NEED—I need Thee every hour (334)
SOMETHING FOR JESUS—Saviour, Thy dying love (400)

Luke, Jemima Thompson (b. Islington, London, Eng., Aug. 19, 1813; d. Newport, Isle of Wight, Eng., Feb. 2, 1906), was the daughter of one of the founders of the British and Foreign Sailors' Society, among whose activities was the supplying of floating chapels for the use of sea men. Serious illness prevented her from a missionary career, but did not decrease her interest in this work. She served as editor of *The Missionary Repository* (1841-45), the first missionary magazine in England for children. In 1843 she married a Congregational minister, Samuel Luke, and after his death in 1868 she continued her literary and charitable activities. Later in life she retired to Newport, Isle of Wight.

I think when I read that sweet story of old (506)

Luther, Charles Carroll (b. Worcester, Mass., May 17, 1847; d. Farmingdale, L.I., N.Y., Nov. 4, 1924), after graduation from Brown University in 1871, was a journalist and quite active as a lay evangelist. He was ordained by the First Baptist Church, Worcester, in 1886, and in 1889 moved to Mansfield, Pennsylvania, where he was engaged in evangelistic work. After two years he accepted the pastorate of the First Baptist Church, Bridgeport, Connecticut, 1891-1893. Following his pastorate he resumed his evangelistic activity, and for a number of years he was associated with the state Baptist Mission Board of New Jersey. He is the author of about twenty-five hymns and the compiler of *Temple Chimes,* a collection of hymns and songs.

Must I go, and empty-handed (430)

Luther, Martin (b. Eisleben, Saxony, Nov. 10, 1483; d. Eisleben, Feb. 18, 1546), was educated at Magdeburg and Eisenach, and studied law at the University of Erfurt. In 1505 he became an Augustinian monk, and was ordained a priest in 1507. The following year he became a member of the faculty of the University of Wittenberg. It was at Wittenberg on October 31, 1517, that he posted his now famous ninety-five theses or articles against papal abuses and corruption. In 1519 he denied the Pope's supremacy, which resulted in the condemnation of Luther and his writings. Luther's influence increased and the Reformation spread throughout the Continent. His greatest literary achievement was his scholarly translation of the Bible into the German language. He completed the New Testament in 1521 and the Old Testament in 1834. Under Luther's leadership the music of the church service became once again a matter of congregational participation. He wrote thirty-seven hymns and paraphrases, and strongly advocated the singing of hymns in homes, schools, and churches. Regarding his role as a composer of chorale melodies, there is considerable uncertainty. At least two tunes are generally credited to him, including the one given here. There is less agreement regarding other tunes which sometime bear his name. No other man of the sixteenth century exerted so widespread an influence as Martin Luther, who gave the German people in their own tongue the Bible and the hymn book.

A mighty fortress is our God—EIN' FESTE BURG (40)

Lutkin, Peter Christian (b. Thompsonville, Wis., Mar. 27, 1858; d. Evanston, Ill., Dec. 27, 1931), received his early education in the public schools of Chicago and the choir school at St. James's Cathedral, where he became organist at the age of fourteen. After four years study in Europe, 1881-84, he returned to Chicago and served as organist and choirmaster at St. Clements' Church, 1884-91, and at St. James's Church, 1891-96. During this time he also taught theory at the American Conservatory of Music. He became the first dean of the School of Music established by Northwestern University in 1896. In this position he exerted a profound influence on music education, as his students went forth to teach in high schools and colleges in America. He earned a widespread reputation as a choral conductor and lecturer on sacred music. Syracuse University awarded him the Mus.D. degree in 1900. He was one of the founders of the American Guild of Organists, and a leader in the Music Teacher's National Association, serving as president in 1911 and 1920. He was one of the editors of the Methodist *Hymnal* (1905) and the Episcopal *Hymnal* (1918). Among his musical compositions are a number of anthems, hymn tunes, and instrumental works.

LANIER—Into the woods my Master went (90)
Response (542)

Lwoff, Alexis Feodorovich (b. Reval (now Tallinn), Est., June 6, 1798; d. Romanovo, near Kovno, Lith., Dec. 28, 1870), received his early education from his father, who was the director of the Imperial Court Chapel at St. Petersburg. After graduating from the Institute of Road Engineering in 1818, he served in the Russian army, advancing to the rank of major general. In 1837 he succeeded his father at the Imperial Chapel, a position he held for twenty-four years. During this time he edited a collection of service music for the ecclesiastical year of the Greek Orthodox Church. He was an excellent violinist, and his string quartet toured Europe with great success. He composed three operas, several violin works, and considerable chamber music. Deafness caused his retirement in 1867.

Russian Hymn—God the almighty One! wisely ordaining (42)

Lyra Davidica. This small collection by an anonymous compiler was published in London by J. Walsh in 1708, with its full title: *Lyra Davidica, or a Collection of Divine Songs and Hymns, Partly New Composed, Partly Translated from the High German and Latin Hymns; and Set to Easy and Pleasant Tunes.* Consisting of approximately eighty pages, it contained thirty-one hymns and twenty-five tunes. As to the sources of tunes, Lightwood notes that nine are German chorales, among which were Ein' Feste Burg, Eisenach, and Wachet Auf; two are Latin melodies; and nine are English, probably written for this work. The remainder of the tunes are probably English, but were taken from other sources. In the Preface, the compiler sets forth his purpose to introduce

a little freer air than the grave movement of the Psalm-tunes, as being both seasonable and acceptable. . . . In Germany, where they have abundance of divine songs and hymns, set to short and pleasant tunes, the peasant at his plow, the servants at their labour, the children in the street . . . make use of these for the expression of their mirth; and have no such custom as we unhappily labour under, of ballads and profane songs.

Apparently this effort to introduce to England the sturdy German melodies was a private venture and only a few copies were ever printed. The only extant copy is in the British Museum.

Easter Hymn—Christ the Lord is risen today (115)

Lyte, Henry Francis (b. Ednam, Kelso, Scot., June 1, 1793; d. Nice, Fr., Nov. 20, 1847), was educated at Portora Royal School, Enniskillen, Ireland, and at Trinity College, Dublin. Abandoning his plans for a medical career, he was ordained in 1815, and after serving several churches, was appointed perpetual curate at Lower Brixham, Devonshire. He ministered patiently among the people of this fishing village for twenty-three years. He was never in robust health, and later suffered from asthma and consumption. Among his works are *Tales on the Lord's Prayer* (1826); *Poems, Chiefly Religious* (1833); and *The Spirit of the Psalms* (1836).

Abide with me: fast falls the eventide (295)
Jesus, I my cross have taken (387)
Praise, my soul, the King of heaven (18)

Mackay, William Paton (b. Montrose, Scot., May 13, 1839; d. Portree, Scot., Aug. 22, 1885), was educated at the University of Edinburgh and

343

practiced medicine for a number of years. Feeling called to the ministry, he abandoned his medical practice, was ordained, and became pastor of the Prospect Street Presbyterian Church, Hull, in 1868. Seventeen of his hymns appeared in W. Reid's *Praise Book* (1872).

We praise Thee, O God! for the Son of Thy love (205)

MacMillan, Ernest Campbell (b. Mimico, Ont., Aug. 18, 1893), the son of Alexander MacMillan, D.D., Mus.D., editor of the *Hymnary of the United Church of Canada* (1930), was educated at the University of Toronto, University of Edinburgh, and Oxford University. He visited Bayreuth in the summer of 1914 to attend the Wagner Festival, and when war broke out was interned at Ruhleben prison camp, 1914-18. After the armistice he returned to Canada, became director of the Toronto Conservatory of Music, 1926-52, and conductor of the Toronto Symphony Orchestra 1931-56. He was knighted in 1935 by King George V for his services to music in Canada as organist, teacher, conductor, and composer. In addition to his many compositions, he has published several educational works, and *Music in Canada* (Toronto, 1955). Since his retirement, Sir Ernest has continued to make his home in Toronto.

Tempus Adest Floridum (arr.)—Gentle Mary laid her Child (73)

Main, Hubert Platt (b. Ridgefield, Conn., Aug. 17, 1839; d. Newark, N.J., Oct. 7, 1925), was the son of Sylvester Main, a singing school teacher, who was associated with I. B. Woodbury and William B. Bradbury in their publishing endeavors. He gained invaluable experience through his association with Philip Phillips in Cincinnati and with the music firm of F. J. Huntington & Company, New York. In 1866 he assisted Phillips in the compilation of the *Methodist Episcopal Hymn and Tune Book*. In 1867 he accepted a position with the William B. Bradbury Co., New York. Following Bradbury's death in 1868, the new firm of Biglow and Main was formed, with Sylvester Main as junior partner, and this became Bradbury's successor. Young Main remained with the new firm throughout his lifetime and, with but few exceptions, every publication of this firm passed through his hands in the making, compiling, editing, proofreading and so on. Because of his intimate knowledge of music copyrights, his counsel was frequently sought by other publishers in this regard. While he is credited with having written more than a thousand compositions, his greatest contribution to American hymnody was through his role as a publisher and hymnologist. His personal collection of old music books now is a part of the Newberry Library, Chicago, and is known as the Main Library. The publishing interests of Biglow and Main were purchased by the Hope Publishing Company of Chicago in 1920.

ELLESDIE (arr.)—Jesus, I my cross have taken (387)
　　　Hark, the voice of Jesus calling (440)

Maker, Frederick Charles (b. Bristol, Eng., 1844; d. Bristol, 1927), spent his entire life in Bristol, where he began his musical career as a chorister in the Bristol Cathedral. After studying organ with Alfred Stone, he served as organist at the Milk Street Methodist Free Church, Clifton Downs Congregational Church, and finally at the Redland Park Congregational Church from 1882 until his retirement in 1910. He was a visiting professor at Clifton College and conductor of the Bristol Free Church Choir Association. He contributed a number of hymn tunes to the 1881 edition of *The Bristol Tune Book,* compiled by his former teacher, Alfred Stone, and these established his reputation as a hymn tune composer.

INVITATION—Come to the Saviour now (226)
REST (ELTON)—Dear Lord and Father of mankind (335)
　　　O Thou whose gracious presence blest (375)
ST. CHRISTOPHER—Beneath the cross of Jesus (345)

Malan, Henri Abraham César (b. Geneva, Switz., July 7, 1787; d. Vandoeuvres, near Geneva, May 18, 1864), was educated at the College of Geneva, where his father, Jacques Imbert Malan, was a member of the faculty. He was ordained to the ministry in the Reformed Church in 1810 and became pastor of the Chapelle du Temoignage in Geneva. His fervent evangelical preaching attracted large congregations, but his outspoken criticism regarding the spiritual apathy and empty formalism into which the Reform Church had degenerated aroused strong opposition and resulted in his resignation. He built a chapel in his own garden and preached there for forty-three years. His evangelistic tours made him well known throughout France, Belgium, and Great Britain. Julian notes that "the distinguishing characteristic of these tours was his dealing with individuals. On the steamboat or the diligence [stagecoach], in the mountain walk, at the hotel, no opportunity was lost." In addition to his fame as a preacher, poet, and musician, he was an artist, mechanic, carpenter, blacksmith, and printer. He wrote more than one thousand hymns and tunes, and published *Chants de Sion* (1841). On this contribution to hymnody rests his fame. The Rev. H. Leigh Bennett, a prebendary of Lincoln Cathedral, said:

The greatest name in the history of French hymns is that of Cesar Malan of Geneva. The general store of hymns has grown up almost entirely from a number of small contributions; Malan alone emulates the wealth of production exhibited by Watts and Wesley. Like Watts, he gave the first great impulse toward the general recognition of hymns in public worship; like Charles Wesley, he was the poet and interpreter of a great religious movement craving devotional expression.

HENDON—Ask ye what great thing I know (161)
    Take my life, and let it be (357)

Mann, Arthur Henry (b. Norwich, Eng., May 16, 1850; d. Cambridge, Eng., Nov. 19, 1929), was educated at Norwich Cathedral and at New College, Oxford (Mus.B. 1874; Mus.D. 1882). He became organist at St. Peter's Wolverhampton, 1870; Tettenhall Parish Church, 1871; and Beverley Minster, 1875. After only a few months in this latter position he went to King's College Chapel, Cambridge, where he remained until his death, serving as organist for fifty-three years in the same church. During this time he contributed much to the great musical traditions which exist there. He was considered an authority on Handel, and a skilful trainer of boys' choirs. He wrote many anthems, a number of hymn tunes, and considerable organ music. He served as musical editor for Charles D. Bell's *The Church of England Hymnal* (1895).

ANGEL'S STORY—O Jesus, I have promised (386)

March, Daniel (b. Millbury, Mass., July 21, 1816; d. Woburn, Mass., Mar. 2, 1909), the son of Samuel and Zoa (Park) March, spent his childhood on his father's farm. At the age of seventeen he enrolled in Millbury Academy, later attended Amherst College, 1834-36, became a traveling book agent, and served briefly as principal of Chester Academy in Vermont. He was graduated from Yale University, 1840, and was principal of the Fairfield Academy (Connecticut), 1840-43. He completed his theological studies at Yale, was ordained to the Congregational ministry in 1845, and became pastor of the Congregational church in Cheshire, Connecticut. In addition to pastorates in Nashua and Brooklyn, N.Y., and Philadelphia, Pennsylvania, he was twice pastor at Woburn, Massachusetts, 1856-64 and 1877-95. He traveled extensively and was greatly interested in missionary endeavors around the world. He frequently lectured on his world travels. He was awarded the D.D. degree by Western University of Pennsylvania. In 1841 he was married to Jane P. Gilson of Proctorsville, Vermont who died in 1857, and in 1859 to Anna B. Laconte of Cheshire, Connecticut, who died in 1878. One son, Frederick William March, was for many years a missionary to Syria. Among his published works are: *Our Father's Home, or, The Unwritten Word; From Dark to Dawn, or, Night Scenes of the Bible; The First*

346

Lessons from the Life of Joseph; Days of the Son of Man; Home Life in the Bible; Walks and Homes of Jesus. The hymn given here seems to be the only one he ever wrote.

Hark, the voice of Jesus calling (440)

Marlatt, Earl Bowman (b. Columbus, Ind., May 24, 1892), graduated from DePauw University and Boston University (S.T.B., 1922; Ph.D., 1929) and did further graduate work at Oxford University and the University of Berlin. He became professor of the philosophy of literature and religious education at Boston University in 1925, and served as dean of the School of Theology, 1938-45. In 1946 he was appointed professor of the philosophy of religion, at Southern Methodist University, and served in this position until his retirement in 1957. Since his retirement he has made his home in Winchester, Indiana. Always keenly interested in hymnology, he has been an active and helpful member of the Hymn Society of America, presently serving as curator of the Treasure Room and Hymn Museum at the Interchurch Center, New York City. He served as the associated editor of *The American Student Hymnal* (1928).

"Are ye able," said the Master (351)

Marriott, John (b. Cottesbach, near Lutterworth, Eng., Sept. 11, 1780; d. Broadclyst, near Exeter, Eng., Mar. 31, 1825), was educated at Rugby and Christ Church College, Oxford. Following his ordination he served as private tutor and chaplain in the family of the Duke of Buccleuch at Dalkeith, where he became a close friend of Sir Walter Scott. The second canto of Scott's *Marmion* was dedicated to him. In 1808 he was appointed to the rectory of Church Lawford, Warwickshire, which he retained until his death. However, his wife's illness made residence there impossible, and he lived in Devonshire where he served several curacies. He wrote a number of hymns but modesty prevented his permitting publication of them during his life time. A few were published but without his permission.

Thou, whose almighty word (461)

Marsh, Charles Howard (b. Magnolia, Iowa, Apr. 8, 1886; d. La Jolla, Calif., Apr. 12, 1956), was born a few months after his father and mother, Rev. and Mrs. George Marsh, arrived from England and his father became pastor of the Congregational Church in Magnolia, Iowa. His extraordinary talent as a pianist was evident during his high school years in Pittsburgh, and upon his graduation he was invited by J. Wilbur Chapman to play at the Winona Lake Chautauqua and Bible Conference in Indiana. After several years of private and conservatory teaching he taught at the Bible Institute of Los Angeles, 1915-19, and at the University of Redlands, 1919-26. During the summer of 1924 he was a student at the Fontainebleau Conservatory in France, studying organ with Charles-Marie Widor and Henri Libert. From 1926 to 1928 he was in Paris, a pupil of Philipp and Camille Decreaus in piano, of Marcel Dupre in organ, and of Nadia Boulanger in composition and orchestration. Upon his return to America, he became president of the European School of Music and Art, Fort Wayne, Indiana, and organist and choirmaster of the First Presbyterian Church, 1928-32. In 1932 he went to Florida as professor of organ at the Orlando College of Music, later becoming university organist at the University of Florida, Gainesville, and organist-choirmaster of the First Baptist Church. In 1935 he moved to California and served as district supervisor of the Federal Music Project, San Diego, California, until 1939. From 1936 until his death he served as organist-choirmaster for the St. James-by-the-Sea Episcopal Church, La Jolla, California. He was a fellow of the American Guild of Organists and was quite well known for his poetry and painting, as well as his music. His creative ability in music is evidenced by the considerable amount of solo songs, instrumental works, and anthem literature which he produced.

CHAPMAN—One day when heaven was filled with His praises (85)

Marsh, Simeon Butler (b. Sherburne, N.Y., June 1, 1798; d. Albany, N.Y., July 14, 1875), in 1814 attended his first singing school and became such an enthusiastic student that three years later he was a singing school teacher himself. In 1818 he attended the singing school of Thomas Hastings at Geneva, New York, and received great encouragement and help from Hastings. Following this experience he began teaching singing schools in the churches of the Albany Presbytery, an activity he continued for thirty years. In 1837 he founded a newspaper at Amsterdam, New York, *The Intelligencer* (later named *The Recorder*), which he edited for seven years. Later he began another newspaper, *The Sherburne News,* in his home town. He was a devoted Presbyterian layman and, in addition to his musical interests, was active in Sunday school work. After the death of his wife in 1873 he made his home with his son, John Butler Marsh, Albany, where his death occurred in 1875.

MARTYN—Jesus, lover of my soul (156)

Martin, Civilla Durfee (b. Jordan, N.S., Aug. 21, 1866; d. Atlanta, Ga., Mar. 9, 1948), was the daughter of James N. and Irene (Harding) Holden. After teaching village schools for several years and a brief period of music study, she married Walter Stillman Martin (*q.v.*). Her musical talents were most helpful in the evangelistic campaigns of her husband. She was a loyal and devoted wife, and was of great assistance to her husband in his work as teacher, evangelist, and pastor. She collaborated with him in the writing of a number of gospel songs.

Be not dismayed whate'er betide (274)

Martin, Walter Stillman (b. Rowley, Essex Co., Mass., 1862; d. Atlanta, Ga., Dec. 16, 1935), was educated at Harvard University. He was ordained to the Baptist ministry, but later became a member of the Christian Church (Disciples of Christ). In 1916 he became professor of Bible at the Atlantic Christian College, North Carolina. He was married to Civilla Durfee Holden, a native of Nova Scotia. In 1919 he moved to Atlanta, Georgia, and made this his residence until his death, as he conducted Bible conferences and evangelistic meetings throughout the nation.

GOD CARES—Be not dismayed whate'er betide (274)

Mason, Harry Silvernale (b. Gloversville, N.Y., 1881), graduated from Syracuse University in 1911 and later attended Boston University School of Theology. For twenty-five years he was on the faculty of Auburn Theological Seminary, Auburn, New York. He is an Episcopalian, but a major portion of his fifty-four years as a church organist was spent in Presbyterian churches, his longest term of service being in the Second Presbyterian Church, Auburn, New York.

BEACON HILL—"Are ye able," said the Master (351)

Mason, Lowell (b. Medfield, Mass., July 8, 1792; d. Orange, N.J., Aug. 11, 1872). Among those who contributed to Mason's early musical training were Amos Albee, the local schoolmaster, and Oliver Shaw, a musician living at Dedham, Massachusetts. By the time Lowell was sixteen he was leading the village choir and teaching singing schools. From 1812 to 1827 he lived in Savannah, Georgia, where he worked as a bank clerk and studied harmony and composition with F. L. Abel. For seven years during this time he served as organist of the First Presbyterian Church. In 1827 he returned to Boston, became president of the Handel and Haydn Society, 1827-32, and served for fourteen years as choir director of Bowdoin Street Church, where his choir earned widespread recognition for the quality of its singing. In an effort to improve music in both choir and congregation, he began music classes for the children of his church and published *The Juvenile Psalmist, or The Child's Introduction to Sacred Music* (1829). To fur-

\ther implement this cause, he established the Boston Academy of Music in 1832. By 1838 he had gained approval for the teaching of vocal music in the public schools of Boston in "preparation for making the praise of God glorious in families and churches." In his zeal for music education in the schools, he pioneered in the area of teacher training for nearly twenty-five years, and, as Arthur L. Rich comments,

through teachers' classes, musical conventions, lectures on the pedagogy of music, teachers' institutes, and musical normal institutes, he provided the United States for more than a generation with most of its trained public school music teachers, as well as a large proportion of its trained church musicians and other professional musicians.

He was prolific in his publication of collections of music for church and school, and Rich lists at least eighty collections with which Mason was associated either as sole compiler or in collaboration with others. To his collections of sacred music he contributed many original hymn tunes, as well as many adaptations and arrangements of tunes from other sources, largely European. His grandson, Henry L. Mason, in *Hymn-Tunes of Lowell Mason* (1944) gives the names of 1,126 original tunes and 497 arrangements. Of unusual interest in the fact that a majority of tune names chosen by Mason for his tunes were taken from the Old Testament, thirty-five of which may be found in the fifteenth chapter of Joshua.

An intensive treatment of Mason and his work and publications has been written by Arthur L. Rich, head of the Music Department, Mercer University, entitled, *Lowell Mason: The Father of Singing Among Children* (Chapel Hill: The University of North Carolina Press, 1946).

ARIEL (arr.)—Let all on earth their voices raise (7)
　　　　　O could I speak the matchless worth (146)
AZMON (arr.)—O for a thousand tongues to sing (129)
　　　　　The head that once was crowned with thorns (117)
BETHANY—Nearer, my God, to Thee (322)
BOYLSTON—The Holy Ghost is here (168
　　　　　A charge to keep I have (358)
DENNIS (arr.)—Blest be the tie that binds (366)
HAMBURG (arr.)—When I survey the wondrous cross (99)
HARWELL—Hail, Thou long-expected Jesus (70)
　　　　　Hark, ten thousand harps and voices (145)
LABAN—A parting hymn we sing (397)
　　　　　My soul, be on thy guard (420)
MENDEBRAS (arr.)—O day of rest and gladness (36)
MISSIONARY HYMN—From Greenland's icy mountains (449)
　　　　　The light of God is falling (442)

OLIVET—My faith looks up to Thee (257)
SABBATH—Safely through another week (37)
UXBRIDGE—Be present at our table, Lord (396)
WESLEY—Hail to the brightness of Zion's glad morning (453)
WORK SONG—Work, for the night is coming (424)

Matthews, Timothy Richard (b. Colmworth, near Bedford, Eng., Nov. 4, 1826; d. Tetney, Lincolnshire, Eng., Jan. 5, 1910), was educated at Bedford Grammar School and at Gonville and Caius College, Cambridge (B.A., 1853). He became a private tutor at Windsor, and while here studied organ under George Elvey (*q.v.*), with whom he enjoyed a lifelong friendship. Ordained in 1853, after a curacy at Nottingham he became curate at North Coates in 1859—ten years later becoming rector—where he remained until his retirement in 1907. He composed more than one hundred hymn tunes and edited *Tunes for Holy Worship* (1859), *The Village-Church Tune-Book* (1859), *Congregational Melodies* (1862), *Hymn Tunes* (1867), *North Coates Supplemental Tune Book* (1878), and *The Village Organist* (1877).

MARGARET—Thou didst leave Thy throne (82)
SAXBY—Father in heaven, who lovest all (460)

Matheson, George (b. Glasgow, Scot., Mar. 27, 1842; d. North Berwick, Scot., Aug. 28, 1906), in spite of impaired vision, which, by the age of eighteen had made him almost blind, he was a brilliant student at Glasgow Academy and Glasgow University. He was licensed to preach in 1866, was assistant at Sandyford Church, Glasgow, and minister of Clydeside parish, Innellan, Argyllshire. In 1886 he became minister of St. Bernard's Church, Edinburgh, and remained there until ill health forced his resignation in 1899. He wrote many books of theology and devotion and one volume of verse, *Sacred Songs* (1890). Widely known and greatly respected, he was one of the outstanding Scottish Presbyterian ministers of his day. The University of Edinburgh awarded him the D.D. degree in 1879, and the University of Aberdeen, the LL.D. in 1902.

O love that wilt not let me go (290)

McAfee, Cleland Boyd (b. Ashley, Mo., Sept. 25, 1866; d. Jaffrey, N.H., Feb. 4, 1944), graduated from Park College, Parkville, Missouri, in 1884, and studied at Union Theological Seminary. He returned to Park College to teach, serve as pastor of the college church, and direct the church choir, 1881-1901. He entered pastoral work, serving the Forty-first Street (now First) Presbyterian Church, Chicago, 1901-04, and the Lafayette Avenue Presbyterian Church, Brooklyn, 1904-12. At McCormick Theological Seminary, Chicago, he served as professor of systematic theology, 1912-30, and was then elected secretary of the Presbyterian Board of Foreign Missions, 1930-36. After his retirement he made his home at Jaffrey, New Hampshire but remained active with his writing, lecturing, preaching, and teaching.

There is a place of quiet rest—McAfee (301)

McConnell, James Edwin (b. Atlanta, Ga., Jan. 12, 1892; d. Newport Beach, Calif., July 24, 1954), the son of J. Lincoln and Mary (White) McConnell, was educated at Webb Preparatory School, Bell Buckle, Tennessee, and William Jewell College, Liberty, Missouri. For a number of years he served as pianist, evangelistic singer, and choir director in the evangelistic meetings conducted by his father, a Baptist minister, at one time pastor of the First Baptist Church, Oklahoma City, Oklahoma. In 1922 he began a successful radio career, known as "Smilin' Ed McConnell," and his program, "Hymn Time," was carried by the National Broadcasting Company. He was also well known in the medium of television.

I am happy today and the sun shines bright—McConnell (209)

McCutchan, Robert Guy (b. Mount Ayr, Iowa, Sept. 13, 1877; d. Claremont, Calif., May 15, 1958), the son of Erastus Gilmore and Margaret (Edie) McCutchan, was educated at Park College, Parkville, Missouri, Simpson College, Indianola, Iowa, and later studied in Berlin and Paris. In 1904 he began teaching at Baker University, Baldwin, Kansas, and two years later became the head of the newly established Music Department there. In 1911 he was appointed dean of the School of Music, DePauw University, Greencastle, Indiana, and remained in this position until his retirement in 1937. He was a member of the Commission on Church Music of the Methodist Episcopal Church, 1924-28; the Joint Commission for the Revision of the Methodist Hymnal, 1928-35; and for a number of years following 1937 a member of the General Conference Committee on Music of the Methodist Church. He was a devoted churchman and served his denomination with distinction as an educator, church musician, and hymnologist. His keen wit, sparkling humor, and magnetic personality endeared him to all who knew him. Bishop G. Bromley Oxnam, in a personal tribute says:

Dean McCutchan was a man who passionately loved human beings. Nevertheless, he appraised them with uncanny accuracy. He recognized worth and talent in rich and poor, cultured and untutored alike. He knew there was more wisdom in the mind and heart of an uneducated and hard-working mother than in many a Ph.D. oral, and more understanding in a coal pit than in some faculty rooms. He penetrated sham like an X-ray, and was unafraid to speak the frank and at times critical word.

Following his retirement in 1937 he moved to Claremont, California, and remained active as a lecturer on hymnology and conducted church music conferences. For eighteen months, 1954-55, he was visiting professor at the Perkins School of Theology, Southern Methodist University, Dallas. In 1904 he was married to Carrie Burns Sharp, who died in 1941. In 1944 he was married to Helen Laura Cowles, reference librarian at Claremont University College, who was born in the Union of South Africa, the daughter and granddaughter of Congregational missionaries. Dean McCutchan was music editor of the *American Junior Church and Church School Hymnal* (1928), and *Standard Hymns and Gospel Songs* (1929), and was the author of *Better Music in Our Churches* (1925), *Music in Worship* (1927), *Hymns in the Lives of Men* (1945), and *Hymn Tune Names* (1957). His greatest contribution to hymnody was his role as editor of the *Methodist Hymnal* (1935) and as the author of its handbook, *Our Hymnody* (1937). His valuable personal library of over three thousand volumes was given to Claremont College, Claremont, California, and is housed in the Honnold Library.

CAMPMEETING (harm.)—Prayer is the soul's sincere desire (336)
Response (521)

McDaniel, Rufus Henry (b. near Ripley, Brown Co., Ohio, Jan. 29, 1850; d. Dayton, Ohio, Feb. 13, 1940), attended school at Bentonville, Ohio, and at Parker's Academy, Claremont County, Ohio. He was licensed to preach at the age of nineteen and ordained in the Christian church in 1873. He was married to Margaret Dragoo, and they had three children: Clarence, a Christian minister; Minnie (Mrs. Frank R. Liesenhoff, of Dayton, Ohio); and Herschel, who died in 1913. He served many charges in the Southern Ohio Conference of the Christian Church, including Hamersville, Higginsport, Centerburg, and Sugar Creek. Following a pastorate in Cincinnati, he retired to Dayton. He is credited with having written more than one hundred hymns, many of which were published by the Rodeheaver Company. Only the one given here has survived in common usage.

What a wonderful change in my life has been wrought (310)

McDonald, William (b. Belmont, Me., Mar. 1, 1820; d. Monrovia, Calif., Sept. 11, 1901), was of Scottish descent. He became a local preacher in the Methodist Episcopal Church in 1839, joined the Maine

Conference in 1843, transferred to the Wisconsin Conference in 1855, and to the New England Conference in 1859. For fifteen years he was editor of the *Advocate of Christian Holiness*. He published ten volumes on religious subjects and was associated as editor or coeditor of seven collections of sacred music. Among these were *Western Minstrels* (1840), *Wesleyan Sacred Harp* (1855), *Beulah Songs* (1870), and *Tribute of Praise* (1874).

I am coming to the cross (243)

McGranahan, James (b. near Adamsville, Pa., July 4, 1840; d. Kinsman, Ohio, July 7, 1907), at the age of nineteen, began teaching singing classes. During the summer of 1861-62 he attended Bradbury's Normal Music School at Geneseo, New York. He became associated with J. G. Towner and conducted musical conventions and singing schools throughout Pennsylvania and New York, 1862-64. Later he studied under George F. Root, and was a member of the faculty of Root's Normal Musical Institute at Somerset, Pennsylvania, 1875, and at Towanda, Pennsylvania, 1876. Following the death of P. P. Bliss (*q.v.*), in December 1876, he became song leader for the evangelist, Major D. W. Whittle (*q.v.*). They conducted evangelistic meetings throughout the United States, and twice visited England, 1880 and 1883. Among the song leaders of his day, he pioneered in the use of men's choirs in his meetings and published *The Gospel Male Choir* (two volumes, 1878, 1883). As an editor and compiler he was associated with many publications, the most important of which are: *The Choice*; *Harvest of Song* (with C. C. Case); *Gospel Choir* (with Ira D. Sankey); and *Gospel Hymns,* Nos. 3, 4, 5, and 6 (with Sankey and George C. Stebbins). His Most successful songs appeared in this latter series. His health broke down in 1887 and he settled in Kinsman, Ohio, living in semi-retirement and continuing his writing.

CHRIST RETURNETH—It may be at morn, when the day is awaking (120)
EL NATHAN—I know not why God's wondrous grace (275)
McGRANAHAN—Hallelujah! hallelujah! (114)
MY REDEEMER—I will sing of my redeemer (143)
NEUMEISTER—Sinners Jesus will receive (195)
ROYAL BANNER—There's a royal banner given for display (408)
SHOWERS OF BLESSING—There shall be showers of blessing (264)

McGregor, Ernest Frank (b. Alexandria, N.H., Oct. 7, 1879; d. Clinton, Conn., May 31, 1946), was educated at the University of Minnesota and at Yale Divinity School (B.D., 1904; M.A., 1907; Ph.D.,

1911). While a graduate student at Yale, he held pastorates at two Congregational churches in Connecticut: Avon, 1904-07; and Clinton, 1907-12. In 1912 he became pastor of the First Congregational Church, Norwalk, Connecticut, where he served with distinction for thirty-two years until his retirement in 1944. Many of his seventeen hymns were written in connection with his sermons for special occasions.

O blessed day of motherhood (504)

McIntosh, Rigdon McCoy (b. Maury Co., Tenn., Apr. 3, 1836; d. Atlanta, Ga., July 2, 1899), was the son of Hector and Mamie (Biggs) McIntosh, and was educated at Jackson College, Columbia, Tennessee. He received his musical training under L. C. and Asa B. Everett (*q.v.*), and for several years was associated with the Everetts, composing and editing books, and teaching in their musical normals and singing schools throughout the South. He was married to Sallie McClasson of Farmville, Virginia, and through her influence was converted and joined the Methodist Episcopal Church, South.

In 1875 he became head of the Music Department, Vanderbilt University, Nashville. Two years later he accepted a similar position at Emory College, Oxford, Georgia, and made his home here the rest of his life. He resigned his teaching position in 1895 and, having established The R. M. McIntosh Publishing Company, devoted his time exclusively to his company. In the 1860's he became music editor for the publishing house of the Methodist Episcopal Church, South, Nashville, and maintained this relationship for about thirty years.

He was one of the most outstanding musicians in the southern states during his day. He excelled as a choral director, teacher, composer, and editor. He published the following collections for church and Sunday school use: *Tabor* (1866); *Herman, the Methodist Hymn and Tune Book*; *Prayer and Praise*; *Christian Hymns*; *Gospel Grace*; *McIntosh's Anthems*; *Glad Tidings*; *Amaranth*; *Emerald*; *The Gem*; *Good News*; *Light and Life*; *New Life, No. 1*; *New Life No. 2*; *Living Songs*; *Pure Words*; and *Songs of Service*. He frequently used the psuedonym "Emilius Laroche."

PROMISED LAND (arr.)—On Jordan's stormy banks I stand (479)
THE KINGDOM IS COMING—From all the dark places (409)

McKinney, Baylus Benjamin (b. Heflin, La., July 22, 1886; d. Bryson City, N.C., Sept. 7, 1952), the son of James Calvin and Martha (Heflin) McKinney, was educated at Mt. Lebanon Academy, Louisiana; Southwestern Baptist Theological Seminary; Siegel-Myers Correspondence School of Music (B.M., 1922); and Bush Conservatory,

Chicago. He was awarded the Mus.D. degree by Oklahoma Baptist University in 1942. He was a member of the faculty of the School of Sacred Music, Southwestern Baptist Theological Seminary, Fort Worth, Texas, 1919-32. In addition to his teaching responsibilities and church work, he served as music editor for Robert H. Coleman (*q.v.*), 1918-35. During this time he became a prolific composer of gospel songs.

When the financial difficulties caused by the depression of the early thirties forced the Seminary to reduce its faculty, McKinney resigned to become assistant pastor of the Travis Avenue Baptist Church, Fort Worth, 1931-35. At the invitation of Dr. T. L. Holcomb, he came to the Baptist Sunday School Board, Nashville, in December, 1935, first as music editor, and in 1941 he became secretary of the newly organized Church Music Department. In this capacity he compiled and published *Songs of Victory* (1937), *Broadman Hymnal* (1940), and *Voice of Praise* (1948). He served as the first editor of *The Church Musician,* a monthly periodical for Southern Baptist musicians, the first issue appearing in October, 1950.

McKinney wrote both words and music for about one hundred fifty gospel songs and composed tunes for about one hundred fifteen texts by other authors. In 1918 he married Leila Routh, and they had two sons. B. B. McKinney, Jr., is a lieutenant colonel in the United States Air Force. Gene McKinney, known for his playwriting, teaches drama and playwrighting at Trinity University, San Antonio, Texas, and at the Dallas Theater Center, Dallas, Texas. Dr. McKinney's death occurred as the result of an automobile accident near Bryson City, North Carolina, as he and Mrs. McKinney were returning to Nashville following the 1952 Church Music Leadership Week at Ridgecrest Baptist Assembly, Ridgecrest, North Carolina.

Arise, O youth of God (alt.)—LEAVELL (423)
Blessed Saviour, we adore Thee—GLORIOUS NAME (138)
Coming now to Thee, O Christ my Lord—TRAVIS AVENUE (342)
God, give us Christian homes—CHRISTIAN HOME (377)
Have faith in God when your pathway is lonely—MUSKOGEE (253)
Have you failed in your plan of your storm-tossed life—LUBBOCK (231)
Holy Spirit, breathe on me (alt.)—TRUETT (174)
I am satisfied with Jesus—ROUTH (436)
I know the Bible was sent from God—GRICE (184)
Lord, lay some soul upon my heart—LEILA (332)
Send a revival, O Christ, my Lord—MATTHEWS (333)
Serve the Lord with gladness—LEE (434)

Speak to my heart, Lord Jesus—HOLCOMB (331)
"Take up thy cross and follow Me"—FALLS CREEK (347)
While passing through this world of sin—COLEMAN (348)
BY AND BY (arr.)—Trials dark on every hand (473)
Response (arr.) (523)
Responses (540, 541)

McNeely, Edwin Martin (b. Gorman, Tex., Apr. 26, 1891), the son of a Baptist minister, attended Haskell State School of Agriculture and Southwestern Baptist Theological Seminary. During World War I he was a corporal in the 141st Infantry, serving in France as a runner, carrying information to the troops at the front, 1918-19. After the war he returned to the seminary and received the diploma of gospel music in 1922, and the B.S.M. in 1932. He studied voice with Herbert Witherspoon, Charles Farwell Edson, and Horatio Connell, and has done graduate study at the Cincinnati Conservatory of Music and Union Theological Seminary, School of Sacred Music. In 1946 he was awarded the honorary Mus.D. degree by the Boguslawski School of Church Music, Chicago. He began teaching in the School of Church Music, Southwestern Baptist Theological Seminary, Fort Worth, in 1921, while a student, and retired in 1961 after forty years of distinguished service on the music faculty. During this time he served as minister of music for the Evans Avenue Baptist Church, Fort Worth, Texas, for more than twenty-five years. He has written a considerable amount of poetry, and wrote the libretto for the unpublished sacred music drama, *Ruth*, by Isham E. Reynolds (*q.v.*). He is the author of *Evangelistic Music* (1959). He has led the music for numerous conferences and conventions, and conducted many music schools in local churches. In 1920 he was married to Wayne Walker, who died in 1957, and the following year he was married to Addie Wilson Heritage. He retired in 1961 and makes his home in Newton, Mississippi.

Jehovah the Lord, our Saviour and King (494)

Medley, Samuel (b. Cheshunt, Hertfordshire, Eng., June 23, 1738; d. Liverpool, Eng., July 17, 1799), as a youth served in the Royal Navy and was severely wounded off Port Lagos, 1759. His schoolteacher father was a friend of Isaac Newton. He was converted after reading a sermon by Isaac Watts and joined the Eagle Street Baptist Church (now Kingsgate Church), London. He was pastor of the Baptist church, Watford, Hertfordshire, 1767-72, then moved to the Byron Street Baptist Church, Liverpool, 1772-99. His ministry in Liverpool was immensely successful, and the congregation became so large that a new edifice was erected in 1790. His hymnic writings were published in his *Hymns* (1785; 2nd ed., Bristol, 1785; enlarged ed. 1787) and *Hymns: The Public Worship and Private Devotion of True Christians Assisted in some Thoughts in Verse* (London, 1800). *A Memoir,* written by his daughter, Sarah, in 1833, contained forty-four additional sacramental hymns.

Awake, my soul, in joyful lays (26)
O could I speak the matchless worth (146)

Meineke, Charles (b. Germany, 1782; d. United States, 1850), in 1810 left Germany and spent some time in England. He had established his residence in Baltimore, Maryland, by 1822, and is mentioned as being organist at St. Paul's Episcopal Church of that city in 1836. He published *Music for the Church, containing Sixty-two Psalm and Hymn Tunes in Four Parts Together with Chants, Doxologies, and Responses . . . Composed for St. Paul's Church, Baltimore, by C. Meineke, Organist* (Baltimore, 1844), and the date of this publication would indicate that he served this church for at least eight years.

Response (524)

Mendelssohn, Felix (b. Hamburg, Ger., Feb. 3, 1809; d. Leipzig, Ger., Nov. 4, 1847), was the son of Abraham Mendelssohn, a Jewish banker, and the grandson of the famous Jewish philosopher, Moses Mendelssohn. His mother was an artist, pianist, and singer, and gave her children their first music training. In 1811, during the French occupation of Hamburg, the family moved to Berlin, and were baptized in the Lutheran church. At this time Abraham Mendelssohn added to the family name that of Bartholdy (a family property on the Spree) to indicate that they were Christians. Young Felix revealed his extraordinary musical talents at an early age. At the age of nine he made his first public performance as a pianist, and by the time he was twelve he had composed many works, including five symphonies. As a youth he discovered the music of J. S. Bach, and this became a great influence in his life. In 1829 he conducted a performance of Bach's *St. Matthew Passion,* the first performance of this work since Bach's death. He traveled extensively throughout Europe and England, and became widely known as a a composer and performer. Other details of his life and lists of his works are readily available in other sources and space does not permit their inclusion here. He left an enormous number of musical works: symphonies, overtures, chamber music, concertos, organ and piano works, much vocal music, and two oratorios, *St. Paul* and *Elijah.* (Cf. *The Hymn,* XI, No. 4, 110-113.)

CONSOLATION—Still, still with Thee, when purple morning breaketh
(25)
We would see Jesus, for the shadows lengthen (324)
MENDELSSOHN—Hark! the herald angels sing (81)
MUNICH (harm.)—O Word of God incarnate (183)
NUN DANKET (harm.)—Now thank we all our God (491)
Response (529)

Mercer, William (b. Barnard Castle, Durham, Eng., 1811; d. Leavy
Greave, Sheffield, Eng., Aug. 21, 1873), was educated at Trinity College,
Cambridge (B.A., 1835). In 1840 he was appointed incumbent of St.
George's Church, Sheffield. This was the church James Montgomery
(*q.v.*) attended in his later years. While Mercer made several translations
and paraphrases of Latin and German hymns, his principle contribution
to hymnody was his *Church Psalter and Hymn Book* (1854). Its four
hundred hymns were a skilful blending of the Wesleyan hymns and German translations, and no doubt part of its popularity can be attributed
to the musical editing of John Goss. Mercer's hymnal was the first used in
the Church of England to effectively include tunes, and it marked the
transition to the modern type of Church of England hymnal.

God, that madest earth and heaven (30—stanza 2)

Meredith, Isaac Hickman (b. Norristown, Pa., Mar. 21, 1872; d.
Orlando, Fla., Nov. 2, 1962), the youngest of eleven children, began
singing alto at thirteen in the adult choir of the Oak Street Methodist
Church, Norristown, and was elected Sunday school chorister when he
was nineteen. In the summer of 1892 he attended the Ocean Grove Assembly in New Jersey, where John J. Lowe was music director. The inspiration of this experience was a deciding factor in turning his interests
to sacred music. He began his career as an evangelistic singer at South
River, New Jersey, and for a time was associated with Rev. George L.
Barker. His first song was composed at South River, and it was purchased and published by John J. Hood of Philadelphia. Subsequent song
compositions were purchased by Sankey, Excell, Bilhorn and others, until he established his own publishing firm, the Tullar-Meredith Company,
New York, 1893, in association with Grant Colfax Tullar (*q.v.*). During
World War I he served for two years with the YMCA in France. Following the war, in addition to his publishing business, he was music director
at various times at the Bushwick Avenue Methodist Church, Brooklyn,
the Peddie Memorial Baptist Church and the Centenary Methodist
Church, Newark, New Jersey. As song leader, he was at various times associated with such evangelists as Billy Sunday and Gypsy Smith. He

composed over four thousand songs, principally gospel songs, festival songs for the Sunday school, and several anthems and cantatas.

Seal us, O Holy Spirit—CARSON (175)

Merrill, William Pierson (b. Orange, N.J., Jan. 10, 1867; d. New York, N.Y., June 19, 1954), was converted at the age of eleven and joined the Belleville Congregational Church, Newburyport, Massachusetts. Two years later he joined the Second Dutch Reformed Church, New Brunswick, New Jersey. He was educated at Rutgers College (A.B., 1887; M.A., 1890) and Union Theological Seminary (B.D., 1890). He was ordained to the Presbyterian ministry in 1890. Following pastorates in Philadelphia and Chicago, he became pastor of the Brick Presbyterian Church, New York City, in 1911, where he remained until his retirement in 1938. He was a successful pastor and his reputation as a preacher was widely known. In addition to several hymns, he was the author of a number of books, among which were: *Footings for Faith* (1915), *Christian Internationalism* (1919), *The Common Creed of Christians* (1920), *The Freedom of the Preacher* (1922), *Liberal Christianity* (1925), *Prophets of the Dawn* (1927), *The Way* (1933), and *We See Jesus* (1934).

Rise up, O men of God (445, 423 alt.)

Messiter, Arthur Henry (b. Frome, Somersetshire, Eng., Apr. 12, 1834; d. New York, N.Y., July 2, 1916), received his early education from private tutors. He studied music for four years at Northampton under McKorkell and later under Derfell. He came to America in 1863, and for a time sang in the choir at Trinity Church, New York City. After some months as organist at Poultney, Vermont, and Philadelphia, he became organist at Trinity Church, New York, in 1866. When the news of his appointment was announced, one music critic wrote. "We hear that the authorities at Trinity Church have appointed an organist from Philadelphia. We suppose that at the next vacancy they will try Coney Island." During his thirty-one years of distinguished service in this position, he maintained the highest standards of the English cathedral tradition; and his choir of men and boys served as a model for many other Episcopal churches in this country. In addition to composing a number of anthems, he edited a *Psalter* (1889), *Choir Office Book* (1891), and *Hymnal with Music as Used in Trinity Church* (1893). He was the author of *A History of the Choir and the Music of Trinity Church* (New York, 1906).

MARION—Rejoice, ye pure in heart (17)

Miller, William. No information has been found to identify this composer. Many collections of the late nineteenth century give his name as "Dr. William Miller." Since this hymn has been frequently found among the "early Adventist hymns," it seems possible that this composer could be William Miller, the leader of the "Millerites," who looked for the second coming of Christ in the 1840's. However, no information has been found to substantiate this theory.

LAND OF REST—O land of rest, for thee I sigh (284)

Mills, Elizabeth King (b. Stoke Newington, Eng., 1805; d. London, Eng., Apr. 21, 1829), was the daughter of Philip King and married Thomas Mills, a member of parliament. No other information has been found concerning this author.

O land of rest, for thee I sigh (284)

Milman, Henry Hart (b. London, Eng., Feb. 10, 1791; d. Sunninghill, Berkshire, Eng., Sept. 24, 1868), was the son of Sir Francis Milman, physician to King George III. Educated at Eton and Brasenose College, Oxford, he was an outstanding student winning the Newdigate, Latin Verse, Latin Essay, and English Essay prizes. Ordained in 1817, he was vicar at St. Mary's, Reading, 1816-35, and served as professor of poetry at Oxford University, 1821-31. Canon of Westminister Abbey and rector at St. Margaret's, Westminster, 1835-49, he was appointed Dean of St. Paul's Cathedral in 1849. He wrote thirteen hymns for Reginald Heber's *Hymns* (1827); and these were included in his *Hymns for the Use of St. Margaret's, Westminster* (1837). In addition to his fame as a churchman, poet, and scholar, he was perhaps best known as a historian. Among his most significant works in this field are *Christianity from the Birth of Christ to the Abolition of Paganism in the Roman Empire* (1840) and *A History of Latin Christianity* (1854).

Ride on! ride on in majesty (102)

Milton, John (b. London, Eng., Dec. 9, 1608; d. London, Nov. 8, 1674), was educated at St. Paul's School and at Christ's College, Cambridge (B.A., 1629; M.A., 1632). After graduation he lived for six years in his father's home at Horton, Buckinghamshire, where he wrote *Il Penseroso, L'Allegro, Comus,* and *Lycidas.* During the rule of Cromwell, he was appointed Secretary for Foreign Tongues in the Council of State, 1649, in which position he translated letters of the British Government to foreign states and rulers. He became blind in 1653, but continued his work until Cromwell's abdication in 1659. The fact that he escaped the scaffold was a tribute to his fame and reputation. He published *Paradise Lost* in 1677, and *Paradise Regained* and *Samson Agonistes* in 1671. In a strict sense, he should not be considered a hymn writer, for his nineteen metrical psalms were not intended to be sung, although a few have been included in various collections. Perhaps the greatest significance to hymnological development was his influence on Watts and Wesley. In the preface to *Horae Lyricae* (1709) Watts refers to his poetic style. Of his influence on the Wesleys, Henry Bett, in his *Hymns of Methodism,* says that it "is visible everywhere in the hymns. The great Puritan poet is the source of many of their striking phrases, and his influence upon the poetic style of the Wesleys is greater, perhaps, than that of any other writer."

The Lord will come and not be slow (126)

Minor, George A. (b. Richmond, Va., Dec. 7, 1845; d. Richmond, Jan. 29, 1904), was educated in a military academy in Richmond, and served in the Confederae Army during the Civil War. For several years following the war, he was engaged in teaching vocal music and conducting singing schools and musical conventions. Sometime after 1875 he was one of the founders of the Hume-Minor Company of Richmond and Norfolk, manufacturers of pianos and organs. On November 10, 1886, he was married to Mrs. Jennie B. Pope, daughter of Captain J. H. Prince of Green Plain, Southampton County, Virginia. For many years he was a devoted member of the First Baptist Church of Richmond, where he was chairman of the music committee and music leader for the Sunday school. His death occurred at his home in Barton Heights, Richmond, and he was buried in Hollywood Cemetery. Among his several published collections are *Golden Light, No. 1* (1879); *Golden Light No. 2; Golden Light No. 3* (1884); *Standard Songs* (1896); and *The Rosebud,* a collection for small children.

HARVEST—Sowing in the morning, sowing seeds of kindness (432)

Mohr, Joseph (b. Salzburg, Aust., Dec. 11, 1792; d. Wagrein, Aust., Dec. 4, 1848), as a boy was a chorister in the cathedral choir at Salzburg. He was ordained a priest in the Roman Catholic Church in 1815, and from August 25, 1817, until October 19, 1819, he served as assistant priest at St. Nicholas Church, Oberndorf, where he wrote the carol which made him famous. After several other appointments, he became vicar at Hintersee in 1828, and at Wagrein, near St. Johann, in 1837, where he remained until his death.

Silent night, holy night (72)

Monk, William Henry (b. London, Eng., Mar. 16, 1823; d. London, Mar. 1, 1889), received his musical training under Thomas Adams, J. A. Hamilton, and G. A. Griesbach. After serving as organist for six years at various London churches, he was appointed choir director at King's College, London, in 1847, and two years later became organist. In 1852 he became organist at St. Matthias Church, Stoke Newington, a position he held until his death. During this same time he was professor of vocal music at King's Collge, London, 1874; professor of music at the School for the Indigent Blind, the National Training School for Music, and Bedford College, London. Durham University awarded him the Doctor of Music degree in 1882. Of extraordinary significance was his editorial work on musical editions of a number of hymnals, the most important of which was *Hymns Ancient and Modern* (1861, 1875, 1889). In addition to his editorial work, he composed fifty tunes for this work. This monumental work is a bench mark in the development of English hymnody, and no other hymnal has had so great an influence on congregational song, both in England and America. (Cf. *The Hymn* XII, No. 2, 37-41.)

EVENTIDE—Abide with me: fast falls the eventide (295)
VICTORY (adapted)—The strife is o'er, the battle done (107)

Monsell, John Samuel Bewley (b. St. Columb's, Londonderry, Ire., Mar. 2, 1811; d. Guildford, Eng., Apr. 9, 1875), was educated at Trinity College, Dublin (B.A., 1832) and was ordained in 1834. After several appointments in Ireland, he came to England where he was vicar of Egham, Surrey, 1853, and rector at St. Nicholas, Guildford, 1870. He was accidently killed by a stone which fell when repairs were being made on the roof of St. Nicholas Church. He published eleven volumes of poetry, including nearly three hundred hymns. A strong advocate of vigorous congregational singing, he urged that hymn singing should be "more fervent and joyous. We are too distant and reserved in our praises; we sing, not as we should sing to Him who is Chief among ten thousand, the Altogether Lovely."

Fight the good fight with all thy might (406)
Light of the world, we hail Thee (454)

Montgomery, James (b. Irvine, Ayrshire, Scot., Nov. 4, 1771; d. Sheffield, Eng., Apr. 30, 1854), was the son of John Montgomery, who was for many years the only Moravian minister in Scotland. His parents left him at the Moravian settlement at Bracehill near Ballymena, County Antrim, Ireland, when they went to Barbados Island as missionaries and died there. Educated at Fulneck Seminary, Yorkshire, he intended to study for the ministry. However, the school authorities were dissatisfied with his scholastic record and apprenticed him to a baker. He ran away in 1787 and eventually settled in Sheffield in 1792, gaining employment with a Mr. Gales, owner and publisher of the *Sheffield Register.*

Because of political opposition caused by his editorials, Gales left the country in 1794 to avoid prosecution and certain imprisonment. Montgomery took over the newspaper, changed its name to the *Sheffield Iris,* and served as editor for thirty-one years. During this time he was twice imprisoned for expressing his opinions in his newspaper, once for printing a song to celebrate the fall of the Bastille, and again for his account of a riot in Sheffield. He was a public-spirited man and a champion of humanitarian causes. His was a strong voice for the abolition of slavery, and equally strong was his support of foreign missions and the British Bible Society.

In 1814 he became a member of the Wesleyan Society in Sheffield. However, a few years later he became involved in the controversy over the hymnal compiled by Thomas Cotterill, vicar of St. Paul's Church, Sheffield, which finally gained approval in 1820, and won acceptance for hymn singing in the Church of England. His support of Cotterill was of great significance and it increased his own interest in hymnody. Later in life he became a communicant member of St. George's Church, Sheffield, where William Mercer (*q.v.*) was vicar. He wrote about 360 hymns, which appeared in his *Songs of Zion* (1822); *The Christian Psalmist* (1825); and *Original Hymns for Public, Private, and Social Devotion,* (1853). (Cf. *The Hymn,* V, No. 3, 73).

> Angels, from the realms of glory (76)
> Be known to us in breaking bread (398)
> Go to dark Gethsemane (105)
> In the hour of trial (317)
> Prayer is the soul's sincere desire (336)
> Stand up, and bless the Lord (16)
> The Lord is my Shepherd, no want shall I know (57)

Moore, George D., was an itinerant evangelist who was active in New Jersey and Pennsylvania in the latter part of the nineteenth century. No other information has been found concerning this composer.

HAVEN OF REST—My soul in sad exile was out on life's sea (228)

Moore, James Cleveland (b. Draketown, Paulding Co., Ga., May 2, 1888; d. Ashburn, Ga., June 1, 1962), the son of Charles Robert and Mary Ellen (Hesterley) Moore, was educated at Draketown Baptist Institute, Mercer University, and the University of Florida. He received his musical training under B. B. Beall and J. Henry Showalter. He was ordained to the Baptist ministry and was pastor at Funstron, Alma, Moultree, Glenwood, Willacoochee, and Abbeville, Georgia, and also Hawthorne, Florida. He served for two years as president of the Georgia-Florida-Alabama Tri-State Singing Convention, and also was president of the Southern Singers' Association of Georgia. Throughout the years he engaged in writing songs, and estimated that he had written more than five hundred. Perhaps the most widely known of his songs is "Where We'll Never Grow Old." His son, James C. Moore, Jr., is a Baptist minister in Georgia.

Thou, O Christ of Calvary—MOORE (189)

Moore, Thomas (b. Dublin, Ire., May 28, 1779; d. Sloperton, Devizes, Eng., Feb. 25, 1852), was educated at Trinity College, Dublin, and studied law at the Middle Temple, London. In 1804 he went to Bermuda as registrar to the Admiralty Court. Finding this position extremely monotonous, he appointed a deputy and returned to England. Later the deputy's embezzling of funds caused him financial ruin and forced him into temporary exile on the Continent. He returned to England in 1822, after the indebtedness had been repaid. His prolific literary writings and his social graces made him a popular favorite in London. He was a member of the Roman Catholic Church.

Come, ye disconsolate, where'er ye languish (297)

Moore, William. No biographical information has been found regarding this composer. He compiled *The Columbian Harmony*, which was registered in the District of West Tennessee on April 2, 1825, and was printed in Cincinnati by Morgan, Lodge, and Fisher for the compiler. The book contains seventeen pages of introductory material—rudiments, instructions, observations, and so on—and one hundred eighty pages of music. On the final page of the introductory material appears the line, "William Moore, West Tennessee, Wilson County, March, 1825." The compiler claimed authorship of eighteen tunes, at least three of which, HOLY MANNA, SWEET RIVERS, and CONVERTED THIEF, were widely adopted by subsequent compilers in the South. Two of his tunes, WILSON and LEBANON, bear names of his home county and its county seat town.

HOLY MANNA—Brethren, we have met to worship (368)

Morris, Lelia Naylor (Mrs. Charles H.) (b. Pennsville, Morgan County, Ohio, Apr. 15, 1862; d. Auburn, Ohio, July 23, 1929), shortly after her father's return from the Civil War in 1866, moved to Malta,

Ohio, just across the Muskingum River from McConnelsville. Upon the death of her father, she, her mother, and one of her sisters opened a small millinery shop in McConnelsville. With her family, she had been a member of the Methodist Protestant Church, but following her marriage to Charles H. Morris in 1881 she joined the Methodist Episcopal Church with her husband and was active in every phase of church life.

In the 1890's she began writing songs—both words and music. In these early efforts she was greatly encouraged and assisted by Dr. H. L. Gilmour (*q.v.*), whom she first met at the camp meeting at Mountain Lake Park, Maryland. She was a frequent attendant at various summer camp meetings—Old Camp Sychar, Mt. Vernon, Ohio, Sebring Camp, Sebring, Ohio, and others. In 1913 her eyesight began to fail, and to help her continue her song writing, her son erected a large blackboard twenty-eight feet long with music staff lines on it. Within a year her sight was gone, but she continued to write music with the help of devoted friends. A year before her death she and her husband moved to Auburn, Ohio, to live with their daughter, Mrs. W. R. Lunk.

> If you are tired of the load of your sin—McConnelsville (230)
> Jesus is coming to earth again—Second Coming (125)
> Nearer, still nearer, close to Thy heart—Morris (281)

Mote, Edward (b. London, Eng., Jan. 21, 1797; d. Southwark, Eng., Nov. 13, 1874). Mote's parents kept a public house, and as a youth he was apprenticed to a cabinetmaker. In 1813 he was greatly influenced by the preaching of John Hyatt of Tottenham Court Road Chapel. He later settled at Southwark, a suburb of London, where he became a successful cabinetmaker and was a devoted churchman.

Mote wrote more than one hundred hymns, and these were included in his *Hymns of Praise, A New Selection of Gospel Hymns, Combining All the Excellencies of Our Spiritual Poets, with many Originals* (London, 1836). Of unusual interest in the fact that here marks the first use of the term "gospel hymn." Theologically he was a Calvinist, and his collection of hymns was largely an anthology of Calvinistic praise. In 1852 he became pastor of the Baptist church at Horsham, Sussex, where he ministered for twenty-one years. Because the building in which this church worshiped was secured largely through his efforts, the church members, out of gratitude to him, offered to give him the deed to the property. He refused the gift, saying. "I do not want the chapel, I only want the pulpit; and when I cease to preach Christ, then turn me out of that." Because of failing health he resigned in 1873, and died the following year. He was buried in the churchyard.

> My hope is built on nothing less (283)

Moultrie, Gerard (b. Rugby, Eng., Sept. 16, 1829; d. Southleigh, Eng., Apr. 25, 1885), was the son of an Anglican minister, Rev. John Moultrie. According to Haeussler, his great-grandfather Moultrie went back to England from South Carolina after the outbreak of the Revolutionary War. Fort Moultrie at Charleston, South Carolina, was named for General William Moutlrie, a great-granduncle, who was elected governor of South Carolina in 1785. He was educated at Rugby and Exeter College, Oxford (B.A., 1851; M.A., 1856), and became assistant master and chaplain of Shrewsbury School, 1852-55. After various chaplaincies he became vicar of Southleigh in 1869 and warden of St. James' College, 1873, where he remained until his death. He is the author of much religious verse, and numerous hymns, including translations from the Greek, Latin, and German. Among his publications are *Hymns and Lyrics for the Seasons and Saints' Days of the Church* (1867) and *Cantica Sanctorum* (1880).

Let all mortal flesh keep silence (tr.) (80)

Mountain, James (b. Leeds, Yorkshire, Eng., 1844; d. Tunbridge Wells, Kent, Eng., June 27, 1933), after attending Gainford Academy near Darlington, was educated for the ministry of the Countess of Huntingdon's Connexion at Rotherham College, Nottingham Institute, and Cheshunt College. He was ordained and became pastor of Great Marlow in Buckinghamshire. Because of a breakdown in health, he resigned and spent some time on the Continent, studying at the universities of Heidelberg and Tübingen. He was greatly influenced by the visit of Moody and Sankey in the early 1870's, and his *Hymns of Consecration and Faith* (London, 1876), reflect the impact of Sankey's music. He conducted missions throughout the United Kingdom, 1874-82, and made an evangelistic world tour, 1882-89. After serving as pastor of the Countess of Huntingdon's church at Tunbridge Wells, 1889-97, he changed his views regarding baptism, resigned his pastorate, and became a Baptist. Remaining at Tunbridge Wells, he founded St. John's Free Church, serving as pastor until his retirement. He was well known as a writer of books and a contributor to religious periodicals. While he wrote a number of hymns, he is perhaps far better known for his tunes. *The Keswick Hymn-Book* (London, *ca.* 1940), contains fourteen of his tunes, while the *Baptist Hymn Book* (London, 1962) includes only one.

WYE VALLEY—Like a river glorious (294)

Mozart, Wolfgang Amadeus (b. Salzburg, Aust., Jan. 27, 1756; d. Vienna, Aust., Dec. 5, 1791), as a child revealed extraordinary musical talent. By the age of four he was playing the harpsichord and clavier with amazing skill, and composing pieces at age five. His sister, Maria Anna, was almost equally talented. In 1762 his father, Leopold Mozart, official musician of the archbishop of Salzburg, took the two children on an extended tour of the principal cities of Europe, and also London, where they continued their music studies and gave public concerts.

The ensuing years found him engaged in performances and the production of fantastic compositions. The details of these years and the listing of his works are easily available and need not be given here. In later years he became interested in Freemasonry and joined this order, although he did not renounce the Roman Catholic Church to which he belonged. In 1782 he was married to Constanze Weber, a cousin of Carl Maria von Weber (*q.v.*). Poor management of the meager income he received resulted in poverty and hardship. Prolonged overwork undermined his health and his premature death came at the age of thirty-six. He left some six hundred musical compositions covering every area of musical performance. A number of hymn tunes have been arranged by adapting melodies from his works, and while the tune given here usually appears with his name, its source has never been traced.

ELLESDIE—Jesus, I my cross have taken (387)
Hark, the voice of Jesus calling (440)

Murray, James Ramsey (b. Andover, Mass., Mar. 17, 1841; d. Cincinnati, Ohio, Mar. 10, 1905). Murray's parents, Walter and Christine (Morrison) Murray, arrived in America from Scotland the year before his birth. After his early musical training, he studied under Mason, Root, Bradbury, and Webb, and the Musical Institute, North Reading, Massachusetts, 1856-59. After serving in the Union Army during the Civil War, he was employed by Root & Cady of Chicago, and served as editor of *The Song Messenger,* a monthly periodical published by this firm. When the Chicago fire of 1871 destroyed Root & Cady, he returned to Andover and taught music for several years. In 1881 he became associated with the John Church Company of Cincinnati as head of the publishing department and editor of *The Musical Visitor*, this firm's monthly periodical, and remained in this position until his death. He composed a large number of Sunday school songs, gospel songs, and anthems. Among the most popular of the numerous collections which he edited are: *The Prize, Royal Gems, Pure Diamonds* (1872), and *Murray's Sacred Songs.*

MUELLER—Away in a manger, no crib for a bed (77)

Murray, Robert (b. Earltown, near Truro, N.S., Dec. 25, 1832; d. Halifax, N.S., Dec. 10, 1910), was educated at Free College, Halifax, and was ordained to the Presbyterian ministry. He became one of the most influential ministers of the Presbyterian church in Canada in the Maritime Provinces. Because of his literary skill, he was appointed editor of the *Presbyterian Witness*, and for more than fifty years served in this position. He wrote a number of hymns, some of which first appeared anonymously in the columns of his periodical.

From ocean unto ocean (450)

Nägeli, Johann (Hans) Georg (b. Wetzikon, near Zürich, Switz., May 26, 1773; d. Wetzikon, Dec. 26, 1836), established a music publishing firm in Wetzikon in 1792, and was the founder and president of the Swiss Association for the Cultivation of Music. A pioneer music educator, he applied the principles of the Pestalozzian system to music instruction, and through this activity he influenced Lowell Mason, who used his methods in the United States. Nägeli published *Gesangsbildungslehre nach Pestalozzischen Grundsätzen* (1810).

DENNIS—Blest be the tie that binds (366)

Nares, James (b. Stanwell, Middlesex, Eng., 1715; d. London, Eng., Feb. 10, 1783). It is not known why John Wesley credited the tune named below to this English composer and organist in his *Foundery Collection* (1742). (See discussion of tune.)

AMSTERDAM—Rise, my soul, and stretch thy wings (122)

Neale, John Mason (b. London, Eng., Jan. 24, 1818; d. East Grinstead, Sussex, Eng., Aug. 6, 1866), was educated at Trinity College, Cambridge, and ordained in the Anglican church. Through the influence of the Oxford Movement, he became a High Churchman, and because of his spirit of independence regarding his belief and religious exercises, he was in disfavor with ecclesiastical authorities. In 1846 he was appointed warden of Sackville College, East Grinstead, a home for indigent old men. In this position he became merely a caretaker, for the Bishop of Chichester forbad his administering in the religious services, and this restriction remained in effect from 1847 until 1863, three years before his death. He received no honors or recognition from his own country, and his D.D. degree was granted him by the University of Hartford, Connecticut. A scholarly student of the liturgies and practices of the early church, he was one of the first to translate ancient Latin and Greek hymns. His strong attachment to the old Breviary hymns caused him to urge the omission of the Protestant hymns from the Anglican service in favor of the translations of medieval hymns. Among his principal collections which contain his original hymns and translations are: *Mediaeval Hymns and Sequences* (1851); *The Hymnal Noted* (1851); *Hymns of the Eastern Church* (1862); and *Original Sequences, Hymns and other Ecclesiastical Verses* (1866).

All glory, laud and honor (tr.) (151)
Art thou weary, heavy laden (245)
Come, ye faithful, raise the strain (tr.) (109)
Good Christian men, rejoice (tr.) (74)
Jerusalem, the golden (tr.) (477)
The day of resurrection (tr.) (111)

Neander, Joachim (b. Bremen, Ger., 1650; d. Bremen, May 31, 1680), the eldest child of Johann Joachim and Catharina (Knipping) Neander, was educated at the Pädagogium at Bremen, where his father was a teacher, and at the Academic Gymnasium. He became engulfed in the rebellious, riotous student atmosphere and, when he was twenty, joined a group of students to attend a service at St. Martin's Church, Bremen, to criticise and scoff. The forceful preaching of the pastor, Theodore Under-Eyck, greatly impressed him, and subsequent conversations with Under-Eyck led to his conversion. After tutoring at Frankfurt-am-Main and at Heidelburg, in 1674 he was appointed rector of the Latin School at Düsseldorf, a school operated by the German Reformed (Calvinistic) Church. He had come under the influence of the Pietists and was a close friend of their leader, Jakob Spener. His association with the Pietists and his activities in their behalf aroused strong opposition and he was suspended from the school. He lived for some months in a cave near Mettman on the Rhine, which is still known as "Neander's Cave." In 1679 he returned to Bremen and became assistant preacher at St. Martin's Church. He died of consumption the following year at the age of thirty. He wrote about sixty hymns for which he also provided the tunes. These were first circulated privately among his friends in Düsseldorf, and were first published in *A und Ω Joachimi Neandri Glaub-und Liebesübung* (1680). He is regarded as the outstanding hymn writer of the German Reformed Church, and has been called the "Paul Gerhardt of the Calvinists."

Praise to the Lord, the Almighty, the King of creation (6)

Needham, John (d. *ca.* 1787), was the son of John Needham, pastor of the Baptist church, Hitchin, Hertfordshire. Nothing is known of his early life, but it is supposed that he entered the ministry under his father's association. In 1746 he moved to Bristol and was associated with John Beddome in the pastorate of the Baptist church in the Pithay, Bristol. He was ordained in 1750 and became copastor of the church. Upon Beddome's retirement two years later, a Mr. Tommas was invited to be copastor with Needham. Tommas accepted on the condition that he be the pastor and Needham the assistant. An unhappy controversy arose, and in the end the majority of the congregation passed a resolution stating that Needham was no longer either a minister or a member of the church. From November, 1752 to June, 1755 Needham and his friends used the meetinghouse of a Baptist congregation in Callowhill Street, in another section of Bristol. After almost three years of meetings at different hours on each Lord's Day, the two congregations united, and the two pastors became copastors. It is known that this arrangement continued until 1784, but beyond this the history of the church is almost a blank. It is known that by 1787 both pastors had died, and the Callowhill church became extinct. Needham wrote two hundred sixty-three hymns and these were published in his *Hymns, Devotional and Moral, on Various Subjects, etc.* (Bristol, 1768).

Awake, my tongue, thy tribute bring (24)

Neumeister, Erdmann (b. Uchteritz, Ger., May 12, 1671; d. Hamburg, Ger., Aug. 18, 1756), the son of Johann Neumeister, schoolmaster and organist, was educated at the University of Leipzig (M.A., 1695). In 1698 he became pastor at Bibra, and assistant superintendent of the Eckartsberg District. In 1704 he became tutor to Duke Johann Georg's daughter, and assistant court preacher, at Weissenfels, and two years later moved to Sorau as senior court preacher. In 1715 he became pastor of St. James's Church in Hamburg, where he remained until his death. Neumeister was well known as an eloquent preacher, and an ardent champion of the older, conservative Lutheranism. He was outspoken in the pulpit and press against the influences of the Pietists and Moravians, as he sought to "preserve the simplicity of faith from the subjective novelties of this period." In addition to his fame as the author of about six hundred fifty hymns, he is recognized as the originator of the church cantata. About 1700 he began publishing annual sets of cantata texts, largely poetic paraphrases of Scripture appropriate for the various feasts of the church year. J. S. Bach and other composers quickly sized upon these timely and popular texts. He published *Der Zugang zum Gnadenstuhle Jesu Christo* (Weissenfels, 1705) and *Evangelischer Nachklang* (Hamburg, 1718). *Fünffache Kirchen-Andachten* (Leipzig, 1716) was a collected edition of his cantata texts.

Sinners Jesus will receive (195)

Newell, William Reed (b. Savannah, Ohio, May 22, 1868; d. De-Land, Fla., Apr. 1, 1956), was educated at Wooster College (A.B., 1891), and attended Princeton and Oberlin Seminaries. After holding several pastorates, he went to Chicago in 1895 as pastor of Bethesda Congregational Church, and later the same year he became assistant superintendent of the Moody Bible Institute. At the suggestion of Dwight L. Moody, the evangelist, he conducted interdenominational Bible classes in Chicago, Detroit, Toronto, and St. Louis. The success of these classes led him to extensive writing, and his published works included expositions on the books of Romans, Hebrews, and Revelation, and Old Testament studies. At the time of his retirement he moved to DeLand, Florida.

Years I spent in vanity and pride (96)

Newhall, Charles Stedman (b. Boston, Mass., Oct. 4, 1842; d. Berkley, Calif., Apr. 11, 1935), was educated at Amherst College and at Union Theological Seminary. Ordained to the Congregational ministry, he served as a pastor for more than twenty-five years. In 1898 he became associated with the United States Forestry Service in California, and became recognized as an outstanding naturalist. Following his retirement in 1905 he made his home in Berkeley until his death.

O Jesus, Master, when today (466)

Newman, John Henry (b. London, Eng., Feb. 21, 1801; d. Edgbaston, near Birmingham, Eng., Aug. 11, 1890), the eldest son of a prosperous London banker, was educated at Great Ealing, a private school, and at Trinity College, Oxford. Ordained in 1824, he became a curate of St. Clement's Church, Oxford, and served as vicar of St. Mary's Church, Oxford, 1828-43. At first he was an intense evangelical, but became an ardent leader of the Oxford Movement and contributed many tracts issued by this group. During 1832-33 he traveled abroad, and most of his hymns, including "Lead, kindly light," were written during this time. Tract 90, which he wrote in 1841, was repudiated by Anglican church leaders, and two years later he resigned his post at Oxford. In 1845 he became a Roman Catholic, and was ordained a priest at Rome the following year. From 1847 to 1852 he was the principal of the Oratory of St. Philip Neri, which he founded at Edgbaston, near Birmingham. He became rector of the newly organized Dublin Catholic University in 1854, and four years later returned to Edgbaston. In 1879 he was made a cardinal in the Roman Church. (Cf. *The Hymn*, II, No. 1, 5.)

Lead, kindly Light, amid th'encircling gloom (60)

Newton, John (b. London, Eng., July 24, 1725; d. London, Dec. 21, 1807). Newton's mother, who died when he was seven, was a devout Christian; but his father, a sea captain, did not share her religious interests. He went to sea with his father when he was eleven, and later served in the Royal Navy on a British man-of-war. He joined the crew of a slave-trading ship, where he was cruelly treated by the captain. The turning point in his Christian experience came through his reading of Thomas a Kempis' *The Imitation of Christ,* and his experience of a stormy night in 1748 on a waterlogged ship, when he faced iminent death. He remained a slave-trader and became captain of his own ship. Throughout his early turbulent life the memory of his mother and his love for Mary Catlett, who later became his wife, served as restraining influences. In 1854 he left the sea and became tide surveyor in Liverpool, where he came under the influence of Whitefield and Wesley, and by 1758 had begun to preach. He was ordained in the Church of England and was appointed curate of Olney, Buckinghamshire, in 1764. William Cowper (*q.v.*), came to Olney in 1767, and together they published *Olney Hymns* (1779), to which Newton contributed 280 texts. In 1780 he became vicar at St. Mary Woolnoth, London, and continued to preach until after his eightieth year. In his last years a servant would stand by his side in the pulpit and help him find the headings in his manuscript. When he was no longer able to read and was advised to give up preaching, he replied, "What, shall the old African blasphemer stop while he can speak!" He was buried in the churchyard, and the gravestone bears the epitaph which he himself wrote:

> John Newton, Clerk
> Once an infidel and libertine,
> A servant of slaves in Africa:
> Was by the rich mercy of our Lord and Saviour, Jesus Christ,
> Preserved, restored, pardoned,
> And appointed to preach the Faith
> He had laboured long to destroy.
> Near sixteen years at Olney in Bucks;
> And twenty-seven years in this church.

Amazing grace! how sweet the sound (188)
Glorious things of thee are spoken (381)
How sweet the name of Jesus sounds (160)
How tedious and tasteless the hours (306)
May the grace of Christ our Saviour (538, 540)
Safely through another week (37)

Nichol, Henry Ernest (b. Hull, Eng., Dec. 10, 1862; d. Hull, 1928), abandoned his intended career as a civil engineer to study music and received his Bachelor of Music degree from Oxford University in 1888. He wrote a large number of tunes, mainly for Sunday school anniversary services. He used the pseudonym, "Colin Sterne," a rearrangement of the letters in his name, in signing those hymn texts for which he wrote the music.

We've a story to tell to the nations—MESSAGE (455)

Nicholson, James (b. Ireland, *ca.* 1828; d. Washington, D.C., Nov. 6, 1876). Nothing is known of Nicholson's early years in Ireland. He came to the United States in the early 1850's, settled in Philadelphia, where he lived for almost twenty years, and was an active member of the Wharton Street Methodist Episcopal Church. About 1871 he moved to Washington, D.C., where he worked as a clerk in the Post Office Department. In his spare time he remained active in religious work, teaching Sunday school classes, leading singing, and assisting in evangelistic endeavors. His death occurred at Washington and he was buried at Philadelphia.

Lord Jesus, I long to be perfectly whole (201)

Norris, John Samuel (b. West Cowes, Isle of Wight, Eng., Dec. 4, 1844; d. Chicago, Ill., Sept. 23, 1907), the son of John and Harriet (Chalk) Norris, was educated in Canada, and ordained to the Methodist ministry in Oshawa, Canada, 1868. For ten years he served Methodist churches in Canada, New York, and Wisconsin. In 1878 he became a Congregationalist and for five years held pastorates in Wisconsin at Mondovi, Hixton, Grand Rapids, and Shullsburg. From 1882 to 1901 he pastored in Iowa at Ames, Webster City, Parkersburg, Peterson, Tripoli, and served for a while as state evangelist. He moved to Chicago in 1901, where he remained until his death. He was married in 1870 to Elizabeth Ann Hurd in Sunderland, Canada, and seven children were born to this home. Of the more than one hundred hymns which he wrote, only the one given here remains in common usage. He published one collection, *Songs of the Soul.*

NORRIS—I can hear my Saviour calling (361)

North, Frank Mason (b. New York, N.Y., Dec. 3, 1850; d. Madison, N.J., Dec. 17, 1935), was educated at Wesleyan University, Connecticut (A.B., 1872; M.A., 1875). He was ordained to the ministry of the Methodist Episcopal Church in 1872, and for twenty years served churches in Florida, New York, and Connecticut. From 1892 to 1912 he served as editor of *The Christian City* and as corresponding secretary of the New York Church Extension and Missionary Society of the Methodist Episcopal Church. In 1912 he became corresponding secretary of the Board of Foreign Missions. He was president of the Federal Council of Churches of Christ in America, 1916-1920. He wrote about twelve hymns, most of them for special occasions. (Cf. *The Hymn,* I, No. 3, 5.)

Where cross the crowded ways of life (464)

Nusbaum, Cyrus Silvester (b. Middlebury, Ind., July 27, 1861; d. Wichita, Kan., Dec. 27, 1937), after completing high school in Middlebury, Indiana, began teaching school in Marion County, Kansas, in 1885. The following year he was ordained to the Methodist ministry, and for nine years pastored churches in Douglass, Goddard, Wichita, and Kingman, Kansas. After serving as educational secretary of Southwestern College, Winfield, Kansas, 1895-97, he was pastor at Ottawa, Kansas, 1897-1903; presiding elder of the Independent District, 1903-7; and pastor at Parsons, Kansas, 1908-14, and was appointed conference evangelist in 1914. During World War I, he was appointed by President Woodrow Wilson as an inspector of the American Red Cross in France, and held the rank of captain in the U.S. Army.

Following the war he lectured on the Redpath Lyceum circuit, and traveled throughout the United States. He enjoyed the reputation of being an eloquent and convincing speaker, and was best known as an evangelist, conducting meetings throughout Kansas, Nebraska, Oklahoma, and Texas. He was awarded the D.D. degree by Southwestern College. He was married in 1886 to Harriett E. Erwin, and two children, Bertha E. and Mark E., were born to this home. The latter part of his life he spent with the smaller churches in Kansas, and was serving as supply preacher at Lost Springs and Antelope at the time of his last illness. He was buried at Kingman, Kansas. He wrote both words and music for a number of hymns, but only the one given here survives in common usage.

Would you live for Jesus, and be always pure and good—NUSBAUM (239)

Oakeley, Frederick (b. Shrewsbury, Eng., Sept. 5, 1802; d. London, Eng., Jan. 29, 1880), was educated at Christ's Church, Oxford, and was made a fellow of Balliol in 1827. He took an active part in the Oxford Movement. He was ordained in 1826, and after several appointments was made the incumbent of Margaret Chapel, London, 1839. During this time, in collaboration with his organist, Richard Redhead (*q.v.*), he sought to reform the church services and published several collections for this purpose. As one of the Tractarian authors he published several pamphlets supporting Roman Catholic doctrine which caused great controversy and led to his resignation from the Church of England in 1845.

He then joined the Roman Catholic Church, and in 1852 was made a canon of Westminster Procathedral.

O come, all ye faithful, joyful and triumphant (tr.) (66)

Oatman, Johnson, Jr. (b. near Medford, N.J., Apr. 21, 1856; d. Norman, Okla., Sept. 25, 1922), the son of Johnson and Rachel Ann (Cline) Oatman, was educated at Herbert's Academy, Vincentown, New Jersey, and the New Jersey Collegiate Institute, Bordentown. At the age of nineteen he joined the Methodist Episcopal Church and was ordained to the ministry, but he remained a local preacher without a pastoral assignment. He was associated with his father in the mercantile business and after his father's death established an insurance business at Mount Holly, New Jersey. Beginning about 1892, he wrote many sacred poems which proved highly successful as texts for gospel songs. His poetical talents were in great demand by such composers as John R. Sweney, William J. Kirkpatrick, Charles H. Gabriel, and E. O. Excell.

I am so happy in Christ today (194)
I'm pressing on the upward way (319)
When upon life's billows you are tempest tossed (318)

Ogden, William Augustine (b. Franklin Co., Ohio, Oct. 10, 1841; d. Toledo, Ohio, Oct. 14, 1897), received his early musical training in community singing schools. During the Civil War, he served in the 30th Indiana Volunteer Infantry for four years. He resumed his music education after the war, studying under Lowell Mason, Thomas Hastings, E. E. Bailey, and B. F. Baker. He became widely known as a teacher of normal music schools, and a conductor of musical conventions. He wrote many tunes and published a large number of Sunday school collections. In 1887 he was appointed supervisor of music for the public schools of Toledo, Ohio, a position he held until his death.

'Tis the grandest theme through the ages rung—DELIVERANCE (198)
SHEPHERD—Hark! 'tis the Shepherd's voice I hear (429)

O'Kane, Tullius Clinton (b. Fairfield Co., Ohio, Mar. 10, 1830; d. Delaware, Ohio, Feb. 10, 1912), was educated at Ohio Wesleyan University (A.B., 1852; A.M., 1855). After he served as tutor in mathematics at Ohio Wesleyan University, he became a public school principal in Cincinnati in 1857. In 1864 he became associated with the piano firm of Philip Phillips & Company, where he remained for three years. In 1867 he moved to Delaware, Ohio, and for the following six years traveled the state of Ohio as a representative of the Smith American Organ Company of Boston. During this time he became a regular attendant at the state and county Sunday school conventions and began publishing his Sunday school collections. Among these publications were *Fresh Leaves* (1868), *Dew Drops of Sacred Song, Songs of Worship* (1873), and *Jasper and Gold* (1877). He assisted with the compilation of *Joy to the World* (1878; with McCabe and Sweney); and *Songs of Redeeming Love No. 1* (1882) and *No. 2* (1887; with McCabe, Sweney, and Kirkpatrick). Of his many tunes, only the two given here remain in popular usage.

HOME OVER THERE—O think of the home over there (480)
O'KANE—On Jordan's stormy banks I stand (478)

Oliver, Henry Kemble (b. Beverly, Mass., Nov. 24, 1800; d. Salem, Mass., Aug. 12, 1885), was educated at the Boston Latin School and at Phillips Andover Academy, spent two years at Harvard, and graduated from Dartmouth in 1818. He served as church organist for thirty-six years and a schoolteacher for twenty-four. In addition to these activities, he was active in civic affairs, serving as mayor of both Salem and Lawrence, and also state treasurer of Massachusetts, 1861-65. He was awarded the honorary A.B. and M.A. degrees by Harvard in 1862, and the Mus.D. degree by Dartmouth in 1883. He wrote many hymn tunes, which were included in his *The National Lyre* (1848; with Tuckerman and Bancroft), *Oliver's Collection of Hymn and Psalm Tunes* (1860), and *Original Hymn Tunes* (1875).

FEDERAL STREET—My dear Redeemer and my Lord (83)

Olivers, Thomas (b. Tregynon, Montgomeryshire, Wales, 1725; d. London, Eng., Mar., 1799), left an orphan at the age of four, was reared on the farm of a distant relative. Apprenticed to a shoemaker at the age of eighteen, he was fired because of bad conduct. Olivers was converted by a sermon preached by George Whitefield at Bristol on the text, "Is not this a brand plucked from the burning?" For twenty-two years he served as an intinerant Methodist preacher, traveling throughout England and Ireland. Upon the separation of Whitefield and the Wesleys, Olivers remained with the Wesleys, and in 1775 became supervisor of all publications. However, he was discharged by John Wesley in 1789 and spent his retirement in London.

O Thou God of my salvation (164)

Owens, Priscilla Jane (b. Baltimore, Md., July 21, 1829; d. Baltimore, Dec. 5, 1907), was the daughter of Isaac and Jane (Stewart) Owens. Her entire life was spent in Baltimore, where she was a public schoolteacher for forty-nine years. She was a member of the Union Square

Methodist Episcopal Church, and was particularly interested in the work of the Sunday school. Her literary efforts, both prose and poetical, appeared in such religious periodicals as the *Methodist Protestant* and the *Christian Standard*.

We have heard the joyful sound (191)

Oxenham, John (b. Manchester, Eng., Nov. 12, 1852; d. London, Eng., Jan. 24, 1941). "John Oxenham" is the pseudonym of William Arthur Dunkerly. He was educated at Old Trafford School and Victoria University, Manchester. For several years he was engaged in business with his father, a wholesale merchant, and during this time he traveled in Europe and the United States. After two years in the United States, he returned to England and published the London edition of the *Detroit Free Press*. His early literary adventures, for which he used the pseudonym "John Oxenham," were so successful that he devoted his full time to his writing and adopted his pseudonym. He published more than forty novels and twenty other volumes in verse and prose. He was a devout Christian and an active churchman, serving as a deacon in the Ealing Congregational Church, where he taught a Bible class.

In Christ there is no East or West (443)

Palestrina, Giovanni Pierluigi da (b. Palestrina, It., 1525; d. Rome, It., Feb. 2, 1594), was the son of a well-to-do citizen of Palestrina, and after the custom of the day, he was called "da Palestrina," after his birthplace. Information concerning his early life and training is obscure. In 1544 he became organist and choirmaster in his native town, and seven years later accepted the position as master of the children at the Julian chapel in Rome. During the rest of his life he served in various positions in Roman churches and devoted much time to extensive composition. Among his works are about one hundred masses, two hundred motets, hymns, offertories, and other liturgical material, together with some secular music. His complete works, in thirty-three volumes, were published by Brietkopf & Härtel (1862-1903).

VICTORY—The strife is o'er, the battle done (107)
O Lord of love, Thou light divine (520)

Palmer, Horatio Richmond (b. Sherburne, N.Y., Apr. 26, 1834; d. Yonkers, N.Y., Nov. 15, 1907), after early music instruction from his father and his aunt, studied in New York, Berlin, and Florence. In 1857 he was head of the music department of Rushford Academy, New York, and served as organist and choir director in Rushford's Baptist church. After the Civil War, he settled in Chicago, where he edited a monthly musical journal, *The Concordia*, wrote books, and conducted festivals and conventions with great success. He organized the Church Choral Union of New York City, which gave massive concerts of sacred music. In one concert at Madison Square Garden he conducted four thousand singers. From 1877 to 1891 he was dean of the summer school of music at Chautauqua, N.Y. Among his more popular collections were *The Song Queen, The Song King, The Song Herald,* and *Concert Choruses.*

Yield not to temptation—PALMER (364)
VINCENT—Lord, for tomorrow and its needs (339)

Palmer, Ray (b. Little Compton, R.I., Nov. 12, 1808; d. Newark, N.J., Mar. 29, 1887), the son of Judge Thomas Palmer, was educated at Phillips Academy and Yale University. He was ordained to the Congregational ministry in 1835 and served as pastor at Bath, Maine (1835-50), and Albany, New York (1850-65). In 1865 he was appointed corresponding secretary of the American Congregational Union with headquarters in New York, where he remained until his retirement in 1878. He contributed fifteen hymns, original and translations from the Latin, to Park and Phelps' *The Sabbath Hymn-Book* (1858). He is the author of several volumes of religious verse and devotional essays, among which are *Spiritual Improvement* (1839); *Hymns and Sacred Pieces, with Miscellaneous Poems* (1865); *Hymns of My Holy Hours and Other Pieces* (1868); and his complete *Poetical Works* (1876).

Jesus, Thou joy of loving hearts (tr.) (136)
My faith looks up to Thee (257)

Park, John Edgar (b. Belfast, Ire., Mar. 7, 1879; d. Cambridge, Mass., Mar. 4, 1956), was educated at Queen's College, Belfast, Royal University, Dublin, Edinburgh, Leipzig, and Oxford Universities, and came to the United States to study at Princeton University. He was ordained to the Presbyterian ministry in 1902 and worked in the lumber camps of the Adirondacks. He then became a Congregational minister, and for nineteen years served as pastor of the Second Congregational Church, West Newton, Massachusetts. In 1926 he became president of Wheaton College, Norton, Massachusetts, where he remained until his retirement in 1944. He is the author of a number of hymns and several volumes of religious and devotional works.

We would see Jesus; lo! His star is shining (89)

Parker, Edwin Pond (b. Castine, Me., Jan. 13, 1836; d. Hartford, Conn., May 28, 1925), was educated at Bowdoin College and Bangor Theological Seminary. Ordained to the Congregational ministry, he became pastor of the Center Church, Hartford, Connecticut, where he remained for fifty years. Aside from his pastoral duties, his greatest interest was in hymnology. He wrote more than two hundred hymns, composed a number of original tunes and arrangements, and assisted with the compilation of several hymnals.

Come to Jesus, ye who labor (246)
Master, no offering, costly or sweet—LOVE'S OFFERING (401)
MERCY (arr.)—Holy Ghost, with light divine (170)

Parker, William Henry (b. New Basford, Nottingham, Eng., Mar. 4, 1845; d. Nottingham, 1929), as a youth was apprenticed in the machine construction department of a large lace-making plant in New Basford and remained with the same company for a number of years. Later he became the head of an insurance company. An active member of the Chelsea Street Baptist Church, Nottingham, he was greatly interested in Sunday school work and most of his hymns were written for Sunday school anniversaries. The National Sunday School Union acquired his hymns, and fifteen appear in the *Sunday School Hymnary* (1905).

Tell me the stories of Jesus (505)

Parry, Joseph (b. Merthyr Tydfile, Wales, May 21, 1841; d. Cartref, Penarth, Wales, Feb. 17, 1903), was born into a poor family. Before he was ten years old, he was working in the puddling furnaces smelting iron ore. In 1854 the family moved to Danville, Pennsylvania, and he had his first music training in classes conducted by the Welsh workers in the ironworks. He attended the Normal Music School at Genesco, New York, in the summer of 1861. Returning to Wales, he competed successfully in several Eisteddfod contests, winning prizes at Swansea in 1863, at Llandudno in 1864, and at Chester in 1866. He studied at the Royal Academy of Music, 1868-71, where his teachers included William Sterndale Bennett and Charles Stegall. From Cambridge he received the B.Mus. degree in 1871 and the D.Mus. in 1878. He conducted a private music school in Danville, Pennsylvania, 1871-73 and then returned to Wales where he became professor of music at the Welsh University College at Aberystwyth, 1873-79. After teaching privately for nine years, first at Aberystwyth and later at Swansea, he taught at the University College, Cardiff, from 1888 until his death. At the National Eisteddfod of 1896 he was given an award of £600 in recognition of his great service to Welsh music. He wrote a considerable amount of music: three oratorios, light operas, eleven cantatas, anthems, piano numbers, and more than four hundred hymn tunes.

ABERYSTWYTH—Jesus, lover of my soul (158)

Partridge, Sybil F. The only information the writer has found concerning this author is in an article entitled "The Catholic Author of a Protestant Hymn" by Frederick M. Steele in *The Continent* (Nov. 11, 1920), which describes an interview with the author, who had been identified previously as "S. M. X."

As a result of extensive correspondence, . . . I received an invitation to call upon S. M. X. in the convent of Notre Dame, on Mount Pleasant, Liverpool.

I found her a charming, sweet-faced nun of the Roman Catholic faith who had given her life to teaching in that ancient school for girls. She was perhaps 60 years of age, small of stature, most gracious in demeanor, of attractive personality and withal most unassuming and retiring.

I told her I had come to pay my respects to the author of "Lord, for tomorrow and its needs," and to tell her how much we thought of it in America. She modestly disclaimed what she assumed to be praise, and said she knew little of the world outside of her four walls, and did not know that her little fugitive had traveled so far. I told her I was a Presbyterian living in Chicago, and that we Americans loved her hymn, and wanted to know of its author and her real name. . . .

Finally, the nun answered my original query directly, "Yes, I'll give you my name. It is Sybil F. Partridge. But it would be my preference that the great world outside should not know it till after I am gone." She had a hectic cough, and I learn she recently has passed away, so I am at liberty now to tell the story.

. . . [She] was good enough to give to me, in her own handwriting, the full poem of nearly a dozen stanzas, to which as an addendum, she appended the verse following, written for me in remembrance of the visit I am describing.

> Since "Today" gave to me in you a friend,
> Unknown, unseen for long, so to the end
> I pray you let me, too, that title borrow;
> And keep, I pray you, in your mindful prayer
> The name which you discovered with such care—
> Till we shall see and know, in God's tomorrow!
>
> S. M. X.

Lord, for tomorrow and its needs (339)

Peace, Albert Lister (b. Huddersfield, Eng., Jan. 26, 1844; d. Liverpool, Eng., Mar. 14, 1912), was a child prodigy in music and at the age of nine became organist at the parish church at Holmfirth, Yorkshire. He was educated at Oxford University (B.Mus., 1870; D.Mus., 1875). In 1879 he became organist at the Glasgow Cathedral and in 1897 succeeded W. T. Best as organist at St. George's Hall, Liverpool, where he remained until his death. He was one of the most prominent of Scottish organists, and after the ban on organs in the churches was removed by the Church of Scotland in 1865, he enjoyed tremendous popularity as a recitalist, playing opening services for new organs. In addition to composing cantatas, service music, organ pieces, and hymn tunes, he edited several collections for the Church of Scotland: *The Scottish Hymnal* (1885), *Psalms and Paraphrases with Tunes* (1886), *The Psalter with Chants* (1888), and *The Scottish Anthem Book* (1891).

ST. MARGARET—O Love that wilt not let me go (290)

Peek, Joseph Yates (b. Schenectady, N.Y., Feb. 27, 1843; d. Brooklyn, N.Y., Mar. 17, 1911), was a carpenter, farmer, and druggist's clerk prior to serving with the Union forces in the Civil War. From 1881 to 1904 he worked as a florist and achieved considerable fame in this occupation. In 1904 he became a Methodist lay preacher and his engagements took him to Maine, Florida, and California. For many years he was a member of the Nostrand-DeKalb Methodist Episcopal Church, Brooklyn. His dream of becoming an ordained minister was realized in January 22, 1911, less than sixty days before his death. Although he had no formal musical training, he maintained a keen interest in music throughout his life, playing the violin, banjo, and piano. Biographical information concerning Peek was unknown until the late Reginal L. McAll, executive secretary of the Hymn Society of America, with the co-operation of Edgar M. Doughty of Brooklyn, uncovered these facts through careful research.

PEEK—I would be true, for there are those who trust me (315)

Perronet, Edward (b. Sundridge, Kent, Eng., 1726; d. Canterbury, Eng., Jan. 2, 1792), belonged to a family of Huguenot refugees who fled from Switzerland to England in 1680. His father, Vincent Perronet, was vicar of Shoreham, and was greatly esteemed by the Wesleys. Edward was an intimate friend of both Charles and John Wesley and was closely associated with them for a number of years. However, his poem, *The Mitre,* published in 1757, attacking the abuses of the Church, aroused Wesley's anger. His differences with Wesley over his right to administer the ordinances and his hostility toward the Church of England finally forced his separation from the Wesleys. He joined the Countess Huntingdon's connexion, but she also resented his violent attitude toward the Church of England, and he spent his last years as pastor of a small independent chapel at Canterbury. He published several hymns, but only the one given here survives.

All hail the power of Jesus' name (132, 133, 134)

Phelps, Sylvanus Dryden (b. Suffield, Conn., May 15, 1816; d. New Haven, Conn., Nov. 23, 1895), was educated at the Connecticut Literary

Institute, Brown University (A.B., 1844), and Yale Divinity School. He was ordained to the Baptist ministry and was pastor of the First Baptist Church, New Haven, Connecticut, 1846-74; and Jefferson Street Baptist Church, Providence, Rhode Island, 1874-76. He resigned the church in Providence to become editor of a religious journal, *The Christian Secretary*. Brown University awarded him the honorary D.D. degree in 1854. He published a number of books of both verse and prose, the most popular of which was his *Holy Land, with Glimpses of Europe and Egypt, a Year's Tour* (1862). His son, William Lyon Phelps, became famous as an author and professor of English at Yale University, and in his autobiography gives the following incident about his father.

In 1892 I was reading aloud the news to my father. My father was an orthodox Baptist minister; he was a good man and is now with God. I had never heard him mention a prize fight and did not suppose he knew anything on that subject, or cared anything about it. So when I came to the headline CORBETT DEFEATS SULLIVAN, I read that aloud and turned over the page. My father leaned forward and said earnestly, "Read it by rounds!"[1]

Saviour, Thy dying love (400)
This rite our blest Redeemer gave (384)

Pierpoint, Folliott Sanford (b. Bath, Eng., Oct. 7, 1835; d. Newport, Monmouthshire, Eng., Mar. 10, 1917), was educated at the Grammar School, Bath, and at Queen's College, Cambridge, where he was graduated in 1857. He was for some time classical master at Somersetshire College. After resigning this position, he lived at Babbicombe, Devonshire, and other places, doing occasional teaching. He wrote a number of hymns and published several volumes of verse.

For the beauty of the earth (153)

Plumptre, Edward Hayes (b. London, Eng., Aug. 6, 1821; d. Wells, Eng., Feb. 1, 1891), was educated at King's College, London, and University College, Oxford. He was ordained in 1846, and soon won fame as a scholar, theologian, and preacher. He served as chaplain of King's College, 1847-68; professor of pastoral theology, 1853-63; and professor of New Testament exegesis, 1864-81. His numerous literary works include the classics, history, theological, biblical criticism, biography, and poetry. He was a member of the Old Testament Company for the Revision of the Authorized Version of the Holy Scriptures. He became dean of Wells in 1881 and remained there until his death.

Rejoice, ye pure in heart (17)

[1] *Autobiography with Letters* (New York: Oxford University Press, 1939), p. 356.

Plunket, William Conyngham (b. Dublin, Ire., Aug. 26, 1828; d. Dublin, Apr. 1, 1897), was educated at Trinity College, Dublin, and took holy orders in the Church of Ireland in 1857. He was precentor of St. Patrick's Cathedral, Dublin, 1869-76, and was elected Bishop of Meath. In 1884 he was appointed to the Archdiocese of Dublin. The hymn given here seems to be his only contribution to hymnody.

Our Lord Christ hath risen (112)

Pollard, Adelaide Addison (b. Bloomfield, Iowa, Nov. 27, 1862; d. New York, N.Y., Dec. 20, 1934), was the daughter of James and Rebecca (Smith) Pollard, and her name was Sarah Addison Pollard. However, because of her dislike for the name Sarah, she adopted Adelaide. She attended the Denmark Academy, Denmark, Iowa, also a school in Valparaiso, Indiana, and then took a three years' course in elocution and physical culture at the Boston School of Oratory. She moved to Chicago and taught in several girls' schools for a number of years in the 1880's.

Through the influence of a friend, Lily L. Waller, Miss Pollard became interested in the evangelistic work of Alexander Dowie, assisting him in his healing services, and claimed that she herself was healed of diabetes in this manner. Later, she and Miss Waller went to New England and were associated with the evangelist, Sanford, who predicted the imminent return of Christ. She became greatly interested in becoming a missionary, and when her plans to go to Africa failed she spent eight years teaching at the Missionary Training School at Nyack-on-the-Hudson. Presumably this was prior to 1901, for the existing records of this school do not reveal her name after that date.

Prior to the outbreak of World War I Miss Pollard spent several months in Africa, and after hostilities began she was transferred to Scotland, where she remained during the war years. After the war she returned to New York and continued her religious work throughout New England. Always in frail health and strangely attracted to extreme religious sects and groups, she lived the life of a mystic. Her devout Presbyterian family had little contact with her except for infrequent visits home, usually to regain her strength. She wrote a number of hymns, but only the one given here remains in common usage.

Have Thine own way, Lord (355)

Poole, William Charles (b. Easton, Talbot Co., Md., Apr. 14, 1875; d. Lewes, Del., Dec. 24, 1949), the son of William Charles and Rachel (Leonard) Poole, grew up on the family farm, and was converted at the age of eleven. He was educated at Washington College, Chestertown, Maryland. In 1900 he was ordained in the Methodist ministry and served in the Wilmington Conference in various pastorates for thirty-five years. Largely through the inspiration of Charles H. Gabriel (*q.v.*) he began writing gospel song texts, and in addition to the present listing, his most widely-known songs are: "The Church by the Side of the Road" (1925) and "Sunrise" (1924).

Just when I need Him, Jesus is near (267)

Pott, Francis (b. Southwark, London, Eng., Dec. 29, 1832; d. Speldhurst, Kent, Eng., Oct. 26, 1909), was educated at Brasenose College, Oxford (B.A., 1854; M.A., 1857). Ordained in 1856, after several appointments he became rector of Northill, Bedfordshire, in 1866. Increasing deafness caused his resignation in 1891, and he retired to Speldhurst and devoted his energies to study and research. His keen interest in hymnology turned his attention to translating Latin and Syriac hymns. He was a member of the original committee for the preparation of *Hymns Ancient and Modern* (1861). He published *Hymns Fitted to the Order of Common Prayer* (1861) and *The Free Rhythm Psalter* (1898).

The strife is o'er, the battle done (tr.) (107)

Pounds, Jessie Brown (b. Hiram, Ohio, Aug. 31, 1861; d. 1921), at the age of fifteen, began to write regularly for religious periodicals. For more than thirty years she wrote religious poetry for James H. Fillmore (*q.v.*). In 1897 she was married to Rev. John E. Pounds, who was then pastor of the Central Christian Church, Indianapolis, Indiana. Among her published works are nine books, fifty cantata librettos, and more than four hundred gospel song texts. In addition to the two hymns given here, she is the author of "Anywhere with Jesus," "The Touch of His Hand on Mine," and "Beautiful Isle of Somewhere."

I know that my Redeemer liveth (127)
I must needs go home by the way of the cross (196)

Prentiss, Elizabeth Payson (b. Portland, Me., Oct. 26, 1818; d. Dorset, Vt., Aug. 13, 1878), after education in the public schools of Portland, taught school for a number of years. In 1845 she married George Lewis Prentiss, a Congregational minister, who later became professor of Homiletics and polity at Union Theological Seminary, New York, and from 1851 on they made their home in New York. At the age of sixteen she contributed the first of many articles to the *Youth's Companion*. Among her published works are: *Stepping Heavenward* (1869), *Religious Poems* (1873), and *Golden Hours, or Hymns and Songs of the Christian Life* (1874). Her *Life and Letters* was published shortly after her death.

More love to Thee, O Christ (292)

385

Prichard, Rowland Hugh (b. Graienyn, near Bala, North Wales, Jan. 14, 1811; d. Holywell, Wales, Jan. 25, 1887), a man of humble station, spent most of his life in Bala. At the age of sixty-nine he became a loom tender's assistant at the Welsh Flannel Manufacturing Company at Holywell. He was a well-known amateur musician and regularly led the singing in his church. HYFRYDOL, his most famous hymn tune, was written when he was about twenty years old. Other tunes which he composed were published in Welsh periodicals. In 1844 he published *Cyfailly Cantorion* (The Singer's Friend), a children's songbook made up largely of his own tunes.

HYFRYDOL—Praise the Lord! ye heavens, adore Him (9)

Prior, Charles Edwin (b. near Moosup, Conn., Jan. 27, 1856; d. Bridgeport, Conn., June 27, 1927), the son of Erastus L. and Sarah (Burleson) Prior, moved with his family to Jewett City, Connecticut, where he became an official in the Jewett City Savings Bank, and later held responsible positions in the Security Company of Hartford. In 1870 he became organist at the Congregational church of Jewett City, and in 1878 was organist and music director of the Baptist church. At Hartford he was an active member of the Baptist church, serving as president of the Baptist Union and music director at several of the annual assemblies of the Baptist Sunday School Union at Crescent Beach. In addition to writing a number of songs, he published several collections of Sunday school songs: *Spicy Breezes* (1883); *Sparkling and Bright* (with J. H. Tenney, 1890); and *Our Best Endeavor* (with W. A. Ogden, 1892).

It may not be on the mountain's height (425—stanzas 2 and 3)

Pruden, Edward Hughes (b. Chase City, Va., Aug. 30, 1903), was educated at the University of Richmond, Southern Baptist Theological Seminary (Th.M.), and the University of Edinburgh (Ph.D.). He has done further graduate study at Yale University and was given the honorary D.D. degree by the University of Richmond. Ordained to the Baptist ministry, he served as pastor of the First Baptist Church, Petersburg, Virginia, 1930-31, and since 1936 has been pastor of the First Baptist Church, Washington, D.C. His church is jointly affiliated with the American and Southern Baptist Conventions, and he has held positions of leadership in both conventions. In 1950 he was elected president of the American Baptist Convention. During 1935-36 he was guest professor of English at the University of Shanghai, China. In addition to numerous contributions to religious books and magazines,. he is the author of *Interpreters Needed* (1951).

O God of our fathers, we praise and adore Thee (500)

Psalmodia Evangelica, was a tune book compiled by Thomas Williams with the full title, *Psalmodia Evangelica: A Collection of Psalm and Hymn Tunes in Three Parts for Public Worship* (2 Vols.; London, 1789).

TRURO—Ride on! ride on in majesty (102)
Lift up your heads, ye mighty gates (247)

Quaile, Robert Newton (b. County Limerick, Ire., 1867; d. ?), the son of an Irish Methodist minister, was an amateur musician and was engaged in business at Mallow, County Cork. As a result of the political and economic difficulties in Ireland, all of his possessions were burned in 1920. He composed several tunes, three of which were included in the English *Methodist Sunday School Hymnal* (1910).

OLDBRIDGE—For all the blessings of the year (495)

Rankin, Jeremiah Eames (b. Thornton, N.H., Jan. 2, 1828; d. Cleveland, Ohio, Nov. 28, 1904), following education at Middlebury College and Andover Theological Seminary, was ordained to the Congregational ministry in 1855. He served pastorates in New York, Vermont, and Massachusetts before he became pastor of the First Congregational Church, Washington, D.C., in 1869. In 1884 he was called to the Valley Congregational Church, Orange, New Jersey, and five years later became president of Howard University, Washington, D.C., where he remained until his death. He compiled and edited a number of gospel songbooks, including the *Gospel Temperance Hymnal* (1878) and *Gospel Bells* (1883). He also published *German-English Lyrics, Sacred and Secular* (1897).

God be with you till we meet again (372)

Rawson, George (b. Leeds, Eng., June 5, 1807; d. Clifton, Eng., Mar. 25, 1889), was educated at Manchester and for many years maintained a legal practice in Leeds. He was a devoted Congregational layman, and in 1853 assisted a group of Congregational ministers in the compilation of *Psalms, Hymns, and Passages of Scripture for Christian Worship, the Congregational Collection,* commonly known as the *Leeds Hymn Book.* He also assisted in the compilation of *Psalms and Hymns for the Use of the Baptist Denomination* (1858). He was extremely modest about his own hymn writing and his early hymns were signed, "A Leeds Layman." He published *Hymns, Verses, and Chants* (1876), which contained eighty of his own hymns, and most of these were reprinted in his *Songs of Spiritual Thought* (1885). Following his retirement he made his home at Clifton where his death occurred.

Cast thy burden on the Lord (254)

Reed, Andrew (b. London, England, Nov. 27, 1787; d. Cambridge, Heath, Hackney, England, Feb. 25, 1862). Reed's father was a watchmaker and also a Congregational lay preacher. After learning his father's trade, he decided to become a minister and entered Hackney College in 1807. He was ordained to the Congregational ministry and served as pastor of the New Road Chapel, St. George's-in-the-East, London, 1811-1861. Under his ministry the congregation increased and built the Wycliffe Chapel in 1831. An ardent philanthropist, he was largely instrumental in founding the London Orphan Asylum at Clapton; the Reedham Orphanage at Coulsdon, Surrey; an asylum for idiots at Earlswood, Surrey; the Royal Hospital for Incurables, Putney, Surrey; and the Eastern Counties Asylum at Colchester, Essex. In 1817 he published the *Hymn Book* as a supplement to Watts's *Psalms and Hymns,* and this was revised and enlarged in 1825 and again in 1842. He contributed twenty-one hymns to these volumes. His hymns, together with those of his wife, Eliza Reed, were published in the *Wycliffe Supplement* (1872). In 1834, while visiting Congregational churches in the United States, he was awarded the D.D. degree by Yale College.

Holy Ghost, with light divine (170)

Spirit divine, attend our prayers (172)

Reed, Eliza Holmes (b. London, Eng., Mar. 4, 1794; d. London, July 4, 1867), the daughter of Jasper Thomas Holmes of Castle Hill, Reading, England, she was married to Andrew Reed (*q.v.*) in 1816. She wrote twenty hymns, all of which were contributed to her husband's collections.

O do not let the Word depart (234)

Redhead, Richard (b. Harrow, Eng., Mar. 1, 1820; d. Hellingly, Eng., Apr. 27, 1901), was educated as a chorister at Magdalen College, Oxford, and studied organ with Walter Vicary. From 1839 to 1864 he was organist at Margaret Chapel, London, which became All Saints' Church, Margaret Street, in 1859, and was known as the "Tractarian Cathedral." In 1864 he became organist at St. Mary Magdalene, Paddington, where he served for thirty years. He was greatly influenced by the Tractarian Movement and his plain song psalter, *Laudes Diurnae* (1843), and his *Ancient Hymn Melodies and Other Church Tunes* (1853) contributed significantly to the revival of interest in Gregorian plain song in the Anglican church.

GETHSEMANE—Go to dark Gethsemane (105)

Redner, Lewis Henry (b. Philadelphia, Pa., Dec. 15, 1830; d. Atlantic City, N.J., Aug. 29, 1908), was educated in the public schools of Philadelphia and became a wealthy real estate broker in that city. He was a devoted churchman and maintained a keen vocational interest in music throughout his life, serving as organist of four churches in Philadelphia. In addition to his responsibilities as organist at Holy Trinity Episcopal Church, he also served for nineteen years as superintendent of the Sunday school, during which time the attendance increased from thirty-six children to over a thousand. He remained a bachelor throughout his life, making his home with his sister, Mrs. Sarah H. Sagers. His death occurred at the Hotel Marlborough, Atlantic City, New Jersey, after an illness of only three days.

ST. LOUIS—O little town of Bethlehem (75)

Reinagle, Alexander Robert (b. Aug. 21, 1799, Brighton, Eng.; d. Apr. 6, 1877, Kidlington, near Oxford, Eng.), came from a distinguished family of musicians. His grandfather, Joseph Reinagle, Sr., was "trumpeter to the King," presumably in Scotland, and his father, Joseph, Jr., was an outstanding cellist. His uncle, Alexander Reinagle, came to the United States in 1786 and was a leading conductor, composer, teacher, and theatrical manager in Baltimore and Philadephia for more than two decades. Alexander Robert Reinagle was organist of St. Peter's-in-the-East, Oxford, 1822-1853. He composed a considerable amount of music and published *Psalm Tunes for the Voice and the Pianoforte* (1830).

ST. PETER—In memory of the Saviour's love (393)
    In Christ there is no East or West (443)

Reitz, Albert Simpson (b. Lyons, Kan., Jan. 20, 1879), the son of a Methodist minister, was a YMCA worker in Topeka, Kansas, 1903-8, then traveled for seven years with the evangelist, Henry Ostrom. After two years at Moody Bible Institute, he was ordained to the Baptist ministry, and served as pastor of the First Baptist Church, Berlin, Wisconsin, 1918-21; Rosehill Baptist Church, Los Angeles, California; and Fairview Heights Baptist Church, Inglewood, California, 1926-52. Since his retirement in 1952, he has made his home in Inglewood. His hymn writing began in 1911, and over one hundred of his hymns have been published.

Teach me to pray, Lord, teach me to pray—REITZ (330)

Rees, John P. (b. Jasper County, Ga., 1828; d. near Newnan, Ga., 1900), began teaching singing schools when he was about twenty; for more than thirty-five years he was a leading figure in this activity throughout middle and north Georgia and eastern Alabama. Active in both the Southern Musical Convention and the Chattahoochee Musical Convention, he was appointed a member of the committee to prepare the appendix for the third edition (1859) of *The Sacred Harp*. To this appendix he contributed sixteen tunes, both originals and arrangements. His brother, Rev. H. S. Rees (1827-1922), also a *Sacred Harp* musician, teacher, and composer, was a Baptist minister in Georgia.

Amazing grace! how sweet the sound (188—stanza 4)

Reynolds, Isham Emmanuel (b. Shades Valley, near Birmingham, Ala., Sept. 27, 1879; d. Fort Worth, Tex., May 10, 1949), was the son of Winfield Pinkney and Mary (Eastis) Reynolds. His education included study at Mississippi College, 1905-6; Moody Bible Institute, 1907-8; voice, theory, and composition under private tutors; Siegel-Myers University Correspondence School of Music (B.M., 1918); Chicago Musical College, 1920. He was given the Mus.D. degree by the Southern School of Fine Arts, Houston, Texas, in 1942.

Converted at the age of nine years, he joined the Cumberland Presbyterian Church. In 1902-3 he attended Normal Singing Schools conducted by J. Henry Showalter and J. B. Herbert. In 1904 he joined the Highland Baptist Church, Birmingham, and the following year began work as an evangelistic singer, serving under the Mississippi Baptist State Mission Board and the Southern Baptist Home Mission Board, at various times from 1907-15.

He was married to Velma Burns in 1900, who passed away in 1906. While leading the singing for the Southern Baptist Convention in Oklahoma City, Oklahoma, in May 1912, he met Lura Mae Hawk, whom he married eight weeks later.

In 1915 at the invitation of Dr. L. R. Scarborough, he joined the faculty of the Southwestern Baptist Theological Seminary, Fort Worth, Texas, as head of the Department of Gospel Music, which became the School of Sacred Music, 1921. During his thirty years in this position he became recognized for his leadership in Southern Baptist church music. He conducted schools of music in many states, associations, and local churches. He lectured and taught at Ridgecrest Baptist Assembly (North Carolina), pioneering the present-day church music leadership conferences conducted there annually. His significance as a church music leader among Southern Baptists is further evidenced by his efforts, beginning in the 1920's, to establish organizational activities at both state and convention levels.

In addition to five mimeographed textbooks prepared for his own classes, he composed two sacred music dramas, four cantatas, miscellaneous anthems, hymns, and gospel songs. He is the author of *A Manual of Practical Church Music* (1923), *The Ministry of Music in Religion* (1928), *Church Music* (1935; the first church music study course text prepared for Southern Baptists), *The Choir in the Non-Liturgical Church* (1938), and *Music and the Scriptures* (1942).

When the sun shines bright and your heart is light—LURA (214)
VENTING—Like radiant sunshine that comes after rain (285)

Reynolds, William Jensen (b. Atlantic, Iowa, Apr. 2, 1920), is the son of George Washington and Ethel (Horn) Reynolds. When he was five months old his parents moved to Oklahoma where his father, a younger brother of Isham E. Reynolds (*q.v.*), was a church music director and evangelistic singer. He was educated at Oklahoma Baptist University, Southwest Missouri State College (A.B., 1942), Southwestern Baptist Theological Seminary (M.S.M., 1945), North Texas State College (M.M., 1946), Westminster Choir College, and George Peabody College for Teachers (Ed.D., 1961).

After seven years as a part time church music director during student days, he served as minister of music, First Baptist Church, Ardmore, Oklahoma, 1946-47; and First Baptist Church, Oklahoma City, Oklahoma, 1947-55. He was employed by the Church Music Department of the Baptist Sunday School Board, Nashville, Tennessee, in 1955, and the following year became music editor. Since 1962 he has been director of editorial services of the Church Music Department. A composer and arranger of sacred choral music, he is a member of ASCAP and a member of the executive committee of the Hymn Society of America. He was music director for the Baptist World Youth Conferences, Toronto, 1958, and Beirut, Lebanon, 1963, and for the Baptist World Alliance, Rio de Janeiro, 1960.

He is the author of *A Survey of Christian Hymnody* (1963). He was a member of the Hymnal Committee for the *Baptist Hymnal* (1956) and is the author of this handbook.

CLONMEL (arr.)—Thy Word is like a garden, Lord (182)
Responses (518, 528)

Rimbault, Edward Francis (b. London, Eng., June 13, 1816; d. London, Sept. 26, 1876), was a student of Samuel S. Wesley and William Crotch. He served as organist at the Swiss church, Soho; St. Peter's Church, Vere Street, London; St. John's Wood Presbyterian Church, and at St. Giles-in-the-Fields. A highly respected music scholar, he served as editor of the Motet Society and founded the Musical Antiquarian Society in 1840. The universities of Harvard, Stockholm, and Göttingen awarded him honorary doctorates, and he was made a fellow of the Society of Antiquaries in 1842.

HAPPY DAY—O happy day that fixed my choice (389)

Rinkart, Martin (b. Apr. 23, 1586, Eilenburg, Saxony; d. Eilenburg, Dec. 8, 1649), was educated in the Latin school at Eilenburg, at St. Thomas' School in Leipzig, where he was a foundation scholar and a chorister, and at the University of Leipzig. After serving appointment as Eisleben, Erdeborn, and Lyttichendorf, he became archdeacon at Eilenburg in 1617. Like many other communities in Saxony, Eilenburg suffered greatly during the Thirty Years' War, 1618-1648. Because it was a walled city, it became a haven for refugees, and more than eight thousand persons died there because of the famine and pestilence. At one time during this period he was the only minister in the town, and during the great pestilence of 1637 he is said to have buried nearly five thousand people, including his own wife, who died May 8, 1637. In spite of the privations and sufferings of these days, Rinkart was a prolific writer of both prose and verse, which reveal the stalwart character of this man whose faith was steadfast and strong.

Now thank we all our God (491)

Rippon, John (b. Tiverton, Devonshire, Eng., Apr. 29, 1751; d. London, Eng., Dec. 17, 1836), joined the Baptist church at Tiverton at the age of sixteen and the following year enrolled at the Baptist College, Bristol, to study for the ministry. When John Fawcett (*q.v.*) declined the call to succeed John Gill as pastor of the Baptist church at Carter Lane, London, in 1772, Rippon, then only twenty-one years of age, was called as interim pastor. The following year he became the permanent pastor and served there for sixty-three years. Since John Gill's pastorate had encompassed fifty-four years, this Baptist church had had only two pastors in 117 years.

Rippon was a successful pastor, and one of the most popular and influential ministers of his day. He edited the revised edition of John Gill's monumental *Exposition of the Old and New Testaments,* published in nine volumes. He published many of his sermons, and served as editor and publisher of the *Baptist Annual Register* (1790-1802). His most significant contribution to hymnody was his *Selection of Hymns from the Best Authors, Intended As an Appendix to Dr. Watts's Psalms and Hymns,* (1787). Many editions of this collection were published both in England and in America, and it became a source book for subsequent compilers. He also published *A Selection of Psalms and Hymn Tunes* (1791).

All hail the power of Jesus' name (alt.) (132, 133, 134)
How firm a foundation, ye saints of the Lord (from his *Selection*)
(262, 263)

Roberts, Daniel Crane (b. Bridgehampton, L.I., N.Y., Nov. 5, 1841; d. Concord, N.H., Oct. 31, 1907), was educated at Kenyon College, Gambier, Ohio, and served as a private with the 84th Ohio Volunteers during the Civil War. He was ordained a deacon in the Protestant Episcopal Church in 1865, and a priest in 1866. After serving appointments in Vermont and Massachusetts, he became vicar of St. Paul's Church, Concord, New Hampshire, where he served almost thirty years. For a number of years he was president of the New Hampshire State Historical Society. Norwich University conferred on him the D.D. degree in 1885.

God of our fathers, whose almighty hand (54)

Robinson, Robert (b. Swaffham, Norfolk, Eng., Sept. 27, 1735; d. Birmingham, Eng., June 9, 1790). His father died while he was a child, and at the age of fourteen Robinson went to London and was apprenticed to a barber. In 1752 he heard George Whitefield preach a sermon on Matthew 3:7 which greatly impressed him, and after almost three years of spiritual turmoil, he made his confession of faith. He began to preach and became pastor of a Calvinistic Methodist chapel in Mindenhall, Suffolk. Shortly after this he organized an Independent congregation at Norwich, and in 1761 changed denominational affiliation for the third time as he became pastor of the Stone Yard Baptist Church, Cambridge, where he served until his retirement in 1790.

In many respects he was an unusual man and, while lacking formal education, he rose to great prominence as a preacher, scholar, and theologian. He wrote many theological works and published a *History of the Baptists* (1790). In his later years he became an intimate friend of Dr. Joseph Priestly, the well-known Unitarian philosopher and theologian, who became a strong influence in his life. He was succeeded at Cambridge by Robert Hall, the spiritual father of Charles Haddon Spurgeon. (Cf. A biography, Graham Hughes, *With Freedom Fired.*)

Come, Thou fount of every blessing (313)
Mighty God, while angels bless Thee (4)

Rooper, W. J. The identity of this author is unknown.

Dare to be brave, dare to be true (411)

Root, George Frederick (b. Sheffield, Mass., Aug. 30, 1820; d. Bailey's Island, Me., Aug. 6, 1895), at the age of nineteen, became associated with A. N. Johnson, a Boston music teacher, and was his assistant organist at both Winter and Park Street churches. In 1841 he assisted Lowell Mason as a music teacher in the Boston city schools. Three years later he moved to New York, where he taught at Abbott's School for Young Ladies, Rutgers Female Institute, Union Theological Seminary, and the New York Institute for the Blind, where Fanny Crosby was one of his students. In 1850 he spent a year studying music in Paris. On his return he composed a cantata. *The Flower-Queen,* for which Fanny Crosby wrote the text.

Under the pseudonym, "G. Friedrich Wurzel," he wrote a number of ministrel songs for Christy's minstrel troupe, the most popular of which were "Hazel Dell" and "Rosalie, the Prairie Flower." In 1858 he moved to Chicago and became associated with the music firm of Root & Cady (his brother, E. T. Root, and C. M. Cady.) Because of losses incurred in the Chicago fire of 1871, the firm was dissolved and he became associated with the John Church Company of Cincinnati, but maintained his residence in Chicago. He composed several hundred songs and was associated with the publication of about seventy-five collections.

Why do you wait, dear brother—SHEFFIELD (220)
ELLON—The wise may bring their learning (513)
Response (515)

Rosser, John L. (b. near Rustburg, Campbell Co., Va., Dec. 1, 1875), was educated at Roanoke College, Salem, Virginia, and at Southern Baptist Theological Seminary. Ordained to the Baptist ministry, he was pastor of the following churches: Memorial Baptist Church, Hampton, Virginia; First Baptist Church, Selma, Alabama; First Baptist Church, Bristol, Virginia; Riverside Baptist Church, Jacksonville, Florida; Ancient City Baptist Church, St. Petersburg, Florida. In 1927 he served as president of the Baptist General Association of Virginia. In 1944 he wrote the history of Florida Baptists. Since his retirement he had made his home in Bristol, Tennessee.

To Him who hallows all our days (499)

Rounsefell, Carrie Esther (b. Merrimack, N.H., Mar. 1, 1861; d. Durham, Me., Sept. 18, 1930), was the daughter of James A. and Clara A. Parker, who moved to Manchester, New Hampshire, when she was still a child. She was married to William E. Rounsefell, a bookkeeper for a paint and wallpaper firm in Manchester. For a number of years she traveled throughout New England and eastern New York State as a singing evangelist, always using a small autoharp to accompany her singing. In her latter years she seems to have become a member of the Church of God. In 1928 she moved to Durham, Maine, where she died at the age of sixty-nine.

MANCHESTER—It may not be on the mountain's height (425)

Rousseau, Jean Jacques (b. Geneva, Switz., June 28, 1712; d. Ermenonville, near Paris, Fr., July 3, 1778), was brought up in a haphazard fashion, and during his early years developed a marked leaning toward an erratic and irregular manner of living. After moving to Paris he became acquainted with Diderot and contributed articles to his *Encyclopédie*. For a number of years he earned his living as a music copyist, and much of his musical knowledge came from this experience. He became involved in the controversy over French music, known as the "Guerre des Bouffons," and composed an opera, *Le Devin du Village* (1752) and wrote *Lettre sur la musique francaise* (1753). Through his writings he became increasingly influential in the life, thought, and literature of his day. He is generally accredited with having inspired the French Revolution and is frequently referred to as the father of romantic literature. Many of his ideas contributed significantly in the development of elementary education. As a philosopher, he left a mark on the world of the eighteenth century which remains to the present day. Except as a musicological curiosity, his musical compositions—three operas and miscellaneous songs—have long been forgotten. His philosophical writings, which may be found in any library, remain virtually unnoticed by the masses of humanity. The work of his pen which has been most frequently published and is perhaps the widest known, is this hymn tune, GREENVILLE, which has appeared in American hymnals in every generation since 1823. In the present use it is sung to a baptismal hymn, but in most collections it is the setting for Joseph Hart's "Come, Ye Sinners, Poor and Needy." In this latter usage, as an invitation hymn inviting sinners to faith in Christ Jesus, it rather mocks the life of this liberal freethinker of the era of eighteenth-century enlightenment who, by his own accounts, seems never to have experienced a vibrant Christian faith.

GREENVILLE—Thou has said, exalted Jesus (390)

Rowe, James (b. Devonshire, Eng., Jan. 1, 1865; d. Wells, Vt., Nov. 10, 1933), the son of John and Jane (Gillard) Rowe, came to the United States in 1890, settled at Albany, New York, and was married to Blanche Clapper. After working as a employee of a railroad and being superintendent of the Hudson River Humane Society, Albany, he devoted the rest of his life to literary pursuits. Writing song texts and editing music journals, he was successively associated with the Trio Music Company, Waco, Texas; A. J. Showalter Music Company, Chattanooga,

Tennessee; and James D. Vaughan Music Company, Lawrenceburg, Tennessee. In his later years he made his home in Wells, Vermont, and devoted his time to writing serious and humorous verse for greeting card publishers. His daughter, Louise Rowe Mayhew, a gifted artist, was associated with him in this work. By his own record, he wrote more than nineteen thousand song texts, among the best known of which are "I Walk with the King," and "I Would Be like Jesus."

I was sinking deep in sin (212)

Rowley, Francis Harold (b. Hilton, N.Y., July 25, 1854; d. Boston, Mass., Feb. 14, 1952), the son of Dr. John R. and Mary Jane (Smith) Rowley, was educated at the University of Rochester (A.B., 1875), and Rochester Theological Seminary (B.D., 1878). Ordained to the Baptist ministry, he served Baptist churches in Titusville, Pennsylvania, 1879-84; North Adams, Massachusetts, 1884-92; Oak Park, Illinois, 1892-96; Fall River, Massachusetts, 1896-1900; and First Baptist Church, Boston, 1900-1910. In 1910 he was elected president of the Massachusetts Society for the Prevention of Cruelty to Animals, which operates the Angell Memorial Animal Hospital in Boston. In this capacity he served with distinction until 1945, when at the age of ninety-one, he was made chairman of the Board. Because of his intense interest in humanitarian activity, he was widely known and highly respected. The Rowley School of Humanities at Oglethorpe University, Atlanta, Georgia, was named in his honor.

I will sing the wondrous story (144)

Runyan, William Marion (b. Marion, N.Y., Jan. 21, 1870; d. Pittsburg, Kan., July 29, 1957), was the son of William White and Hannah (Orcutt) Runyan. In 1884 his Methodist preacher father moved the family to Marion, Kansas. As a youth he studied music and became quite successful as a music teacher while still in his teens. Ordained to the Methodist ministry in 1891, he held various pastorates in Kansas for twelve years. In 1903 he was appointed evangelist for the Central Kansas Methodist Conference. Because of increasing deafness, he resigned his work in Kansas and became associated with John Brown University, Sulphur Springs, Arkansas, as pastor of the Federated Church, editor of the *Christian Workers' Magazine,* and songbook compiler and editor, 1923-25. From 1925 until his retirement in 1948 he made his home in Chicago, where he was associated with Moody Bible Institute, and for several years served in an editorial capacity with the Hope Publishing Company.

FAITHFULNESS—Great is Thy faithfulness, O God my Father (47)

Russell, Anna Belle (b. Pine Valley, Chemung Co., N.Y., Apr. 21, 1862; d. Corning, N.Y., Oct. 29, 1954), the daughter of Chancey and Jane (Denson) Russell, spent most of her life in Corning, New York, where she was an active member of the First Methodist Church. She made her home with her sister, Cora C. Russell, and they both wrote a number of hymns.

There is never a day so dreary (142)

Sammis, John H. (b. Brooklyn, N.Y., July 6, 1846; d. Los Angeles, Calif., June 12, 1919), moved to Logansport, Indiana, in 1869, where he became a successful businessman. For several years he was a YMCA worker, during which time he felt the call to the ministry. He attended McCormick and Lane Theological Seminaries, graduating from the latter in 1881. He was ordained to the Presbyterian ministry in 1880, and held pastorates in Glidden, Iowa, Indianapolis, Indiana, Grandhaven, Michigan, Red Wing, Minnesota, and Sullivan, Indiana. After many years as a successful pastor, he joined the faculty of the Los Angeles Bible Institute, where he taught until his death.

When we walk with the Lord (260)

Sandys, William (b. London, Eng., Oct. 29, 1792; d. London, Feb. 18, 1874), was educated at Westminster School and was admitted to the bar in 1814. He maintained a successful legal practice and from 1861 to his retirement in 1873 was head of the law firm of Sandys & Knott, Gray's Inn Square, London. Sandys' pioneering work in the revival of interest in carols resulted in his publication of *Christmas Carols, Ancient and Modern, Including the Most Popular in the West of England, and the Airs to Which They Are Sung; also Specimens of French Provincial Carols: with an Introduction and Notes* (1833). This was followed by *Festive Songs, Principally of the 16th and 17th Centuries* (1848), and *Christmas-tide, Its History, Festivities, and Carols, with Their Music* (1852).

THE FIRST NOEL—The first Noel the angel did say (From his *Christmas Carols*) (63)

Sankey, Ira David (b. Edinburgh, Pa., Aug. 28, 1840; d. Brooklyn, N.Y., Aug. 13, 1908), following early life on the family farm in western Pennsylvania, moved to Newcastle, Pennsylvania, in 1857. Here he joined the Methodist Episcopal Church, where he became Sunday school superintendent and leader of the choir. After serving in the Union Army during the Civil War he returned to Newcastle and assisted his father who was collector of internal revenue.

In 1870, as a delegate to the YMCA convention in Indianapolis, Indiana, he met Dwight L. Moody, and six months later joined him as his music leader. He led the singing and sang gospel solos, accompanying himself on a small reed organ placed on the rostrum. In the years that followed Moody and Sankey conducted meetings throughout the United States and England. On their first visit to England in 1872, Sankey used Philip Phillips' *Hallowed Songs,* together with some additional songs in manuscript he had brought with him. The immediate demand for these manuscript songs prompted him to request of Phillips' publishers a new edition of *Hallowed Songs* to which these songs might be appended. When this request was refused, an English publisher, Morgan & Scott, published a twenty-four page pamphlet entitled *Sacred Songs and Solos* in 1873. Additional songs were added in subsequent editions until the 1903 edition contained twelve hundred songs.

In the first fifty years following its appearance, Sankey's *Sacred Songs and Solos* is reported to have sold more than eighty million copies. Upon his return to America, Sankey discovered Bliss's *Gospel Songs* (1874), and proposed to Bliss that they merge their songs and publish a joint collection. *Gospel Hymns and Sacred Songs* appeared in 1875, and was followed by *Gospel Hymns No. 2* (1876), *No. 3* (1878), *No. 4* (1883), *No. 5* (1887), and *No. 6* (1891). *Gospel Hymns Nos. 1-6 Complete,* containing 739 hymns, was published in 1894. The *Gospel Hymn* series had an extraordinary influence on Christian song in its day, and many gospel songs still in common usage became popular by inclusion in these collections. Although no longer in print, its English counterpart, *Sankey's Sacred Songs and Solos,* is still published and used in England today.

HIDING IN THEE—O safe to the rock that is higher than I (271)
INTERCESSION—I have a Saviour, He's pleading in glory (232)
NEWCASTLE—He is coming, the "Man of Sorrows" (121)
SANKEY—Encamped along the hills of light (256)
TRUSTING JESUS—Simply trusting every day (259)

Schmolck, Benjamin (b. Brauchitzchdorf, Silesia, Ger., Dec. 21, 1672; d. Schweidnitz, Ger., Feb. 12, 1737), educated at the Gymnasium at Lauban and at the University of Leipzig, was ordained to the Lutheran ministry in 1701. After a year as assistant to his father at Brauchitzchdorf, he was appointed to the Friedenskirche at Schweidnitz, where he remained until his death. Under the terms of the Peace of Westphalia, 1648, all of the churches in this district were turned over to the Roman Catholics and the Lutherans were subjected to many restrictions. The church at Schweidnitz had to serve thirty-six villages, and Schmolck was not permitted to administer communion to the dying without the consent of the Catholic authorities. He is credited with the authorship of over nine hundred hymns. While he was not of the Pietistic group, his hymns reveal the warmth of practical Christianity. He published more than a dozen collections, some of which ran into many editions and were widely used. He was the most popular German hymn writer of his day.

My Jesus, as Thou wilt (251)

Schneider, Friedrich (b. Alt-Waltersdorf, Saxony, Jan. 3, 1786; d. Dessau, Ger., Nov. 23, 1853), was educated at the University of Leipzig. He became organist at St. Paul's Leipzig, 1807; conductor of the Seconda Opera Company, 1810; organist at St. Thomas' Church, 1812; and director of the Municipal Theatre, 1817. After 1821 he became court conductor in Dessau, where he established a widely celebrated music school. His works include seventeen oratorios, seven operas, twenty-three symphonies, cantatas, masses, and overtures.

Lischer—Welcome, delightful morn (21)

Schnyder (von Wartensee), Xavier (b. Lucerne, Switz., Apr. 16, 1786; d. Frankfurt, Ger., Aug. 27, 1868), after early music training, taught at the Pestalozzian Institute, Yverdun. In 1817 he settled in Frankfurt, where he taught music and composed and took an active part in the musical life of the city. At the Swiss music festivals his compositions won him a place of high honor. His works include cantatas, sacred and secular songs, and Swiss songs for men's chorus.

Horton—Come, says Jesus' sacred voice (244)

Scholfield, Jack P. (b. Beulah, near Pittsburg, Kan., July 17, 1882), was educated at Baker, graduating in 1906. After teaching school for a time, he became an evangelistic singer and was associated with Mordecai F. Ham, T. T. Martin, and other evangelists. About 1918 he became associated with the Home Mission Board of the Southern Baptist Convention. In 1931 he retired from evangelistic work and entered the real estate business in Fort Scott, Kansas. In recent years he had made his home in Poplar Bluff, Missouri. He has written a number of gospel songs, most of which were purchased by Robert H. Coleman.

His brother, J. Fred Scholfield (1880-1945), was also active in evangelistic and church music, working with the evangelist T. T. Martin, 1905-15; First Baptist Church, Birmingham, Alabama, 1922-27; First Baptist Church, Atlanta, 1927; and Bellevue Baptist Church, Memphis, Tennessee, 1928. J. Fred Scholfield's son, Fred G. Scholfield, for many years music director for the First Baptist Church, Gainesville, Florida, was a member of the committee which compiled the *Baptist Hymnal.*

I've found a friend who is all to me —RAPTURE (197)

Schuler, George S. (b. New York, N.Y., Apr. 18, 1882), was educated at the Chicago Musical College, Cosmopolitan School of Music, and Moody Bible Institute. For forty years he was a member of the faculty of Moody Bible Institute, and since his retirement he serves on the editorial staff of The Rodeheaver Company. He has composed many gospel songs, and has publishd a number of collections of piano and organ music.

SCHULER—Out in the highways and byways of life (431)

Schumann, Robert Alexander (b. Zwickau, Saxony, June 8, 1810; d. Endenich, near Bonn, Prus., July 29, 1856). Schumann's father was a bookseller and publisher, and the literary atmosphere in which he was reared influenced his musical development. His unusual musical ability was evident at an early age, as he began composing at the age of seven, and was writing for chorus and orchestra at eleven. He became a pupil of Friedrich Wieck, whose daughter, Clara, later became his wife, and, as one of the most accomplished pianists of her time, was largely responsible for the world's knowledge of her husband's music. Tendencies toward insanity became increasingly evident and, after he attempted to take his own life by drowning in 1854, he was committed to an asylum where he remained until his death. He wrote symphonies and chamber music, but is best known for his piano works and solo songs. He was an early leader in the Romantic school of nineteenth century music.

CANONBURY—How beauteous were the marks divine (84)
Lord, speak to me, that I may speak (340)
Bless Thou the gifts our hands have brought (533)

Schwedler, Johann Christoph (b. Krobsdorf, Silesia, Dec. 21, 1672; d. Niederwiesse, Silesia, Jan. 12, 1730), was educated at the Gymnasium at Zittau and the University of Leipzig. During the thirty years of his pastorate at Niederwiese he became famous for his preaching. Great throngs attended his church and it is said that sometimes beginning a service at five or six in the morning, he would continue the service to relays of worshipers, who in succession filled the church until two or three in the afternoon. He wrote more than five hundred hymns, the principal theme being the grace of God through Christ and the joyful confidence imparted to the believer.

Ask ye what great thing I know (161)

Scott, Clara H. (b. Elk Grove, Cook Co., Ill., Dec. 3, 1841; d. Dubuque, Iowa, June 21, 1897), was the daughter of Abel Fiske and Sarah (Rockwell) Jones. In 1856 she attended the first musical institute in Chicago, conducted by C. M. Cady. Three years later she began teaching music in the Ladies' Seminary at Lyons, Iowa. In 1861 she was married to Henry Clay Scott. She became an acquaintance of Horatio R. Palmer (*q.v.*), who greatly encouraged her in creative writing. She contributed a large number of songs to his collections, as well as numerous piano music in sheet music form. She published *The Royal Anthem Book* (1882), the first collection of anthems published by a woman, *Happy Songs, Truth in Song for Lovers of Truth* (1896), and *Short Anthems* (1897). While visiting in Dubuque, Iowa, she was tragically killed when thrown from a buggy by a runaway horse.

Open my eyes that I may see—SCOTT (312)

Scriven, Joseph Medlicott (b. Seapatrick, County Down, Ire., Sept. 10, 1819; d. Bewdley, Rice Lake, Ont., Aug. 10, 1886). Scriven's father was Captain John Scriven of the Royal Marines; and his mother was a sister of the Rev. Joseph Medlicott, an English vicar, whose parish was at Pottern, Wiltshire. In 1835 he entered Trinity College, Dublin, but deciding upon an army career, he became a cadet at Addiscombe Military College, Surrey, in 1837. Poor health forced him to abandon his military ambitions, and he returned to Trinity College, where he received his B.A. degree in 1842. Two years later he moved to Canada, taught school for a while at Woodstock and Brantford and served as a tutor to the family of Lieutenant Pengelley, a retired naval officer, near Bewdley.

Twice tragedy cut short his plans for marriage. In his younger days in Ireland, his bride-to-be was accidentally drowned the evening before their wedding. In Canada, Miss Eliza Roche, a relative of the Pengelley family, died suddenly after a brief illness shortly before they were to have been married. He was a member of the Plymouth Brethren and devoted much of his time to performing menial work for those who were physically handicapped and financially destitute, taking no pay for his labor. In later years he experienced considerable hardship. With failing health, meager income, and fear of becoming physically helpless, he became greatly depressed. It was never ascertained whether or not his death by drowning was suicidal or accidental. *Hymns and Other Verses,* a small collection of his poems, was published in 1869. In 1919 a monument was erected to his memory at Rice Lake, ten miles north of Port Hope, Ontario, which stands as a tribute to this Irish-born emigrant whose hymn of the comforting friendship of Jesus is known around the world.

What a friend we have in Jesus (328)

Seagrave, Robert (b. Twyford, Leicestershire, Eng., Nov. 22, 1693; d. *ca.* 1759), educated at Clare College, Cambridge, was ordained in the Church of England in 1715. He became greatly interested in the work of the Wesleys and Whitefield. Between 1731 and 1746 he issued a series of pamphlets designed to awaken in the clergy a deeper earnestness in their work. He was appointed Sunday evening lecturer at Loriner's Hall, London, 1739-50, and during this time he also frequently preached at Whitefield's Tabernacle. He published *Hymns for Christian Worship* (1742), to which he contributed fifty hymns. The place and date of his death are not known.

Rise, my soul, and stretch thy wings (122)

Sears, Edmund Hamilton (b. Sandisfield, Mass., Apr. 6, 1810; d. Weston, Mass., Jan. 16, 1876), educated at Union College (Schenectady), and Harvard Divinity School, was ordained to the Unitarian ministry and held pastorates at Wayland and Lancaster, Massachusetts. He is the author of a number of books which reveal his great spiritual depth. He once wrote to Bishop Bickersteth, "Though I was educated in the Unitarian denomination, I believe and preach the divinity of Christ." Among his published works are: *Regeneration* (1854); *Pictures of the Olden Time* (1857); *Athanasia, or Foregleams of Immortality* (1858); *The Fourth Gospel, the Heart of Christ* (1872); and *Sermons and Songs of the Christian Life* (1875).

It came upon the midnight clear (71)

Sellers, Ernest Orlando (b. Hastings, Mich., Oct. 29, 1869; d. Eola, La., Oct. 19, 1952), was the son of William A. and Kate (Armstrong) Sellers. After completing high school in Lansing, Michigan, he became an apprentice to a surveyor and civil engineer, and five years later was appointed city engineer and superintendent of public works. He was converted in the Lansing YMCA, and in 1895 enrolled as a student at Moody Bible Institute, Chicago. From 1901 to 1905 he served as YMCA secretary in Macon, Georgia; Washington, D.C.; and Wilmington, Delaware. With the Euclid Avenue Baptist Church, Cleveland, Ohio, he served as director of men's work and assistant pastor, 1905-7. He returned to Moody Bible Institute as assistant director of the Music Department and professor of Sunday school pedagogy, 1908-19. During this time he was active in evangelistic work, leading the singing for such evangelists as R. A. Torrey, Gipsy Smith, A. C. Dixon, and J. Wilbur Chapman. During World War I he was a member of the YMCA Speakers Bureau in France and Germany, 1918-19. In 1919 he became director of the Music Department of the Baptist Bible Institute, New Orleans. Affectionately known as "Uncle Fuller," he was respected and admired by both faculty and student body. Throughout his years at the Seminary, in addition to his teaching responsibilities, he wrote many articles and poems and composed a number of hymn tunes. After his retirement in 1945, he made his home at Eola, Louisiana, and the discovery of oil on his property greatly added to the financial security of his later years. He died at his home, "Bayou Grove," at Eola, and was buried in the Pythian Cemetery, Bunkie, Louisiana.

Among his published works are *Personal Evangelism* (1923); *How to Improve Church Music* (1928); *Elements of Music Notation and Conducting* (1938); and *Worship, Why and How* (1941). He was a member of the committee which compiled *The New Baptist Hymnal* (1926). The School of Sacred Music in the New Orleans Baptist Theological Seminary was named for Sellers after his death.

Thy Word is a lamp to my feet—EOLA (180)

NEW ORLEANS—There is never a day so dreary (142)

Sewell, Hampton Haygood (b. near Atlanta, Ga., Jan. 7, 1874; d. Temple, Ga., Mar. 11, 1937), the son of Plinny Ivey and Mary Annie Sewell, was educated in the grammar schools of Georgia, and studied music with A. J. Showalter (*q.v.*). After several years as a merchant and a farmer, he became an evangelistic singer, beginning his work with Rev. Charles Dunaway in 1909. For more than twenty-five years he was engaged in evangelistic work throughout the South. He wrote about five hundred songs and published three collections: *Hymns of Glory* (1909); *Hymns of Glory, No. 2* (1914); and *World Revival Hymns* (1918).

SEWELL—I am so happy in Christ today (194)

Shaw, Knowles (b. Butler Co., Ohio, Oct. 13, 1834; d. near McKinney, Tex., June 7, 1878). Shaw's parents, Albin and Huldah (Griffin) Shaw, were of Scotch descent. When Knowles was a few months old, they moved from Ohio to Rush County, Indiana, where his father was a farmer and tanner, and later became a merchant. He was converted in 1852 and after teaching school for a brief time began preaching. As an evangelist Shaw became widely known in many states and because of his musical talents was called the "Singing Evangelist." In 1874 he served as pastor of a Christian church in Chicago. Resigning to return to his evangelistic work, he made his home at Rushville, Indiana. After concluding a successful five-week revival in the Commerce Street Christian Church, Dallas, Texas, he left by train for another meeting in McKinney, Texas. Two miles south of McKinney, a broken rail caused derailment of the car in which Shaw was riding, and he was killed instantly. He published five collections of Sunday school songs: *Shining Pearl* (1868), *Sparking Jewels* (1871), *The Golden Gate* (1874), *The Gospel Trumpet* (1875), and *The Morning Star* (1877).

Sowing in the morning, sowing seeds of kindness (432)

Shepherd, Thomas (b. England, 1665; d. Bocking, Essex, Eng., Jan. 29, 1739), the son of William Shepherd, was ordained in the Church of England. However, he left the Anglican church and in 1694 became pastor of the independent Castle Hill Meeting House at Nottingham, where Philip Doddridge later was pastor. In 1700 he moved to Bocking, near Braintree, Essex, where he preached in a barn for seven years before a small chapel was erected for his congregation. He remained as pastor of this church until his death.

Must Jesus bear the cross alone (stanza 1)—(428)

Sheppard, Franklin Lawrence (b. Philadelphia, Pa., Aug. 7, 1852; d. Philadelphia, Feb. 15, 1930), was educated at the University of Pennsylvania. In 1875 he was sent to Baltimore in charge of the foundry of his father's firm, Isaac A. Sheppard & Co., manufacturers of stoves and heaters. He was a member of the Zion Protestant Episcopal Church, Baltimore, where he served as organist and was vestryman. Later he joined the Second Presbyterian Church of Baltimore, where he was music director and became an active Sunday school worker. He served as a lay delegate to the General Assembly, and was a member and later president of the Presbyterian Board of Publication. He was always interested in music, and edited a Presbyterian Sunday school songbook, *Alleluia* (1915), which was widely used. He also served on the editorial committee for the Presbyterian *Hymnal* (1911).

Terra Patris—This is my Father's world (59)

Sherwin, William Fiske (b. Buckland, Mass., Mar. 14, 1826; d. Boston, Mass., Apr. 14, 1888), received his music education under Lowell Mason and other teachers of his day, and he later taught at the New England Conservatory of Music in Boston. He possessed extraordinary ability in the organizing and directing of amateur choruses, and because of this he was chosen to be the musical director at Chautauqua Assembly in New York. He was a Baptist layman.

Bread of Life—Break Thou the bread of life (178)
Here at Thy table, Lord (392)
Chautauqua—Day is dying in the west (29)
Cutting—Christ for the world we sing (458)

Shirreff, Emily (1814-1897). The identity of this author is unknown.

Gracious Saviour, who didst honor (503)

Showalter, Anthony Johnson (b. Rockingham Co., Va., May 1, 1858; d. Chattanooga, Tenn., Sept. 16, 1924), the son of John A. and Susanna (Miller) Showalter, received his early music training from his father. Later he attended singing schools and studied under B. C. Unseld, H. R. Palmer, George F. Root, and F. W. Root. In 1880 he began teaching and published that year his first book, *Harmony and Composition.* In 1884 he moved to Dalton, Georgia, to establish a branch office of the Ruebush-Kieffer Music Company of Dayton, Virginia. Shortly afterward he founded his own publishing operation and published about sixty books, of which it is said that more than two million copies were sold. For more than twenty years he edited *The Music Teacher,* the monthly periodical of his company. For his normal music schools at Dalton, he secured the services of the leading teachers in the nation. He himself conducted singing schools in more than a dozen southern states, and was widely known and respected. In 1895 he spent a year studying music in England, France, and Germany. He was an elder in the First Presbyterian Church, Dalton, and for many years served as music director.

SHOWALTER—What a fellowship, what a joy divine (371)

Shrubsole, William (b. Canterbury, Eng., 1760; d. London, Eng., Jan. 18, 1806), the son of a blacksmith, began his music training as a chorister in Canterbury Cathedral. At the age of twenty-two, he was appointed organist at Bangor Cathedral, but was dismissed less than two years later because of his sympathies with the Dissenters outside the Church of England. He taught music privately in London, and in 1784 secured a position as organist at Spa Fields Chapel, Clerkenwell, one of Lady Huntingdon's chapels, where he remained until his death. He was a close friend of Edward Perronet (*q.v.*), for whose hymn he wrote the tune for which he is remembered.

MILES LANE—All hail the power of Jesus name (133)

Shurtleff, Ernest Warburton (b. Boston, Mass., Apr. 4, 1862; d. Paris, Fr., Aug. 24, 1917), was educated at the Boston Latin School, Harvard University, New Church Theological Seminary, and Andover Theological Seminary. Ordained to the Congregational ministry, he held pastorates at Ventura, California, Old Plymouth and Palmer, Massachusetts, and the First Congregational Church, Minneapolis, Minnesota, 1898-1905. In 1905 he organized the American Church at Frankfurt, Germany, and the following year became director of student activities in the Academy

Vitti, and did a remarkable work among the American students in Paris. With his wife, the former Helen S. Cramer of Cameron, Texas, he did relief work during World War I. Among his published works are: *Poems* (1883), *New Year's Peace* (1885), *Song of Hope* (1886), and *Shadow of the Angel* (1886).

Lead on, O King eternal (417)

Simpson, Robert (b. Glasgow, Scot., Nov. 4, 1790; d. Greenock, Scot., 1832), a weaver by trade, was always greatly interested in music. He led the singing at the Albion Street Congregational Church, Glasgow, and in 1823 was sessions clerk and led the singing at the East Parish Church, Greenock. He died in the summer of 1832 during an epidemic of cholera.

BALERMA (arr.)—Come, Holy Spirit, heavenly Dove (169)
Oh, for a closer walk with God (365)

Sims, Walter Hines (b. Urania, La., Sept. 30, 1907), the son of Walter Heiman and Annie Elizabeth (Rogers) Sims, was reared in Louisiana and Texas, where his father held various pastorates of Baptist churches. He was educated at Hardin-Simmons University (A.B., 1928), Centenary College (B.Mus., 1937), George Peabody College for Teachers (M.A., 1946), he has done graduate work at Southwestern Baptist Theological Seminary, University of Nebraska, and Northwestern University. He was director of instrumental music in the public schools of Shreveport, Louisiana, 1935-45, and during this same period was minister of music, Queensboro Baptist Church, Shreveport. In 1945-46 he was a member of the faculty of George Peabody College for Teachers, Nashville, and served as minister of music, First Baptist Church, Nashville. He came to the Church Music Department of the Sunday School Board, Nashville, as associate secretary in 1946, and became secretary of the Church Music Department in 1952. He was awarded the honorary Mus.D. degree by Hardin-Simmons University in 1948. In his present position he gives guidance to the program of church music ministry, which includes publication, curriculum development, and field promotion for more than thirty-two thousand Southern Baptist churches. He serves as director of the annual Southern Baptist Music Leadership Conferences at Ridgecrest, North Carolina, and Glorieta, New Mexico. In addition to serving as editor of *The Church Musician,* the monthly periodical for Southern Baptist musicians, he has compiled and edited several hymnals and choral collections published by Broadman Press. He is the author of *Instrumental Music in the Church* (1947), *Song Leading* (1959), and *Church Music Manual.* He was the editor of *Baptist Hymnal* (1956), for which this handbook was written, and served as chairman of the Hymnal Committee.

McComb—This rite our blest Redeemer gave (384)
Response (539)

Slade, Mary Bridges Canedy (b. Fall River, Mass., 1826; d. Fall River, 1882), was a schoolteacher and served for a time as assistant editor of *The New England Journal of Education*. The wife of a clergyman, she spent her entire life in her home town. She is the author of a number of gospel song texts, of which only the present two remain in common usage.

From all the dark places (409)
Sweetly, Lord, have we heard Thee calling (362)

Sleeper, William True (b. Danbury, N.H., Feb. 9, 1819; d. Wellesley, Mass., Sept. 24, 1904), the son of Jonathan and Mary (Parker) Sleeper, was educated at Phillips-Exeter Academy, the University of Vermont, and Andover Theological Seminary. After his graduation he was ordained to the Congregational ministry, engaged in mission work in Worcester, Massachusetts, and later was a home missionary in Maine, where he established three churches. In 1876 he returned to Worcester to accept the pastorate of the Summer Street Congregational Church, which he had served years earlier when it was a mission, and enjoyed a successful pastorate of more than thirty years. His three children distinguished themselves in their fields of service. William W. Sleeper was a Congregational minister and was pastor at Wellesley for many years, Henry Dyke Sleeper was professor of music at Smith College, and Mary Sleeper Ruggles was a well-known contralto soloist in Boston. Helen Joy Sleeper, daughter of William W. Sleeper, was music librarian at Wellesley College and widely respected as a scholarly researcher. In 1883 he published a book of poems, *The Rejected King, and Hymns of Jesus*.

A ruler once came to Jesus by night (215)
Out of my bondage, sorrow, and night (233)

Small, James Grindlay (b. Edinburgh, Scot., 1817; d. Renfrew-on-the-Clyde, Scot., Feb. 11, 1888), was educated at the University of Edinburgh, ordained in the Free Church of Scotland in 1847, and became pastor of the Free Church at Bervie, near Montrose. He was greatly interested in hymnology and published *Hymns for Youthful Voices* (1859), and *Psalms and Sacred Songs* (1859), as well as two volumes of poems.

I've found a friend, Oh, such a friend (261)

Smart, Henry Thomas (b. London, Eng., Oct. 26, 1813; d. London, July 6, 1879), was educated at Highgate, and later abandoned the study of law in favor of music. Largely self-taught in music, he became one of the finest organists of his day. He served as organist at the parish church, Blackburn, Lancashire, 1831-36; St. Philip's Church, Regent Street, London, 1838-39; St. Luke's Church, Old Street, 1844-64; and at St. Pancras Church, London, from 1865 until his death. Troubled with poor eyesight for a number of years, he became totaly blind about 1865. However, his memory and skill made it possible for him to continue playing.

His advice and counsel were frequently sought for new organ installations both in England and Scotland, and the organs in City and St. Andrew's Halls, Glasgow, and the Town Hall, Leeds, were designed by him. He wrote a great deal of church music, both choral and organ. In addition to publishing his *Choral Book* (1856) and Collection of *Sacred Music* (1863), he served as musical editor for *Psalms and Hymns for Divine Worship* (1867) and the *Presbyterian Hymnal* (1875), the hymnbook of the United Presbyterian Church of Scotland.

LANCASHIRE—Lead on, O King Eternal (417)
    From ocean unto ocean (450)
PILGRIMS—Hark, hark, my soul! angelic songs are swelling (469)
REGENT SQUARE—Praise, my soul, the King of heaven (18)
    Angels, from the realms of glory (76)
    Lo, He came with clouds descending (123)
    Look, ye saints! the sight is glorious (148)
    O Thou God of my salvation (164)

Smith, Henry Percy (b. England, 1825; d. 1898), was educated at Balliol College, Oxford, and ordained in the Church of England. At Eversley, 1849-51, he was curate to Charles Kingsley, one of the leaders of the Christian Socialism Movement. He was appointed curate of St. Michael's, Yorktown, Camberley, Surrey, 1851-68, and vicar of Great Barton, Suffolk, 1868-82. From 1882 to 1895 he was chaplain at Christ Church, Cannes, France, and from 1892 he was canon of the cathedral of Gibraltar.

MARYTON—Come, Holy Spirit, Dove divine (385)
    O Master, let me walk with Thee (426)

Smith, Howard E. (b. July 16, 1863; d. Norwalk, Conn., Aug. 13, 1918). Very little is known about Smith, except that he was an active musician throughout his life and served many years as a church organist in Connecticut. He composed a number of hymn tunes, but only the present one remains in common usage.

SAFETY—I was sinking deep in sin (212)

Smith, John Stafford (b. Gloucester, Eng., 1750; d. London, Eng., Sept. 21, 1836), was an English organist and composer who received his early training from his father, Martin Smith, and from William Boyce. He gained a high reputation as a tenor singer, organist, antiquarian, and composer of catches, glees, part songs, and anthems. The fact that the tune which has become our national anthem appeared in his fifth collection of glees, 1799, arranged for three voices and entitled "Anacreon in Heaven," has led to his being mistakenly regarded as the composer of this tune, which apparently had been known before this date. Percy Scholes in *The Oxford Companion to Music,* though erroneously crediting this tune to Smith, astutely remarks, "the nation defied has furnished the music for the defiance—a proceeding happily unresented by either party."

NATIONAL ANTHEM—Oh, say, can you see, by the dawn's early light (486)

Smith, Samuel Francis (b. Boston, Mass., Oct. 21, 1808; d. Boston, Nov. 16, 1895), was educated at the Boston Latin School, Harvard University, and Andover Theological Seminary. After a year and a half service as editor of the *Baptist Missionary Magazine,* he was pastor of the Baptist church at Waterville, Maine, 1834-42. During this time he was also professor of modern languages at Waterville College (now Colby College). He was pastor of the Baptist church at Newton, Massachusetts, 1842-54, and resigned to become editorial secretary of the American Baptist Missionary Union. In 1880 he visited the mission field in Asia and Europe, and his experiences and impressions were published in *Rambles in Mission Fields* (1884). During his student days he became keenly interested in missionary work through the work of Adoniram Judson in Burma, and throughout his life the spark of missionary zeal burned brightly. His son, Dr. A. W. Smith, became a Baptist missionary to Burma, and served as president of the theological seminary at Rangoon. Together with Baron Stow, he compiled *The Psalmist* (1843), the most widely used Baptist hymnal of its day in America. He was keenly interested in hymnology and is credited with writing about one hundred hymns. At a class reunion at Harvard University his close friend and classmate, Oliver Wendell Holmes, read a poem which said of Smith:

> And there's a nice youngster of excellent pith,—
> Fate tried to conceal him by naming him Smith;
> But he shouted a song for the brave and the free,—
> Just read on his medal, "My country, of thee!"

My country, 'tis of thee (487)
The morning light is breaking (448)

Smith, Walter Chalmers (b. Aberdeen, Scot., Dec. 5, 1824; d. Kinbuch, Perthshire, Scot., Sept. 20, 1908), was educated at the Grammar School and University of Aberdeen and at New College, Edinburgh. He was ordained a minister in the Free Church of Scotland and was pastor of the Free Church, Chadwell Street, Islington, London, 1850-57; Roxburgh Free Church, Edinburgh, 1857-76; and then became pastor of the Free High Church, Edinburgh, where he remained until his retirement in 1894. He was elected moderator of the Free Church of Scotland in 1893. His hymns were published in his *Hymns of Christ and the Christian Life* (1876).

Immortal, invisible, God only wise (43)

Smyth, Harper G. (b. New York, N.Y., Mar. 16, 1873; d. Cleveland, Ohio, Aug. 25, 1945), received his musical training at the Institute of Musical Art, New York, and for two years was a member of the Metropolitan Opera Company. For a brief time he directed church choirs in Atlanta, Georgia, and Indianapolis, Indiana, and served as song leader on tours with Maud Ballington Booth of the Salvation Army and Evangelist J. Wilbur Chapman. In 1913 he became music director of the Euclid Avenue Baptist Church, Cleveland, Ohio, where he made his home until his death. During World War I he earned a reputation for writing and directing pageants which he continued for many years.

Smyth was the official song leader for the National Republican Convention in Cleveland in 1924, and served in the same capacity for the Rotary International conventions. He published *Let's Adventure in Personality,* 1941, and gave frequent lectures on this subject. Until a few years before his death he maintained a voice studio in Cleveland and was active in the musical life of the city. In April, 1945, he suffered a stroke while leading the singing for a group of inductees at the Army Induction Center in Cleveland and died four months later. He wrote about twenty-five songs, but only the one given here remains in common usage.

Is your life a channel of blessing—EUCLID (438)

Spafford, Horatio Gates (b. North Troy, N.Y., Oct. 20, 1828; d. Jerusalem, Oct. 16, 1888), after early life in New York, moved to Chicago in 1856, where he established a successful legal practice and served as professor of medical jurisprudence of Lind University, later Chicago Medical College. A Presbyterian layman, he was a Sunday school teacher, and active in YMCA work. He served as a director and trustee for the Presbyterian Theological Seminary of the Northwest, established in Chicago by Cyrus McCormick. In 1870 he spent four months in England and Scotland. In Edinburgh he met Dr. Piazza Smith, Astronomer Royal for

Scotland, and became greatly interested in the archaeology of the Bible.

Some months prior to the Chicago fire in 1871, Spafford had invested heavily in real estate on the shore of Lake Michigan, and his holdings were wiped out by the fire. The tragic deaths of his four daughters (see discussion of the hymn) was compounded by the death of his son in 1880. The unsympathetic attitude of Christian friends in the midst of their sorrow caused the Spaffords to decide to leave Chicago, and the interest in the Holy Land which began a decade before, turned their attention to Jerusalem. In 1881, with a group of friends, they settled in Jerusalem where they established the American Colony. The unusual experiences of this extraordinary family and the significant work of the American Colony in Jerusalem is vividly told by his daughter, Bertha Spafford Vester, in her book, *Our Jerusalem*. On July 24, 1963, the writer visited with Mrs. Vester in her apartment at the American Colony in Jerusalem, Jordan.

When peace, like a river, attendeth my way (265)

Spitta, Carl Johann Philipp (b. Hanover, Ger., Aug. 1, 1801; d. Burgdorf, Ger., Sept. 28, 1859), was of a Huguenot family which fled from France during the Roman Catholic persecution. They changed their name from de l'Hopital to the German equivalent, Spital or Spittel, later modified to Spitta. His father was a bookkeeper and a teacher of French, and his mother was a Christian Jewess. He was apprenticed to a watchmaker, but later studied for the ministry at the Gymnasium at Hanover and at the University of Göttingen. He was ordained to the Lutheran ministry in 1828 and became assistant chaplain to the garrison and to the prison at Hameln. He would have become permanent chaplain, but the military authorities refused to sanction this promotion because of reports that he was a Pietist and a mystic.

Spitta became pastor at Wechold, near Hoya, Hanover, in 1837, Lutheran superintendent of Wittingen, in 1847, and chief pastor of Peine in 1853. A few weeks after his appointment to Burgdorf in 1859, he died very suddenly. One son, Friedrich Spitta, became a well-known Lutheran theologian, and another son, Johann August Spitta, is the author of the authoritative treatise on J. S. Bach. While serving as tutor to a private family, 1824-28, he passed through a deep spiritual experience, and while he had written secular verse before this, he now turned his attention to the writing of hymns. In 1826 he wrote to a friend:

In the manner in which I formerly sang I sing no more. To the Lord I consecrate my life and my love, and likewise my song. His love is the one great theme of all my songs; to praise and exalt it worthily is the desire of the Christian singer. He gave to me song and melody; I give it back to Him.

His *Psalter und Harfe* (Pirna, 1833), containing sixty-one hymns, became exceeding popular and a second edition, adding five more hymns, was published at Leipzig, 1834. A second volume of forty hymns using the same title, was published at Leipzig in 1843.

O happy home where Thou art loved the dearest (373)

Spohr, Louis (Ludwig) (b. Brunswick, Ger., Apr. 5, 1784; d. Cassel, Prus., Oct. 22, 1859). Spohr's father, a physician, was a flute player, and his mother a singer and pianist. In this musical atmosphere, his musical talents developed early. He was a student of Riemenschneider, Dufour, Maucourt, and Eck, and became a violin virtuoso of great renown. His concerts throughout Europe and England were widely acclaimed. As a composer he wrote oratorios, operas, violin concertos, and chamber music which obtained excellent success in Germany. An extremely self-centered musician, he was highly critical of the works of other composers and saw little virtue in the compositions of Beethoven, Weber, and others. Yet, he was an early champion of Wagner, producing two Wagnerian operas in Cassel in 1842 and 1853, despite opposition.

SPOHR—All things bright and beautiful (8)
I heard a voice of Jesus say (302)

Spratt, Ann Baird (1829-?). No information has been found to identify this composer.

KEDRON—No, not despairingly (206)

Spurgeon, Charles Haddon (b. Kelvedon, Essex, Eng., June 19, 1834; d. London, Eng., Jan. 31, 1892). Spurgeon's family was of Dutch origin which sought refuge in England during the persecution of the Duke of Alva, 1567-73. His father, John Spurgeon, was a Congregational minister. After studying at Colchester and at the Agriculture College at Maidstone, he was for a few years an assistant teacher at Newmarket and Cambridge. Although reared in a Congregational family and converted in a Methodist chapel, he joined the Baptist church at Isleham, May, 1850. In 1851 he became pastor of the Baptist church at Waterbeach, near Cambridge, and in 1854 was called as pastor of the Baptist church at New Park Street London, (formerly Carter Lane Chapel), where John Gill and John Rippon (*q.v.*) had served. His preaching attracted such throngs that the congregation soon outgrew the building, and in 1861 the Metropolitan Tabernacle was erected which seated six thousand. For the use of his congregation, he compiled *Our Own Hymnbook* (1866), which included his twenty hymns.

The Holy Ghost is here (168)

Stainer, John (b. London, Eng., June 6, 1840; d. Verona, It., Mar. 31, 1901), the son of a schoolmaster, became a chorister at St. Paul's Cathedral, London, and was educated at Christ Church, Oxford, and St. Edmund Hall. He became organist at Magdalen College in 1860 and at University College, 1861. In 1872 he succeeded Sir John Goss as organist at St. Paul's Cathedral and served with distinction in this position until failing eyesight forced his retirement in 1888. He was knighted by Queen Victoria in 1888, and returned to Oxford University where he taught until his death. He wrote over 150 hymn tunes, many anthems, an oratorio, and several cantatas, including the well-known *Crucifixion* (1887). He was coeditor of *The Dictionary of Musical Terms* (1879) and author of *The Music of the Bible* (1879). His textbook on organ playing remained a classic for more than half a century. He was the musical editor for the *Church Hymnary* (1898). As a skilful and effective choir trainer, organist, editor, composer, and teacher, he stands as one of the most eminent of the Victorian church musicians.

Responses (546, 547)

Stead, Louisa M. R. (b. Dover, Eng., *ca.* 1850 [?]; d. Penkridge, near Umtali, Southern Rhodesia, Jan. 18, 1917), born of Christian parents in England, was converted at the age of nine, and as a teen-age girl felt the call of God to be a foreign missionary. She came to America in 1871 and for a time lived with friends in Cincinnait, Ohio. At a camp meeting in Urbana, Ohio, she surrendered her life for missionary service in China, but her frail physical condition prevented her from securing appointment. About 1875 she was married to a Mr. Stead, and to this home was born a daughter, Lily. When Lily was four years old, Mr. Stead accidentally drowned while trying to rescue a child in the waters off Long Island, New York. With her daughter, Lily, Mrs. Stead went to South Africa about 1880, where she worked as a missionary in the Cape Colony for fifteen years. During this time she was married to Robert Wodehouse, a native of South Africa. In 1895 her poor health made necessary their return to America, and Mr. Wodehouse became a local Methodist pastor. The cooler climate of her homeland and skilful medical attention restored her physical strength and again their thoughts turned to the mission field that they loved. She and her husband were delegates to the Ecumenical Missionary Conference in New York in 1900, and out of the inspiration of this experience they offered themselves again for mission work. They received their appointment to the Methodist Mission at Umtali, Southern Rhodesia. They arrived in Umtali on April 4, 1901, and a few months later in her report to the East Central Africa Mission of the Methodist Church, she wrote:

In connection with this whole mission there are glorious possibilities, one cannot in the face of the peculiar difficulties help saying, "Who is sufficient for these things?" but with simple confidence and trust we may and do say, "Our sufficiency is of God."

She retired in 1911 after ten years of service. Lily, who became Mrs. D. A. Carson, served for many years as a missionary in Southern Rhodesia, and cared for her mother in her retirement. After several years of prolonged illness, Mrs. Wodehouse died at her home in Penkridge, near Mutambara Mission, about fifty miles from Umtali, and was buried in a grave hewn out of solid rock on the side of Black Mountain near her African home.

The writer is indebted to Ernest K. Emurian, who provided the initial information identifying this hymn writer in his *Famous Stories of Inspiring Hymns* (1956). Further documentation has been kindly provided by the Board of Missions of the Methodist Church, New York City.

'Tis so sweet to trust in Jesus (258)

Stebbins, George Coles (b. Orleans Co., N.Y., Feb. 26, 1846; d. Catskill, N.Y., Oct. 6, 1945), studied music in Buffalo and Rochester, New York, and at the age of twenty-three moved to Chicago where he was associated with Lyon & Healy Music Company, and was music director of the First Baptist Church. During this time he became acquainted with the leading musicians of Chicago—Root, Bliss, Palmer, and Sankey. In 1874 he became music director of the Clarendon Street Baptist Church, Boston, Massachusetts. He accepted a similar position with the Tremont Temple in January, 1876, but during that summer Dwight L. Moody persuaded him to enter evangelistic work, and for twenty-five years he was associated with Moody and other leading evangelists. In addition to his work as a song leader, he composed hundreds of songs, and assisted in compiling numerous gospel song collections. After the death of Bliss, he and James McGranahan assisted Sankey in editing and compiling the third, fourth, fifth, and sixth editions of the *Gospel Hymns* series. His *Memoirs and Reminiscences* (1924), provides an interesting insight into his life and work.

BORN AGAIN—A ruler once came to Jesus by night (215)
CALLING TODAY—Jesus is tenderly calling thee home (229)
EVENING PRAYER—Saviour, breathe an evening blessing (34)
FRIEND—I've found a friend, oh, such a friend (261)
GREEN HILL—There is a green hill far away (98)
HOLINESS—Take time to be holy (367)
JESUS I COME—Out of my bondage, sorrow, and night (233)

LIFELINE (arr.)—Throw out the lifeline across the dark wave (217)
POLLARD—Have Thine own way, Lord (355)
PROVIDENCE—Must I go, and empty-handed (430)
TRUEHEARTED—Truehearted, wholehearted (410)

Stennett, Samuel (b. Exeter, Eng., 1727; d. London, Eng., Aug. 24, 1795). At the time of Stennett's birth his father, Joseph Stennett, was pastor of the Baptist church at Exeter. Ten years later the father moved to London to serve as pastor of the Baptist church at Little Wild Street, Lincoln's Inn Fields. Stennett was educated under Rev. John Hubbard of Stepney and Dr. John Walker of the Academy at Mile End. He became assistant to his father in 1747, and after his father's death he became pastor in 1758. In 1736 he received a call from the Sabbatarian Baptist church in London, where his grandfather had been pastor for twenty-three years. Although he did not accept the call as pastor, he preached for the church every Saturday morning for twenty years. He was one of the outstanding dissenting preachers of his day, and used his influence in support of the principle of religious freedom. He was a personal friend of George III, and John Howard, the noted English philanthropist and prison reformer, was a member of his congregation. He was given the D.D. degree by King's College, Aberdeen, in 1763. He contributed thirty-nine hymns to John Rippon's *Selection of Hymns* (1787).

Majestic sweetness sits enthroned (118)
On Jordan's stormy banks I stand (478, 479)

Stites, Edgar Page (b. Cape May, N.J., Mar. 22, 1836; d. Cape May, Jan. 7, 1921), was a direct descendant of John Howland, who came to America on the *Mayflower*. During the Civil War, he was stationed at Philadelphia, and was in charge of feeding the troops that passed through that city. Following the war he was a Delaware River pilot. He became a local preacher in the Methodist church, and for a time was a missionary in Dakota. For more than sixty years he was a member of the First Methodist Episcopal Church of Cape May, New Jersey, and regularly attended the annual Methodist Assembly at Ocean Grove. He was a cousin of Eliza E. Hewitt (*q.v.*). Frequently he used the pseudonym, "Edgar Page," for his hymns. In addition to the hymn given here, he is also the author of "Beulah Land," which was exceedingly popular for many years.

Simply trusting every day (259)

Stocking, Jay Thomas (b. Lisbon, N.Y., Apr. 19, 1870; d. Newton Center, Mass., Jan. 27, 1936), was educated at Amherst College, Yale

Divinity School, and the University of Berlin. Ordained to the Congregational ministry in 1901, he held several pastorates in New England, New Jersey, Missouri, and Washington, D.C. He was active in interdenominational affairs, and vitally interested in the work of the Federal Council of Churches, serving on the Commission on International Justice and Good Will. In 1934 he was elected moderator of the Congregational Council.

O Master Workman of the race (441)

Stockton, John Hart (b. New Hope, Pa., Apr. 19, 1813; d. Philadelphia, Pa., Mar. 25, 1877), was converted at a Methodist camp meeting at Paulsboro, New Jersey, in the summer of 1832, and was ordained to the Methodist ministry, uniting with the New Jersey Conference. During his pastorates, though often in feeble health, he devoted considerable time and strength to church music. He wrote a number of hymns, and published *Salvation Melodies* (1874), and *Precious Songs* (1875).

Come every soul by sin oppressed—STOCKTON (235)
GLORY TO HIS NAME—Down at the cross where my Saviour died (95)
GREAT PHYSICIAN—The great Physician now is near (86)

Stone, Samuel John (b. Whitmore, Staffordshire, Eng., Apr. 25, 1839; d. Charterhouse, Eng., Nov. 19, 1900), was educated at Charterhouse and at Pembroke College, Oxford (B.A., 1862; M.A., 1872). Ordained in the Church of England in 1862, he became curate at Windsor, and in 1870 was curate at St. Paul's Church, Haggerston, London, succeeding his father as vicar there in 1874. In 1890 he was appointed rector of All-Hallows-on-the-Wall, London, where he remained until his death. He published *Lyra Fidelium* (1866); *The Knight of Intercession, and Other Poems* (1872); *Sonnets of the Christian Year* (1875); *Hymns* (1886); and *Order of the Consecutive Church Service for Children, with Original Hymns* (1883). His *Collected Poems and Hymns* were published posthumously by F. G. Ellerton. He was a member of the committee which prepared the 1909 edition of *Hymns Ancient and Modern*.

The church's one foundation (380)

Storer, John (b. Hulland, near Derby, Eng., May 18, 1858; d. Berwick-on-Tweed, Eng., May 1, 1930), was educated at Oxford University (Mus.B., 1878). In 1891 he became music director of the old Globe Theater, London, and later became organist of the Roman Catholic Cathedral, Waterford, Ireland, and was professor of plainchant at St. John's Ecclesiastical College. He composed three operas, one oratorio, two symphonies, several masses, church services, songs, and organ pieces.

Amens (551, 552, 554)

Stowe, Harriet Beecher (b. Litchfield, Conn., June 14, 1811; d. Hartford, Conn., July 1, 1896), was the daughter of Lyman Beecher, and the sister of Henry Ward Beecher. In 1832 her family moved to Cincinnati, Ohio, where her father was president of Lane Seminary. Four years later she was married to Calvin E. Stowe, professor of language and biblical literature at Lane Seminary. Her husband later taught at Bowdoin College and Andover Theological Seminary. She became intensely interested in the abolition of slavery and her *Uncle Tom's Cabin* (1852) brought her national fame. In addition to her writings for periodicals, she published more than forty volumes of prose, and one volume of poetry, *Religious Poems* (1867).

Still, still with Thee, when purple morning breaketh (25)

Stowell, Hugh (b. Douglas, Isle of Man, Eng., Dec. 3, 1799; d. Salford, Eng., Oct. 8, 1865), was educated at St. Edmund's Hall, Oxford (B.A., 1822; M.A. 1826). He was ordained in the Church of England in 1823, and after several curacies he was appointed rector of Christ Church, Salford, in 1831, where he remained until his death. He was a fervent and powerful preacher, and his large Sunday school revealed his intense love for children. He was one of the outstanding evangelical leaders in the Church of England during his day. In 1831 he published *A Selection of Psalms and Hymns Suited to the Services of the Church of England*. To this collection and subsequent editions he contributed approximately fifty hymns.

From every stormy wind that blows (296)

Sullivan, Arthur Seymour (b. Bolwell Terrace, Lambeth, Eng., May 13, 1842; d. Westminster, England, Nov. 22, 1900), at the age of twelve became a chorister at the Royal Chapel under Thomas Helmore. He was educated at the Royal Academy of Music where he studied under Sterndale Bennett and John Goss. He also studied under Hauptmann, David, and Moscheles at the Leipzig Conservatory. After his return to England he held several organist positions and became professor of composition at the Royal Academy of Music in 1866. He wrote a great deal of church music, but it is by his music composed for the Savoy Operas, in which he was associated with Sir W. S. Gilbert, that he received international fame, and the Gilbert and Sullivan operettas became a part of English life and tradition. Most of his hymn tunes were written between 1867 and 1874, appeared in *The Hymnary* (1872) and *Church Hymns* (1874). He strongly opposed the making of hymn tunes from popular melodies, and declined numerous requests for his permission to make hymn tune adaptations from his operettas.

St. Edmund—Draw Thou my soul, O Christ (314)
St. Gertrude—Onward, Christian soldiers (412)
Forward through the ages (463)
St. Kevin—Come, ye faithful, raise the strain (109)

Sumner, John B. (b. Lime Hill, Pa., Mar. 25, 1838; d. Binghamton, N.Y., May 9, 1918), was the son of George and Lydia (Bunnell) Summer and was educated at Wyoming Seminary, Pennsylvania. For a number of years he was a music teacher, holding singing schools in the Susquehanna Valley. Ordained to the Methodist ministry, he entered the Wyoming Conference in 1869, and held numerous pastorates until his retirement in 1908. He had a rich tenor voice, and with two other Methodist ministers in the area organized the Wyoming Conference Trio, which became quite popular at Methodist conferences at Chautauqua meetings. Of the eleven hymn tunes which he composed, only the present one is known today.

Binghamton—My Father, is rich in houses and lands (270)

Sweney, John R. (b. West Chester, Pa., Dec. 31, 1837; d. Chester, Pa., Apr. 10, 1899), at the age of twenty-two taught music at Dover, Delaware. After the outbreak of the Civil War, he directed the band of the Third Delaware Regiment. Following the war he became professor of music at the Pennsylvania Military Academy, where he remained for twenty-five years. For more than ten years of this time he was music director of the Bethany Presbyterian Church, and song leader of the Sunday school of which John Wanamaker was superintendent. His unusual ability as a song leader is evidenced by the demand for his leadership at summer assemblies at Ocean Grove, New Jersey; Lake Bluff, Illinois; New Albany, Indiana; Old Orchard, Maine; Round Lake, New York; Thousand Islands, New York, and many others. He composed over one thousand gospel songs and was associated with the compilation of more than sixty collections of gospel songs, Sunday school music, and anthems.

I Shall Know Him—When my life-work is ended, and I cross the
swelling tide (472)
Stars in My Crown—I am thinking today of that beautiful land (470)
Story of Jesus—Tell me the story of Jesus (211)
Sunshine—There is sunshine in my soul today (273)
Sweney—More about Jesus would I know (321)

Tappan, William Bingham (b. Beverly, Mass., Oct. 24, 1794; d. West Needham, Mass., June 18, 1849). Tappan's father died when he was twelve, and he was apprenticed to a clockmaker in Boston. In 1815 he moved to Philadelphia where he made and repaired clocks. He became greatly interested in the Sunday school movement, and in 1822 secured employment with the American Sunday School Union and remained with this organization until his death. In 1840 he was licensed as a Congregational minister and engaged in evangelistic work in many states, all the while promoting the work of Sunday schools. He was quite prolific as a poet, publishing ten volumes of verse.

'Tis midnight, and on Olive's brow (104)

Tarrant, William George (b. Pembroke Dock, South Wales, July 2, 1853; d. Wandsworth, Eng., Jan. 15, 1928), was the son of Matthew and Mary (Lane) Tarrant. His father died when he was one year old, and his mother died when he was six. He was sent to an orphanage in Birmingham and his early schooling was in the Free Industrial School there. He was apprenticed to a silversmith, and later became a student at the Unitarian Home Missionary College in Manchester and the Manchester New College, London. He was ordained to the Unitarian ministry and pastored the Unitarian Christian Church, Wandsworth, London, for thirty-seven years. He was one of the leading ministers of his denomination, and in addition to his pastoral work he edited the Unitarian weekly paper, *The Inquirer*, 1887-97, 1918-27. He was keenly interested in literature and fond of writing verse. He also provided tunes for many of his hymns. His published works include *The Story and Significance of the Unitarian Movement* (1910), and *Songs of the Devout* (1912).

With happy voices ringing (507)

Tate, Nahum (b. Dublin, Ire., 1652; d. Southwark, London, Eng., Aug. 12, 1715), the son of an Irish clergyman, Faithful Teate [the original spelling], was educated at Trinity College, Dublin. After his graduation in 1668 he went to London to seek literary fame. He wrote much for the stage, and, lacking unusual creative talent of his own, he adapted works of others. He was appointed poet laureate in 1692 and royal historiographer in 1702. His chief claim to fame is his collaboration with Nicholas Brady in the *New Version of the Psalms of David* (1696), which was thoughtfully dedicated to the King William III. Failing to achieve financial success, and because of his own intemperance and carelessness, he was frequently in dire circumstances. His death occurred in the mint at Southwark, at the time a refuge for debtors.

While shepherds watched their flocks by night (79)

Taylor, John Prentice (b. Hamilton, Scot., Sept. 28, 1871; d. Hamilton, Feb. 14, 1936). Taylor's family originally came from the Island of Sanda off the coast of Southend Kintyre, Argyll. His early education was in Hamilton and as a young man he took up pharmacy. His musical interest caused him to study at the Athenaeum and Technical College, Glasgow, and the Midland Institute, Birmingham. He lead the singing for a time at the Chapel Street United Presbyterian Church [now Avon Street United Free Church], Hamilton, and afterwards served as organist of Kirn Parish Church.

KIRN—Our Lord Christ hath risen (112)

Taylor, Sarah E. (b. Stockport, Eng., 1883; d. Central Falls, R.I., Oct. 5, 1954), was the daughter of William B. and Sarah (Wood) Taylor. Her father, a Primitive Methodist preacher, brought his family to America in 1892. After her graduation from Brown University (A.B., 1904; M.A., 1910), she spent the rest of her life as a schoolteacher. First teaching in mission schools in Alabama and Virginia, she later taught in Methuen, Massachusetts, and for thirty-two years she taught in the high schools of Central Falls and Pawtucket, Rhode Island. After her retirement in 1949, she made her home in Central Falls until her death. She wrote a number of poems, and is the author of the Rhode Island state song.

O God of light, Thy Word, a lamp unfailing (185)

Tearne, T. S. The identity of this composer is unknown.

Response (553)

Tennyson, Alfred (b. Somersby, Lincolnshire, Eng., Aug. 6, 1809; d. Aldworth, Surrey, Eng., Oct. 6, 1892), the son of the G. C. Tennyson, rector of Somersby, was educated at Louth Grammar School and at Trinity College, Cambridge. His poetical talent became widely known during his student days at Cambridge, and after the publication of *In Memoriam,* he was made poet laureate, succeeding William Wordsworth. He was elevated to peerage, becoming Lord Tennyson in 1884. He produced about twenty major works, among which were *Maud* (1855), *Idylls of the King* (1859), and *Poems* (1842). He died at his country home, Aldworth, and was buried in Westminster Abbey.

Ring out the old, ring in the new (496)

Tersteegen, Gerhard (b. Mörs, Rhenish Pruss., Nov. 25, 1697; d. Mühlheim, Rhenish Pruss., Apr. 3, 1769). Tersteegen's parents had intended that he should be a Reformed Church minister, but his father died when he was six and a university education was financially impossible. At the age of sixteen he was apprenticed to a merchant, and four years later had his own business. For nearly five years he experienced seasons of deep spiritual despondency. After an unusual experience of grace in 1724, he wrote out a solemn covenant with God and signed it with his own blood. From this time until the end of his life he devoted his energies to religious work and literary activities. It is said that he worked at his loom ten hours each day, prayed for two hours, and spent two hours writing and discussing spiritual matters with friends. Finally he gave up his business and his home, known as the "Pilgrim's Cottage," became a refuge where he ministered to the physical and spiritual needs of many. He prepared food and simple medicines for the poor. He shared with Neander the feeling that the Reformed Church had become too engrossed in mechanics, and had lost its evangelical fervor. While he lived apart from the Reformed Church, he made no effort to set up a new sect, and he lived the quiet life of a celibate and ascetic.

God calling yet! shall I not hear (223)

Teschner, Melchior (b. Fraustadt, Silesia, 1584; d. Oberprietschen, Posen, Dec. 1, 1635), was appointed cantor of the Lutheran church at Fraustadt in 1609 and taught in the parish school. In 1614 he became pastor at Oberprietschen, and was succeeded in this position by his son and later his grandson.

ST. THEODULPH—All glory, laud, and honor (151)

Theodulph of Orleans (d. 821), apparently a native Italian, became abbot of a monastery in Florence. Emperor Charlemagne brought him to France and he was appointed Bishop of Orleans, 781-818. He ruled with strictness and founded schools for the education of his people. He was one of Charlemagne's counselors and became his chief theologian. After the death of Charlemagne he fell into disfavor with his son and successor, Emperor Louis the Pious, was accused of conspiracy, and imprisoned at Angers in 818. He died three years later, probably from poison.

All glory, laud, and honor (151)

Thomas, Alexcenah. The identity of this author is unknown.

Hark! 'tis the Shepherd's voice I hear (429)

Thompson, Will Lamartine (b. East Liverpool, Ohio, Nov. 7, 1847; d. New York City, Sept. 20, 1909), was educated at Mt. Union College, Ohio, and at the Boston Conservatory of Music, and later studied in

Leipzig, Germany. While he wrote many secular and patriotic songs, his major interest was in the writing of sacred songs. He established the Will L. Thompson & Co., a successful music publishing firm in East Liverpool and Chicago, Illinois. The story is told of a visit Thompson made to Dwight L. Moody at a time when Moody was quite ill. Visitors had been forbidden, but when Moody heard that Thompson was there, he insisted that he be admitted to the room. Moody greeted him most cordially and said, "Will, I would rather have written 'Softly and tenderly Jesus is calling,' than anything I have been able to do in my whole life."

Jesus is all the world to me—ELIZABETH (155)
Softly and tenderly Jesus is calling—THOMPSON (236)

Thomson, Mary Ann (b. London, Eng., Dec. 5, 1834; d. Philadelphia, Pa., Mar. 11, 1923), spent her early life in England. She came to America and became the wife of John Thomson, who served as the first librarian of the Free Library in Philadelphia. For many years she was a member of the Church of the Annunciation, Philadelphia, where her husband was the accounting warden. Many of her poems and hymns appeared in *The Churchman,* New York, and *The Living Church,* Chicago.

O Zion haste, thy mission high fulfilling (451)

Thring, Godfrey (b. Alford, Somerset, Eng., Mar. 25, 1823; d. Shamley Green, Guildford, Eng., Sept. 13, 1903), was educated at Shrewsbury School, and Balliol College, Oxford (B.A., 1845). Ordained in the Church of England in 1846, he held several curacies, and in 1858 succeeded his father as rector of Alford. He became prebendary of East Harptree in Wells Cathedral in 1876, where he remained until his retirement in 1893. His publications include *Hymns and Other Verses* (1866); *Hymns Congregational and Others* (1866); and *A Church of England Hymn Book, Adapted to the Daily Services of the Church Throughout the Year* (1880; rev. ed., 1882).

Crown Him with many crowns (in part—152)
The radiant morn hath passed away (32)

Thrupp, Dorothy Ann (b. London, Eng., June 20, 1779; d. London, Dec. 14, 1847). Very little is known about this hymn writer. Under the pseudonym, "Iota," she contributed some hymns to W. Carus Wilson's *Friendly Visitor* and *Children's Friend.* Mrs. Herbert Mayo's *Selection of Hymns and Poetry for the Use of Infant Schools and Nurseries* (1838), contained several hymns signed "D.A.T." She was the editor of *Hymns for the Young,* (*ca.* 1830), in which all the hymns were unsigned.

Saviour, like a shepherd lead us (344)

Tillman, Charles Davis (b. Tallassee, Ala., Mar. 20, 1861; d. Atlanta, Ga., Sept. 2, 1943), was the youngest son of James Lafayette and Mary (Davis) Tillman. After traveling with his preacher father in evangelistic work, he worked as a house painter, a traveling salesman for a Raleigh, North Carolina, music company, sang comic songs on a traveling wagon advertising Wizard Oil, and sang first tenor in a male quartet. In 1887 he began his career as an evangelistic singer. He established his own publishing company in Atlanta, Georgia, and published about twenty gospel song collections which were quite popular throughout the South. About 1891, while he was assisting his father in a tent revival in Lexington, South Carolina, a group of Negroes borrowed the tent for a Sunday afternoon service. Their singing of "The Old Time Religion" so impressed Tillman that he wrote it down, later publishing it for the first time in any form. Two of his songs which became immensely popular were: "My Mother's Bible," and "Life's Railway to Heaven."

TILLMAN—Ready to suffer grief or pain (439)

Tindley, Charles Albert (b. Berlin, Md., July 7, 1851; d. Philadelphia, Pa., July 26, 1933), a Negro Methodist preacher, was the son of slave parents, Charles and Esther Tindley. His mother died when he was four years old, and the following year he was separated from his father. By his own determination he learned to read and write when he was seventeen. Shortly afterward he moved to Phliadelphia, worked as a hod carrier, was janitor of a small church, and attended night school. He took a correspondence course from the Boston School of Theology.

Ordained to the Methodist ministry, he joined the Delaware Annual Conference in 1885 and served the following charges: South Wilmington, Delaware, 1885-86; Cape May, New Jersey, 1886-87; Odessa, Delaware, 1887-89; Pocomoke Circuit, Maryland, 1889-92; Fairmount, Maryland, 1892-95; Ezion, Delaware, 1895-97; Wilmington, Delaware, 1897-99; presiding elder of the Wilmington District, 1899-1902.

In 1902 he became pastor of the Calvary Methodist Episcopal Church of Philadelphia, the church where he had once been janitor. So successful was his leadership that in 1907 a new building was needed for the growing congregation. A new building was erected at Broad and Fitzwater Streets in 1924, and, in spite of his protests, the church was renamed the Tindley Temple Methodist Church. Here he preached to great throngs of people. Both Negroes and whites were represented in the leadership of the church, along with Italians, Jews, Germans, Norwegians, Mexicans, and Danes. He wrote both words and music for many gospel songs, among the most popular of which are "Nothing Between," "Leave It There,"

"I Have Found at Last a Saviour," "Stand by Me," and the present hymn. It was Tindley's song, "I'll Overcome Some Day," written in 1901, that served as a basis, more in spirit and thought than in actual words or melody, for "We Shall Overcome," a theme song of the present-day civil rights movement.

Trials dark on every hand—BY AND BY (473)

Tomer, William Gould (b. Oct. 5, 1833; d. New Jersey, Sept. 26, 1896), during the Civil War, served in the 153rd Pennsylvania Infantry and was detailed at the headquarters of General O. O. Howard. After the war he spent twenty years as a government employee in Washington, D.C., and during this time he served as music director at the Grace Methodist Episcopal Church there. He spent the last years of his life in New Jersey as a schoolteacher.

GOD BE WITH YOU—God be with you till we meet again (372)

Toplady, Augustus Montague (b. Farnham, Surrey, Eng., Nov. 4, 1740; d. London, Eng., Aug. 11, 1778), was educated at Westminster School, London, and at Trinity College, Dublin. While in Dublin he was converted by a sermon by James Morris, a Methodist lay preacher, at a service in a barn. Ordained in the Church of England in 1762, he was curate at Blagdon and Farleigh, and appointed vicar at Broadhembury, Devonshire, in 1766. He moved to London in 1775, and preached at the French Calvinist church in Leicester Fields. An ardent Calvinist, he was an outspoken critic of Wesleyan theology, and bitter feelings existed for many years. Among his published works are: *Poems on Sacred Subjects* (1796), *Historic Proof of the Doctrinal Calvinism of the Church of England* (1774), and *Psalms and Hymns for Public and Private Worship* (1776).

Rock of Ages, cleft for me (103)

Tourjée, Lizzie Shove (1858-1913), was the daughter of Dr. Eben Tourjée, founder of the New England Conservatory of Music. She was educated in the high school of Newton, Massachusetts, and at Wellesley College, 1877-78. In 1883 she was married to Franklin Estabrook.

WELLESLEY—There's a wideness in God's mercy (48)

Tours, Berthold (b. Rotterdam, Neth., Dec. 17, 1838; d. Fulham, London, Eng., Mar. 11, 1897), the son of a distinguished Dutch organist, Barthelemy Tours, was educated in the conservatories at Brussels and Leipzig. He settled in London in 1861, taught music privately and played in various orchestras, and the following year became organist of the Swiss Church, Holborn. He joined the editorial staff of Novello & Company in 1878, and wrote a considerable amount of music.

BERTHOLD—With happy voices ringing (507)

Towner, Daniel Brink (b. Rome, Pa., Mar. 5, 1850; d. Longwood, Mo., Oct. 3, 1919), received his early musical training from his father, Professor J. G. Towner, a singer and music teacher of considerable reputation. Later he studied with John Howard, George F. Root, and George J. Webb. He served as music director of the Centenary Methodist Episcopal Church, Binghamton, New York, 1870-82; York Street Methodist Episcopal Church, Cincinnati, Ohio, 1882-84; and the Union Methodist Episcopal Church, Covington, Kentucky, 1884-85. Because of his fine baritone voice and his skill as a choral conductor, Dwight L. Moody invited him to become associated with his evangelistic work in the fall of 1885. In 1893 he became head of the Music Department of Moody Bible Institute, Chicago. In this position he exerted an unusual influence in church music throughout the Midwest as he trained evangelical church music leadership and evangelistic singers. He was awarded the Mus.D. degree by the University of Tennessee in 1900. More than two thousand songs have been credited to him, and he was associated with the publication of fourteen collections. His death occurred while he was leading the music in an evangelistic meeting in Longwood, Missouri.

CALVARY—Years I spent in vanity and pride (96)
MOODY—Marvelous grace of our loving Lord (200)
TRUST AND OBEY—When we walk with the Lord (260)

Tuckerman, Samuel Parkman (b. Boston, Mass., Feb. 11, 1819; d. Newport, R.I., June 30, 1890), studied church music and organ with Carl Zeuner in Boston. In 1840 he became organist and choirmaster at St. Paul's Episcopal Church, Boston. He spent four years in England studying English cathedral music, and returned to Boston in 1853, giving lectures in early cathedral music and church music. Three years later Tuckerman returned to England where he lived from 1856 to 1864. He also spent several years in Switzerland. He compiled and edited *The Episcopal Harp* (Boston, 1844), *The National Lyre* (Boston, 1848), *Cathedral Chants* (1858), and *Trinity Collection of Church Music* (Boston, 1864).

HUMILITY—O Jesus, Master, when today (466)

Tullar, Grant Colfax (b. Bolton, Conn., Aug. 5, 1869; d. Ocean Grove, N.J., May 20, 1950), the son of Austin M. and Rhoda (Maine) Tullar, was born when Ulysses S. Grant and Schuyler Colfax were president and vice-president of the United States, which accounts for his name. His mother died when he was two years old, and he was reared by unsympathetic relatives. At the age of ten he worked in a woolen mill. Later, in Hartford, he clerked in a shoe store until he was fifteen. He was converted at a Methodist camp meeting near Waterbury, Connecticut, at the age of nineteen. His only formal education was at Hackettstown Academy, New Jersey, 1889-91. Ordained to the Methodist ministry, he served as pastor for one year at Dover, Delaware, resigning to enter evangelistic work. He became song leader for the evangelist, Major George A. Hilton, with whom he worked for ten years. In 1893, with Isaac H. Meredith (*q.v.*), he founded the Tullar-Meredith Publishing Company, New York, which became a successful business enterprise, publishing church and Sunday school music.

FACE TO FACE—Face to face with Christ, my Saviour (475)
TULLAR—Hear ye the Master's call (437)

Turner, H. L. The identity of this author is unknown.

It may be at morn, when the day is awaking (120)

Turner, Herbert Barclay (b. Brooklyn, N.Y., July 17, 1852; d. Washington, Conn., May 1, 1927), was educated at Amherst College and at Union Theological Seminary. Ordained to the Congregational ministry, he held pastorates in Massachusetts and Connecticut before becoming chaplain of Hampton Institute, Virginia, 1892-1925. He edited three compilations of hymns and tunes, one of which was *Hymns and Tunes for Schools* (1905).

CUSHMAN—We would see Jesus; lo! His star is shining (89)

Turner, M. Elmore (b. Richmond, Va., Aug. 16, 1906), was educated at Lynchburg College, Virginia (A.B., 1928), and The College of the Bible, Lexington, Kentucky (B.D., 1936). He was ordained to the ministry in the Disciples of Christ Church, taught in the Department of Religion, Lynchburg College, and was pastor for two years at Cape Town, Union of South Africa. After holding pastorates in Corbin, Kentucky, and Washington, North Carolina, he became pastor of the Broad Street Christian Church, New Bern, North Carolina, in 1952.

Revealing Word, thy light portrays (177)

Tuttiett, Lawrence (b. Colyton, Devonshire, Eng., 1825; d. St. Andrews, Scot., May 21, 1897), the son of a surgeon in the Royal Navy, was educated at Christ's Hospital and at King's College, London. He was ordained in the Church of England in 1848, and was appointed vicar of Lea Marston, Warwickshire, 1854-1870. In 1870 he became rector of St. Andrews, Fife, Scotland, ten years later was named an honorary canon of St. Ninian's Cathedral, Perth. Among his published works are: *Hymns for Churchmen* (1854), and *Hymns for the Children of the Church* (1862).

Father, let me dedicate (498)

Ufford, Edward Smith (b. Newark, N.J., Feb. 10, 1851; d. Union, Me., Dec. 8, 1929), was educated at Stratford Academy, Connecticut, and Bates Theological Seminary, Maine. He was licensed to preach in 1878 by the First Baptist Church, Portland, Maine, and ordained by the First Baptist Church, East Auburn, Maine, in 1879, where he first served as pastor. Later he was pastor of Baptist churches in Alna, Maine; Canton, Dedham, Hingham, Winchendon, and Willimansett, Massachusetts. He published four collections of songs: *Convert's Praise, Life-Long Songs, Wonderful Love,* and *Gathered Gems.*

Throw out the lifeline across the dark wave—LIFELINE (217)

Vail, Silas Jones (b. Brooklyn, N.Y., Oct. 6, 1818; d. Brooklyn, May 20, 1884), after working as a hatmaker in Danbury, Connecticut, settled in New York and became a successful businessman. Maintaining an avid interest in music as a hobby, he composed a number of hymn tunes and was associated in editing a number of collections, one of which was *Songs of Grace and Glory* (1874), in collaboration with William F. Sherwin.

CLOSE TO THEE—Thou my everlasting portion (354)

Van DeVenter, Judson W. (b. near Dundee, Mich., Dec. 5, 1855, d. Tampa, Fla., July 17, 1939), the son of John W. and Eliza (Wheeler) Van DeVenter, was educated in the public schools of Dundee and at Hillsdale College (Mich.). He received his musical training in numerous singing schools. He studied art and in 1885 toured Europe, visiting the famous art galleries and studying painting. For several years he taught art and penmanship in public schools, and became supervisor of art in the high school at Sharon, Pennsylvania. During this time he was an active member of the Methodist Episcopal Church and sang in the choir. After experiencing a definite call to the ministry, he was licensed as a local preacher. He began evangelistic work, preaching throughout the United States, England, and Scotland. He was assisted for many years by W. S. Weeden (*q.v.*), an evangelistic singer. During the last years of his life, he resided at Tampa, Florida.

All to Jesus I surrender (363)

Van Dyke, Henry (b. Germantown, Pa., Nov. 10, 1852; d. Princeton, N.J., Apr. 10, 1933), was educated at the Brooklyn Polytechnic Institute, Princeton University, and Princeton Theological Seminary. Ordained to the Presbyterian ministry, he began his pastoral work in the United Congregational Church, Newport, Rhode Island, 1879-83, then became pastor of New York City's Brick Presbyterian Church, 1883-1899. In 1899 he was appointed professor of English literature at Princeton, and continued this association for twenty-three years. His friend, Woodrow Wilson, whom he had known when Wilson was president of Princeton University, appointed him as the United States minister to the Netherlands and Luxemburg, where he served from 1913 to 1916. In 1917 he was a lieutenant commander in the United States Navy Chaplain Corps. He served his denomination with distinction, being elected moderator of the General Assembly, and chairman of the committee which prepared the *Book of Common Worship,* 1905, and its revision in 1932. He published a number of books, among which were *The Reality of Religion* (1884), *The Story of the Psalms* (1887), *Sermons to Young Men* (1893), *The Story of the Other Wise Man* (1896), and *The Gospel for an Age of Doubt* (1896).

Joyful, joyful, we adore Thee (44)

Vories, William Merrell (b. Leavenworth, Kan., Oct. 28, 1880), as a student at Colorado College, became a student volunteer for foreign missions. In 1905-7 he taught at Omi-Hachiman, Japan, and was greatly impressed with the need for Christian missionary work there. During this time he founded the Omi Mission, later the Omi Brotherhood. He returned to America and studied architecture that with this knowledge he might help the Japanese build more substantially and economically. Through the years the work of the Omi Brotherhood has become a vast organization, employing more than five hundred workers. The Omi Brotherhood Foundation conducts the evangelistic, medical, and social activities. The Omi Brotherhood School Foundation operates a kindergarten, primary school, junior high, and senior high school. The Omi Brotherhood, Ltd., is the business organization consisting of the Mentholatum and Air-Wick Department, the Architectural Department, and the Importing and Exporting Department. The founder of the Mentholatum Company, A. A. Hyde, was one of the early supporters of the Omi Brotherhood, and gave this organization the sole rights and profits from the manufacture and sale of these products in Japan. The Architectural Department has designed and built more than two thousand churches, schools, and other buildings in Japan, including the International Christian University, Tokyo. In 1919 he married Maki Hitotsuyanagi, daughter of a Japanese noble family. About 1940 he became a Japanese naturalized citizen. He dropped his first name, added his wife's family name, and today is known as Merrell Vories-Hitotsuyanagi. Dr. Hitotsuyanagi remains active in his adopted country, serving God and his fellow man in the many activities of his work.

Let there be light, Lord God of hosts (444)

Wade, John Francis (b. *ca.* 1710; d. Aug. 16, 1786), was an English layman who lived in Douay, France, a Roman Catholic center in which was located an English college, and was a haven for English religious and political refugees of the Jacobite rebellion of 1745. Here he made his living copying and selling plain chant and other music for use in the chapels and homes of the community. He also was a teacher of music.

O come, all ye faithful (66)—ADESTE FIDELES (66, 262)

Walch, James (b. Edgerton, near Bolton, Eng., June 21, 1837; d. Barrow-in-Furness, Eng., 1901), studied music with his father, John Walch, and later with Henry Smart. He became organist at Duke's Alley Congregational Church, Bolton, in 1851, Walmsley Church, 1857, and Bridge Street Wesleyan Chapel in 1858. In 1863 he became organist at St. George's Parish Church, Bolton. From 1870 to 1874 he was conductor of the Bolton Philharmonic Society. In 1877 he moved to Barrow-in-Furness where he maintained a music business and was honorary organist of the parish church. Of the church music he composed, only the present tune remains in common usage.

TIDINGS—O Zion haste, thy mission high fulfilling (451)

Walford, William (b. Bath, Somerset, Eng., 1772; d. Uxbridge, Eng., June 22, 1850). The evidence presented in discussing the hymn named below indicates that possibly it should be credited to William Walford of Homerton. Educated at Homerton Academy, 1793-98, he was ordained to the Congregational ministry. He served as pastor at Stowmarket, Suffolk, 1798-1800; Great Yarmouth, Norfolk, 1800-13; and was classical tutor at Homerton, 1814-31. He was pastor at Uxbridge, Middlesex for two terms, 1824-31 and 1833-48, after which he retired. Possibly the interval from 1831 to 1833 corresponds to the period of illness referred to in the discussion of the hymn. He is the author of *The Manner of Prayer* (1836); *The Book of Psalms, a New Translation; Curae Romanae; A Catechism on Christian Evidences,* and other works. His *Autobiography,* edited by John Stoughton, was published in 1851.

Sweet Hour of prayer, sweet hour of prayer (327)

Walker—*see* "Coghill."

Wallace, William Vincent (b. Waterford, Ire., June 1, 1812; d. Château de Bages, France, Oct. 12, 1865), of Scotch descent, received his early musical training from his father, a bandmaster and bassoon player. He became an accomplished violinist, giving his first concert at the age of fifteen in Dublin. After an unhappy marriage which ended in divorce, he spent some time in Australia, New Zealand, India, and South America. Returning to England, he presented two operas at Drury Lane, London, *Maritana* (1845), and *Matilda of Hungary* (1847). Following this he made an extensive concert tour of the United States, Mexico, and South America, after which he settled in London. He led an adventurous life and achieved considerable success as a concert violinist and composer. He composed seven operas, one cantata, and a great deal of piano music. In his later years he was afflicted with poor eyesight, and he returned to France for his health.

SERENITY—Immortal Love, forever full (277)

Walter, Howard Arnold (b. New Britain, Conn., Aug. 19, 1883; d. Lahore, India, Nov. 1, 1918), was educated at Princeton University, Hartford Theological Seminary, and did further study at the universities in Edinburgh, Glasgow, and Göttingen. He taught English at Waseda University, Tokyo, Japan. Returning to the United States, he served as assistant pastor at the Asylum Hill Congregational Church, Hartford, Connecticut, 1910-13. He joined the executive staff of the YMCA for India and Ceylon to work with Mohammedan students, and set up his headquarters at Lahore, the capital city of Punjab in India.

I would be true, for there are those who trust me (315)

Walton, James George (1821-1905). Other than the dates of his birth and death, the only information known about this composer is that he edited *Plain Song Music for the Holy Communion Office* (1874), which contained the tune given below.

ST. CATHERINE (adapted)—Faith of our fathers! living still (252)
Jesus, Thy boundless love to me (288)

Ward, Samuel Augustus (b. Newark, N.J., Dec. 28, 1847; d. Newark, Sept. 28, 1903), the son of George Spencer and Abbie Ann (Tichenor) Ward, received his musical training in New York City, one of his teachers being Jan Pychowski. He settled in Newark, New Jersey, established a successful retail music store and was active in the musical life of the city. He was married to Virginia Bell Ward [no relation] in 1871.

In 1880 he succeeded Henry S. Cutler (*q.v.*) as organist at Grace Episcopal Church, Newark, and held this position for a number of years. He founded the Orpheus Club of Newark in 1889, and served as its director until 1900. In 1934 a brass plaque was erected to his memory on the exterior wall of the Parish House of Grace Church by the Schoolmen's Club, assisted by the public school children of Newark.

MATERNA—O beautiful for spacious skies (489)

Ware, Henry, Jr. (b. Hingham, Mass., Apr. 21, 1794; d. Framingham, Mass., Sept. 25, 1843), after graduation from Harvard in 1812, taught at the preparatory school at Exeter, New Hampshire. He was ordained to the Unitarian ministry and became pastor of the Second Unitarian Church, Boston, where his assistant, in 1829, was Ralph Waldo Emerson. For twelve years he was professor of pulpit eloquence and pastoral care at the Cambridge Theological School. He was also editor of *The Christian Disciple* [later *The Christian Examiner*]. To avoid confusion with his father, Dr. Henry Ware of the Harvard Divinity School, he is sometimes referred to as Henry Ware, the Younger.

Happy the home when God is there (374)

Waring, Anna Laetitia (b. Plas-y-Velin, Neath, Glamorganshire, South Wales, Apr. 19, 1823; d. Clifton, near Bristol, Eng., May 10, 1910), the daughter of Elijah Waring of Plas-y-Velin, Neath, was brought up in the Society of Friends. However, she abandoned her Quaker background, joined the Church of England, and was baptized in 1842. Her *Hymns and Meditations by A.L.W.* (1850), contained nineteen hymns and was enlarged to thirty-nine hymns in the tenth edition (1863). During her later years she lived at Clifton and spent much of her time visiting prisoners in the jails.

In heavenly love abiding (303)

Warner, Anna Bartlett (b. Long Island, N.Y. 1820; d. Constitution Island, near West Point, N.Y., 1915), was a daughter of Henry W. Warner, a New York lawyer, and after 1837 she made her home with her father and her older sister, Susan, on Constitution Island, near the United States Military Academy at West Point. While she did not achieve the literary fame accorded her sister, she wrote a number of novels under the pseudonym "Amy Lothrop," and published two collections of verse, *Hymns of the Church Militant* (1858), and *Wayfaring Hymns, Original and Translated* (1869). She and her sister conducted Sunday school classes for the cadets at West Point for many years. Their home, "Good Crag," was willed to the Academy and has been made a national shrine. Anna died at the age of ninety-five and was buried with military honors.

Jesus loves me! this I know (512)
We would see Jesus, for the shadows lengthen (324)

Warren, George William (b. Albany, N.Y., Aug. 17, 1828; d. New York, N.Y., Mar. 17, 1902), was educated at Racine College, Wisconsin. As an organist, he was largely self-taught. An outstanding American organist of his day, he served as organist at St. Peter's Episcopal Church, Albany, 1846-58, St. Paul's Church, Albany, 1858-60; Holy Trinity Church, Brooklyn, 1860-70; and at St. Thomas' Church, New York City, 1870-90. In addition to composing anthems and service music, he edited *Hymns and Tunes as Sung at St. Thomas' Church* (1888).

NATIONAL HYMN—God of our fathers, whose almighty hand (54)
Heralds of Christ, who bear the King's commands (452)

Wartensee—see "Schnyder"

Watts, Isaac (b. Southampton, Eng., July 17, 1674; d. Stoke Newington, Eng., Nov. 25, 1748). Watts's father, Isaac Watts, a clothier by trade, was a deacon at the Above Bar Congregational Church in Southampton, and was imprisoned several times for his beliefs. His wife, of French Huguenot descent, carried Isaac as a baby to visit her husband in jail. Isaac Watts was educated at the Free School, Southampton, and in the Nonconformist academy of Thomas Rowe at Stoke Newington near London. In 1699 he became assistant pastor at Mark Lane Independent Chapel, London, and three years later became pastor. During a serious illness in 1712 he was invited to stay in the home of Sir Thomas Abney at Theobalds, near Cheshunt, Hertfordshire. The illness lasted for four years, but he remained with the Abney family for the rest of his life, acting as tutor to the children and chaplain to the household. During this time he devoted much of his time to writing, producing about sixty books dealing with a wide range of subjects. His *Logic* was used as a textbook at Oxford University for many years. He died in the Abney home and was buried at Bunhill Fields. A monument to his memory was erected in Westminster Abbey.

Universally accepted as the "father of English hymnody," Watts wrote about six hundred hymns, and many of the best of these were written in his early twenties. Most of his hymns appeared in his three now famous collections: *Hora Lyricae* (1706); *Hymns and Spiritual Songs* (1707); and *The Psalms of David Imitated in the Language of the New Testament and Applied to the Christian State and Worship* (1719). As stated in the title of this latter collection, Watts believed that the New Testament church should sing praise to God in the "language of the New Testament," and on this principle laid the foundation for the transition from the singing of metrical psalms to hymns of "human composure" throughout the English-speaking world. Bernard Manning in *The Hymns of Wesley and Watts* (1942), says, "To Watts more than to any other man is due the triumph of the hymn in English worship. All later hymn-writers, even when they excell him, are his debtors."

Alas, and did my Saviour bleed (94, 101)
Am I a soldier of the cross (405)
Begin, my tongue, some heavenly theme (49)
Come, Holy Spirit, heavenly Dove (169)
Come, we that love the Lord (308)
Jesus shall reign where'er the sun (116)
Joy to the world! the Lord is come (65)
Let all on earth their voices raise (7)
My dear Redeemer and my Lord (83)
Now to the Lord a noble song (19)
O God, our help in ages past (286)
So let our lips and lives express (323)
The heavens declare Thy glory, Lord (187)
This is the day the Lord hath made (39)
When I can read my title clear (468)
When I survey the wondrous cross (99)

Watson, Lawrence White (b. Charlottetown, Prince Edward Island, May 2, 1860; d. Charlottetown, July 17, 1925), after musical study at the Roman Catholic convent in his home town, became organist at St. Peter's Episcopal Church at the age of eighteen and served in this position until 1920. In addition to his musical activities, he was greatly interested in painting, botany, geology and natural history. In his botanical research on Prince Edward Island, he discovered a new species of violet, and this was named for him by the government, *Viola Watsoni.*

SALVE DOMINE—Light of the world, we hail Thee (454)

Weaver, Mack. The identity of this author is unknown.

Lord, lay some soul upon my heart (332—stanzas 2 and 3)

Webb, George James (b. Wiltshire, near Salisbury, Eng., June 24, 1803; d. Orange, N.J., Oct. 7, 1887), after studying music under Alexander Lucas of Salisbury, became organist at Falmouth. In 1830 he came to the United States, settled at Boston, and became organist of the

Old South Church, a position which he held for forty years. He was active in the musical affairs of the city of Boston, and became associated with Lowell Mason in the Boston Academy of Music, the establishing of music conventions to train music teachers, and also in the editing and compiling of music collections. He became widely known and respected as a choral and orchestral conductor. His publications include *The Massachusetts Collection of Psalmody* (1840); *The American Glee Book* (1841); *The Psaltery* (1845; coedited with Mason); *The National Psalmist* (1848); *Cantica Laudis* (1850); and *Cantica Ecclesiastica* (1859). For a brief time he edited two music periodicals, *The Music Library,* 1835-36, and *The Musical Cabinet,* 1837-40.

WEBB—O Thou whose hand hath brought us (379)
Stand up, Stand up for Jesus (415)
The morning light is breaking (448)

Webbe, Samuel (b. London, Eng., 1740; d. London, May 25, 1816), after completing apprenticeship as a cabinet maker, decided at the age of twenty to become a musician and began as a music copyist for the London publisher, Welcker. His work so impressed Carl Barbandt, that he gave him music lessons. He became organist at the chapels of the Sardinian and Portuguese embassies in London, two of the few respectable organ positions then open to a Roman Catholic organist. He published *A Collection of Sacred Music As Used in the Chapel of the King of Sardinia in London* (ca. 1793), *A Collection of Masses for Small Choirs* (1792), *A Collection of Motetts and Antiphons* (1792; compiled with his son, Samuel Webbe, the Younger), *Antiphons in Six Books of Anthems* (1818), and nine collections of glees and catches.

CONSOLATION (WEBBE)—Come, ye disconsolate, where'er ye languish (297)

Weber, Carl Maria von (b. Eutin, Ger., Nov. 18, 1786; d. London, Eng., June 4, 1826). Weber's father was a traveling theatrical impresario and during his boyhood his family lived in many places. He studied with Michael Haydn at Salzburg and later with Abt Vogler. In 1804, through Vogler's influence, he became the conductor of the Municipal Theater at Breslau, and later held similar positions at Stuttgart, Prague, and Dresden. He gained great fame for the operatic writing: *Der Freischütz, Preciosa, Euryanthe,* and *Oberon.* In addition to his operas, he wrote symphonies, masses, cantata, chamber music, and other miscellaneous compositions. He died suddenly in London of tuberculosis.

JEWETT—My Jesus, as Thou wilt (251)

SEYMOUR—Softly now the light of day (33)
    Holy Spirit, from on high (171)
    Depth of mercy! can there be (242)
    Cast thy burden on the Lord (254)
    Gentle Jesus, meek and mild (510)

Webster, Joseph Philbrick (b. Manchester, N.Y., Mar. 22, 1819; d. Elkhorn, Wis., Jan. 18, 1875), was educated at the academy at Pembroke, New Hampshire, and studied music under Lowell Mason in Boston. He spent a number of years in New York and Connecticut, teaching music and giving concerts. He was a talented musician, playing the flute, violin and piano. Some time before the Civil War, because of his antislavery convictions, he settled at Elkhorn, Wisconsin. It is said that he composed more than one thousand musical compositions. His most popular secular song was "Lorena." He compiled *The Signet Ring* (Chicago, 1868).

SWEET BY AND BY—There's a land that is fairer than day (471)

Weeden, Winfield Scott (b. Middleport, Ohio, Mar. 29, 1847; d. Bisby Lake, N.Y., July 31, 1908), the son of Isaac and Sarah (Faar) Weeden, was educated in the public schools of his home town. For a number of years he taught singing schools, and later entered evangelistic work. He had a fine solo voice and was a talented leader, frequently invited to lead the music at YMCA, Christian Endeavor, and Epworth League conventions. In addition to composing numerous gospel songs, he compiled several collections, among which were *The Peacemaker* (1894), *Songs of Soverign Grace* (1897), *Songs of the Peacemaker* (1895). During the last years of his life he lived in New York, where he owned a small hotel in lower Manhattan. He was buried in New York City's Woodlawn Cemetery, with the title of his best-known hymn, "I Surrender All," engraved on the gravestone.

SURRENDER—All to Jesus I surrender (363)

Weissel, Georg (b. Domnau, Pruss., 1590; d. Königsberg, Pruss., Aug. 1, 1635), the son of Johann Weissel, burgomeister of Domnau, near Königsberg, was educated in the Universities of Königsberg, Wittenberg, Leipzig, Jena, Strassburg, Basel, and Marburg. In 1623 he became pastor of the Altrossgart Church at Königsberg, where he remained until his death. One of the most important early hymn writers of Prussia, he wrote about twenty hymns.

Lift up your heads, ye mighty gates (247)

Wells, Marcus Morris (b. Otsego, N.Y., Oct. 2, 1815; d. near Hardwick, N.Y., July 17, 1895), as a youth was converted in a mission in Buffalo. He spent most of his life near Hardwick, where he farmed and made farm implements.

Holy Spirit, faithful guide—FAITHFUL GUIDE (165)

Wesley, Charles (b. Epworth, Lincolnshire, Eng., Dec. 18, 1707; d. London, Eng., Mar. 29, 1788), was educated at Westminster School and at Christ Church College, Oxford, where, after his graduation, he became a tutor. There he founded the "Holy Club," a group of young Oxford students who were called "Methodists" because, as Wesley stated, they pledged themselves "to observe with strict formality the method of study and practice laid down in the statutes of the University." Following his ordination in the Church of England in 1735, he accompanied his brother, John, on a trip to the English colony in Georgia, arriving in Savannah in February, 1736. On this trip he served as private secretary and chaplain to Governor James E. Oglethorpe.

In a few months he returned to London, became associated with a group of Moravians there, and on Whitsunday, May 20, 1738, he experienced his spiritual conversion. Shortly afterward he accepted a curacy at Islington, London, but within a few months he was forbidden to preach in the parish. From this time on he was closely associated with his brother, John, and devoted his energies and talents to their evangelistic work. He traveled throughout England, riding on horseback, preaching to throngs in the out-of-doors, and founding societies for prayer and Bible study. In all this activity he remained loyal to the Church of England and was not in sympathy with those of the "Methodist" group who wanted to leave the Anglican church. Following his marriage in 1749, he confined his work largely to Bristol and London.

A prolific hymn writer, he wrote more than sixty-five hundred hymns which covered the broad scope of Christian experience in subjective expression, revealing a new evangelical emphasis in Christian song. He greatly expanded existing metrical form using thirty different meters for his hymns. He wrote with great ease and extraordinary facility on the slightest provocation. His hymns were written at home, at church, in the fields, on horseback, and while walking in the street. Of this rare talent, McCutchan wrote:

Like Schubert with his melodic instinct, every thought that came to the mind of Charles Wesley seemed to shape itself in poetic form. Not only was he merely the "sweet singer" of Methodism, but more than any other he was successful in presenting religion and religious experiences in lyrical form.

His hymns appeared in the fifty-six collections which the Wesleys published over a period of fifty-three years.

A charge to keep I have (358)
Blow ye the trumpet, blow (250)
Christ the Lord is risen today (115)
Christ, whose glory fills the skies (22)
Depth of mercy! can there be (242)
Father, I stretch my hands to Thee (46)
Gentle Jesus, meek and mild (510)
Hail, thou long-expected Jesus (70)
Hark! the herald angels sing (81)
Jesus, lover of my soul (156, 157, 158)
Lo, he comes with clouds descending (123)
Love divine, all loves excelling (2)
O for a thousand tongues to sing (129, 140)
Rejoice, the Lord is King (108)
Soldiers of Christ, arise (416)
Ye servants of God, your Master proclaim (147)

Wesley, John (b. Epworth, Lincolnshire, Eng., June 17, 1703; d. London, Eng., Mar. 2, 1791). Charles Wesley's older brother, John, was educated at Charterhouse and at Christ Church College, Oxford. He was ordained in the Church of England in 1724. After serving for a brief time as curate to his father, Rev. Samuel Wesley, rector of Epworth, 1727-29, he was a tutor at Lincoln College, Oxford, 1729-35. In 1736 he went to the English colony of Georgia, under appointment of the Society for the Propagation of the Gospel, to minister to the colonists. He became quite friendly with a group of Moravian missionaries on board ship and was impressed by their hymn singing. He learned German on the voyage and began translating some of the German hymns into English. Some of these translations, together with hymns of Watts, Austin, and Herbert which he had brought with him, were published at Charlestown as *A Collection of Psalms and Hymns* (1737). Henry Wilder Foote, in *Three Centuries of American Hymnody,* comments:

It is interesting to reflect that both the beginning of Wesleyan hymnody and the opening to the English-speaking world of the treasury of German worship-song took place in Georgia in the fourth decade of the eighteenth century, when that colony was still only an outpost in the wilderness.

After an unpleasant two years in Georgia, he returned to England, and at a meeting at Aldersgate Street in May, 1738, he felt his heart "strangely warmed," and dated his spiritual conversion from that experience. For the

437

rest of his life he devoted himself to evangelistic activity, traveling two hundred and twenty-five thousand miles and preaching more than forty thousand sermons. When churches were closed to him, he preached out-of-doors, on occasions preaching to many thousands at one time. To the body of Wesleyan hymnody he contributed only about twenty-seven original hymns and translations, but as leader, administrator, teacher, publisher, admonisher, and counselor he made a significant contribution to the development of Christian hymnody.

Jesus, Thy boundless love to me (tr.) (288)

Wesley, Samuel Sebastian (b. London, Eng., Aug. 14, 1810; d. London, Apr. 19, 1876), the son of Samuel Wesley, and the grandson of Charles Wesley (*q.v.*), was the greatest musical genius of the Wesley family, and one of the most significant English church musicians of the nineteenth century. His early music training was from his father, who was himself the greatest English organist of his day. He was a chorister at the Chapel Royal, and in 1839 received both the B.Mus. and D.Mus. degrees from Oxford University. He served as organists at five parish churches, including that of Leeds, and four cathedrals—Hereford, Exeter, Winchester, and Gloucester. In 1850 he became professor of organ at the Royal Academy of Music.

He was extremely fond of fishing, and it is said that he accepted or rejected organist positions offered him according to the fishing advantages of the vicinity. One of his assistants recorded that on one occasion, while driving with him to play the opening service for a new organ, Wesley could not resist the temptation of the fishing opportunities afforded by a river they crossed. He sent his assistant ahead to play the service, instructing him to say that he was unavoidably detained. He became recognized as the outstanding English organist of his time, and was ever an ardent advocate for improving English cathedral music. K. L. Parry states that he was "one of the most distinguished, venturesome, original-minded, and passionate for reform among nineteenth-century church musicians." He composed a great deal of service music and published *The European Psalmist* (1872), a compilation of 733 hymn tunes, of which 130 were his own.

AURELIA—I lay my sins on Jesus (210)
   I need Thee, precious Jesus (221)
   The church's one foundation (380)
   Another year is dawning (497)
Response (522)

West, Robert Athow (b. Thetford, Eng., 1809; d. Georgetown, D.C.,

Feb. 1, 1865), after early life in England, came to America in 1843 and served as official reporter for the General Conference of the Methodist Episcopal Church in 1844. He was one of a committee of seven appointed by the General Conference to compile *Hymns for the Use of the Methodist Episcopal Church* (1849). He served as editor of the *Columbia Magazine,* 1846-49, and of the *New York Commercial Advertiser* following 1858. He published *Sketches of Methodist Preachers* (1848), and *A Father's Letters to His Daughter* (1865).

Come, let us tune our loftiest song (128)

Weston, Rebecca J. The identity of this author is unknown.

Father, we thank Thee for the night (341)

Whately, Richard (b. London, Eng., Feb. 1, 1787; d. Dublin, Ire., Oct. 8, 1863), was educated at Oriel College, Oxford, where he had a brilliant career as a student, and was ordained in the Church of England in 1814. In 1825 he became principal of St. Alban's Hall, Oxford, and in 1831 was made bishop of Dublin. He is the author of a number of literary works, among which is his *Historic Doubts Relative to Napoleon,* a clever answer to Hume's contention that no amount of evidence can prove a miracle. His famous *Elements of Logic* (1826) went through many editions.

God, that madest earth and heaven (30—stanza 3)

Whelpton, George (b. Redbourne, Eng., May 17, 1847; d. Oxford, Ohio, Nov. 25, 1930), at the age of four was brought to the United States and at sixteen enlisted in the Union Army during the Civil War. He studied music under Horatio R. Palmer (*q.v.*), and later became a choral director of considerable reputation in Buffalo, New York. In 1903 he joined the editorial staff of the Century Publishing Company, New York, where he compiled *Hymns of Worship and Service, The Church Hymnal,* and other collections. In 1916 he accepted a similar position with A. S. Barnes Company, where he remained until his retirement in 1925.

Response (530)

White, Lewis Meadows (b. London, Eng., 1860; d. South Croydon, Eng., Dec., 1950), the son of Rev. L. B. White, vicar of St. Mary Aldermary, was ordained in the Church of England in 1884 and became curate of Cromer. In 1934 he was made honorary canon of Norwich Cathedral. An accomplished organist, he frequently gave organ recitals.

MOTHERHOOD—Gracious Saviour, who didst honor (503)

Whitefield, George (b. Gloucester, Eng., Dec. 16, 1714; d. Newburyport, Mass., Sept. 30, 1770), educated at St. Mary le Crypt School and Pembroke College, Oxford, was ordained in the Church of England in 1736. The following year he began preaching for the "Society of Methodists," which he had joined in 1735. From this time until his death he divided his time between England and America where he first visited in 1738, and became the connecting link of the evangelical movement on both sides of the Atlantic. In 1741, because of doctrinal differences, he separated from the Wesleys; and his followers and those of Wesley were to a certain extent rivals.

A popular and powerful preacher, he made much use of hymn singing in his meetings, and he was influential in the transition from psalm singing to hymn singing in the American colonies as he introduced the hymns of Watts in the days of the Great Awakening. For use in his Tabernacle in Tottenham Court Road, he published *Hymns for Social Worship* (1753). He brought this collection to America and several American reprints were published. In 1769 he made his final voyage to America and died the following year. He was buried under the pulpit of the Old South Presbyterian Church, Newburyport, Massachusetts.

Hark! the herald angels sing (alt.) (81)

Whitfield, Frederick (b. Threapwood, Shropshire, Eng., Jan. 7, 1829; d. Croyden, Eng., Sept. 13, 1904), was educated at Trinity College, Dublin (B.A., 1859). Ordained in the Church of England, he became curate of Otley, vicar of Kirby-Ravensworth, senior curate of Greenwich, and vicar of St. John's Bexley. In 1875 he was appointed to St. Mary's Church, Hastings. He published about thirty volumes of prose and verse.

I need Thee, precious Jesus (221)
I saw the cross of Jesus (190)
There is a name I love to hear (131)

Whiting, William (b. Kensington, Eng., Nov. 1, 1825; d. Winchester, Eng., May 3, 1878), was educated at Clapham and Winchester Colleges. For over twenty years he was master of Winchester College Choristers' School. He published *Rural Thoughts and Other Poems,* 1851. The present hymn is the only one he ever wrote.

Eternal Father, strong to save (61)

Whittier, John Greenleaf (b. Haverhill, Mass., Dec. 17, 1807; d. Hampton Falls, N.H., Sept. 7, 1892), was the son of Quaker parents and he worked on the family farm until he was twenty. His early poetical writings attracted the attention of William Lloyd Garrison, who persuaded his father to send him to Haverhill Academy. After the publication of his first book, *Legends of New England,* he became editor of the *Pennsylvania Freeman,* an antislavery newspaper published at Philadelphia. He was an ardent abolitionist, and employed his pen and his influence without restraint against slavery. As a poet, he ranks among the distinguished company of America's greatest poets. His works, too numerous and too well known to list here, may be found in any library. Hymns which bear his name have been taken from his poetical works, and he has said of himself: "I am really not a hymn writer, for the good reason that I know nothing of music. Only a very few of my pieces were written for singing. A good hymn is the best use to which poetry can be devoted, but I do not claim to have succeeded in composing one." Congregations which heartily sing his hymns would not agree with his final statement! (Cf. *The Hymn,* VIII, No. 4, 105-110.)

All things are Thine; no gift have we (403, 536)
Dear Lord and Father of mankind (335)
Immortal Love, forever full (277)
O brother man, fold to thy heart thy brother (447)

Whittle, Daniel Webster (b. Chicopee Falls, Mass., Nov. 22, 1840; d. Northfield, Mass., March 4, 1901), during his youth moved to Chicago, where he became a cashier of the Wells Fargo Bank. In 1861 he joined the 72nd Illinois Infantry, Company B, serving as a second lieutenant. He became provost marshal on the staff of General O. O. Howard, was with General Sherman on his march to the sea, and was wounded at Vicksburg. At the close of the war he was promoted to the rank of major and was known by this title the rest of his life. Returning to Chicago, he became treasurer of the Elgin Watch Company, but resigned in 1873, under Moody's influence, to become an evangelist. He was greatly successful in his evangelistic work and was fortunate to have successively the assistance of three outstanding singers—P. P. Bliss, James McGranahan, and George C. Stebbins. He wrote a number of hymns, most of which bore the pseudonym "El Nathan."

I know now why God's wondrous grace (275)
There shall be showers of blessing (264)
There's a royal banner given for display (408)
While we pray and while we plead (218)

Wigner, John Murch (b. King's Lynn, Norfolk, Eng., June 19, 1844; d. London, Eng., Mar. 31, 1911). At the time of Wigner's birth, his father, Rev. John Thomas Wigner, was pastor of the Baptist church at King's Lynn, Norfolk, England. He was educated at London University,

441

and in 1867 was appointed to the India Home Office, London, where he served until his retirement in 1909. An active Baptist, he was well known as a children's evangelist and a lay preacher. He was a member of the Council of the Children's Special Service Mission.

Come to the Saviour now (226)

Williams, Aaron (b. London, Eng., 1731; d. London, 1776), taught music in London, and was a music engraver and publisher. He served as clerk at the Scottish Church, London Wall. Among his publications are: *Universal Psalmodist* (1763), *The Royal Harmony* (1766), *New Universal Psalmodist* (1770), *Harmonia Coelestis* (6th ed., 1775), and *Psalmody in Minature* (1778). His 1763 collection was reprinted in many editions. An American edition was published at Newburyport, Massachusetts, by Daniel Bailey, *The American Harmony* (1769).

ST. THOMAS—I love Thy kingdom, Lord (382)
Rise up, O men of God (445)

Williams, Loren Raymond (b. Billings, Mo., Nov. 16, 1909), the son of Oscar T. and Caroline (Garbee) Williams, was educated at Southwest Baptist College, Bolivar, Missouri, William Jewell College, Liberty, Missouri, Southwest Missouri State College, Springfield (B.S., 1936); Kansas State College, Pittsburg (M.A., 1940); and Mount Vernon University (Ed.D., 1949). From 1931 to 1948 he was a public schoolteacher and music supervisor in Missouri, during which time he served as music director in several churches. He was minister of music, First Baptist Church, Owensboro, Kentucky, 1948-50, and First Baptist Church, Tulsa, Oklahoma, 1950-52. In 1952 he became associated with the Church Music Department of the Baptist Sunday School Board, Nashville, Tennessee, as editor of church music materials. Since 1962 he has served as director of field services in the Church Music Department. He is the author of *Familiar Hymns to Play and Sing* (1955), *Graded Choir Handbook* (1958), and *Hymn Playing* (1959). He was a member of the Hymnal Committee for the *Baptist Hymnal*.

DEDICATION (arr.)—What can I give to Jesus (508)

Williams, Peter (b. Llansadurnin, Carmarthenshire, Wales, Jan. 7, 1722; d. Llandyfeilog, Wales, Aug. 8, 1796), was educated at the Carmarthen Grammar School, and while there was converted under the preaching of George Whitefield. He was ordained in 1744 and appointed to the parish of Eglwys Cymmyn, where he started a school. However, the fervor of his preaching brought much opposition, and he was compelled to leave the Established Church. In 1746 he joined the Calvinistic

Methodists, and as an itinerant preacher became one of the most prominent leaders of the Methodist Revival in Wales. However, he was later expelled by the Methodists on the grounds of heresy. He then built a chapel of his own in Water Street, Carmarthen, on land which belonged to him. He published a Welsh hymnbook in 1759, a Welsh Bible with annotation (1767-70), a *Concordance* (1773), and *Hymns on Various Subjects* (1771).

Guide me, O Thou great Jehovah (tr.) (55, 56)

Williams, William (b. Cefn-y-coed, near Llandovery, Wales, Feb. 11, 1717; d. Pantycelyn, Wales, Jan. 11, 1791), was educated at Llwyn-llwyd Academy, Carmarthen, for the medical profession. He was so impressed by a sermon preached by Howell Harris, that he decided to enter the ministry. He was ordained deacon at the age of twenty-three, and served as a curate for three years. After he was refused ordination as a priest, because of his evangelical ideas, he left the Established Church and became an evangelist of the Welsh Calvinistic Methodist Church. He was an exceedingly popular preacher throughout Wales. He wrote about eight hundred hymns in Welsh and one hundred in English. Of his hymns, H. Elvet Lewis has said:

What Paul Gerhardt has been to Germany, what Isaac Watts has been to England, that and more has William Williams of Pantycelyn been to the little principality of Wales. His hymns have both stirred and soothed a nation for more than a hundred years; they have helped to fashion a nation's character and to deepen a nation's piety.

Guide me, O Thou great Jehovah (55, 56)

Willis, Richard Storrs (b. Boston, Mass., Feb. 10, 1819; d. Detroit, Mich., May 7, 1900), was educated at Chauncey Hall, Boston Latin School, and Yale College, (A.B., 1841). Six years were spent in Germany studying with Xavier Schnyder (von Wartensee) (*q.v.*) and Moritz Hauptmann. During this time he became an intimate friend of Mendelssohn who was greatly interested in his compositions. He returned to the United States in 1848, was music critic on the *New York Tribune, The Albion,* and *The Musical Times.* From 1852 to 1864 he edited *The Music Times, The Musical World,* and *Once a Month.* After 1861 he made his home in Detroit, Michigan, but spent four years in Nice, Italy, 1874-78, to educate his daughter. He published *Church Chorals and Choir Studies* (1850), *Our Church Music* (1856), *Waif of Song* (1876), and *Pen and Lute* (1883).

CAROL—It came upon the midnight clear (71)
CRUSADERS' HYMN (arr.)—Fairest Lord Jesus (159)

443

Wilson, Emily Divine (b. Philadelphia, Pa., May 24, 1865; d. Philadelphia, June 23, 1942), was the daughter of John and Sarah (Lees) Divine, her father a native of Ireland, and her mother a native of England. In 1887 she was married to Rev. John G. Wilson, a Methodist minister, who served as district superintendent of the Philadelphia Conference, and at the time of his death, August 2, 1933, was pastor of the Wharton Memorial Methodist Church, Philadelphia. Both she and her husband were well known at Ocean Grove, New Jersey, where they regularly attended the summer assemblies. Leon T. Moore, writing in the Philadelphia Conference Minutes, says:

Mrs. Wilson was the acknowledged inspiration of her esteemed husband. She was beloved by the congregations of the churches served. Her musical ability was a great contribution to the work of the local church, together with her ability in dramatic art.

HEAVEN—Sing the wondrous love of Jesus (483)

Wilson, Hugh (b. Fenwick, Ayrshire, Scot., 1766; d. Duntocher, Scot., Aug. 14, 1824), after education in the village school, learned the shoemaking trade from his father, John Wilson, and in his spare time studied mathematics, music, and designed sundials. One of his sundials may still be seen in Fenwick. Frequently he led the psalm singing in the Secession Church, and he supplemented his income by teaching some of the villagers reading, writing, arithmetic, and music. About 1800 he moved to Pollokshaws where he became calculator and draftsman in the mills of William Dunn. Later he moved to Duntocher where he held a similar post. He was elected the manager of the Secession Church in the village and, with the help of James Slimmond, founded the first Sunday school there. He composed and arranged many psalm tunes, but only the one given below remains in common usage.

AVON—Alas, and did my Saviour bleed (101)

Wilson, Ira Bishop (b. Bedford, Taylor Co., Iowa, Sept. 6, 1880; d. Los Angeles, Calif., Apr. 3, 1950), received his early music training from an older sister, learning to play the violin and organ, and had begun the study of harmony before he left home. About 1902 he entered Moody Bible Institute to train himself for evangelistic music work. However, in 1905 he accepted an editorial position with the Lorenz Publishing Company, Dayton, Ohio; also as composer of choral music. His many works have appeared in the Lorenz publications as he was a contributing editor to *The Choir Leader* and *The Choir Herald,* and was editor in chief of *The Volunteer Choir.* For his writing he employed numerous pseudonyms, the major one being "Fred B. Holton." He was particularly successful in the composition of seasonal choir cantatas which have had sales of more than one and a half million copies. After 1930, while continuing his work with Lorenz, he made his home in Los Angeles, California. His son, Roger C. Wilson, well-known composer, is also a member of the Lorenz editorial staff.

Out in the highways and byways of life (431)

Winkworth, Catherine (b. London, Eng., Sept. 13, 1827; d. Monnetier, Savoy, Fr., July 1, 1878), lived in the neighborhood of Manchester until she settled with her father and sisters in Clifton in 1862. Always interested in educational and social problems, she was a pioneer in the higher education of women. She was governor of the Red Maids' School, Bristol, and was one of the founders of Clifton High School for Girls. She is regarded as one of the best translators from the German, and her *Lyra Germanica* (two series, 1855 and 1858) was widely known. She also published *The Chorale Book for England* (1863), and *Christian Singers of Germany* (1869).

Lift up your heads, ye mighty gates (tr.) (247)
Now thank we all our God (tr.) (491)
Praise to the Lord, the Almighty, the King of creation (tr.) (6)

Witt, Christian Friedrich (b. Altenburg, Ger., 1660; d. Altenburg, Apr. 13, 1716), was a student of Wecker at Nuremberg and became court capellmeister at Gotha. He composed music for several dramatic productions presented before the court of Saxe-Gotha. His *Passacaglia in D minor* was published as the work of J. S. Bach. He composed a number of instrumental works and several cantatas which appear to have been lost. He published his *Psalmodia Sacra* in Gotha in 1715.

STUTTGART—God is love; His mercy brightens (50)
O my soul, bless God the Father (51)
Grant us, Lord, the grace of giving (537)

Wolcott, Samuel (b. South Windsor, Conn., July 2, 1813; d. Longmeadow, Mass., Feb. 24, 1886), was educated at Yale College, 1833, and Andover Theological Seminary, 1837. He did missionary work in Syria, 1840-42, but poor health forced him to return to America, and he was pastor of Congregational churches in Providence, Rhode Island; Chicago, Illinois; and Cleveland, Ohio. He later served as secretary of the Ohio Home Missionary Society. He wrote his first hymn when he was fifty-six, and during the remaining seventeen years of his life he wrote more than two hundred hymns. Of these only the present remains in common use.

Christ for the world we sing (458)

Wolfe, Aaron Robarts (b. Mendham, N.J., Sept. 6, 1821; d. Montclair, N.J., Oct. 6, 1902), was educated at Williams College (A.B., 1844), and at Union Theological Seminary. He was a licensed Presbyterian minister, but decided to devote his life to educational work. From 1852 to 1855 he conducted a school for young women in Tallahassee, Florida, and in 1859 established the Hillside Seminary for Young Ladies at Montclair, New Jersey, serving as its principal until his retirement in 1872. In 1858 he contributed eight hymns signed "A.R.W." to Thomas Hastings' *Church Melodies*.

A parting hymn we sing (397)

Woodbury, Isaac Baker (b. Beverly, Mass., Oct. 23, 1819; d. Charleston, S.C., Oct. 26, 1858), at the age of thirteen, moved to Boston and began the study of music. In 1838 he spent a year in music study in Paris and London. Upon his return to Boston he spent several years teaching music there. In 1849 he moved to New York, where he directed the music at Rutgers Street Church, and later was editor of *The Musical Review* and *The Musical Pioneer*. In 1858, due to overwork, his health broke down, and he decided to spend the winter in the South, hoping to regain his strength. Three days after his arrival in Charleston, South Carolina, he died at the age of thirty-nine. He edited a number of tune books which were exceedingly popular and widely used. Among these were *The Choral* (1845), *The Timbrel* (1848), *The Dulcimer* (1850), *The Lute of Zion* (1853), *The Harp of the South* (1853), *The Cythera* (1854), *The Casket* (1855; published by the Southern Baptist Society, Charleston, S.C.), and *The New Lute of Zion* (1856). He also assisted in the compilation of the *Methodist Hymn Book* of 1857.

DORRNANCE—May the grace of Christ our Saviour (538)

Wordsworth, Christopher (b. Lambeth, Eng., Oct. 30, 1807; d. Harewood, Eng., Mar. 21, 1885), was educated at Winchester School and Trinity College, Cambridge, where he had a distinguished career as a scholar and was equally well known for his athletic ability. Ordained in the Church of England in 1833, he served as headmaster at Harrow, 1836-44, and then became canon of Westminster. He was appointed vicar of Stanford-in-the-Vale, Berkshire, 1850-69, after which he was made bishop of Lincoln. He was a nephew of the poet, William Wordsworth, and became recognized as one of the outstanding Greek scholars of his day. He published many works, including a commentary on the whole Bible. Of hymnological interest is his *The Holy Year, or Hymns for Sundays and Holy Days, and Other Occasions* (London, 1862), which contained 117 original hymns with a supplement of 82 hymns from other sources. In the 1863 edition ten additional original hymns were added.

Hallelujah! hallelujah! (114)
O day of rest and gladness (36)

Wyeth, John (b. Cambridge, Mass., Mar. 31, 1770; d. Philadelphia, Pa., Jan. 23, 1858), before he was twenty-one, learned the printer's trade and was engaged as a printer and publisher throughout his life. He was a printer in Santo Domingo at the time of the Haitian insurrection, and while he lost all of his property, he escaped to the United States disguised as a sailor. Settling at Harrisburg, Pennsylvania, he became joint owner and coeditor of *The Oracle of Dauphin,* a Federalist paper, with which he was associated for thirty-five years. He was appointed postmaster of Harrisburg in 1793 under President George Washington, but was removed from office in 1798 by President John Adams because of "the incompatibility of the office of postmaster and editor of a newspaper." He published *Repository of Sacred Music* (Harrisburg, Pa., 1810). A supplement to this collection appeared in 1813.

NETTLETON—Come, Thou Fount of every blessing (313)

Yates, John Henry (b. Batavia, N.Y., Nov. 21, 1837; d. Batavia, Sept. 5, 1900), was the son of John H. and Elizabeth (Taylor) Yates, both originally from England. After completing his studies at Batavia Union School, he was engaged in the retail shoe business, and in 1871 became a department manager for the E. L. & G. D. Kenyon Store, a hardware firm, where he worked for fifteen years. In 1886 he became editor of a local paper which he served for ten years. Licensed to preach in the Methodist church in 1858, he was ordained later in life in the Baptist ministry, and served seven years as pastor of the West Bethany Free Will Baptist Church. His poetic ability attracted the attention of Ira D. Sankey, who, in 1891, engaged him to write a gospel hymn text. He is the author of *Poems and Ballads* (1897).

Encamped along the hills of light (256)

Young, John Freeman (b. Pittston, Kennebec Co., Me., Oct. 30, 1820; d. New York, N.Y., Nov. 15, 1885), the son of John and Emma (Freeman) Young, was educated at the Wesleyan University, Middletown, Connecticut. He joined the Episcopal church and received his theological training at the Virginia Theological Seminary at Alexandria. Ordained in 1845, he was transferred to the Diocese of Florida, serving at Jacksonville and Tallahassee. From 1848 to 1855 he served in Texas, Mississippi, and Louisiana. Then for twelve years he served in New York City. In

1867 he was elected second bishop of Florida and for eighteen years served diligently the cause of Christ on the frontier.

His keen interest in architecture resulted in the erection of many church buildings of distinctive appearance. His concern for educational opportunities led him to establish a boys' school in Jacksonville and a girls' school in Fernandina. He was active in the reopening in 1869 of the University of the South, Sewanee, Tennessee, and was a frequent lecturer at this school. He published *Hymns and Music for the Young* (1860-1861), and his *Great Hymns of the Church* was published posthumously by John Henry Hopkins, Jr., in 1887.

For the above biographical data, the writer is indebted to information contained in the splendid presentation made in "Bishop John Freeman Young, Translator of 'Stille Nacht'," by Byron Edward Underwood, which appeared in *The Hymn,* Vol. 8, No. 4, October, 1957, pp. 123-30.

Silent night, holy night (tr.) (72)

Zundel, John (b. Hochdorf, Ger., Dec. 10, 1815; d. Cannstadt, Ger., July, 1882), began his musical career in Russia at St. Petersburg (now Leningrad), where he was organist at St. Anne's Lutheran Church and bandmaster of the Imperial House Guards. In 1847 he arrived in America, and after brief service at the First Unitarian Church, Brooklyn, and St. George's Episcopal Church, New York, he became organist at Henry Ward Beecher's Plymouth Congregational Church, Brooklyn, January 1, 1850. His organ playing became also as popular as Beecher's preaching, and "we will go hear Beecher and Zundel," became a common expression as the services became widely known for great preaching, skilful organ playing, and thrilling congregational singing. He published *The Choral Friend* (1852), *Psalmody* (1855), and *Christian Heart Songs* (1870). He assisted Beecher in the editing of *Temple Melodies* (1851), and the *Plymouth Collection* (1855). To this latter collection he contributed twenty-eight tunes. In 1863 he founded the *Monthly Choir and Organ Journal,* but ceased publication after a year. In 1873 he became editor of *Zundel and Brandt's Quarterly,* which contained twelve pages of music in each issue. Upon his retirement in 1880, he returned to his native Germany and his death occurred two years later.

LOVE DIVINE—Love divine, all loves excelling (2)
God, our Father, we adore Thee (5)

Index of Tunes

451